THE
FOUNDATION
CENTER'S

GUIDE TO
Grantseeking
on the
Web

THE
FOUNDATION
CENTER'S

GUIDE TO

Grantseeking
on the
Web

2000 EDITION

CONTRIBUTING STAFF

The creation and operation of the Foundation Center's Web site is truly a team effort. Similarly, this edition of *The Foundation Center's Guide to Grantseeking on the Web* is the result of the hard work of the following staff, and of their considerable experience exploring the World Wide Web.

Jonathan Chan	Christine Innamorato
Ray Chan	Rebecca Kopf
Lai Lee Chau	Cheryl Loe
David Clark	Beverly McGrath
Sarah Collins	Mitchell Nauffts
Mirek Drozdzowski	Janice Rosenberg
Phyllis Edelson	Suzanne Scarola
Andrea Feld	Frederick Schoff
Caroline Herbert	Renée Westmoreland

Library of Congress Cataloging-in-Publication Data
The Foundation Center's guide to grant seeking on the WEB.
    p. cm.
  Originally published, c1998.
  Includes bibliographical references and index.
  ISBN 0-87954-865-7
    1. Fund raising—Computer network resources—Directories.
2. Endowments—Computer network resources—Directories. 3. Web sites—Directories. I. Title: Guide to grantseeking on the web.
II. Title: Guide to grant seeking on the web. III. Title: Grantseeking on the web. IV. Foundation Center.

HV41.2.F68   2000
025.06´65815224—dc21   00-023142
                                             CIP

TABLE OF CONTENTS

FOREWORD

Like other important popular media, such as the telephone and the television, the Internet has demonstrated great power not only as a communication tool but also as a reshaper of culture. The World Wide Web is both a reflection of and an impetus for our increasingly global society. As we entered the new millennium, various groups estimated that the number of people using the Internet worldwide would reach 300 million by 2005, with almost 100 million people in the United States online.

As the Web took off in 1995, we heard fears expressed that the medium would be captured by commercial, for-profit, .com ("dot com") interests, that the communal, sharing ethos and culture of the Internet would be destroyed. There is no question that by 1999 "e-commerce" appeared to be driving the Web bus. However, the limited concept of e-commerce as secure credit card transactions taking place over the Web was supplanted by the more comprehensive concept of "e-business." And the broader issue of individuals' privacy quickly overshadowed the narrow concept of secure credit card transactions. The original issue concerning the logistics of secure funds transfer became an issue about social policy and practice.

Despite the ability of large commercial interests to dominate public discourse about the World Wide Web, it is still true that the very technology of the Web does not permit outright monopolization. (See Appendix A for a discussion of the technology underlying the Internet.) Tim Berners-Lee, the acknowledged inventor of the Web, is now head of the World Wide Web Consortium (WC3). His goal is to keep the Web open and universal. He believes, now that we have the Web, that our next task is to develop a "web of trust." He believes we can develop Web technology that, for example, will allow e-business to take place without unseen manipulation by large commercial interests, and that will safeguard our children without at the same time facilitating government censorship. While it is true that large commercial interests have the resources to be the most visible players, many people and groups are working to ensure that any community of interest can find a place on the Web so long as it has conviction, energy, and the basic resources needed to place itself there.

To echo this point, in a November 1999 interview, management guru Peter Drucker declared, "The 20th century was the century of business. The next century is going to be the century of the social sector." We will see if this bold prediction comes true, but it is true that the media are now full of news of the nonprofit world in general, and of philanthropy in particular. And, as a result of a number of factors, "cyber-giving" arose as a phenomenon during 1999, with many Web sites facilitating the giving by individuals to charitable causes. It may be that some of these efforts are just a new form of "cause-related marketing" (that is, created to serve commercial interests ultimately), but they also hold great potential to reshape our culture through the continued convergence of Web technology—and perhaps the commercial sector itself—with the charitable sector.

It is clear that this increased interest in the nonprofit sector and philanthropy is due, at least in part, to years of a strong U.S. economy and the creation of new wealth, much of it fueled by technology companies, including those focused specifically on the Internet. Whether you take Peter Drucker literally or not, the social sector is being recognized widely as a major locus of economic activity. And people want to know where philanthropic dollars go.

When the Web was brand new there was much talk about its potential for disintermediation; that is, individuals now could transact any kind of business without relying on traditional middlemen. Interestingly, by 1999 it was clear —in both the commercial and the social sectors—that many companies and groups were striving mightily to become intermediaries for economic exchange.

A very encouraging counterpoint to the emphasis on e-business has been the rapid rise of the concept and practice of "distance learning." The interactivity of the Web holds out significant promise that this use of it will take root and flourish. In late 1999 a Department of Education study reported that by 1997–98, the percentage of colleges with distance learning programs offering Internet classes had reached 60 percent.

The possibilities for education worldwide are breathtaking. We have the instructive lessons of television to guide us, and so many groups, including a number of private foundations, are studying issues concerning a potential "digital divide" forming between those who do/don't have full access to Internet technology.

However the interplay of these major social and economic forces unfolds—and the "network effect" of the Web makes accurate prediction difficult—the original culture of the Web still seems ideally suited to embrace and serve the nonprofit community. With our Web site and the second edition of this work, the Foundation Center is both documenting and contributing to the creation of a fully networked philanthropic community. In doing so we are making use of the Web's primary strengths: the broad distribution of useful information and search tools to find the *most* useful information, and the ability for people and groups to readily communicate with each other. We continue to develop Your Gateway to Philanthropy on the World Wide Web. We hope it opens many doorways for you as you pursue your goals.

Frederick Schoff
December 1999

The Foundation Center: Your Gateway to Philanthropy on the World Wide Web

The primary goal of the second edition of this work is to save you time, to help you use the World Wide Web for finding information relevant to grantseeking. The Foundation Center decided to produce this work to help people seek grants on the Web simply because, for all its wonders, the World Wide Web will chew up an extraordinary amount of your time. Using this book to become familiar with the Web resources available to grantseekers prior to logging on will help you make the most of your time spent online.

Foundation Center staff have been scanning the Web since 1994, when Netscape Navigator 1.0 was released and the Center launched its own Web site (www.fdncenter.org). A primary goal of the Web site is to fulfill our organizational mission of fostering public understanding of the foundation field by collecting, organizing, analyzing, and disseminating information on foundations, corporate giving, and related subjects. By serving the information needs of both grantseekers and grantmakers, the Foundation Center is ideally positioned to satisfy the growing interest in the nonprofit sector and philanthropy. In addition to demystifying the operation of foundation philanthropy and quantifying and describing the contributions of U.S. foundations to society, our Web site has given us the ability to provide grantseekers direct access to a tremendous variety of available Web resources, to be Your Gateway to Philanthropy on the World Wide Web.

Since 1994, Foundation Center staff have been cataloging Web sites of potential value to grantseekers interested in any and all potential sources of support—

whether foundation funding, corporate giving programs, government grant and aid programs, or wealthy individuals identified through what is known as prospect research—and putting links to these sites on our Web site.

This work presents in linear form the results of our continuous scanning of the Web. In many ways the presentation tracks the organization of our Web site.

Be forewarned. We fully expect that there will be some "broken links" in this version of Your Gateway to Philanthropy on the World Wide Web (broken links are Web addresses that are no longer accurate). These only reflect the incredible dynamism of this new medium. A static version can only be a snapshot of the Web at a particular moment in time. Links change for any number of reasons. Sometimes individuals or small organizations cannot sustain the effort required to maintain a vital Web site and so they disappear from view. Some Web addresses will change because what was once a small effort hosted on someone else's computer has grown into a full-fledged site that is moved to a larger or dedicated host computer. In preparing this second edition, we were excited to see the stability and indeed growth of sites concerned with philanthropy and the nonprofit world. The energy and dynamism of the nonprofit world is plainly visible on the Web.

With our Web site and this work, the Foundation Center has created a specialty portal for grantseekers and others interested in philanthropy. We continue to develop and expand the offerings of this gateway, trying to keep pace with the burgeoning Web. Once you have become familiar with the Web resources available in your areas of interest, we invite you to log onto (www.fdncenter.org) and follow the paths that open up to you.

Appendix A reviews the history of the Internet and the World Wide Web from a technology perspective. Below we present a brief overview of how people's ability to access and interact with the World Wide Web has evolved in just a few short years. Our hope is that it serves to demonstrate for those new to the Web some of the trends driving the composition of Web services being offered at the close of 1999.

From Surfing to Searching, From Portals to Communication

When the Web was young, proprietary networks like Prodigy, Compuserve, America Online, and the Microsoft Network offered a collection of specific content modules they created and designed for you, in addition to Internet e-mail services. Many people first got on the Internet through these few proprietary doors. However, with the arrival of easy-to-use "browsers" (see Chapter 1), users soon opted for plain vanilla Internet access that allowed them to surf the Web on their own. Going through a proprietary network to get to the Web had become unnecessary. In response, the various proprietary networks began offering direct Internet access as an additional service in order to compete with a growing number of Internet Service Providers (ISPs), those companies that connect individual customers to the Internet.

Soon after, the proprietary networks began offering unlimited-use pricing (doing away with charging for time online) so that they could continue to compete with the ISPs. And at the turn of the millennium, some services were offering free Internet access as a way to do business with a growing Web audience and an evolving and even more competitive business environment. (AOL was the only remaining service successfully charging fees for proprietary content, albeit with Internet connectivity included.)

SEARCH ENGINES

With broad distribution of easy-to-use browsers and direct access to the Web, people could "surf" the Web to their heart's content, or at least to the limits of their patience. The appearance of search engines available to anyone through a standard Web address was a great advance. Digital's AltaVista search engine was perhaps the most visible early entry. People could begin to actively seek out the information available on the Web themselves, rather than rely only on hyperlinks or word-of-mouth referrals to particular Web sites. However, using a simple search engine across something as large and diverse as the Web has its drawbacks. Users were thrilled that they could surf the Web on their own, but they found themselves sifting through long search results lists that contained a lot of irrelevant material. As the Web expanded rapidly, containing more and more information, much of it frivolous, this problem grew worse. Hybrid search services arose that let users search the Web, but across indexes that had been prepared through editorial research, human beings reviewing and classifying Web sites. Yahoo! is probably the best known and most successful example.

The number of Web sites and pages continued to grow rapidly and, despite claims of superior technology and results, search engine functionality became a commodity. In addition, it was widely believed that none of the search engines could do a good job of indexing such a vast amount of material. By the summer of 1999, people estimated there were 800 million searchable Web pages and that the largest search engine index included less than 20 percent of them. A number of "open directory" efforts were begun, in which the Web user community participated in indexing and classifying Web sites and pages. In this way more search services began following the Yahoo! model of categorizing Web sites as a way to better organize and make available so much material. The trick was to enlist considerable volunteer labor to accomplish this.

THE ADVENT OF PORTALS

Whatever their limitations, stand-alone search engines and services were a great boon to Web users. However, many service providers saw the need to being aggregating a number of Internet services in order to create and/or maintain high traffic rates for their sites. Free e-mail accounts became readily available at a number of sites. Capturing "eyeballs" was considered key to supporting the Web site advertising revenue streams developed to make up for dropping (or nonexistent) revenues from connection or content-delivery fees. These full-service sites were dubbed "portals." The term describes a Web page offering a variety of Web services, which people can use as a home base for all of their Web explorations, the page they choose as the first page they see when they log onto the Web and open their browser.

Many of the full-service portals that survive the millennium developed from search service sites. Most now offer search services, free e-mail services, and the ability to customize your own search site "home page." Local weather, specific stock market quotations, particular news or sports feeds, and individual horoscopes all can greet you when you open up these sites, as well as links to related or co-branded Web offerings, either free or fee-based services.

The fact is, there are now many portal sites offering the same combination of services and links, even though they may have started out providing individual services quite distinct from each other.

BEYOND PORTALS TO COMMUNICATION

User preferences and behavior evolved rapidly as the population became more sophisticated about the Web. Portals themselves rapidly have become an undifferentiated commodity, with some analysts speculating that they won't survive, that the model of a generalized portal won't be viable as users become more and more skilled at finding what they want on their own.

In response, by late 1998, Excite, Yahoo!, Infoseek, Lycos, America Online, and others were trying to create "portal loyalty" by offering the ability for people with common interests to create their own private networks within their suite of services. The goal was to retain users, create loyalty to their portals by capitalizing on the relationships that already exist in the real—as opposed to the virtual—world. They had begun offering more sophisticated communication tools, rather than just offering Web destinations.

The Foundation Center's Web site fills this role for its particular community by serving and indeed strengthening the relationships that exist within philanthropy. Since 1956 the Foundation Center has helped build effective bridges between grantseekers and grantmakers by providing information that can help people identify their common goals and interests, and by educating grantseekers about the need to build relationships with grantmakers. The Center's World Wide Web site is a powerful tool with which to further this goal of connecting the vital and important ideas of the nonprofit world with the resources that can help advance them. In fact, over time, the Center's Web presence will become less of a Web site per se, and more of a communication system for use by the field of philanthropy and those interested in it.

Arrangement of the Book

Chapter 1 briefly discusses the genesis and development of Web "browsers," the software tools whose arrival fueled the tremendous growth of the Web and accelerated its evolution. After this brief discussion, this chapter presents the features and operation of a fully developed browser product, using current versions of both Netscape Navigator and Internet Explorer as the leading examples. Those people new to Web, or those who may be upgrading their browser versions, can get a comprehensive introduction to the full set of tools these software products offer.

Chapter 2 is a survey of the range of information and services available at (www.fdncenter.org), the Foundation Center's Web site. We reorganized and redesigned our Web site in late 1998 (our second major redesign) to accommodate the growing amount of information and number of services provided, and to make navigating through the site easier for both first-time and repeat visitors. Especially for first-time visitors, reviewing this chapter may make navigating our site even easier than we have tried to make it. And remember, the Web is vast; if you get lost following a trail of links, you can always return to (www.fdncenter.org),Your Gateway to Philanthropy on the World Wide Web, and pick up the trail afresh.

In Chapter 3 we discuss various approaches that independent private foundations are taking in using the World Wide Web within their operations. From simply providing basic information to actively championing the use of new communication technologies and trying to ensure equal access for all, foundations are increasingly getting involved with the Web. As in many chapters of this work, we list the many links to foundations that can be found at (www.fdncenter.org), along with brief abstracts of what can be found at these foundation sites. This static version cannot, of course, offer the ability to search the text of these abstracts that we offer at our Web site, nor provide the other search tools and searchable databases available there, but readers can familiarize themselves with the world of foundations on the Web prior to going online, as well as learn about the programs of individual foundations.

The Foundation Center takes pains to accurately present a picture of U.S. philanthropy, to define the field. In doing so we stress the legal distinctions between private foundations and public charities, sometimes known as "public foundations." In Chapter 4 we present separately the U.S. public charities on the Web we have identified as having grantmaking programs. This group includes community foundations, a growing segment of U.S. philanthropy. As we did with foundations in Chapter 3, we present the many links to grantmaking public charities to be found at (www.fdncenter.org) as well as the abstracts to these we have prepared. (We write abstracts continually, so check the "Grantmaker Information" area of (www.fdncenter.org) for the latest listings.) Information is not as systematically available for the great variety of public charities as it is for private foundations, so it is our hope that highlighting grantmaking public charities in this way will stimulate more of them to provide us with detailed information about their grantmaking activities. In this chapter, we list grantmaking public charities alphabetically by name, but we present all community foundations in a separate listing by individual states.

Chapter 5 surveys the field of corporate philanthropy, in addition to reviewing strategies for finding corporate funding information on the Web. Corporations present their giving programs in a variety of ways and to varying degrees, so creativity and persistence come into play when doing corporate giving research. This chapter stresses the need to consider the different motivations and goals of corporate givers, and how this can affect your funding approach. The annotated list of links in this chapter combines those of corporate foundations and of direct giving programs. Similar to the situation with community foundations versus other grantmaking public charities, you will often find more detailed information for corporate foundations than you will for direct company giving programs.

There is a tremendous amount of government information on the World Wide Web. Chapter 6 attempts to make sense of this vast amount of information by pointing you to those sites, at many levels of governement, that describe assistance programs. Researching government sources of support is different than researching corporations, described in Chapter 5, where you may need to sift through general company information to find information specifically about giving programs. Since historically one of the major activities of government has been to provide assistance, there is a wealth of information. People both within and without government have tried to organize this information for you. This chapter reviews the many sites describing specific support programs, as well as sites that can lead you to more specific information. Reviewing these sites can help you understand how government agencies and programs are organized and can be revealing of their relationship to the nonprofit sector.

Chapter 7 has a functional focus, in recognition that the World Wide Web distributes interactive software capability as well as information and hyperlinks. This chapter surveys a variety of sites—housed in a variety of settings—that offer searchable databases which may help Web users identify potential sources of assistance or general information. Whereas in the first edition of this work we divided the world of searchable databases into the two major categories of "for-free" and "for-fee," significant blurring of the line between them has occurred as older Web services evolve and newer ones are created. In this edition we don't rely on that distinction, and your Web explorations will reveal where service fees come into play. There is some overlap of this chapter with others in the book because these databases are offered within corporate, government, and nonprofit organization—including foundation—settings.

Chapter 8 chronicles Web sites, many of them housed at nonprofit organizations, that Foundation Center staff have found to be the most useful and descriptive of the nonprofit sector and philanthropy, including some sites concerned with philanthropy in other countries. Many of the sites in this chapter can, like (www.fdncenter.org), provide you with links to other resources you may find useful. We survey some of our staff's picks in detail. The full listing of sites is organized under the various subject categories used at the Center's Web site to provide ready access to this growing number of resources.

Chapter 9 is a comprehensive listing of online publications (with abstracts for each) concerned with philanthropy and the nonprofit sector. Included are many field-specific newsletters and other online publications that can provide the current trends and policy context for various nonprofit activities. Use this chapter to identify the online publications that will keep you up-to-date with your particular field and interests.

Chapter 10 illustrates how two-way communication is used to build community on the World Wide Web. The simple but powerful interactivity of Internet e-mail and electronic mailing lists and bulletin boards allows communities of Web users to define themselves online, and to create dialogs and conversations, both private and public, which can advance their work or inform their interests. This chapter surveys a number of the community-building services available for grantseekers and other nonprofit practitioners, as well as provides tips on how to begin participating in these various forums.

Appendix A provides a brief overview of the technical underpinnings of the Internet. It then tracks the software developments that spurred the initial phenomenal growth of the World Wide Web and that continue to offer a seemingly unlimited potential for the Web to knit together various global communities. The apparent promise of Web technology to break down barriers to communication and to distribute computing resources around the world is truly astounding. The development of software, and as important, the adoption of universally recognized software and data standards, is an ongoing process and will only accelerate.

Appendix B is a bibliography of titles about the Internet that may be of interest to nonprofit practitioners. It is a compilation drawn from the Foundation Center's *Literature of the Nonprofit Sector* database, a bibliographic database you can search for free yourself by visiting http://fdncenter.org/lnps/index.html. (Please note that to reach the Center's Web site you can drop the "www." and just use "fdncenter.org.")

With the new edition of this work, we took the time to create an index. The Web is so dynamic we had to fight the urge to get "our Web book" out sooner by skipping this step. However, the number of resources listed here has grown considerably, and so we hope you find this addition useful.

The Foundation Center's Web site, described in detail in Chapter 2, is a specialty portal that we call "Your Gateway to Philanthropy on the World Wide Web." It has been designed for those interested in the nonprofit world, particularly the world of U.S. grantmakers. This work is in one sense a static version of this specialty portal. It is full of specific information about where to find Web sites that may be useful in your grantseeking efforts. We invite you to use both formats of Your Gateway to Philanthropy on the World Wide Web as a way to get your Web grantseeking efforts off to a flying start.

CHAPTER ONE

The Web Browser: Your Cyberspace Viewer

Birth of the Browser

Around 1993, while a staff member of the National Center for Supercomputing Applications (NCSA) at the University of Illinois, a fellow named Marc Andreessen created a software program called Mosaic. It was the first true graphical user interface (GUI) to the World Wide Web, making access to the World Wide Web much simpler. A GUI providing ready access to the Web was dubbed a "browser." This one development is arguably the single biggest factor in the subsequent phenomenal growth of the Web. Several versions of Mosaic were released, but along the way Marc Andreessen and others involved in its original development left NCSA to join Jim Clark and form Mosaic Communications Corp., which soon changed its name to Netscape Communications. A *Wall Street Journal* article described the situation in May of 1994 this way:

> But his new company will have to move fast to provide added features and functions that will separate its product from a horde of similar offerings. Many companies are seeking licenses to develop commercial versions of Mosaic, or are developing knockoffs of the concept. . . . Most of the companies are developing products that will facilitate initial access to the Internet as well as provide a Mosaic-like look and feel. . . . "There's lots of competition," notes Marc Porat, chief executive officer of General Magic Inc., a software consortium based in Mountain View, Calif. Eventually, he says, software giant Microsoft Corp., could join the fray, bundling an Internet navigator with its best-selling Windows operating system "and undermining everyone."

> *("Silicon Graphics' Clark Sets Up Firm to Provide Internet Operating System,"* Wall Street Journal, *Monday May 9, 1994, page B2)*

A couple of these were truly prophetic comments. But generally, in the same way GUIs had made personal computing accessible to millions of people, GUI access to the Web brought the global connectivity offered by the Internet to millions of people around the world. Also, in the same way that GUIs had made it possible for personal computer users to be ignorant of operating system file structures and specialized computer languages, GUI access to the Web rendered some of the basic, ground-breaking functionality of the original Internet quaint, if not obsolete, particularly as these earlier developments work more transparently within browsers (see Appendix A for a summary of pre-browser Internet development). With an Internet connection established, browser installed, and mouse in hand, all it took for millions of people to enter cyberspace was the ability to type a Web address known as a URL.

What Is a URL?

URL stands for "Uniform Resource Locator." It is the standard form for specifying an address on the Internet, such as a file, newsgroup, or Web site home page or document. URLs look like this:

- file://wuarchive.wustl.edu/doc/gutenberg/standard.new
- ftp://wuarchive.wustl.edu/graphics/mirrors/avalon/ITIndex.zip
- http://www.w3.org:80/Consortium/
- news://alt.hypertext
- telnet://dra.com

The first part of the URL, before the colon, specifies the access method and indicates the type of file represented by the address. In general, two slashes after the colon indicate that a machine name (or "port") follows. The domain name, including the appropriate domain suffix, is often used here. (The third format in the above list is the most common.) It used to be necessary to precede that with "www" to indicate a hypertext Web document, but that is often assumed now (given the "http" designation, which stands for "hypertext transfer protocol") and can be omitted. Additional address information after the domain name refers to specific Web pages or files on a particular Web server. URLs are either typed into browser address boxes or operate behind the scenes when the user clicks on a hyperlink.

Browser Development

Netscape Navigator 1.0 shipped in December 1994, just as the Foundation Center put its first home page on the Web. The arrival of a Web browser used easily by anyone with a mouse brought a Star-Trek-like capability to a tremendous number of desktops. Since that time, browser development and the acceptance of developing standards have allowed more and different kinds of content to be provided on the Web. At various times, key browser enhancements have altered the mix of available Web content, and spurred the continued evolution of the culture of the Web. Netscape Communications in particular played a key role in the development of the Web.

The "Browser War"

In December 1994, in order to issue a browser of its own that could compete with Netscape, Microsoft licensed Spyglass Mosaic, added some features to it, and released a new browser named Microsoft Explorer. The so-called "browser war" had officially begun. Although it is well known that for quite a while the various releases of Netscape Navigator were more technically advanced than Microsoft's browser offerings, the gap had narrowed considerably by the time they each had released their 3.0 versions. Giving Explorer away for free was a big help, and, in 1996, America Online chose a version of Explorer as their default browser in exchange for prime real estate on the Windows desktop. Also in 1996, Opera Software AS, based in Oslo, Norway, released its Opera browser, which gained recognition for its speed, ease of use, and adherence to open standards. It seemed to be the first non-Netscape or Microsoft browser to achieve even a small measure of popularity.

In January 1997 it was estimated that Netscape still had a nearly 80 percent share of the browser market. However, almost two years later, by November 1998, it was reported that use of Internet Explorer had overtaken that of Netscape Navigator (with a big leg up from a growing AOL membership). Microsoft's apparent market advantage of having Explorer ship with the Windows operating system software, as well as other Microsoft business practices, had attracted the attention of the Justice Department. In addition, in late 1998 it was already being reported that parts of Netscape's business would merge or be acquired by America Online or Sun Microsystems, Inc.

AOL bought Netscape in November 1998 (the deal also involved Sun Microsystems). People began talking about potential competition for Microsoft's Windows desktop operating system from the new and evolving companies. People were very curious to see whether AOL would continue to use Explorer as its default browser. Around the same time, a Unix-like operating system called Linux was gaining popularity and support for its "open systems" approach. Microsoft was ordered to start supporting the Java standard, rather than only its proprietary version of the open standard. The plot had thickened considerably.

Irrespective of the more general issue of whether anyone could compete effectively against the dominance of Microsoft's Windows desktop, by March 1999 Explorer users outnumbered Navigator users by 2 to 1. By August it was 3 to 1. Explorer 5.0 had shipped earlier in the year, well ahead of Navigator 5.0, slated to be released in December 1999. (Just as with IE4, it caused the usual consternation when people loaded it and reckoned with Microsoft's free hand with their desktops and applications.) In October the AOL flavor of IE5 was released worldwide. Current contractual agreements between AOL and Microsoft concerning Explorer run until 2001.

This all may be moot, as it is unclear whether it is the browser market that the software giants care about, except perhaps as a way to gain advantage in other markets—perhaps the portal-driven e-commerce aggregation for which Amazon.com is so well known. In any case, you will find people as opinionated about the respective merits of the various versions of these two browsers as people are about their Macs or PCs. You also will find knowledgeable people who declare the browser war over, saying that browsers are a commodity, that they all do basically the same things. Each person can and will make up their own mind.

Whatever the final outcome of the browser war, in 1997, Jones Digital Century (http://www.jii.com) explained the future of browsers this way:

> As a result of [Netscape's] technological and business innovations, virtually all players in the Internet software industry now envision a future of "distributed computing resources," within which people will use the Internet in ways analogous to their present use of computer hard drives. Perhaps even more importantly, as more and more information becomes digitized, stored in enormous databases, and made available on the Internet or on closed networks, the browser will become an increasingly important tool for the organization, access, and preservation of the world's knowledge.

It is possible to get as deeply involved with the Web and its various technologies as it is (for any enthusiast) to become absorbed in the details of any particular passion. However, the focus of this book is the content available via the Web that is useful for grantseekers. Our goal is to help those grantseekers fairly new to the Web get past the technology involved, to bring them closer to the information of value to them. The latest versions of both the Netscape and Microsoft browsers now include additional features that go beyond basic browser functioning. Below we reference these added features briefly so that you will know what they are and can recognize them on your screen, but the browser function is your true window onto the World Wide Web. E-mail is the other function essential to doing research on the Web (see Chapter 10 in particular), and its use is now closely integrated with routine browser operation.

Browser Suites

The leading creators of browser software envision a future where all of your desktop computing—whether you are creating a personal document or spreadsheet, working collaboratively in a networked workplace environment, or communicating throughout the world via the Web—takes place in a single screen window on your computer. Netscape Communications paved the way for this by creating the Netscape Communicator suite. Microsoft followed suit by adding a clustered suite of tools to its Internet Explorer browser.

We try to ensure that the pages we post at our Web site display correctly in various browsers and browser versions. Netscape Navigator was the browser of choice in December 1994 when the Foundation Center launched its original Web site. Reflecting the current dominance of Internet Explorer, in the remaining chapters of this book all graphic examples of Web pages will be shown within the Explorer 5.0 browser window. (Although even IE4 may still be quite popular, we are assuming that more and more Navigator users will migrate to IE5.) Of course, as is obvious when comparing the descriptions of the menus, toolbars, and functionality of the two leading browsers below, they can be used interchangeably.

NETSCAPE COMMUNICATOR 4.61

This software suite contains the following functions:

Navigator 4.61 Browser
This works very much like Navigator 3.0, although certain menu items were rearranged.

Messenger
This is your Internet e-mail capability. (In Navigator 3.0, the e-mail function was accessible from the Window Menu; in Navigator 4.61, it is accessible from the Component Bar or the Communicator Menu. See below.) Messenger also allows you to access Web newsgroups and forums.

Composer
This feature lets you create your own HTML documents.

AOL Instant Messenger Service
This feature allows you to have real-time chats with other Internet users while surfing the Web. The AOL Instant Messenger Service function can be opened from the drop-down Communicator Menu on the Menu Bar, and from the Personal Toolbar, which will be described below.

When you first click on the Communicator icon on your desktop, the Navigator browser window opens as the default. If you are connected to the Internet you will be taken to Netscape's homepage, called Netcenter.

You can use the option available under "Preferences" (see more on Preferences further on in this chapter) to choose any Web page as your default, to appear any time you launch the browser.

Most of the functions in the Communicator suite are accessible from the Component Bar (shown below), which can stay on your desktop or be minimized to appear in the "status line" at the bottom of the Navigator window.

LAUNCHING NAVIGATOR 4.61

A while back, prior to the AOL-Netscape merger, Netscape revamped its own
home page by creating the Netcenter portal, admitting that they were slow to provide a multi-service home base for Navigator users (*Business Week*, April 1998).
Before this makeover, the Netscape home page had looked primarily like a place
to buy software. Since then, Netscape has tried to be a more active partner in your
Internet experience with Netcenter appearing as your default home page when
you first install and open the browser. However, changing your default home page
is very easy. Click "Edit" on the Menu Bar, then click on "Preferences," the last
item in the drop-down list. You will see the following window:

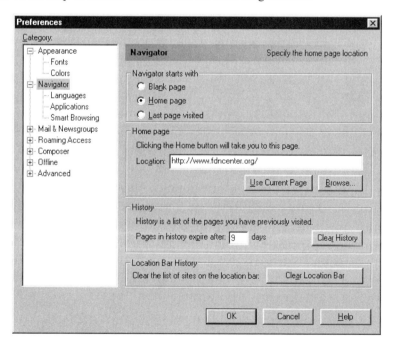

Click on "Navigator" in the topic list displayed in the window (if it isn't already
the default). There is a box labeled "Location," under the heading "Home Page,"
on the right-hand side of the window in which you can type the URL of your

choice. Click "OK" and, unless you change it at another time, whenever Navigator opens, it will take you to that Web page. (You can also use the "Browse" feature to locate an HTML file on your local drive to use as your default home page.)

"Preferences" is a useful place to remember, and we will talk about it more fully later. In Navigator 3.0, "Preferences" was under "Options" on the Menu Bar. In the Communicator suite, there are fewer separate pull-down menus than in Navigator 3.0. Other items from the old "Options," "Directory," and "Window" menus are now part of the new "Communicator" menu. Putting "Preferences" on the Edit Menu may seem like a strange choice for those who associate "Edit" with the basic cut, copy, and paste functions offered in Windows. When you first begin using Navigator 4.61, it may be handy to think in terms of "editing your preferences" as a reminder of the location for "Preferences."

TOOLBARS

We will review the most important of the various pull-down menus later, but the various toolbars available in Navigator 4.61 are the most useful tools for browsing the Web. There are three of them: the Navigation Toolbar, the Location Toolbar, and the Personal Toolbar. We will discuss them all, but before you make any of them disappear by accident, we'll show you how to customize their arrangement in the blank Navigator window shown below. (To get a blank window, just open Navigator without connecting to the Internet.)

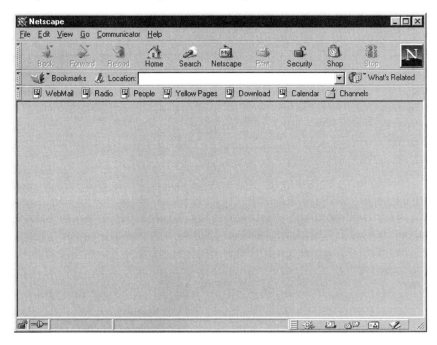

The three toolbars are stacked one on top of the other in the above order: Navigation, Location, Personal. Note the narrow vertical bars containing little triangle arrows that appear at the left of each of these toolbar areas. Click on one of them to see how that toolbar is now hidden. You can hide all of them if you wish at any time during your Web browsing. To restore them, simply click on the narrow bars again (which are horizontal when the toolbars are hidden). You can also change the "stacking" order of the toolbars. Just click (and hold) on one of the narrow bars and drag that toolbar past the others to put it where you prefer. For instance, you might want to have the Location Toolbar up top. In any case, we are going to discuss that one first, because getting to the home pages containing the information you seek is likely to be your top priority.

Location Toolbar

The Location Toolbar is the one containing the long box into which you type URL (Uniform Resource Locator) addresses. A URL is text used for identifying and addressing an item in a computer network. A URL provides location information, and Navigator displays it in the location field. Most often you don't need to know a page's URL because the location information is included automatically as part of a highlighted link or a toolbar link. However, if you have learned of a URL from some other source than surfing the Web itself (getting such a tip is often the best way to learn of something really useful), you will have to type it into the Location Box on the Location Toolbar. After you type in a URL and before you hit "Enter," the word "Location" changes to "Go to" in the Location Toolbar. If you are viewing a page that comes from a Netscape server, the word "Location" changes to "Netsite."

With a URL address typed into this box, just press "Enter" to bring that particular Web page to your Navigator window. (You will soon discover that even one incorrectly typed character in a URL address will prevent your browser from finding that Web resource.) Once you bring up any page that has blue hyperlinks on it, you can be off and surfing the Web simply by clicking on the links provided. However, you can start over again at any time by typing in a different URL or by clicking on a URL already stored within any of several places within Navigator.

One of the places to store URLs you want to remember (and therefore won't have to type again) is your "Bookmarks" function, the link to which appears directly to the left of the Location Box on this toolbar. Creating your own list of URLs to remember and never type again is a very useful capability, and we will discuss creating your own list of "bookmarks" more thoroughly later. For now, while viewing the blank Netscape Navigator page offline, click on the Bookmark icon on the Location Toolbar to see a list of default categories that Netscape has provided. Pick a category and put your cursor on it. Another list will appear containing the names of specific Web pages in that category. These names each represent an Internet URL address. When you click on a name in one of these lists, behind the scenes the URL for the Web page it represents is inserted automatically into the address box in the Location Toolbar, and Navigator takes you to that page (if you are connected to the Internet, that is, and not just learning browser functions while offline).

One other interesting capability on the Location Toolbar: if you click on the "drop-down arrow" at the right-hand side of the address box, you will see a drop-down list of those URL addresses you visited recently by typing them directly into the address box. This is another place where Navigator stores URLs which you can click on to revisit frequently viewed Web pages. The important thing to remember about this particular list is that it only contains URLs that were *typed* in recently. It won't store the URLs you chose by clicking on links or that you have stored as bookmarks.

Navigation Toolbar

This is the toolbar to use for navigation and page control. The buttons described below provide quick access to the most commonly used Web-surfing features.

Back. Click on this button to display the page you were viewing just previously. Holding down the button, or clicking on it with right mouse button, will display a window containing a history list, which we will discuss more later.

Forward. If you have used the "Back" button (or made use of its history list), clicking on this button will bring you to what you were viewing before. It will be "grayed out" (i.e., disabled) if you have returned to the most recently viewed page.

Reload. Click this button to redisplay the current Navigator page, reflecting any changes made since the original loading. To reload, Navigator checks the network server to see if any change to the page has occurred. If no change has occurred, the original page is retrieved from the cache (see more about caching later in this chapter). If there has been a change, the updated page is retrieved from the server. If you hold down the Shift key and then press the Reload button, Navigator will retrieve the page from the server, bypassing the cache.

Home. Click this button to display the home page designated in the "Navigator" panel in "Preferences" (under "Edit" on the Menu Bar). If you haven't designated a particular home page to use as your default, clicking on Home will take you to the Netscape home page.

Search. Click on "Search" to visit a Netscape server and retrieve a Web page that offers access to a number of ways to explore the Web. On this page you will find a list of direct links to what people initially called "search engines." However, as discussed in the Introduction, with the further development of these Web services, that terminology has become too limited. So, on the Netscape "Search" page you will find links to some of the major search services displayed prominently. You will also find sub-menus listing some search service links under the heading "Search the Web," while others are listed under the heading "Explore by Topic." The fact is, the major Web search services take different approaches, both technical and philosophical, trying to "index" the contents of the World Wide Web.

Images. This button is available on the Navigation Toolbar only if you have turned off the "Automatically load images" option found within the "Advanced" panel of the "Preferences" section (found in the Edit Menu). If you had turned off automatic image loading, clicking on this button will load the images for the page you are viewing.

My Netscape. Clicking this button takes you to the customizable Netcenter portal launched in mid-1998 (see the Introduction for more on the advent of "portals"). Netcenter contains a menu of category links which will in turn take you to pages with more specific links that help you find information in those categories.

Print. Just as you would expect, clicking on this button takes you to a dialog box that lets you select printing characteristics.

Security. The options available concerning Internet security are numerous, and we won't go into them in this book. Briefly, clicking on this button takes you to a page where you can establish encryption status, personal and site certificates, passwords, and other security-related applications.

Stop. Clicking this button halts any ongoing transfer of page information. It is often used to stop downloading a particular page that seems to be taking too long.

Clicking "Stop" and then "Reload" can sometimes bring down the page you are seeking more quickly.

The Personal Toolbar

The Personal Toolbar isn't really a toolbar in the way the Navigation Toolbar is. Basically, the Personal Toolbar displays icons of your favorite bookmarks. We will discuss how to customize it when we talk more about Navigator's Bookmarks feature. When you first install Navigator, you will see that, as a default, Netscape has placed some potentially useful bookmarks within easy reach on your Personal Toolbar. The Personal Toolbar also contains a button for AOL Instant Messenger Service.

THE BROWSER WINDOW

Page Content Area

The content area contains the current page corresponding to the most recently requested URL. Vertical and horizontal scroll bars should be present if the page is larger than the screen area. The title bar at the very top of the browser window shows the title of the currently loaded page. You can open multiple Navigator windows to view multiple pages of information. You might want to do this, for instance, if you are doing specific research and have found different Web sites that you wish to compare. You can open separate windows to look at them side by side. Also, if a page you are trying to load is for some reason loading very slowly, you can continue to surf while you wait for it to appear in its own window.

Web pages can contain a lot of text which requires scrolling to view them in their entirety. However, it is easy to search Web pages for particular words and phrases. You can click on "Edit" on the Menu Bar and then click on the "Find in Page" menu item. This opens a "Find" dialog box that lets you type the string of characters you wish to find on a Web page. Within this dialog box you can choose to search up or down. You can access this dialog box in an even easier way: simply hit "Control-F" on your keyboard.

A Word about Frames

Some pages are designed to be a patchwork of separate pages called "frames." Each frame is a smaller page within the larger page. (Together, a group of frames forms a top-level page called a frameset.) Individual frames may have different characteristics. Each frame may contain a scroll bar to let you view more information within that frame. Individual frames can be resized by positioning your cursor in the border between frames and dragging them to the desired size. Generally, toolbar and menu items affect the top-level page. However, some menu items, such as printing or saving, might apply only to individual frames. Many people have been surprised after clicking "Print" and then receiving only a portion of the full Web page on their screen.

Status Message

The status message area is located at the bottom of the browser window. It contains text describing a page's location. When you position your cursor over highlighted words serving as a link to a page, the status message will show the URL that will be used to bring that page to the screen. When you position your cursor over an image with "hotspots" (active links within an image area), the status message will show a description for the active area. When you click on a link, the status message will tell you what is happening: whether Navigator made a connection with the server, what percentage of a file has been downloaded, etc. It's always nice to (finally) get the "Document: Done" message, which shows that the complete file has been downloaded.

Progress Bar

Also located at the bottom of the browser window, the Progress Bar animates to show the progress of the current operation. It displays graphically the percentage done as a page loads. When the amount of time necessary to load a page cannot be estimated accurately, a segment of the Progress Bar "bounces" between its boundaries.

Component Bar

If you have closed the Communicator Component Bar we showed earlier, it will appear in minimized form in the status line at the bottom right-hand side of the browser window. You can click any of the icons to access other Communicator features, such as e-mail. Click the Mailbox icon to display the mail Inbox folder and retrieve new messages. The Mailbox icon will show a question mark (?) if Communicator cannot automatically check the mail server for new messages (for example, if you have not yet supplied your password to access messages). The Mailbox icon will include a down-arrow if the mail server has new messages for you.

Security Indicator

At the bottom left-hand side of the status line a padlock icon indicates security information. A closed padlock shows that a page is encrypted. An open padlock shows that a page isn't encrypted. Clicking the padlock icon displays the same security information window accessible by clicking the Security button on the Navigation Toolbar.

LINKS AND IMAGES

It's usually easy to tell what's a link. When using the default "Appearance" settings (found in "Preferences," which of course you will recall is under the Edit Menu), text links are underlined and appear in blue. When you put your cursor on a link, your cursor arrow will change to a friendly pointing hand and the status line will show you the URL for that link. After you follow a link, when you return to the page you linked from, that link appears in purple to show that you've already visited there. (You can always use the link again; the change in color is just a reminder for you.) "Hotspots," mentioned earlier, are just like links except that they are embedded within graphic displays. Hotspots perform an action when you click on them. Sometimes hotspots are small, or "thumbnail," versions of larger graphic images that you can download or view. Hotspots are often used as graphic menu items that take you to a different part of a site.

RIGHT-CLICKING THE MOUSE

In general, desktop software has gotten sophisticated enough that "right-clicking" the mouse should become a new habit. The right mouse button is often used now to provide additional information or access to additional functions on your desktop. Navigator 4.61 takes advantage of the right mouse button. By right-clicking on the links and images you encounter on Web pages, you have access to a wide range of functions concerning those items. As an example, go to the Netscape home page at (home.netscape.com). Right-click while your cursor is on any of the many links on the Netcenter page. A menu will display, as shown.

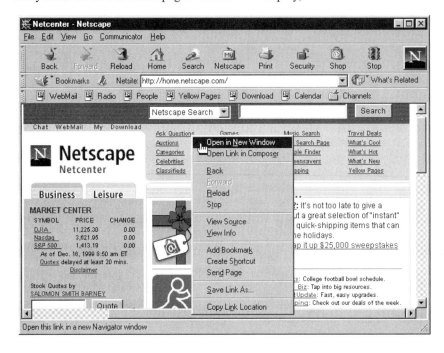

The "Back," "Forward," "Reload," and "Stop" commands on this menu work just like their counterpart buttons on the Navigation Toolbar. However, there are a number of other things you can do from this pop-up menu.

Open in New Window. This opens a new browser window that displays the document specified in the link. Your original window stays open.

Open Link in Composer. This opens the linked page in Netscape Composer so that you can modify the document contents.

View Source. Click here to see the HTML code for the current document.

View Info. Click here to view information about the current document, including the various graphic components and when it was created.

Add Bookmark. More about bookmarks later, but by clicking here you can add the link to your bookmark list without visiting the actual page. You can look at it later.

Create Shortcut. Similar to adding a bookmark, without having to visit the page, you can add an icon to your desktop that will link you directly to this page.

Send Page. When you click on this item, a New Message window appears so that you can address an e-mail to any recipient. The e-mail message will automatically include the currently displayed document as an attachment.

Copy Link Location. This copies the link to your Windows clipboard.

When you right-click on an image hotspot or a graphic, you will see many of the menu items listed above, plus a few similar ones that are more pertinent to image files.

MENU BAR

We've mentioned various "menu items" a number of times so far in our tour of Navigator 4.61. While the toolbars let you do most of what you need to do to simply browse the Web, there are a few specific menu items that may be helpful during your Web research. In this section we will briefly describe some of the most useful. (We will skip entirely the ones that are self-evident or that are familiar as standard computing functions.)

File Menu

New. Click here and you get a sub-menu which lets you open a new Navigator window, open the e-mail message composition window, or perform actions in Composer.

Open Page. This feature lets you type a URL or select a file using the "Choose File" button to display a page in the content area, either in the Navigator or Composer window. With this feature you can view HTML documents within your browser that are stored on your local hard drive or network.

Save (Frame) As. In the File Menu, one of the most useful functions is called "Save As." The "Save Frame As" feature does the same thing, except for an individual frame rather than a top-level page. Clicking here will open a standard window that lets you choose where on your hard drive or network to save the frame you are viewing. Simply specify the location where you want the document saved and then choose whether to save the document as an HTML file (for viewing in your browser at a future time) or as an ASCII text file. As you search the Web and find documents useful for your work, you'll find yourself making good use of this feature to save valuable documents to view offline later.

Send Page (or *Send Frame* if you are within a frame). This feature lets you create and send an e-mail message with the page you are currently viewing as an attachment. When you click on this feature, the message composition window is displayed with the current page's URL automatically inserted into the message area. You can add more text to the message. The window doesn't display the page you are sending, but the recipient will see your additional message followed by a display of the attached page.

Edit Page/Edit Frame. This feature lets you modify the underlying HTML source text that determines the page's/frame's content and display.

Edit Menu

Preferences. The Edit Menu contains the "Find in Page" (or "Find in Frame") utility already mentioned (don't forget the Control-F shortcut to this utility) and the "Search Internet" and "Search Directory" features, which take you to lists of different services to do those very things. Explore these at your leisure. In this brief overview, the only feature in the Edit Menu that needs emphasizing is the aforementioned "Preferences" feature. (In Navigator 3.0, "Preferences" was found under "Options.")

Preferences panels. Click on "Preferences" in the Edit Menu to display a dialog box containing a list of separate preference panels. There are seven main panels: Appearance, Navigator, Mail & Newsgroups, Roaming Access, Composer, Offline, and Advanced. These have additional sub-panels listed under them. Click on the plus sign ("+") next to these main category names to see the complete list of preference panels available. The default settings in most of these panels are just fine unless you want to customize Navigator, so we recommend experimenting with them at your leisure. However, there are a couple of panels you should be familiar with because they have a direct influence on the performance of your browsing and Internet e-mail functions.

Mail & Groups. E-mail is becoming more and more integrated with browser functioning and the Web pages you will be visiting. Underneath the Mail & Groups main preference panel are a number of sub-panels. Two of these sub-panels need to be filled out correctly for Internet e-mail to work for you as it should: "Identity" and "Mail Server." Click on the "Identity" sub-panel under Mail & Groups. Your e-mail address needs to be in the appropriate box. Next, click on the "Mail Server" sub-panel. Your e-mail account name (your e-mail address minus the @_____ part) needs to be in the "Mail server user name" box. There may already be a default called "mail" in the boxes for both "Outgoing mail (SMTP) Server" and "Incoming mail server." These won't necessarily work and you won't be able to send or receive Internet e-mail until you specify your own server names, which in most cases will be the same. You may need to know the exact name of the mail server used at your e-mail service provider, as well as the protocols it uses. Chances are it is using POP3 (Post Office Protocol, version 3). IMAP (Internet Message Access Protocol) is becoming more prevalent. If your service provider offers a choice between these two, choose IMAP. In this sub-panel you can elect to have your POP3 messages left on the server if that is allowed. That way you can retrieve them again later or access them from a different computer if you sometimes travel or work from home.

Advanced. The Advanced preference panel has three additional sub-panels, entitled "Cache," "Proxies," and "Disk Space." The Cache panel can possibly be of help to you in optimizing your computer for Web use.

Caching

Each time your computer has to connect to a remote server to pull down a Web page, you are entering the packet-switching maelstrom which is the Internet. Especially if the pages you wish to view have graphic elements or are large files for other reasons, you are competing with all the other file transfer traffic on the Internet. The concept of caching was developed to artificially improve the performance in this environment. With caching, the files that compose Web pages viewed recently within your browser window are stored on your local computer, either in memory or on your hard drive. If you revisit those pages, your browser first checks the remote server to see if the requested pages have changed at all since you last viewed them. If they haven't, the browser pulls the files down from the local source, thereby obviating the need to connect again to the remote server. Each page file pulled down from your own computer will be visible within your browser window faster than if it is sent anew over the Internet. (When you use the "Back" button or choose an item from its history list, Navigator does not check the network to see if the page has changed. It will automatically look to see if a cached version of the page is still available. Click the "Reload" button to make sure you are using the most recent version of a Web page.)

In the "Cache" sub-panel of the Advanced preferences panel you can increase or decrease the size of the memory cache and the disk (hard-drive) cache on your computer. Navigator retrieves a page from the memory cache more quickly than from the disk cache, but retrieving from the disk cache is still faster than retrieving a page from a remote server. Another difference: the memory cache is cleared each time you exit Communicator. The disk cache is maintained between sessions (and so takes up space on your hard drive). Click on "Cache" and you will see the following sub-panel.

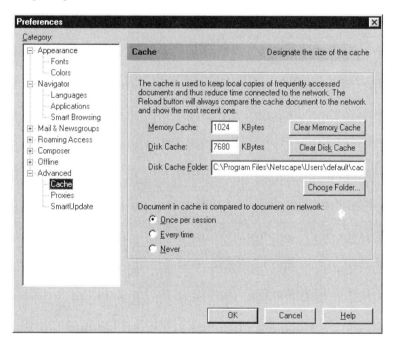

The default for the memory cache is probably set at 1024K. The default for the disk cache is probably set at 7680. These are simple to change; just type in new numbers. A larger cache may increase performance, although allocating too much space will constrict other applications. Netscape recommends increasing your memory cache conservatively, to whatever units of memory your system routinely doesn't use. Depending on the amount of space left unused on your hard drive, allocating more megabytes for the disk cache is less problematic. However, you may find that a large disk cache increases the time required to quit Communicator. If cache maintenance is causing noticeable delay when exiting the program, consider reducing the size of the disk cache.

View Menu

Items in the View Menu are mainly redundant with toolbar functioning or are self-evident. For the curious, however, clicking "Page Source" will display a window showing the current page in HTML format. This HTML source text includes all the commands used to create the content of the page as you see it. Clicking "Page Info" will display a window with details about the current page's structure and composition, including (if available) the title, location (URL), MIME type, source, local cache file, date of last modification, content length, expiration, character-set encoding, and security status. Pages with security features will also show the type of encryption used and certificate information. Is this more than you want to know? Probably.

Go Menu

The Go Menu contains the same "Back," "Forward," and "Home" commands readily available on the Navigation Toolbar. However, it has one other interesting feature: a history list slightly different than the one you can pull down from the Location Toolbar. Whereas that one showed only the URLs you had typed directly into the Location Box recently, the history list that is accessible from the Go Menu shows all the URLs you have used in your current session, whether you visited those pages by typing in the URLs or by clicking on links. For that reason, it may prove more useful to you. This list can be also accessed by right-clicking or clicking and holding the "Back" button on the Navigation Toolbar.

Communicator Menu

The Communicator Menu lets you access all the components of the Communicator suite. Assuming that, besides the Navigator browser itself, you most often will use the e-mail component that is available on the minimized Component Bar (in the status line at the bottom of the browser window), you won't need to use this menu very often. However, it does give access to yet another level of your Web-browsing history. Click on "History" on the Communicator Menu/Tools and you will see a window displayed like this one:

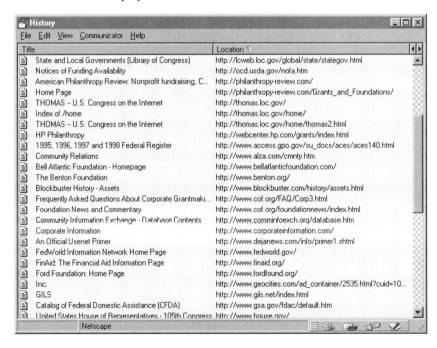

This history list contains all the URLs you have visited in the current as well as all earlier sessions, going back as many days as is indicated in the main Navigator preference panel (Remember that? Click on "Preferences" in the Edit Menu and then highlight "Navigator"). At the bottom of this panel you can set the number of days' activity that you want this comprehensive history list to remember for you. Or you can wipe out the entire list and start again by choosing the "Clear History" button.

BOOKMARKS

So far we have described three different places where Navigator 4.61 remembers Web pages you have visited recently. These various history lists can be very useful for the active user who becomes familiar with them. But perhaps one of the most useful features of Navigator is Bookmarks. This function lets you *selectively* store and then organize the history of your Web travels, remembering those sites you never want to forget until you choose to. The Bookmarks feature is available from the Communicator Menu, but it is so useful that Netscape put an icon for it (the Bookmarks QuickFile icon) right on the Location Toolbar, just to the left of the Location Box.

The Bookmarks feature offers an easy way to retrieve pages you want to visit over and over again. You store bookmarks in a list that's saved on your hard drive. Clicking on them sends the URL to your browser, which automatically goes out and retrieves that page. Try clicking on one of the default bookmark categories that Netscape includes with the initial installation of Navigator 4.61.

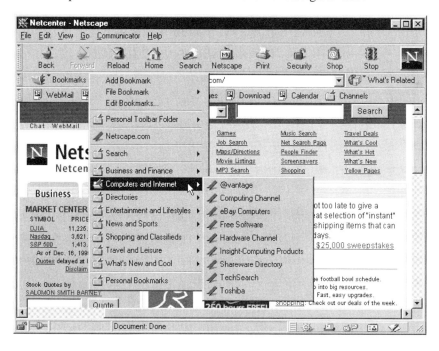

Simply put your cursor on one of these default categories and then click on one of the links appearing in the list of bookmarks displayed for that category. Navigator goes out and retrieves that page and places the URL associated with that bookmark into the Location Box on the Location Toolbar.

Adding Bookmarks to Your Lists

There are a number of ways to add bookmarks of your choosing to your list. You can click on the Bookmarks QuickFile icon on the Location Toolbar and then click "Add Bookmark" from the menu that appears. A name for the page you are viewing will be added to your list, identified behind the scenes with the appropriate URL. You can also right-click while your cursor is on the page you are viewing and choose the same "Add Bookmark" command in the menu that appears. You can also hit "Control-D" and the bookmark for the page you are viewing gets added to your list behind the scenes. It is important to note that when using any of these three methods, the new bookmark is simply added to the bottom of your list of bookmarks. This is fine when you have just a short list stored, but your list will get unwieldy very quickly when you start bookmarking all the good pages you find.

Filing Bookmarks

You can actually file your new bookmarks right when you first create them. When you find a page you will want to return to often, click on the Bookmarks QuickFile icon on the Location Toolbar and then put your cursor on "File Bookmark," rather than clicking on "Add Bookmark." Your list of bookmark categories will appear. Just select the category in which you want to put your new bookmark and it will be added to the bottom of the list within that specific category. You can perform this same operation in another way. When viewing a page you wish to bookmark, put your cursor on the Page icon just to the left of the Location Box on the Location Toolbar. (If you look closely the Page icon looks like an open book with a bookmark lying on it.) When you do this your cursor changes into a little hand. Now click and drag the Page icon to the Bookmark QuickFile icon directly to the left. The same list of bookmark categories will appear, and you can drag your cursor to the appropriate category and drop your new bookmark there. This method takes a little more dexterity, but with either of these two methods you can file a new bookmark in the appropriate place at the same time that you initially save it.

Note that if you file a bookmark in your Personal Toolbar Folder, that bookmark becomes an icon displayed on your Personal Toolbar whenever you have it activated.

Once you add a bookmark to your list, unlike the automatic history lists, it stays there until you remove it (or change lists). The permanence and accessibility of bookmarks make them a tremendous resource for customizing your Web-browsing experience.

Bookmark Window

Even if you file all your new bookmarks conscientiously when you first create them, pretty soon you will want to edit them even more, delete ones that weren't as valuable as you thought, rename them so that even your over-worked, multi-tasked brain can remember what they are—whatever rethinking is generated by your continued Web-browsing experience. When you feel the need to further refine your list of bookmarks, click on the Bookmark QuickFile icon and select "Edit Bookmarks." The Bookmark Window will appear in a slightly different format (see below). Once again we show the default list of bookmarks loaded with the initial installation of Netscape Navigator 4.61. You can see that Netscape thoughtfully included a Personal Bookmarks category at the very bottom of the bookmark list, so that even if you thoughtlessly add bookmarks without filing them, they will clutter up only your own catch-all category.

This Bookmark Window offers a full set of menu items to help you organize the list by creating your own hierarchical menus, different menu displays, even multiple bookmark files. You can drag and drop bookmark icons or use the menu items provided in the window to arrange the display of your bookmarks and folders. These menus work a lot like the standard Windows menus you see elsewhere, so we won't review their functioning. However, one very useful function again depends on that new habit, right-clicking.

Highlight a specific bookmark folder or an individual bookmark and right-click. A menu will appear that duplicates some of the menu functions available on the Bookmark Window's own menu. However, the last item on the list is called "Bookmark Properties." Click on this and you will come to the panel that lets you rename a bookmark or bookmark folder as well as type in a description of what it is. This proves a handy feature when that clever mnemonic device you chose as a bookmark name six months ago doesn't ring a bell.

The Bookmark Window is worth exploring and experimenting with as a way to enhance your research work on the World Wide Web. You can download additional software applications that soup up your bookmark editing capabilities, but the capabilities provided in Navigator itself will help you remember and locate again the most useful Web sites you find in the course of your browsing. By the way, if you decide to install IE5 in addition to Netscape, IE5 will copy your Netscape "bookmarks" into its listing of "favorites."

INTERNET EXPLORER 5

This software suite contains the following functions:

Internet Explorer 5.0 Browser (IE5)

The ability to subscribe to "channels" is integrated with the basic browser function. Through the "Settings" area on the "Start Menu" of the Windows 98 operating system, you will be able to choose the "active desktop," the more Web-integrated way of computing.

Outlook Express

This integrated mail program gives you access to Internet e-mail and newsgroups.

FrontPage Express

This is the Web-page authoring tool that is integrated into the Internet Explorer suite.

When you first click IE5 on your desktop, the Internet Explorer browser window opens as the default.

IE5 lets you customize your own "start" page, which you can then choose as your default. Or, as in Navigator, you can choose any Web page as your default, so that it appears automatically any time you launch the browser.

LAUNCHING INTERNET EXPLORER 5

Internet Explorer 5 has become a more common choice of browser as the benefits of its integration in the Windows desktop have become more evident. E-mailing, chatting, and receiving regularly updated streams of information have become basic elements of being a member of the online community. Microsoft has made all of these options only a few mouse clicks away when working in Explorer.

To open this program you can either double-click the Explorer icon on your desktop or hold your mouse down over your "Start" button and choose "Programs," the "Internet Explorer" folder and, finally, "Internet Explorer," the program. Your browser window will appear, initially with the Microsoft Web site open. One way to make your browser serve you best, is by setting your "start" page to a Web site of interest. Once you have become comfortable surfing the Web and have discovered a site that you would like to automatically open when you start your program, you can choose your home page. It is a simple process that introduces you to a helpful area—your "Internet Options."

First, open the Web page that you have selected as your start-up page. Then click on "Tools" at the top of your screen. Select "Internet Options" in the pull-down menu. Make sure the "General" tab appears to be raised. Then click the button that reads "Use Current." Make sure that the address appearing in the text box above is the one you mean to select. Then click "OK" to finalize the process.

"Internet Options" is now found in the Tools menu, a change from Internet Explorer 4.0 (IE4), which had it listed in the View menu. The Tools option has replaced the Go menu as the fifth listing on that toolbar.

TOOLBARS

There are four toolbars appearing at the top of IE5's browser among which you can select most actions you need to easily navigate the Web. Before explaining their uses, we will review how to arrange these toolbars to your liking. Most importantly, we will begin by going over how to display and hide the different toolbars. By right-clicking anywhere on the toolbar area you will pull up a short-cut menu. The check displayed next to the toolbar name determines that the toolbar will be displayed on the top of your window. If at any point you would like to hide a toolbar, remove the check by clicking on it, and when you want the toolbar to reappear, replace the check.

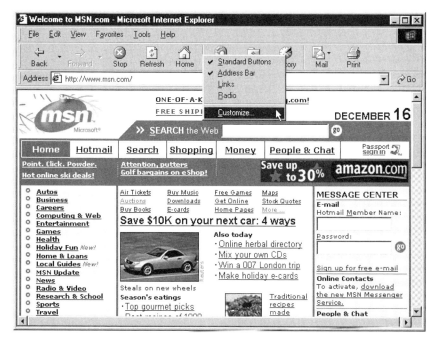

You also can customize the location of the different toolbars. Once you are familiar with their functions, you will be able to decide which you use the most and where you would like them to be placed. When you have determined this, the move itself is easy. Just put your mouse above the vertical line on the left of a toolbar. When the line changes to a horizontal double arrow, hold the mouse button down as you move the mouse and drag the toolbar to your preferred location. You may also use the "click and drag" technique by selecting the horizontal line separating the toolbars and the browser window to make the toolbar area smaller. If you choose the do this, the toolbar whose space is being eliminated will move and be placed to the right of the toolbar above it. It will be displayed by the name of the toolbar. The following introductions to the different toolbars will help you decide what order you prefer.

Address Bar

The Address Bar is Explorer's equivalent to Netscape's Location Toolbar—the long box into which you type your URL (Uniform Resource Locator) addresses. As described earlier, a URL is text used for identifying and addressing an item in a computer network. A URL provides location information, and Explorer displays it in the address field. When linking to a page from another site or a toolbar link, you don't need to type in the address—Explorer will automatically display it. You need to make sure that any address you do type in is accurate to the last character or the browser will not be able to locate the site you want. Once you become an old hand at entering addresses, stay alert as to what the first series of characters are, not all addresses begin with "www"!

When you want to enter a URL, use your mouse to click in the Address Bar text box. When the cursor appears type in the full address and press "Enter." An Explorer icon will appear when the browser has found a responding site. You may type in a new address at any point during an Internet session, regardless of what site you are on and how many links you followed to get there. As we continue, you will discover that there are many different ways to go to a new site and to return to a site you have visited.

Take a moment and click "Best of the Web" in the Links Bar and you will see how Explorer automatically places the new address in the text box as soon as the site has responded. This will occur when you follow a link on any Web site, when you select one of your Favorite sites (which we will discuss later), and when you want to return to a site that you recently visited but had left by following a link. To return to one of the most recent pages in your current session, you can click the "File" menu and select one of the last couple of pages you visited. This means that you don't have to worry about constantly writing down the addresses that appear when you link to a site you envision exploring later in your session. This is in addition to your ability to store your favorite sites for as long as you want and to access the addresses you have recently typed in manually by selecting the arrow at the end of the text box and choosing from the drop-down window.

This text box will also serve as a search tool. Enter a question mark, then a space, then the topic you want to search for and a list of hyperlinked results will appear in the window.

Explorer Bar

This is the toolbar that is used to navigate through Web sites and for page control. The following descriptions of these buttons' functions will provide you with the most basic ability to navigate the Web.

Back. Click on this button to display the page you were viewing just previously. Clicking on the triangle on the right side of the button, or right-clicking on it, will bring up the history list discussed earlier.

Forward. If you have used the "Back" button (or made use of the history list mentioned earlier), clicking this button will bring you to what you were viewing before. This button will appear gray (i.e., disabled) and will not respond to a click if you are starting a session or have returned to the most recently viewed page.

Stop. Clicking this button halts any ongoing transfer of information. It is often used to stop downloading a particular page that seems to be taking too long. Hint: clicking "Stop" and the "Refresh" can sometimes bring down the page you are seeking more quickly if you already have part of the page.

Refresh. Click this button to redisplay the current Explorer page, reflecting any changes made since the original loading. To refresh, Explorer checks the network server to see if any change to the page has occurred. If no change has occurred, the original page is retrieved from the cache (see more about caching earlier in this chapter). If there has been a change, the updated page is retrieved from the server.

Home. Click this button to display the home page that has been designated in "Internet Options" as your start-up page. If setting is "Default Page" then you will be sent to the Microsoft Network Web site (www.msn.com).

Search. Clicking this button will activate a Search Bar that will appear in the left side of your browser window. If you are searching for anything other than a Web site (addresses, phone numbers, etc.) make sure you click the appropriate radio button. Enter the topic you are searching for in the text box and click on the "Search" button. A list of hyperlinked search results will appear which you can scroll through and from which you can select a page.

Favorites. When you click this button a Favorites list will appear in the left half of your browser window with a list of the different folders that hold saved Web site addresses, both pre-set and the ones that you have compiled. You can click on any of folders to open them and then select a site to link to, or click on one of the sites that are listed when the bar first appears. Any title that follows an Explorer icon is a link. We will discuss later how to add pages into your Favorites Bar.

History. Selecting this button calls up a History list in the left side of the browser window. First you are able to select the time period in which you are interested. Once you choose a time frame—a week or a day—a list of the sites you went to then will appear. When you select a site, you will then see the pages that you visited within the site and you may click one of them to return to that page.

Mail. Click this button to go directly to your Outlook Mailbox and check your mail.

Print. Clicking this button will take you to a dialog box that lets you select printing characteristics.

Edit. This button allows you to edit the current Web page.

Discuss. Clicking this button will take you to a dialog box where you can set up a discussion server and have live chats with friends while surfing the Web.

You may choose which of these buttons you would like displayed and what order you want them to be placed by right-clicking on an empty spot on this toolbar. Select "Customize" from the menu that appears. You can click on any of the buttons in the "Current toolbar options" column and use the "Move up" or "Move down" box to change the order. You can also peruse the icons in the "Available toolbar buttons" column to add other common toolbar functions to your toolbar. When you click on "Close," your changes will be applied and you will immediately see the results.

Links Toolbar

This toolbar is not a collection of functionality keys, but a display of the various folders that contain saved Web addresses. The program comes with some potentially useful sites already categorized and suggested divisions of topics. Later on we will discuss how to save your own Favorites.

THE BROWSER WINDOW

Page Content Area

This is the primary window of the browser; it displays the content of the page whose URL is in the Address Bar, either entered manually or selected through a link. If the page is longer or wider than the window, there will be scroll bars displayed which allow you to move beyond the screen area. The title bar at the very top of the window shows the title of the open page. This does not necessarily mirror the address, but describes the content of the specific page you are viewing. As with Netscape Navigator, you can open multiple Explorer windows to view multiple pages of information. You might want to do this, for instance, if you are doing specific research and have found different Web sites that you wish to compare. You can open separate windows to look at them side by side. Also, if a page you are trying to load is for some reason loading very slowly, you can continue to surf while you wait for it to appear in its own window.

The amount of text on a Web site is often overwhelming, especially when you are looking for something very specific, but there is a way to locate the exact subject that you are looking for. Once again, similar to Navigator, you can search Web pages for particular words and phrases. You can click on "Edit" on the Menu Bar (not to be confused with the "Edit" button on the Explorer toolbar!) and then click on the "Find on This Page" menu item. This opens a "Find" dialog box that lets you type the string of characters you wish to find on the page you have opened. Within this dialog box you can choose to search up or down. You can also access this dialog box more directly: simply hit "Control-F" on your keyboard.

Status Bar

The bottom strip of the browser window makes up the Status bar. The far left-hand corner finds the text section. There is a small Explorer icon that is followed by text describing a page's location or just blank space when a page is fully loaded and the cursor is not on a link. When your cursor is above a link, usually either highlighted text, a directive icon or a hotspot, the address of that site will appear in this area. When you click a link or press Enter after typing in a URL in the Address Bar, a message will appear describing the status of the browser's attempt to load that page. It will tell you when it is looking for the site, when it has found it, and then follows the progress in loading all the different elements of the page. Finally, to your relief, the very important "Done" will appear and the page will be displayed.

Alongside the text, there is another bar that serves a similar function through a graphic. This shows you how far the browser is in its current operation. It shows how much of the page has been loaded through a growing bar, which fills the area when 100 percent of the operation had been completed.

If you are working offline (to be addressed later), there will be an icon specifying this in the progress bar. The next small spot displays a padlock when you are viewing a secure Web site. You want to make sure this icon is there before using your credit card or submitting confidential information.

The far right of the Status bar identifies in which Security Zone the page you are viewing is categorized. These categories—Internet, Local intranet, Trusted sites, and Restricted sites—can be set by you in the "Internet Option" under Tools in the Menu Bar, by selecting the "Security" tab.

LINKS AND IMAGES

When viewing a Web site through any browser, it is usually easy to identify a link to another page. Text is often underlined and a different color from the other words and images can illustrate the subject that they lead to. If you are not sure whether a link is present or not, just place your cursor above the questionable area. You will see the URL displayed in the Status bar if it is a link. If it is hyperlinked text, it will change colors. Text links will appear in a third color if you have already visited this site, although that doesn't stop you from using the link. You will also often be able to easily identify hotspots. These are links that produce graphic displays, often looking like smaller versions of what they lead to. You click these with the cursor, just like a link.

RIGHT-CLICKING THE MOUSE

There are often many more options available to a computer user than are displayed on the screen at any one moment. This is true with IE5. There are additional functions of the browser that can be accessed through various paths. Many of these are presented when a user right-clicks when visiting a Web site. Right-clicking is just what it sounds like—place the cursor on any element and press the right button of the mouse to discover your many options for that element. The following menu will appear when you right-click and the described options will appear:

Back, Forward, Print, and *Refresh* are all the same as the standard buttons of the same name.

Save Background As. This option will be grayed-out unless the selected element has a background image. If it does, then this allows you to save the image that the Web site you are on is using as its background. The Save dialog box will appear and you will need to direct the file into the directory you want it saved in and name the image.

Set as Wallpaper. This option is also frequently grayed-out, but will be available if you have selected a specific part of a page. This function allows you to choose anything and have that appear as the background on your computer screen.

Copy Background. This is the last option that is normally grayed-out. But, when it is available you will be able to copy the background of the selected page. This does not save the image in your computer, but just makes it available to be pasted where you want it.

Select All. This is the equivalent to the Select All option in a word processing system. When you pick this option from the menu, all of the different elements of the page you are on are selected and highlighted. This way you can copy or save everything that you are looking at without needing to highlight each thing separately.

Create Shortcut. This is an option you won't want to use often, but when you do choose to use it, it can be invaluable. When you select this, an icon will appear on your desktop, alongside your other programs, that will take you directly to the site you are visiting. When you use this desktop item, Internet Explorer will automatically start and take you directly to this page.

Add to Favorites. This allows you to add a Web site to your list of Favorites, which we will discuss in detail soon, with only a few clicks of the mouse.

View Source. Selecting this option will pull up a basic text screen of the HTML coding that instructs the browser on how to present the information inside it. This is helpful if you want to learn how a certain Web page, or part of a page, was designed so that you can emulate it. It also allows you to look at the raw text in case there is something wrong with the site and the text is illegible.

Encoding. Clicking this will allow you to change the alphabet that is displayed to one the you have selected as your primary alphabet. This means that your computer can apply your color, font, and size preferences to a Web site, although it can affect the layout. This will also allow you to view a Web site that offers another language alternative if you have selected that language in "Internet Options."

Properties. Finally, you can have important characteristics of the site that you are viewing displayed in a comprehensive manner.

If you have selected an image, your right-click menu will be slightly different, with a few additions specific to graphics or links.

MENU BAR

Another place to look for options that aren't obvious on the toolbars is in the different menus listed across the top of the browser window, below the three main toolbars. Many of the choices within these options are functions that we have already come across in different locations, but there are some interesting ones that are most easily found through these drop-down menus.

File Menu

New. This lets you open another window of IE5, so that you can use it in side-by-side situations, like those described earlier. You can also open new message and contact sheets from Outlook, if you would like to record something you have found on a Web site.

Open. You can open any Web site by entering its address in this box, but it is especially helpful when you want to view an HTML document that exists on your computer or your network by allowing you to browse your files.

Page Setup. This gives you an opportunity to set what a print copy of the page will look like. The dialog box is similar to page setup boxes in other programs.

Save As. This is how you can save a Web site to your hard drive so that you can look at it when you are offline. You are given an option within the Save As dialog box of how much of the site you want to save, which can save you memory.

Send. This option allows you to send a copy of a whole page or an element of a page to an e-mail address.

The recipient will know that the copy came from you, as it will come from your Outlook e-mail address.

Import and Export. This addition to the File Menu allows you to send or receive an HTML file to or from your Favorites folders. When you choose this option, you will enter the Import/Export Wizard. You will be able to follow the explicit instructions to make your Favorite folders into files that can be e-mailed as attachments or to take a folder that has been sent to you and place it directly into your Favorites.

Work Offline. Choosing this option allows you to view Web pages that you have downloaded without being connected to your ISP or the Internet.

Edit Menu

Find (on This Page). It is important to remember that this very helpful tool we discussed earlier can be found here.

View Menu

Status Bar. This allows you to remove and add the Status bar from the bottom of your browser window, just as we saw earlier that "Toolbars" does for the three toolbars on the top.

Explorer Bar. This is a second way of opening the different sidebars that are listed in the Explorer Bar, in case you have chosen to hide that toolbar.

Text Size and *Encoding.* Formerly "Font," the elements of the old option have been separated into their own topics. This is where you can set the size and alphabet that you prefer. You can then use the "Language" in the right-click menu to apply these choices to different Web sites.

Full Screen. Choosing this will expand the content window to fill your whole screen. The most essential options in the toolbar are changed into small icons along the top and many of the other features are not visible. To switch back to the original layout of Explorer, just click on the sizing icon in the upper right-hand corner.

Java Console. Only in the Advanced Internet Options in the last version of Explorer, it is now much easier to enable your computer to read Java script, a special coding language. Once you change this setting, you will have to reset your computer for it to be effected. This will allow you to view some very interesting and advanced Web sites.

Favorites Menu

It is finally time to address a major feature of Web browsers that we have repeatedly alluded to: the ability to store and organize an extensive collection of Web site addresses that you would like to store for easy retrieval. The Favorites Menu offers you functionality options, but also one touch access to your collection of preferred sites.

Add to Favorites. This is yet another quick and easy way to add a Web site to one of your Favorites folders. When you choose this option while at the desired Web site, a dialog box will appear. First, you need to think about how you are going to use this page. If you would like to be able to return to the page at the touch of the mouse, then you only need to choose a name for the site—although a default name will automatically appear—and then choose the folder you want to place it in by clicking the "Create in:" option. Your newest Favorite will automatically appear at the bottom of the list you have added it to. If you would like to look at the site offline, meaning that you would be able to look at what was currently on the site without being connected to the Internet, be sure to place a check in the box marked "Make available offline."

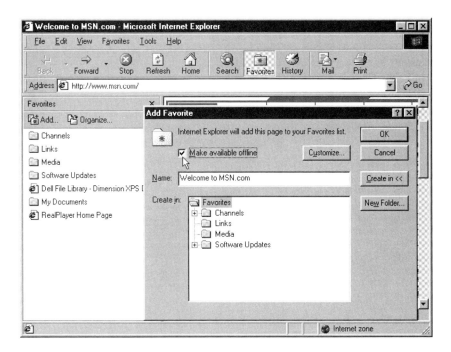

Note the folder "Links" in the Favorites folder. Items inside "Links" will appear on the Links toolbar, which we discussed earlier. If you want instant access to some sites, this is the best way to do it. But remember, a toolbar is only as wide as the window, and overloading it will cause some links to be not visible. Make sure that the items in this folder are really the ones you will be using frequently.

Organize Favorites. The dialog box that will appear when you select this topic has the four main functions on buttons in the middle: "Create Folder," "Move to Folder," "Rename," and "Delete." There is also a window that shows you all of your existing folders so that you can choose the folder you want to work with or be able to review existing titles. When you have ordered the folders and placed all of the pages, just click "Close" and your changes will be enacted.

Tools Menu

Mail and News. This option allows you to pull up other programs within the Explorer suite. By choosing "Mail" you will open your Outlook inbox. If the program is already open, then a second window will appear, as opposed to just pulling up the window of the inbox you already had opened. This is nothing to be concerned about, as anything you do in either window will immediately appear in the other. When you choose "News" you are given easy access to any newsgroups that you have subscribed to in Outlook Express. This is a simple process that you are guided through by the Internet Connection Wizard when you choose "Accounts" in the Tools Menu in that program. You are able to quickly access any updates since the last time you logged on.

Synchronize. An "Items to Synchronize" dialog box will appear when this is chosen. This gives you an opportunity of having your computer check and make sure that any data you have stored on your computer is current with data on your network. For your purposes, you will be able to use this to save Web sites and view them offline. When the box appears, click on the check box next to the name of the site that you would like updated or downloaded for the first time. Click "Synchronize" and watch the status box to see the progress of the download. When the box disappears, the action has been completed.

Windows Update. As we all know, the speed of development in technology is awesome and the advancements in the Explorer suite are on that rapid pace. This choice allows you easy access to the Microsoft web site's page with the newest version of Internet Explorer. Once you are on the page, you are only a few clicks away from having an updated version of the program installed on your machine. Be sure to read the small print carefully and pay attention to which programs you want updated. Be warned that a complete download of all the programs can now take over two hours, so plan accordingly.

Internet Options. We have referred to this dialog box in earlier discussions because of the many various and important options that can be found in it.

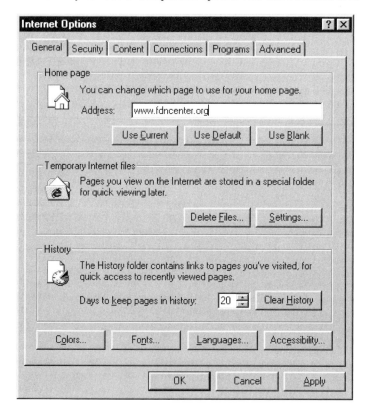

General. This tab, which will usually appear when you open "Internet Options," has options for some tasks that are automatically performed. As we mentioned earlier, this is where you set your start-up page and it is also where you are given the opportunity to delete the record of the Web sites you have visited.

Security. This tab has been significantly updated from the last version of Explorer. You can now specify different levels of security for sites in various categories. You choose a category by highlighting its image in the window along the top of the box. If you have had a bad experience in downloading a virus from a certain Web site or you have heard that other people have, you should highlight "Restricted sites" and click on "Sites." You can then add the URL of the page from which you want to be protected from downloading. Back on the main security page you can also adjust the level of security with the new slider created for this purpose. This will allow you to protect your computer from all sites on the Internet, or even on your intranet, while loading any you have designated as "Trusted Sites."

Content. This tab allows you to determine parameters for the content being downloaded onto your computer. By clicking "Enable" in the Content Advisor section, you will activate another dialog box. Here you can adjust what users are allowed to see with another slide. When you press "OK" the first time, you will need to create a Supervisor Password. You must have this password to adjust these levels in the future. Back on the main "Content" page you can also set how you would like to be identified when communicating from Explorer, and specify personal information that can be drawn from whenever, for example, you want to buy something with a credit card on the Web.

Connections. This tab you will find different options for connecting your computer to the Internet. If you normally connect through a network at work, but would like to connect by a modem at home, this is where you can change that setting.

Programs. Here you can choose what other programs you would like IE5 to call on when necessary. You can tell Explorer whether you use Outlook or Outlook Express for e-mail and what address book you use. This way you will be able to send e-mails when visiting a Web site (when you click on an e-mail address and a black message screen pops up) and easily add interesting finds into your contacts list.

Advanced. This tab brings a long list of options for how the browser should run. The default choices are often satisfactory, but once you are comfortable surfing, you might want to spend some time changing these settings. You might prefer that your browser open and fill the whole screen or that printing include background color and images. This is somewhere to experiment with what makes your searching most efficient.

Help Menu

Finally, you have the Help menu, which is similar to help options in most programs. You can request online help, essentially a user's manual. You can either look for your topic in the table of contents that immediately appears or use the "Search" tab to find your topic in the contents. You can also take the "Web Tutorial" which takes you step-by-step through some of the actions we have described. This is also where you want to look if you have forgotten what version you are using and need to know!

"A Browser Is a Browser"

Analogous features can be found in Netscape Navigator 4.61 and Internet Explorer 5.0 (IE5), confirming one pundit's general statement that "a browser is a browser." This is particularly true if you are doing specific Web-based research, instead of looking to be entertained or intrigued by evolving Web technology.

To get close to the information on the Web you find valuable for your work, using your browser of choice should become automatic, something you don't have to think about. The newer versions of the leading browsers come with a lot of functionality. This can appear daunting if you try to learn it all at once. The good news is that you can begin browsing the Web very quickly, without understanding all the capabilities right at the beginning. We hope that this admittedly selective tour of Navigator 4.61 and Internet Explorer 5.0 (IE5) helps you discover the wide world that awaits you on the Web.

CHAPTER TWO

A Guided Tour of the Foundation Center's Web Site

The Role of the Web Site in Fulfilling the Mission of the Foundation Center

The Foundation Center's mission is to foster public understanding of the foundation field by collecting, organizing, analyzing, and disseminating information on foundations, corporate giving, and related subjects for use by grantseekers, grantmakers, researchers, policymakers, the media, and the general public. The Center uses various media, increasingly electronic, to achieve its mission. The Center's Web site opens virtual doors to Foundation Center libraries for audiences not reached in the past, and makes foundation information more accessible to audiences already familiar with the Center.

Technology Used on the Center's Web Site

In order to reach the widest possible audience, the Foundation Center's Web site was designed for almost everyone, from high-level computer users to novices, including those using older, slower computer equipment. The file size of the home page is just 30 K, and major directory pages range from 40–42 K, allowing them to download quickly on most platforms. The site design uses frames only in locations where the technology can ease navigation and help to incorporate large volumes of information into the confined area of the computer screen. JavaScript is used to generate floating windows and graphical effects, and to enhance site navigation. And interactive features, such as specialized search engines, automatic listserv subscription forms, and secure ordering forms are used to expedite the delivery of information and goods to our visitors. While the site has been designed to accommodate as many visitors as possible, across as many computer platforms as possible, we recommend using the latest version of either Microsoft's Internet Explorer or Netscape's Communicator to browse the site.

An Overview of the Foundation Center's Web Site

First, go to the home page of the Foundation Center. In the location window of your browser, enter the URL (Uniform Resource Locator) or Web address (http://www.fdncenter.org) for the Center's Web site.

The Foundation Center's Web site greets you with an attractive and informative home page that will quickly guide you to the information you seek, living up to its tag line, "Your gateway to philanthropy on the World Wide Web." Links to the four main directories of the site—Grantmaker Information, Online Library, Marketplace, and About Us—and a link to the *Digest* (abbreviated from *Philanthropy New Digest)* are located just below our logo.

From the left side of the home page, you will find a link to answers to frequently asked questions entitled "FAQ"—a common Web feature which first-time visitors will find especially valuable, and a link to the "Site Map," an image map of the directory structure of the site that can deliver you directly to your destination when you click on the map's individual elements.

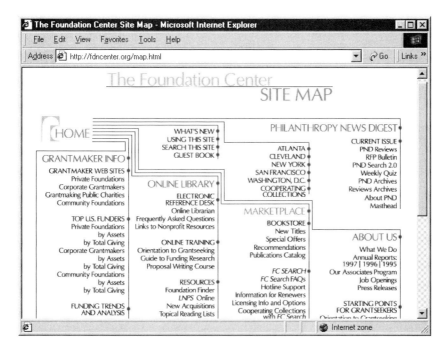

You will also find a link to the "Search Zone." The Search Zone provides access to all search mechanisms at the Center's Web site from one central location, along with recommendations for the best search to conduct in order to find the information you seek. In addition to providing visitors with the ability to search our entire Web site with the Sitewide Search, we have created a number of specialized searches to aid you in your research.

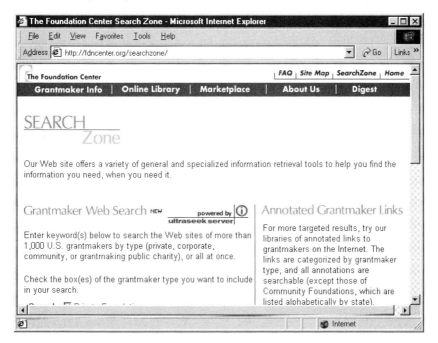

With our newest search feature, you can search grantmaker Web sites using an engine that has gone out and "spidered" a comprehensive list of grantmaker sites selected by the Foundation Center. When you use this tool you will be searching all the contents of just those sites, rather than the entire Web. Or, you can use a separate mechanism to search the text of our annotated links to those Web sites. If you use these indexes you perform a more controlled search guaranteed to bring you at least some results. The searchable annotations have been divided by grantmaker type (private foundations, corporate grantmakers, and grantmaking public charities) and written by staff who have personally visited each grantmaker Web site.

Also available are true searchable databases. Contact information and other basic information about a particular foundation can be found with Foundation Finder, a tool used by entering a foundation's name to start your search. More detailed information about the nation's largest foundations can be obtained by subscribing to *The Foundation Directory Online,* a searchable database offered by subscription. The link to *The Foundation Directory Online* will deliver you to a page where you can find out more information about the service, subscribe, or log in once you've subscribed.

Other search functions that can be accessed through the Search Zone include *PND* Search, which searches all back issues of *Philanthropy News Digest,* and a search of the Center's *Fact of the Day* archives.

From the left column of the home page, you also can link directly to customized home pages for each of the five Foundation Center field office libraries.

Click on the words "Did you know" to access a pop-up window with a fascinating fact about philanthropy which includes links to sites that expand on the topic covered. An archive of these facts, searchable by keyword or date, can be reached from the pop-up window.

The right column of the home page offers "news notes" about current features on the site and events and news from the Center, and an excerpt from a *Philanthropy News Digest* (*PND*) abstract. New items are posted here daily.

The center of the home page offers a window with "Quick Links" to the most interactive and frequently accessed features of the site: What's New, FAQ, Publications Catalog, Training and Seminars, Cooperating Collections, Foundation Finder, Top U.S. Funders, Foundation Profiles, Trends and Analysis, Foundation Folders, Online Library, Guide to Funding Research, Proposal Writing Course, Literature of the Nonprofit Sector, For Grantmakers, Job Corner, and RFP Bulletin.

If you have an immediate fundraising question, you can link directly from the bottom of the home page to the Online Librarian, 24 hours a day, seven days a week, and expect a response generally within two business days. And, if you are a first-time visitor to the site or have an observation to share with the Center's Web Services staff, click on Guest Book and fill out the interactive form.

The Web site's main directories are designed to aid grantseekers and grantmakers by providing specific tools and directed information according to the needs of each visitor. Clicking on the name of each directory on the top navigation bar will take you to the main page of that directory, which provides an index of links for the content within the directory.

On the main page of each directory, you will find a paragraph summarizing the overall content within, as well as direct links to the FAQ, Site Map, and Search Zone. The main navigation bar at the top of each directory page will take you to any of the other main directory pages, to the *Digest,* or back to the home page. The four main directory pages (as well as the individual library home pages) also offer the same Quick Links provided on the home page. In the deeper levels of the site, almost every page provides a common navigation bar to take you to the main directories, the *Digest,* the home page, the FAQ, the site map, or the site-wide search engine.

At the top of almost every page of the Center's Web site, a navigation bar will quickly deliver you to the main directories, the home page, site map, or search engine.

Let's briefly go through the four main areas of the Web site.

ABOUT US

It is the nature of the Web that there are no real beginning, middle, or end points, but About Us is a good place to start if you are new to the Foundation Center and its services. As its title suggests, the "What We Do" area found here provides basic information about the Foundation Center, its mission, and services. Within About Us you will find also annual reports for the past three years, contact information, and a complete description of the benefits and services offered by the Center's Associates Program, a membership program offered by the Center for a fee to professional grantseekers. And you will find listings of current job openings at the Center, recent press releases about new products or upcoming events, and a general FC Calendar of Events. There are also links to the Orientation to Grantseeking and the *User-Friendly Guide to Funding Research and Resources* (two key starting points for grantseekers), and to grantmaker services such as the Foundation Folders project (a service for grantmakers without a previous presence on the Web). You can also link to both fee-based and free training information, and to each of the individual library home pages.

About Us also provides information on the Center's "Electronic Grant-Reporting Initiative." Although it likely sounds intriguing to grantseekers and will ultimately benefit them, it is, in fact, a vehicle for grantmakers to report their grants to the Foundation Center electronically, to facilitate putting this information into the Center's publishing database. There is also a link to the Internet Edition of the *Grants Classification System Indexing Manual*, which details how the Center adds value to database information through its grants-indexing procedures.

You can also link directly from the left column to information about the Center's 200+ Cooperating Collections—public or special libraries holding the core set of Foundation Center publications in their collections. (You should be sure to find out if there is a Center Library or Cooperating Collection located near you.)

ONLINE LIBRARY

The Online Library holds a wealth of information for anyone new to the Foundation Center or the novice grantseeker. The Electronic Reference Desk, like the reference desk in an actual library, answers questions and refers visitors to specific

resources. The Electronic Reference Desk directs visitors to the answers of frequently asked questions about the Center and the grantseeking process, allows
visitors to ask questions of an Online Librarian via e-mail, and provides annotated
links to hundreds of Web sites providing nonprofit resources, categorized as they
would be if found in a Foundation Center Library.

Within the Online Library are two resources that new grantseekers will find particularly useful. These are the Orientation to Grantseeking and the Guide to
Funding Research, formally known as *The Foundation Center's User-Friendly
Guide to Funding Research and Resources.* The Orientation is a step-by-step
guide to the grantseeking process for true beginners to grantseeking and the
Internet. The Orientation is designed in a linear fashion to guide grantseekers
through each step of the process. For those who want to jump right into the fundraising process, the *User-Friendly Guide* is the Internet version of a book by the
same name. The online version has a hyperlinked table of contents and is presented in frames for quick navigation directly to the questions you need answered.
The entire guide can also be downloaded as one file for future reference. Both the
Orientation and the *User-Friendly Guide* offer an introduction to proposal writing, which is elaborated on in the Proposal Writing Short Course, also found in
the Online Library. A prospect worksheet, which can be printed and copied, is
available to keep track of potential funders as you progress with your research.

More experienced researchers will find the *Literature of the Nonprofit Sector*
(LNPS) Online a useful tool. The LNPS Online is a searchable database of the literature of philanthropy, incorporating the contents of the Center's five libraries. A
supplementary list of new acquisitions is updated on a bimonthly basis.

The Online Library also houses Topical Reading Lists, User Aids for specific
categories of individuals and nonprofits, the answer to a weekly reference question, an interactive news quiz (based on the current issue of *Philanthropy News
Digest*), and a series of common grant application forms.

Finally, the Online Library provides links directly to the home pages of the Center's five libraries and to information about Cooperating Collections—those
libraries throughout the country that make the core titles of the Center's collection
of reference products available to the public. The Collections are listed by state
and provide the name of the library, address, phone number, whether or not the
library has a copy of *FC Search: The Foundation Center's Database on CD-ROM*,
and whether or not the library holds private foundation information returns (IRS
Forms 990-PF) for their state and/or neighboring states. Links are provided to
Cooperating Collections that have Web sites.

GRANTMAKER INFORMATION

The Center's Grantmaker Information directory provides you with the most current and accessible information about grantmakers. This information takes several
forms and is based either upon information culled from grantmaker Web sites or
data collected from information reported by grantmakers to the IRS, through their
publications, or in response to questionnaires sent to them by the Center. The different presentations of grantmaker information accommodate different research
styles and different needs.

The first is our annotated links to grantmaker Web sites, which itself has a three-
tiered presentation—approximately 1,000 hot links, alphabetized links with annotations, and the ability to search annotated links by geography or subject keyword.

This link library can truly serve as "your gateway to philanthropy on the World Wide Web." Each grantmaker site is explored by Foundation Center staff, who then write annotations for each. Searches of our annotated links will provide you with a list of grantmakers whose Web sites might warrant a visit in the course of your research. These grantmakers are organized within four areas: private foundations, corporate grantmakers, grantmaking public charities, and community foundations. The first three categories offer searchable annotations, and the fourth, community foundations, is organized by state. Grantmaker Web site annotated links are updated at regular intervals and dated individually, providing you with a sense of how current the information is.

We also give you the ability to search grantmaker Web sites themselves. The Foundation Center has created a search application using software from InfoSeek that indexes only information gathered from grantmaker Web sites. Instead of trying to retrieve useful information from a search of the entire Web, we have programmed this software to search only the Web sites of grantmakers, thus significantly increasing your chances of finding the information you are looking for. You can search across all categories of grantmakers, or narrow your search to one category.

If you need information about a particular foundation, follow the link to Foundation Finder. This is a tool that allows you to look up basic information on a foundation by entering its name or a portion of its name. Foundation Finder holds information extracted from the Center's database of grantmakers, such as address, contact person, telephone number, e-mail address, fax number, hot-linked Web address (URL), basic financial information, and type of foundation. More than 50,000 foundations are listed in Foundation Finder. The Finder also provides an update form allowing foundations to correct any outdated or erroneous information in their entry.

The final presentation of grantmaker data is *The Foundation Directory Online,* a searchable database of the 10,000 largest U.S. foundations, available by subscription. This searchable, online version of *The Foundation Directory,* the definitive reference book for information on the largest foundations in the U.S. for nearly 40 years, allows searches across six separate fields of data to return targeted lists of funding prospects, as well as plain text searching. Searches return foundation profiles including address and contact information, Web site links, donors, fields of interest, types of support, officers and trustees, staff, financial information, and more. To make this resource accessible to a wide audience, *FD Online* is offered at a low monthly rate as well as a yearly subscription.

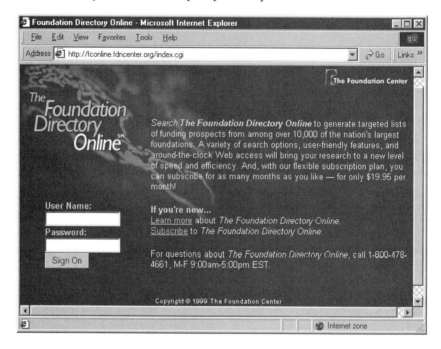

Grantmaker Information also links you to lists of the nation's top funders and to the Funding Trends and Analysis section of the site. If you are new to this sort of research, you may find this area instructive in becoming more familiar with the foundation world and giving trends. The Center lists the top U.S. funders by assets and total giving, using the most current audited financial information received from the foundations themselves.

Finally, in Grantmaker Information, you will find a description of the Center's Foundation Folder initiative. It is the Center's goal to encourage more foundations to develop a Web presence and to put more foundation information before a wider audience. Any domestic independent, community, or company-sponsored foundation can have a folder—that is, a virtual Web site—on the Center's Web server at no charge. The Foundation Center has created folders for more than 50 foundations, a few of which have used their folders as stepping stones to creating and maintaining Web sites of their own. Foundation Folders are included in our library of links to grantmaker Web sites.

The highlights and excerpts from Foundation Center publications provided in Funding Trends and Analysis will put some of this data into a useful context and give you some sense of how, why, and to whom foundations are giving grants. Adobe PDF files of selected research materials can be downloaded from this area of the site.

MARKETPLACE

In addition to operating libraries that provide directories of grantmaker information, nonprofit literature collections, and other tools to aid grantseekers, the Foundation Center publishes and sells books and CD-ROMs about foundations and fundraising.

The Marketplace directory offers the Center's Publications Catalog in its entirety, and revolving book titles are conveniently featured within New Titles, Special Offers, and Recommendations (for beginners, individuals, or international grantseekers). Grantseekers can read detailed descriptions about the Center's directories of grantmakers, grants, and subject areas of grantmaking, as well as descriptions of books about nonprofit management, fundraising, and philanthropy. The books in the catalog can be ordered online, using either an interactive form or a form that can be printed and then faxed or mailed. The catalog is updated three times a year, in conjunction with the Center's print catalog.

The Publications Catalog also offers information about ordering *FC Search: The Foundation Center's Database on CD-ROM, FC Scholar: The Foundation Center's Database of Education Funding for Individuals,* or subscribing to DIALOG, a service through which Foundation Center databases can be accessed on the Internet.

From the Marketplace main directory page, you can access the Electronic Resources area, which includes information on *FC Search, FC Scholar,* and *The Foundation Directory Online.*

You'll also find information on the Center's Fax-on-Demand service, available 24 hours a day, seven days a week, through which you can order profiles of the top 100 foundations included in the print work *The Foundation 1000.*

Finally, under Seminars and Training Registration you will find links to detailed information on the Center's fee-based seminars and training, which include Proposal Writing Seminars, *FC Search* training programs, *Grantseeking on the Web* training programs, and Meet the Grantmakers programs. Online registration is available for selected programs. In the left column of the Marketplace directory main page, you will find a link to Free Workshops, which include Grantseeking Basics, weekly introductions to library resources providing an overview of the funding research process; Beyond the Basics, a series of seminars for nonprofit grantseekers who are acquainted with the Center's resources and want to enhance their understanding of specific aspects of funding research; Electronic Resources Overview, a weekly introduction to the Center's electronic research tools; and other workshops on special topics.

PHILANTHROPY NEWS DIGEST

Philanthropy News Digest (PND) is a weekly online news service of the Foundation Center. You will find it by clicking "Digest" from almost any page on the site. *PND* is a compendium, in digest form, of philanthropy-related articles and features culled from print and electronic media outlets nationwide. The most recent issue of *PND* is posted to the Web site and delivered via e-mail every Tuesday evening.

The front page of each issue of *PND* features a quote of the week and lists news headlines. Clicking on a headline takes you to a page with one abstracted news story, as well as links to the other stories in the issue, PND Search, and the Front Page.

Besides keeping grantseekers and others abreast of the recent and significant developments in the world of philanthropy, the abstracts in *PND* are accompanied by FCNotes, information from the Center's database regarding grantmakers mentioned in each article. This is the most current information available and may not yet be published in print form.

From the left column of the *PND* Front Page, you can also link to PND Reviews—Off the Shelf (book reviews) and On the Web (Web site reviews); the RFP Bulletin, a listing by category of active grantmaker "requests for proposals," complete with posting dates and deadlines; the Weekly Quiz, an interactive test of what you've learned from *PND;* the Job Corner, which lists job openings at U.S. foundations; and the NPO Spotlight, which highlights the interests and activities of a different nonprofit each week.

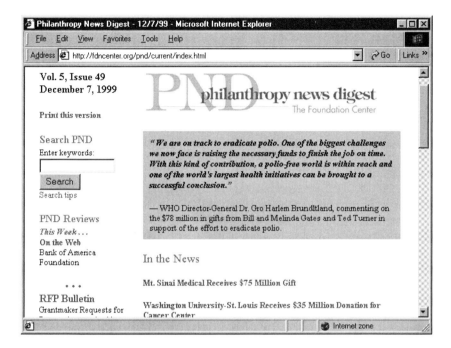

All issues of *PND* from January 1995 to the present are archived on the Web site, and can be viewed by going to the *PND* Archives and selecting the issue date. Past issues can also be searched by entering a keyword in the search form on *PND*'s Front Page. Results of your search will list the titles of abstracts, in date order, in which your search terms appear.

If you would like *PND* delivered to your e-mail box every Tuesday evening, just enter your e-mail address into the subscription box on the Front Page and click "Add me!"

Grantseeker Research Using the Center's Web Site

With its ever-growing sources of information the Web is an excellent place for you to begin your fundraising research. Once you are generally acquainted with the Foundation Center's Web site, you will want to explore the tools specifically designed to aid grantseekers with their research. Bear in mind that the Foundation Center is not going to find grants for you. However, the Web site will prove to be an invaluable resource in your research.

LEARNING THE PROCESS

A logical place to start your research on the Web is in our Online Library. The Online Library offers excellent guides to grantseeking and proposal writing, and it is the place to find answers to questions that will crop up as you proceed with your research. In the Online Library, you will also find a prospect worksheet and common grant application forms.

Online Orientation

For new grantseekers with little experience on the Web, the Online Orientation is the ideal resource. The Orientation to the Grantseeking Process introduces you to the process of seeking funding from private foundations step by step, as you will see if you choose this as a starting place. One of the most exciting aspects of the Web is its non-linear design, allowing you to see an interesting link and jump to it in an instant, within one Web site or among the myriad Web sites that exist. However, the somewhat chaotic nature of the Web can be overwhelming. Unlike other resources on the Web that offer a jumble of links to choose from, the Orientation is designed in a linear format with a clear beginning and end with links that guide you through it page by page.

From the home page, click on the Online Library tab. This will take you to the table of contents of that directory. From this page, you can view all that the Online Library comprises. You will find the link called Orientation to Grantseeking that will take you there. The Orientation will acquaint you with the following topics:

- What the Foundation Center is and the services we offer.
- What a foundation is, and how foundations typically operate.
- Three approaches to funding research.
- Who gets foundation grants.
- What funders look for in a grantee.
- What types of support grantmakers typically give.
- How to establish a nonprofit organization.
- How to find support available to individuals.
- Effective tools for funding research.
- Hints on proposal writing.

After a general introduction, the Orientation follows two main paths: grant-seeking for individuals and grantseeking for nonprofit organizations. Within those paths, it branches further into specific tools, skills, and topics of interest. The Orientation provides several resources for further research on the Internet, but the bulk of its listings for additional resources are printed materials. Other areas of the Web site, which we discuss later in this chapter, have extensive lists of links to Internet resources.

The Foundation Center's User-Friendly Guide to
Funding Research and Resources

If you are familiar with the Web and the grantseeking process or have completed the Center's orientation, the Internet edition of *The Foundation Center's User-Friendly Guide to Funding Research and Resources* is a good refresher and reference as you conduct your research. Click on the link "Guide to Funding Research" in the Online Library. The *User-Friendly Guide* contains much of the same information as the Orientation but offers it in more standard Web format. From its table of contents and navigation frames, you can choose just the subjects you want to review and jump around if you like, without going through the material in linear fashion.

The *User-Friendly Guide* also has a glossary of common terms you will likely encounter in your research. You might want to print it out or bookmark it in your browser. As you conduct your research on the Web, it is a good idea to bookmark pages that you think you will return to again. If you are using Netscape, you will find the heading Bookmarks at the top of the screen; if you are using Internet Explorer, you will find the heading Favorites. When you find a page you'd like to bookmark, click on Bookmarks/Favorites and then select Add Bookmark/Add to Favorites from the pull-down menu.

In the table of contents of the *User-Friendly Guide*, you will see that you can print or save to your computer a single text file of the entire *Guide*. If you don't have regular access to a computer, you may want to consider printing the file for future reference.

Electronic Reference Desk

Although you will find a wealth of information about the grantseeking process in the Orientation and the *User-Friendly Guide,* you will certainly have additional questions. And if you don't have questions now, you are likely to once you have begun your research. At that time you will want to go to the Electronic Reference Desk in the Online Library. Here you will find the answers to frequently asked questions—FAQ, in Web parlance. If you have gone through the FAQ and still don't have an answer, you can pose your question to the Online Librarian by e-mail. There are links to the Online Librarian from the home page, the Online Library, and other strategic locations throughout the Web site. The Online Librarian will respond to your question usually within 48 hours.

Philanthropy News Digest (PND)

While you are conducting your grantseeking research, read the Center's online newsletter weekly, or have it e-mailed to you every Tuesday. *PND* will keep you abreast of major developments in philanthropy, and provide you with information that will help you with your research. *PND* will also alert you to new requests for proposals posted in the RFP Bulletin. If you would like more information about a potential funder, you might search the *PND* archives for any past news items on that funder.

GETTING TO WORK

Now that you know what you need to do to begin researching and applying for grants to fund your project, the Web is a good place to start your research. However, since there are many foundations and grantmakers without a presence on the World Wide Web, assume that you will also have to explore some of the printed directories and CD-ROMs the Center and other organizations publish about fundraising. The fundraising research you will conduct on the Web primarily will involve exploring the Web sites of grantmakers.

The Foundation Center has incorporated into its broader mission the collection of information about grantmakers' Web sites. Because the information on the Web is not organized, you could easily spend a great deal of time just finding out whether or not various grantmakers have Web sites at all. The Center has done this legwork for you by providing links to virtually every grantmaker with a Web presence. But the Center's Web site does not just provide you with blind links. The grantmaker Websites are organized by type of grantmaker. Each Web site has been individually explored and annotated, and those annotations can be searched by subject or geographic keyword (a keyword is a descriptive term, e.g. "health" or "Southeast," entered into a search program).

Before beginning your research, you should become familiar with the Prospect Worksheet found within the Online Library.

Prospect Worksheet

This is a simple form to print out and copy before starting your research. It will help keep your research organized and focused. As you locate funders whose priorities closely match your project, fill out a prospect worksheet for each funder. The prospect worksheet will help you match the properties and needs of your project with the properties and interests of funders. Use this simple tool to record financial data; subject focus; geographic limits; types of support; populations served; foundation officers, donors, trustees, and staff; application information; sources from which you gathered information about the foundation; notes; and follow-up communications.

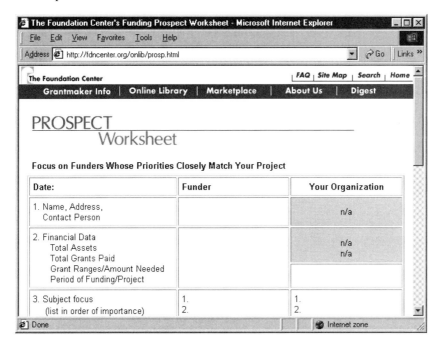

Grantmaker Information

With your prospect worksheet in hand, click on Grantmaker Information (a link provided at the top of almost every page on the site, including the Prospect Worksheet itself). Start with grantmaker Websites. The links to grantmaker Web sites fall into four categories: private foundations, corporate grantmakers, grantmaking public charities, and community foundations. (You can select "no-frames" versions of the first three to assist your navigation if you have a browser that doesn't support frames.)

The directories for the Web sites of private foundations, corporate grantmakers, and grantmaking public charities are organized in a similar fashion. The main page for each of these directories contains a list of hot links, a program to search the annotations, links to keyword lists to help you focus your search, and links to the alphabetized annotated links.

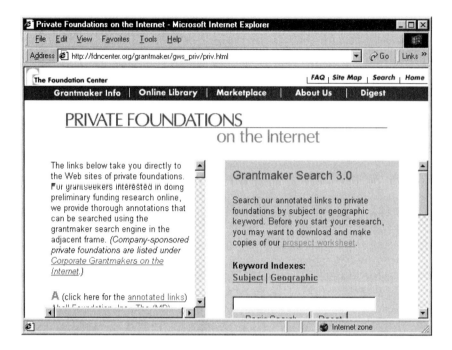

There are three ways to use these directories. If you are familiar with a grantmaker and would like to go directly to the grantmaker's Web site, the list on the left side of the screen provides direct links to those grantmakers' Web sites. If you have heard of a grantmaker, but would like some preliminary information before visiting its Web site, find the grantmaker in the list on the left side of the screen. Instead of selecting the name of the grantmaker, select "annotated links" for the letter of the alphabet under which the grantmaker falls. You will find a list of grantmakers, links to their Web sites, and descriptions of what you will find at each Web site.

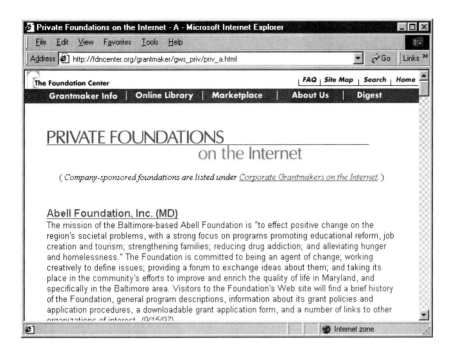

If you are looking for funders focusing in a particular subject area or geographic location, you will find the Grantmaker Search the most helpful. Go to the right side of the screen. In the box enter a word or words that describe the type of project you are trying to fund, or enter the geographic location of the project. To make your search more successful, click on Subject or Geographic to retrieve the lists of known words the search engine will find. Find the word or words that fit your project and enter them in the box. Now click Begin Search. You will receive a list of grantmakers for which the Center has annotated links. When you click on a grantmaker name in the search results list, you will find a description of the grantmaker and its Web site. There will also be a link to that Web site. The Grantmaker Search searches only one directory of grantmakers (private, corporate, or public) at a time. Grantmakers are broken into these categories to provide more information about them and how they operate—private foundations operate quite differently than corporate grantmakers—and this will help grantseekers to better understand prospective funders.

The directory for community foundations is not searchable in the same fashion; rather, the foundations are organized by state. You should be able to identify easily those foundations in your geographic location.

You may also want to search the actual Web sites of foundations using our search engine programmed to index sites the Foundation Center has identifies as those of legitimate grantmakers. This automated spider crawls Web sites we've instructed it to visit, so that your search will return results only from Web sites related to the research you are conducting. Since this will likely return broader results than the previous search method, you may need to narrow your search terms when using this engine.

For the greatest number of results, use broad search terms and conduct your search across all grantmaker categories. To narrow your search, use more specific search terms and select one category of grantmaker within which to conduct your search.

Both of these search mechanisms will provide you with a list of grantmakers on the Web that are possible funders for you, although a final determination about that will likely require additional research.

To compile a more comprehensive and targeted list of potential funders, you might consider subscribing to *The Foundation Directory Online*, our searchable database of the nation's 10,000 largest foundations. Offered at a reasonable price to ensure broad accessibility to this service, *The Foundation Directory Online* allows searching across six categories of data extracted from the Foundation Center's database.

FD Online searches return foundation profiles including address and contact information, Web site links, donors, fields of interest, types of support, officers and trustees, staff, financial information, and more.

When visiting the grantmaker Web sites your search returned in the first two search methods, or reading the records in *FD Online*, you will look for the following things:

Does the grantmaker fund projects similar to yours? Most Web sites state explicitly the sort of projects that are funded, or if the foundation gives grants at all. Go through the Web site thoroughly to get a sense of its mission, founders, and history.

Does the Web site offer a listing of grants that have been awarded? If such a list is not apparent, see if the grantmaker has posted its annual report on the Web site. Often annual reports will contain grants lists. Some Web sites provide links to the Web sites of their grantees. Exploring these Web sites will also provide you with additional information about the kinds of projects and organizations funded by the grantmaker.

Does the grantmaker accept applications? Some grantmakers consider projects by invitation only.

What are the application guidelines? This area, provided on most grantmaker Web sites, will tell you in the clearest terms whether or not a project such as yours would be considered for funding. The application guidelines will provide you with application procedures and deadlines, and whether you should apply directly or first send a letter of inquiry. Some grantmaker Web sites have application forms, which you can download or print from the screen. A few will allow you to apply online.

Look through the annual report. If there is one available, it should contain financial data on the Grantmaker.

Look for funding restrictions. These are usually stated explicitly, often in the application guidelines.

Locate the contact information for the grantmaker. Note the correct address, phone number, and e-mail address. Before you contact a grantmaker, become familiar with that grantmaker's application guidelines. Some accept e-mail inquiries and online applications, but the majority will require that you send a formal letter or proposal by post.

Find out the names of officers, trustees, and staff. If this information is available, when you contact the grantmaker you will be able to address your inquiry to the correct person, not the foundation at large.

Note: As mentioned earlier, it is important to try to ascertain how recently the information was posted to the Web site. If the information is vague or not dated, you will need to confirm the information you have gathered from another source or directly from the grantmaker.

Fill out a prospect worksheet for each grantmaker Web site you visit. You will have concrete results from your research on the Web, and you will know what information you must find from other sources.

Links to Nonprofit Resources

To complement our links to grantmaker Web sites, the Center has a great many links—also annotated—to other nonprofit resources. Links to Nonprofit Resources is located in the Online Library. You may want to look through sites listed here for information from organizations doing work related to philanthropy or the Internet, or for nonprofit organizations with projects similar to yours. You will find scores of links in the following categories:

- General Resources (Business & Industry, the Internet, Library Links, Policy Institutes, and Reference)
- Nonprofit Resources, General
- Nonprofit Resources, by Program Area
- International Resources
- Philanthropy Resources
- Nonprofit Management Resources
- Nonprofit Fundraising Resources
- Government Resources

Other Valuable Online Resources

If you are searching for quick contact information for a particular foundation, you can access the Foundation Finder from the Quick Links on the Center's home page, or from the Online Library directory page. The Foundation Finder is a free look-up tool that allows users to search for a foundation by name (or partial name), further narrowing by city or state, and then receive the address, phone number, contact information, and basic financial information for that grantmaker.

If you are searching for a particular book or publication, enter the *Literature of the Nonprofit Sector* (LNPS) Online. This is a searchable database of the literature of philanthropy, incorporating the unique contents of the Center's five libraries, containing tens of thousands of full bibliographic citations, many of which have descriptive abstracts. It is updated on a regular basis.

To further assist you in your research, there are New Acquisitions lists—including books, articles, and other resources recently added to LNPS Online. You'll also find Topical Reading Lists—annotated bibliographies in the areas of Fundraising Ethics, State and Local Funding Directories, and Working in Nonprofits. And finally, you can access the Center's User Aids—created by Center librarians to guide visitors (individuals or nonprofit organizations) with particular interests (e.g., artists, students, job seekers) to use effectively the resources in the Center's library collection.

Foundation Center Resources

If you need to conduct more research to complete your fundraising search, whether to fill in gaps of information about grantmakers, or to locate information about grantmakers who haven't yet developed a Web presence, the Center's Web site has yet more information for you. Using Quick Links from the home page or a main directory page, or directly from the site map, go to Cooperating Collections. Here you can find out if there is a Cooperating Collection nearby where you can continue your research. As you may recall, Cooperating Collections are libraries that house the core collection of Foundation Center publications as well as *FC Search: The Foundation Center's Database on CD-ROM* and *FC Scholar: The Foundation Center's Database of Education Funding for Individuals.* So, our materials may be available to you even if you do not have access to one of the Center-operated libraries located in New York, Washington, D.C., Atlanta, Cleveland, or San Francisco.

If you are not near a library or Cooperating Collection, or if you are a professional grantseeker, you may want to purchase Center publications or our CD-ROMs to continue your research. Or you can log onto the Center's Web site and subscribe to *The Foundation Directory Online.* To review detailed descriptions of titles published by the Foundation Center, go to the Publications Catalog in the Marketplace directory. As mentioned earlier, you can order all Foundation Center publications—including CD-ROMs—online.

If you live in the geographical region where a Foundation Center field office library is located, you may want to visit that library's own home page to find out about library hours, local services, and upcoming events, including training seminars and workshops. At these five field office libraries, the Foundation Center offers educational programs on the fundraising process, proposal writing, grantmakers and their giving, and related topics.

The individual home pages of Center-operated libraries can be accessed from the Center's home page, the Online Library, and About Us.

FINISHING THE JOB

Once your research is complete, and you've identified grantmakers to whom you would like to apply for your grant, you will begin the process of writing your proposal. The Center's Web site will guide you through this process.

A Proposal Writing Short Course

Both the Online Orientation and the *User-Friendly Guide* will give you an overview of the key elements of proposal writing, but the Center's Web site also has a Proposal Writing Short Course, which will give you more detailed instruction in writing a proposal. You will find links to this tutorial from the home page, the Online Library, the Orientation, and the *User-Friendly Guide.* Use this tutorial to get you through what can be a daunting process, and consider bookmarking it so that you can refer to it each time you have to write a new proposal. Remember: even though far more time should be spent developing your program or project and researching and cultivating appropriate funders than on actual proposal preparation, you do want to approach the proposal process with care.

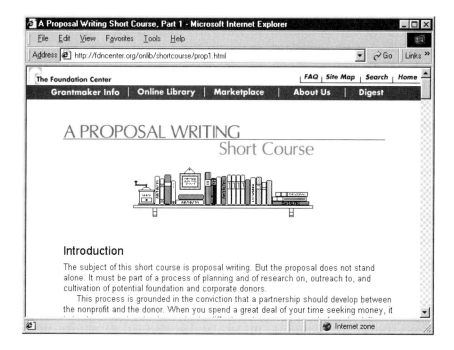

Common Grant Application Forms

The common grant application format has been adopted by groups of grantmakers to allow grant applicants to produce a single proposal for a specific community of funders, thereby saving time. Before applying to any funder that accepts a common grant application form, be sure to check that your project matches the funder's stated interests, and ascertain whether the funder would prefer a letter of inquiry in advance of receiving a proposal. Also be sure to check whether the funder has a deadline for proposals, as well as whether it requires multiple copies of your proposal.

Links to the following common grant applications and guidelines are available in the Online Library:

- Associated Grantmakers of Massachusetts (hosted by AGM)
- Association of Baltimore Area Grantmakers
- Connecticut Council for Philanthropy (CT) (hosted by CCP)
- Council of Michigan Foundations (hosted by CMF)
- Delaware Valley Grantmakers (PA) (hosted by DVG)
- Grantmakers of Western Pennsylvania (hosted by Carnegie Mellon University)
- Minnesota Common Grant Application Form (hosted by MCF)
- National Network of Grantmakers (hosted by NNG)
- New York/New Jersey Area Common Application Form (hosted by NYRAG)
- Rochester Grantmakers Forum
- Washington Regional Association of Grantmakers (hosted by WRAG)
- Wisconsin Common Application Form (hosted by Marquette University)

Conclusion

The Foundation Center's Web site, like the Foundation Center itself, is a multiple-door gateway to the foundations and other grantmakers who share your interest in a common cause. You should leave the Center's Web site closer to your goal of finding the funds you seek to carry out your work. The Center's site also, through its information resources and organized Web link libraries, will inform a variety of audiences about the philanthropic field generally. In addition, with an ever-increasing number of interactive features, the Foundation Center's Web site is being conceived as a communication system for the field of philanthropy. Before you leave the Center's Web site, remember to bookmark the pages you will likely return to the next time you visit. And please sign our Guest Book and share your impressions of the Foundation Center's Web site and its many features and functions.

CHAPTER THREE

Independent Foundations on the Web

With $330 billion in combined assets and total annual giving in excess of $15 billion, the 44,000-plus independent foundations in the United States comprise a national resource of considerable importance. Freed from constraints imposed by shareholders and the bottom line, foundations are able—and, historically, have demonstrated a willingness—to fund new, innovative, and sometimes controversial approaches to a range of seemingly intractable problems, from soaring population growth and endemic disease in the developing world to drug addiction and homelessness in our own backyard.

But foundations can also be insular and cautious in their approach to change. As Michael Porter and Mark Kramer, writing in the *Harvard Business Review* ("Philanthropy's New Agenda: Creating Value," Nov.–Dec. 1999), note: "Whether foundations are fulfilling their potential…is an open question. Not enough foundations think strategically about how they can create the most value with society at their disposal. Little effort is devoted to measuring results. On the contrary, foundations often consider measuring performance to be unrelated to their charitable mission."

As society stands on the threshold of an era that promises rapid, discontinuous change, Porter, Kramer, and others argue that foundations must rethink the way they go about their business or risk becoming irrelevant.

Perhaps nowhere is this more true than in the areas of communications and information technology. Driven by unprecedented rates of adoption and relentless innovation, the Internet and World Wide Web have in a few short years transformed the financial markets, retailing, the gathering and distribution of news, the distribution of hardware and software, and business-to-business commerce. Even more profound changes lie ahead. Education, health care, politics, work, warfare—in the next 20 years, all will be transformed virtually beyond recognition by information technologies and the digital revolution.

The prospect is at once exhilarating and sobering. As Zoe Baird, president of the Markle Foundation (http://www.markle.org/) wrote in July 1999, a year after assuming leadership of the New York City-based foundation: "[W]e are now entering a time in which new commercial, cultural, social, and institutional norms will begin to be established for the long term. This is a period of definition for the communications industry and its influence on society at large. The decisions made today will have lasting impact."

The increasing commercialization of the Internet—which was spawned by the public sector and whose early growth was nurtured by government and academia—is of particular concern to Baird. Radio and television, she reminds us, serve as cautionary tales about what can happen to promising communications media— and society's expectations for them—when market forces and entrepreneurial energy alone are allowed to shape a new mass medium. In both cases, writes Baird, experimentation and innovation were squeezed out once profitable business models had been identified by for-profit entities. Unfortunately, as a new century dawns the odds of the Internet escaping the fate of its predecessors seem to grow longer with each passing month.

In response to this challenge, Baird and the Markle Foundation announced a five-year, $100 million initiative in the summer of 1999 aimed at ensuring that public needs would continue to be served by emerging communications media and information technologies. At the same time, the foundation unveiled four new areas of funding—Public Engagement through Interactive Technologies, Policy for a Networked Society, Interactive Media for Children, and Information Technologies for Better Health; announced the creation of an Opportunity Fund to support public interest initiatives that fall outside these areas; and signaled its intent to partner with a range of nonprofit, academic, and commercial entities in order to leverage its financial contributions in these areas over the next few years.

The announcement of Markle's new direction was widely applauded and, half a year later, continues to generate positive coverage in the mainstream media. The reason, one suspects, is because it was so unusual. While the Markle Foundation's interest in communications media goes back 30 years, foundations in general have been slow to formulate a coherent response to the rapidly changing communications landscape of the 1990s or to integrate new information technologies into their work. One need only look as far as the World Wide Web, where 70 percent of the 100 largest foundations and roughly 400 of the more than 50,000 independent foundations in the United States have a Web site or "presence"—and only a handful of these accept proposals or applications online—to see that the field lags the rest of society.

In the next few pages, we'll take a look at Web development and practice, foundation-style, particularly as it relates to the subject of this book, grantseeking on the Web. Our survey isn't meant to be comprehensive, nor is it completely objective. The Foundation Center launched its Web site in December 1994, and the biases we've adopted since then concerning Web site design, performance, and usability occasionally make an appearance in the pages and annotations that follow. Our intent, however, is to inform rather than criticize, while at the same time highlighting practices and trends that seem to hold promise for foundations, the nonprofit sector, and society in general.

Foundations on the Web: From Information to Engagement

In terms of design, Web sites can be placed on a "generational" continuum, a concept originated by David Siegel, creator of the High Five excellence-in-Web-design awards (http://www.highfive.com/) and influential author of *Creating Killer Web Sites* (Indianapolis: Hayden Books). At one end of the scale, says Siegel, are "first-generation" sites, which were designed in the Web's early days for text-only terminals, black-and-white monitors, and low-resolution color displays. First-generation sites are characterized by long lines of unbroken text, default background and hyperlink colors, the liberal use of standard HTML elements such as bulleted lists and horizontal rules, and a hierarchical information architecture. In a first-generation site, form follows function.

Second-generation sites, which began to appear in the spring of 1995 shortly after Netscape Communications announced a set of extensions to HTML (most notably the [table] tag and its offspring), are basically first-generation sites with more color, graphical elements (navigation bars, icons, buttons, pictures, etc.), and a greater reliance on technology. In the best second-generation sites, form is elevated to the same level as function and the user experience is enhanced as a result.

Third-generation sites use metaphor and well-executed graphic design to attract and guide visitors through the site. As Siegel puts it, "Third-generation sites form a complete experience—the more you explore, the more the entire picture of the site comes together. Third-generation design turns a site from a menu into a meal."

Siegel developed his ideas about site design in 1995–1996, long before e-commerce began to drive Web site development in new directions. Today, e-commerce and fourth-generation sites are all the rage, though out of the reach of most organizations and businesses. While still stylish and pleasing to the eye, fourth-generation sites add a layer of technology that provides, among other things, database integration, on-the-fly page generation, transactional and streaming multimedia capabilities, and, increasingly, personalization.

One of the more endearing aspects of the Web, however, is its democratic nature. Examples of each type of site abound and are rarely more than a click or two away from the site you happen to be visiting at the moment. It's as if the Web were a freeway, crowded with vehicles of every shape and size, from energy-efficient subcompacts to SUVs with the latest bells and whistles. For businesses and, to a lesser extent, nonprofits and foundations, the question is, Can we avoid the freeway and still get where we want to go? And if we're already on the freeway, at what point do we trade in the Honda for a Suburban?

The Foundation Center has been helping foundations answers those questions through its Foundation Folder program since 1998. From the beginning, the program has had two goals: to provide private, community, and company-sponsored foundations with an immediate, low-cost presence on the Web and, in the process, help them become familiar with some of the issues surrounding the rapid evolution of communications technologies and media; and to put more information about foundations in front of a wider audience by making that information available on the World Wide Web.

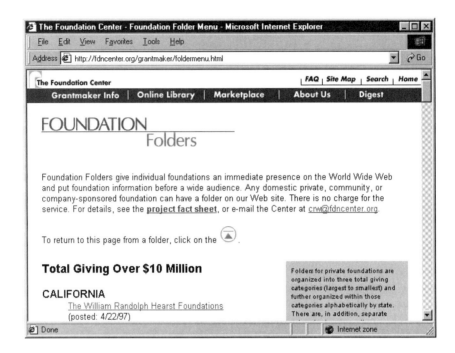

The service enables eligible grantmakers (more than 50 as of December 1999) to post public information materials (mission statements, program descriptions, application guidelines, grants lists, financial statements, contact information, and the like) to a "folder" in the Grantmaker Information area of the Center's Web site (http://www.fdncenter.org/grantmaker/). Once a grantmaker in the program decides to establish a more permanent presence on the Web (typically, under its own unique domain name—for example, http://www.myfoundation.org/), its folder on the Center's site is "retired" and a link to and description of the new site is added to the appropriate section (e.g., Private Foundations on the Net) of the Grantmaker Information directory.

Folders come in all shapes and sizes, from one-page fact sheets—see the folders for the van Ameringen Foundation (http://fdncenter.org/grantmaker/vanameringen/) or the Scholarships Foundation (http://fdncenter.org/grantmaker/scholarships/), both based in New York City—to fairly elaborate, multi-tiered mini-sites. Examples of the latter include the folders for the St. Paul-based Otto Bremer Foundation (http://fdncenter.org/grantmaker/bremer/), the New York City-based William T. Grant Foundation (http://fdncenter.org/grantmaker/wtgrant/), and the Chicago-based Retirement Research Foundation (http://fdncenter.org/grantmaker/rrf/).

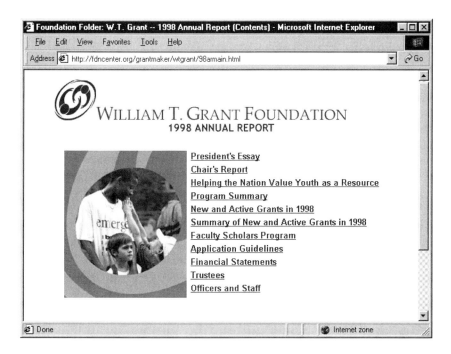

But whether a folder comprises a single page or an entire annual report, the end result is the same: the informational materials "in" the folder can be viewed by anyone, anywhere, who has Internet access and a Web browser. The reality of this fact presents foundations—especially smaller foundations—with a host of challenges, and is likely to profoundly reshape the way most foundations communicate with their constituencies in the next decade. At a minimum, posting public information materials to the Web ensures that those materials can be found and indexed by Web-based search engines. The search engines, in turn, retrieve that information (with varying degrees of effectiveness) whenever it's requested. As the information in a folder is disseminated in ever wider circles, the chances of other individuals and organizations finding and creating links to it increases. (The Foundation Center Online, for instance, offers links to thousands of Web sites and resources, and at last count was linked to by more than 10,000 individual Web sites.) In the final analysis, it's the very simple but powerful hyperlinking capabilities of the medium that enables webs of common interest to be created – and, ultimately, drives the exponential growth of the Web itself.

As the numbers indicate, most foundations aren't ready to become a node in a web—or on the Web, for that matter. And their reasons for staying on the fence usually boil down to resources, or the lack thereof (Web sites can be expensive to build and maintain), and/or apprehension about being exposed to a broader audience. For foundations that have taken the plunge, on the other hand, the Web is the future. And their responses to it, in terms of design, are as intriguingly diverse as the field itself.

At the first-generation end of the spectrum, for example, you'll find the Andrew W. Mellon Foundation (http://www.mellon.org/) and the Annenberg Foundation. The New York City-based Mellon Foundation, one of the largest private foundations in the country, was created in 1969 by the merger of two smaller foundations established in the 1940s by Paul Mellon and Ailsa Mellon Bruce, son and daughter of Andrew W. Mellon, the formidable American financier and patron of the arts. The Foundation's broadly stated purpose is to "aid and promote such religious, charitable, scientific, literary, and educational purposes as may be in the furtherance of the public welfare or tend to promote the well-doing or well-being of mankind." Its austere Web site offers a selection of public-information materials (mission statement, program descriptions and reports, abridged versions of recent annual reports, basic contact information) and a handful of links to other sites. While there's a good deal of information on the site of interest to grantseekers, anyone hoping to find a grants list or the foundation's application guidelines will be disappointed.

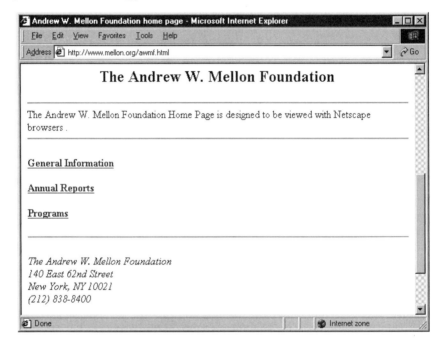

Although fashioned from the same first-generation HTML as the Mellon site, the Annenberg Foundation (http://www.whannenberg.org/) Web site clearly reflects the St. Davids, Pennsylvania-based foundation's willingness to engage grantseekers more directly. The foundation, which was established in 1989 by the publisher (*TV Guide, Seventeen*) and philanthropist Walter H. Annenberg and is best known for its $500 million K–12 Challenge Grant program, has awarded challenge grants to reform-minded school districts, local governments, and/or nonprofit stakeholders in more than a dozen cities, including Atlanta, Baltimore, Boston, Chattanooga, Chicago, Detroit, Houston, Los Angeles, Miami, New York, Philadelphia, Salt Lake City, and San Francisco. With that much money at stake, it's no surprise that one of the goals of the program is to replicate successful school reform programs throughout the country. One way of doing that, as the Annenberg site demonstrates, is to use the Internet's hyperlinking capabilities to connect people in dispersed locations to different ideas and experiences by creating links to other sites—in this case, Web sites created by stakeholders in the various challenge grant locations.

The Annenberg Foundation also operates programs in math and science learning and communications policy studies, and here again it uses its Web site to make its processes more transparent to grantseekers. In addition to posting proposal guidelines, an explanation of its review procedures, and a short list of sample grants at its site, the foundation accepts brief inquiries electronically at a general e-mail box.

In the last year or two, a good many foundations have traded in their first-generation sites for more appealing second-generation sites. Examples of stellar second-generation Web design abound. One of the better examples in the field belongs to the New York City-based Rockefeller Brothers Fund (RBF).

The RBF site (http://www.rbf.org/) incorporates many of the hallmarks of good second-generation design—the judicious use of icons, thumbnail photos, and graphical headers; a "Web-safe" color palette; consistent navigational elements; and a well-thought-out, hierarchical architecture—with a layer of basic interactivity to provide a satisfying, information-rich experience for grantseekers and others. Because a major objective of the Fund is to improve the well-being of all people through the support of efforts that contribute to the transition to global interdependence, the site also is offered in a fast-loading text-only version that minimizes download times and access costs for international users with slow and/ or expensive phone connections.

Grantseekers who visit the RBF site can access a wealth of information, all logically organized and conveniently linked to relevant information located elsewhere on the site. In addition to comprehensive descriptions of Fund programs and strategies (Sustainable Resource Use, Global Security, the Nonprofit Sector, Education, Health, Arts and Culture, New York City, South Africa, and a special Asian Projects fund), the site offers lists of recent grants awarded in each program area, application guidelines, a well-organized set of links to dozens of other sites, and a list of RBF publications available free of charge via a publications order form and, in many cases, as downloadable PDF files.

Grantseekers can see another fine example of second-generation design at the Web site of the John D. and Catherine T. MacArthur Foundation (http://www.macfnd.org/), the Chicago-based foundation known for its MacArthur Fellows Program (the so-called "genius grants"). The Foundation makes grants through two major programs, Human and Community Development and Global Security and Sustainability, and two special programs—the General Program, which undertakes special initiatives and supports projects that promote excellence and diversity in media, and the Fellows Program. Underlying all its programs and policies, however, are several assumptions, one of which is that its effectiveness depends on its capacity to learn from others, including its grantees.

The extent to which this assumption is embraced is underscored by the MacArthur Web site, which melds functional, low-tech design with a service-oriented approach to the Foundation's audiences. Everything about the site—from its flat architecture to its use of Web-safe colors and global navigation elements—is designed to make it easy for grantseekers and other visitors to browse and find the information they're looking for. Of particular interest is the way prime real estate on the home page is used to provide shortcuts to program information, grant deadlines, and information about special grant competitions. And the grouping of links to recent grants lists, program guidelines, and application instructions on most second-level pages only reinforces the idea that, as far as its Web site is concerned, the Foundation is committed to transparency and ease of use.

As 1999 ended, third-generation foundation Web sites were still rare, although their number was on the rise. During the course of the year, large philanthropies such as the Ford Foundation (htttp://www.fordfound.org/), the United Nations Foundation (http://www.unfoundation.org/), and the Open Society

Institute (http://www.soros.org/) unveiled meticulously designed, database-driven third-generation sites. It also was interesting to watch the steady increase in the number of small and medium-sized foundations that were able to leverage modest new media budgets into excellent examples of third-generation site design.

Among these were the Santa Monica, California-based Durfee Foundation (http://www.durfee.org/), whose areas of interest include arts and culture, education, history, and community development, primarily in Southern California; and the Russell Sage Foundation (http://www.russellsage.org/), a New York City-based operating foundation with interests in the future of work, immigration, the social psychology of cultural contact, the 2000 census, and literacy among disadvantaged students (a joint project with the Andrew W. Mellon Foundation).

The Durfee Foundation site combines a muted, Web-safe palette with elegant graphic headers and eye-catching thumbnail graphics. The site is proof that superior Web design can be achieved, albeit on a modest scale, if you are clear at the outset about the goals for the site.

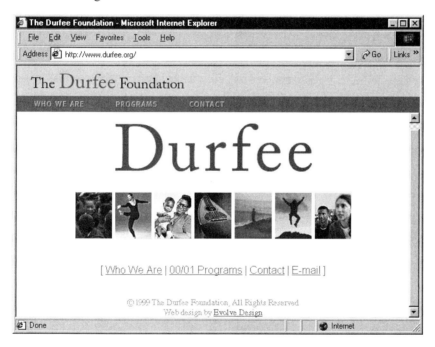

Grants Information on the Web

A number of foundations list some or all of their recent grants on their site. For example, information about grantees of the Seattle-based Bullitt Foundation (http://www.bullitt.org/) can be accessed by alphabetical listing, service area, program priority area, or issue. Grantee profiles include a description of the grantee organization and grant, address, and contact information including phone and fax numbers, email addresses, and URLs.

Several foundations offer grants information through searchable databases accessible directly from their sites. Two examples of searchable online grant databases can be found at the Web sites of the W.K. Kellogg Foundation (http://www.wkkf.org/) and the Graham Foundation for Advanced Studies in the Fine Arts (http://www.grahamfoundation.org/).

The Kellogg Foundation states clearly the goals for their Web site in general: "The purpose of this site is to inform potential grantees and others about the Kellogg Foundation's mission and current programming interests and to communicate and disseminate lessons learned, to people worldwide who share similar interests and concerns and might benefit from the Foundation's knowledge and experience."

The Chicago-based Graham Foundation for Advanced Studies in the Fine Arts (http://www.grahamfoundation.org/) states that it receives approximately 500 applications for support each year, of which about 100 receive awards. Until now, a list of annual grantees was available only in print. The Foundation also states clearly their goals for their new searchable grants feature: "We have put this data online in a searchable form because we intend these abstracts to be utilitarian data rather than only historical records. We seek to inform an interested audience; to connect authors and publishers; to associate like-minded scholars; to inform potential participants about contemplated symposia or exhibitions; and, to remind exhibitors and institutions of creative and experimental work that is underway."

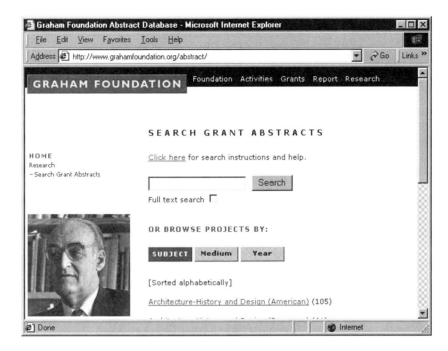

The Ford Foundation (http://www.fordfound.org/), the Charles Stewart Mott Foundation (http://www.mott.org), and the Pew Charitable Trusts (http://www.pewtrusts.com) are other good examples of foundations that offer searchable grants databases on their sites.

Portals, Content Aggregators, and Information-Rich Sites

A number of foundations have developed Web sites that go beyond presenting information only about their own programs. In the field of health care, for example, the Robert Wood Johnson Foundation (http://www.rwjf.org/), the Henry J. Kaiser Family Foundation (http://www.kff.org/), located in Menlo Park, California, and the New York City-based Charles A. Dana Foundation (http://www.dana.org/) use their sites to inform people about the issues addressed by their programs. For example, the Dana Foundation offers extensive information about programs, activities and foundation publications, "as well as material of interest to anyone concerned about brain disorders and about innovative reforms that strengthen early education." The Dana BrainWeb is a directory of links to 4 web sites in 23 categories related to brain disease and disorder; complementary links are added quarterly.

In a another presentation, the Baltimore-based Annie E. Casey Foundation (http://www.aecf.org/) site provides a range of interactive features. The KidsCount interactive database provides profiles, graphs (state indicators graphed over time), maps, rankings, and raw data as Excel or comma-delimited files. The "Family to Family" initiative offers tools for rebuilding foster care, including a one-page fact sheet, multi-page summary, full implementation guide (requires registration), and related links, as well as an online publications order form. Visitors can also access information on a range of other Casey Foundation initiatives—Casey Family Services, Juvenile Detention Alternatives, Mental Health Initiative for Urban Children, Education reform, Jobs Initiative, State and Local Systems Reform, Rebuilding Communities, Neighborhood Transformation/Family Development, Reforming City-Level Systems, Baltimore, Assessing the New Federalism.

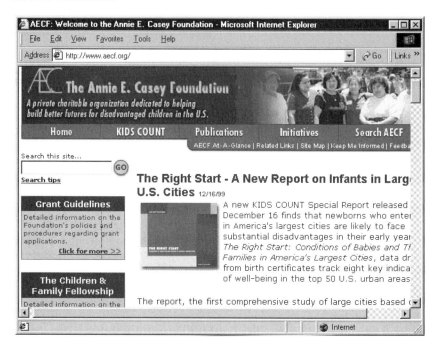

The entire site of the Washington, D.C.-based Benton Foundation (http://www.benton.org/) is designed to connect people to the information and resources they need to make a difference in their communities and to use information technologies more effectively. Their programs include Communications Policy + Practice; Connect for Kids; Open Studio: The Arts Online (a partnership with the National Endowment for the Arts; Destination Democracy; Sound Partners for Community Health; "Casting the Net: Creative Fundraising for Communications technology"; and "The Digital Divide and the US Hispanic Population."

The Gill Foundation (http://gillfoundation.org/), in Denver, Colorado, takes information provision a step further by providing sample grant proposals in three formats (HTML, PDF, MS Word). The site also provides grantwriting workshop handouts (sponsored by the Gay and Lesbian Fund for Colorado); sample policy documents concerning Employment Non-Discrimination Policy, Non-Piracy Software Policy, and Fiscal Sponsorship. The OutGiving area of the site provides organizational audit tools for NPOs, a sample corporate sponsorship package, and a list of 25 ideas for publicity about corporate sponsorship.

The Application Process Online

A number of foundations have in fact taken the plunge and begun using their sites to enable the application process. The Grant Program of the J. Paul Getty Trust (http://www.getty.edu/grant/view2.html#con) makes available online download-able copies of its application forms for Postdoctoral Fellowships (12 pages), Col-laborative Research grants (6 pages), and Curatorial Research fellowships (4 pages).

The California Endowment (http://www.calendow.org/), in Woodland Hills, California, offers an applicant cover sheet and a sample budget format in PDF for-mat, online forms for ordering publications (including their annual report), and a mechanism for sending feedback.

The Edward E. Ford Foundation (http://www.eeford.org/), in Washington, D.C., offers a password-protected area on its site to facilitate the proposal process, stat-ing that "Schools and Associations which have secured a place on an Agenda for consideration by the Board of the Foundation will be issued a password to be entered below to access specific directions and necessary forms for submitting a proposal."

The Livermore, California-based Fannie and John Hertz Foundation (http://www.hertzfndn.org/) offers interactive an application form through Embrak.com's WebApps service/tool, stating that, "Applications are normally submitted in electronic form via the Internet. Paper application materials for those lacking Internet access may be obtained (without prejudice) from the Foundation by telephonic request."

Foundation for the Future (http://www.futurefoundation.org/), in Bellevue, Washington, makes a preliminary interactive application form available at its site. Another Washington-based grantmaker, the Brainerd Foundation (http://www.brainerd.org/) is dedicated to "protecting the environment of the Pacific Northwest." Their site offers information "about how [the Foundation] supports grassroots-oriented projects in WA, OR, ID, MT, AK, BC, and the Yukon." The site offers lots of information, some interactive forms, an online Opportunity Fund Grant Application Form, and their searchable grants database was recently under construction.

The purpose of the Frank Stanley Beveridge Foundation (http://www.bever-idge.org/) Web site is designed specifically "...to determine if your organization is eligible to receive grants from the Foundation." It presents information under the headings About, Funding Cycle, Funder's Biography, Purpose, Officers and Directors, Recent Grants, Guidelines, and Limitations. The site also includes a privacy statement and asks potential grantees for for their "types of support inter-est." It contains a self-administered survey, Determining Eligibility, which leads to the Preliminary Grants Proposal form, which if approved will be followed by a printed Grant Proposal Abstract and Grant Proposal Guidelines. A Geographic Focus section asks you to indicate state in which your organization is located. If the Foundation doesn't fund in your state, you get a message to that effect.

All of the above are but examples of the foundation Web sites that go beyond offering the most basic information about the foundations themselves. A number growing of foundations have begun using the Web to facilitate and organize their relationships with grantees and potential grantees.

Online Funding Research

Going directly to individual foundation Web sites is most useful if you have already identified them as potential funders of your work. In order to facilitate your online funding research, the Grantmaker Information Directory of the Foundation Center's Web site offers links to and annotations of hundreds of grantmaker Web sites, divided into three searchable categories: private independent foundations, grantmaking public charities, and corporate grantmakers. (See, Chapter 2 for a thorough description of all our Web site features. The list of links and abstracts for those grantmaker sites are included in this and following chapters.) The grantmaker search engine in the Grantmaker Information directory allows you to search the annotations in a specific grantmaker category by subject and geographic keyword, making it possible for you to assemble a list of grantmakers on the Web that may be able to address your specific funding needs. (Using the lists of index terms presented will guarantee you at least some results, as these index lists were compiled in consistent fashion during our review of grantmaker sites.) Remember, however, that even though the Center's Grantmaker Information directory represents the most complete listing of foundations on the Web, it is restricted to those funders with some sort of Web presence—some 1,000 grantmakers of the many thousands currently tracked by the Foundation Center. In other words, unlike the information in the Center's database-driven print directories, the *FC Search* CD-ROM, and *The Foundation Directory Online*, the comprehensiveness of the annotations in our Grantmaker Information directory depends solely on the availability and breadth of the online resources themselves. As more foundations join the online community, the Center will continue to expand its list of searchable site annotations.

The same proviso should be taken into account when using the Foundation Spider available in the Search Zone of the Center's Web site. The accuracy and usefulness of your results depend on what terms or phrases you search for, and how your search strategy works in relation to the information on the Web sites created by individual grantmakers.

This brief introduction to the world of foundations to be found on the Web is designed to show you the various types of sites you are likely to find. We invite you to explore the full range of grantmaker sites available using the various search tools offered at the Foundation Center's Web site, or by following your own knowledge and instincts. The complete list of independent foundation Web sites and their annotations—that is, complete at the time of this writing—follows, organized in alphabetical order.

Links to and Abstracts of Private Foundations on the Web

Listed below, in alphabetical order, are links to and annotations of the independent private foundations on the Web at the time of publication. Check our Grantmaker Information directory (fdncenter.org/gratmaker/priv.html) for the most up-to-date listing.

Abell Foundation, Inc. (MD) (http://www.abell.org/)

The mission of the Baltimore-based Abell Foundation is "to effect positive change on the region's societal problems, with a strong focus on programs promoting educational reform, job creation and tourism; strengthening families; reducing drug addiction; and alleviating hunger and homelessness." The Foundation is committed to being an agent of change; working creatively to define issues; providing a forum to exchange ideas about them; and taking its place in the community's efforts to improve and enrich the quality of life in Maryland, and specifically in the Baltimore area. Funding falls within three areas: economic development, education, and health and human services. Visitors to the Foundation's Web site will find a brief history of the Foundation, general program descriptions, information about its grant policies and application procedures, a downloadable grant application form, a number of links to other organizations of interest, publications and contact info. In addition to grantmaking, the Foundation has a venture fund through which they invest in companies located in Baltimore.

Achelis Foundation (NY) (http://fdncenter.org/grantmaker/achelis/)

Established in 1940 by Elisabeth Achelis, a native of Brooklyn Heights and a founder of the World Calendar Association, the Achelis Foundation today concentrates its grantmaking in the greater New York City area. Areas of foundation interest include youth, rehabilitation, biomedical research, child welfare, science education, major cultural institutions, health and hospitals, social services, alcohol and drug abuse, father absence and responsible fatherhood, and education (including charter schools, public school reform, and parental school choice). Other interests include literacy, volunteerism, homelessness, entrepreneurship and economic development, environment (science education and land conservation), welfare reform, and job training with employment in the private business sector. Visitors to the Foundation's "folder" on the Center's Web site will find a brief history of the New York City-based Foundation; a statement from Foundation president John N. Irwin III; application guidelines and procedures; recent grants lists; a listing of the Foundation's trustees, officers, and staff; and contact information.

The J.A. & Kathryn Albertson Foundation (ID) (http://www.jkaf.org)

Established in 1966 by Joe Albertson and his wife Kathryn, this family foundation based in Boise, Idaho is committed to "fostering the improvement of education in Idaho through the promotion of research, experimentation, and innovation in an educational environment." Funding is focused in five areas: student learning, teaching excellence, preparation and advancement of educational practitioners, performance of educational systems, and early childhood education. In addition to grantmaking, the Foundation has a Center for Educational Excellence committed to the professional development needs of educators and to the promotion of the field of education in Idaho. Points of interest on their Web site include a description of their grantmaking approach; grant guidelines and instructions; a calendar of and contact information for the Center for Educational Excellence events; downloadable publications (newsletters, brochures, and annual reports); an electronic free publications request form; general contact information; and links to related sites. Online event registration for the Foundation's events and activities is currently under construction.

Alcoholic Beverage Medical Research Foundation (MD) (Operating foundation) (http://www.abmrf.org)

The Alcoholic Beverage Medical Research Foundation (ABMRF) states that it "fundamentally exists to improve the quality of people's lives at home and in the workplace" through financial support of innovative biomedical, behavioral and social science research on alcohol consumption and abuse prevention. Headquartered in Baltimore, Maryland, the Foundation was first established in 1969 as the Medical Advisory Group under the administrative auspices of The Johns Hopkins University School of Medicine to provide independent medical advice on the health effects of alcoholic beverages to members of the Beer Institute. It merged in 1982 with a parallel group in Canada to become ABMRF, the largest, independent, nonprofit foundation in North America supporting research on the effects of alcohol on behavior, health, and prevention of alcohol-related problems. Primary research interests include: factors influencing the transition from moderate to excessive use of alcohol; effects of moderate use of alcohol on health and behavior; mechanisms underlying the biomedical effects of alcohol; and alcohol and youth, traffic accidents and work-related issues. Lower priority areas for support are treatment research and complications of advanced alcoholism. Web site contains highlights of ABMRF-funded research, grant information and guidelines, a downloadable grant application and guidelines, abstracts of The ABMRF Journal, annual reports, summaries of recent conferences, highlights of grantee publications in various journals, a list of publications supported in part by ABMRF, contact information, and related links. The site also contains short professional bios of each member of the Foundation's management and board of trustees, and of each member of the Foundation's two advisory boards, which review grant applications and advise the Foundation of research.

Paul G. Allen Charitable Foundation (WA) (http://www.paulallen.com/foundations/)

The purpose of the Bellevue, Washington-based Paul G. Allen Charitable Foundation is to "improve the quality of life in the Pacific Northwest through programs designed to create new opportunities for community service." To that end, the Foundation funds projects in whole or in part in the areas of education, environmental research, youth services, social services, and aid to the disabled and disadvantaged. Ordinarily, the Foundation does not consider grant requests for operating, administrative or overhead expenses; for contributions to general fund drives, annual appeals or federated campaigns; for the benefit of specific individuals; for conduit organizations; to institutions "whose policy or practice unfairly discriminates against race, ethnic origin, sex, creed or sexual orientation"; to sectarian or religious organizations; or to organizations currently funded by any other Paul G. Allen foundation. In addition to a fair amount of biographical information about Microsoft co-founder Allen, "The Wired World of Paul Allen" Web site provides examples of recent grants and projects supported by the Foundation, grant application guidelines, a description of the application process, a downloadable application form, and links to Allen's other charitable organizations.

Paul G. Allen Foundation for Medical Research (WA) (http://www.paulallen.com/foundations/)

The purpose of the Bellevue, Washington-based Paul G. Allen Foundation for Medical Research is to "promote innovative medical research in a variety of fields, including biochemistry, biomedical engineering, virology, immunology, cell and molecular biology, pharmacology and genetics." Projects that "develop new insights into the prevention or successful treatment of cancer" are of special interest. Ordinarily, the Foundation does not consider grant requests for operating, administrative or overhead expenses; for contributions to general fund drives, annual appeals or federated campaigns; for the benefit of specific individuals; for conduit organizations; to institutions "whose policy or practice unfairly discriminates against race, ethnic origin, sex, creed or sexual orientation"; to sectarian or religious organizations; or to organizations currently funded by any other Paul G. Allen foundation. In addition to a fair amount of biographical information about Microsoft co-founder Allen, "The Wired World of Paul Allen" Web site provides examples of recent grants and projects supported by the Foundation, grant application guidelines, a description of the application process, and a downloadable application form.

Allen Foundation for the Arts (WA) (http://www.paulallen.com/foundations/)

The purpose of the Bellevue, Washington-based Allen Foundation for the Arts is to "promote a creative and flourishing arts community in the Pacific Northwest." The Foundation, which is especially interested in the performing and visual arts, also supports entities that sustain artists and art organizations. Ordinarily, the Foundation does not consider grant requests for operating, administrative or overhead expenses; for contributions to general fund drives, annual appeals or federated campaigns; for the benefit of specific individuals; for conduit organizations; to institutions "whose policy or practice unfairly discriminates against race, ethnic origin, sex, creed or sexual orientation"; to sectarian or religious organizations; or to organizations currently funded by any other Paul G. Allen foundation. In addition to a fair amount of biographical information about Microsoft co-founder Allen, "The Wired World of Paul Allen" Web site provides examples of recent grants and projects supported by the Foundation, grant application guidelines, a description of the application process, and a downloadable application form.

Paul G. Allen Forest Protection Foundation (WA) (http://www.paulallen.com/foundations/)

The purpose of the Bellevue, Washington-based Paul G. Allen Forest Protection Foundation—the newest Allen foundation—is to assist in "the acquisition and conservation of forest land in order to preserve needed wildlife habitat and, where possible, to provide public recreational access." Rather than directly acquiring and preserving properties, the Foundation works with established conservancies (e.g.,. the Wilderness Society, the Nature Conservancy) to leverage, through its contributions, the expertise of these organizations to implement programs consistent with the Foundation's purpose. The Foundation is particularly interested in protecting ancient forests or "old growth." Ordinarily, the Foundation does not consider grant requests for operating, administrative or overhead expenses; for contributions to general fund drives, annual appeals or federated campaigns; for the benefit of specific individuals; for conduit organizations; to institutions "whose policy or practice unfairly discriminates against race, ethnic origin, sex, creed or sexual orientation"; to sectarian or religious organizations; or to organizations currently funded by any other Paul G. Allen foundation. In addition to a fair amount of biographical information about Microsoft co-founder Allen, "The Wired World of Paul Allen" Web site provides examples of recent grants and projects supported by the Foundation, grant application guidelines, a description of the application process, and a downloadable application form.

Paul G. Allen Virtual Education Foundation (WA) (http://www.paulallen.com/foundations/)
The mission of the Bellevue, Washington-based Paul G. Allen Virtual Education Foundation is to "advance the development and growth of online learning, especially distance learning that eliminates dependence upon face-to-face contact as the primary context for learning." Funding is primarily given to projects to produce digital content for education, including multimedia instructional materials and software. Support is also given for testing, design, and production of digital materials, and for projects focused on the evaluation of online education in practice. The Foundation does not fund individual faculty projects or capital improvements to information infrastructure or the development of instructional management or delivery technology. Consistent with the policy of all Paul Allen foundations, institutions in the Pacific Northwest are given priority consideration. In addition to a fair amount of biographical information about Microsoft co-founder Allen, "The Wired World of Paul Allen" Web site provides examples of recent grants and projects supported by the Foundation, grant application guidelines, a description of the application process, and a downloadable application form.

Allen Foundation, Inc. (MI) (http://www.tamu.edu/baum/allen.html)
Established in 1975 by agricultural chemist William Webster Allen with the goal of reaching more people with better nutritional information to alleviate malnutrition, the Midland, Michigan-based Allen Foundation makes grants to projects that benefit programs for human nutrition in the areas of education, training, and research. Visitors to the Foundation's Web site will find a brief biography of Mr. Allen, a listing of the Foundation's board of trustees, contact information, and links to other nutrition and food science sites on the Internet. Visitors may also access the Foundation's most recent annual reports.

Alliance Healthcare Foundation (CA) (http://www.alliancehf.org/)
The San Diego-based Alliance Healthcare Foundation funds healthcare programs for medically indigent and underserved populations in California, primarily in San Diego County. Their mission is to improve access to healthcare for all people, especially the medically indigent. Priority is given to programs that address the issues of restricted access to healthcare, substance abuse, communicable diseases, violence prevention, mental health, and other community health problems. The Foundation also performs fundraising, advocacy, and public education. The Foundation's brand-new Web site provides general program descriptions; detailed application guidelines, rules, and procedures; links to related organizations and

resources in the healthcare field; board and staff listings with e-mail links; a brief "News" section; and contact information.

The Herb Alpert Foundation (CA)
(http://www.almosounds.com/herbalpert/secondwind/found.html)
In the 1980's, musician and painter Herb Alpert established the Herb Alpert Foundation, which funds projects in education, the arts, and the environment. Instead of responding to grant proposals, it is "more typical" of the Foundation to "focus on a social need, find qualified organizations that can respond in a healing manner to that need, and then creatively join in the development of responsive programs." The majority of their funding is directed toward the youngest members of American society, "in hopes that the future for them, and for the world, can be improved by an earlier intervention." Other than this, the site mainly contains information on the professional achievements of Herb Alpert. A separate award is mentioned, the "Alpert Award in the Arts", which was created in conjunction with the California Institute of the arts in 1994, and awards $50,000 fellowships to emerging artists in each of five disciplines: dance, theatre, music, film/video, and visual arts. This award is administered by the California Institute of the Arts and funded by the Herb Alpert foundation to enable artists to further pursue creative expression. A link from this Web site (http://www.alpertawards.com) contains detailed information, including a mission statement, a description of the nomination process, statements from Alpert and the California Institute of the Arts, and information on past winners of the award.

Amateur Athletic Foundation of Los Angeles (CA) (http://www.aafla.com)
The Amateur Athletic Foundation of Los Angeles was established in 1985 to manage Southern California's share of the surplus funds generated by the 1984 Olympic Games. The mission of AAF is to serve youth through sport and to increase knowledge of sport and its impact on people's lives. The Foundation focuses its grantmaking activities on sports programs for youth in Southern California's eight counties: Imperial, Los Angeles, Orange, Riverside, San Bernardino, San Diego, Santa Barbara, and Ventura. At the same time, the Foundation gives special attention to women, minorities, the physically challenged or developmentally disabled, and youth in areas where the risk of involvement in delinquency is particularly high. Visitors to the Foundation's Web site will find detailed grant guidelines and application criteria, a list of the Foundation's board of directors, and links to other sports sites. The site also offers information on the Foundation's own youth sports program, historic sports art and artifact collection, sports research library, and special events.

The Amerind Foundation, Inc. (AZ) (Operating foundation)
(http://www.amerind.org)
Presently a nonprofit archaeological research facility and museum devoted to the study and interpretation of Native American cultures, The Amerind Foundation was founded by William Shirley Fulton in 1937 as a private, nonprofit archaeological research institution. Located in the southeastern corner of Arizona known locally as Texas Canyon, the Foundation commits its resources to three main concerns: the conservation and preservation of material culture, research, and education. The Amerind Foundation "strongly promotes the scholarly study and analysis of the materials in its existing collections" and "supports the active

development and participation in archaeological field investigations" to recon-
struct Native American cultures which have disappeared. The Foundation also
"resolves to plan and support educational programs in the form of exhibits and
lectures, adult and children's programs, professional services and publications, as
well as other museum-related activities open to all individuals regardless of ethnic
origin." In addition to the museum, the Foundation also has an archaeological
library open to visiting scholars. Visitors to the Web site will find information on
the history of the Foundation, current museum exhibits, a statement of purpose,
contact information, publications information and online publications request
form, and a list of related links. However, no specific information is provided on
grants.

Amy Foundation (MI) (http://www.amyfound.org)

Named after their daughter, the Amy Foundation was established by W. James
Russell and his wife Phyllis in 1976. The Foundation, based in Michigan, seeks to
restore the spiritual and moral character of the nation and "reclaim" America from
its perceived moral decline. The Web site states: "The Amy Foundation calls all
Christians in the U.S. to the work of teaching obedience to all Christ's commands,
thus making disciples through every means of communication and institutional
influence open to them." To that end, the foundation has writing awards and scholarships, "specifically designed to encourage and equip both professional and non-
professional writers to develop and utilize their skills to the reclaiming of America". The Foundation has other programs designed to carry out their mission, such
as their Church Writing Group program and the dissemination their brochure
titled "The United States—A Discipled Nation in this Generation", which outlines a biblical plan for discipling the nation by the year 2025 and is also available
online. Visitors to this Web site will find writing award and scholarship criteria
and rules, samples of past awarded writing, the Amy Internet Syndicate which
provides editorial opinion columns free of charge for use in any publication, an
online feedback form, an online publications request form (including Amy Award
rules and guidelines brochure and winning entries booklet), a list of resources and
links to other sites.

Annenberg Foundation (PA) (http://www.whannenberg.org/)

The principal grantmaking focus of the St. Davids, Pennsylvania-based
Annenberg Foundation is on pre-collegiate education, specifically public school
restructuring and reform for grades K through 12. Within these broad areas, the
Foundation is particularly interested in early childhood education in relation to
public education at the primary level, and in child development and youth services. Visitors to the Foundation's no-frills Web site will find a brief biography of
founder/donor and former TV Guide publisher Walter H. Annenberg; an overview
of the Foundation's K–12 Challenge Grant program and contact information for
15 challenge grant sites and initiatives; general information about its independent
Foundation-sponsored programs (the Annenberg/CPB math and Science Project
and the Annenberg Washington Program in Communications Policy Studies at the
University of Pennsylvania); a short list of sample grants; application procedures
and proposal guidelines; and basic fiscal information.

Arca Foundation (DC) (http://fdncenter.org/grantmaker/arca/index.html)

Established in 1952 as the Nancy Reynolds Bagley Foundation, the Washington, D.C.- Arca Foundation received its present name in 1968. Domestically, the Foundation's primary concern is "the overwhelming influence of private money in politics and its effect on who runs for public office, who wins, and in whose interest they govern." Arca's funding emphasizes "educational efforts to expose this legal form of corruption and suggest effective remedies at the state and national level." It also funds projects "that address the imbalance of power in society more generally, emphasizing issues of economic equity and labor rights at home and abroad." In the foreign policy field, Arca's grantmaking "reflects a focus on issues that are particularly influenced by U.S. policy in the Western Hemisphere. U.S. policy toward Cuba and Central America continues to be a central concern, alongside the human consequences of globalized production." The Foundation's "folder" on the Center's Web site provides a brief history of the Foundation, grantmaking guidelines and recent grants list organized by area of interest, financial statements, and contact information.

ArtServe Michigan (MI) (Operating foundation)
(http://www.artservemichigan.org/index2.html)

ArtServe Michigan is a synergy of four organizations: Arts Foundation of Michigan, Business Volunteers for the Arts, Concerned Citizens for the Arts in Michigan and Michigan Alliance for Arts Education, that came together on May 1, 1997. Its goals are to serve as the premier advocate for arts and arts education; foster unity within Michigan's cultural community; educate the public about the importance of cultural arts and education; encourage participation and support from all sectors; provide direct support services for arts education, artists, cultural organizations and communities involved in cultural activities; and utilize the latest technologies to communicate with artists and facilitate involvement in the cultural community. With three offices in Lansing, Grand Rapids, and Southfield, ArtServe Michigan has many programs, awards and grants for the promotion of all artistic disciplines in Michigan, as well as an online Virtual Gallery where artists, educators, student artists, and other cultural organizations can display their work. Also of note is an electronic bulletin board for artists and a "Slidebank" where visual artists and craftspeople interested in exhibiting their work can submit samples and resumes to ArtServe, where they can be viewed by individuals or organizations interested in displaying and/or purchasing. Visitors to the Web site will find detailed information and guidelines on grants, awards, programs; information on past grant and award recipients, downloadable forms, applications, and publications; press releases; and contact information.

The Assisi Foundation of Memphis, Inc. (TN)
(http://www.tenethealth.com/about_tenet/at_assisi.html)

When Tenet Health Care, a nationwide provider of heath care services, acquired St. Francis Hospital in 1994 and converted it from a not-for-profit hospital to for-profit status, the Assisi Foundation of Memphis, Inc. was created. Based in Memphis, Tennessee, this community foundation awards grants in the areas of health and human services, education, ethics, community enhancement and other civic and cultural endeavors, with the largest share of funding in 1994 through 1996 awarded to programs in the categories of health and human services and education. Since its founding, the Foundation has committed an excess of $12 million to more than 180 programs. The site contains information on past awarded grants, but has little other information on the foundation itself. However, the rest of the Web site contains plenty of information on Tenet Health Care as well its contact information, and visitors can also find links to Tenet's other health care conversion foundations.

Mary Reynolds Babcock Foundation, Inc. (NC) (http://www.mrbf.org/)

The Babcock Foundation was created in 1953 with a $12 million bequest from Mary Reynolds Babcock, a daughter of the founder of the R. J. Reynolds Tobacco Company. Based in Winston-Salem, North Carolina, the Foundation concentrates its activities on community-building initiatives in the southeastern United States, placing a special emphasis on activities that seek to assure the well-being of children, youth, and families; bridge the fault lines of race and class; and invest in communities' human and natural resources over the long term. The Foundation's current program, Building Just and Caring Communities, comprises four funding areas: the Organizational Development Program, to strengthen the effectiveness and sustainability of organizations throughout the Southeast; the Community Problem Solving Program, which aims to support coalitions working on local community issues in ways that "build lasting capacity in their communities to solve problems"; Grassroots Leadership Development, to build the capacity of grassroots leaders to influence state policy, leverage financial support for leadership development through community foundations, and increase the capacity of organizations that do grassroots leadership development; and Small Grants for Grassroots Organizations, to support operating budgets and organization development goals.. Visitors to the Foundation's Web site will find detailed descriptions of all four programs, a list of recent grants, a brief history of the Foundation and a statement of its purpose and values, listings of the Foundation's board and staff, and contact information.

Helen Bader Foundation, Inc. (WI) (http://www.hbf.org/)

The Milwaukee-based Helen Bader Foundation supports innovative programs that advance the well-being of people and promote successful relationships with their families and communities. The Foundation concentrates its grantmaking in six areas: Alzheimer's disease and dementia (geographic focus: national, with priority given to Milwaukee and Wisconsin), children and youth in Israel (geographic focus: Israel), economic development (geographic focus: Milwaukee), education (geographic focus: Milwaukee), Jewish life and learning (geographic focus: Milwaukee and Delaware River Valley area), and the Sankofa-Neighborhood Revival Initiative (geographic focus: Milwaukee). In addition to background information, press releases, and a biography of founder Helen Bader, the Foundation's elegant, easy-to-navigate Web site provides general program information; application guidelines and online and downloadable application forms; recent grants, grant summaries by program area, and profiles of featured grantees; and contact information.

The Francois-Xavier Bagnoud Foundation (NY) (http://www.fxb.org/ffxb/fxb.htm)

In 1989, the Countess Albina du Boisrouvray, along with family and friends of Francois, created the Bagnoud Foundation in memory of the Countess' only son, a helicopter pilot killed in a crash on a flying mission in West Africa at the age of

24. The Foundation "carries out various philanthropic activities"; among its programs are five fellowships in the College of Engineering at the University of Michigan and the Francois-Xavier Bagnoud Aerospace Prize, consisting of a $250,000 honorarium and sculpture, administered by the Aerospace Engineering Department at the University of Michigan. Also featured on the site is the Association Francois-Xavier Bagnoud, which, although funded by the foundation, is independent of the foundation's philanthropic activities and has a disposal of $5 million for "strictly humanitarian goals". The Association is involved in "more than two dozen initiatives involving children's rights, health and human rights, and pediatric HIV/AIDS in 17 countries". The Web site contains information and guidelines for the Xavier-Bagnoud Aerospace Prize and information on past winners of the prize; detailed information on the Association's work in each region around the world; news and press releases; downloadable application for foundation funds and an online contact form. Also available are a calendar of events, a search engine, and an archive of past news releases and information dating back to 1996, as well as links to related sites.

Baptist Community Ministries of New Orleans (LA) (http://www.bcm.org/)

Baptist Community Ministries (BCM) was endowed with the proceeds from the sale of Mercy + Baptist Medical Center in August of 1995. Their stated mission: "Baptist Community Ministries is committed to the development of a healthy community offering a wholesome quality of life to its residents and to improving the physical, mental, and spiritual health of the individuals we serve". This $150 million private foundation makes grants to qualifying charitable organizations in the five-parish region surrounding New Orleans. Its funding interests are primarily in education, health, public safety and governmental oversight, and grantees and programs are "evaluated considering the religious history and mission of BCM." Awards range from $50,000 for one year to nearly $2 million over four years. BCM's Web site lists goals for each funding area, and provides grant information and guidelines, a summary of the grant review process, a listing of past grant recipients and contact information.

Arnold and Mabel Beckman Foundation (CA)
(http://www.beckman-foundation.com/)

The Arnold and Mabel Beckman Foundation makes grants "to promote research in chemistry and the life sciences, broadly interpreted, and particularly to foster the invention of methods, instruments, and materials that will open up new avenues of research in science." The Irvine, California-based Foundation's no-frills Web site provides brief bios of Arnold and Mabel Beckman; guidelines, printable application forms and a recipient list for the Beckman Young Investigators (BYI) Program, which provides research support to promising young faculty members in the early stages of academic careers in the chemical and life sciences, and information on the Beckman Research Technologies Initiatives, which supports the development of new research technologies, and the Beckman Scholars Program, which recognizes outstanding undergraduate students in chemistry and biological sciences; links to Beckman Institutes/Centers at the University of Illinois at Urbana-Champaign, the California Institute of Technology, Stanford University, the Beckman Laser Institute, and City of Hope; and contact information.

Beldon Fund (NY) (http://www.beldon.org/)

Beldon Fund is an environmental grantmaker headquartered in New York City. Their goals are to build a base of involved and informed activists to protect the environment and to strengthen the capacity of nonprofit organizations to effectively organize environmental activists. The primary interest of the Beldon Fund is in supporting environmental organizations working at the state level, with the following funding categories: state and regional environmental organizations; national organizations' work with state-level constituencies; progressive state-wide coalitions involving a broad spectrum of constituencies; hazardous waste and toxics use reduction; training and technical assistance; and building the organizational capacity of grantees. Beldon Fund focuses on organizations at the state level because it believes that the need is great and that their limited resources can be used most effectively there. The Beldon fund supports a range of approaches to strengthening the environmental movement, including outreach to new constituencies; building coalitions; encouraging greater cooperation between state and national organizations; increasing effective citizen participation in democratic political processes; and diversifying and expanding environmental groups' funding bases. The fund makes both general support and project-specific grants. The Web site features grant guidelines and application procedures, the president's statement and executive director's report, a summary of 1997 grants, and contact information.

Benton Foundation (DC) (http://www.benton.org/)

The Benton Foundation seeks to shape the emerging communications environment and to demonstrate the value of communications for solving social problems. Its mission is to promote communication tools, applications, and policies in the public interest. Through its Communications Policy & Practice arm, the foundation supports nonprofits using communications to solve social problems and strengthen social bonds. Other projects of the Foundation are Connect for Kids (http://www.connectforkids.org/), an online resource for "helping Americans act on behalf of children"; Open Studio: The Arts Online (http://www.openstudio.org/), which provides community access to the arts on the Internet; Destination Democracy (http://www.destinationdemocracy.org/), dedicated to campaign finance reform; and Sound Partners for Community Health (http://www.soundpartners.org), which awards grants to public radio stations that demonstrate how community centered journalism can positively affect the ways in which local health care issues are addressed. The Foundation has created the Virtual Library, which supplies dozens of papers and policy documents online. Visitors to the site will find useful communications technology "best practices"; the Benton Foundation Library; hundreds of annotated links to nonprofit and telecommunications resources on the Internet; and a listing of the Foundation's board members and staff.

H.N. & Frances C. Berger Foundation (CA) (http://www.hnberger.org/)

The H.N. and Frances C. Berger Foundation was created to provide people with the opportunity to improve their own situations, "to help people help themselves." Established as a private family foundation in 1961 by Nor and Frances Berger, the focus of their funding is on children and youth, in keeping with the Bergers' belief that the future rests in their hands. To that end, the establishment of college buildings and scholarships are among their charitable projects. The foundation, located in Palm Desert, California, supports a variety of civic, educational and community projects, with the majority of grants related to programs in the Southern California area. The Berger Foundation prefers to seek out its own projects, and does not solicit grant proposals. However, "those with interest in a potential dialogue" are encouraged to submit a one to two page request for consideration, which should include a concise statement of intent and a brief history of the organization and its activities. The Web site contains an address for contact, and a brief bio of the founders.

Frank Stanley Beveridge Foundation, Inc. (FL) (http://www.beveridge.org/)

The Florida-based Beveridge Foundation was established in Massachusetts in 1947 by Frank Stanley Beveridge, the founder of Stanley Home Products, Inc. Today the Foundation considers grant proposals in some two dozen institutional/program activity areas, including animal related, arts and culture, civil rights, community improvement, conservation/environment, crime, disasters/safety, diseases/medical disciplines, education, employment, food and agriculture, health—general & rehabilitative, housing, human services, mental health—crisis intervention, philanthropy/voluntarism, public affairs and society benefit, recreation, religion, science, social sciences, and youth development. The stated purpose of the Foundation's Web site, however, is to determine whether potential applicants are eligible to receive grants from the Foundation. In addition to a self-administered interactive survey to help grantseekers determine whether they meet the Foundation's basic eligibility requirements, visitors to the site will find a biography of Mr. Beveridge, a recent grants list, a listing of the Foundation's officers and directors, contact information, and links to other funding resources. If you meet the eligibility requirements, a preliminary grant proposal form can be submitted online.

William Bingham Foundation (OH)
(http://fdncenter.org/grantmaker/bingham/index.html)

The William Bingham Foundation was established in 1955 by Elizabeth Bingham Blossom in memory of her brother, William Bingham II, to continue the philanthropic tradition of the family. Initially, the Foundation's grantmaking focused on educational, cultural, and health and human service organizations in the Cleveland area. Over the years, however, the Foundation's objectives have broadened to reflect the needs of the communities in which its trustees reside. Today, the Foundation contributes to a wide variety of organizations in the areas of the arts, education, and health and human services in those communities as well as nationwide. The Foundation's "folder" on the Center's Web site provides a brief history of the Foundation, its program interests and grantmaking procedures, a list of grants with links to grantee organizations, financial statements, contact information, and trustee, officer, and staff listings.

Blandin Foundation (MN) (http://www.blandinfoundation.org/)

The mission of the Blandin Foundation is to strengthen rural Minnesota communities, with a special focus on the Grand Rapids community and Itasca County. To that end, the Foundation sponsors conferences and leadership programs and provides approximately $15 million to Minnesota organizations annually. Outside of Itasca County, Blandin grants are restricted to the focus areas established by the Foundation's board of trustees: education, cultural opportunities, community leadership training, environmental stewardship, safe communities, economic opportunity, and "convening." The trustees commit most of the Foundation's grant dollars to its major partners, who have the responsibility of administering each focus area. Potential grant applicants are encouraged to review the Foundation's current focus areas and then contact the appropriate partner organization, which can be done via e-mail through the Foundation's Web site. The site also provides program descriptions, a list of grants made in January 1998, and detailed grant restrictions.

The Arthur M. Blank Family Foundation (GA) (http://www.BlankFoundation.org)
The Arthur M. Blank Family Foundation is "committed to supporting programs and organizations that create opportunity, enhance self esteem and increase awareness about cultural and community issues among young men and women." The Atlanta-based foundation provides funding in the following areas: arts and culture, athletics and outdoor activities, environment, fostering understanding between young people of diverse backgrounds, helping adolescents learn, and empowering young women and girls. The foundation's geographic focus includes Atlanta, GA; New York, NY; Boston, MA; and Los Angeles, CA; special consideration is given to organizations that are located in Atlanta, reach underserved youth or improve the quality of public education. The Web site includes information about each funding area, grant application instructions and a description of the review process, a downloadable application, and a listing of grant limitations.

Blowitz-Ridgeway Foundation (IL)
(http://fdncenter.org/grantmaker/blowitz/index.html)
Founded in 1984 with the proceeds from the sale of Chicago's Ridgeway Hospital, a psychiatric facility focusing on low-income adolescents, the Blowitz-Ridgeway Foundation continues the hospital's mission by making grants primarily for medical, psychiatric, psychological and/or residential care; and research programs in medicine, psychology, social science, and education. Preference is given to organizations operating within the state of Illinois. Visitors to the Foundation's "folder" on the Center's Web site will find application guidelines and procedures, and a listing of recent grants.

Bodman Foundation (NY) (http://fdncenter.org/grantmaker/bodman/index.html)
The Bodman Foundation was established in 1945 by investment banker George M. Bodman and his wife, Louise Clarke Bodman, to distribute funds in the religious, educational, and charitable fields "for the moral, ethical and physical well being and progress of mankind." Today the Foundation concentrates its grantmaking in New York City, with occasional grants directed to northern New Jersey in memory of the Bodmans. Areas of Foundation interest include funding for youth, rehabilitation, biomedical research, child welfare, science education, major cultural institutions, health and hospitals, social services, welfare reform, alcohol and drug abuse, responsible fatherhood and father absence, and education (including charter schools, public school reform, and parental school choice). Other interests include volunteerism, literacy, homelessness, entrepreneurship and economic development, environment (science education and land conservation), and job training with employment in the private business sector. Visitors to the Foundation's "folder" on the Center's Web site will find a brief history of the Foundation; a statement from Foundation president John N. Irwin III; application

guidelines and procedures; recent grants lists; a listing of the Foundation's trustees, officers, and staff; and contact information.

Corella & Bertram F. Bonner Foundation (NJ) (http://www.bonner.org/)
The Bonner Foundation was established in 1989 by Corella and Bertram Bonner with "the hope and, indeed the expectation, that the impact of their support would be far reaching in the areas of hunger and education." In the years since then, the Foundation has provided $9.5 million in grants to thousands of religious, community-based hunger relief programs across the country through its Crisis Ministry Program. Over the same period the Bonner Scholars Program has awarded more than $12 million in scholarship support to more than 2,500 students at 24 colleges. The Foundation's Web site provides general information on and application guidelines for both programs, including a downloadable grant application cover sheet, as well as highlights from the Foundation's newsletter, a list of recent grants, board and staff listings, and contact information.

Mary Owen Borden Foundation (NJ)
(http://fdncenter.org/grantmaker/borden/index.html)
The Mary Owen Borden Foundation was founded by Bertram H. Borden in 1934 to honor his recently departed wife. In recent decades, the Foundation has limited its new funding to New Jersey's Mercer and Monmouth counties. Its current giving is focused on disadvantaged youth and their families, including needs such as health, family planning, education, counseling, childcare, substance abuse, and delinquency. Other areas of interest for the Foundation include affordable housing, conservation and the environment, and the arts. The Foundation's "folder" on the Center's Web site provides general Foundation information, application guidelines and procedures, a summary of grants, a listing of the Foundation's officers and trustees, and contact information.

Robert Bowne Foundation, Inc. (NY)
(http://fdncenter.org/grantmaker/bowne/index.html)
Established in 1968 by Bowne & Co., Inc., and named in honor of the company's founder, Robert Bowne (1744–1818), the Robert Bowne Foundation concentrates its grantmaking on out-of-school programs in New York City that address the issue of youth literacy. The Foundation provides grants—ranging from $5,000 to $25,000—for special, advocacy, and research projects; for general operating expenses of relevant programs; for technical assistance in program design and reform; and for evaluation studies. The Foundation does not support in-school projects or projects following a traditional remedial model of instruction, nor does it award grants to religious organizations, primary or secondary schools, colleges, or universities (except when some aspect of their work is an integral part of a program receiving funding from the Foundation). Visitors to the Foundation's "folder" on the Center's Web site will find a brief history of the Foundation, a detailed description of its program and application procedures, grants lists, a listing of the Foundation's trustees and staff, and contact information.

Lynde and Harry Bradley Foundation (WI) (http://www.townhall.com/bradley/)
Established to commemorate Lynde and Harry Bradley, successful turn-of-the-century Milwaukee businessmen, the Bradley Foundation furthers the brothers' mutual interest in helping to improve the quality of life in the metropolitan

Milwaukee area and to "preserving and defending the tradition of free representative government and private enterprise which has enabled the American nation...to flourish intellectually and economically." Like the Bradley brothers, the Foundation is "devoted to strengthening American democratic capitalism and the institutions, principles and values which sustain and nurture it. Its programs support limited, competent government; a dynamic marketplace for economic, intellectual, and cultural activity; and a vigorous defense at home and abroad of American ideas and institutions." Recognizing that "responsible self-government depends on enlightened citizens and informed public opinion," the Bradley Foundation also supports scholarly studies and academic achievement. The Foundation's current program interests are projects that focus on cultivating a "renewed, healthier, and more vigorous sense of citizenship among the American people, and among people of other nations, as well." The Foundation's Web site provides passionate descriptions of the Foundation's mission and driving philosophy; general information about its current program interests and grantmaking policies; and listings of the Foundation's board, officers, and staff.

Brainerd Foundation (WA) (http://www.brainerd.org/)

The Brainerd Foundation is dedicated to protecting the environmental quality of the Pacific Northwest—Alaska, Idaho, Montana, Oregon, Washington, and the Canadian province of British Columbia—by supporting "grassroots-oriented projects that motivate citizens to get involved in efforts to protect the environment." The majority of the foundation's grants are awarded within one of three program areas: endangered ecosystems, toxics and communities, and communications and capacity building. The Foundation also makes what it calls Emergency Grants, which range from $250 to $2,000 and are given to "organizations that are confronted with an opportunity to carry out important work—in a hurry." Visitors to the Foundation's Web site will find detailed program guidelines and limitations, application procedures (including an application coversheet, lists of recent grant recipients, biographies of the Foundation's directors and staff, a number of links to community resources in the Pacific Northwest, an online feedback form, grantee profiles, and financial statements.

Otto Bremer Foundation (MN)
(http://fdncenter.org/grantmaker/bremer/index.html)

The mission of the St. Paul-based Otto Bremer Foundation is "to be an accessible and responsible financial resource to aid in the development and cohesion of communities within the states of Minnesota, North Dakota, Wisconsin, and Montana, with preference given to those communities served by the affiliates of Bremer Financial Corporation." Within these geographic areas, the Foundation has chosen to focus on promoting human rights and equality for the year 2000, which involves undoing the barrier of equal access. Visitors to the Foundation's "folder" on the Center's Web site will find program and application guidelines, a summary of the Foundation's 1996 grantmaking activities, recent grants, and comprehensive grants lists in each program area.

The Brookdale Foundation (NY) (http://www.ewol.com/brookdale/)

Based in New York, NY, the Brookdale Foundation Group is comprised of The Brookdale Foundation, the Glendale Foundation, and Ramapo Trust. These three distinct entities have separate officers and Boards of Directors or Trustees, but all are endowed by the Schwartz family and share a common focus: the needs and challenges of America's elderly population. The Foundation Group has three major funding initiatives: The Leadership in Aging Program, a fellowship in the field of gerontology and geriatrics; The National Group Respite Program, which provides small seed grants and technical assistance to foster the development of dementia-specific, social model day-service programs to meet the needs of persons with Alzheimer's and their caregivers; and the Relatives as Parents Program, to establish community-based services to grandparents and other relatives who have assumed the responsibility of surrogate parenting. However, the Foundation Group will also consider new and innovative projects to provide direct services that will improve the lives of older people. Guidelines for the three funding initiatives and instructions for application are provided, as well as contact information for each program. Those interested in the Leadership in Aging program can also find lists of participating institutions, members of the medical advisory and review boards who review applications, past fellows, and senior fellows on the site. For those who wish to submit proposals unrelated to the three major initiatives, the Group provides suggestions for submission as well as a downloadable information cover sheet for general grant applications and contact information.

James Graham Brown Foundation, Inc. (KY)
(http://www.brownfoundation.com/)
Established under a trust agreement in 1943 and formally incorporated in 1954, the James Graham Brown Foundation is dedicated to fostering the well-being, quality of life, and image of Louisville (i.e., Jefferson County) and Kentucky. The Foundation does this by actively supporting and funding projects in the fields of civic and economic development, education, youth, and health and general welfare. Since the death of its benefactor, James Graham Brown, in 1969, the Foundation has awarded approximately 2,100 grants totaling more than $200 million—mainly in Kentucky, with a small percentage awarded in other parts of the Southeast. Visitors to the Foundation's Web site will find information about its proposal requirements and application procedures, a list of grant recipients organized by program area, and contact information.

Kathleen Price Bryan Family Fund (NC)
(http://fdncenter.org/grantmaker/kpbryan/index.html)
Established in 1955, the Kathleen Price Bryan Family Fund serves North Carolinians in building strong and healthy communities. To that end, the Fund is interested in the development of tangible, sustainable results in North Carolina in the following areas: human resources (education, health, safety); economic resources (affordable housing, business development, asset generation and development, income and economic self-reliance); natural resources (environmental concerns); North Carolina cultural resources (preserving distinctive arts, customs, and cultures); public interest; and societal issues. In addition, the Fund takes a special interest "in community-based organizations working to build their own capacities through projects which expand local resources for local concerns, create results that have long-term effects, and link individual, family and community interests," as well as organizations "working to build collaborative action and approaches to statewide issues through public/private partnerships, prevention programs, and advocacy on key issues." Visitors to the Fund's "folder" on the Center's Web site will find a brief history of the Fund, detailed statements of the Fund's

grantmaking policies and interests, answers to FAQs, a 1997 grants list, and contact information.

Bullitt Foundation (WA) (http://www.bullitt.org/)

The Seattle-based Bullitt Foundation is committed to the protection and restoration of the environment of the Pacific Northwest. This commitment includes environmental problems that disproportionately impact lower-economic people in both urban and rural communities. The Foundation invites proposals from nonprofit organizations that serve Washington, Oregon, Idaho, British Columbia, western Montana (including the Rocky Mountain Range), and the rain forest region of southern Alaska. Within these broad parameters, the Foundation focuses its grantmaking activities in the following program areas: energy and climate change; forests and land ecosystems; growth management and transportation; public outreach, education, and capacity building; rivers, wetlands, and estuaries; sustainable agriculture; and toxic substances, mining, and radioactive waste. Visitors to the Foundation's Web site will find program descriptions, grant application and final report instructions, detailed grantee information, a report from the Foundation's president (Denis Hayes, national coordinator of the first Earth Day in 1970), an FAQ section, board and staff listings, preliminary financial statements, and contact information. Application cover sheets can be downloaded from the site.

Burroughs Wellcome Fund (NC) (http://www.bwfund.org/)

Established in 1955 to advance the medical sciences by supporting research and other scientific and educational activities, the Burroughs Wellcome Fund today emphasizes "career development of biomedical scientists and...advancing areas in the basic medical sciences that are underfunded or that have a shortage of qualified researchers." Approximately eight-five percent of the Fund's resources are distributed through seven competitive award programs, and the majority of those programs are open to scientists who are citizens or permanent residents of the United States and Canada. BWF's straightforward Web site offers complete descriptions of the Fund's programs; award eligibility requirements and guidelines; application deadlines; a listing of the Fund's board of directors, officers, and staff; its annual report; and an FAQ section. Application cover sheets for each program can be downloaded from the site.

Edyth Bush Charitable Foundation (FL)
(http://fdncenter.org/grantmaker/bush/index.html)

The mission of the Edyth Bush Charitable Foundation is to "grantmaking designed to help people help themselves." To that end, the Foundation supports programs that "help underprivileged or needy people to improve themselves or relieve human suffering." The Foundation makes grants to nonprofit organizations exclusively located and/or operating within a 100-mile radius of Winter Park, Florida, with special emphasis on Orange, Seminole, Osceola, and Lake counties. The Foundation, which was founded by the widow of Archibald G. Bush, a director and principal shareholder of the Minnesota Mining & Manufacturing Company, also has broad interests in human service, education, and health care, and a limited interest in the arts. Visitors to the Foundation's "folder" on the Foundation Center's Web site will find a detailed account of the Foundation's application policies and procedures, as well as recent grants lists by subject area.

The Morris and Gwendolyn Cafritz Foundation (DC)
(http://www.cafritzfoundation.org/)

The Morris and Gwendolyn Cafritz Foundation was established in 1948 by Morris Cafritz, a civic leader who raised money for numerous charities and community projects. This Washington, D.C. based foundation was created with the goal of "helping others less fortunate make a better life for themselves and their families, and to assist young people in achieving their full potential", and currently funds projects in four areas: arts and humanities, education, health, and community service. The foundation concentrates grants to organizations in the greater Washington area on a project basis, and generally "projects of direct assistance to the District of Columbia and its environs." The Foundation uses the Washington Regional Association of Grantmakers Common Grant Application, which can be viewed on their Web site. Also available on their Web site are grant guidelines and restrictions, the 1997 annual report, a list of email links to certain staff members, information about grantees, and a list of linked resources for grantseekers.

The California Endowment (CA) (http://www.calendow.org/)

Established in 1996 as a result of Blue Cross of California's conversion from a not-for-profit to a for-profit corporation, the California Endowment works to expand access to affordable, quality health care for underserved individuals and communities and to promote fundamental improvements in the health status of the people of California. Within this context, and as a new foundation keenly interested in delivering maximum benefit to its constituents, the Endowment has identified four broad areas of interest: Access, with a focus on expanding and improving access to health systems and related resources for underserved individuals and communities; Community Innovations; Health & Well-Being, especially as it relates to the promotion of prevention strategies for all populations; and Multicultural Health, with a focus on developing the field of multicultural health by supporting the theoretical and applied work of addressing socio-cultural barriers to improved health. The Foundation's Web site offers application procedures, a downloadable application cover sheet and sample budget format, an online publications order form (the Endowment's publications are offered to the public at no charge), staff and board listings, contact information (including an electronic feedback form), and press releases.

California Wellness Foundation (CA) (http://www.tcwf.org/)

The mission of the California Wellness Foundation is to improve the health and well-being of the people of California through health promotion and wellness education, and disease prevention programs. The Foundation concentrates its grantmaking activities in five areas—community health, population health improvement, teenage pregnancy prevention, violence prevention, and work and health—and while it generally supports organizations located in California or projects that directly benefit California residents, national organizations providing services in California are also considered. In addition to information about its general grants program and descriptions of strategic initiatives in each of its five focus areas, the Foundation's Web site provides a listing of 1997 grants, links to related Web sites, and both viewable and downloadable version of its annual report and newsletters.

Iris & B. Gerald Cantor Foundation (CA) (Operating foundation)
(http://www.cantorfoundation.com/)

Established in 1978, the Iris and B. Gerald Cantor Foundation is involved with the support and promotion of the arts. The goal of the foundation, which bears the names of its founders, is to "promote and encourage the recognition and appreciation of excellence in the arts", with an emphasis on the sculptures of Auguste Rodin. They have donated more than 450 Rodin sculptures to institutions throughout the world, funded and organized Rodin exhibitions, created a Rodin Research Fund at Stanford University, and have given numerous endowments to major art museums. The Foundation is also committed to supporting biomedical research; the support of healthcare initiatives for women, with an emphasis on the early diagnosis and treatment of breast cancer, is of particular interest to this Beverly Hills, CA foundation. The Foundation in its support of biomedical research makes significant gifts to endow new patient facilities, laboratories, and research fellowships at hospitals and medical centers. Visitors will find a site mostly devoted to Rodin's life and work (such as a schedule of traveling Rodin exhibitions organized by the Foundation, a suggested reading list on Rodin, the artist's bio, a virtual gallery), but will also find information on the Cantor Foundation's activities and a biography of the founders.

Canyon Research (CA) (Operating foundation)
(http://www.canyonresearch.org)

This San Diego-based foundation seeks to advance communications research and education by funding specialized research projects that focus on three areas of support: advanced computer-related communications technology, public communications policy, and domestic communications regulatory issues. Canyon Research supports these three areas of research through grants and fellowships that allow researchers to develop new and innovative technologies that in turn will create breakthroughs in computer communications capabilities. There are currently no restrictions on grant amounts and no restrictions based on geography, and typical awards are between US$25,000 and US$50,000. Canyon Research periodically issues a call for applications that describe the targeted research and education projects funded; proposals that do not fall within the specified areas of support or are not in response to a specific call for applications are unlikely to be funded. Points of interest on this Web site are the 'call for applications' section where the targeted research project is described, application procedures, grantmaking guidelines, areas of exclusion, contact information, and proposals, final reports and descriptions of past and current projects.

CarEth Foundation (MA) (http://www.funder.org/careth/)

The CarEth Foundation seeks to promote "a compassionate world of enduring peace, with justice, and with social, economic, and political equality for all." In support of its mission, the Foundation is currently funding programs that promote the creation of a global community of peace and justice, a genuine democracy in the United States, and peaceful conflict resolution. The Foundation is also currently interested in projects involving today's youth. Visitors to CarEth's Web site will find general descriptions of program goals, application procedures and limitations, a list of recent grantees with links to those with Web sites, and contact information.

CARLISLE Foundation (MA) (http://www.carlislefoundation.org)

Based in Framingham, MA, the CARLISLE Foundation evolved from CARLISLE Services, Inc., a grantmaking company founded in 1988 that acted as an intermediary between private donors and the human services community, soliciting and reviewing grant proposals and presenting them to donors for consideration. In 1991, those same donors established the CARLISLE Foundation as a more efficient and effective means for continuing their philanthropic endeavors and as a statement of their continuing commitment. CARLISLE Foundation only funds programs operating within the six New England states, and "attempts to promote creative problem solving and interventions." The Foundation prefers to support new and innovative projects, or those that demonstrate potential as models; and though they review a wide range of proposals, several areas have emerged as high priorities: substance abuse, domestic and community violence, homelessness/housing, economic development, and other services for children, youth, and family. In addition to grantmaking, the Foundation provides free technical assistance or consultation to human services organizations, whether it be assistance with proposal development or program development to fiscal or personnel management. More information about this service, and application and grant guidelines are available on their site. Also of interest are descriptions of programs currently funded, a list of organizations that received prior grants, contact information for funded projects and for the CARLISLE Foundation, complete with email, telephone, and fax numbers.

Carnegie Corporation of New York (NY) (http://www.carnegie.org)

In addition to a brief history of Andrew Carnegie and his philanthropies and information about the Foundation itself, the Web site of the Carnegie Corporation of New York gives visitors general information about the Foundation's four currently supported program areas: education reform, international peace and security, international development, democracy, and special projects. The last affords the Foundation an opportunity to make grants and appropriations outside its three defined program areas. Available as well are application guidelines and grant restrictions; a description of the Foundation's six special initiatives; full-text online versions of selected Carnegie publications, including its annual report; grants lists; a listing of Foundation officers and trustees; links to other foundation and nonprofit resources on the Internet; and contact information.

Carnegie Endowment for International Peace (DC) (Operating foundation) (http://www.ceip.org/)

The Carnegie Endowment for International Peace was established with a gift from Andrew Carnegie in 1910. It conducts programs of research, discussion, publication, and education in international affairs and U.S. foreign policy, and publishes the quarterly magazine Foreign Policy. The Endowment and its associates seek "to invigorate and extend both expert and public discussion on a wide range of international issues", such as worldwide migration, nuclear non-proliferation, and regional conflicts. It also "engages in and encourages projects designed to foster innovative contributions in international affairs." The Carnegie Endowment also has a public policy research center in Moscow to promote collaboration among scholars and specialists in the US, Russia, and other post-Soviet states. The Moscow Center holds seminars, workshops, and study groups and provides a forum for international figures to present their views to "informed Moscow audiences."

The Endowment has Junior Fellows Program; Junior Fellows are research assistants to senior associates. Fellows are uniquely qualified graduating seniors and individuals who have graduated during the past academic year and are selected from a pool of nominees. The Web site offers information on this program, as wells as information about the various projects within the Global Policy and Russia/Eurasia programs, and links to the Carnegie Moscow Center and their magazine, Foreign Policy. A media guide, library, downloadable publications and book summaries, and lists of associates and their bios, junior fellows, and board of trustees are also available.

Carnegie Hero Fund Commission (PA) (Operating foundation) (http://trfn.clpgh.org/carnegiehero/)

A coal mine explosion on January 25, 1904 near Harwick, PA and the death of the two men who died trying to rescue those inside the mine inspired industrialist and philanthropist Andrew Carnegie to establish the Carnegie Hero Fund Commission. Within three months after the explosion that claimed 181 lives, Carnegie set aside $5 million under the care of a commission to recognize "civilization's heroes" and to carry out his wish that "heroes and those dependent upon them should be freed from pecuniary cares resulting from their heroism." Ninety-five years later, their mission is still the same: "to recognize acts of civilian heroism throughout the United States and Canada", and "to provide financial assistance to the awardees and the dependents of those awardees who are killed or disabled by their heroic actions." The Pittsburgh, PA-based foundation awards a bronze medal, a $3000 grant, and scholarship eligibility to all cases considered worthy. Visitors to the Web site can read about the history behind the Commission and about past awardees; find award guidelines, application instructions, and contact information; peruse a bibliography for additional information about the Commission; and find links related to Andrew Carnegie.

Roy J. Carver Charitable Trust (IA) (http://www.carvertrust.org/)

The Roy J. Carver Charitable Trust was created in 1982 through the will of Roy J. Carver, an industrialist and philanthropist who died in 1981. Based in Muscatine, IA, "it is the largest private foundation in the state of Iowa", listing five funding areas: medical and scientific research; education; scholarship and awards; youth; and miscellaneous, which are grants that "for various reasons do no fall within the Trust's four primary program classifications" and "in many cases…are grants awarded for projects within the Muscatine area that have received special consideration because of their location." The Trust has an annual grantmaking budget of over $11 million, and the majority of grants are awarded for initiatives in Iowa and a portion of western Illinois. Visitors to the site will find information about each of the five funding areas, grant lists, information about grant guidelines and application procedures, a downloadable application cover sheet, and contact information.

Annie E. Casey Foundation (MD) (http://www.aecf.org/)

Established in 1948 by Jim Casey, one of the founders of United Parcel Service, and his siblings, the Annie E. Casey Foundation is dedicated to fostering "public policies, human-service reforms, and community supports that more effectively meet the needs of today's vulnerable children and families." In general, the grantmaking of the Baltimore-based Foundation is limited to "initiatives that have significant potential to demonstrate innovative policy, service delivery, and community supports for children and families. Most grantees have been invited by the Foundation to participate in these projects. The Foundation does not make grants to individuals, nor does it support capital projects that are not an integral part of a Foundation-sponsored initiative. The Foundation's new Web site is organized into four broad areas: Kid's Count, a national and state-by-state effort to track the educational, economic, social, and physical well-being of children in the United States; Foundation Initiatives; Foundation News; and a listing of Foundation publications. The site also provides proposal instructions and grant guidelines, features a search engine for the site, and an online feedback form.

The Casey Family Program (WA) (Operating foundation) (http://www.casey.org)
Jim Casey, founder of United Parcel Service, created the Casey Family Program in 1966. His father died when he was a young boy, but the "guidance of a strong mother and support of his family kept him grounded." He sought ways to help those without the family life he felt was so important. The Casey Family Program was created to "provide planned, long-term out-of-home care to children and youth, with long-term family foster care as its core." Its mission: to equip "young people with the skills to form and sustain significant positive relationships, to effectively parent their own children, to participate responsibly in their communities, to sustain themselves economically, and to provide support to those children and youth who will follow them into the Program." The Program, "through national and local community partnerships, advocacy efforts, and by serving as a center for information and learning about children in need of permanent family connections…aims to positively impact the lives of children", in addition to those the Program directly helps with foster care. Headquartered in Seattle, Washington, there are field offices in Arizona, California, Colorado, Hawaii, Idaho, Louisiana, Montana, North Dakota, Oklahoma, Oregon, South Dakota, Texas, Washington and Wyoming. Visitors to the Web will find information on their programs, research services, annual reports, their strategic plan, locations, contact information, and links to sister organization and resources.

Samuel N. and Mary Castle Foundation (HI)
(http://fdncenter.org/grantmaker/castle/index.html)
For more than a century, the Samuel N. and Mary Castle Foundation and its precursor, the Samuel N. Castle Memorial Trust, have served the needs of the people of Hawai'i. Over the years, the Foundation's grantmaking has focused primarily on the support of early education and child care, private education (elementary and high schools as well as colleges and universities), Protestant churches, and arts and cultural organizations with ties to the Castle family. In addition, through the Henry and Dorothy Castle Memorial Fund, the Foundation supports the health and human services sector, concentrating its funds on agencies directly providing services to young children and their families. Because Hawaii's population is concentrated on O'ahu, preference is given to organizations whose programs are O'ahu-based. The Foundation's "folder" on the Center's Web site provides a history of the Foundation and brief biographies of Samuel N. and Mary Tenney Castle, messages from the Foundation's president and executive director, a rundown of its grantmaking policies and application procedures, a list of grants, and contact information.

Century Foundation (NY) (Operating foundation) (http://www.tcf.org/)
The Century Foundation (formerly the Twentieth Century Fund) was founded in 1919 and endowed by Edward A. Filene to "undertake timely and critical analyses of major economic, political, and social institutions and issues." The Foundation is an operating rather than grantmaking foundation and does not award fellowships or scholarships, support dissertation research, or make grants to individuals or institutions. Similarly, it almost never supports large-scale data-gathering efforts or research designed primarily to develop theory or methodology. Currently, it welcomes proposals in four areas: improving living standards, restoring civil society and respect for government, reinvigorating the media, and identifying new foundations for American foreign policy. In addition to information on and excerpts from current and recently completed projects, visitors to the Foundation's Web site will find a mission statement and history of the Foundation, detailed program descriptions, proposal submission guidelines, the Foundation's 1995–96 annual report, press releases and a publications catalog, listings of the Foundation's board and staff, including e-mail links to staff members, links to sites of interest, and contact information.

The Champlin Foundations (RI) (http://fdncenter.org/grantmaker/champlin/)
The aim of the Champlin Foundations is to "provide funds to tax-exempt organizations in Rhode Island who serve—or are able to serve—the broadest possible segment of the population." The Warwick, Rhode Island, foundation makes direct grants for capital needs such as the purchase of equipment, construction, and purchases of real property. They do not provide funds for facilities or equipment for agencies who engage in "program activities", such as counseling, and day care, and do not rely solely on applications to allocate grants. They identify and make grants to many organizations that have not applied, or may encourage those who have not to apply. Grantseekers can consult the Web site for guidelines and funding criteria, and find contact information, a list of members of the Distribution Committee, and a breakdown of 1998 grants.

The Chiang Ching-kuo Foundation for International Scholarly Exchange (VA) (Operating foundation) (http://www.cckf.org/)
The Chiang Ching-kuo Foundation for International Scholarly Exchange (the CCK Foundation) is headquartered in Taipei, Taiwan, ROC, with a regional office in McLean, Virginia. CCK Foundation was established in 1989 in memory of the late President of the Republic of China, Chiang Ching-kuo, who died in 1988. Its purpose is to promote the study of Chinese culture and society, to promote understanding between the Chinese and other people of the world, with the "ultimate goal of encouraging the integration of the best of Chinese culture with an emerging global culture." The scope of their programs includes Chinese cultural heritage, classical studies, the Republic of China, Taiwan area studies, and China-related comparative studies. Grants are made to institutions and individuals, for institutional enhancement, research, conferences and seminars, subsidies for publication, and fellowships for graduate students and post-doctoral research. Visitors to the Web site will find details of each of their funding categories and programs, grant guidelines and deadlines, downloadable applications, contact information, a list of the board of directors and offices, and grant recipient lists.

Chiesman Foundation For Democracy, Inc. (SD) (http://www.chiesman.org)

Allene R. Chiesman founded the Chiesman Foundation for Democracy to pro-mote and support the "greater awareness of the meaning of democracy and demo-cratic ideals by its citizens." She was a philanthropist whose beliefs "were rooted in the fundamentals of hard work and giving back to society a fair share of what one gains through living in a democratic society." Based in Rapid City, South Dakota, the Chiesman Foundation supports: institutes and programs which assist citizens to understand the meaning of American democracy; the importance of participatory citizenship; the principles of economic competitiveness and devel-opment and the role of government; scholars who research and publish results on sound government policy options that promote economic growth and productivity, participatory government, and U.S. constitutional law; and universities and col-leges that establish centers for civic education and law-related education, and establish forums for the education of students, faculty and citizens. Visitors to the Web site will find more detailed information about their goals and purposes and their programs and endowments. Other points of interest are descriptions of their grant programs, application criteria and instructions, a bio of the founder, online viewing of their publication, Chiesman Quarterly, a listing of civic education resources, and contact information. In the future, their Web site will feature a Vir-tual Classroom, an online education center, where meetings, conferences, and classrooms will take place.

Edna McConnell Clark Foundation (NY)
(http://fdncenter.org/grantmaker/emclark/index.html)

The Edna McConnell Clark Foundation seeks to improve conditions and opportu-nities for people who live in poor and disadvantaged communities. Through its grantmaking, the Foundation "assists nonprofit organizations and public agencies committed to advancing practices and policies that better the lives of children and families, [while supporting] initiatives that promise to help systems and institu-tions become more responsive to the needs of the people they serve." The current interests of the Foundation fall into four separate program areas, each with spe-cific goals, strategies, and grantmaking priorities: the Program for Children, the Program for New York Neighborhoods, the Program for Student Achievement, and the Program for Tropical Disease Research. Applicants may want to read the Foundation's latest annual report to ensure that their projects fit within the above programs' very specific, site-based grantmaking strategies. Visitors to the Foun-dation's "folder" on the Center's Web site will find detailed program descriptions, application guidelines, a 1997 grants list organized by program area, a report from Foundation president Michael A. Bailin, a list of Foundation-sponsored publica-tions that can be obtained free of charge, board and staff listings, and contact information.

Robert Sterling Clark Foundation, Inc. (NY)
(http://fdncenter.org/grantmaker/rsclark/index.html)

Incorporated in 1952, the Robert Sterling Clark Foundation has provided financial assistance to a wide variety of charitable organizations over the years. At present, it is concentrating its resources in the following fields: improving the performance of public institutions in New York, strengthening the management of New York City cultural institutions, and ensuring access to family planning practices. While most of its support will be allocated for these purposes, the Foundation has also begun to make funds available to protect artistic freedom and to educate the pub-lic about the importance of the arts in our society. Visitors to the Foundation's "folder" on the Center's Web site will find program guidelines, application proce-dures, annual report, and contact information.

The Clipper Ship Foundation (MA) (http://www.agmconnect.org/clipper1.html)
The Clipper Ship Foundation, based in Boston, MA offers financial assistance to fulfill the goals and broaden the scope of human service organizations. Priority is given to organizations devoted to helping the homeless and ill-housed, the desti-tute, the handicapped, children, the elderly, or supplying special needs of minor-ity, low-income individuals and families. The foundation favors grants that will be matched or will stimulate giving by other donors, and grants for the construction or renovation of physical facilities or other capital projects over operating grants. In general, grants are limited to human service organizations whose majority of individuals served reside in the Greater Boston area; but special consideration will be given to emergency disaster situations worldwide. Grants in support of the arts will be limited to those that expose children or disabled individuals to the arts without charge or at a significantly reduced cost. Visitors to the Web site will find some more information about the Foundation, application information, and con-tact information to get copies of grant guidelines and annual reports.

The Coleman Foundation, Inc. (IL) (http://www.colemanfoundation.org/)
The Chicago, Illinois-based Coleman Foundation was established in 1951 by Mr. and Mrs. J. D. Stetson Coleman, entrepreneurs with various holdings which included Fannie May Candies. Their desire was to "make the community aware of opportunities which could improve the quality of Life." The Coleman Foundation has four program areas: entrepreneurship awareness education; cancer research, care and treatment in the Midwest; housing and education for the handicapped; and a wide range of other educational programs. The Coleman Foundation also considers "special needs associated with poverty and unemployment." Support is generally focused on organizations within the Midwest and particularly within the state of Illinois and the Chicago Metropolitan area, although programs outside of this geographic area but within the United States are considered. Proposals are not solicited and grantseekers should first make contact through an inquiry letter. Their Web site contains information about their programs, grant eligibility, grant applications and procedures, grant lists, financial statements and contact information.

The Colorado Trust (CO) (http://www.coloradotrust.org)
The mission of the Colorado Trust is to promote the health and well-being of the people of Colorado through the support of accessible and affordable health care programs and the strengthening of families. The Trust employs an initiative framework in which it identifies objectives, establishes workable approaches, and recruits interested organizations to implement programs. Visitors to the Trust's easy-to-navigate Web site will find descriptions of its initiatives in each of Colo-rado's counties as well as information about its approaches to grantmaking. Spe-cial features of the site include a funding opportunities mailing list and a program evaluation section entitled "Lessons Learned at the Colorado Trust."

Columbia Foundation (CA) (http://www.columbia.org)

Madeleine and her brother, William Haas, established the Columbia Foundation in 1940 "for the furtherance of the public welfare". This San Francisco-based foundation has had a long-standing interest in world peace, human rights, the environment, cross-cultural and international understanding, the quality of urban life, and the arts, though the board of directors set new priorities within these areas as conditions change. Currently, there are four program areas: arts and culture, whose goal is to enhance the quality of life through arts and cultural programs, with a geographic focus in the San Francisco Bay Area and London; human rights, whose goal is the protection of basic human rights for all, with a focus in the San Francisco Bay area and national programs; preservation of wildness eco-systems and biological diversity, whose goal is to protect and restore wild ecosys-tems, with a focus on Northern California; and sustainable urban community development, with the goal of promoting the viability and quality of life over time without using up the natural processes and products on which life depends, with a geographic focus on the San Francisco Bay Area. The foundation also considers media projects. Their Web site provides grant and application guidelines, a sum-mary of their screening process, information about their funding and project prior-ities, a printable application cover sheet, grant lists, and contact information.

Common Counsel Foundation (CA) (Operating foundation) (http://www.commoncounsel.org)

The Common Counsel Foundation is an Oakland, CA-based public charity that offers strategic philanthropic advisory services to a small group of family founda-tions and individual donors. Proposals are submitted to Common Counsel and are reviewed by staff members who keep in mind the member fund for which the pro-posal may be appropriate. Common Counsel also develops grantmaking programs that reflect the objectives of the member funds and individual donors. This group of family foundations and individual donors are committed to funding economic, environmental and social justice initiatives, seeking to "give voice" to the needs of low-income people, women, youth, people of color, and others working for jus-tice, equity and a healthy, sustainable environment. The member funds of Com-mon Counsel have a special interest in organizations that are committed to the empowerment of their members through community organizing. Current member funds of the foundation are the Abelard Foundation, the Acorn Foundation, and the Penney Family Fund. Common Counsel Foundation also administers the Grantee Exchange Fund and coordinates two retreat programs, one for writers and one for social-change community organizers and activists. The Web site contains information about the goals and funding areas of each of its member funds and retreat programs, contact information for developing your own grantmaking pro-gram, proposal guidelines, printable applications, grant lists, printable applica-tions for the two retreat programs, and contact information.

The Commonweal Foundation, Inc. (MD) (Operating foundation) (http://www.commonweal-foundation.org)

The Commonweal Foundation supports education and programs in the Maryland and Washington, D.C. metropolitan area, with a focus on educational assistance for disadvantaged, at-risk youth. Current programs of the foundation are: Path-ways to Success Boarding School Scholarship Program, which awards scholar-ships to boarding schools; Afterschool and Summer Skills centers in low-income housing complexes; "I have a dream" class; and the small grants program. The Pathways to Success Boarding School Scholarship program has its own separate Web site describing the program and procedures for applying, but no other information about the other programs is provided on this Web site. However, contact information is provided for this Silver Spring, Maryland-based organization, complete with phone and fax numbers, street and email addresses.

Commonwealth Fund (NY) (http://www.cmwf.org)

The Commonwealth Fund, a national New York City-based foundation, undertakes independent research on health and social issues. Its programs focus on improving health care services, bettering the health of minority Americans, advancing the well being of elderly people, and developing the capacities of children and young people. The Fund also offers several international fellowships in health and public policy. Information is available at the Fund's Web site, which also provides a history of the organization, descriptions of its most recent initiatives and related publications, grant guidelines, a listing of its board and staff, and a financial summary.

Connelly Foundation (PA) (http://www.connellyfdn.org)

Based in West Conshohocken, PA, the Connelly Foundation develops programs with and directs its support to educational, human services, health, cultural, and civic organizations. Established in 1955 by Mr. and Mrs. John F. Connelly, who rose from the working class to prominent industrialists and philanthropists, its mission is to enhance the quality of life in the greater Philadelphia area. The foundation focuses its philanthropy on nonprofit organizations and institutions based in and serving the city of Philadelphia and the surrounding Delaware Valley region, and prefers to support projects that receive funding from several sources. Of note is the founders' mandate, which specifies that a minimum sixty percent of funding be granted each year to organizations affiliated with the Roman Catholic Church or toward programs impacting its members. Visitors to the Web site will find application guidelines, grant summaries and breakdown of grants by geographic concentration, short bios of its founders and contact information.

Conservation, Food & Health Foundation (MA)
(http://www.fdncenter.org/grantmaker/cf&hf/)

The primary purpose of the Massachusetts-based Conservation, Food & Health Foundation is "to assist in the conservation of natural resources, the production and distribution of food, and the improvement and promotion of health in the developing world." The Foundation is especially interested in supporting projects that lead to the transfer of responsibility to the citizens of developing countries for managing and solving their own problems and in supporting self-help initiatives. Preference is given to organizations located in developing countries or to developed country organizations whose activities are of direct and immediate benefit to developing countries. The Foundation does not consider the states of the former Soviet Union or former eastern bloc countries as within its geographic focus, however. Visitors to the Foundation's "folder" on the Center's Web site will find detailed application guidelines and eligibility requirements, a grants list, a form for submitting a concept paper to the Foundation (in advance of a final proposal), and contact information.

Cooper Foundation (NE) (http://www.cooperfoundation.org/)

The Nebraska-based Cooper Foundation restricts it support to organizations within its home state, primarily in Lincoln and Lancaster County. The Foundation's mission is to support innovative ideas that "promise substantial impact and encourage others to make similar or larger grants." To that end, it funds programs in education, human services, the arts, and the humanities. It does not fund individuals, endowments, private foundations, businesses, health or religious issues, travel, or organizations outside of Nebraska, and most of its grants are for program funding rather than general operating support. In addition, the Foundation accepts formal applications only from organizations that have already communicated with them and been asked to complete an application form. Visitors to the Foundation's Web site will find a brief history of the foundation, an equally brief description of program priorities, an application guide, description of the application process, an online contact form, financial reports, grants lists, and personnel listing. The Foundation uses the Lincoln/Lancaster County Grantmakers Common Application Form, which can be downloaded at the site.

The Cooper Institute for Advanced Studies in Medicine and the Humanities (FL) (Operating foundation) (http://www.cooperinstitute.org)

The Cooper Institute for Advanced Studies in Medicine and the Humanities, based in Naples, FL, is a nonprofit educational foundation established in 1974 by Irving S. Cooper, who was an internationally renowned neurosurgeon, teacher, and author. The Institute is focused on the interests and well-being of health care-consumers and dedicated to bringing "clarity to the increasingly complex health care environment by organizing health care information in a manner that provides consumers with the tools to make informed decisions", thereby preparing and empowering patients for their "enhanced role as more active and assertive partners in the management of their health care." The Institute's goal is that patient education will create choice and also encourage patient input in the debate over medical quality improvement. Visitors to the Web site will find information about the institute and its founder, links to databases of physician profiles, links to sites about health care policy, a survey, in-depth interviews with authorities in health care, and contact information.

The Aaron Copland Fund for Music, Inc. (NY) (http://www.amc.net/resources/grants)

The Aaron Copland Fund for Music, Inc. is one of the grant programs administered by The American Music Center (AMC), based in New York City, NY. Aaron Copland was one of the founders of AMC in 1939, whose original mission was "foster and encourage the composition of contemporary (American) music and to promote its production, publication, distribution and performance in every way possible throughout the Western Hemisphere", and whose contemporary mission now is "building a national community for new American music." There are two programs under The Aaron Copland Fund for Music, the Performing Ensembles Program, and the Recording Program. The objective of the Performing Ensembles Program is to support organizations whose performances encourage and improve public knowledge and appreciation of serious contemporary music, with grants ranging from $1,000 to $20,000. The objectives of the Recording Program are: to document and provide wider exposure for the music of contemporary American composers; to develop audiences for contemporary American music through record distribution and other retail markets; and to support the release and dissemination of recordings for previously unreleased contemporary American music and the reissuance of recordings no longer available. Grants range from $2,000 to $20,000. Visitors to the Web site will find eligibility, funding provisions, criteria, review procedures, application instructions, downloadable brochures and applications, and contact information for these two programs. Visitors will also find links to other grant programs administered by AMC and information about AMC.

Jessie B. Cox Charitable Trust (PA) (http://www.agmconnect.org/cox.html)
Jessie B. Cox, noted for her philanthropy, established the Jessie B. Cox Charitable Trust to continue that tradition following her death in 1982. The Boston, MA-based Trust funds projects in New England in the areas of health, education, environment, and philanthropy, with a particular interest in projects that will primarily benefit underserved populations and disadvantaged communities, as well as projects that focus on prevention rather than remediation. They also have an interest in fostering collaboration among nonprofit organizations in New England and welcome collaborative concept papers. Their goals are to improve the level of health, enhance educational opportunities and achievement, especially for underserved children and youth, protect and enhance the natural and urban environment and to conserve New England's natural resources, and to increase philanthropy in the area. Their Web site provides grant guidelines and policies, exclusions, application procedures, annual reports and grant lists and contact information.

Crail-Johnson Foundation (CA) (http://www.crail-johnson.org/)
The Crail-Johnson Foundation of San Pedro, California, seeks to "promote the well being of children in need, through the effective application of human and financial resources." Priority is given to organizations and projects of benefit to residents of the greater Los Angeles area. In addition to awarding cash grants, the Foundation also provides technical assistance to select community-based projects benefiting children and families. No grants are made directly to individuals, or for programs and projects benefiting religious purposes, university-level graduate and post-graduate education, research, cultural programs, sporting events, political causes, or programs attempting to influence legislation. Current areas of emphasis are health and human services, education programs, and neighborhood and community. Visitors to the CJF Web site can access the Foundation's annual report, which provides detailed grant application guidelines and limitations, a financial statement, information on selected grants, and a listing of officers and staff. The Web site also provides links to other grantmakers online, detailed descriptions of special Foundation projects, and contact information, including e-mail links to staff members.

Crotched Mountain Foundation (NH) (http://www.cmf.org/)
The Crotched Mountain Foundation is an umbrella organization comprised of the Crotched Mountain School and Rehabilitation Center and the Crotched Mountain Community Based Services, which extends throughout New Hampshire and into Maine and New York. Founded by businessman and philanthropist Harry Alan Gregg, the foundation traces its origins back to the NH Society for Crippled Children, established in 1936. Its mission is to "promote, encourage, and sponsor charitable health, rehabilitative, and educational services on behalf of children,

adults, and elderly persons." Their foundation "enables and empowers persons with physical, developmental, emotional or other health-related considerations to pursue their highest degree of physical, emotional, and social independence as may be individually possible." Based in Greenfield, NH, the Foundation's Web site contains its history, its programs for the disabled and elderly, a search engine for the Web site, links, and contact information.

Nathan Cummings Foundation, Inc. (NY) (http://www.ncf.org/)
Established by noted philanthropist and founder of the Sara Lee Corporation, Nathan Cummings, the Nathan Cummings Foundation is "rooted in the Jewish tradition and committed to democratic values, including fairness, diversity, and community. [The Foundation seeks] to build a society that values nature and protects ecological balance for future generations; promotes humane health care; and fosters arts to enrich communities." To that end, the Foundation focuses its grantmaking activities in five program areas: arts, environment, health, Jewish life, and "interprogram," which reinforces connections among the Foundations core areas. Visitors to the Foundation's Web site will find detailed guidelines, grant lists for each program area, and links to grantee Web sites; application procedures; staff and trustee listings; and various reports and publications, including the Foundation's annual report.

Charles A. Dana Foundation, Inc. (NY) (http://www.dana.org/)
The Charles A. Dana Foundation is a private philanthropic foundation with principle interests in brain research and public-education initiatives. The Foundation's Web site contains a statement of the Foundation's grantmaking policies and procedures; detailed application and program information; information on active grant projects; information about the Charles A. Dana Awards, which honor innovators in neuroscience and education reform; information about the Dana Clinical Hypotheses in Neuroscience Research, which supports pilot testing of innovative and experimental ideas that have potential of advancing clinical applications of neuroscience research; the Dana Alliance for Brain initiatives, a nonprofit dedicated to educating the public about the benefits of brain research; a publications archive (including the Foundation's annual report); Dana BrainWeb (annotated links to Web sites devoted to specific brain disorders, general health, and neuroscience); a listing of the Foundation's directors, officers, and staff; and press and contact information.

The Davidson Foundation (NV) (http://www.davidsonfoundation.org/)
Located in Incline Village, Nevada, the Davidson Foundation was founded in 1997 by Bob and Jan Davidson and their children, Liz, Emilie, and John. Its mission is to "advance learning, enhance human potential and empower people to live lives of achievement and service", with a focus on supporting exceptionally gifted young people. To that end, one of their programs is the Davidson Young Scholars Pilot Program, whose mission is to "recognize, nurture and support the special needs of exceptionally gifted children." The program was launched in the spring of 1999 and provides a variety of resources, such as needs-assessment, personal planning, funding, mentoring, and fellowship to children between the ages of 4 and 12. The Foundation states that it is proactive in its grantmaking, and that the Foundation seeks out and investigates grantmaking opportunities with nonprofit organizations whose work supports their mission. They do not accept unsolicited

grant proposals. Consult their Web site to learn more about their foundation, their focus on exceptionally gifted children, the Davidson Young Scholars Pilot Program, application procedures, information on exceptionally gifted children, annual report, grant list, and contact information.

Arthur Vining Davis Foundations (FL) (http://www.jvm.com/davis/)

The Arthur Davis Vining Foundations provide support nationally for five primary program areas: private higher education, secondary education, religion (graduate theological education), health care (caring attitudes), and public television. The Foundations do not make grants to individuals; institutions or programs outside the United States and its possessions; publicly governed colleges, universities, and other entities that are supported primarily by government funds (except in health care and secondary education programs); or projects incurring obligations extending over several years. Visitors to the Foundation's Web site will find descriptions of each program area, recent grants lists organized by program area, application procedures, a brief FAQ, and contact information.

Dr. G. Clifford & Florence B. Decker Foundation (NY) (http://www.spectra.net/~deckerfn/index.html)

Dr. G. Clifford Decker established the Decker Foundation in 1979 with his wife, Florence, to assist charitable organizations servicing the residents of Broome County, New York. Located in Binghampton, New York, the Foundation focuses grantmaking on education, medical and medical research institutions, and cultural and human service organizations. Grants may be used for capital projects or new and innovative projects and programs. In general, they do not provide continuing or regular operating support, as their efforts are "directed toward helping organizations provide programs to earn income and thus become self-sufficient." Grant applications can be requested by phone, mail, or email. They state that "interest in the Decker Foundation is welcome". Visitors to the Web site will find grant application guidelines, the Decker's and Foundation's history, annual reports, a list of their Board of Directors, links to institutions that have received Decker Foundation grants, and contact information.

The Dekko Foundation, Inc. (IN) (http://www.dekkofoundation.org)

Chester E. Dekko created the Dekko Foundation in 1981 as a way to give back to the communities that had bred his success. He learned that education, hard work, and leadership could provide economic freedom for any individual that desired it; accordingly, the mission of his foundation is to "foster economic freedom through education." The Foundation's two broad program areas are education and community, with a geographic focus on communities that Group Dekko International had plants or where Mr. Dekko had a presence prior to his death in 1992. Grant proposals are considered from counties in Indiana, Iowa and Alabama. Based in Kendallville, IN, its educational priorities are public and private schools and early childhood education; its community priorities are community foundations, libraries, museums, parks, festivals, summer camps, youth organizations, and organizations for the needy and disabled. In addition to these funding areas, Dekko Foundation also has four proactive programs in supporting education and community: Einstein Grants, for ideas that will stimulate excitement for education; Youth Initiative, to empower young people to serve their community and school through grantmaking; Early Education Programs, which develops partnerships with early childhood programs; and the Dekko Award for Teaching Excellence. Visitors to the Web site will find further information on the funding areas, proactive programs, geographic focus, grant guidelines and application instructions, the history of the foundation and its founder, and contact information.

Gladys Krieble Delmas Foundation (NY) (http://www.delmas.org/)

The Gladys Krieble Delmas Foundation promotes "the advancement and perpetuation of humanistic inquiry and artistic creativity by encouraging excellence in scholarship and in the performing arts, and by supporting research libraries and other institutions that preserve the resources which transmit this cultural heritage." The Foundation sponsors four distinct grantmaking programs: in the humanities, in the performing arts, for research libraries, and for Venetian research. Foundation trustees may also award discretionary grants outside of these specific programs. Visitors to the Foundation's Web site will find descriptions and grants lists for each program area, as well as recent grants for Independent Research in Venice and the Veneto; application procedures and eligibility requirements; and a listing of the Foundation's trustees, staff, and advisory board members. The site also features an online information and application request form and contact information.

William Orr Dingwall Foundation (CA) (http://www.wod.org/index.html)

Established in 1994 by Dr. William Orr Dingwall, the San Francisco-based Dingwall Foundation has two primary goals: to provide financial assistance to persons of Korean ancestry to pursue undergraduate or graduate studies devoted to any subject offered by well-established universities throughout the world; and to provide financial assistance to persons of any national origin to pursue graduate studies devoted to the neural bases of language. Every year the Foundation distributes one or more grants of up to $18,000 per year to students who meet its goals. The normal duration of the grant is three years, but may be extended for up to one additional year. The Foundation's Web site provides a brief description of its one program and an electronic application form, in both English and Korean.

DJ & T Foundation (CA) (http://www.djtfoundation.org)

Television personality Bob Barker, of "Price is Right" fame, established the Beverly Hills, CA-based DJ & T Foundation in 1995, which was named in memory of his wife, Dorothy Jo, and his mother, Matilda (Tilly) Valandra, who both loved all animals. Its goal is to help relieve animal overpopulation by funding low cost or free spay/neuter clinics all over the United States. The Foundation assists all qualified spay/neuter clinics, but is most committed to making grants at the grassroots level to under-funded clinics that provide free or low cost spay/neuter services. Grants are only awarded to organizations operating a stationary and/or mobile clinic, or who are in the process of creating one. Grant seekers can download an application or request one in writing after checking out grant guidelines and the FAQ sheet on their Web site.

Geraldine R. Dodge Foundation, Inc. (NJ) (http://www.grdodge.org/)

The Geraldine R. Dodge Foundation makes grants in five major areas: 1) elementary and secondary education; 2) arts, with a primary focus on New Jersey and on programs that seek to establish and improve education in the arts, foster conditions that promote public access to the arts, recognize the critical role of the individual artist, enable developing institutions to gain stability, and help major institutions realize long-term goals; 3) welfare of animals, especially projects with national implications that encourage a more humane ethic and lower the violence in the way we treat animals; 4) critical issues, with a particular interest in New Jersey and the Northeast and focusing on ecosystems preservation, energy conservation, pollution prevention and reduction, education and communication efforts that lead to enlightened environmental policy, and projects that address population growth and family planning; and 5) local projects in Morris County, New Jersey. The Foundation's Web site provides concise program descriptions, grants lists, application guidelines, a brief history of the Foundation, and contact information. The site also provides information on Foundation-initiated programs.

The Patrick and Catherine Weldon Donaghue Medical Research Foundation (CT) (http://www.donaghue.org)

The Patrick and Catherine Weldon Donaghue Medical Research Foundation, based in West Hartford, CT, was created in the will of Ethel Frances Donaghue in memory of her parents. One of three trusts provided for in her will when she died in 1989 at the age of 93, the Medical Research Foundation was funded in May 1991 with over $50 million, the bulk of the proceeds of two generations of successful family endeavors in Hartford commerce and investment. One of Connecticut's first woman lawyers, she dedicated her substantial fortune to providing " financial assistance for research in the fields of cancer and heart disease and/or other medical research to promote medical knowledge which will be of practical benefit to the preservation, maintenance and improvement of human life." The Medical Research Foundation began in 1991 with three grant programs that focused on postdoctoral fellows and new investigators doing basic and pre-clinical research in cancer and heart disease, and has since expanded to include research in community health, epidemiology and health services. The also "invite grant applications from investigators in mental health and neurodegenerative illnesses." There are currently three types of grant awards: Research in Clinical and Community Health Issues, Donaghue Investigator Program, and the Practical Benefits Initiatives. The Foundation focuses funding of research to health-related institutions and organizations located in Connecticut. Visitor to their Web site will find downloadable applications; information on their funding areas, grant award types, and grant guidelines and instructions; the founder's and the foundation's history; highlights of their grantmaking and financial information; members of their advisory boards; a downloadable newsletter, FAQ sheet and contact information.

William H. Donner Foundation, Inc. (NY) (http://www.donner.org/)

The William H. Donner Foundation, a small, family foundation based in New York City, was created in 1961 with the endowment originally established by Mr. Donner for the International Cancer Research Foundation, which he founded in 1932 to honor his son's memory after his death from cancer. In January 1999, the foundation adopted a policy that it would no longer accept unsolicited proposals; only applications invited by the Foundation are considered. In its grantmaking, the Foundation follows two philanthropic principals of its founder: "acceptance of clearly defined risks and the judicious use of incentive grants to advance thoughtful, creative projects." The Foundation's Web site contains a biography of its founder, a statement of its grantmaking policy, a listing of Foundation officers and staff, and contact information. A link to application forms is provided, but requires a password for entry.

Do Right Foundation (CA) (http://www.doright.org/)

The broadly stated goal of the Do Right Foundation is to "address some of the current obstacles to a more joyful and rewarding society," and the Foundation's Web site is devoted to explaining this philosophy as it relates to the grantseeking process. Funding areas are: reducing violent crime, fighting joblessness, increasing productivity of our legal system, encouraging transition from welfare to work, developing ever-improving generations of children, improving integrity and efficiencies of government, alleviating homelessness, promoting fire safety and prevention, and promoting quality management. The Foundation gives priority to grantseekers who focus on the application of new and improved management theories. Visitors to the site will find a biography of Dr. W. Edwards Deming, upon whose management concepts the Foundation's philosophies are based. Grants lists, a downloadable application, and contact information are also available. Prospectors are encouraged to submit a pre-grant inquiry by e-mail before applying formally.

J.C. Downing Foundation (CA) (http://www.jcdowning.org/)

The San Diego-based J.C. Downing Foundation supports innovative efforts and original projects in five program areas: education and human development, environmental research and preservation, fine arts, sports and athletics, and technology and communications. The Foundation awards grants to qualified nonprofit organizations with explicit, identifiable needs, and does not place geographic or dollar restrictions on its grants (although the typical award falls between $5,000 and $50,000). The Foundation's Web site provides grantmaking guidelines and areas of exclusion, application procedures, a list of selected grants the Foundation has made since 1990, and a "General Guidance" section, which includes information about the grantseeeking process, a recommended reading list, and links to Web sites of interest.

Camille and Henry Dreyfus Foundation, Inc. (NY) (http://www.dreyfus.org/)

The principal aim of the Camille and Henry Dreyfus Foundation is to "advance the science of chemistry, chemical engineering and related sciences as a means of improving human relations and circumstances around the world." To that end, the Foundation makes grant awards to academic and other eligible institutions for the purposes of sponsoring qualified applicants in their education and research. The Foundation's Web site provides detailed descriptions of the Foundation's various programs, including eligibility requirements and application and nomination procedures, and a listing of recent grantees. As an added convenience, some application and nomination forms can be submitted online; online submission of application and nomination forms for all programs will be available in the future.

Joseph Drown Foundation (CA) (http://www.jdrown.org)

Joseph Warford Drown was involved with the hotel industry, notably as owner of Hotel Bel-Air in Los Angeles. He formed the Los Angeles, CA-based Joseph Drown Foundation in 1953 to provide an organized means of charitable giving, both during his lifetime and after his death in 1982. The goal of his foundation is to assist individuals to becoming successful, self-sustaining, contributing citizens, and the foundation is interested in programs that break down barriers that prevent growth and learning. The Foundation has five main funding areas: education, community, health and social services, arts and humanities, medical and scientific research, and special projects, which are at discretion of the board but still related to the mission of the foundation. Programs in the area of medical and scientific research are initiated by the Foundation; arts and humanities programs are a lesser priority and concentrate on outreach and education. Most of their grantmaking is limited to programs and organizations in California. Consult their Web site for more information about each funding area, as well as the grant application procedure, a list of sample grants, contact information and related links.

The Peter F. Drucker Foundation for Nonprofit Management, Inc. (NY)
(Operating foundation) (http://www.pfdf.org/)

Frances Hesselbein founded the Peter F. Drucker Foundation for Nonprofit Management in 1990, named for and inspired by the "acknowledged father of modern management." The mission of the New York City-based foundation is "to lead social sector organizations toward excellence in performance", through the presentation of conferences, the annual Peter F. Drucker Award for Nonprofit Innovation, the Frances Hesselbein Community Innovation Fellows Program, and the development of management resources, partnerships, and publications. The Foundation considers itself "a broker of intellectual capital, bringing together the finest leaders, consultants, authors and social philosophers in the world with the leaders of social sector voluntary organizations." The Peter F. Drucker Award for Nonprofit Innovation is given to a nonprofit organization in recognition of an innovative program, and is accompanied by a $25,000 prize and a professionally-produced short video documentary of the winning project or program. The Frances Hesselbein Community Innovation Fellows Program recognizes the accomplishments and supports the professional development of social sector leaders who have a demonstrated record of leadership and entrepreneurial performance, and who are engaged in projects or programs that demonstrate community innovation. Visitors to their Web site will find guidelines and instructions for these two programs; downloadable applications, conference reports, quarterly newsletters and annual reports; schedules and printable registration forms to their events; an online feedback and information request form; descriptions of the Foundation's leadership publications, reader's guides, and links to order their publications; and contact information. The Foundation makes clear that they only provide programs and resources, and does not make grants and does not accept funding proposals.

Doris Duke Charitable Foundation (NY)
(http://fdncenter.org/grantmaker/dorisduke/)

The New York-based Doris Duke Charitable Foundation was created in 1996, in accordance with the terms of the will of Doris Duke, to improve the quality of people's lives by preserving natural environments, seek cures for diseases, and nurture the arts. The Foundation currently pursues its mission through three grantmaking programs supporting performing artists in the creation and public performance of their work; the protection and restoration of the environment, and promotion the sustainable use of land and other natural resources; and medical research leading to the prevention and cure of heart disease, cancer, AIDS, and sickle cell anemia and other blood disorders. The Foundation's Web site—a

Foundation Folder on the Center's site—describes these programs in detail and provides guidelines to the grantmaking process. Visitors to the site will also find grants lists for the last three years, information about the Foundation's three non-grantmaking operating foundations, and a listing of trustees and staff.

The Duke Endowment (NC) (http://www.dukeendowment.org/)

The Duke Endowment, a charitable trust established in 1924 by North Carolina industrialist James Buchanan Duke, continues its founder's philanthropic legacy of giving to "educate students and teachers, to heal minds and bodies, to nurture children, and to strengthen the human spirit." As a trust, the Duke Endowment differs from a private foundation in that its principle donor named specific organizations or individuals eligible to receive funding. In the case of the Endowment, these are: not-for-profit health care organizations in North and South Carolina; not-for-profit child care institutions in North and South Carolina; rural United Methodist churches and retired ministers in North Carolina; and Duke, Furman, and Johnson C. Smith universities, and Davidson College. Program areas are education, health care, child care, and rural churches. The Endowment's Web site provides general program descriptions and application procedures, a grants list organized by area of interest, links to resources and grantee organizations, a searchable online catalog of library materials (the Endowment's library houses a Foundation Center Cooperating Collection), financial statements, a listing of Endowment trustees and staff, and contact information.

Jessie Ball duPont Fund (FL) (http://www.dupontfund.org/index.html)

The Jessie Ball duPont Fund, a national foundation having a special, though not exclusive, interest in issues affecting the South, makes grants "to a defined universe of eligible institutions"—that is, any institution that received a contribution from Mrs. duPont between January 1,1960, and December 31, 1964 (approximately 350 in total). Proof of eligibility is determined by the Fund from examination of Mrs. duPont's personal or tax records or by the applicant presenting written verifiable evidence of having received a contribution during the eligibility period. The Fund's mission, "to address broad-based issues of communities and of the larger society that have regional, national, and international relevance," is achieved through programs in arts and culture, education, health, historic preservation, human services, and religion. Visitors to the Fund's Web site will find detailed program information and eligibility guidelines, a statement of the Fund's mission and core values, a biography of Mrs. DuPont, and contact information. The Fund also plans to post to excerpts from Notes from the Field, its publication devoted to philanthropic "best practices," in the following areas: access to health care, affordable housing for low-income families, inclusiveness in institutions of higher education, taking action and seeking justice, and creating healthy outcomes for children.

Durfee Foundation (CA) (http://www.durfee.org/)

Named in honor of the late Dorothy Durfee Avery who, with her husband, the late R. Stanton Avery, founded the Avery Dennison Corporation, a multinational manufacturing concern, the Durfee Foundation has awarded more than $13 million in grants since 1960 in the areas of arts and culture, education, history, and community development, primarily in Southern California. Programs currently supported by the Foundation include the American/Chinese Adventure Capital Program, the

Durfee Community Fund, the Durfee Sabbatical Program, Student Challenge Awards, the Student Service and Philanthropy Project, and Durfee Artist and Music Fellowships. Although as a rule the Foundation does not review unsolicited proposals, one-page letters of introduction are welcome. Visitors to the Foundation's Web site will find program descriptions and criteria; project proposal guidelines; financial statements and a summary of grants from the Foundation's most recent annual report; a listing of the Foundation's trustees, and contact information.

The John and Genevieve Dyer Educational Foundation (VA)
(http://www.dyeredu.com)
The Arlington, Virginia-based John and Genevieve Dyer Educational Foundation was established by Dr. Timothy J. Dyer, "recognized worldwide as a leader in education", in memory of his parents. He started the foundation in gratitude to them for instilling in him "the beauty and power of education." The Foundation's purpose is to instill in others an appreciation of the value of education and teaching, and to annually recognize and award individuals or institutions that have achieved excellence in those areas. It will also contribute to individuals, groups, or organizations that work against discrimination, and that provide training and education that furthers a respect for diversity. Visitors to their sparse Web site will find information about their award program, application instructions, and contact information.

Echoing Green Foundation (NY) (http://echoinggreen.org)
New York City-based Echoing Green Foundation was founded by venture capitalist Ed Cohen, who along with a group of investors created an organization that "applies venture capitalist principles to a social change sphere." echoing green, named after one of the poems of Eighteenth Century poet and artist William Blake, is a nonprofit foundation that offers full-time fellowships to emerging "social entrepreneurs", and applies a venture capital approach to philanthropy by providing seed money and technical support to individuals creating innovative public service organizations or projects with goals of positive social change. Investing in organizations and projects at an early stage where most funders are unwilling to do so, echoing green also provides them with support to help them grow beyond a start-up. The fellowship includes a two-year $60,000 stipend, health care benefits, online connectivity, access to their network of social entrepreneurs, training, and technical assistance. Proposed organizations and projects can be domestic or international and in all public service areas, including but not limited to the environment, arts, education, youth service, civil and human rights, and community and economic development. Consult the echoing green Web site for information about the foundation and how to become a fellow, news and events related to the foundation, a resource center covering topics from organizational development to attracting resources to people development and for related links, a public forum for dialogue about fellows and projects, a database of profiles of fellows, and contact information.

El Pomar Foundation (CO) (http://www.elpomar.org/)
Founded in 1937 by copper mining magnate Spencer Penrose, El Pomar Foundation today has assets in excess of $350 million, making it one of the largest and oldest foundations in the Rocky Mountain West. The Foundation makes grants

throughout the state of Colorado in the areas of human services, community development, the arts, health care, amateur athletics, and education. In addition to grant application guidelines and summary financial information for the year ended December 31, 1996, visitors to the Foundation's Web site will find general information about the Foundation and its many operating programs: Fellowship in Community Service, a program designed to develop future leaders among recent college graduates; El Pomar Youth in Community Service (EPYCS); El Pomar Awards for Excellence, which reward outstanding nonprofit organizations in Colorado; the Foundation's Education Initiative; Resource Library; and El Pomar Center, which is dedicated to the recognition and promotion of excellence within the nonprofit community.

Energy Foundation (CA) (http://www.ef.org/)
Created in 1991 under the auspices of the MacArthur Foundation, The Pew Charitable Trusts, and the Rockefeller Foundation, the mission of the Energy Foundation is "to assist in the nation's transition to a sustainable energy future by promoting energy efficiency and renewable energy." Visitors to the Foundation's Web site will find program descriptions, application guidelines, lists of recent grant recipients, and printable application forms for each of the Foundation's program areas: utilities, buildings, transportation, renewable energy, clean energy, and integrated issues. Also available online are essays devoted to the realities surrounding the Foundation's mission, a section for special Foundation reports, and a list of annotated links to energy-related Web sites.

Lois and Richard England Family Foundation, Inc. (DC) (http://fdncenter.org/grantmaker/england/index.html)
Created in 1994, the Lois and Richard England Family Foundation is "committed to improving the lives of those in need in the Washington metropolitan area." Toward that end, the Foundation's grantmaking focuses on local human services, education, and arts and culture. The Foundation also supports programs to strengthen Jewish life and institutions locally, nationally, and in Israel. In addition to mission and goal statements, the Foundation's "folder" on the Center's Web site provides grant guidelines, grants lists, a listing of the Foundation's trustees, and contact information.

Esquel Group Foundation, Inc. (DC) (http://www.esquel.org)
Esquel Group Foundation, Inc. (EGF) is the US-based member and coordinator for regional programs of the Grupo Esquel Network, a group of nonprofit, nongovernmental organizations dedicated to promoting "alternative policies and programs which strengthen the role of civil society" and to promoting sustainable and equitable development in South America. The Washington, DC-based EGF provides a variety of services, including research, advocacy, technical cooperation and extensive advice regarding development in Latin America to nongovernmental organizations, foundations, private corporations, and international development agencies working in Latin America and the Caribbean. EGF also works in collaboration with private sector entities to improve public policy for sustainable development, with political, economic, social, and natural resource considerations in mind. Grupo Esquel has five priority areas: legal framework for civil society; environment, especially in Semi-Arid and Arid Zones; rural development and agriculture; children and youth at risk; and "microenterprise

development". Visitors to the EFG site will find reports on their work, list of publications and conferences participated in and organized by EGF, contact information for members of the EGF network, board and staff member profiles, a history of EGF, and information on their internship program.

Lettie Pate Evans Foundation, Inc. (GA) (http://www.lpevans.org)

Lettie Pate Evans was the wife of Joseph Whitehead, one of the original bottlers of Coca-Cola. She became one of the first American women to serve as a director of a major American corporation when she was appointed to the Board of Directors of the Coca-Cola Company in 1934, a post she held for 20 years. In 1945, Lettie Pate Evans created a foundation in her own name, for the "promotion of charity," with a grant program reflecting a strong emphasis in private secondary and higher education, arts and culture, and museums and historic preservation. Grants awarded by this Atlanta, Georgia-based foundation are generally limited to institutions in Georgia and, from time to time, institutions in Virginia favored by Lettie Pate Evans during her lifetime. Preference has traditionally been given to one-time capital projects. Grant proposals submitted to the Foundation may be also be considered by one or more of the four other foundations sharing staff and offices with the Lettie Pate Evans Foundation; therefore, it is unnecessary to communicate separately with more than one of these foundations when seeking information or grant support. Points of interest on the Web site include grant application guidelines, analysis of 1998 grants, financial information, a list of officers and trustees, contact information, including an email link, a link to other foundations, and a short biography of the founder.

Samuel S. Fels Fund (PA) (http://www.dvg.org/Fels/)

Samuel S. Fels was a Philadelphia philanthropist and civic leader who was president of Fels & Company, which manufactured Fels Naptha, a popular household soap. On December 17, 1935, the Samuel S. Fels Fund was incorporated to initiate and support projects of "a scientific, educational or charitable nature which tend to improve human daily life and to bring the average person greater health, happiness, and a fuller understanding of the meaning and purposes of life". Their mission is also to support projects "which prevent, lessen or resolve contemporary social problems". Based in Philadelphia, PA, the foundation had four funding categories: arts and humanities, education, community programs, and health. Grants are restricted to organizations located in the city of Philadelphia or focused on local issues, and an "ideal proposal to Fels is one that addresses positive social change." Grants range from $1000 to $30,000, though larger grants are occasionally made in exceptional situations. Visitors to the Web site will find detailed grant application guidelines, a printable proposal cover sheet, 1998 grants list, list of trustees and staff, President's message, and contact information.

Flinn Foundation (AZ) (http://aspin.asu.edu/flinn/index.html)

The Phoenix-based Flinn Foundation primarily awards grants in the fields of health and health care, but also sponsors a scholarship program for higher education and supports Arizona's arts organizations (by invitation only). The Foundation takes a proactive approach in its grantmaking; most grant recipients are chosen through Requests for Proposals or by invitation. The Foundation's activities are limited to the state of Arizona. In addition to brief biographies of Foundation founders Dr. Robert Flinn and his wife, Irene Pierce Flinn, visitors to the

Foundation's Web site will find program descriptions, grant application procedures, a downloadable annual report, links to online resources, a publications order form, a listing of the Foundation's trustees and staff, and an online contact/grant proposal inquiry form.

Ford Foundation (NY) (http://www.fordfound.org)
Founded in 1936 by Henry and Edsel Ford and operated as a local philanthropy in the state of Michigan until 1950, the Ford Foundation has since expanded to become a leading force in the world of national and international philanthropy. The Foundation's broadly stated goals are to "strengthen democratic values, reduce poverty and injustice, promote international cooperation, and advance human achievement." To better realize its goals, the Foundation implemented a new program and organizational structure in October 1996 that, among other things, consolidated its grantmaking into three program areas: asset building and community development; education, media, arts, and culture; and peace and social justice. In addition to providing visitors with program guidelines, application procedures, a listing of recent grants, and worldwide contact information, the Foundation's comprehensive Web site also contains a grants database, press releases, and its annual report.

Edward E. Ford Foundation (RI) (http://www.eeford.org/)
Established by Edward E. Ford, an IBM director and independent businessman, in 1957, the Edward E. Ford Foundation is dedicated to encouraging and improving secondary education as provided by independent schools in the United States. To that end, the Foundation has awarded 1,796 grants totaling almost $58 million since its inception—the vast majority of them to National Association of Independent School member schools or NAIS member state and regional associations. The Foundation does not make grants to individuals. The initial step in the process of filing an application with the Foundation is to contact the Office of the Executive Director in Washington for a preliminary telephone interview. The Foundation's Web site provides a brief history of the Foundation, proposal guidelines for schools and associations, a list of recent grants, a one-page financial statement, and contact information.

Thomas B. Fordham Foundation (DC) (http://www.edexcellence.net)
Thomas B. Fordham was a successful industrialist and prominent civic leader in Dayton, Ohio who passed away in 1944. In 1953, his widow, Thelma Fordham Pruett, established the Thomas B. Fordham Foundation in his memory. During her lifetime, the Foundation aided diverse charitable organizations and educational institutions in the Dayton area; but upon her death in 1995, the trustees determined that reform of elementary/secondary school education would be their sole focus, as it was a long-time interest of Thelma Pruett. To that end, the Thomas B. Fordham Foundation supports research, publications, and action projects of national significance in elementary/secondary education reform, and significant education reform projects in Dayton, Ohio and vicinity. The Washington, DC-based foundation is pro-active in approach, designing and conducting projects and seeking out partners to "further its mission of public awareness and education reform"; it does not support unsolicited projects or consider unsolicited proposals. It is primarily interested in "projects leading to information that advances knowledge of effective education reform strategies consistent with the Foundation's

principles". Visitors to the Web site will find further information on the Foundation's mode of operation, information on their national reform issues, links, viewable and downloadable publications and articles, ordering information, bibliographies of recommended books, and contact information.

Foundation for Child Development (NY) (http://www.ffcd.org/)

The New York City-based Foundation for Child Development is dedicated to the principle that all families should have the social and material resources to raise their children to be healthy, educated, and productive members of their communities. The foundation makes grants nationally to nonprofit institutions for research, policy analysis, advocacy, leadership development, and a small number of program development projects. Three cross-cutting themes guide FCD's work: linking research on children and families to formation of relevant programs and policies; identifying fresh approaches to crafting sound social strategies for children and families; and nurturing new generations of leaders in child development research and policy. The Foundation does not consider requests for scholarships or grants to individuals; capital campaigns; or the purchase, construction or renovation of buildings. The Foundation's Web site offers a brief history of the Foundation, its mission statement and application instructions, a searchable grants database, the FCD Working Paper Series in PDF format, listings of the Foundation's board and staff, and contact information.

The Foundation for College Christian Leaders (CA) (http://collegechristianleader.com)

Formerly known as the Eckmann Foundation, The Foundation for College Christian Leaders was formed in 1988. The San Diego, CA-based Foundation's purpose is to "assist Christian individuals with identified leadership history, high academic achievement and financial need with academic, vocational, and ministry training to further the kingdom of Jesus Christ". The Foundation awards scholarships for undergraduate studies, and occasionally for graduate studies. Consult their Web site for guidelines, application information, electronic submission of application forms and contact information.

Foundation for the Future (WA) (http://www.futurefoundation.org)

In 1996, Walter Kistler established Foundation for the Future, located in Bellevue, Washington. He is founder of Kistler Instruments Corporation, a world leader in the development of quartz sensors, and is also the co-founder and Chairman Emeritus of Kistler Aerospace Corporation. The Foundation is focused on the long-term survivability of humanity and supports research and symposia whose purpose is to identify the most critical factors that may affect future human life on Earth. To that end, the Foundation has a research grant award program, the biannual Kistler Prize, and the Humanity 3000 symposium and seminars. The research grant award program provides financial support to scholars for research that is directly related to a better understanding of the factors affecting the quality of life for the long-term future of humanity. The Kistler Prize is awarded every other year to individuals and organizations for "outstanding achievement in identifying the genetic factors that may have a decisive impact on the survivability of a human population", and includes a $100,000 prize. The Foundation is also planning Humanity 3000, a major international symposium of "approximately 100 of the world's most prominent scholars" for discussion and debate of the factors affecting quality of human life in the future. Visit the Web site for more information about the foundation's programs, application procedures, newsletter, links to other futurist organizations, and contact information. The site also has online submission of preliminary applications and an online feedback and information request form.

Foundation for Microbiology (NY) (http://www.tiac.net/users/waksman/)

The purpose of the New York City-based Foundation for Microbiology is "to promote, encourage, and aid scientific research in microbiology; [and] to provide and assist in providing the funds and facilities by which scientific discoveries, inventions, and processes in microbiology may be developed." The Foundation does not offer conventional research, fellowship, or travel grants. Instead, its funds are used "for the support of lectureships, prizes, or courses related to the field of microbiology, as well as for unusual publications or other activities in this field poorly supported by the usual Government agencies. To qualify for support, any of these activities must be expected to address a national or an international audience. Innovative educational programs dealing with microbiological topics and making use of contemporary communication techniques are a special focus of interest, as are programs concerned with enhancing public awareness of science, including K–12 teaching programs that make use of microorganisms. Visitors to the Foundation's Web site will find financial information; concise application guidelines and limitations; a list of grants and contributions made by the Foundation; and a directory of officers and trustees (complete with phone, fax, and e-mail info).

Foundation for Seacoast Health (NH) (http://www.nh.ultranet.com/~ffsh)

The mission of the Foundation for Seacoast Health, the largest private charitable foundation in the State of New Hampshire, is to support and promote health care in the New Hampshire/Maine Seacoast area, which includes Portsmouth, Rye, New Castle, Greenland, Newington, and North Hampton, New Hampshire; and Kittery, Eliot, and York, Maine. The Foundation awards grants to nonprofit agencies and public entities addressing the health-related needs of persons residing in the Seacoast communities. It also offers annual scholarships ranging from $1,000 to $10,000 to assist qualified students who are residents of the Seacoast area and are pursuing health-related fields of study. Visitors to the Foundation's Web site will find general background and contact information, and grant application guidelines with time tables for both general grants and individual scholarships.

Freedom Forum, Inc. (VA) (http://www.freedomforum.org)

Dedicated to "free press, free speech and free spirit for all people," the mission of the Freedom Forum is to help the public and the news media understand one another better. Primary areas of interest include First Amendment rights, journalism education, newsroom diversity, professional development of journalists, media studies and research, and international journalism programs. The Forum does not accept unsolicited grant applications and only makes limited grants in connection with its programs. Its Web site offers a range of information and features, including detailed descriptions of the Forum's programs and history; articles drawn from various Freedom Forum publications; links to the Gannett Center for Media Studies as well as dozens of related online resources; an online version of the Forum's 1997 annual report, with grant "highlights" organized by month; and a listing of the Foundation's trustees and officers.

Frey Foundation (MI) (http://www.freyfdn.org)

As heir to Union Bank and Trust and founder of Foremost Insurance Company, Edward Frey accumulated considerable wealth, which he and his wife Francis believed should be reinvested in the community. As a means to carry out their charitable interests, they established the Frey Foundation, based in Grand Rapids, Michigan. The Frey Foundation is "committed to working together to make a difference in the lives of individuals, families, organizations, and communities", and states that "as we strive to make a meaningful impact on the lives of people, we encourage creativity and excellence and expect accountability of ourselves and others." The Foundation has five funding categories: Enhancing the lives of children and their families, Protecting the Environment, Nurturing Community Arts, Encouraging Civic Progress, and Strengthening Philanthropy; and two special initiatives: Revitalizing Our Community, and Supporting Our Children. Support is primarily given to the western side of Michigan's lower peninsula, with special emphasis on the greater Grand Rapids area and Charlevoix and Emmet counties. Consult their Web site for more details about each funding category, grant application instructions, financial statements, available publications, contact information including an email link, and links to other organizations in the community.

Friedman-Klarreich Family Foundation (OH) (http://members.aol.com/klarff/index.htm)

Established in 1992 by Susan Friedman Klarreich and her four daughters, Karin, Betsy, Kathie, and Beth, the Los Altos, California-based Friedman-Klarreich Family Foundation awards grants to innovative nonprofit organizations or properly qualified individuals dedicated to achieving educational and economic equality for girls and women and/or to enhancing the stability of families. The Foundation's simple Web site provides application guidelines and requirements, schedule for application submission, examples of previous grants, links to related sites of interest, and contact information.

The Frist Foundation (TN) (http://www.fristfoundation.org)

Formerly known as the HCA Foundation, the Nashville-based Frist Foundation was established in 1982 by Hospital Corporation of America. Following the merger of HCA with Columbia Healthcare Corporation in 1994, the Foundation became fully independent of the company, and in 1997 changed its name to honor the philanthropic influence of its founding directors Dr. Thomas F. Frist, Sr., gifted cardiologist, businessman, and philanthropist, and Dr. Thomas F. Frist, Jr., who still serves as chairman. The Frist Foundation continues its mission to invest its resources in select not-for-profit organizations in Metropolitan Nashville in order to strengthen their ability to provide services. The Foundation's activities are mostly grantmaking, but they have also initiated special programs to enhance the community, some of which awards grants. Grants are awarded to a variety of organizations in the fields of health, human services, civic affairs, education, and the arts, and generally fall into three categories: sustaining (operating support), project and program, and capital. Consult their Web site for more information on their special programs guidelines, funding guidelines, lists of directors and staff members, annual report, grant recipient lists, and contact information, including an email link.

Helene Fuld Health Trust (NY) (http://www.fuldtrust.org)

Dr. Leonhard Felix Fuld and his sister, Florentine, created a foundation in honor of their mother in 1935, which was converted to the Helene Fuld Health Trust in 1965. This New York City-based Trust, dedicated to the support and promotion of the health, welfare, and education of student nurses, is the nation's largest private funder devoted exclusively to nursing students and nursing education. The Trust has three program areas: Curriculum and Faculty Development in Community-based Care, to prepare nursing students to work in a community or outpatient setting; Leadership Development, to develop the leadership ability of a new generation of nurses to provide inspiration and direction in the uncertain and "dramatically changing future" of the health care industry and of the "nursing profession in particular"; and Educational Mobility, to aid nursing students to earn higher degrees in nursing . Grants are made not to individuals, but to nursing schools and educational programs or nonprofit organizations with programs that benefit nursing students and relate to nursing education. Visitors to the Web site can learn more about their program guidelines, application instructions, recent grants list, and contact information.

The Fuller Foundation (NH) (http://www.agmconnect.org/fuller1.html)

Alvan T. Fuller, state legislator, member of Congress, Lieutenant Governor, and two-time Governor of Massachusetts, founded the Fuller Foundation in 1936 so that his legacy of philanthropy would continue. This Rye Beach, New Hampshire-based Foundation's purpose is to support nonprofit agencies that improve the quality of life for people, animals and the environment. It also funds the Fuller Foundation of New Hampshire, which supports horticulture and education programs for the public at Fuller Gardens, which is what remains of Fuller's summer estate. The Fuller Foundation seeks proposals in three focus areas of grantmaking: Youth at Risk, "Wildlife, Endangered Species—Their Environment, and Animals Helping People", and the Arts. Geographic focus area of their grantmaking is predominantly the Boston area and the immediate seacoast area of New Hampshire. New and "seed" organizations that do not have financial history will also be considered for support, as long as they have sound financial plans. Consult their Web site for more details on focus areas, guidelines, application procedures, grant list, and contact information.

Fund for the City of New York (NY) (Operating foundation) (http://www.fcny.org/)

The Fund is an independent private operating foundation whose mandate is "to respond to the opportunities and problems of New York City; to improve the performance of the city's government and the quality of life of its citizens." The Fund concentrates its effort in three areas: youth, government, and technology, but it also makes a limited number of grants that do not fall neatly into any of the above categories. Grants awarded are generally between $5,000 and $10,000, and the Fund provides both general and project support. It also operates the Cash Flow Loan Program, the Nonprofit Computer Exchange, Incubator Program, and Internet Academy, which are core organizational assistance programs for government and nonprofit organizations. The Fund also has two award programs, one to recognize individuals for public service, and the other for projects in the areas of homelessness and hunger, economic self-sufficiency, conflict resolution, youth and family development, and HIV/AIDS. The Fund welcomes nominations for these awards. Visitors to the Fund's Web site will find detailed information on all of the Fund's programs and initiatives, as well as contact information.

The G & P Charitable Foundation (NY) (http://www.gpcharity.com)

The G & P Charitable Foundation, based in New York City, supports research that will lead to advances in the treatment of hematologic malignancies, such as leukemia, lymphoma, and other such cancers. The following general approaches are funding priorities: Genetic abnormalities, Signal Transduction Pathways, Cell Death Programs, Clinical Trial Research, Epidemiology and Prevention, Early Diagnosis, and Immune Prevention of Malignancy. The G&P Charitable Foundation seeks: improvement of treatment through the development of novel therapeutic approaches that could replace or be used in conjunction with existing therapies; collaborative efforts between select leaders in different areas of biology and integrative medical research; to improve efficacy and reduce toxicity of cancer treatments; and improve quality of life for patients. The Foundation was the vision of Gabrielle Rich Aouad, who died at the age of 27 from AML Leukemia. Her last wish was to create a foundation, named for herself and her husband, that would invest in research to find better treatment for leukemia and spare others from the suffering she endured. To that end, her husband, Philip Aouad, and her mother, Denise Rich, formed The G&P Charitable Foundation for Cancer Research. Consult the Web site for more information about each funding priority, goals, medical advances, and an online contact form.

Gates Family Foundation (CO) (http://members.aol.com/Gatesfdn/)

In 1911, Charles C. Gates, Sr., educated as a mining engineer, bought the Colorado Tire and Leather Company for $3500 in response to a newspaper ad, and founded the company known today as the Gates Corporation. By the time he transferred presidency to his son in 1961, the Gates Corporation had annual sales totaling $137 million. Charles C. Gates, Sr., along with members of the Gates family, established The Gates Foundation on November 6, 1946, whose name was later changed in December 1995 to the Gates Family Foundation. Its purpose is to "aid, assist, encourage, initiate, or carry on activities that will promote the health, well-being, security, and broad education of all people." Among their varied interests are the growth and development of independent schools and private colleges, historic preservation, the arts, urban and mountain parks and U.S. Forest Service trail systems, supporting organizations that promote free enterprise, and supporting programs that encourage individuals to improve and maintain their physical well-being. This Denver, Colorado Foundation invests primarily in institutions, projects and programs that will affect the people of Colorado, with special attention paid to the Denver metropolitan area. Consult their Web site for further details on the Foundation's major areas of funding interest, guidelines, application instructions, 1996 annual report with grant list, projects funded, resource links, and contact information.

Bill and Melinda Gates Foundation (WA) (http://www.gatesfoundations.org/)

The William H. Gates Foundation and the Gates Learning Foundation merged in August 1999 to become the Bill and Melinda Gates Foundation, which encompasses those two foundations and the Gates Center for Technology Access. The Gates Foundation ranks as one of the wealthiest private foundations in the world. Established by the Microsoft co-founder and CEO, the Seattle-based Foundation is led by Bill Gates's father, William Gates Sr., and supports initiatives in education, technology and global health, and community giving in the Pacific Northwest. The Foundation requests that grantseekers submit letters of inquiry before submitting formal funding proposals. Visitors to the Foundation's Web site, will find descriptions of the Foundation's various initiatives, grantmaking guidelines, press releases, a PDF version of the Foundation's most recent annual report, links to recent grantees, and contact information.

Gebbie Foundation, Inc. (NY) (http://www.gebbie.org/)

The Gebbie Foundation was established in 1964 by the daughters of Frank and Harriett Louise Gebbie as a memorial to their parents. Since its inception, the Foundation has paid out more than $55 million in grants to support its "focus on children/youth/education, arts, human services, and community development." The Foundation primarily supports activities in the Jamestown/ Chautauqua County region of New York State but will consider making grants elsewhere, provided the requests meet the broad criteria outlined in the Foundation's mission. Grants are not made to individuals or to sectarian or religious organizations, and funds are not usually available for general support, endowment purposes, or national appeals. Visitors to the Foundation's Web site will find biographies of the Gebbies and their daughters, brief descriptions of the Foundation's policies and guidelines, application procedures, and contact information.

Carl Gellert and Celia Berta Gellert Foundation (CA) (http://fdncenter.org/grantmaker/gellert/index.html)

Based in San Francisco, the Gellert Foundation promotes religious, charitable, scientific, literary, and educational activities in the nine counties of the greater San Francisco Bay Area (i.e., Alameda, Contra Costa, Marin, Napa, San Francisco, San Mateo, Santa Clara, Solano, and Sonoma counties). Visitors to the Foundation's "folder" on the Center's Web site will find a mission statement, application guidelines, a list of grants and contributions, and contact information.

Wallace Alexander Gerbode Foundation (CA)

(http://fdncenter.org/grantmaker/gerbode/index.html)
The Wallace Alexander Gerbode Foundation supports programs in the San Francisco Bay Area and Hawaii in the areas of arts and culture, environment, population, reproductive rights, citizen participation/building communities/inclusiveness, and strength of the philanthropic process and the nonprofit sector. The Foundation generally does not support direct services, deficit budgets, general operating funds, building or equipment funds, general fundraising campaigns, religious purposes, private schools, publications, scholarships, or grants to individuals. In addition to general application and fiscal information, the Foundation's "folder" on the Center's Web site provides grants lists by program area.

J. Paul Getty Trust (CA) (Operating foundation) (http://www.getty.edu/)

The J. Paul Getty Trust, a private operating foundation dedicated to the visual arts and humanities, comprises a museum, four institutes, and a grant program. The purpose of the latter is to strengthen the fields in which the Trust is active by funding exceptional projects throughout the world that promote research in the history of art and related fields, advancement of the understanding of art, and conservation of cultural heritage. Grants may fund conceptual projects that take intellectual risks, or they may support more basic resources and activities. Funded projects include a wide variety of methodologies and subject matter, ranging through all historical periods and geographic regions. The Trust's Web site provides a general overview of the Trust's grantmaking activities, extensive program information and guidelines, a list of grants recently awarded, and application and contact information. Applications for some Getty programs can be downloaded from the site.

The Gill Foundation (CO) (http://www.gillfoundation.org)

Headquartered in Colorado Springs, Colorado, the Gill Foundation "serves as a catalyst and provides resources for communities in pursuit of justice and equality, while building awareness of the contributions gay men and lesbians make to American society." The Gill Foundation was established in 1994 by Tim Gill, one of two openly gay individuals on the 1997 Forbes 400 list and founder, Chairman, and Chief Technology Officer of Quark, Inc., a successful desktop publishing software company. It currently has three program areas: Gill Foundation Grantmaking, which funds organizations nationwide serving gay men, lesbians, bisexuals, transgendered individuals and people living with HIV/AIDS; the Gay and Lesbian Fund for Colorado, which funds nonprofits in Colorado in the areas of social justice, children and youth, leadership development, arts and culture, public broadcasting and excellence in communications; and the OutGiving Project, which aims to expand the base of support for gay, lesbian, bisexual, and transgender organizations by providing organizational development and fund-raising training, and training for donors on how to give effectively, through both workshops and online resources. Visitors to the Web site will find more details about each program area, guidelines, application instructions, a sample of a successful grant proposal (downloadable and viewable), downloadable handouts from their OutGiving Project, online request forms (including one for borrowing publications from the foundation), links to other resources, and contact information.

Irving S. Gilmore Foundation (MI) (http://www.isgilmorefoundation.org/)

Irving Gilmore, a lifelong resident of Kalamazoo, Michigan, established the Irving S. Gilmore Foundation in 1972 as a way of giving back to the community he loved in perpetuity. The Foundation strives to sustain and, whenever possible, to improve the cultural, social, and economic life of greater Kalamazoo, with a focus (in order of importance) on the arts, culture and humanities, human services, education and youth activities, community development, and health and well-being. The Foundation's trustees make all decisions concerning the funding of proposals and encourage grant applications from Kalamazoo area nonprofits whose work does, or will, benefit the community. The Foundation does not make grants to individuals. The Foundation's Web site provides a brief history of the Foundation and a description of its involvement in the community, grant application guidelines and procedures, and contact information.

Glenn Foundation for Medical Research, Inc. (CA) (Operating foundation) (http://www.glenn.deco.net/)

The purpose of the Glenn Foundation is "to extend the healthful productive years of life through research on the mechanisms of biological aging." The Foundation neither solicits nor accepts charitable contributions, and it does not consider unsolicited grant applications or fellowship nominations. Programs are supported through the American Federation of Aging Research, and grant applications can be obtained from its site at http://www.afar.org. The Glenn Foundation's Web site, which was developed as a resource and point-of-access for scientists whose primary interest is the biology of aging, offers brief descriptions of the Foundation's programs, conferences, and workshops, as well as numerous links to other organizations involved in aging research.

Global Environmental Project Institute, Inc. (ID) (http://www.gepifoundation.org/)

The Global Environment Project Institute, Inc. (GEPI) is a family foundation created in 1986 to educate the public about global environmental issues. The Ketchum, Idaho-based GEPI is grantmaking foundation that "selects projects or actions that will affect life on this planet for generations to come", in order to fulfill its mission of promoting the conservation of biodiversity and the sustainability of life on earth. Its areas of funding are Environmental Education, Citizen Participation, Sustainable Development, Environmental Advocacy/Wilderness Protection (Northern Rockies only), and International, which is limited to specific proposals solicited by GEPI. GEPI does not accept proposals for publications, conferences, specific-species related work, scientific research, capital campaigns, and land trusts or other land acquisition programs. Grant applications are accepted by email and by mail. Consult the GEPI Web site for application guidelines, grant lists, descriptions of projects initiated, and contact information.

The Arnold P. Gold Foundation (NJ) (http://www.humanism-in-medicine.org/cgi-bin/start.cgi/AB/missionframe3.htm)

Drs. Arnold and Sandra Gold, to "foster humanism in medicine" and emphasize the tradition of compassion in the doctor-patient relationship, established the Arnold P. Gold Foundation in Englewood, New Jersey in 1988. The founders are colleagues at the Columbia University College of Physicians and Surgeons, where Dr. Arnold P. Gold is Professor of Clinical Neurology and Professor of Clinical Pediatrics. The Foundation raises funds that have resulted in significant advances in the development, implementation, evaluation and replication of innovative medical educational programs and projects that are influencing the way physicians are trained. There are medical student, resident, educator, and research programs, through which the Gold Foundation supports annual commencement awards, provides assistant and associate professorships, sponsors student-initiated programs, and conduct research of medical students' attitudes toward humanism. Grant applications will be considered from medical schools and organizations, and will not be accepted from individuals. Visit their Web site for information about their programs, grant application procedure, printable grant request form, past award recipients, public forum and bulletin board, and contact information.

Richard & Rhoda Goldman Fund (CA) (http://www.goldmanfund.org/)

The Goldman Fund was established in 1951 by Richard and Rhoda Goldman to improve the quality of life in the San Francisco Bay Area, to protect the environment, and to promote a more just and sustainable world. The Fund is interested in supporting programs that will have a positive impact in an array of fields, including the environment, population, Jewish affairs, children and youth, the elderly, social and human services, health, education, and the arts. While the Fund is primarily interested in organizations and projects that have an impact on San Francisco and local Bay Area communities, it will consider inquiries from domestic organizations that provide support to Israel and national and international projects that address environmental and population issues. The Fund does not accept applications for research, grants or scholarships to individuals, conferences, documentary films, fundraisers, deficit budgets, or endowment campaigns; unsolicited proposals for support of arts organizations or institutions of primary, secondary, or higher education; or applications for the Goldman Environmental Prize, a program for grassroots environmentalists. The Fund's Web site provides detailed application guidelines, limitation statements, recent grants lists organized by subject area, answers to frequently asked questions, summaries of recent Fund initiatives, a letter from board chair Richard Goldman, financial statements, and a link to the Goldman Environmental Prize Web site (http://www.goldmanprize.org/).

Graham Foundation for the Advanced Studies in the Fine Arts (IL)
(http://www.GrahamFoundation.org/)
The Graham Foundation was established by a bequest from Ernest R. Graham, a prominent Chicago architect who died in 1936. Since Graham died in the depths of the depression, the value of his estate was "severely depressed", and it took twenty years to rebuild his estate and implement his legacy. In 1956, the Graham Foundation for the Advanced Studies in the Fine Arts was established in Chicago, Illinois. The Foundation supports individuals and institutions undertaking work in architecture and with other arts and academic disciplines that are "immediately contributive to architecture." In the past, the Foundation has supported a variety of endeavors, including grants to sponsor fellowships, seminars and symposia at universities, architectural publications, and grants for exhibitions. In addition to its general grantmaking program, there is also the Carter Manny Award, to support doctoral candidates in their research for academic dissertations directly concerned with architecture. Points of interest on their Web site are grant descriptions and application instructions, list of past supported projects and publications, annual report, list and bios of trustees, list of and contact information for staff members, schedule of lectures and exhibitions, and a searchable database of past grantees.

William T. Grant Foundation (NY)
(http://fdncenter.org/grantmaker/wtgrant/index.html)
Established in 1936 to "assist research, education, and training through the sciences," the William T. Grant Foundation has pursued that goal over the years through its support of postdoctoral research projects on the development of children, adolescents, and youth, and for service projects in the New York City area. Prospective applicants should note that the Foundation does not support or make contributions to conferences and meetings; fellowships and scholarships; building funds; fund-raising drives; operating budgets of ongoing service agencies or educational institutions; or endowments. The Foundation's "folder" on the Center's Web site offers a good deal of general information about the Foundation and its programs; detailed application procedures; a downloadable cover sheet for letters of inquiry; a list of grants; officer, staff, and trustee listings; and an online version of the Foundation's annual report.

Green Mountain Fund, Inc. (VT) (http://homepages.together.net/~gmfps/)

Located in Westford, Vermont, the Green Mountain Fund for Popular Struggle supports organizations that actively organize for radical social change in Vermont and the Champlain Valley watershed of New York. The Fund is "committed to revolutionary transformation toward a socialist-feminist society", a society that "requires the elimination of all oppressions (such as oppressions by race, sex, class, sexual orientation, age, ability or species) and their basis in patriarchal, capitalist and imperialist structures." The Fund was set up with a one-time donation of $500,000, and "recognizing that income-producing investments require the exploitation of labor, the fund has placed the money with nonprofit organizations…in the form of no-interest loans." The loans are repaid on an annual basis over a period of ten years and these repayments provide funds to be granted to other groups. Therefore, barring unsolicited donations, the Fund expects to dissolve by the year 2000. To be eligible, organizations have to be eligible for tax-exempt status and no significant portion of their budget can come from government agencies, religious institutions or "establishment foundations" such as United Way and the Rockefeller Foundation. Consult their Web site for a complete listing of the causes they support, application guidelines and instructions, application form and coversheet, contact information for each board member, grant lists, links to other resources.

Greenville Foundation (CA) (http://fdncenter.org/grantmaker/grnville/)

The Sonoma, California-based Greenville Foundation provides support for special projects in the following areas: education, the environment, human and social issues, international, and religion. The Foundation does not make grants for scholarships, individuals, venture capital, capital improvements, endowments, general classroom-based environmental education programs, individual species preservation, health, food banks, or temporary shelter. Because it is located in the West, "practicality dictates that proposals for domestic projects be located west of the Rockies" (although a limited number of grants may be made outside the region). Grants for international programs are made only through U.S.-based or affiliated nonprofit organizations, and for projects as specifically defined by the Foundation's international and environment programs. The Foundation's "folder" on the Center's Web site provides program descriptions, recent grants lists in each program area, application guidelines and procedures, a downloadable application cover sheet, a financial report, and contact information.

The Grotto Foundation, Inc. (MN) (http://www.grottofoundation.org/)

The Grotto Foundation, Inc. was established on December 31, 1964 by Louis Warren Hill Jr., eldest grandson of James J. Hill, the railway baron known as the "Empire builder." Believing that people were capable of improving their own lives in their own ways, the foundation he created supports projects and programs that "empower people to chart their own course". Located in St. Paul, Minnesota, the Foundation works with communities of different ethnic groups and cultures who are "inspired by their sense of vision and possibility" and assists these communities as they move forward in the course they have determined themselves. Its formal mission statement is "to benefit society by improving the education and the economic, physical, and social well-being of citizens, with a special focus on families and culturally diverse groups." It is further interested in "increasing public understanding of the American cultural heritage, the cultures of nations, and the individual's responsibility to fellow human beings." Visit the Web site for grant guidelines and instructions, link to download the Minnesota Common Grant Application, bios of the founder and founding director, 1997 grant list, financial information, list of board and staff members, contact information, and links to other resources. A printable version of their entire Web site is also available.

Harry Frank Guggenheim Foundation (NY) (http://www.hfg.org/)

The Harry Frank Guggenheim Foundation sponsors scholarly research on problems of violence, aggression, and dominance and encourages related research projects in neuroscience, genetics, animal behavior, the social sciences, history, criminology, and the humanities. The Foundation also awards research grants to established scholars and dissertation fellowships to graduate students. (Institutions, programs, and pure interventions are not supported.) Visitors to the Foundation's Web site will find a section on its research priorities, detailed application guidelines and procedures, a comprehensive listing of recent Foundation grants and fellowships, and a form for requesting written application guidelines and/or the Foundation's annual report.

John Simon Guggenheim Memorial Foundation (NY) (http://www.gf.org/)

The John Simon Guggenheim Memorial Foundation awards fellowships for advanced professionals in all areas of the natural sciences, social sciences, humanities, and creative arts (except the performing arts). The Foundation selects its Fellows on the basis of two separate competitions, one for the United States and Canada, the other for Latin America and the Caribbean. Only professional individuals are eligible for awards; the Foundation does not support students, organizations, or institutions. The Foundation's Web site provides general information about its programs, fellowship eligibility requirements, and application deadlines in English, Spanish, and Portuguese. Also available in English only is a listing of recent Guggenheim Fellows, a helpful FAQ, an interactive form for ordering application forms, a listing of Foundation officers and trustees, and contact information.

George Gund Foundation (OH) (http://www.gundfdn.org/)

The George Gund Foundation was created in 1952 by Cleveland banker and businessman George Gund, who believed the private foundation structure provided the most positive, far-sighted vehicle for intelligent underwriting of creative solutions to social ills in a manner which would not be limited to his own lifetime. Today, the Foundation makes grants quarterly in the areas of education, economic development and community revitalization, human services, arts, environment and civic affairs. The Foundation's Web site offers a biography of George Gund, program descriptions, grant application instructions and grant restrictions, contact information (including e-mail links for each program area), press releases, grants lists, and links to a handful of related Web sites.

Gunk Foundation (NY) (Operating foundation)
(http://www1.mhv.net/~gunk/welcome.html)

The Gunk Foundation is a charitable operating foundation established in 1994 "to provide a counterbalance to the recent, disturbing trends in funding for intellectual endeavors...." It does this by supporting two types of projects—public arts projects, which are funded through the Foundation itself, and scholarly/artistic publications, which are funded through Critical Press, the Foundation's publishing arm. Grant amounts are small and usually fall in a range between $1,000 and $5,000. Visitors to "GunkWeb" will find grant application guidelines (for the Foundation), proposal guidelines (for Critical Press), and a grant archive. Grant applications for public arts projects can be printed from the site.

Luke B. Hancock Foundation (CA) (http://www.lukebhancock.org)

Established in 1948 with a donation from pioneering oilman Luke B. Hancock, the Hancock Foundation received its principal assets from his estate in 1963 and later changed its name to the Luke B. Hancock Foundation in order to recognize its founder and first president. Because of limited resources and the large number of requests it receives, the Foundation focuses its support on the South Bay of the San Francisco Bay area, in particular San Jose, and on grassroots neighborhood initiatives that benefit youth as well as the entire community. Historically, the Foundation has considered some cultural grants and special projects, but these are primarily initiated by the Foundation itself. In addition to a 1996/1997 grants list and financial statements, the Foundation's "folder" on the Center's Web site provides application guidelines, a look at three community organizations funded by the Foundation that are "changing their world," a brief biography of Luke Hancock, board and staff listings, and contact information.

Phil Hardin Foundation (MS) (http://www.philhardin.org/)

The Hardin Foundation was created in 1964 by Mississippi businessman Phil Hardin, who wanted to give something back to the people of the state. From the outset, the focus of the Foundation was on education. In 1997 it decided to further concentrate its efforts and resources on four goals: strengthening the capacity of communities in the state to nurture and educate young children; strengthening the capacity of higher education institutions to renew communities and their economies; strengthening the capacity of communities for locally initiated educational improvement and economic development; and strengthening policy and leadership at local and state levels. In addition to pursuing these goals, the Foundation also operates four programs: the Thomas R. Ward Fellows Program, which provides fellowships for experienced principals and those aspiring to principalship to attend the Harvard University School of Education's Principals' Center; the S.A. Rosenbaum Earthwatch Mississippi Teaching Fellows Program, which provides faculty of Mississippi schools (K–12) and community colleges the opportunity to participate in Earthwatch Expeditions to further their personal and professional development; the Mississippi Geography Education Fund, which is designed to improve the teaching of geography in Mississippi; and, with the John M. Olin Foundation, the George Washington Scholars Institute, which provides a one-week educational study program at Mount Vernon, in northern Virginia, for as many as 20 teachers from public and non-public schools. Visitors to the Hardin Foundation Web site will find detailed information about the Foundation's goals, programs, and strategies; application guidelines and a printable application form; a comprehensive set of links to related education resources; and contact information.

John A. Hartford Foundation, Inc. (NY) (http://www.jhartfound.org/)

Established in 1929 by John A. and George L. Hartford, former chief executives of the Great Atlantic and Pacific Tea Company (A&P), the John A. Hartford

Foundation is concerned with the improvement of health care in America. The Foundation focuses its grantmaking activities in the areas of aging and health and healthcare cost and quality, and generally makes grants by invitation. Grant-seekers are encouraged to familiarize themselves with the Foundation's program areas and guidelines—detailed information about which can be found at its Web site—before submitting a letter of inquiry in writing. The Web site also provides the Foundation's finances, a report from the chairman, Foundation trustees and staff, and contact information.

Walter and Elise Haas Fund (CA) (http://www.haassr.org/welcome.htm)

The Walter and Elise Haas Fund was created in 1952. Walter Haas was president and later chairman of Levi Strauss and Co. The Haas' shared a commitment to the "basic values and pluralism of American culture, quality, ethical conduct, creative approaches to meeting human needs, leadership, public participation, and joining public good and individual initiative." The San Francisco-based foundation was created to provide support for the charitable causes consistent with these values, and is interested in projects that demonstrate an ability to have wide impact and which demonstrate creative approaches toward meeting human needs. An overall goal is the development of leadership and professional competence in the fields of funding support, which are: human services; arts; environment; professional ethics; education; Jewish life; citizenship and civic education; and the Creative Work Fund, where the Haas Fund along with three other funders support the collaboration between artists and nonprofit organizations to create new work. Each field of support has funding and geographic priorities, which are listed in the grant guidelines. Consult their Web site for grant guidelines, application instructions, grant request cover sheet, link to the Creative Work Fund, which has its own separate site and application instructions; grant list, President's statement and Executive Director's report, list of staff, and contact information.

Charles Hayden Foundation (NY)
(http://fdncenter.org/grantmaker/hayden/index.html)

The New York City-based Hayden Foundation seeks to promote the mental, moral, and physical development of school-aged youth in the New York and Boston metropolitan areas—the former defined as New York City and Nassau County, the southern portion of Westchester County and, in New Jersey, all of Hudson and Essex Counties and the contiguous urban portions of Union, Passaic, and Bergen counties, the latter as the City of Boston and adjacent municipalities located on the east side of an arc from Salem to Quincy that is roughly delineated by Route 128. Priority is given to institutions and programs serving youth most at risk of not reaching their full potential, especially youth in low-income communities, and that continuously provide opportunities and supports over many years. Visitors to the Foundation's "folder" on the Center's Web site will find a mission statement, recent grants lists, detailed application guidelines, and contact information.

John Randolph Haynes and Dora Haynes Foundation (CA)
(http://www.haynesfoundation.org/)

Established in 1926, the Haynes Foundation supports study and research in political science, economics, public policy, history, social psychology, and sociology, favoring projects with specific application to California and, more particularly, the Los Angeles region. The Foundation also provides undergraduate scholar-ships, graduate fellowships, and faculty research fellowships in the social sci-ences to colleges and universities in the greater Los Angeles area. All support is made directly to institutions; no grants are awarded to individuals. A searchable bibliography of publications resulting from 70 years of Foundation support is available at the Foundation's Web site, along with detailed program information, application guidelines, a listing of the Foundation's board of trustees, and a his-tory of the Foundation and the Haynes family.

Healthcare Foundation of New Jersey (NJ)
(http://fdncenter.org/grantmaker/hfnj/)

The Healthcare Foundation of New Jersey is firmly rooted in the strong tradition of delivering the highest standards of medical care, a tradition established by the Jewish community in Newark, New Jersey and that began with the inauguration of the Newark Beth Israel Hospital in 1901. Formerly known as the NBI Healthcare Foundation, the private grantmaking foundation was founded in 1996 to alleviate the suffering of the most vulnerable members of the community. Its goal is to strengthen existing healthcare programs and provide seed money for innovative projects that address unmet healthcare needs. The foundation is interested in health-related proposals that address one of their four priority areas: vulnerable children and families of Newark, especially the South Ward; vulnerable members of the MetroWest Jewish community of Northern New Jersey; medical education and humanism in medicine; and clinical research, especially at the Newark Beth Israel Medical Center. The foundation also has the Humanism in Medicine Award, which recognizes graduating medical students and faculty members who best exemplify humanism and compassion in medical care delivery, and the Humanistic Patient Care Awards, which recognizes healthcare workers at area hospitals and nursing homes for compassionate caregiving. Consult their Web site for grant guidelines, instructions, information on their programs, grant lists, finan-cial information, and contact information.

William Randolph Hearst Foundations (NY)
(http://fdncenter.org/grantmaker/hearst/index.html)

The Hearst Foundation, Inc., was founded in 1945 by publisher and philanthropist William Randolph Hearst. In 1948, Hearst established the California Charities Foundation, the name of which was changed to the William Randolph Hearst Foundation after Mr. Hearst's death in 1951. The charitable goals of the two Foun-dations are essentially the same, reflecting the philanthropic interests of William Randolph Hearst—education, health, social service, and culture. The Founda-tions' proposal evaluation process is divided geographically: organizations east of the Mississippi River must apply to the Foundations' New York offices, while organizations west of the Mississippi are asked to apply through the Foundations' San Francisco offices. In addition to their grantmaking activities in the four pro-gram areas mentioned above, the Hearst Foundations make grants to students through the Hearst Journalism Awards Program and the United States Senate Youth Program. Visitors to the Foundations' "folder" on the Center's Web site will find program guidelines, funding policies and limitations, application procedures, and descriptions of both awards programs.

Heathcote Art Foundation, Inc. (CT)
(http://www.artswire.org/ArtsWire/heathcote)
The Heathcote Art Foundation was established in New York in 1964 by Jose-phine Mercy Heathcote Haskell. Its was originally an exhibiting foundation for Haskell's personal collection of English 18th Century art and furnishings, but since its conversion to a grantmaking foundation in 1986, its purpose has been to support arts organizations that directly assist emerging artists of promise and that promote the creation of new and innovative work in all artistic disciplines. Located in Old Greenwich, Connecticut, the Foundation prefers to restrict its grantmaking to organizations in the New York City area with annual operating budgets no greater than $1 million, though exceptions are made at the discretion of the executive committee. Whenever possible, grants are passed through spon-soring organizations to benefit individual artists. Visitors to the Web site will find grant guidelines and instructions, printable application form, some financial infor-mation, grants list, and contact information.

The Heinz Endowments (PA) (http://www.heinz.org/)
The Pittsburgh-based Heinz Endowments support the efforts of nonprofit organi-zations active in the areas of arts and culture, education, children, youth and fami-lies, economic opportunity, and the environment, with an emphasis on programs either in southwestern Pennsylvania or of clear benefit to the region. A model of functional design, the Endowments' Web site offers a range of information, including broad and program-specific statements of philosophy; information about goals, grants, projects, and staff in each program area; application guide-lines; news; and brief biographies of Howard Heinz and Vira I. Heinz as well as various program officers and directors.

Hershey Foundation (OH)
(http://fdncenter.org/grantmaker/hershey/index.html)
Founded in 1986 by Jo Hershey Selden, the Hershey Foundation was established in honor of her late husband, Alvin A. Hershey. Located in Concord Township, Ohio, the Foundation is dedicated to providing "bridges of opportunity for the children of Northeast Ohio". The Foundation aims to help schools, museums, cul-tural institutions, and other nonprofits develop and implement innovative pro-grams that will improve quality of life, build self-esteem, enhance learning, increase exposure to other cultures and ideas, and encourage the develop-ment of independent thinking and problem-solving skills. Support is given to pilot projects that can be replicated in other settings, with priority given to alternative educational programs, arts, cultural, and science programs, and early childhood education programs. A particular funding focus is Montessori education and pro-grams embodying the Montessori child-centered approach to learning. Grants are given for program development and special projects, equipment that brings new capabilities to an organization (but not computers), capital campaigns and endow-ment of special projects. Visitors to the Web site will find grant guidelines and procedures, grants list, financial information, and a history of the Hershey Foundation.

Fannie and John Hertz Foundation (CA) (http://www.hertzfndn.org/)
The Fannie and John Hertz Foundation was founded in 1957 by John Daniel Hertz, an Austrian emigrant who lived the American Dream. The Foundation,

based in Livermore, California, is an expression of his gratitude for the country that afforded him so many opportunities. He sensed that the nation, "in order to survive, prosper, and lead, had to increase substantially the ranks of its most competent engineers and applied scientists", and felt that that Foundation could "perform a notable service to the nation by fostering the education and training of out tanding students in these areas". To that end, the Foundation provides fellowships for graduate work leading to a Ph.D. degree from three dozen universities in applications of the physical sciences: applied physics, chemistry, mathematics, modern biology, and all areas of engineering. Although a list of fields of study is provided on the Web site, it is up to the individual applicant to advocate his or her specific field of interest as an "applied physical science". Consult their Web site for information and application instructions for the Graduate Fellowship program. Visitors to the Web site will also find a history of the foundation and a biography of John Hertz and his wife Fannie, a soon-to-be available FAQ page, links to other resources, and contact information. Applications may be submitted online and through traditional means.

William and Flora Hewlett Foundation (CA) (http://www.hewlett.org/)

The broadly stated mission of the Hewlett Foundation, established by Palo Alto industrialist William R. Hewlett (of Hewlett-Packard fame), his late wife, Flora Lamson Hewlett, and their eldest son, Walter B. Hewlett in 1966, is "to promote the well-being of mankind by supporting selected activities of a charitable nature, as well as organizations or institutions engaged in such activities." The Foundation concentrates its resources on activities in the areas of education, performing arts, population, environment, conflict resolution, family and community development, and U.S.-Latin American relations, the latter an outgrowth of the Foundation's long-standing interest in U.S.-Mexico relations. The Foundation's Web site provides program descriptions and application guidelines, a list of grant authorizations organized by program area, an online version of the Foundation's annual report, and contact information.

Hoblitzelle Foundation (TX) (http://home.att.net/~hoblitzelle/)

The Hoblitzelle Foundation, based in Dallas, Texas, was founded by Karl Hoblitzelle in 1942. Karl Hoblitzelle had a successful entertainment business and investments in the oil, gas, real estate and banking industries in Texas. The Foundation focuses its grantmaking on specific, non-recurring needs of the educational, social service, medical, cultural, and civic organizations in the state of Texas only, and particularly within the Dallas Metroplex. Consult the Web site for application guidelines, links to additional information, a short bio of its founder, a listing of directors, grant list, and contact information.

The Hoglund Foundation (TX) (http://www.hoglundfdtn.org)

Established in 1989, the Hoglund Foundation uses the "resources and abilities of the extended family of Forrest E. Hoglund and Sally R. Hoglund to generate and/or support activities that can make a positive difference in the lives of others." The primary focus of the Dallas-based foundation is to "promote interests and entities in education, health science and services, social services, and children's health and development." Priorities are organizations and programs that nurture, recognize, and reward individual initiative and responsibility; are innovative and promote creative solutions; have sound management and are efficient in the management of funds; and are collaborative in nature so that resources are shared and the impact of the grant is multiplied in the community. The Foundation's geographic focus is primarily Dallas and Houston, Texas, but grants are made outside of this area. Check out their Web site for grant application guidelines, contact information, and links to other resources.

Hutton Foundation (CA) (http://www.huttonfoundation.org)

The Betty L. Hutton founded the Hutton Foundation in 1980. She was the widow of Harold C. Hutton, with whom she had built an international oil-refining business empire. The Foundation supports educational, health and community organizations and acts as a catalyst to encourage development of new programs and services for future generations. Primary areas of focus include education, health and human services, child, youth and family services, arts and culture, women's services, and civic and community development. Funding is primarily awarded to organizations in Orange, Riverside, and Santa Barbara Counties in California, with select international awards. In addition to donations and grants, the Foundation also offers Program Related Investments (PRI), which are loans to purchase buildings, make major tenant improvements on buildings owned by nonprofit organizations, and to refinance existing real estate or construction loans. The Foundation is headquartered in Santa Barbara, California, with an additional office in Orange. Visit the Web site for grant application guidelines and instructions, further information about PRIs, information about the review and selection process, 1998 grants list, and contact information.

Houston Endowment, Inc. (TX) (http://www.hou-endow.org/)

Founded in 1937 by Jesse H. Jones and Mary Gibbs Jones, and today the largest private philanthropic foundation in Texas, the Houston Endowment is dedicated primarily to the support of charitable undertakings serving the people of the greater Houston area and the state of Texas, and contributes to a broad spectrum of programs in education, health care, human services, cultural arts, and other areas. An endowment valued in excess of $1 billion at the end of 1995 allows annual giving of approximately $45 million. In addition to general information about the Foundation and its founders, visitors to the Web site will find descriptions of the Foundation's programs and grant eligibility criteria, application procedures, grants lists, board and staff listings, and contact information.

Hyde and Watson Foundation (NJ)
(http://fdncenter.org/grantmaker/hydeandwatson/)

Formerly the Lillia Babbitt Hyde Foundation and the John Jay and Eliza Jane Watson Foundation which were consolidated in January 1983, the New Jersey-based Hyde and Watson Foundation supports capital projects such as purchase or relocation of facilities, building improvements, capital equipment, instructive materials development, and certain medical research areas. Broad fields include health, education, religion, social services, arts, and humanities. Currently grant support is focused primarily in the New York City Metropolitan area, and Essex, Union, and Morris Counties in New Jersey. The typical grant range is $5,000–$25,000. The foundation's Web site, hosted through the Center's Foundation Folder program, provides a history of the foundation, grant guidelines, grants list, financial statements, and information about the foundation's management.

I Have a Dream Foundation (NY) (Operating foundation) (http://www.ihad.org)
The "I Have a Dream Foundation" (IHAD) was started by Eugene Lang, a New York businessman who in 1981 made an extraordinary offer to a group of six-graders at the east Harlem elementary school he had once attended: he promised partial college scholarships if they finished high school. Four years later, all the children were still in school, and widespread national attention and interest began to develop. In 1986, Eugene Lang organized the national "I Have a Dream Foundation" to help launch a new generation of IHAD projects across the country. Today, IHAD helps "children from low-income areas become productive citizens by providing a long-term program of mentoring, tutoring, and enrichment, with an assured opportunity for higher education." Its goal is to see that all the Dreamers, as the children are called, graduate from high school "functionally literate and prepared either for fulfilling employment or further education." IHAD provides partial financial assistance for college, university, or accredited vocational school. Local IHAD project usually have 60 to 79 Dreamers who are either entire grade levels from elementary school or entire age groups from public housing projects, determined in consultation with local school officials, community-based organizations, and the national IHAD foundation. For this reason, students can not apply to be Dreamers. Visit the Web site for further information on the IHAD program. Visitors will find a history of the foundation, a FAQ sheet, locations and contact information for local IHAD projects, and information about how to get involved.

International Science Foundation (NY) (Operating foundation)
(http://www.isf.ru/index-isf.html)
The International Science Foundation (ISF), based in New York City, was established in 1992 by George Soros, a financier, philanthropist and social thinker. Its goal was to help the scientists of the former Soviet Union "weather the economic crisis in the region without having to leave science or their countries and to encourage new approaches to funding and managing scientific research in the former Soviet Union." ISF had several grant programs, but over the course of 1996 ISF gradually merged its operation with those of the Open Society Institute (OSI), part of the Soros Foundation network. As of 1997, it has discontinued all of its grantmaking programs, and as of 1998, had discontinued its Grant Assistance Program (GAP). Under the GAP, ISF offered its "extensive banking and shipping network to donor organizations that have typically faced numerous roadblocks and prohibitive costs in implementing their grant or charitable activities in the former Soviet Union or Baltic countries." Eligible organizations and government agencies sent funds and equipment to the region tax-free. ISF had also negotiated "various other discounts and exemptions throughout the FSU and Baltic countries to ensure that grants and donations transferred through the GAP infrastructure will have the greatest possible impact." However, as of January 1998, that program has been discontinued by ISF, although the United States Civilian Research and Development Foundation for the Independent States of the Former Soviet Union (CRDF) has launched its own GAP. Information and grant applications forms for GAP are available on their Web site (http://www.crdf.org/). An archive of ISF materials is available at http://www.soros.org/gap/isf.html. Visit the Web site of the Open Society Institute for more information about the OSI's activities, as well as the activities of other foundation in the Soros Foundations network.

James Irvine Foundation (CA) (http://www.irvine.org/)
The San Francisco-based Irvine Foundation was established in 1937 as trustee of the charitable trust of James Irvine, a California agricultural pioneer, to promote the general welfare of the people of California. Today, it is dedicated "to enhancing the social, economic, and physical quality of life throughout California, and to enriching the State's intellectual and cultural environment." Within this broad mandate, the Foundation makes grants in seven program areas: the arts; children, youth and families; civic culture; health; higher education; sustainable communities; and workforce development. Visitors to the Foundation's Web site will find detailed program information, including priority goals and recent grants in each funding area; application guidelines; board and staff listings; numerous links to grantee organizations; an interesting feedback area; and contact information.

Irvine Health Foundation (CA) (http://www.ihf.org/)
Established in 1985, the Irvine Health Foundation provides support for prevention, service, research, and policy activities related to the health and wellness of the Orange County, California, community. The Foundation's Web site offers a mission statement, a listing of directors and staff, FAQs, press releases, grant highlights, a "For Your Health" feature, highlights from the IHF lecture series, grant application procedures with FAQs, and links to numerous related sites.

Ittleson Foundation, Inc. (NY) (http://www.IttlesonFoundation.org)
Henry Ittleson, founder of CIT Financial Corporation, established the Ittleson Foundation in 1932. The New York City-based Foundation seeks to fund pilot projects, test and demonstration projects and applied research that would inform public policy, and "such projects should have significance beyond the local area of implementation and should result in an outcome of some consequence in the real world." Areas of particular interest are mental health, AIDS, and the environment; although they fund broadly in each area, there are specific concerns of interest. In the area of mental health, the Foundation prefers projects that "cut across the entire field and those that address underserved populations." In the area of environment, they seek to educate a new generation of environmentalists, and have interest in urban environmental issues and efforts at resource protection. And for AIDS, the Foundation focuses on prevention and mental health consequences of the disease. Visit the Web site for further information on each grantmaking area, application guidelines, viewable grant lists and summary, downloadable annual report, guidelines, grant lists and summary, and contact information.

Martha Holden Jennings Foundation (OH)
(http://fdncenter.org/grantmaker/jennings/index.html)
The Martha Holden Jennings Foundation is dedicated to fostering "the development of young people to the maximum possible extent through improving the quality of education in secular elementary and secondary schools in Ohio." To that end, the Cleveland-based Foundation is eager to explore new frontiers in Ohio schools and to promote more effective teaching in those schools. Visitors to the Foundation's "folder" on the Center's Web site will find a statement of purpose, a brief biography of Martha Holden Jennings, application guidelines, and contact information.

Jerome Foundation (MN) (http://www.jeromefdn.org/)

The St. Paul-based Jerome Foundation promotes the careers and work of emerging artists in Minnesota and New York City through its support of programs in dance, literature, media arts, music, theater, performance art, visual arts, multidisciplinary work, and arts criticism. The Foundation places the emerging creative artist at the center of its grantmaking and gives funding priority to programs and projects that are artist-driven. The Foundation's Web site, sections of which are still under construction, comes in two versions, Java-flavored (a little buggy) and Java-free (our recommendation), and provides program guidelines; application requirements and procedures; grants listed by program area or by date; answers to frequently asked questions; financial statements; contact information; and enough multimedia bits to keep you busy for hours.

Jewish Healthcare Foundation (PA) (http://www.jhf.org)

The Jewish Healthcare Foundation (JHF) continues the tradition of its predecessor, Montefiore Hospital, a high-quality teaching hospital that pioneered advancements in medicine and public health, and provided medical care in a kindly environment with an understanding of Jewish people and their needs. It was founded in 1908 by the Jewish community of Southwestern Pennsylvania. In 1990, the Board of Trustees of Montefiore Hospital adopted a "plan of division" that separated the newly created Jewish Healthcare Foundation from the hospital. The mission of JHF is to "foster the provision of healthcare services, healthcare education, and when reasonable and appropriate, health care research, and it shall respond to the health-related needs of the elderly, underprivileged, indigent and underserved populations in Western Pennsylvania." The Pittsburgh, PA-based JHF also supports and sometimes produces the research and publications necessary to inform others about new approaches to health problems. Grantmaking priorities are: giving children the physical and mental health to succeed; preventing disease and disability; building healthy neighborhoods and communities; and improving public policies and systems of care. Visit the Web site for specific information on each grantmaking priority and for funding guidelines and application instructions. The Web site also features an online feedback form, site search function, a media contact center, a research report on foundations and philanthropy, online publications order form and contact information.

Johnson Foundation, Inc. (WI) (Operating foundation)
(http://www.johnsonfdn.org/)

The primary activity of the Wisconsin-based Johnson Foundation is planning and co-sponsoring conferences of public interest at Wingspread, its Frank Lloyd Wright-designed headquarters and conference center in Racine. The Foundation encourages conference proposals from nonprofit organizations in six areas of interest: supporting sustainable development; enhancing learning productivity at all educational levels; building civil and civic community; encouraging constructive adult engagement in the lives of children and youth; Keland Endowment conferences on the arts, the environment, and persons with disabilities; and southeastern Wisconsin. The Foundation does not award grants; fund programs; sponsor retreats or fundraisers; or rent its facilities. Visitors to the Foundation's elegant, earth-toned Web site will find a brief history of the Foundation and its mission; general descriptions of its program interests; a searchable "Virtual Library" with online versions of recent annual reports and conference proceedings, articles (both HTML and .PDF versions) from back issues of the Wingspread Journal, and dozens of links organized by program interest; an Online Discussion area with both "open" and "closed" discussions; and detailed information about proposing a conference.

Robert Wood Johnson Foundation (NJ) (http://www.rwjf.org/)

The mission of the Robert Wood Johnson Foundation is to improve the health and health care of all Americans. The Foundation's main funding goals are to assure that all Americans have access to basic health care at reasonable cost; to improve the way services are organized and provided to people with chronic health conditions; and to reduce the harm caused by substance abuse—tobacco, alcohol, and elicit drugs. The Foundation's comprehensive Web site is a guide to its programs and activities and a substantial resource for the health care field. Visitors will find detailed program descriptions and application guidelines, grant outcomes and related publications, information about the Foundation's own programs and projects, a library of publications, current calls for proposals, and press releases and other media-related information. Visitors to the site will also find links to the Foundation's special resource sites: Last Acts (http://www.lastacts.org/), a call-to-action campaign designed to improve care at the end of life, and ChronicNet (http://www.chronicnet.org/), a resource for reporting on chronic health conditions and disabilities.

Walter S. Johnson Foundation (CA) (http://www.wsjf.org/)

The Walter S. Johnson Foundation supports programs in Northern California and Washoe County, Nevada, that "help children and youth meet their full potential and rise to the challenges of our diverse and changing society." The Foundation's grants program is focused on three primary goals: ensuring the well-being of children and youth, strengthening public education, and assisting young people in the transition to adulthood. Within these broad goals, the majority of grants are likely to focus on positive youth development, the professional development of educators, or the transition from school to career. Grants are also made for families in crisis, and for integrated services, family support, and neighborhood development. The Foundation's straightforward Web site provides grantmaking guidelines and grants lists for each program area, as well as application procedures and a listing of the Foundation's trustees and staff.

W. Alton Jones Foundation, Inc. (VA) (http://www.wajones.org/)

Established in 1944 by millionaire oilman "Pete" Jones, the W. Alton Jones Foundation "focuses on global environmental protection and the prevention of nuclear war [or disaster]." At present, the Foundation concentrates its efforts in two main areas: a Sustainable World Program, which "supports efforts that will ensure that human activities do not undermine the quality of life of future generations"; and a Secure World Program, which "seeks to build a secure world, free from the nuclear threat." The Foundation's Web site combines a smartly efficient architecture with an array of features and content, including program descriptions; grants lists and links to grantee Web sites; grantee publications; application procedures; a listing of trustees, officers, and staff; and contact information.

The Joyce Foundation (IL) (http://www.joycefdn.org)

Beatrice Joyce Kean, whose family wealth came from the lumber industry, established the Joyce Foundation in 1948. The Foundation supports efforts to protect the natural environment of the Great Lakes, to reduce poverty and violence in the region, and to ensure that its people have access to good schools, decent jobs, and a diverse and thriving culture. It also support efforts to reform the system of financing election campaigns. Currently, the Foundation's program areas are education, employment, environment, gun violence prevention, money and politics, and culture. The Chicago-based foundation gives preference to organizations based in or who have a program in the Midwest, specifically the Great Lakes region: Illinois, Indiana, Iowa, Michigan, Minnesota, Ohio and Wisconsin. A limited number of grants are made to organizations in Canada, and culture grants are restricted to the Chicago metropolitan area. Consult the Web site for further information on each program area and for grant application information and deadlines. The Web site also features downloadable application form and guidelines, downloadable newsletter and annual report, grants list, links to grantee organizations, a site search function, announcements and press releases, listing of officers, directors and staff, and contact information.

Henry J. Kaiser Family Foundation (CA) (http://www.kff.org)

The Kaiser Family Foundation is an independent philanthropy that seeks to be an independent, trusted, and credible source of information, analysis, and balanced discussion on the field of health, which the foundation recognizes as being otherwise dominated by large interests. The foundation seeks to be this source of information to policymakers, the media, and the general public. The Foundation's work is focused on four main areas: health policy, reproductive health, HIV policy, and health and development in South Africa, and its Web site is primarily designed to be an information resource in its program areas, and as such provides a wealth of health-related news, reports, and fact sheets. The Foundation makes few grants, but information about applying can be found in the "About KFF" section of the site.

Kansas Health Foundation (KS) (http://www.kansashealth.org/)

Established with the proceeds from the sale of the Wesley Medical Center in 1985, and with an endowment of more than $200 million, the Kansas Health Foundation makes grants to health organizations throughout the state aimed at improving the quality of health in Kansas. Although the majority of the Foundation's activity centers around Foundation-initiated partnerships and programs, it does provide $500,000 in funding each year through its Recognition Grant program "to support grass-roots organizations doing creative and innovative work to improve the health of Kansans." Recognition Grants fall into six primary funding categories: children, leadership, rural health, public health, health promotion and disease prevention, and health policy and research. In addition to general information about the Foundation and its programs, visitors to the Foundation's Web site will find grant program descriptions, application guidelines with downloadable application forms, news, publications, information on the Foundation's health campaigns, and contact information.

The Karma Foundation (NJ) (http://fdncenter.org/grantmaker/karma/)

The New Jersey-based Karma Foundation was established in 1996 to provide grants to support organizations engaged in activities and programs in the areas of arts and culture, education and literacy, health and human services, and the development and enrichment of Jewish life. The foundation's Web site, hosted through the Center's Foundation Folder program, provides grant guidelines, application procedures, restrictions, sample grants, and foundation trustees.

Ewing Marion Kauffman Foundation (MO) (http://www.emkf.org/)

The Kansas City-based Kauffman Foundation is an operating and grantmaking foundation with a special interest in entrepreneurial leadership and youth development. In making grants, the Foundation aims to support "sustainable programs and projects that will lead to individual, organizational and community self-sufficiency." The Foundation accepts direct inquiries but does not seek unsolicited proposals. Its Web site includes extremely detailed information about its many youth- and entrepreneurship-related areas of interest of funding, funding guidelines, programs and partners, research reports, press releases, FAQs, contact information, and a biography of Ewing Kauffman.

The Calvin K. Kazanjian Economics Foundation, Inc. (PA) (http://www.kazanjian.org)

Calvin K. Kazanjian established the Economics Foundation in his own name in 1947. A business owner for thirty years, he believed that social and political difficulties could be traced to economic illiteracy and that if people understood the basic facts of economics, "the world would be a better place in which to live." Therefore the mission of the foundation is "to help bring greater happiness and prosperity to all through better understanding of economics." Based in Dallas, Pennsylvania, the Foundation is interested in projects that: present economics in an effective, thoughtful, and understandable way; encourage measurement of economic understanding more often, and/or more effectively; help otherwise disenfranchised youth and/or adults learn to participate in the economic system; and distribute high-quality economic education materials to regions of the world with emerging markets, though such projects represent a small portion of the annual grants budget. The Kazanjian Foundation is primarily interested in proposals that are national in scope, and usually does not support regional or statewide programs. Visitors to the Web site will find application guidelines and procedures, information about the founder, links to other economic education resources, descriptions of some projects funded and contact information.

The W.M. Keck Foundation (CA) (http://www.wmkeck.org/)

Established in 1954 by William Myron Keck, founder of the Superior Oil Company, the W.M. Keck Foundation focuses its grantmaking on the areas of medical research, science, and engineering. The Foundation also maintains a program for liberal arts colleges and a Southern California Grant Program that provides support in the areas of civic and community services, health care and hospitals, precollegiate education, and the arts. According to the Foundation's guidelines, eligible institutions in the fields of science, engineering, medical research, and liberal arts are "accredited universities, colleges, medical schools, and major, independent medical research institutions." In the Southern California program, "only organizations located in and serving the population of Southern California are eligible for consideration." Visitors to the Foundation's Web site will find general program descriptions, application criteria and guidelines, excerpts from the Foundation's 1996 annual report, 1995 and 1996 grants lists organized by program area (no dollar amounts), a page devoted to the W.M. Keck Observatory on Hawaii's Mauna Kea volcano, and contact information.

W.K. Kellogg Foundation (MI) (http://www.wkkf.org/)

The mission of the W.K. Kellogg Foundation is to "help people help themselves through the practical application of knowledge and resources to improve their quality of life and that of future generations." The Foundation awards grants in three primary global regions: the United States; five southern Africa countries, including Botswana, Lesotho, South Africa, Swaziland, and Zimbabwe; and Latin America and the Caribbean. In addition to thorough program descriptions, application guidelines, and the Foundation's 1997 annual report, the Foundation's sophisticated Web site offers a variety of useful features, including a state-of-the-art searchable grants database; an electronic version of the International Journal of the W.K. Kellogg Foundation; and individual listings of resources of interest in the Foundation's various program areas.

Joseph P. Kennedy, Jr. Foundation (DC)
(http://www.familyvillage.wisc.edu/jpkf/)

The Joseph P. Kennedy, Jr. Foundation has two major objectives: "to improve the way society deals with its citizens who have mental retardation, and to help identify and disseminate ways to prevent the causes of mental retardation." To that end, the Foundation provides seed funding that encourages new methods of service and supports, and through the use of its influence to promote public awareness of the needs of persons with mental retardation and their families. The Foundation does not participate in capital costs or costs of equipment for projects, or pay for ongoing support or operations of existing programs. Visitors to the Foundation's Web site will find information on the Foundation's various funding and award programs, application guidelines, and an extensive listing of links to other online resources for mental retardation.

Kentucky Foundation for Women (KY) (http://www.kfw.org/)

The mission of the Kentucky Foundation for Women is "to change the lives of women by supporting feminist expression in the arts in Kentucky." The primary goal of the Foundation's grants program is to support the work of individual artists who live or work in Kentucky and "whose work embodies a feminist consciousness." Grants may also be awarded to organizations and for special collaborative projects that share the Foundation's goals. In addition to general Foundation information, application guidelines and procedures, and a list of grant recipients, visitors to the KFW Web site can learn about the Foundation's literary journal, The American Voice, and Hopscotch House, its rural retreat for women.

Charles F. Kettering Foundation (OH) (Operating foundation)
(http://www.kettering.org/)

Established in 1927 by inventor Charles F. Kettering, the Kettering Foundation's objective is "to understand the way bodies politic...function or fail to function." The Foundation does not make grants, but rather sponsors its own programs and participates in collaborative research efforts with other organizations to address the roles of politics and institutional structures as a dimension of everyday life. The results of the Foundation's research are published in study guides, community workbooks, and other exercises to help the public act responsibly and effectively on its problems. In addition to general information about the Foundation's activities and publications, a listing of Foundation trustees, and e-mail and contact information, visitors to the Foundation's Web site can access a searchable database of more than 2,000 non-evaluative summaries of books and articles in the subject areas of governing, community, education, international, science, policy, and political philosophy.

John S. and James L. Knight Foundation (FL) (http://www.knightfdn.org/)

Established in 1950, the John S. and James L. Knight Foundation focuses its grantmaking activities on journalism, education, and arts and culture. The Foundation also supports organizations in 27 communities where the communications company founded by the Knight brothers publishes newspapers, and it "remains flexible enough to respond to unique challenges, ideas and projects that lie beyond its identified program areas, yet would fulfill the broad vision of its founders." Visitors to the site can access an array of information about the Foundation and its programs; application guidelines, restrictions, and application forms; news and publications, including grants lists and the Foundation's annual report; and an informative FAQ section.

Kongsgaard-Goldman Foundation (WA) (http://www.kongsgaard-goldman.org)

The Kongsgaard-Goldman Foundation was formed in 1988 by Martha Kongsgaard and Peter Goldman. The Seattle-based private foundation supports a wide range of nonprofit organizations in the Pacific Northwest, specifically Washington, Oregon, Idaho, Alaska, Montana, and British Columbia, Canada. Primary funding areas are: environmental conservation and restoration in the Pacific Northwest; civic development and civil rights in the Pacific Northwest; and artistic expression in the state of Washington. Another funding area, but of low priority, is Technical Assistance. Within these funding areas, the Foundation favors projects that reflect "a deep and broad level of citizen participation and leadership." Their priority is to help "fund the building of grassroots organizations with the power to change their communities and improve their lives." Visitors to the Web site will find further information on each funding area, downloadable guidelines, application instructions, grants lists with links or email addresses of grantee organizations, links to related sites, and contact information.

Kopp Family Foundation (MN) (http://www.koppfamilyfdtn.org)

Lee and Barbara Kopp established the Kopp Family Foundation in 1986. The Edina, Minnesota Foundation, focused on youth, women, and the aging population, runs a grant's management program and a scholarship program. Through their grant's management program, they support nonprofit organizations mainly within the Twin Cities, though they have donated to organizations throughout Greater Minnesota, in several other states, and internationally as well. Their scholarship program provides funds directly to participating high schools for graduating seniors, enabling them to continue education at a post-secondary school of their choice. Their other scholarship program is the Random Acts of Kindness (RAK) program, which provides funds to participating high schools for students who need help for unexpected emergencies. Visit the Web site for grant

application instructions, scholarship program information, links to other foundation Web sites, annual report and contact information. The site also features
online reporting forms for schools that participate in the scholarship and Random
Acts of Kindness programs.

Kresge Foundation (MI) (http://www.kresge.org)

Sebastian S. Kresge, founder of the S.S. Kresge Company that is now known as
Kmart, established the Kresge Foundation in 1924. Its mission statement is simple: "to promote the well-being of mankind." The Kresge Foundation makes
grants to build and renovate facilities, challenge private giving, and build institutional capacity among nonprofits, with goals of strengthening the capacity of
charitable organizations to provide effective programs of quality. Located in Troy,
Michigan, the Foundation has national geographic scope, occasionally international, and supports a range of organizations "reflecting almost the entire breadth
of the nonprofit sector." Currently, there are five programs: Bricks and Mortar,
which is grant program to build facilities and challenge private giving, and makes
up about 80% of their grantmaking; Science Initiative, a challenge grant program
to upgrade and endow scientific equipment; Detroit Initiative, grant program to
support strategic investment in Detroit and Southeastern Michigan; The Kresge
Foundation Partnership to Raise Community Capital, a five-year grant program to
develop permanent endowment assets for community foundations and nonprofit
organizations; and The Kresge Foundation HBCU initiative, a five-year grant program that helps develop fundraising capacity at historically Black colleges and
universities. Visit their Web site for detailed information on each of their programs and application guidelines, 1997 annual report, FAQ page, history of the
foundation, staff listing, and contact information.

Samuel H. Kress Foundation (NY) (http://www.shkf.org)

Samuel H. Kress, who made his fortune from S.H. Kress & Co. variety stores,
established the Samuel H. Kress Foundation in 1929. With his fortune from his
stores, Samuel Kress amassed a collection of over 3000 works of art, which he
then donated to more than 90 institutions in 33 states. At the time of distribution,
completed over three decades ago, the collection was valued at $100 million.
Beyond its endowment of works of art, the Foundation has several Grant Programs, for projects or programs focused on European art from antiquity through
the early nineteenth century: the Resources of Scholarship, for development of
essential resources for art historical research and the practice of art conservation;
the Sharing of Expertise, projects in which art historians and conservators share
their professional skills and experience; Art Conservation Research, scientific
investigation of problems in art conservation; Conservation and Restoration Projects, which supports the care and conservation of works of art and the preservation of European monuments; and its Special Initiatives Program, which are projects that the Foundation takes an active role in development and implementation.
To advance the academic discipline of the history of art, the Foundation developed
four Kress Fellowships: Conservation, Curatorial, Travel, and Two-Year Fellowships in the History of Art, which are for the completion of dissertation research.
Further information and application information for its grant and fellowship programs is available on the Web site, along further information on the Foundation
and samples and locations of works from the Kress Collection.

Kronkosky Charitable Foundation (TX) (http://www.kronkosky.org)
The Kronkosky Charitable Foundation was established by a Trust Agreement in 1991 but did not receive its principle funding until 1997, some $295 million from the estate of Albert Kronkosky, Jr. The Kronkosky family was a significant shareholder in Merck stock and was involved in a number of successful local business ventures. Based in San Antonio, Texas, the Foundation's mission statement is "to produce profound good that is tangible and measurable in Bandera, Bexar, Comal, and Kendall counties in Texas by implementing the Kronkosky's charitable purposes." The focus of the Foundation is to "support programs, projects, and collaborative efforts that reach as many people as possible; involve the persons served in developing solutions; raise expectations; build self-esteem; develop personal and organizational capacity; encourage innovation; and make use of technology." Its funding areas are: health and human services, including the elderly, youth, child abuse and neglect, and persons with disabilities; cultural activities; and other areas, such as wildlife preservation and animal issues. Consult the Web site for detailed information on each funding area, application information, a FAQ area, grants lists, tax information and annual reports, online feedback/contact form, and contact information.

The Lalor Foundation (RI) (http://www.lalorfound.org)
The Lalor Foundation, based in Providence, Rhode Island, was established in 1935 from bequests from members for the Lalor Family. The goal of the Foundation is to give assistance and encouragement to capable investigators who have teaching and research careers in universities and colleges. The principal areas of support have been branches of life sciences "wherein applications of chemical and physical methods of research could be expected to give useful and fruitful results." Since 1960, however, the Foundation has concentrated its support on special aspects of reproductive physiology, which the Foundation considers of "pressing importance"; their Web site states that since resources must be conserved, "a finer understanding of all aspects of reproduction and the means to control population growth is an imperative." The program of research grants offered in 1999 were grants to institutions for "basic postdoctoral research in mammalian reproductive biology as related to the regulation of fertility". Visit their Web site for more information about their foundation and grant program, application instructions and printable application form, links to related sites, current grant awardees and their projects, and contact information.

Jacob and Valeria Langeloth Foundation (NY) (http://www.langeloth.com)
The Jacob and Valeria Langeloth Foundation has its roots in a bequest in 1914 from Jacob Langeloth, Chairman of the American Metal Co., Ltd. Langeloth left instructions for a convalescent home for professionals of modest means. Called Valeria Home in honor of his wife, it was open for six decades until it was closed and sold in 1977. Proceeds from the sale passed to the newly-named Jacob and Valeria Langeloth Foundation, which continues in the tradition of Langeloth's commitment to convalescence. The Foundation "supports programs designed to improve, speed, make more cost effective, and in other ways promote physical and emotional recovery from illness and accident." The New York City-based Foundation seeks proposals that include one or more of the following: innovative approaches or model programs that can be replicated; new community models that reach out to empower communities that may normally be beyond the reach of

good medical care; interdisciplinary and interagency collaboration; programs that promote among patients greater knowledge of their illnesses, paths to recovery, and rights as consumers of medical care, as well as involving families in the convalescent process; applied research which holds the promise of developing new knowledge and understanding about the field; and humanization of relations between medical professionals and those in their care. Consult their Web site for application procedures, sample budget template, history of the foundation and its founder, listing of staff, and contact information.

Albert & Mary Lasker Foundation, Inc. (NY) (Operating foundation) (http://www.laskerfoundation.com)

The Albert & Mary Lasker foundation is known for its Albert Lasker awards. Philanthropists Albert and Mary Woodard Lasker first inaugurated these awards in 1946. The mission of the foundation is "to elevate and sustain medical research as a universal priority so that the foundation's goals—to eradicate life threatening disease and disabilities and improve health standards—are strongly supported by national and international policies and resources." An international jury of top medical researchers annually selects the Lasker Award recipients, who are scientists, physicians and public servants who have made major advances in the understanding, diagnosis, treatment, prevention and cure of human disease. Currently, three awards are presented each year: the Albert Lasker Basic Medical Research Award, Clinical Medical Research Award, and Award for Special Medical Research Achievement. In addition to its awards program, the Foundation also has a program of public education aimed at encouraging federal financial support for biomedical research. The primary beneficiary of their support has been the National Institutes of Health. Visit the Lasker Foundation Web site for more information about their award programs, past recipients, a searchable library of materials related to the awards and its past recipients, and press releases.

The LEF Foundation (CA) (http://www.agmconnect.org/lef.html)

The LEF Foundation assists the "innovative efforts of individuals and organizations seeking to expand the boundaries of artistic expression and create new ideas and opportunities that affirm the constructive link between the arts and contemporary life." Funds are given for projects, programs, and services that encourage "a positive interchange between the arts and the natural urban environment", and may involve visual, media, performing and literary art. Projects may also involve public and environmental art, architecture and landscape architecture, and be design and interdisciplinary collaborations. Within these areas, the Foundation also considers projects that address critical community needs. Located in Cambridge, MA and St. Helena, CA, the Foundation primarily sponsors projects in New England and Northern California, although application may be open to relevant proposals outside of those areas. Consult the Web site for application instructions and guidelines, and contact information.

Leeway Foundation (PA) (http://www.leeway.org/)

The Leeway Foundation was established in 1993 by artist Linda Lee Alter to promote the welfare of women and to benefit the arts. The Foundation's primary grantmaking program supports individual women artists in the Philadelphia area and encourages their increased recognition and representation in the community. The Foundation makes grants each year in a selected visual or literary discipline.

Grants are awarded to artists who demonstrate exceptional creativity and vision in a body of work. In addition, two special grants recognizing artists at particular stages in their careers are available each year at the jurors' discretion. The Bessie Berman Grant acknowledges the accomplishments of a woman artist fifty years or older. The Edna Andrade Emerging Artist Grant encourages a woman artist who exhibits great promise early in her artistic career. The Foundation's Web site provides information about these programs as well as the Foundation's general program, application instructions (including the dates and locations of Foundation-sponsored application workshops in the five-county Philadelphia metro region), the names of recent grantees and examples of their work, listings of the Foundation's board and staff, and contact information.

The Lifebridge Foundation, Inc. (NY) (http://www.lifebridge.org)
The Lifebridge Foundation's role is to bridge the "chasm between the spiritual and the so-called mundane", and "facilitating the integration of an emerging holistic consciousness into daily action." It believes that people all over the world, particularly in industrialized western societies, are searching for meaning, for "what is missing" in their lives. Lifebridge Foundation believes that this missing part is the "ability to perceive our existence as part of the same life as the Earth and the Universe; as integral parts of an ever-evolving co-creation." The Foundation, located in New York City, seeks to promote the concept of "One Humanity and the Interconnectedness of all Life" and to foster a spirit of "inclusiveness and global vision leading to transformative action". Grantees cover a wide range of disciplines and social concerns, and can be roughly divided into the following fields: arts and culture, youth/education, environment, science, community service, world goodwill, and 'interdimensional'. The Foundation generally pre-selects grantees but accepts letters of introduction. Visit the Web site for grant guidelines, list of grantees and their email and/or web addresses, newsletter, links to related sites and projects, and contact information.

Franklin Lindsay Student Aid Fund (TX) (http://www.franklinlindsay.org)
The Franklin Lindsay Student Aid Fund was provided for in the Will of Franklin Lindsay, who died on May 3, 1954. He believed that "the greatest good that could be done for the country and the world was to educate its people." Accordingly, he arranged for his $2 million estate to be held and managed in a Trust for loans to be provided for students to further their education. Located in Austin, Texas, the Fund makes loans to "worthy and deserving" students of either sex who wishes to pursue an education at an institute of higher learning within the state of Texas. Loans are up to $3000 per academic year, and are non-interest bearing for up to four months after the student's graduation, provided they maintain certain terms and conditions. Consult the Web site to learn more about the their loan program, its terms and conditions and application procedures, and for contact information. The site also features online forms to start the application process and for feedback about the site.

Albert A. List Foundation, Inc. (NY)
(http://fdncenter.org/grantmaker/listfdn/index.html)
The New York City-based List Foundation achieves its mission of supporting and enhancing citizen participation within our pluralistic society through grantmaking in three major program areas: Democracy and Citizen Participation, Freedom of

Expression, and New Problems/New Solutions. The Foundation currently funds organizations that foster citizen participation in the democratic process and share its commitment to a society free of ageism, classism, homophobia, racism, religious prejudice, sexism, and discrimination against those who are physically or mentally challenged; community involvement; economic justice; involving youth in the process of social change; alliances that go beyond traditional, short-term coalition building around a specific action; progressive, proactive policies that speak to the needs of broad sectors of society; and solutions to ongoing and emerging problems that enable us to live more harmoniously with our natural environment and with each other. The Foundation's "folder" on the Center's Web site provides descriptions of its three main programs, eligibility requirements, application procedures, and contact information.

The John Locke Foundation (NC) (Operating foundation) (http://www.johnlocke.org)

The John Locke Foundation is a non-partisan public policy institute that opened its doors in 1990. Based in Raleigh, North Carolina, the Foundation was named for the 17th Century English philosopher whose writings on government and political freedom inspired the founding documents of this country, and who played a major role in drawing up the Fundamental Constitution of Carolina in 1665. Locke was also a "great believer in the value of public debate and policy research." The name is fitting since the Foundation's purpose is to "conduct research, disseminate information, and advance public understanding of society based on the principles of individual liberty, the voluntary exchange of a free market economy, and limited government." The Foundation also seeks to "foster a climate of innovative thinking and debate on issues facing North Carolinians." It operates a number of programs and services to provide information and observations to legislators, policymakers, business executives, citizen activists, civic and community leaders, and the news media. Among its activities are producing newsletters, journals, and policy research reports, holding public policy events, making speeches, and responding to requests for information. Visit their Web site to learn more about the services the Foundation offers, the history of the Foundation and its namesake, and its goals and purposes and position on issues. The Foundation also has its publications online.

Edward Lowe Foundation (MI) (Operating foundation) (http://www.lowe.org/elf/index.htm)

The focus of the Edward Lowe Foundation, a private operating foundation, is "to champion the entrepreneurial spirit by providing information, research and education experiences which support small business people and the free enterprise system." Although the Foundation makes limited grants, guidelines and a grantee list are provided at its Web site. Additionally, the site provides information on the Foundation's programs; biographies of it founder and chair; a link to Entrepreneurial Edge Online (http://edge.lowe.org/); a peer-learning community for growing companies, where they can find peers, share experiences and grow; and contact information.

George Lucas Educational Foundation (CA) (http://glef.org/)

The George Lucas Educational Foundation uses various media, including its Web site, to promote and share the latest strategies to change the K–12 educational system, especially those that integrate technology with teaching or learning. Those strategies are based on the filmmaker's belief that "education is the most important investment we can make to secure the future of our democracy." Visitors to the site can access Edutopia, the Foundation's newsletter and "Learn & Live," the Foundation's educational resource guide. Although the Foundation is a private operating entity and does not make grants, visitors are encouraged to contact the Foundation if they know of a program or resource that can advance the Foundation's mission.

Henry Luce Foundation, Inc. (NY) (http://www.hluce.org/)
Established in 1936 by the late Henry R. Luce, co-founder and editor-in-chief of Time Inc., the New York City-based Henry Luce Foundation today focuses its activities on the interdisciplinary exploration of higher education; increased understanding between Asia and the United States; the study of religion and theology; scholarship in American art; opportunities for women in science and engineering; and contributions to youth and public policy programs. Higher education has been a persistent theme for most of the Foundation's programs, with an emphasis on innovation and scholarship. The Foundation's elegant, bandwidth-friendly Web site provides detailed information about a range of programs, including the Luce Fund in American Art, the American Collections Enhancement Initiative, the Clare Booth Luce Program, the Henry R. Luce Professorships, the Luce Scholars Program, the United States-China Cooperative Research Program, and the Asia Project; general application guidelines, guidelines for specific programs, and grant restrictions; recent grants list organized by program area; a helpful FAQ; listings of the Foundation's board and staff; and contact information.

Christopher Ludwick Foundation (PA)
(http://www.libertynet.org/athena/ludwick.html)
The Christopher Ludwick Foundation was founded by Christopher Ludwick (1720–1801), a Baker General of the Army of the United States during the American Revolution. His bequest of $13,000 was to be put in a trust for "the schooling and gratis, of poor children of all denominations, in the city and liberties of Philadelphia, without exception to the country, extraction, or religious principles of their parents and friends…" The origins of the Foundation can be traced back to the founding of the Philadelphia Society for Free Instruction of Indigent Boys in 1799, which over the course of two centuries bore different names until it became the Christopher Ludwick Foundation in 1995. The trust has grown to over $5 million over the intervening two hundred years, and approximately $250,000 in grants are awarded each year, with secondary school children a current funding priority. Programs must target children who reside in Philadelphia in order to receive funding. Visit their Web site for application information, further information on the foundation, listing of trustees and grants list.

Lumpkin Foundation (IL) (http://www.lumpkinfoundation.org)
The mission of the Illinois-based Lumpkin Foundation is "to provide leadership, individually and collectively, both locally and globally, to enrich [family members'] respective communities and in so doing preserve the tradition and goals of the [Lumpkin] family." The Foundation is dedicated to supporting education, preserving and protecting the environment, and fostering opportunities for

leadership, and gives special consideration to its heritage in East Central Illinois. In addition to a mission statement and officer and committee listings, the Foundation's Web site provides grant application procedures and restrictions, a letter of conditions (for grant recipients), downloadable versions of its grant application cover sheet and post-evaluation grant report, and contact information.

John D. and Catherine T. MacArthur Foundation (IL) (http://www.macfdn.org/)

The Chicago-based MacArthur Foundation recently revised most of its programs and guidelines, and unveiled a redesigned Web site to help get the message out. With a broad goal of fostering lasting improvement in the human condition, the Foundation seeks the development of healthy individuals and effective communities; peace within and among nations; responsible choices about human reproduction; and a global ecosystem capable of supporting healthy human societies. The Foundation makes grants through two major integrated programs—Human and Community Development and Global Security and Sustainability—and two special programs. The former supports national research and policy work and—in Chicago and Palm Beach County, Florida—direct local efforts. The program on Global Security and Sustainability focuses on arms reduction and security policy, ecosystems conservation, and population, and on three cross-cutting themes: concepts of security and sustainability; new partnerships and institutions; and education about United States interests and responsibilities. The Foundation's two special programs are the General Program, which undertakes special initiatives and supports projects that promote excellence and diversity in the media, and the MacArthur Fellows Program, which awards fellowships to exceptionally creative individuals, regardless of field of endeavor. Visitors to the Foundation's well-organized, bandwidth-friendly Web site will find a great deal of information, including brief biographies of John D. Catherine T. MacArthur, detailed program descriptions and application guidelines, recent grants, annual report, links to philanthropy resources, contact information, and a variety of other materials.

The Maclellan Foundation, Inc. (TN) (http://www.maclellanfdn.org)

Dora Maclellan Brown, Robert J. Maclellan, and Robert L. Maclellan established the Maclellan Foundation, located in Chattanooga, Tennessee, in 1945. The original principle of the Foundation and its related trusts was in the form of Provident Life and Accident Insurance Company stock, a company founded by Thomas Maclellan, father of Robert J. Maclellan and Dora Maclellan Brown. The purpose of the Foundation is "to contribute to and otherwise serve strategic national and international organizations committed to furthering the Kingdom of Christ; to contribute to and otherwise serve select local organizations which foster the spiritual welfare of the community; and to serve by providing financial and leadership resources to extend the Kingdom of God in accordance with the Great Commission." The Foundation prefers to make project or seed grants, not operating grants. Visit the Web site for application instructions; information about their philosophy, policies, and guidelines; the grantmaking process, from board meetings to a site meeting checklist used by the Foundation; grantee responsibilities; and contact information. The site also features a letter from one of its founders on the ideals the Foundation was established upon, a grantmaking manual prepared by the Foundation, a public discussion forum and multimedia clips.

Maddie's Fund (CA) (http://www.maddies.org/)
Established in 1994 by David and Cheryl Duffield to honor the memory of their beloved miniature schnauzer, Maddie's Fund (formerly known as the Duffield Family Foundation) hopes "to revolutionize the status and well being of companion animals" by spending more than $200 million to help build, community by community, a "No-Kill Nation" in which "healthy, adoptable dogs and cats in animal shelters across the country are guaranteed loving homes." The Fund is particularly interested in supporting animal welfare organizations capable of building alliances and developing collaborative pet-related projects within their communities. Successful projects will set forth comprehensive life-saving strategies that involve the participation of cooperating animal shelters, rescue groups, volunteer foster organizations, local animal control agencies, veterinarians, and others. In addition to a clear articulation of the Fund's philosophy and goals, the Maddie's Fund Web site provides detailed grant proposal guidelines and requirements, a hypothetical funding scenario, a downloadable application form in PDF format, a letter from the Fund's president, and contact information.

A. L. Mailman Family Foundation, Inc. (NY) (http://www.mailman.org)
Headquartered in White Plains, New York, the A. L. Mailman Family Foundation focuses its grantmaking activities on children and families, with a special emphasis on early childhood. The Foundation's current program is focused in the following areas: early care and education, family support, and moral education and social responsibility. Foundation grants generally range from $30,000 to $35,000, but are not awarded for ongoing direct services, general operating expenses, individuals, capital expenditures, endowment campaigns, or for local services or programs. Visitors to the Foundation's Web site will find general information and 1997 grant summary lists for each program area; grant application guidelines; a listing of directors, officer and staff; and contact information.

Manitou Foundation, Inc. (CO) (http://www.manitou.org/mf_homepage.html)
The Manitou Foundation offers land grants in the Crestone/Baca area of Colorado to qualified U.S. nonprofit organizations in the following categories: religious organizations and spiritual projects, ecological and environmental sustainability projects, and related educational endeavors (youth and adult). The Foundation also administers a land preservation program and seeks to network with individuals and organizations locally, nationally, and internationally to facilitate its mission objectives. Visitors will find program guidelines and application procedures for the program, information on its programs and projects, and contact information with e-mail addresses.

John and Mary R. Markle Foundation (NY) (http://www.markle.org/)
The John and Mary R. Markle Foundation was established in 1927 "to promote the advancement and diffusion of knowledge and the general good of mankind." Today the Foundation focuses its activities on the ways that emerging communications media and information technology create unprecedented opportunity to improve people's lives. Most of the Foundation's current work is through following programs: Public Engagement through Interactive Technologies, Policy for a Networked Society, Interactive Media for Children, and Information Technologies for Better Health. Visitors to the Foundation's Web site will find lots of information on its focus on communications and technology and current

programs, grant guidelines, the history of the Foundation, board and staff listings, grants and investments since 1990, news, and contact information.

Edmund F. Maxwell Foundation (WA) (http://www.maxwell.org)

The Edmund F. Maxwell Foundation, located in Seattle, Washington, "believing in the importance of acknowledging the fine accomplishments of high-achieving young people", offers the Edmund F. Maxwell Foundation Scholarships to residents of Western Washington who require financial assistance to attend independent colleges or universities. The Foundation's namesake, Edmund Maxwell, was the head of Blyth & Co., a premier investment firm in the region. Students who are residents of Western Washington, with combined S.A.T. scores of over 1200 and demonstrated financial need, and who meet other criteria are eligible for the scholarship, which is $3500 for the 1999–2000 school year. Consult the Web site for a brief biography, application guidelines, printable forms, recipient list, and contact information. Forms are also available by mail.

McCarthy Family Foundation (CA) (http://fdncenter.org/grantmaker/mccarthy/index.html)

The San Diego-based McCarthy Family Foundation makes grants in five primary program areas: secondary school science education; AIDS research, education and support; assistance to homeless people; support for children and families in need; and environmental protection. The Foundation makes grants exclusively within California, with the typical grant award between $5,000 and $15,000. The Foundation does not make grants for individuals, scholarship funds, sectarian religious activities, general fundraising drives, or programs supporting political candidates or to influence legislation. The Foundation's "folder" on the Center's Web site provides visitors with program guidelines, application instructions, and a grants list.

Robert R. McCormick Tribune Foundation (IL) (http://www.rrmtf.org)

The Robert R. McCormick Tribune Foundation was established as a charitable trust in 1955 upon the death of Colonel Robert R. McCormick, longtime editor and publisher of the Chicago Tribune, and was restructured as a foundation in 1991 with an emphasis on four grantmaking areas: communities, journalism, education, and citizenship. Because each program has its own guidelines, geographic restrictions, and application procedures, grantseekers are encouraged to read carefully all information pertaining to their particular program of interest. In addition to the four program areas, the Foundation also provides annual support to Cantigny, the Colonel's former estate in Wheaton, Illinois, which is now operated as a park for the "education, instruction and welfare of the people of Illinois." The Foundation's Web site provides program descriptions, grant summaries, and grant guidelines where applicable.

McCune Charitable Foundation (MN) (http://www.nmmccune.org/)

Perrine D. McCune founded the McCune Charitable Foundation in Sante Fe, New Mexico in 1989, to continue the philanthropic legacy that she and her husband, Marshall Lockhart McCune, had established during their lifetime. The couple was a significant part of the cultural and artistic life in the Sante Fe area, and helped establish many organizations and institutions there. The mission of the Marshall L. and Perrine D. McCune Charitable Foundation is "to memorialize the donors through grants which enrich the cultural life, health, education, environment and spiritual life of the citizens of New Mexico." Funding is targeted for community-based, community-driven projects, with preference given to organizations that operate programs in Sante Fe or northern New Mexico. Visitors to the Web site will find grant application guidelines, staff listing, short descriptions of sample funded projects and contact information.

James S. McDonnell Foundation (MO) (http://www.jsmf.org/)

The McDonnell Foundation was established in 1950 "to explore methods for developing a stable world order and lasting peace." Today the Foundation funds internationally primarily in the areas of biomedical and behavioral sciences research. Its web site contains program information, application guidelines, and a listing of the most recent grants and awards made by the Foundation.

R.J. McElroy Trust (IA) (http://www.cedarnet.org/mcelroy)

R. J. McElroy was a pioneer Iowa broadcaster who founded the Black Hawk Broadcasting Company, put KWWL radio station, KWWL TV and several other radio and television stations on the air. When he died in 1965, a provision in his will provided for the establishment of a trust fund for the educational benefit of deserving young people. Located in Waterloo, Iowa, the R.J. McElroy Trust has since then funded a broad range of educational programs, such as scholarships, fellowships, internships, student loan funds and other projects to benefit youth of all ages. Organizations located in the KWWL viewing area are preferred, and organizations located in Black Hawk County and the rural counties in that viewing area will receive higher priority. The Trust will also give higher priority to grants that fund program rather than capital projects. Consult their Web site for grant application guidelines, policies, and contact information, including an email link.

McGregor Fund (MI) (http://comnet.org/mcgregor/)

Founded in 1925 by Michigan philanthropists Tracy and Katherine Whitney McGregor, the McGregor Fund was established to "relieve the misfortunes and promote the well being of mankind." The Fund presently awards grants in the areas of human services, education, health care, arts and culture, and public benefit. Only organizations located in the metropolitan Detroit area, or projects which significantly benefit that area, are eligible for support. The Fund does not award grants for individuals or student scholarships and generally does not support travel, conferences, seminars or workshops, film or video projects, or disease specific organizations. Visitors to the Fund's Web site will find brief descriptions of each program area, application procedures and guidelines, a grants list organized by program area, financial statements, a listing of Fund trustees and staff, and contact information.

The McKnight Endowment Fund for Neuroscience (MN) (http://www.mcknight.org/neuroscience)

The McKnight Endowment Fund for Neuroscience is an independent organization established and funded by the McKnight Foundation in 1986 to oversee their neuroscience research awards program, which dates back to 1977, due to the success of the awards program and the recognition attained by the participants. The Fund has its own board of directors but is administered by the Foundation. This research program is a direct legacy of founder William L. McKnight, who was interested in the biology of the brain, particularly diseases affecting memory. The Endowment Fund has the following awards for research on memory: McKnight Scholar Awards, for scientists in the early stages of their research careers; McKnight Investigator Awards, for mid-career scientists exploring new ideas about the basic mechanisms of memory and disorders affecting memory; McKnight Technological Innovations in Neuroscience Awards, which provides seed funding for highly innovative projects to stimulate the development of novel approaches to exploring and understanding how the brain functions; and McKnight Senior Investigator Awards, of which 10 were given every three years from 1977 to 1999 to established neuroscientists and their associates. The Board of Directors makes on the basis of recommendations by review committees. Visitors to their Web site will find downloadable application forms and guidelines, list of awardees, announcements, a search engine for the site, and contact information.

The McKnight Foundation (MN) (http://www.mcknight.org)

The McKnight Foundation was established and endowed by William L. McKnight and Maude L. McKnight in 1953. William McKnight was one of the early leaders of 3M, as president and chief executive; however, the Foundation is independent of that corporation. The McKnight Foundation seeks to improve the quality of life for present and future generations; "supports efforts to improve outcomes for children, families, and communities; contributes to the arts; encourages preservation of the natural environment; and promotes scientific research in selected fields." The Foundation has the following funding areas: Children, Families, and Communities; Arts; Environment; Initiatives; International; and Research and Applied Science. Located in Minneapolis, Minnesota, its primary geographic focus in its human services and arts grantmaking is the state of Minnesota. Consult their Web site for more information on grant and award programs for each funding area; downloadable guidelines (can also be ordered by phone); conditions and limitations; grants lists; financial information; online free publications request, including their annual report; and an online contact form.

Meadows Foundation, Inc. (TX) (http://www.mfi.org/)

The Meadows Foundation was established in 1948 by Algur H. and Virginia Meadows to benefit the people of Texas by "working toward the elimination of ignorance, hopelessness and suffering, protecting the environment, providing cultural enrichment, encouraging excellence and promoting understanding and cooperation among people." The Foundation provides grants in the areas of art and culture, civic and public affairs, education, health, and human services. In addition to examples of grants awarded in each area of giving, visitors to the Foundation's Web site can access grant guidelines (in Spanish and English), the Foundation's financial information, a listing of officers, directors, and staff, and links to local and national nonprofit organizations. The site also describes the Foundation's Wilson Historic District housing restoration project as well as its Awards for Charitable School project, which supports youth voluntarism.

Medina Foundation (WA) (http://www.medinafoundation.org/)

The Medina Foundation seeks to "aid in improving the human condition in the greater Puget Sound community by fostering positive change, growth and the improvement of people." The Foundation makes grants to qualified charitable organizations, particularly those offering direct service delivery. No grants are made to individuals. The Foundation's Web site includes program descriptions, application guidelines, FAQs, and contact information.

Andrew W. Mellon Foundation (NY) (http://www.mellon.org)

Under its broad charter, the New York City-based Andrew W. Mellon Foundation currently makes grants on a selective basis in the following areas of interest: higher education; cultural affairs and the performing arts; population; conservation and the environment; and public affairs. Although the Foundation reviews proposals on a rolling basis throughout the year, "prospective applicants are encouraged to explore their ideas informally with Foundation staff (preferably in writing) before submitting formal proposals." The Foundation does not make grants to individuals or to primarily local organizations. In addition to a range of general information, visitors to the Foundation's no-frills Web site will find program descriptions, a list of Foundation trustees and staff, and online versions of some two dozen Foundation reports from 1987 to present.

Richard King Mellon Foundation (PA) (http://fdncenter.org/grantmaker/rkmellon/)

Founded in 1947, the Pittsburgh, Pennsylvania-based Richard King Mellon Foundation funds efforts to improve the quality of life in southwestern Pennsylvania, and for national land and wildlife conservation. In southwestern Pennsylvania, the foundation supports programs that relate to human services, education, medicine, civic affairs, and cultural activities. The foundation will consider support for operations, capital projects, programs, and start-up. Visitors to the foundation's Web site, hosted by the Center's Foundation Folder program, will find the foundation's history, program interests, geographic focus, a letter from the president, recently approved grants, grant guidelines, an application form, and a listing of trustees, officers, and program staff.

Merck Family Fund (MA) (http://www.merckff.org/)

Established in 1954, Merck Family Fund is a private family foundation with two goals: to restore and protect the natural environment and ensure a healthy planet for generations to come; and to strengthen the social fabric and the physical landscape of the urban community. There are two areas of priority to help achieve a healthy planet: the protection of vital ecosystems in eastern United States, and supporting the shift towards environmentally sustainable economic systems, incentives, and behaviors. The two areas of priority for strengthening the urban community are creating green and open space, and supporting youth as agents of social change. The Milton, Massachusetts-based Fund limits grants to grassroots programs in New York City, Providence, RI, and Boston, MA. Visit the Web site for more information on their funding areas and priorities, grant application guidelines, financial information, grant lists with links to grantee organizations, related links, and contact information. The Fund urges grantseekers to use the common proposal format (for invited proposals only) and provides a link to site where it can be downloaded.

Joyce Mertz-Gilmore Foundation (NY) (http://www.jmgf.org/)

The Joyce Mertz-Gilmore Foundation makes grants to nonprofit organizations active in the areas of the environment, human rights, peace and security, and New York City civic and cultural life. The Foundation currently sponsors five grant-making programs: environment/energy, human rights, peace and security, New York City human and built environment, and arts in New York City. Visitors to the Foundation's Web site will find program guidelines and restrictions, a listing of selected grants by program area, Foundation history, financial statements, application instructions, and a listing of the Foundation' staff and board of directors.

Meru Foundation (MA) (Operating foundation) (http://www.meru.org)

The Meru Foundation is a private nonprofit research and educational corporation founded in 1983 to "study ancient alphabets and texts from a modern mathematical perspective, with emphasis on their self-organizing whole systems." Its work is based on 20 years of research by Stan Tenen into the origin and nature of the Hebrew alphabet, and the mathematical structure underlying the sequence of letters of the Hebrew text of Genesis. Visit their Web site for articles and papers describing his work.

Meyer Memorial Trust (OR) (http://www.mmt.org/)

Founded by retail-store magnate Fred G. Meyer, the Portland-based Meyer Memorial Trust operates three grantmaking programs—General Purpose Grants, Small Grants, and Support for Teacher Initiatives—to benefit qualified tax-exempt applicants in Oregon and Clark County, Washington. Visitors to the Trust's Web site will find updates about Trust operations, grant application guidelines, searchable grants lists, frequently asked questions, annual report studies of selected trust grants, links to other Internet resources, and direct e-mail access to the Trust.

Milbank Memorial Fund (NY) (http://www.milbank.org)

The Milbank Memorial Fund, based in New York City, supports nonpartisan analysis, study, research and communication on significant issues in health policy, and makes the results of its work available in meetings with decision-makers, reports, books, and the Milbank Quarterly, a peer-reviewed journal of public health and healthcare policy. Access book titles, abstracts, and articles online on its Web site.

Milken Family Foundation (CA) (http://www.mff.org/index.html)

Established in 1982 by Lowell and Michael Milken, the California-based Milken Family Foundation advances its mission of "helping people help themselves and those around them to lead productive and satisfying lives" by focusing its activities on education and medical research. The Foundation's Web site describes these focus areas and provides detailed information on its initiatives. Where applicable, the descriptions of the Foundation's initiatives may include recipient lists or selection criteria. The Foundation's site also provides news, a publications request form and a form to contact the Foundation.

American Epilepsy Society/Milken Family Foundation Epilepsy Research Award Grants and Fellowship Program, recognizing outstanding physicians and scientists working to improve the lives of people with epilepsy; Mike's Math Club, a mentoring program for fifth- and sixth-graders; and the Milken Family National Educator Awards, offering financial recognition to outstanding educators in schools affiliated with the Bureau of Jewish Education of Greater Los Angeles.

Morino Foundation/Institute (VA) (http://www.morino.org)

Founded by business leader and "social entrepreneur" Mario Marino, the Morino Foundation/Institute is dedicated to "opening the doors of opportunity—economic, civic, health and education—and empowering people to improve their lives and communities in the communications age." Grants are normally made from the Morino Foundation, on behalf of the Institute, in support of initiatives or focus areas in which the Institute is actively engaged—youth advocacy and services, entrepreneurship, social networking, and community services. In all of its grantmaking activities, the Institute, which does not accept unsolicited proposals, emphasizes the emerging medium of electronic communications and how it can be applied to further positive social change and community improvement. The Institute's Web site offers a good deal of interesting information about the Institute's core beliefs and funding philosophy, general program and grant information, links to a variety of Institute-sponsored projects and partners, and contact information.

Charles Stewart Mott Foundation (MI) (http://www.mott.org/)

Established in 1926 by industrialist Charles Stewart Mott, the Flint, Michigan-based Mott Foundation makes grants in the United States and, on a limited geographic basis, internationally, in four broad program areas: civil society, the environment, Flint, and poverty. These programs, in turn, are divided into more specific areas: the civil society program focuses on the United States, South Africa, Central/Eastern Europe, Russia, and the newly created Republics; the environment program is devoted to reform of international lending and trade policies, prevention of toxic pollution, protection of the Great Lakes ecosystem, and special initiatives; the Flint program concentrates on institutional capacity building, arts and recreation, economic and community development, and education; and the poverty program focuses on building communities, strengthening families, improving education, economic opportunity, and cross-cutting initiatives. In addition to detailed application guidelines and a biography of Charles Stewart Mott, the Foundation's well-organized Web site offers a searchable grants database, dozens of links to grantee Web sites, a list of publications available through the Foundation, and related stories in each broad program area.

M.J. Murdock Charitable Trust (WA) (http://www.acgilbert.org/murdock.htm)

The Murdock Charitable Trust was created by the will of the late Melvin J. (Jack) Murdock, a co-founder of Tektronix, Inc. of Beaverton, Oregon, in 1975. The Trust's mission is "to strengthen the region's educational and cultural base in creative and sustainable ways." Although the Trust's major funding interests are education and scientific research, grants are also given to a wide variety of organizations, including those that serve the arts, public affairs, health and medicine, human services, and people with disabilities. This simple Web site provides a description of the Trust and a telephone number to call for application information.

The Murray Foundation, Inc. (NY) (http://www.murrayfoundation.org)

Founded in 1986 by Mr. And Mrs. John P. Murray, Jr., The Murray Foundation is a family foundation dedicated to providing a source of funding for medical research and innovative treatment and therapies in the area of oncology and familial disease. This New York City-based foundation has a special focus on Von Hippel-Lindau disease (VHL); their primary goal is to assist in finding a genetic cure for VHL. In the meanwhile, it will fund research and non-invasive techniques to "hold the line on tumor growth", in order to give VHL patients a "higher quality of life without forcing them to undergo traumatic and debilitating conventional surgery." Visitors to the Web site will find information on VHL, online submission of grant request forms, online submission of contact forms, and a listing of some currently funded programs with grantee web or email addresses.

The Mustard Seed Foundation (VA) (Operating foundation) (http://www.msfdn.org)

Dennis and Eileen Harvey Bakke established the Mustard Seed Foundation in 1983 as "an expression of their desire to advance the Kingdom of God through faithful stewardship." The Foundation provides grants to Christians who are engaged in or preparing for evangelism, stewardship, ministry, education, and relieving human suffering. Individuals and organizations receiving Mustard Seed grants must demonstrate personal faith in Christ and must desire "to serve and witness in His name". For the Foundation, "the gospel of Jesus Christ and the advance of His Kingdom are central to all that we are and all that we do." They place highest priority on funding projects that "seek to draw disciples to Jesus from every 'unreached' community, city, and culture and which attempt to redeem society's structures and institutions." The Foundation has the following funding categories: Acts of Mercy, Church Parenting, Empowerment, Unreached peoples, and Christian Discipleship; and the following scholarships: Theological Scholarships, Bakke Scholars, and Harvey Fellows. Consult the Web site for more detailed information on each area of their grant program and scholarship programs. The site features a downloadable application form, and online contact forms. Visitors to the Web site will also find a description of their principles, their annual report and financial information.

Needmor Fund (CO) (http://fdncenter.org/grantmaker/needmor/index.html)

Established in Toledo, Ohio, in 1956, the Colorado-based Needmor Fund today works to change the social, economic, and political conditions that bar access to participation in a democratic society. The Fund is committed to the idea that "citizens should be free and equal to determine the actions of government and the terms of public policy" and thus assure their right to justice, political liberty, the basic necessities of life, an education that enables them to be contributing members of society, and the opportunity to secure productive work with just wages and benefits and decent working conditions. Visitors to the Fund's "folder" on the Center's Web site will find a statement of the Fund's mission and values, detailed application guidelines and restrictions, and a list of grants.

New England Biolabs Foundation (MA) (http://www.nebf.org/)

Established in 1982, NEBF supports grassroots organizations working in the areas of the environment, social change, the arts, elementary education, and limited scientific research. Ordinarily, NEBF limits its domestic grantmaking to the greater

Boston/North Shore area. But the Foundation does encourage proposals from or about developing countries with an emphasis on assisting community organizations in their endeavors. Due to its size, it restricts these activities to specific countries. Visitors to the NEBF site will find detailed application guidelines and reporting requirements, proposal tips from the Foundation's director, a list of, and contact information. NEBF accepts the common grant application form sponsored by the National Network of Grantmakers.

New York Foundation (NY) (http://fdncenter.org/grantmaker/nyfoundation/)

The New York Foundation was established in 1909 and supports groups in New York City working on problems of urgent concern to residents of disadvantaged communities and neighborhoods, and is particularly interested in start-up grants to new, untested programs that have few other sources of support. Grants are not limited to specific issue areas, although half the foundation's grants are reserved for projects involving youth or the elderly. Visitors to the foundation's Web site, hosted through the Center's Foundation Folder program, will find a history of the foundation, a listing of trustees and staff, mission statement, grant program guidelines, application procedures, and grants lists.

Samuel Roberts Noble Foundation (OK) (http://www.noble.org/)

Established in 1945 by oil industrialist Lloyd Noble in honor of his father, the Samuel Roberts Noble Foundation seeks "to assist humanity in reaching its maximum usefulness." To that end, the Ardmore, Oklahoma-based Foundation focuses on basic plant biology and agricultural research, consultation, and demonstration projects that enable farmers and ranchers to achieve their goals, enhancing plant productivity through fundamental research and applied biotechnology and assisting community, health, and educational organizations through grants and employee involvement. Among other offerings, the Foundation's Web site provides grant guidelines and procedures; an overview of activities in the Foundation's Plant Biology and Agricultural divisions; links to a variety of local, regional, and Internet resources; and contact information.

Norcross Wildlife Foundation, Inc. (MA) (Operating foundation)
(http://www.norcrossws.org/)

The Norcross Wildlife Foundation, Inc. was established in 1965 by Arthur D. Norcross, a native of Massachusetts and founder and manager of the Norcross Greeting Card Company. He established the Wales, MA-based Foundation to ensure the future well being of the Norcross Wildlife Sanctuary, which presently covers 4000 acres, but had its beginnings with a 100-acre family woodlot-pasture Arthur Norcross inherited from his father in 1916. Around 1930, he began gathering nearby wooded acres, farmland, wetlands and other parcels with the goal of establishing the Sanctuary. It was formally dedicated in 1939 as "a place where wildlife may be encouraged not just to survive but also to propagate and spread naturally, so that specific species, threatened with extinction, might again attain more normal distribution". In addition to maintaining the Sanctuary, the Foundation also has a grantmaking program. The Foundation prefers to place grants with organizations that ask for specific amounts, for example, to purchase and protect land, build nature centers and walkways, print and distribute educational materials—generally projects that have finite completion dates. Consult their Web site for grant request guidelines and contact information. Visitors to the Web site will also find a history of the Foundation and Sanctuary, descriptions of the programs and exhibits at the Sanctuary, schedules, and horticultural and animal facts.

Nord Family Foundation (OH) (http://www.kellnet.com/nordf)

The Nord Family Foundation was originally the Nordson Foundation, a trust created in 1952 by Walter G. Nord, founder of the Nordson Corporation in Ohio. The Nordson Foundation was dissolved in 1988 and the Nord Family Foundation was created. In the tradition of its original founders Walter and Virginia Nord, the Foundation, located in Elyria, Ohio, seeks to build community by supporting projects that bring opportunity to the disadvantaged, strengthen family bonds, and improve quality of life. Grants are awarded in the fields of social service, health, education, the arts, and civic affairs. High priority is given to programs that address the needs of economically or socially disadvantaged families, and projects that address the root causes of problems are of special interest. Most grants are made to organizations or for projects in Lorain County, Ohio, with a small number of grants to organizations in Cuyahoga County, Ohio; Denver, Colorado; Columbia, South Carolina; and to national organizations that address the Foundation's priorities. Consult their Web site for application instructions and contact information. As the site is presently under construction, they intend to post additional information in the future, such as copies of annual reports, press releases, and other public statements.

Norman Foundation (NY) (http://www.normanfdn.org/)

The New York-based Norman Foundation is committed to a strategy of seeking and supporting grassroots efforts that strengthen the ability of communities to determine their economic, environmental and civic well-being; promote community-based economic development efforts that are trying out new ownership structures and financing mechanisms; work to prevent the use of toxics and their disposal into the environment; build bridges across issues and constituencies and organize to counter the "radical right" in all its forms; promote civil rights by fighting discrimination and violence and working for ethnic, religious, and sexual equity and for reproductive freedom; challenge the power of money over our political process; and/or seek to improve governments' and businesses' accountability to the public and especially to those affected by their actions. The Foundation also seeks to address "the profound civic disengagement in society," and is particularly interested in strategies "on how to engage more Americans in their civic lives and how to increase their faith and involvement in community institutions." The Foundation's Web site provides a description of the application process, grant guidelines and restrictions, basic financial information, a list of grants, listings of the Foundation's officers, directors, and staff, and contact information.

The Kenneth T. and Eileen L. Norris Foundation (CA) (http://www.ktn.org)

The Kenneth T. and Eileen L. Norris owned Norris Stamping and Manufacturing Companies, later called Norris Industries. Kenneth Norris was a metallurgist who discovered a way to make steel casings for bullets, which led to a key role for the family business during World War II. The Norrises believed they had an obligation to give back to the community, so they established the Kenneth T. and Eileen L. Norris Foundation in 1963. The Foundation funds in the categories of medicine, education and science, youth, community and cultural arts. Located in Long Beach, California, the Foundation funds organizations in he Los Angeles County area. Visitors to the Web site will find information about the founder, application guidelines, downloadable annual report, downloadable proposal information sheet, and contact information including email links.

Northwest Area Foundation (MN) (http://www.nwaf.org/)

The Northwest Area Foundation was established in 1934 by Louis W. Hill, son of James, J. Hill, the founder of the Great Northern Railroad, and renamed in 1975 to reflect its "commitment to the region that provided its original resources and its growth beyond the scope of the traditional family foundation." Recently, it announced a new mission: to help communities most in need create positive futures economically, ecologically, and socially." In addition to contact information, a brief history of the Foundation, and staff and trustee listings, the Foundation's Web site provides an overview of its new direction and the decision-making process that led to it.

Northwest Fund for the Environment (WA) (http://www.wolfenet.com/~nwfund)

The Northwest Fund for the Environment was established in 1971 with the initial purpose of functioning as a "pass-through" organization to allow small groups to receive tax deductible funding from grassroots supporters. When tax laws changed in the eighties, the Foundation's purpose was to evaluate requests and make grants from an annual donation. In 1994, the Fund received a major bequest and became a private foundation with an endowment. The endowment is designated for "promoting change in the uses of natural resources which will increase their protection and preservation in the State of Washington", with special emphasis placed on "the protection of wild fish, native wildlife, natural forests, wetlands and shorelines, and the preservation of pure and free-flowing waters." Located in Seattle, Washington, the Fund supports actions to preserve threatened and endangered species and/or ecosystems, implement and enforce environmental laws and regulations, fund research directly relevant to Washington state on a limited basis, and strengthen the effectiveness of nonprofit environmental groups. Visit the Web site for grant guidelines, printable and downloadable application forms, selections from annual reports, a report of their grantmaking trends, and contact information.

Jessie Smith Noyes Foundation, Inc. (NY) (http://www.noyes.org)

The Jessie Smith Noyes Foundation was established in 1947 by Charles F. Noyes as a memorial to his wife. Charles F. Noyes owned a real estate brokerage firm in New York City, and his most famous deal was the 1951 sale of the Empire State Building, "previously regarded as a white elephant", for the largest price at the time in real estate history. Located in New York City, the Foundation is committed to "protecting and restoring Earth's natural systems and promoting a sustainable society by strengthening individuals, institutions and communities pledged to pursuing those goals." Currently, the Foundation makes grants primarily in the areas of environment and reproductive rights, with the following program areas: toxics; sustainable agriculture; sustainable communities; reproductive rights; metro New York environment; and related interests, which are activities outside of the five areas but still further the Foundation's goals. Projects that receive preference are ones that address the connections between these concerns and their broader implications, have potential for widespread impact or applicability, and that address the connections between environmental issues and social justice issues. Visit the Web site for program and application guidelines, grants lists, annual reports, financial information, staff listing, and contact information.

John M. Olin Foundation, Inc. (NY) (http://www.jmof.org/)

The John M. Olin Foundation was established in 1953 by the industrialist John Merrill Olin (1892–1982). Mr. Olin was committed to "the preservation of the principles of political and economic liberty as they have been expressed in American thought, institutions and practice." Accordingly, the purpose of the John M. Olin Foundation is to provide support for projects that "reflect or are intended to strengthen the economic, political and cultural institutions upon which the American heritage of constitutional government and private enterprise is based." Within this context, the Foundation has authorized grants in the areas of American institutions, law and the legal system, public policy research, and strategic and international studies. In each of these areas, it attempts to advance its objectives through support of research, institutional support, fellowships, professorships, lectures and lectures series, books, scholarly journals, journals of opinion, conferences and seminars, and, on occasion, television and radio programs. The Foundation's straightforward Web site provides general information about its programs, grant-making policies, and application procedures; a schedule grants; listings of the Foundation's trustees and staff; and contact information.

Onan Family Foundation (MN) (http://www.onanfamily.org/foundation.htm)

The Onan Family Foundation was founded by David Warren Onan, an entrepreneur in Minneapolis who wanted to give back to the community where his business thrived and where he lived. Located in Minneapolis, MN, the Foundation has a strong interest in programs that focus on Minneapolis and St. Paul, MN. Funding areas are education, social welfare, cultural and civic affairs, and religion. Consult the Web site for grant guidelines, grants list, staff listing, financial information and contact information. Grant requests are to be made using the Minnesota Common Grant Application form, and a link is provided to the site where the form can be downloaded or printed.

Ottinger Foundation (MA) (http://www.funder.org/ottinger/)

The Ottinger Foundation, a private family foundation based in Amherst, Massachusetts, supports organizations that promote "democratic participation, economic justice, environmental preservation, and energy conservation." The Foundation encourages the "submission of innovative proposals that address causes rather than symptoms of problems," and it supports the common grant application form sponsored by the National Network of Grantmakers. Most of the projects funded by the Foundation include a strong component of grassroots activism and have national significance. At this writing, however, the Foundation was undergoing an administrative reorganization and not accepting proposals. It expects to post new guidelines, staff, and location information by the end of 1999 at its Web site.

David and Lucile Packard Foundation (CA) (http://www.packfound.org/)

The David and Lucile Packard Foundation was created in 1964 by David Packard (1912–1996), a co-founder (with his Stanford classmate William Hewlett) of the Hewlett-Packard Company, and his wife, Lucile Salter Packard (1914–1987). From its relatively modest beginnings—over the first dozen years of its existence the Foundation had only one employee and awarded just over $1 million in grants—the Packard Foundation has grown into one of the largest private grant-making foundations in the country, with assets approaching $9 billion as of the end of 1997. The Foundation continues "to support nonprofit organizations with the hope that [it] can help people through the improvement of scientific knowledge, education, health, culture, employment opportunities, the environment, and quality of life." To that end, the Foundation makes grants nationally and internationally (with a special focus on the Northern California counties of San Mateo, Santa Clara, Santa Cruz, and Monterey) in the following broad program areas: science; conservation; population; children, families, and communities; arts; organizational effectiveness; philanthropy; andPueblo, Colorado (David Packard's hometown). In addition to a history of the Foundation and a biography of David Packard, the Foundation's Web site provides detailed program descriptions and application guidelines, recent grants in a number of program areas, a listing of the Foundation's officers and trustees, Foundation contact names by program area, and the Foundation's annual report.

Alicia Patterson Foundation (DC) (Operating foundation) (http://www.aliciapatterson.org)

The Alicia Patterson Foundation was established in 1965 in memory of Alicia Patterson, editor and publisher of Newsday for 23 years before her death in 1963. The Washington, D.C.–based Foundation has a fellowship program, in which one-year grants are awarded to working journalists to pursue independent projects of "significant interest". They spend that year traveling, researching, and writing articles based on their investigations for The APF Reporter, a quarterly magazine published by the Foundation. A stipend of $35,000 is provided for each fellow. The application form and instructions are available for downloading from their site, and past APF Reporters are available on line. Visitors to the Web site will also find two biographies of Alicia Patterson, grant application instructions, listings of past fellows, related links and contact information.

William Penn Foundation (PA) (http://fdncenter.org/grantmaker/wmpenn/)

The William Penn Foundation, a private grantmaking organization created in 1945 by Otto Haas and his wife, Phoebe, strives to improve the quality of life in the greater Philadelphia area, particularly for its neediest residents. The Foundation makes grants ranging from a few thousand dollars to several million dollars in four main categories: Children, Youth and Families; Communities; Arts and Culture; and the Natural Environment. Within the first three categories, the Foundation's grantmaking is limited to the six-county Philadelphia area (Bucks, Chester, Delaware, Montgomery, and Philadelphia counties in Pennsylvania and Camden County, especially the City of Camden, in New Jersey) unless initiated by the Foundation. Grants for school-based programs in Philadelphia are generally limited to the Martin Luther King, Jr. and West Philadelphia clusters. Grants in the Natural Environment category are awarded throughout a larger region extending from the Delaware Water Gap southeast along the northern border of Warren, Hunterdon, Mercer, and Ocean counties in New Jersey to the Atlantic coast at Manasquan; south along the coast to the mouth of the Delaware Bay; west along the C & D Canal and the Susquehanna River to the Appalachian trail; and north along the trail to the Delaware Water Gap. The Foundation's "folder" on the Center's Web site provides detailed program descriptions, application guidelines and restrictions, grants lists, statements of the Foundation's mission and grant-making values, a history of the Foundation, board and staff listings, and contact information.

Pew Charitable Trusts (PA) (http://www.pewtrusts.com/)

The Philadelphia-based Pew Trusts are a group of seven individual charitable funds established by the children of Sun Oil Company founder Joseph N. Pew and his wife, Mary Anderson Pew. Each year, the Trusts make grants of about $180 million to between 400 and 500 nonprofit organizations in the areas of culture, education, the environment, health and human services, public policy, and religion, and through its Venture Fund. In addition to a strong national giving program, the Trusts maintain a particular commitment to their local community. The Trusts' well-organized Web site provides visitors with program guidelines and limitations, application procedures, searchable grants lists, grantee Web links, publications, news, and a staff list with phone numbers and e-mail addresses.

Pickett & Hatcher Educational Fund, Inc. (GA) (http://www.pickettandhatcher.org)

The Pickett & Hatcher Educational Fund was established in 1938 through the generosity of Claud A. Hatcher, president of the Nehi Corporation that later became the Royal Crown Cola Company. Located in Columbus, Georgia, the Fund is a private foundation that grants student loans to help students who otherwise might not be able to attend college. To be eligible, students should be United States citizens and legal residents of one of the following states: Alabama, Florida, Georgia, Kentucky, Mississippi, North Carolina, South Carolina, Tennessee, and Virginia. They should also have a minimum ACT of 20 or a combined SAT I of 950. Loans of up to $5500 are made per academic year. Consult the Web site for complete eligibility requirements, loan limits, interest rates, renewal requirements, application instructions and contact information. (Due to the success of this program, and the demand for student loans, applications for the 1999–2000 academic year are no longer available. The distribution of applications will resume January 3, 2000 for the 2000–2001 academic year.)

Plan for Social Excellence, Inc. (NY) (Operating foundation) (http://www.netsurftech.com/pfse)

The Plan for Social Excellence, located in Mt. Kisco, New York, creates and supports innovative pilot projects in education in the United States that are fluid and responsive to the needs of individual schools and communities instead of programs that attempts to address needs through a system-wide process of reform. Supported projects take place at various levels, including early childhood education and higher education. The Plan pursues its goals through five major activities: grantmaking, 'coinvestments' (collaboration and co-investment with other foundations and corporations in funding programs), technical assistance, scholarships, and dissemination. The Plan is primarily interested in funding replications of certain pilot programs, but also considers grant requests for innovative projects that are designed for easy evaluation and can be replicated. Along with its grant-making, technical assistance is provided to grantees and other educational organizations, and includes providing information and resources to support or enhance project goals. In addition, the Plan publishes and disseminates the results of many funded projects to organizations that may be candidates for replicating the project.

The Plan also administers a last-dollar scholarship program for high school students who have participated in select Plan-supported projects. Consult the Web site for more complete information on their activities and programs, and for application information and instructions. A grant guideline request form is available online. Visitors to the site will also find downloadable quarterly newsletters, scholarship recipient lists, links to related resources, and contact information.

Pollock-Krasner Foundation, Inc. (NY) (http://www.pkf.org/)

Established by Lee Krasner, widow of the painter Jackson Pollock and a celebrated artist in her own right, the Pollock-Krasner Foundation's mission is "to aid, internationally, those individuals who have worked as professional artists over a significant period of time." Potential grant recipients must demonstrate a combination of recognizable artistic merit and financial need, relating to either work, living, or medical expenses. The Foundation provides support exclusively to visual artists—painters, sculptors, and artists who work on paper, including printmakers—and will not accept applications from commercial artists, photographers, video artists, performance artists, filmmakers, crafts-makers, or any artist whose work primarily falls into one of these categories. Nor does the Foundation fund academic study or make grants to pay for past debts, legal fees, the purchase of real estate, relocation to another city, or the costs of installations, commissions, or projects ordered by others. The Foundation's Web site provides visitors with a brief history of the Foundation, application and selection procedures, a downloadable application form, a listing of recent grantees, a listing of officers and staff, and contact information.

The Prospect Hill Foundation (NY) (http://fdncenter.org/grantmaker/prospecthill/)

The Prospect Hill Foundation was established in New York in 1960 by William S. Beinecke, former president and chairman of the Sperry and Hutchinson Company. In 1983, the Prospect Hill Foundation merged with the Frederick W. Beinecke Fund. The foundation has a broad range of philanthropic interests, but recently has made grants to support organizations active in environmental conservation, nuclear weapons control, and family planning in Latin America, as well as selected social service, arts, cultural, and educational institutions. The foundation's Web site, hosted through the Center's Foundation Folder program, provides an introduction to the foundation, grants program description, grants list, and application guidelines.

Public Welfare Foundation, Inc. (DC) (http://www.publicwelfare.org/)

Established and incorporated in Texas in 1947 and reincorporated in Washington, D.C., in 1960, the Public Welfare Foundation is dedicated "to supporting organizations that provide services to disadvantaged populations and work for lasting improvements in the delivery of services that meet basic human needs." The Foundation's wide-ranging interests include community support (homelessness, low-income housing, low-income community and economic development, global security, countering hate-motivated activity and discrimination, immigration and refugees, international human rights, technical assistance to grassroots community development efforts); criminal justice (community-based correctional options, institutional programming, legal representation of low-income persons, violence prevention); the disadvantaged elderly (community-based long-term care), disadvantaged youth (early intervention; employment, training, and alternative education; teen parents and their children; violence prevention; youth empowerment and leadership development); the environment (global climate change, sustainable development, direct support and technical assistance to grassroots organizations); health (health advocacy and reform, hunger and nutrition, mental health advocacy and services, occupational health and safety, preventive and primary services); and population and reproductive health (AIDS prevention, education, and advocacy; international family planning; reproductive rights; reproductive health for teens; emerging issues). A model of uncluttered, functional design, the Foundation's Web site provides a short history of the Foundation, answers to frequently asked questions, detailed program information, financial statements, application procedures, grants lists organized by specific funding area, contact information, and more.

The Puffin Foundation, Ltd. (NJ)
(http://www.angelfire.com/nj/PuffinFoundation)

The Puffin Foundation was established in 1987, with the mission of "continuing the dialogue between art and the lives of ordinary people." The Foundation seeks to "open the doors of artistic expression to those who are often excluded because of their race, gender, or social philosophy", and "ensure that the arts not merely survive, but flourish at all levels of our society." The Foundation provides seed grants to artists and arts organizations across the entire spectrum of visual and performing arts. It has established two exhibition, performance, and discussion spaces, the Puffin Room in Soho, and the Puffin Cultural Forum in Teaneck, NJ, where the Foundation is located. It also a publishing branch to produce books that "otherwise might not come to life." Consult their Web site for instructions on obtaining an application packet. Their site also contains a link to the site of the Puffin Cultural Forum, which provides a schedule of upcoming events.

Bernard and Audre Rapoport Foundation (TX) (http://www.rapoportfdn.org/)

The mission statement of the Bernard and Audre Rapoport Foundation is "meeting basic human needs while building individual and social resiliency." Located in Waco, Texas, the Foundation's current program priorities are: Education, in all its broad areas, but with a focus on early learning; Cultural Enrichment, especially programs that encourage the participation of children and the disadvantaged; Healthcare, to improve the quality and delivery of services to all citizens, but especially women, children and the disadvantaged; Community Building, to improve quality of life and foster the growth and development of children; and Building Democratic Opportunities and Encouraging Democratic Citizenship, to make government more responsive and encourage citizens to take a more active interest and role in political life. Consult the Web site for grant application instructions, an update on the Foundation's activities, and contact information, including an email link.

A.C. Ratshesky Foundation (MA) (http://www.agmconnect.org/ratshes1.html)

A.C. Ratshesky celebrated his 50th birthday in 1916 by establishing this charitable foundation in his own name. Currently, the Boston, MA-based Foundation has three program areas: human services, focusing on the well-being of children and families in inner-city neighborhoods; education/training/advocacy, including adult vocation, GED and literacy programs, school enrichment, parenting skills, reproductive freedom and reproductive health education, prevention of discrimination and racism, and community organizing and promotion of citizenship skills; and arts/culture, supporting school enrichment, performing arts, youth programs, and performance opportunities for young artists. Support is generally limited to Boston and adjacent communities, and is focused on children, teens, immigrants, "linguistic minorities", the gifted and talented, and the Jewish community; support for programs that service disadvantaged Jewish populations or Jewish cultural institutions are of special interest, in accordance with the original declaration of trust. From time to time, the trustees may also give consideration to programs that fall outside of the usual geographic or program limitations. Visit the Web site for application procedures, grants list, and contact information.

Michael Reese Health Trust (IL)
(http://fdncenter.org/grantmaker/reese/index.html)
The Michael Reese Health Trust seeks to improve the health of people in Chicago's metropolitan communities through effective grantmaking in health care, health education, and health research. The Trust, which funds exclusively in metropolitan Chicago, with an emphasis on the city of Chicago, seeks to address the needs of the most vulnerable in society, particularly programs that serve the medically indigent and underserved, immigrants, refugees, the elderly, mentally and physically disabled, children and youth. To emphasize the Trust's Jewish heritage, special consideration will be given to programs that serve those in the Jewish community who fall within these populations. The Trust does not fund programs operating outside of metropolitan Chicago; capital needs (such as buildings, vehicles, and equipment); endowment; fundraising events; debt reduction; individuals; or scholarships. The Trust's "folder" on the Center's Web site includes a mission statement, program guidelines, application procedures, and contact information.

Research Corporation (AZ) (http://www.rescorp.org/)
Established in New York in 1912, making it one of the first private foundations in the United States, the Research Corporation is the only domestic foundation wholly devoted to the advancement of science and technology. Its unique philanthropic mission is to make inventions and patent rights "more available and effective in the useful arts and manufactures," and to devote any new resources there from "to provide means for the advancement and extension of technical and scientific investigation, research and experimentation" at scholarly institutions. The Foundation makes between 200 and 300 awards annually for original research in chemistry, physics, and astronomy at colleges and universities throughout the U.S. and Canada. Visitors to the Web site will find guidelines for Foundation-supported programs (Cottrell College Science Awards, Cottrell Scholars, Partners in Science, Research Opportunity Awards, Research Innovation Awards, Department Development Program, and General Foundation Awards); recent news releases; contact information; and the Research Corporation Bulletin in Adobe Acrobat (PDF) format.

Retirement Research Foundation (IL)
(http://fdncenter.org/grantmaker/rrf/index.html)
The Chicago-based Retirement Research Foundation is the nation's largest private foundation exclusively devoted to aging and retirement issues. Founded by the

late John D. MacArthur, it makes approximately $8 million in grants each year to nonprofit and educational organizations to support programs, research, and public policy studies to improve the quality of life of older Americans. The Foundation operates a general grants program, two award programs (ENCORE and the Congregation Connection Program) open to Chicago-area nonprofits only, and the National Media Owl Awards, a national film and video competition. Visitors to RRF's "folder" on the Foundation Center's Web site will find a variety of materials, including an overview of the Foundation and its funding interests, program descriptions, grants lists, program-related FAQs, application information, and a number of press releases.

Kate B. Reynolds Charitable Trust (NC) (http://www.kbr.org)

Located in Winston-Salem, North Carolina, the Kate B. Reynolds Charitable Trust is named after the late Kate Gertrude Bitting Reynolds, wife of William Neal Reynolds, chairman of R.J. Reynolds Tobacco Company. She created the Trust in 1947 in her will, designating that one-fourth of the income from the Trust be used for the poor and needy in Winston-Salem and Forsyth County, and that the remaining three-fourths be used for charity patients in North Carolina hospitals. These designations have become the Trust's two divisions, the Health Care Division and the Poor and Needy Division, which has an emphasis on those who need assistance with basic necessities. The Trust's grantmaking is limited to the state of North Carolina. Guidelines, applications, expenditure and program report forms (for grantees) are available for downloading, and there is an online contact form on their site. The Trust also has Satellite offices in different areas of the state, to make themselves more accessible to those who can benefit most from their grantmaking and help the Trust gather information on different areas of the state. Another component of their outreach effort is technical workshops, where organizations can learn about the Trust's objectives, the grant process, preparation of grant requests, and ask questions. Consult their Web site for information on their two divisions, their outreach programs, and special initiatives. Visitors will also find grant lists, advisory board and staff listings, FAQ sheet, press releases, and contact information.

Donald W. Reynolds Foundation (NV) (http://www.dwreynolds.org)

The Donald W. Reynolds Foundation was established in 1954 by Donald W. Reynolds, pioneer in the American communications industry and founder of Donrey Media Group. The Foundation's current programs, however, did not begin taking shape until 1993, when Mr. Reynolds died and left a generous bequest. The mission statement of the Las Vegas-based Foundation is to make grants in "Arkansas, Nevada, and Oklahoma to qualified charitable organizations which demonstrate a sustainable program, exhibit an entrepreneurial spirit, and assists those served to be healthy, self-sufficient and productive members of the community." The Foundation has five programs: Capital Grants, Aging and Quality of Life Initiative, Clinical Cardiovascular Research, Community Services Center Program, and Donald W. Reynolds Special Initiatives. Some solicit applications and others are driven exclusively by Trustee Initiative. Guidelines for the Capital Grants and Community Services Center programs are available. Consult the Web site for more information on their programs, for annual reports, grant lists (including brief descriptions and contact information for grantee organizations), staff listings, and contact information, including email links to staff members.

Z. Smith Reynolds Foundation (NC) (http://www.zsr.org/)

Created almost 60 years ago to serve the people of North Carolina, the Z. Smith Reynolds Foundation is the country's largest general purpose foundation with a mandate to make grants within a single state. The Foundation focuses its activities in the areas of pre-collegiate education, community economic development, environmental interests, minority issues, and women's issues, but will consider proposals that fall outside these areas as long as they are consistent with the Foundation's mission. The Foundation's Web site provides general information about the Foundation, detailed grant application procedures, information on special publications and programs, and links to grantee Web sites.

RGK Foundation (TX) (http://www.rgkfoundation.org)

Ronya and George Kozmetsky established the RGK Foundation in 1966 to support medical and educational research. Since then, the Austin, Texas-based Foundation has broadened its focus over the years and 'community' is now the third component to their grantmaking. Grants in these three areas support research (the Foundation has sponsored studies in several areas of national and international concern, including health, corporate governance, energy, economic analysis, and technology transfer); conferences, which are designed to enhance information exchange as well as maintain an "interlinkage" among business, academia, community, and government; and programs that promote academic excellence in institutions of higher learning, raise literacy levels, attract minority and women students into the math, science, and technology fields, and promote the well being of children. There are no geographic limitations to their grantmaking. Visitors to the Web site will find application guidelines; a printable and downloadable application form; online contact form; grant lists; related links; a list of publications resulting from Foundation-sponsored research; financial data; staff listing; and contact information.

Smith Richardson Foundation, Inc. (CT) (http://www.srf.org)

H. Smith Richardson and his wife, Grace Jones Richardson, created the Smith Richardson Foundation in 1935. H. Smith Richardson helped build a "world-wide medicinal empire" with Vicks Family Remedies. Located in Westport, CT, the Smith Richardson Foundation seeks to "help ensure the vitality of our social, economic, and governmental institutions", and "assist with the development of effective policies to compete internationally and advance US interests and values abroad." The Foundation has two grant programs: the International Security and Foreign Policy Program, which supports research and policy projects on issues central to the strategic interests of the United States; and the Domestic Public Policy Program, which supports research, writing, and analysis that informs the thinking of policy makers and the public on domestic issues. The Foundation also makes small grants to organizations in North Carolina and Connecticut that provide innovative services for children and families at risk, though the Foundation's Governors customarily solicit these grants. Consult the Web site for information about their grant programs, grant guidelines, proposal templates (for those who are invited to submit a proposal after an initial inquiry has been made), grant reporting requirements, FAQ sheet, staff listing, and contact information, including an email link.

Sid W. Richardson Foundation (TX) (http://www.sidrichardson.org)

The Ft. Worth, Texas-based Sid W. Richardson Foundation was established in 1947 for the purpose of supporting organizations that serve the people of Texas. The Foundation provides grants primarily in the areas of education, health, human services, and the arts and humanities. Funding is limited to programs and projects within the state of Texas. Visit the Web site for grant guidelines, grants lists, a short bio of its founder, information on ordering annual reports and Foundation-sponsored reports, and contact information. Links are also provided to related resources, Sid W. Richardson's collection of western art, and to the Lee and Ramona Bass Foundation.

The Riordan Foundation (CA) (http://www.riordanfnd.org/)

Richard J. Riordan founded The Riordan Foundation in 1981 "to ensure that all children become successful readers and writers while they are still young." The Foundation also seeks to use its funds as a "catalyst to encourage a broad base of support for early childhood education." The Foundation charted Rx for Reading in 1989, a public foundation through which many donations are distributed, to enhance and support the goals of the Riordan Foundation. Through Rx for Reading, the Foundation makes challenge grants to schools who wish to participate in Writing to Read, Computers in the Classroom, and English Language Development grants. Outside donations are used to meet the terms of the challenge grants, and since the Foundation funds all administrative expenses, 100% of the contributions to Rx for Reading go directly toward funding projects. The Riordan Foundation also provides mini-grants, only available in Los Angeles County: Safe Place to Play, which are small grants to develop, improve, or enhance play areas; and Easy Access To Books For Recreational Reading, to develop or enhance classroom lending libraries. Visit the site for more information on their grant programs, grant guidelines, FAQ sheet, and contact information. Schools interested in applying for grants administered through Rx for Reading can print application forms from the site or call to request applications.

Fannie E. Rippel Foundation (NJ) (http://fdncenter.org/grantmaker/rippel/index.html)

The Fannie E. Rippel Foundation's objectives are to support the relief and care of aged women, the erection and maintenance of hospitals, and the treatment of and/ or research concerning heart disease and cancer. Although strict geographic limitations are not imposed, emphasis is given to institutions located in New Jersey and the greater New York metropolitan area, the general Northeast, and the Middle Atlantic Seaboard. The Foundation's "folder" on the Center's Web site serves as an online version of the Foundation's current annual report, offering application guidelines, messages from the Foundation's president and chairman, grants listings, statements of financial position and activities, and a listing of its trustees and staff.

Rockefeller Brothers Fund (NY) (http://www.rbf.org/index.html)

Since 1984, the main part of the Rockefeller Brother Fund's grantmaking program has been organized around the theme of One World, with two major components: sustainable resource use and world security. The Fund's program areas are sustainable resource use, global security, the nonprofit sector, health, education, arts and culture, New York City, South Africa, Potanico Historic Area, and the Ramon

Magsaysay Award Foundation in Manila, Philippines. Visitors to the Fund's Web site will detailed guidelines and information for each program area, including grants lists and application procedures. The site also provides news, annual reports, affiliations, and links.

Rockefeller Foundation (NY) (http://www.rockfound.org/)

Endowed by John D. Rockefeller and chartered in 1913 for "the well-being of people throughout the world," the Rockefeller Foundation is one of America's oldest private foundations and one of the few with strong international interests. The Foundation focuses its activities on the arts and humanities, equal opportunity, agricultural sciences, health sciences, population sciences, global environment, and special African initiatives including female education. The balance of the Foundation's grant and fellowship programs support work in building democracy, international security, international philanthropy, and other special interests and initiatives. Visitors to the Foundation's comprehensive Web site will find information about the Foundation's programs, funding priorities, fellowships, and recent grants, along with the annual reports, a listing of the Foundation's trustees, and a letter from the Foundation's president.

Rosenberg Foundation (CA) (http://www.rosenbergfdn.org/)

The Rosenberg Foundation was established in 1935 by relatives and associates of Max L. Rosenberg, a San Francisco businessman and philanthropist. Since the 1940s, the Foundation has emphasized the health, education, and recreation of California's children and communities. Today, the Foundation accepts grant requests in three priority areas: the Changing Population of California, which includes activities that "promote the full social, economic, and cultural integration of immigrants and minorities into a pluralistic society"; Children and their Families in Poverty, which includes activities that "reduce dependency, promote self-help, create access to the economic mainstream, or address the causes of poverty among children and families"; and Child Support Reform, a multi-year initiative aimed at increasing "economic security for children, particularly children in low-income families, through the development of a public system that is effective in establishing paternity, fair in awarding support, efficient and effective in collecting and distributing payments, and build[s] toward a national program of child support assurance." Visitors to the Foundation's user-friendly Web site will find thorough program descriptions and recent grants lists by program area; application guidelines and procedures; current financial information; a brief history of the Foundation; and contact information.

The Judith Rothschild Foundation (NY)
(http://fdncenter.org/grantmaker/rothschild/)

The Judith Rothschild Foundation was created in New York by the will of the painter Judith Rothschild to stimulate interest in recently deceased American painters, sculptors and photographers whose work is of the highest quality but lacks wide recognition. The foundation makes grants to present, preserve, or interpret work of the highest aesthetic merit by lesser known American artists who have died after September 12, 1976, a date set in Judith Rothschild's will. The primary emphasis is to promote public awareness of the scope of the artists' achievements as well as direct aesthetic experience of their work. The foundation's Web site, hosted through the Center's Foundation Folder program, states its mission and grant guidelines and provides grants lists, a biography of Rothschild, and a staff/board list.

Russell Sage Foundation (NY) (Operating foundation)
(http://www.russellsage.org/)
The Russell Sage Foundation is dedicated "to strengthening the methods, data, and theoretical core of the social sciences as a means of improving social policies." It does this by conducting a Visiting Scholars program and by funding studies by scholars at other academic and research institutions. The Foundation currently is focusing on four areas: the future of work, immigration, literacy and disadvantaged children, and the psychology of cultural contact. Offerings on its Web site include brief biographies of the Foundation's Visiting Scholars for academic years 1994–1995 through 1997–1998; examples of recent project awards; general application and proposal guidelines; and brief excerpts from recent Foundation-sponsored publications.

Salomon Family Foundation (NY) (http://fdncenter.org/grantmaker/salomon/)
The New York-based Salomon Family Foundation supports the treatment of child abuse, with special emphasis on sexual abuse and programs that provide the intensive and extensive treatment needed. The foundation's Web site, hosted through the Center's Foundation Folder program, states the foundation's purpose, and provides grant proposal guidelines and grant cycles.

The Sasakawa Peace Foundation (Japan) (Operating foundation)
(http://www.spf.org)
The Sasakawa Peace Foundation (SPF) was established in 1986 to promote international understanding, exchange and cooperation. The Foundation, located in Tokyo, Japan, carries out a "diverse program of public-interest activities and initiatives steadfastly aimed at making tangible contributions to world harmony and peace." Their programs are both self-initiated and grant-funded, and are classified under two major categories: "Regular Projects", which address specific fields of nternational issues and concerns such as global policy issues and international networking concerns; and area-specific projects (Pacific Island Nations, China, Central Europe, and Southeast Asia) conducted by special regional funds operating with SPF. Visitors to their Web site will find program information; grant guidelines and application instructions; downloadable application cover sheet and organization information sheet; online feedback and information request forms; annual reports and financial information; newsletters; calendar of upcoming events; and contact information.

The Scholarships Foundation (NY)
(http://fdncenter.org/grantmaker/scholarships/)
The Scholarships Foundation, founded in 1921 by Maria Bowen Chapin, is based in New York and awards grants to undergraduate and graduate students enrolled in academic programs either full-time or part-time. Priority is given to students who do not fit into defined scholarship categories, and grants are based on merit and need. The foundation's Web site, hosted through the Center's Foundation Folder program, states its mission provides the answers to frequently asked questions, including who should apply for a grant and how to do so.

The Arthur B. Schultz Foundation (NV) (http://www.absfoundation.org)
Located in Incline Village, Nevada, the Arthur B. Schultz Foundation supports "improved understanding between nations of previously differing political systems through trade in an interdependent global economy; education of a new generation of students within the framework of an interdependent global economy and environment; and organizations and initiatives promoting environmental protection and natural resource conservation." Grants support improved facilities and specific programs in "visionary educational institutions", and also support environmental conservation, with priority given to habitat protection. Visit the Web site for program areas, grant guidelines, grants lists, financial information, and contact information.

Charles and Lynn Schusterman Family Foundation (OK) (http://www.schusterman.org)
Located in Tulsa, Oklahoma, the Foundation was established by Lynn and Charles Schusterman in 1987 to support programs that enhance Jewish life in the United States, Israel, and the former Soviet Union. It also funds Oklahoma-based, non-sectarian charitable groups that focus on education, children, and community service. Visit the Web site for grant guidelines, online preliminary application form, news and media stories about the Foundation, contact information and related links.

Schwab Foundation for Learning (CA) (Operating foundation) (http://www.perc-schwabfdn.org)
The Schwab Foundation for Learning is a nonprofit operating foundation founded by discount brokerage pioneer Charles R. Schwab and his wife, Helen O'Neill Schwab in 1988. They established a resource center in San Mateo, California that is dedicated to raising awareness and providing parents and teachers with information, resources and support to improve the lives of children with learning differences. Questions about learning differences can be asked online for free, and more extensive help is offered if you become a member, which gives you access to personalized resources and addresses your specific concerns. The Web site also features a list of resources for parents and educators, online bulletin boards, an online feedback form, online membership sign-up, and contact information.

SDMS Educational Foundation (TX) (http://www.sdmsfoundation.org)
The SDMS Educational Foundation is dedicated to improving access to quality education and information for the global sonographic community. Located in Dallas, Texas, the Foundation was established in 1988 by the Society of Diagnostic Medical Sonographers (SDMS) to support and encourage the highest standards in the field of sonography through educational assistance. It provides scholarships for the education of student sonographers and practicing sonographers. Visit their Web site for scholarship and grant information, application instructions, printable grant applications and contact information. A link to provided to their scholarship applications, which is also available by calling or emailing the Foundation.

The Self Family Foundation (SC) (http://www.selffoundation.greenwood.net)
The Self Family Foundation has its roots in the Self Foundation, incorporated by James C. Self, founder of Greenwood mills, in 1942. Its goal then was primarily to build a hospital, which he referred to as a "debt of gratitude to the community

that [had] been so good to [him]." Today, the Foundation's mission is "to encourage self-sufficiency in people and the communities in which they live." Its grant-making program is concerned with enhancing life, encouraging self-sufficiency, and "providing cures rather than treatments", and has the following target areas: education, health care, and arts, culture, and history. The Foundation's primary geographic area of interest is Greenwood, South Carolina, where the Foundation is located, and the surrounding counties followed by the Upper Piedmont region. The Foundation will consider providing seed money for creative and innovative projects in other regions in South Carolina, if they have the potential to be replicated in or have a positive impact on the Greenwood area. Visit their Web site for grant guideline and application procedures, grants lists, and contact information.

Sierra Health Foundation (CA) (http://www.sierrahealth.org)

The Sierra Health Foundation, headquartered in Sacramento, California, awards grants in support of health and health-related activities in a 26-county region of northern California. It was established in 1984 when Foundation Health Plan, now part of Health Net of California, converted from nonprofit to for-profit corporate status. The Sierra Health Foundation was created and endowed with the proceeds from the sale. The Foundation seeks to provide monetary support for local and regional health-related programs and services, influence public health policy and choices, and stimulate improvement in California's health care system. Currently, there are four grant programs: Health Grants, Community Partnerships for Healthy Children, the Conference Program, and brightSMILES, a special dental health grant for the Foundation's northern California region. Visit the Web site to view program information, grant guidelines, and recent awards; download applications; view and download publications; request information on line; and for contact information.

William E. Simon Foundation, Inc. (NJ) (http://www.wesimonfoundation.org)

The William E. Simon Foundation, Inc., located in Morristown, New Jersey, is named after its principal benefactor. It supports programs that strengthen the free enterprise system and "the moral and spiritual values on which it rests: individual freedom, initiative, thrift, self-discipline, and faith in God." The main charitable purpose of the Foundation is to assist those in need by providing the means through which they may help themselves; accordingly, the Foundation seeks to fund programs that promote independence and personal responsibility among those in need. Its funding areas include, but are not limited to, education, religion, youth welfare, athletics, social welfare, and special awards, which recognizes outstanding achievement and excellence in selected fields. Visit the Web site for information about funding areas and for contact information. Application procedures and instructions can be downloaded from the site.

Harry Singer Foundation (CA) (http://www.singerfoundation.org/)

The California-based Harry Singer Foundation focuses on promoting "responsibility and involv[ing] people more fully in public policy." As a private operating foundation, it supports and administers active programs but does not make grants. Current programs focus on government spending, personal responsibility, values, and emotional intelligence. The Foundation's Web site provides information about a range of Foundation programs, including current and past essay contests, a teacher's mentor program, a workbook series, and offers an electronic lending library. The site's archives have an interactive feature called "Match Maker," an electronic bulletin board designed to match worthy grantseekers with sponsors.

Skillman Foundation (MI) (http://www.skillman.org/)
Founded in December 1960 by Rose P. Skillman, widow of 3M vice president and director Robert H. Skillman, the Skillman Foundation seeks to improve the well-being of residents of Southeastern Michigan and, in particular, the Metropolitan Detroit area (Wayne, Oakland, and Macomb counties). Developing children and youth to their maximum potential is the Foundation's primary goal, and to that end it makes grants in the areas of child and family welfare, child and family health, education, juvenile justice, youth development, basic human needs, culture and the arts, and strengthening community and civic institutions. The Foundation's nicely laid out, no-frills Web site provides information about the Foundation's grantmaking policies and procedures, a list of 1996 and 1997 grants organized by subject area, online versions of its most recent newsletter and reports and publications (under construction), an evaluation guide, a listing of the Foundation's trustees and staff, and contact information.

Alfred P. Sloan Foundation (NY) (http://www.sloan.org/)
Established in 1934 by longtime General Motors chairman and CEO Alfred P. Sloan, the New York City-based Sloan Foundation today concentrates its activities in four main areas: science and technology; standard of living, competitiveness, and economics; education and careers in science and technology; and selected national issues. Visitors to the Foundation's Web site will find detailed program descriptions, application procedures, a directory of Foundation officers and staff, and a brief biography of founder Alfred P. Sloan, Jr.

The Christopher D. Smithers Foundation (NY) (http://www.aaw.com/smithers)
R. Brinkley Smithers established the Christopher D. Smithers Foundation in 1953 in memory of his father, who was one of the founders of IBM and a major stockholder. A recovered alcoholic, R. Brinkley Smithers made alcoholism the focus of the Foundation's efforts. The Foundation, located in Mills Valley, New York, seeks to educate the public that alcoholism is a "respectable, treatable disease from which people can and do recover." It also encourages prevention programs and activities, with an emphasis on high-risk populations, and aims to reduce and eliminate the stigma associated with alcoholism. Visitors to the Web site will find a history of the Foundation and several biographies of its founder, related links, and contact information.

The William Snyder Foundation for Animals (MD) (http://www.wsfanimals.org)
The Web site currently contains no information on the Foundation or its grant making programs, as it was being updated. However, it does have their address, phone and fax numbers, and email links to their staff and for foundation and grant application information.

Sobrato Family Foundation (CA) (http://www.sobrato.com/foundation)
Ann and John A. Sobrato, and his wife, Susan, established the Sobrato Family Foundation in 1996. The Sobratos are owners of the Sobrato Development Companies that has led the real estate industry in innovation by developing and building facilities for more than 200 high-technology companies in Santa Clara Valley

in California. The mission of the Cupertino, California-based Family Foundation is "to build a strong and healthy local community by creating opportunities that empower individuals to reach their full potential." Giving is focused on the following program areas: community and economic development, education, health and human services, and youth development. Grants are limited to three counties in northern California: Santa Clara, San Mateo, and the cities of Newark and Fremont in Alameda County, since their goal is to meet the needs of the communities from which the Sobrato family business has benefited. Visit their Web site for grant guidelines, grant program information, grant lists with links to grantee organizations when available, printable proposal abstract form, and contact information.

The Paul & Daisy Soros Fellowships for New Americans (NY) (Operating foundation) (http://www.pdsoros.org)

Operating out of New York City, New York, the Paul & Daisy Soros Fellowships for New Americans was named after the founders who are "New Americans" themselves. The Fellowship was established "in recognition of the contributions New Americans have made to American life and in gratitude for the opportunities the United States has afforded the donors and their family." It provides opportunities to "continuing generations of able and accomplished New Americans to achieve leadership in their chosen fields and to partake of the American Dream." Annually, thirty fellowships consisting of grants for two years of graduate study in the United States are awarded to "New Americans" who have shown at least two of the following three attributes: potential in the fields for which they seek further education; a capacity for creativity, persistence and work; and a commitment to the values of the United States Constitutions and the Bill of Rights. A "New American" is an individual who is a resident alien or has been naturalized as a U.S. citizen or is the child of two parents who are both naturalized citizens. Visit the Web site for further program information and requirements, application instructions, printable application forms (application forms are also available by contacting them directly), profiles of past fellows, related links, and contact information, including email links to staff members.

Soros Foundations Network (NY) (http://www.soros.org)

Supported by financier-turned-philanthropist George Soros, the Soros Foundations Network comprises 26 national foundations located in the countries of Central and Eastern Europe, the former Soviet Union, South Africa, and Haiti; and the Open Society Institute, which promotes connections and cooperation among the various Soros-sponsored foundations. The SFN's member organizations "help build the infrastructure and institutions necessary for open societies" by supporting programs for education, children and youth, media and communications, civil society, human rights and humanitarian aid, science and medicine, arts and culture, and economic restructuring. SFN's Web site, which serves as the information clearinghouse for the network, offers a wide range of information, including general program categories and application guidelines, annotated bibliographies, newsletters, press releases, and contact info. Also of interest is the manner in which the SFN site integrates a Web interface with a central gopher database to allow for meaningful access by the broadest possible online constituency.

Spencer Foundation (IL) (http://www.spencer.org/)

Established by Lyle M. Spencer, founder of the educational publishing firm Science Research Associates Inc., the Spencer Foundation investigates "ways in which education, broadly conceived, can be improved around the world." To this end, the Foundation supports "high quality investigation of education through its research programs... [and] strengthens and renews the educational research community through fellowship programs and related activities." Since 1968, the Foundation has made grants totaling approximately $180 million. Visitors to the Foundation's Web site will find descriptions, eligibility guidelines, and application instructions or contact information for each research grant program. The Foundation's 1996 and 1997 annual report (in Adobe .PDF format) and a listing of its directors, advisors, and staff are also available.

The Stanley Foundation (IA) (Operating foundation)
(http://www.stanleyfdn.org)

The Stanley Foundation is a non-partisan operating foundation based in Muscatine, Iowa. C. Maxwell and Elizabeth Stanley created the foundation in 1956 to pursue their long-time commitment to the effective management of global problems. The Foundation strives toward "provoking thought and encouraging dialogue on world affairs" and "striving for a secure peace with freedom and justice". It serves policy professionals through policy conferences, congressional staff programs and conference reports; involved citizens through conferences, seminars, resource materials and networking; and the wider public through Common Ground, a weekly news radio program on world affairs, World Press Review, a monthly magazine, the Courier, a newsletter, and the foundation's Web site. Current topics are arms control and security, global economy and society, global education, human rights, regions and countries, United Nations, and US Foreign Policy. Visitors to the Web site will find conference reports, radio transcripts and live broadcasts, online publications, publications ordering information and an online contact form.

Stern Family Fund (VA) (http://www.essential.org/stern/)

The Arlington, Virginia-based Stern Family Fund "supports policy oriented government and corporate accountability projects....[T]he Fund is committed to aiding citizens striving to guarantee the responsiveness of public and private institutions that wield substantial power over their lives." The Stern Fund seeks to achieve these goals through two distinct grant programs: the Public Interest Pioneer Program, which provides large seed grants ($50,000 to $100,000) to spark the creation of new organizations; and Strategic Support Grants, which are awarded to projects or organizations "at critical junctures in their development..." With the exception of campaign finance reform proposals, the Fund generally limits its grants to organizations with annual operating budgets of less than $500,000. The Fund's Web site provides detailed program information, a list of grantees (with grant descriptions and amounts) going back to 1995, application guidelines and procedures, questions and answers on the Stern Grant Program, and a listing of the Fund's board members.

The Stuart Foundation (CA) (http://www.stuartfoundation.org)

The Stuart Foundation's "overarching purpose" is to help the children and youth of California and Washington states become responsible citizens. Based in San

Francisco, California, the Foundation's approach to this purpose is to help strengthen the public systems and community supports that contribute to children's development. There are three grant program areas: Strengthening the Public School System, Strengthening the Child Welfare System, and Strengthening Communities to Support Families. Visit to the Web site for funding guidelines and program information; application guidelines and instructions; grant statistics and lists with short project descriptions and email links to grantee organizations; lists of related links; an online feedback form; and contact information.

The Sudbury Foundation (MA) (http://www.agmconnect.org/sudbury1.html)

Longtime residents Herbert J. and Esther M. Atkinson established the Sudbury Foundation in 1952 to benefit the people of Sudbury, Massachusetts and the organizations that serve them. The Atkinsons operated the Sudbury Laboratory, a successful business specializing in marine products and soil testing kits. Their Sudbury-based Foundation was one of the ways through which they shared their good fortune as the laboratory prospered. The Foundation operates two programs: the Atkinson Scholarship Program, which recognizes and assists local, college-bound students; and the Charitable Grants Program, which supports not-for-profit organizations whose work improves the quality of life for Sudbury residents and their neighbors in surrounding towns. Eligible students for the $5000 per-year scholarship should have ties to Sudbury, have financial need, academic promise, and desire and capacity to contribute to society. Preference in funding for the Charitable Grants Program is given to projects that foster individual and organizational self-sufficiency, help those in need, encourage volunteerism, and/or engender a spirit of pride and a greater sense of community. The Foundation also supports environmental programs of direct benefit to the Sudbury area, and also has a Regional Environmental Program which supports organizations based in or active in the New England area working on issues of regional significance. Visitors to the Web site will find funding guidelines for the two main programs, grant lists with descriptions, application instructions, links to other sites of interest, and contact information.

Surdna Foundation, Inc. (NY) (http://www.surdna.org/surdna/)

Established in 1917 by businessman John E. Andrus, the New York City-based Surdna Foundation concentrates its grantmaking activities in four programmatic areas: the environment, community revitalization, effective citizenry, and "a small program in the arts" (which is not accepting applications at this time). The Foundation's Web site offers general information about the Foundation and its approach to grantmaking, as well as detailed program information, application guidelines, and grant restrictions.

John Templeton Foundation (PA) (http://www.templeton.org/)

The Templeton Foundation was established in 1987 by international investment manager John Templeton "to explore and encourage the relationship between science and religion." The Foundation's programs, which are primarily operating in nature, focus on five areas: spiritual information through science, spirituality and health, free enterprise, character development, and the John Templeton Prize for Progress in Religion. In addition to general program and contact information, the Foundation's Web site offers visitors a listing of the Foundation's officers and trustees; winners of the Templeton Prizes for Progress in Religion; information about other awards given by the Foundation; a list of recent grants; and a Request for Proposals for scientific studies in the area of forgiveness, with RFP application packets available for downloading as PDF or Word for Windows files.

Tinker Foundation, Inc. (NY)
(http://fdncenter.org/grantmaker/tinker/index.html)
Created in 1956 by Dr. Edward Larocque Tinker, the Tinker Foundation has long focused its grantmaking activities on Latin America, Spain, and Portugal. More recently, it has included in its mandate the support of projects concerning Antarctica, "a region of significant interest on an international scale." The Foundation has two main programs: Institutional Grants are awarded to organizations and institutions "that promote the interchange and exchange of information within the community of those concerned with the affairs of Spain, Portugal, Ibero-America and Antarctica." Within these parameters, the Foundation looks for innovative projects in the areas of environmental policy, governance, or economic policy that have a strong public policy component. The Foundation also awards Field Research Grants to recognized institutes of Ibero-American or Latin American Studies with graduate doctoral programs at accredited United States universities. The Foundation's "folder" on the Center's Web site offers descriptions of both programs; application instructions, reporting requirements, and a downloadable proposal cover sheet; a selected 1997 grants list for the Institutional Grants program; and a listing of Foundation officers and staff.

The Randall L. Tobias Foundation, Inc. (IN) (http://www.rltfound.org)
The Randall L. Tobias Foundation, Inc. is a family foundation located in Indianapolis, Indiana. Established in 1994, the Foundation's primary emphasis is on providing support for its own initiatives, but grant proposals are "welcomed and encouraged." The Foundation is receptive to proposals in all areas, other than those that are excluded in their policy (consult Web site for list of exclusions). However, there are areas of funding priority: education, at all levels but with particular interest in K–12 education and education reform; culture and the arts, particularly enhancing its quality and availability in selected communities and developing the broadest possible interest in culture and the arts among individuals and groups of all ages; community development, to significantly advance the quality of life in selected communities; and innovation, to support and encourage new ideas and solutions to important issues of public interest in virtually any area of human endeavor. Consult their Web site for funding guidelines, priorities, and contact information. The site features online grant application and a printable brochure on the Foundation.

Tocker Foundation (TX) (http://www.tocker.org/)
The Tocker Founder was established in 1964 to implement the philanthropic interests of Phillip Tocker, a Texas businessman and attorney, and his wife, Olive. In 1992 the Foundation decided to focus its grantmaking on small rural libraries serving a population of 12,000 or less. The Foundation partners with community libraries to make their services more accessible to individuals who by reason of distance, residence, handicap, age, literacy level, or other disadvantage are unable to receive the benefits of public library services. In recent years the Foundation has made grants for outreach and "shut-in" programs, library automation, enhancement of services, adult reading classes, after school projects, bilingual

material, and a variety of other projects initiated by community public libraries. Visitors to the Foundation's Web site will find a brief history of the Foundation, detailed grant proposal guidelines, a downloadable grant application form in PDF format, recent grants lists, a list of library automation projects in progress, and contact information.

Tucson Osteopathic Medical Foundation (AZ) (Operating foundation) (http://www.docenter.org/about.html)

The Tucson Osteopathic Medical Foundation, based in Tucson, Arizona, is a 'conversion" foundation that resulted from the sale of Tucson General Hospital to Summit Health, Ltd. Established in 1986, it is an operating foundation serving the seven counties of southern Arizona whose mission is to advance postgraduate osteopathic medical education, improve the public's understanding of osteopathic medicine, and 'to elevate through education' the health and well-being of the community. It has two grant programs, the Founders Award, which are loans to osteopathic medical students that become scholarships if the students graduate and practice in southern Arizona for a specific period of time, and Trustee Awards, which are grants to local charitable organizations which can achieve significant results with a small grant (it is unclear from their Web site whether grant proposals are accepted). Applicants to the Founders Award must be Arizona residents, and applicants from southern Arizona will be given special consideration. A printable application, criteria, and instructions for the Founders Award are available on their Web site. Visitors to their site will also find information on its operating programs, information on osteopathic medicine, related links, a searchable directory of physicians, and a continuing education event calendar.

Turner Foundation, Inc. (GA) (http://www.turnerfoundation.org/)

The Turner Foundation supports activities directed toward preservation of the environment, conservation of natural resources, protection of wildlife, and sound population policies. The Foundation supports organizations that "provide education and activism on preservation activities and seek to instill in all citizens a sense of common responsibility for the fate of life on Earth." It does not customarily provide support for buildings, land acquisition, endowments or startup funds. Nor does it normally fund films, books, magazines, or other specific media projects. The Foundation's Web site provides detailed program guidelines; lists of recent grants awarded in four main program areas (i.e., water/toxics, energy, forests/habitat, and population); application procedures and limitations; messages from Ted Turner and the Foundation's executive director; and an interactive form for feedback.

Turrell Fund (NJ) (http://fdncenter.org/grantmaker/turrell/index.html)

The main purpose of the New Jersey-based Turrell Fund is "to support social and educational activities that will contribute to the development of young people from families which could not afford these services without help." Programs that focus on children under the age of twelve are given highest priority; requests for capital support, while considered, are of secondary priority. The Fund supports programs in Vermont and in Essex, Hudson, Passaic, and Union counties in New Jersey. Visitors to the Fund's "folder" on the Foundation Center's Web site will find a brief description of its program interests, application instructions, a listing of officers, trustees, and staff, FAQs, and a downloadable summary request form.

United Nations Foundation (DC) (http://www.unfoundation.org)
The United Nations Foundation, located in Washington, D.C., was founded by Ted Turner "to support the goals and objectives of the United Nations and its Charter, in order to promote a more peaceful, prosperous and just world—with special emphasis on the UN's work on behalf of economic, social, environmental and humanitarian causes." The Foundation has four areas of particular interest: women and population; children's health; the environment; and humanitarian causes. The Foundation engages in four primary activities in pursuit of its mission: providing additional funding for programs and people served by UN agencies; strengthening UN institutions and encouraging support for the UN and UN causes; sponsoring or conducting outreach efforts aimed at educating the public about the UN; and raising new funds to support UN programs and purposes. The Foundation works collaboratively with the UN in program development and does not accept unsolicited proposals. Visitors to the Web site will find information about the United Nations Foundation's priority issues, projects, grant lists, on line news briefings about the UN, links to the UN and its agencies, and an online contact form.

United States-Japan Foundation (NY)
(http://www.japanese.com/nonprofit/foundation.html)
The principal mission of the United States-Japan Foundation, a private nonprofit grantmaking organization incorporated in 1980 in the State of New York, is "to promote greater mutual knowledge between the United States and Japan and to contribute to a strengthened understanding of important public policy issues of interest to both countries." The Foundation currently focuses its grantmaking in the areas of pre-college education and policy studies. It does not award grants as contributions to capital campaigns, endowment funds, or deficit operations, or for the construction or maintenance of buildings or for the purchase of equipment. Visitors to the Foundation's Web site will find basic program descriptions, application procedures, a limitations statement, and contact information.

W.E. Upjohn Institute for Employment Research (MI) (Operating foundation)
(http://www.upjohninst.org/grantann.html)
The W.E. Upjohn Institute for Employment Research has its roots in the W.E. Upjohn Unemployment Trustee Corporation, which maintained a cooperative farm for laid-off workers to maintain their income and their dignity. Dr. W.E. Upjohn, founder and head of the Upjohn Company, had conceived of the idea during the Depression in 1932, when he was concerned about the prospects of laying off his workers and the broader problem of the hardships of the unemployed. The farm program did not last long, but concern over unemployment remained a top priority. So in 1945 the Trustees established the W.E. Upjohn Institute, located in Kalamazoo, Michigan, today a research organization devoted to finding, evaluating and promoting solutions to employment-related problems. The Foundation's grant program funds proposals to conduct policy-relevant research on employment issues. Although proposals on any policy-relevant labor market issue will be considered, the Foundation gives higher priority to proposals addressing employment relationships, low wages and public policy, and social insurance. Grants made under this program are expected to result in "research of a rigorous nature and a book published by the Institute that will be of interest to policy makers, practitioners, and academics." The Foundation also invites submissions for its

Dissertation Award, an annual prize for the best Ph.D. dissertation on employment-related issues. Visit the Web site for grant and award program information, application instructions, a history of the foundation, information and publications on employment issues, and contact information.

Valley Foundation (CA) (http://www.valley.org/)

Formed in 1984 from the proceeds of sale of the Community Hospital of Los Gatos, California, and Saratoga, Inc., the Valley Foundation provides funding for nonprofit organizations in Santa Clara County, with an emphasis in the medical field. Although the Foundation's primary interest is in medical services and health care for lower-income households, it also supports programs in the areas of youth, the arts, seniors, and general medical services. Visitors to the Foundation's Web site will find a listing of sample grants awarded in each of the program areas mentioned above, application procedures and limitations, a financial summary of the Foundation's activities in 1995, a listing of the Foundation's board, and, for visitors with a forms-capable browser, an electronic application form.

van Ameringen Foundation (NY)
(http://fdncenter.org/grantmaker/vanameringen/)

The New York-based van Ameringen Foundation provides general/operating support, program development, seed money, and matching funds to promote mental health through preventive measures and treatment and rehabilitation. The foundation also provides support for the field of psychiatry. Funding is generally confined to the Northeast—Washington, DC, to Boston, Massachusetts. The foundation's Web site, hosted through the Center's Foundation Folder program, is a one-page fact sheet stating contact information, financial data, purpose and activities, fields of interest, types of support, limitations, publications and application information.

Wallace Global Fund (DC) (http://www.wgf.org)

The mission of the Washington, DC-based Wallace Global Fund is "to catalyze and leverage critically needed global progress towards an equitable and environmentally sustainable society". The Fund is guided by the vision of the late Henry A. Wallace, former Secretary of Agriculture and Vice-President under Franklin D. Roosevelt. It supports initiatives that advance globally sustainable development in some fundamental way. Grants have been made to a wide range of projects that address obstacles to a sustainable future, including but not limited to population growth, over-consumption, global climate change, imperfect economic policies and inadequate analytic tools, and deforestation. Visitors to the Web site will find program information, application procedures, grants lists with links to grantee organizations, financial information, staff and trustee listing, and contact information.

DeWitt Wallace-Reader's Digest Fund, Inc. (NY) (http://www.dewittwallace.org)

The mission of the DeWitt Wallace-Reader's Digest Fund, a private philanthropic foundation located in New York City, is to foster fundamental improvement in the quality of educational and career development opportunities for all school-age youth, and to increase access to these improved services for young people in low-income communities. The Fund's grantmaking activities, which are limited to nonprofit organizations in the United States, are designed to improve services to children and youth in three areas: elementary and secondary schools, youth serving organizations, and school-community collaboration. Visitors to the Fund's Web site will find information about the Fund's mission, grantmaking strategies, and programs; application guidelines and restrictions; descriptions of grants given in 1997; and the Fund's new directions in grantmaking. The Fund's Web site also has a useful FAQ section, a newsletter focusing on one area of grantmaking, and an interactive form for ordering the 1996 annual report.

Lila Wallace-Reader's Digest Fund, Inc. (NY) (http://www.lilawallace.org)

The mission of the Lila Wallace-Reader's Digest Fund, a private philanthropic foundation located in New York City, is to invest in programs that enhance the cultural life of communities and encourage people to make the arts and culture an active part of their everyday lives. The Fund's grantmaking activities, which are limited to nonprofit organizations in the United States, support leading nonprofit arts and cultural organizations, innovative adult literacy programs, and urban parks programs that encourage community involvement. Visitors to the Fund's Web site will find information about the Fund's mission, grantmaking strategies and programs; application guidelines and restrictions; descriptions of grants given in 1996 and 1997; answers to frequently asked questions about the Fund; and an online newsletter focusing on one area of grantmaking.

Walton Family Foundation, Inc. (AR)
(http://www.wffhome.com/background.html)

The Bentonville, Arizona-based Walton Family Foundation was established by Sam M. (founder of Wal-Mart stores) and Helen R. Walton. The Foundation is principally involved in programs of its own initiative and does not accept unsolicited proposals, but from time to time grants are made to organizations whose work embodies one or more of the goals of the Foundation. Applicants are asked to send a brief letter of inquiry to the Foundation prior to submitting a complete application. The Foundation has a primary focus on education, specifically systemic reform, with special emphasis on primary and secondary education. The Foundation funds three scholarship programs, all for higher education (one for children of Wal-Mart Associates, one for high school seniors interested in pursuing a career in teaching, and one for low-income Central American students to study at three private Arkansas universities). Another Foundation program is the Charter School Grantmaking Program, whose purpose is to improve the quality of charter schools, strengthen the charter school movement, and bring the qualities of the 'charter' concept to more public schools. Its geographic focus is on the state of Arkansas, where the founders lived, although the Foundation also has a particular interest in the economic development and in the enhancement of educational opportunities for students and adults in the Mississippi River's delta region of Arkansas and Mississippi. Consult the Web site for program and scholarship information, funding guidelines, application procedures, links to programs they support and to other resources, and contact information.

The Andy Warhol Foundation for the Visual Arts (NY)
(http://www.warholfoundation.org/)

The Andy Warhol Foundation for the Visual Arts was established in 1987 with the mission, in accordance with Warhol's will, of advancing the visual arts. The Foundation is committed to the idea that "arts are essential to an open, enlightened democracy," and seeks to foster innovative artistic expression and the creative process by encouraging and supporting cultural organizations that in turn, directly or indirectly, support artists and their work. Seeking to advance an "inclusive cultural dialogue", support is given for work of "a challenging and often experimental nature" and to organizations that support artists reflecting a diverse society. The Foundation also supports efforts to "strengthen" areas that directly affect the context in which artists work, such as freedom of artistic expression and equitable access to resources. Grants are made on a project basis to curatorial programs at museums, artists' organizations and other cultural institutions to assist in innovative and scholarly presentations of contemporary visual arts. The creation of new work is also supported through "regranting" initiatives and artist-in-residence programs. The work of choreographers and performing artists occasionally receive funding when the visual arts are an inherent element. Consult the Web site of this New York City-based Foundation for grant guidelines, application information, and contact information. Visitors to the site will also find a brief bio of Andy Warhol, a calendar of funded projects, grant lists, a series of papers from its project on the arts, culture and society (whose purpose is to ensure public debate about the global, economic and societal forces affecting the arts), and a FAQ sheet.

Warren Memorial Foundation (ME) (Operating foundation) (http://www.javanet.com/~warren/board.html)

The Warren Memorial Foundation was established in 1929 with a bequest from Susan Warren, who was Samuel Warren's wife. Samuel Warren was the president of S.D. Warren Mill, and in 1879 he established a library in a small room over the company's main office for his employees. It was Susan Warren who carried on the library's work, a library that eventually became the Warren Memorial Library today that is housed in its own building. The Foundation is the sole funder of the Warren Memorial Library, which is free of charge for all residents and nonresidents of Westbrook, Maine, where the Foundation and library is located. The goal of the Warren Memorial Library is "to provide a collection of materials appropriate to meet the informational, educational, cultural and recreational needs of community residents." The Foundation is also a strong advocate of literacy and encourages reading as a family activity. The library has a program of services designed to encourage an interest in reading and learning in children, and to facilitate the use of the library of senior citizens. Visitors to the Web site can read about the library's history, its programs and policies, and collections. Links to related sites and contact information are provided.

Washington Research Foundation (WA) (http://www.wrfseattle.org)

The Washington Research Foundation (WRF), based in Seattle, Washington, was established in 1981 to help Washington State research institutions capture value from their emerging technologies. WRF initially focused on patenting inventions and licensing them to companies. With its proceeds from licensing, WRF built a seed venture fund, managed by WRF Capital, which creates and invests in technology-based start-up companies that have strong ties to the University of Washington and other nonprofit research institutions in Washington state. It also established WRF Venture Center, which leases office space to technology-based start-ups and provides them with business support. The Foundation continues to pursue its licensing activities, and revenues generated from licensing and WRF Capital investments are used to make gifts to support scholarship and research at Washington State research institutions. Visit their Web site for information on the services offered by the Foundation, WRF Capital, WRF Venture Center, and for contact information. A list of the Foundation's past gifts is also on their site.

Weeden Foundation (NY) (http://www.weedenfdn.org/)

From its inception in 1963, the New York City-based Weeden Foundation (formerly the Frank Weeden Foundation) embraced the protection of biodiversity as its main priority. More recently, the Foundation has sought "to equalize distribution of grants between conservation and population programs in order to more fully address the factors driving biological impoverishment." The Foundation's well-organized Web site offers visitors a mission statement, application guidelines, an index to and summary of its grant awards for the FY 1993–FY 1997 period, and contact information.

Kurt Weill Foundation for Music, Inc. (NY) (http://www.kwf.org/Welcome.html)

The Kurt Weill Foundation for Music is chartered to preserve and perpetuate the legacies of composer Kurt Weill (1900–1950) and actress-singer Lotte Lenya (1898–1981). The Foundation awards grants to individuals and not-for-profit organizations "for projects related to Weill or Lenya" in the following categories: research and travel, publication assistance, dissertation fellowships, professional and regional performance and production, college and university performance and production, recording projects, and broadcasts. In addition to detailed guidelines, application information, and a listing of grants awarded by the Foundation from 1984–1997, visitors to the Web site can read about the Weill-Lenya Research Center, the Kurt Weill Edition (a collected critical edition of Weill's works), and the Kurt Weill Prize. Listings of Foundation staff and board members, information about copyright and licensing permissions, and contact information are also provided.

Weingart Foundation (CA) (http://www.weingartfnd.org)

The Weingart Foundation focuses its grantmaking efforts on programs serving children and youth in the Southern California area, with secondary attention paid to institutions and agencies benefiting the Southern California community in general. The Foundation's Web site serves as an online version of their current annual report and offers a bio of founder Ben Weingart, financial statements for both the current and past year, brief profiles of eight grantees, grant guidelines and application procedures, downloadable application forms, and descriptions of grants $25,000 or more paid in the following categories: crisis intervention, education, health and medicine, community youth programs, higher education, culture and the arts, and adult community services. Annual reports also provided.

The Robert A. Welch Foundation (TX) (http://www.welch1.org)

The Robert A. Welch Foundation was established in 1952 with the estate of Robert A. Welch, who made his fortune in oils and minerals. From his association with scientist, geologists, and petroleum engineers, Robert Welch determined over the course of his career and life that that the pursuit of chemistry and chemical research held "great potential for the vast good and would continue to have a valuable impact on business, industry, global leadership and the human condition". Accordingly, his Houston, Texas-based Foundation supports fundamental chemical research at educational institutions within the state of Texas. It has a research grant program, department grant program, and the Welch Award in Chemistry, which recognizes important chemical research contributions that have a significant, positive influence on mankind. Consult their Web site for grant guidelines, application instructions, newsletter, and contact information.

Wenner-Gren Foundation for Anthropological Research, Inc. (NY) (Operating foundation) (http://www.wennergren.org)

The Wenner-Gren Foundation for Anthropological Research, Inc. was created and endowed in 1941 by Axel Leonard Wenner-Gren, and originally was known as The Viking Fund, Inc. Its mission is "to encourage significant and innovative research on the human species and to foster the development of an international community of anthropological scholars." The Foundation supports research in all branches of anthropology, including cultural/social anthropology, ethnology, biological/physical anthropology, archaeology, anthropological linguistics, and closely related disciplines concerned with human origins, development, and variation. It has five grantmaking program areas: Small Grants Program, for basic research in all branches of anthropology; Conference and International Symposium Program, which funds conferences; Developing Countries Training Fellowships, for scholars and advanced students from developing countries seeking additional training in anthropology, to enhance their skills, or to expand or develop their areas of expertise; Historical Archives Program, to encourage the preservation of unpublished records and other materials of value for research on the history of anthropology; and International Collaboration Research Grants, to assist anthropological research projects undertaken jointly by two (or more) investigators from different countries. The New York City-based Foundation also sponsors Current Anthropology, an international journal of general anthropology. Visit their Web site for further program information, application instructions, grant lists, contact information, listing of trustees, staff and advisory council, and list of related links.

Whitaker Foundation (VA) (http://www.whitaker.org/)

The Whitaker Foundation primarily supports research and education in biomedical engineering. Since its inception in 1975, the foundation has awarded approximately $250 million to colleges and universities for faculty research, graduate fellowships and program development. In the field of biomedical engineering, the Foundation funds research grants, graduate fellowships, development awards, special opportunity awards, a teaching materials program, industrial internships, leadership awards, and conference awards. Visitors to the Foundation's Web site will find detailed program announcements and application guidelines with downloadable applications in PDF format (Acrobat Reader); annual reports going back to 1993, including lists of grantees; research grants program abstracts for 1996–97; and news from the Foundation. The site is searchable and provides links to BMEnet, the Biomedical Engineering Network, which is maintained at Purdue University under a grant from the Foundation.

The Ryan White Foundation (IN) (http://www.ryanwhite.org)

Ryan White was a hemophiliac who contracted HIV through blood-clotting products he received to treat his condition. He was ostracized by his community, but his fight against AIDS and against people's ignorance propelled him into the national spotlight before his death in 1990. In 1991, his mother, Jeanne White, and Phil Donahue founded the Ryan White Foundation to carry on his legacy. Located in Indianapolis, Indiana, the Ryan White Foundation was established to increase awareness of personal, family, and community issues related to HIV and AIDS. The Foundation seeks to increase understanding and acceptance of people with HIV/AIDS through education, and to inform and educate target populations and community groups about HIV/AIDS. Its target populations include youth, parents, and schools. The Foundation's mini-grant program awards grants for nonprofit youth organizations across the country to develop HIV/AIDS awareness and education programs. Consult the Web site for grant information and printable application. Visitors to the Web site will also find Ryan White's story, facts on AIDS and HIV, educational materials, links and information on AIDS-related resources, and contact information.

Whitehall Foundation, Inc. (FL) (http://www.whitehall.org)

The Whitehall Foundation, located in Palm Beach, Florida, assists scholarly research in the life sciences. Currently, it is focused exclusively on assisting basic research (excluding clinical) in vertebrate and invertebrate neurobiology in the United States. Research should specifically concern neural mechanisms involved in sensory, motor, and other complex functions of the whole organism as these relate to behavior, and the overall goal should be to understand behavioral output or brain mechanisms of behavior. Funding is provided through the Research Grants and Grants-in-Aid Programs. Research grants are available to established scientists of all ages working at accredited institutions in the US, range from $30,000 to $75,000 a year, and are provided for up to three years. Grants-in-Aid are designed for researchers at the assistant professor level who have difficulties in competing for research funds because they are not yet firmly established, but are also made to senior scientists. These grants are awarded for a one-year period and do not exceed $30,000. Applications will be judged on its scientific merit and innovative aspects. Consult the Web site for further program information, application procedures, grants lists, and contact information.

Joseph B. Whitehead Foundation (GA) (http://www.jbwhitehead.org)

Joseph B. Whitehead, Jr. established the Joseph B. Whitehead Foundation in 1937 as a memorial to his father, one of the original bottlers of Coca-Cola. The Foundation was established to support charitable activities in the Atlanta, Georgia, where the Foundation is located. The Foundation's grant program has a particular interest in basic human services, especially organizations and programs that benefit children and youth in metropolitan Atlanta; a recent focus is improving public education and family, children and youth services. Preference is given to one-time capital projects. The Foundation shares offices and administrative staff with four other foundations (Robert W. Woodruff Foundation, Inc., Lettie Pate Whitehead Foundation, Inc., Lettie Pate Evans Foundation, Inc., and Ichauway, Inc.), so grant inquiries and proposals may be considered by one or more of the other foundations in this arrangement; it is also unnecessary to communicate separately with these foundations. Visitors to the Web site will find grant guidelines and application procedures, grants lists, links to other foundation resources, a brief bio of Joseph B. Whitehead, and contact information.

Lettie Pate Whitehead Foundation, Inc. (GA) (http://www.lpwhitehead.org)

Conkey Pate Whitehead, influenced by the generous example of his parents, provided in his will of the creation of the Lettie Pate Whitehead Foundation as a memorial to its namesake, his mother. The Foundation was chartered in 1946 to aid "poor and needy Christian girls and women" in nine states: Georgia, North Carolina, South Carolina, Virginia, Louisiana, Mississippi, Alabama, Tennessee and Florida. Support is given in the form of grants to educational institutions in the nine states to fund scholarships for the education of women. While most of the grants are used for undergraduate higher education, a significant number of grants are used to support education in the medical, nursing, and allied health care fields. In addition, operating grants are provided to a few select institutions serving the needs of elderly women in Georgia, Virginia, and North Carolina. Applications for individual scholarship aid should be made directly to the institutions. All inquiries from institutions eligible for Foundation support should be made to the President of the Foundation. Visit the Web site for more information about the Foundation's grant programs, a list of participating institutions, a bio of the founder and of its namesake, links to other foundations with which the Lettie Pate Whitehead Foundation shares a common administrative arrangement, links to other resources, and contact information.

Wilburforce Foundation (WA) (http://www.wilburforce.org/)

The Seattle-based Wilburforce Foundation awards grants in the areas of the environment and population stabilization to nonprofit organizations operating in the Pacific Northwest, Alaska, and the Canadian province of British Columbia. The Foundation's well-designed Web site offers detailed information on the types of grants and support awarded; grant proposal guidelines and application information; a list of the Foundation's 1997 grants; a map of the Foundation's funding regions and grants made in each geographic location; and a wide variety of useful links to organizations and online news articles about the planet.

Willary Foundation (PA) (http://fdncenter.org/grantmaker/willary/)

The Willary Foundation, a small family foundation based in Scranton, Pennsylvania, makes grants for organizations and individuals in Lackawanna and Luzerne counties. The Foundation seeks to foster both individuals and groups with unique, innovative, or unusual ideas and efforts, and is disposed to leveraging the impact of its grants by encouraging efforts that could have a ripple effect in the community or by supporting projects in conjunction with other sources of funding. The Foundation is particularly interested in projects that support leadership and the development of leadership in business, the economy, education, human services, government, the arts, media, and research. In addition to a statement of mission, visitors to the Foundation's "folder" on the Center's Web site will find a history of the Foundation's recent grantmaking activities, downloadable grant application and grant evaluation forms, a listing of the Foundation's board and staff, and contact information.

The Windham Foundation, Inc. (VT) (http://www.windham-foundation.org)

The Windham Foundation was established in 1963 by Dean Mathey, a prominent investment banker who had long family ties to Grafton, Vermont. The Grafton-based Foundation was established with "a three-fold purpose: to restore buildings and economic vitality in the village of Grafton; to provide financial support for education and private charities; and to develop projects that will benefit the general welfare of Vermont and Vermonters." Links are provided on the site to some of their restoration projects. The Foundation awards scholarships to Windham County residents who are studying at the undergraduate level or who are high school graduates pursuing a certificate in a trade or technical setting. Application instructions and an electronic scholarship application are available on their Web site. The Foundation also maintains a grants program that supports elementary and secondary educational organizations in Vermont. Prospective applicants will find application instructions and a downloadable grant application cover sheet on their site. Visitors to the Web site will also find a history of the Foundation, their annual report, a search engine for the site, links to Foundation projects and an online contact form.

The Winston Foundation for World Peace (DC)
(http://www.wf.winstonhome.htm)
Robert Winston Scrivner created the Washington, DC-based Winston Foundation for World Peace in 1986 to work for the permanent prevention of nuclear war, a mission now expanded to the prevention of all conflict. The Foundation pursues its goals through public education efforts to encourage progressive shifts in U.S. foreign policy and through the strengthening of non-governmental organizations (NGOs) worldwide. Funding priorities are conflict prevention and resolution, cooperative security, and non-proliferation of weapons. The Foundation, however, closed its doors in August 1999 and is no longer accepting applications for grants. The Winston Foundation Fellowship, which was offered for the final time in spring 1999, will be managed by the Institute for Peacebuilding at Eastern Mennonite University (EMU) beginning in the fall of 1999. The Fellowship encourages upperclass and graduate students to work with NGOs; it provides two or more individuals per year with professional training at the Summer Peacebuilding Institute of the EMU Conflict Transformation Program, followed by an internship of two months minimum with a NGO. Information is provided on the site for application to that program at EMU. Visitors to the Web site will also find information on the Foundation's past funding activities, grants list, links to other resources including the Foundation's Conflict Prevention Resource site, and contact information.

Robert W. Woodruff Foundation, Inc. (GA) (http://www.woodruff.org/)
Known for the first fifty years of its existence as the Trebor Foundation, the Robert W. Woodruff Foundation was renamed in 1985 in honor of the man who, over six decades, guided the Coca-Cola Company from regional soft-drink enterprise to a multinational conglomerate with one of the most recognizable trademarks in the world—and who, through the Foundation, gave generously to a wide range of charitable and cultural organizations in Atlanta, the state of Georgia, and nationwide. Today, the Atlanta-based Woodruff Foundation focuses its giving in the areas of elementary, secondary, and higher education; health care; human services, particularly for children and youth; economic development and civic affairs; art and cultural activities; and conservation of natural resources and environmental protection. It also has been seeking ways in which it can help achieve "systemic improvement in public education, health care access, and family, children, and youth services at the state and local levels." Most, but not all, of the Foundation's grantmaking is limited to tax-exempt organizations operating in

Georgia, and organizations seeking support are encouraged to make an informal inquiry before submitting a proposal. Visitors to the Foundation's no-frills Web site will find general background information and a brief biography of Robert W. Woodruff, grant application guidelines, an analysis of the Foundation's 1997 grants, and contact information.

Woods Charitable Fund, Inc. (NE) (http://www.4w.com/woods/index.html)

Based in Lincoln, Nebraska, the Woods Charitable Fund seeks to "strengthen the community by improving opportunities and life outcomes for all people in Lincoln. . . ." The Fund supports organizations that "are exploring creative alternatives and promoting more just, effective approaches to meet community needs." Within its limited geographic scope, the Fund's special funding interests are in the program areas of children, youth and families; education; community development and housing; and arts and humanities. In addition to a history of the Fund and the affiliated Woods Fund of Chicago, the Fund's Web site provides general information on its funding interests and limitations, a summary of grants by areas of interest, and a listing of the Fund's board of directors.

Wray Trust (TX) (http://wt.org/)

The Wray Trust, a small Texas-based family foundation, "focuses on environmental projects . . . including work on pollution control, natural resources protection, sustainable technologies, and population stabilization." Visitors to its Web site can access basic information on its application guidelines; lists of 1992–1996 grantees by subject area, location, and organization name; and full grant descriptions for the same period, with the amount of the grant and contact information included for each grantee.

The Frank Lloyd Wright Foundation (AZ) (http://www.franklloydwright.org)

Frank Lloyd Wright, recognized as "one of the 20th Century's greatest architects," established the Foundation in 1940 to perpetuate the Taliesen Fellowship, a "self-sustaining community of apprentices and architects who would learn and practice the philosophy of organic architecture by sharing in architectural work, building construction and the related arts." Located in Scottsdale, Arizona, the Foundation is "committed to advancing the ideas and principles of organic architecture, organic education and conservation of the natural environment," and "seeks to preserve and enhance the lifetime contributions and ideas of Frank Lloyd Wright and make available to the public opportunities to study and experience organic architecture." The Foundation provides for the continued operation, maintenance and reservation of Taliesin (Spring Green, WI) and Taliesin West (Scottsdale, AZ), which were Wright residences during his life, as architectural, educational, environmental and cultural centers, where public outreach and apprenticeship programs take place. Taliesen and Taliesen West also serve as the campus of the Frank Lloyd Wright School of architecture. Visit the Web site to learn more about the activities of the Wright Foundation, a bio of its founder's life and works, links to related sites, and contact information.

CHAPTER FOUR

Grantmaking Public Charities on the Web

What Is a Public Charity?

There are upwards of 600,000 public charities registered with the IRS under Section 501(c)(3) of the Internal Revenue Code. This is more than ten times the number of private foundations. Grantmaking public charities, sometimes referred to as "public foundations," differ from private foundations in several ways, but primarily in their sources of support. As described in Chapter 3, private foundations typically draw their funds from a single source, either an individual, a family, or a company. With the exception of those that are endowed, the majority of public charities are supported by contributions from multiple sources, possibly including individuals, foundations, churches, corporations, and government agencies, augmented in some cases with income generated from charitable activities.

Here are two of the most common ways in which a nonprofit organization can meet the IRS definition of a public charity. One way, called the "public support test" is for the organization to a) receive no more than *one-third* of its support from gross investment and unrelated business income and b) receive at least *one-third* of its income from the public in contributions, fees, and gross receipts related to the organization's exempt purpose. A second way is for the organization to claim Automatic Public Charity Status. This status is given to organizations such as schools, churches or hospitals that meet certain criteria. A simple example would be a church that maintains a facility for religious worship.

Because public charities are assumed to be accountable to a broad support base, the regulations and reporting requirements are less stringent than they are for private foundations. Gifts to public charities are commonly eligible for maximum income tax deductibility, whereas those to private foundations are limited in this respect. Furthermore, public charities and private foundations follow different annual IRS reporting requirements: public charities file Form 990 and Schedule A; private foundations file Form 990-PF.

The fact that the IRS uses the "exclusionary definition" of a private foundation as a 501(c)(3) organization that is not a church, school, hospital, or a government or a publicly supported charity has at times been a source of confusion: when a public charity fails the "public support test," it is listed with the IRS as a private foundation. The Foundation Center does not consider these "failed public charities" to be true private foundations and does not count them in its statistics on the foundation field. To further confuse the issue, a few formerly "private" foundations have deliberately qualified for "public charity" status. Perhaps the simplest definition of a public charity is a *publicly supported nonprofit organization that has been classified as "not a private foundation" and is not required to file a Form 990-PF tax return.*

It is important to remember that most grantmaking public charities are by definition grantseekers as well, with the full tax deductibility mentioned earlier. Another characteristic of grantmaking public charities is that their giving interests are typically very specific, addressing a narrow or single field of interest, a specific population group, or a limited geographic community, as is true for community foundations. For the public charities listed here, their grantmaking activity may be only a small part of their overall charitable program.

Community foundations are usually public charities and not required to file a Form 990-PF. Traditionally, the Foundation Center has included community foundations in its statistical analyses and reference works about private foundations because their primary activity is grantmaking. Their more formal grantmaking operations and grant-reporting capabilities allow them to be represented logically and systematically within that group. Now that the Center is identifying and tracking other grantmaking public charities, for definitional clarity we can present community foundations as a group within the grantmaking public charity universe. The Center's links to community foundation Web sites later in this chapter are organized by state, as most community foundations are focused principally on a specific geographic area.

In recent years, the Foundation Center has identified hundreds of public charities that have some sort of grantmaking program. In this chapter we include those that had a World Wide Web presence at the time of writing.

This chapter does not present a comprehensive picture of the grantmaking public charity universe. This is largely because at this time there is no simple way to identify systematically those non-private-foundation charities that in fact do operate clearly defined giving programs. We hope that our continued efforts to gather information on grantmaking public charities will stimulate those organizations that believe they qualify to be included in such listings to contact us and forward information concerning their grantmaking programs.

NEW IRS DISCLOSURE RULES

Regulations regarding the IRS Form 990 took effect on June 8, 1999. This new disclosure rule requires nonprofit organizations to respond to public requests for information by making copies of their 990 forms for the past three years available to any member of the public. An organization is also required to provide a copy of its application for tax exemption (Form 1023 or 1024), if the organization filed for exemption after July 1987 or possessed a copy of its exemption application on that date. All attachments and associated schedules to the forms must be included, although nonprofits do not have to provide the section listing donor names.

Federal law always has required that most tax-exempt nonprofit organizations allow public inspection of recent annual information returns. As a result of this new ruling, however, public access has been expanded. Copies of 990s must be made readily available to anyone making a request in person to management or administrative personnel of an organization. Requests in writing must be answered within 30 days unless the organization makes these documents widely available.

Organizations must comply with the regulations or face penalties. The rules also define in detail the offices of an organization at which a request may *not* be made, list circumstances under which a response can be delayed for several days, and define a circumstance of harassment—requests made to interfere with an organization's work—in which a response can be withheld.

The regulations also provide that nonprofit organizations can satisfy the "widely available" requirement by posting their 990 Forms on the World Wide Web. If an organization posts its tax return on the Web, it is freed from the requirement to provide the form when requests are made in person or by mail. Information must be in the original form. Most documents will thus be in the Adobe PDF file format, making it necessary for people to have the Adobe Acrobat Reader software to view the files.

A 990 tax return and the application for tax-exempt status are not alternatives to an annual report or an accounting audit. They are primarily used to help the IRS determine if an organization qualifies for tax exemption. Secondarily, they are used to fulfill a legal requirement for accurate financial data that is publicly available. These two legal requirements will offer the public the opportunity to examine a nonprofit's financial and operational activities and heighten public accountability.

USEFUL WEB SITES

There are a number of Web sites that aggregate information about the public charity universe. There are often the best starting points for your Web researches because they present lists of useful Web links in one location. Here is a list of specific Web addresses that will help you access information. Sometimes they will take you to a charity Web page, other times to a specific Web site focused on a particular aspect of your search.

Foundation Center (http://www.fdncenter.org)

The Grantmaker Information area of the Foundation Center's Web site includes its own listing of links to grantmaking public charities with a Web presence. It should always be consulted when searching for grantmaking public charities. There are over 600,000 charities, and only a small percentage are grantmakers. All grantmaking public charities listed on the Center's Web site are briefly annotated with information about the charity's mission and Web site content. As discussed below, the text of these abstracts is searchable via comprehensive lists of keywords of subject interests and geographic priorities.

Council on Foundations (http://www.cof.org)

This site contains a community foundation locator. It provides links to Web sites, and carries programs and services for public charities.

990 Online Project (http://www.990online.com)

This site was developed as a result of the new public access law. To fulfill the requirement of the June 1999 IRS Disclosure Law, many public charities will be providing access to 990 forms on the Web.

Nonprofit Locator (http://www.nonprofits.org)

This valuable site provides coded information that will tell you about individual nonprofit organizations. Click on the line at the bottom of the page and "you can learn more about the IRS fields and Codes" for an explanation of the codes.

GuideStar (http://www.guidestar.org/index.html)

This site states the filing requirements of the entity. Financial information is included and at times program information. In late 1999 GuideStar was planning to make all IRS Form 990 tax returns for public charities available on their site as PDF files.

U.S. Nonprofit Organization's Public Disclosure Regulations Site (http://www.muridae.com/publicaccess)

This site provides useful information about the regulations governing public disclosure of IRS forms concerning nonprofit organizations. It explains the different rules governing different nonprofits.

EXAMPLES OF GRANTMAKING PUBLIC CHARITY WEB SITES

Below are examples of well developed Web sites of grantmaking public charities. Please note that these are large organizations whose grantmaking programs have specific subject areas or geographic priorities.

The Howard Hughes Medical Institute (http://www.hhmi.org)

This site contains a wealth of information, but it is necessary to go through several screens to access it. For example, scroll down the homepage. Among many other items, it shows an Annual Report and a New Grants Program. Click on the Annual Report and a listing of other topics appear. Click on the New Grants Program to view complete descriptions of grant programs and the amount of the grants given. There are still more pages to be accessed. This is an example of a deep Web site, which will take some time to explore thoroughly.

The Virginia Beach Foundation (http://fdncenter.org/grantmaker/vbf/index.html)

The Web site of this community foundation was developed at the Foundation Center as part of its "Foundation Folder" initiative. On the left side of the page is a table of contents. It is possible to see at a glance the topics covered. These include information about the Foundation, its history, list of grants, guide for donors, list of supporters, and an FAQ page.

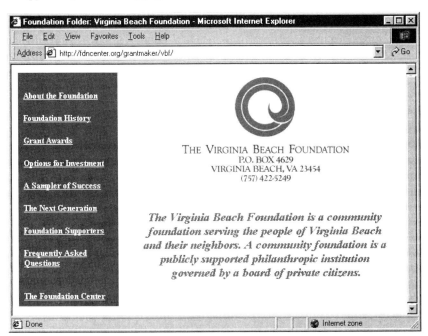

USING SEARCH CAPABILITY AT THE FOUNDATION CENTER'S WEB SITE

At the Foundation Center's Web site it is possible to do structured searching of information concerning grantmaking public charities (as well as other types of grantmakers) that are on the Web.

Every grantmaking public charity listed on the Foundation Center's Web site is annotated with general information about the charity and its Web site. A time-saving search feature lets you search the text of these abstracts to learn the program interests of the charities and become familiar with the contents of their sites without having to take the time to explore them yourself.

Let's say you are interested in environmental issues and are looking for public charities that make grants in those areas. Go to the Foundation Center's Web Site. On top of the home page is a category named Grantmaker Information. Click on that box. On the right side of this next page click on the section named Grantmaking Public Charities. Your search begins here.

To search by subject click on "subject." A subject list will appear on the left side of the page. Scroll down the list. Since you are interested in environmental issues select "environment." Enter this term into the search box. Click the search button to activate the search. A numbered results list will appear. Clicking on a name of any grantmaking public charity will give you a short description of the charity and its Web site. To go to the home page of a particular grantmaking public charity click on the name. Now you are grantseeking on the Web.

You can also search by geographic location. To do this click on "geographic" and follow the same instructions.

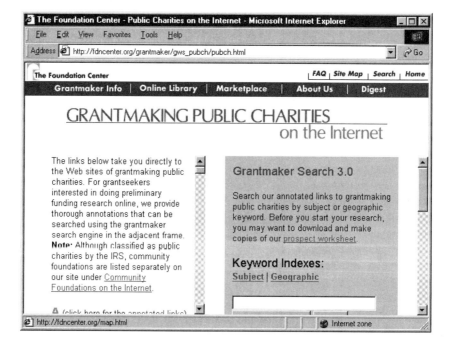

SEARCHING THE INTERNET

There is no substitute for a well-thought-out plan for searching the Web. Discipline is required to navigate through the seemingly endless possibilities available to novice grantseekers. There are, however, several good search engines that can help you define and streamline your searches.

To do a basic search you can use any one of these search engines:

- Alta Vista (http://www.altavista.com)
- Excite (http://www.excite.com)
- Infoseek (http://www.infoseek.com)
- Hotbot (http://www.hotbot.com)
- Yahoo (http://www.yahoo.com)
- Web sites such as Metacrawler (http://www.metacrawler.com) search several search engines at once.

These are some specific words or phrases to include in your search strategies. Include them either separately or with another defining word. In the box next to the search button enter:

- "association"
- "public charity"
- "990 Form"
- "Fund"
- "community foundation"
- "501(c)(3)"

Links and Abstracts of Community Foundation Web Sites

In its general charitable purposes, a community foundation is much like a private foundation; its funds, however, are derived from many donors rather than a single source, as is usually the case with private foundations. Community foundations are usually classified under the tax code as public charities and therefore are subject to different rules and regulations than those which govern private foundations. Community foundations represent a growing segment of the field of philanthropy. Be sure to check the "Grantmaker Information" area of the Foundation Center's Web site for the latest listing.

ALASKA

Alaska Conservation Foundation (http://www.akcf.org/)
Established in 1980, the Alaska Conservation Foundation receives funds and makes grants to protect the integrity of Alaska's ecosystems and to promote sustainable livelihoods among its communities and peoples. New areas of interest for ACF include advocacy, community development, public communications, public policy, and rural affairs; and the Foundation's guidelines favor approaches that convene diverse constituencies, promote citizen participation in public process, provide forums for increasing environmental awareness, and build capacity to implement sustainable futures. The Foundation's Web site offers a mission

statement, a brief history of the Foundation and facts about the state of Alaska, program descriptions, grant guidelines and application procedures, a section on ways to give to ACF, and contact information.

ARIZONA

Arizona Community Foundation (http://www.azfoundation.com/)

The Phoenix-based Arizona Community Foundation was established in 1978 by a trio of local businessmen, and has since become one of the fast-growing public charities in the nation. Through its grantmaking activities, the Foundation aims to improve the lives of children and families and strengthen neighborhoods and communities across the Grand Canyon State. Of special interest to the Foundation are programs that respond to the needs of low income and vulnerable older persons; disadvantaged and underserved children and youth, with an emphasis on "the early childhood years and/or prevention and early intervention strategies that reduce the likelihood or mitigate the severity of negative outcomes for 'at risk' groups"; education; neighborhood- and community-based economic and social development; social justice, with a focus on ways to mediate community conflict and promote appreciation and understanding of cultural diversity in Arizona; and the environment, in particular projects "that preserve and protect habitat for humans, animals, and plant life." In addition to general information about the Foundation's programs, visitors to the ACF Web site will find a listing of its board of directors; information for potential donors, including answers to frequently asked questions and a section called "Estate Planning News"; and contact information for its affiliates in Flagstaff, the Green Valley area, Page, Scottsdale, Sedona, Tempe, and Cochise, Graham, and Yavapai Counties.

ARKANSAS

Foundation for the Mid South (http://www.fndmidsouth.org/)

The Foundation for the Mid South makes grants "to build the capacity of communities, organizations, and individuals" throughout the states of Arkansas, Louisiana, and Mississippi. Grants are made within the three primary program areas of economic development, education, and families and children. In addition to general information about the Foundation, visitors to the Web site will find detailed program descriptions, including types of funding provided within each program area; downloadable application forms in the PDF format; and an interactive bulletin board through which regional grantseekers and grantmakers can communicate. Selections from the Foundation's annual report, including listings of grants by program area, are also available.

CALIFORNIA

California Community Foundation (http://www.calfund.org/)

Established in 1915, the California Community Foundation was Los Angeles's first grantmaking institution and is the country's second-oldest community foundation. The Foundation makes grants to organizations serving the greater Los Angeles region in the following areas: human services, children and youth, community development, civic affairs, community health, community education, arts and culture, the environment, and animal welfare. Visitors to the Foundation's Web site will find a range of general information as well as grant guidelines and a downloadable version of the Foundation's grant application form, a list of recent grants, the annual report and tax returns, and a calendar of upcoming Foundation-related events.

Claremont Community Foundation (http://www.cyberg8t.com/clcomfdn/)
Established in 1989 to serve the philanthropic needs of Claremont, a small town within the larger Los Angeles metropolitan area, CCF seeks to maximize the long-term impact of tax-deductible gifts from individuals, families, small businesses, corporations, and other organizations through careful and prudent oversight of those gifts. In addition to making discretionary grants in the fields of the visual and performing arts, health and general welfare, and history and cultural heritage, the Foundation supports areas of greatest current need in the community through a board-advised fund. The CCF Web site provides very general information about the Foundation and its activities, a list of Foundation board members and officers, and contact information.

The Community Foundation of the Napa Valley (http://www.napanonprofits.org/index.htm)
The Community Foundation of the Napa Valley was established in 1994 to serve the residents of Napa County, California. The Foundation seeks to consolidate charitable giving in the region to include as many nonprofits and sponsors as possible under its umbrella. As a result, it does not specify fields of interest, because potentially all are included. Application information can be downloaded in various formats from the Foundation's Web site. Contact information, a board listing, and links to Napa nonprofits are also provided.

Community Foundation Silicon Valley (http://www.commfdn.org/)
The Community Foundation Silicon Valley (formerly the Community Foundation of Santa Clara County) changed its name in November 1997 to better reflect the entrepreneurial spirit, creativity, and diversity of the community it serves. The Foundation supports programs that benefit the residents of Santa Clara County and southern San Mateo County in the following areas: arts and humanities, community and social services, education, the environment, and health. In addition, the Foundation's Neighborhood Grants Program promotes "the development of healthy and self-reliant neighborhoods by supporting residents to unify for action, actualize their collective power, and create community-based solutions to physical, social, and economic challenges." Low-to-middle-income neighborhoods in Santa Clara County receive priority. The Foundation's Web site provides general program information, application guidelines, a Foundation calendar along with a list of recent grant, an electronic form for ordering copies of the Foundation's print publications, related links, and e-mail contact information.

Glendale Community Foundation (http://www.cwire.com/GCF/)
Founded in 1956 as part of Glendale's 50th anniversary celebration, the Glendale Community Foundation exists to improve the quality of life for the people of the greater Glendale community—Glendale, La Crescenta, La Cañada Flintridge, Montrose, and Verdugo City—by leveraging community assets. The Foundation administers gifts and grants according to donors' wishes and uses the income from

unrestricted gifts to fund hard asset acquisitions (i.e., capital equipment and improvements) and programming for local charities to make them more efficient and effective. Visitors to the Foundation's Web site will find a brief history of the Foundation itself, grant application guidelines and procedures, recent issues of the Foundation's quarterly newsletter, and information on ways to give and the benefits of giving to donors.

Humboldt Area Foundation
(http://www.northcoast.com/~hafound/welcome.html)

The Humboldt Area Foundation was established in 1972 as a vehicle of and for the citizens of the North Coast of California—that is, Humboldt, Del Norte, and parts of Trinity and Siskiyou counties. In addition to general information about the Foundation itself, its Web site provides detailed grant application guidelines and an overview of the resources available to nonprofit organizations at the Foundation-operated William T. Rooney Resource Center.

Marin Community Foundation (http://www.marincf.org/)

The Marin Community Foundation strives to encourage and apply philanthropic contributions to help improve the human condition, embrace diversity, promote a humane and democratic society, and enhance the community's quality of life. The Foundation focuses its grantmaking activities in the following areas: the arts, with an emphasis on arts in the community and arts education; community development; education and training, with an emphasis on drop-out prevention, improving literacy and basic skills, school restructure and redesign, and lifelong learning; the environment; human services; and religion. The MCF Web site provides detailed program descriptions and application guidelines for the above; additional information about the Foundation's various community programs, donor-advised funds, and loan program; answers to questions about MCF's funding reference library; and a handful of links to related sites.

North Valley Community Foundation (http://www.nvcf.org/)

NVCF serves rural communities in Northern California by operating and/or assisting a number of programs dedicated to improvements in those communities. NVCF programs include a Graffiti Eradication program (Chico and Oroville); Leadership Chico, which is dedicated to providing potential and existing community leaders with leadership skills training; Tomorrow's Leaders Today, which provides students in their junior year at Chico schools with leadership skills; Farm-City Celebration, a fall program dedicated to bringing agriculture and related aspects of the agriculture industry to urban residents; P.A.R.T., a collaboration of many groups dedicated to increasing public knowledge of the agricultural industry; and Supporters of V.I.P.S., which provides equipment and supplies to a citizens group that assists local law enforcement. In addition to information about these and other Foundation activities, the NVCF Web site provides a good deal of general information about community foundations and the community foundation movement, a nice set of links to related organizations, and contact information.

Orange County Community Foundation
(http://www.oc-communityfoundation.org/)

In addition to approximately $2 million in donor-advised funds, the Irvine-based OCCF makes discretionary grants in the following areas: children and youth, with a focus on ensuring the safety of young people in their homes and neighborhoods, child and foster care, early childhood development, school preparedness, arts and classical music education, and building self-esteem; family relationships, with a focus on improving family impact on children and youth, parenting, family economic self-sufficiency, and family violence; and diverse communities, with a focus on the promotion of mutual respect and understanding among diverse groups in Orange County. The Foundation also awards a limited number of scholarships to high school juniors and seniors who are continuing their education in an accredited institution and are graduating from an Orange County high school and are residents of Orange County. And it administers something called the XOXO Fund, which was created by an anonymous donor to provide food, health, and social services to those most in need. The OCCF Web site provides information on all its grantmaking activities, application guidelines and recent grants, separate FAQs for grantseekers and potential donors, a summary of Foundation publications, and contact information.

Peninsula Community Foundation (http://www.pcf.org/)

Created by residents of the San Francisco peninsula in 1964, the Peninsula Community Foundation today provides funding for nonprofit groups in San Mateo and Santa Clara counties that address the needs of children, youth and families, or that work in the areas of education, health and human services, housing and homelessness, the arts, or civic and public benefit. Through its Center for Venture Philanthropy, the Foundation is also forging partnerships of donor/investors "to make long-term, focused investments in complex programs… [such] as school reform and welfare reform." In addition to information for potential donors, visitors to the PCF Web site will find general program information, current grantmaking guidelines, a list of recent grants, board and staff listings (including e-mail links), a calendar of deadline and events, a section devoted to the Foundation's "Strategic Philanthropy" initiatives (i.e., the Center for Venture Philanthropy, the Peninsula Partnership for Children, Youth and Families, Every Kid a Start-Up Fund, the Prenatal to Three Initiative, and the Neighborhood Grants program), and contact information.

San Diego Community Foundation (http://www.sdcf.org/html/home.html)

The mission of the San Diego Community Foundation is "to assist donors to build and preserve enduring assets for charitable purposes in the San Diego Region; to monitor and assess changing needs and to meet those needs through financial awards and organizational support." Incorporated in 1975, the SDCF has assets of more than $138 million in some 300 separate funds. Approximately nine percent of the Foundation's endowments generate discretionary income, which is distributed through a community grants program. The Foundation also operates the Funding Information Center, a Foundation Center Cooperating Collection, which provides free access and technical assistance to anyone seeking nonprofit or educational funding. In addition to general information, visitors to the Foundation's Web site will find descriptive lists of its grant awards; staff and board listings; and contact information.

The San Francisco Foundation (http://www.sff.org/)

With more than $500 million in assets and annual giving in excess of $40 million, the San Francisco Foundation is one of the largest community foundations in the country. As the community foundation serving Alameda, Contra Costa, Marin, San Francisco, and San Mateo counties, it partners with diverse donors and organizations to mobilize resources in the promotion of vibrant, sustainable communities throughout the Bay Area. The Foundation, which recently marked its fiftieth anniversary, awards grants to nonprofit organizations in the fields of arts and humanities, community health, education, the environment, neighborhood and community development, social services, and philanthropy. The Foundation's easy to navigate Web site provides a good deal of information about Foundation activities, past and present; its grantmaking, including program priorities, selected grants in each program area, and grantee profiles; information about the Koshland Civic Unity Awards, the Foundation's Special Awards Program, and the Foundation's Community Initiative Funds; information for prospective donors; answers to frequently asked questions; a short list of Foundation publications available upon request; and contact information.

Sonoma Community Foundation (http://www.sonoma.org/)

The Sonoma Community Foundation administers and awards grants from a permanent endowment to eligible nonprofit organizations based and operating in Sonoma County, California, in the areas of health and human services, education, the environment, and the arts. The Foundation also manages and distributes monies from several individual funds established to support the specific philanthropic interests of their donors. The Foundation's Web site provides visitors with detailed grant guidelines and application forms, scholarship information, recent grants lists, and contact information.

Sonora Area Foundation (http://www.sonora-area.org/)

Established in 1989, the Sonora Area Foundation strives "to enhance the community and the quality of life of its residents through facilitating the philanthropic intentions of donors, and the needs of the surrounding communities." The Foundation awards approximately 30 grants annually to nonprofit and public agencies throughout the Tuolumne County, California area. Grants have been made in the past in the areas of recreational services, education, social service programs, and education. The Foundation does not make grants to individuals. The Foundation's Web site offers a short history of the Foundation, brief descriptions of the programs it funds and the individual donor funds administered by the Foundation, a list of the grants the Foundation made recently, grant application policies and instructions, a listing of Foundation board members, and contact information.

COLORADO

Community Foundation Serving Boulder County
(http://bcn.boulder.co.us/community/found/)

Established in 1991, the Community Foundation Serving Boulder County generally supports the community of Boulder County, Colorado; however, "several donors have interests elsewhere which they fund through the Community Foundation." The Foundation's areas of interest include arts, environment, education, health, and human services. The Foundation's Web site is aimed primarily at donors, but basic contact information is included.

The Denver Foundation (http://www.denverfoundation.org/)

The 75-year-old Denver Foundation supports a range of community-based programs that make the metropolitan Denver area a better place to live. The Foundation awards grants in the areas of arts and culture, community development, education, and health and human services to nonprofit organizations in the six-county (Adams, Arapahoe, Boulder, Denver, Douglas, and Jefferson) metropolitan area. In addition, some donor funds help nonprofit organizations throughout Colorado and beyond. The Foundation's Web site provides a mission statement, general program information, grant guidelines and application procedures, an FAQ section for grantees, information for potential donors, an electronic order form for Foundation publications, and extensive contact information.

Yampa Valley Community Foundation (http://www.yvcf.org/)

The Yampa Valley Community Foundation serves the residents of Routt County, Colorado. It was originally established in 1979 under the name of Yampa Valley Foundation to save Alpine College, Colorado. The new name, with the word "community" in it, was adopted in 1994 to reflect reorganization and broadening of focus. The Foundation's present areas of interest include arts and culture, education, health and human services, recreation, and the environment. Detailed application guidelines, frequently asked questions, and a form for requesting more information can be found at the Foundation's Web site.

CONNECTICUT

Community Foundation for Greater New Haven (http://www.cfgnh.org/)

Founded in 1928, the Community Foundation for Greater New Haven manages charitable funds in its 20-town region of Connecticut. The Foundation supports a wide range of interests through many distinct endowments funds. The Foundation's latest annual report, current newsletter, and grant guidelines can be obtained by e-mailing the Foundation from their Web site.

Hartford Foundation for Public Giving (http://www.hartnet.org/~hfpg1/)

Established in 1925 to serve the changing needs of Connecticut's Capitol region, the Hartford Foundation for Public Giving ranks as one of the oldest community foundations in the country. The Foundation's Web site provides general information about the Foundation and its programs, a breakdown of its giving by category and an alphabetical listing of the Foundation's grant recipients, listings of the board and staff, an overview of financial management issues, annual report, and contact information. Organizations interested in applying for a grant are encouraged to call for the Foundation's guidelines and to discuss their interests with a member of the Foundation's program staff prior to planning a grant application.

DELAWARE

Delaware Community Foundation (http://www.delcf.org/)

Established in 1986, the DCF today has over $50 million in charitable assets and distributes close to $2 million annually from more than 200 restricted and unrestricted funds. The Foundation focuses it unrestricted grantmaking resources on building a stronger community, in large part by supporting disadvantaged populations. Program grants have been awarded to address some of Delaware's most pressing challenges, including affordable housing, homelessness, health care, arts stabilization, adolescent needs, and violence prevention. Unrestricted fund grants are distributed to qualified nonprofit organizations twice annually: in the winter for program support, and in the summer for capital needs. The easy-to-navigate DCF Web site provides application guidelines and deadlines for grantseekers; information for potential donors, friends, and supporters; general information on starting an endowment; selections from recent DCF newsletters and an HTML version of the Foundation's most recent annual report; a listing of the Foundation's board and staff; and contact information.

FLORIDA

The Community Foundation for Palm Beach and Martin Counties (http://www.cfpbmc.org/)

Founded in 1972 by Michael and Winsome McIntosh, "a community-conscious couple from New York," the Community Foundation for Palm Beach and Martin Counties today is a thriving enterprise with a $50,000,000 endowment representing the gifts and commitments of many people. The Foundation applies the income from its assets to a wide range of community needs, including human and race relations, arts and culture, education, community development, health, human services, the environment, and the conservation and preservation of historical and cultural resources. In addition to a mission statement, a brief history of the Foundation, and listings of the Foundation's board, officers, and staff, the CFPBMC Web site provides program descriptions and information about the Foundation's Dwight Allison Fellows Program, grant guidelines and eligibility requirements, a selection of recent grants, a section on ways to give to the Foundation, and information about its Funding Resource Center.

The Community Foundation of Sarasota County (http://www.sarasota-foundation.org/)

The Community Foundation of Sarasota County supports a variety of worthy causes throughout the West Coast of Florida, including the arts and culture (increasing audiences for local artistic pursuits), community development (encouraging access to and use of community-based development methods), education (early childhood development, primary education through completion of high school and preparation for employment), the environment (promoting ways to conserve resources, encourage responsible animal welfare, and protect wildlife), health (basic medical, dental, and mental health needs), and human services (families, youth, seniors, the disabled, and the disadvantaged). The Foundation also administers 14 scholarship funds designated for students in Charlotte, Manatee, and Sarasota Counties, Florida. Scholarship recipients are selected on an objective, competitive basis that takes into account academic and non-academic factors plus demonstrated financial need. Visitors to the Foundation's Web site will find application guidelines, scholarship information, and information for donors.

Pinellas County Community Foundation (http://fdncenter.org/grantmaker/pinellas/index.html)

The purpose of the Pinellas County Community Foundation is to distribute the investment income from donated funds (or principal when directed by a donor) to recognized charitable organizations located in Pinellas County, Florida. If designated by a donor, charities located outside of the county can be beneficiaries of donated funds or income earned on those funds. The Foundation carefully screens charities in the county that request funding through discretionary grants and favors those that assist persons with handicaps or who have low or moderate incomes or are trying to become self-sufficient. Also favored are nonprofit organizations that assist persons who have been abused or neglected or have special needs. The Foundation does not make grants to cultural groups, schools, or colleges; to organizations that are largely taxpayer or government funded; or to organizations that have large endowments or have significant fundraising staffs or abilities. The Foundation's "folder" on the Foundation Center's site provides information about the Foundation's structure, guidelines, donor funds, and financials; recent grants lists; reports from the Foundation's chairman and executive director; and contact information.

GEORGIA

The Community Foundation for Greater Atlanta, Inc. (http://www.atlcf.org/)

CFGA was established in 1951 for the purpose of improving the quality of life in the metropolitan Atlanta area. Today the Foundation manages 475 individual funds and more than $300 million in assets for the benefit of residents in a 22-county region (i.e, Barrow, Bartow, Butts, Carroll, Cherokee, Clayton, Cobb, Coweta, DeKalb, Douglas, Fayette, Forsyth, Fulton, Gwinnett, Hall, Henry, Newton, Paulding, Pickens, Rockdale, Spalding, and Walton counties). The Foundation's Unrestricted Grants Program considers and funds proposals in six major program areas: arts and culture, civic affairs, education, health, human services, and community development. The Foundation emphasizes two of these areas each year (children, youth, and families and community capacity building in 1998–99). In addition to its application guidelines, the CFGA Web site provides information about the Foundation's community scholarships, information for donors and professional advisors (including a planned giving design center), press releases, and contact information.

North Georgia Community Foundation (http://www.ngcf.org/)

Established as the Gainesville Community Foundation in 1985, the North Georgia Community Foundation today provides grants and serves donors in an eight-county area (Hall, Banks, Dawson, Forsyth, Habersham, Jackson, Lumpkin, and White counties). The Foundation is interested in organizations that can demonstrate they have planned their projects in light of overall community need, as well as in projects that can be replicated by other nonprofit organizations in other areas. The Foundation generally does not provide funding for annual fund campaigns, lobbying activities, ongoing operating support, or to individuals. Visitors to the NGCF Web site will find very general information about the Foundation and its activities, grant application guidelines, and a few words for potential donors.

ILLINOIS

The Aurora Foundation (http://fdncenter.org/grantmaker/aurora/)
Established in 1948, the Aurora Foundation provides scholarships to students and grants to nonprofit organizations in the greater Aurora, Illinois area, including the Tri-Cities and Kendall County. The Foundation's "folder" on the Center's Web site includes a mission statement and a "letter to the community"; information on ways to give and benefits to donors; a statement of principal transactions for the fiscal year ; a summary of grants awarded; and a listing of directors, officers, and staff.

Oak Park-River Forest Community Foundation (http://www.oprfcommfd.org/)
The Oak Park-River Forest Community Foundation was established in 1958 "to provide a tangible, permanent contribution" to the residents of Oak Park and River Forest, Illinois. The Foundation focuses on supporting educational, cultural, and charitable organizations. The Foundation also provides scholarships and awards. Grant guidelines, answers to frequently asked questions, and contact information can be found at the Foundation's Web site.

INDIANA

Central Indiana Community Foundation (http://www.cicf.org/)
The Central Indiana Community Foundation is the product of a collaborative effort between community foundations serving Marion and Hamilton Counties. The founding partners of CICF—the Hamilton County Legacy Fund and the Indianapolis Foundation—are "committed to a structure that sustains local engagement, leadership and capacity while supporting an expanded level of philanthropic service and growth for the region." In addition to assisting the community in "convening, consensus building and problem solving," the Foundation supports and coordinates a variety of special projects, including the Neighborhood Preservation Initiative, the Youth, Sport and Fitness Network, the Library Fund and Project Hi-Net, the Marion County Education Foundation Network, and the Partnership for National Service. Visitors to CICF's well-organized Web site will find a wealth of information about the Foundation's mission, donor services, programs, and initiatives, as well as links to resources of interest.

Community Foundation of Boone Count
(http://www.bccn.boone.in.us/cf/index.html)
The Community Foundation of Boone County was established in 1992 to serve residents of Boone County, Indiana. The Foundations main areas of interest are education, youth, culture, health and human services, civic affairs, environment and recreation. The Foundation gives both to individual and to nonprofits. Detailed application guidelines are included at the Foundation's Web site, as well as contact information.

Community Foundation of Wabash County (http://www.cfwabash.org)

The Community Foundation of Wabash County serves the residents of Wabash County, Indiana. The Foundation areas of interest include social services, education, civic affairs, cultural affairs, health and medical, recreation, and environment. The Foundation can be contacted directly from its Web site, where one can also find application guidelines and board and staff lists.

Indianapolis Foundation (http://www.cicf.org/About/fsetif.htm)

The Indianapolis Foundation was created in 1916—as one of first such trusts in the United States—to serve the residents in and around Indianapolis, Indiana. The mission of the Indianapolis Foundation is "to help where the needs are greatest and the benefits to our community and its citizens are most substantial; and to provide public spirited donors a vehicle for using their gifts in the best possible way now and in the future as conditions inevitably change." The Foundation funds programs in Marion County, and grants from its unrestricted Community Endowment Fund are made in the areas of arts, culture and humanities, civic and community development, education and libraries, health and human services, and information and technology. Grant guidelines, a list of the board of trustees, and the Foundation's financial statement are provided at its Web site. The Foundation is a partner, with the Hamilton County Legacy Fund, in the Central Indiana Community Foundation, which provides its Web presence.

Kosciusko County Foundation (http://www.kcfoundation.org/)

The Kosciusko County Foundation was first organized in Warsaw, Indiana, in 1968, as the Greater Warsaw Community Foundation under the sponsorship of the Warsaw Chamber of Commerce. In 1973 the Foundation was renamed for the county in which it is located. With help from the Indiana-based Lilly Endowment, the Foundation's assets grew significantly in 1990. Grants are given in civic services, education, health, culture, environment, and social services. Grant guidelines, financial information, and contact information can be found at the Foundation's Web site.

Steuben County Community Foundation (http://www.steubenfoundation.org/)

The Steuben County Community Foundation serves the residents of Steuben County, Indiana. "The Foundation makes grants to support programs and projects arts and culture, community development, education, health and human services and other charitable purposes. It also helps community groups develop and manage resources in the areas of special collaborative projects." Grant guidelines and contact information can be obtained at the Foundation's Web site.

KANSAS

Greater Kansas City Community Foundation (http://www.gkccf.org/)

Established in 1978 and today comprised of more than 500 charitable funds, the Greater Kansas City Community Foundation strives "to make a positive difference in the lives and future of the people in Greater Kansas City"—Jackson, Clay, and Platte counties in Missouri and Johnson and Wyandotte counties in Kansas—"through grant making, advocacy, support of the not-for-profit sector and promotion of philanthropy for the benefit of the community." In addition to a listing of the Foundation's board and officers, contact information, and links to other sites of interest, visitors to the site will find general descriptions of the Foundation's programs, a listing of scholarships available through the Foundation, information about important Foundation initiatives, application guidelines, a section devoted to the services the Foundation provides to donors, upcoming events, Foundation partnerships, grant recipient profiles, and an annual report section.

KENTUCKY

The Community Foundation of Louisville, Inc. (http://www.cflouisville.org/)
With approximately $140 million in assets, the 14-year-old Community Foundation of Louisville promotes philanthropy in the Louisville area by enriching the quality of life of individuals and serving as a catalyst within the local community. In addition to its unrestricted grantmaking, the Foundation awards community grants in support of programs designed to break the cycle of poverty in the Louisville neighborhoods of Algonquin, California Chickasaw, Limerick, Old Louisville, Park DuValle, Park Hill, Parkland Portland, Shawnee, and South Louisville; field of interest grants in the areas of the visual arts, crafts, theater, and historic preservation; donor endowment grants; nonprofit organization endowment grants; and scholarships. The CFL Web site provides a brief overview of the Foundation's activities, general program and application information, a list of recent community grants, an electronic order form for requesting print materials and application forms, a list of the Foundation's board and officers, and contact information.

LOUISIANA

Foundation for the Mid South (http://www.fndmidsouth.org/)
The Foundation for the Mid South makes grants "to build the capacity of communities, organizations, and individuals" throughout the states of Arkansas, Louisiana, and Mississippi. Grants are made within the three primary program areas of economic development, education, and families and children. In addition to general information about the Foundation, visitors to the Web site will find detailed program descriptions, including types of funding provided within each program area; downloadable application forms in PDF format; and an interactive bulletin board through which regional grantseekers and grantmakers can communicate. Selections from the Foundation's annual report, including listings of grants by program area, are also available.

MAINE

Maine Community Foundation (http://www.mainecf.org/)
The Maine Community Foundation administers a variety of individual funds established to support a wide range of organizations and programs within the state of Maine. Funds may be restricted by their donors to support specific programmatic or geographic interests, while others are unrestricted and distributed at the Foundation's discretion. Discretionary grants are not made for lobbying or religious activities, and are not generally awarded for endowment purposes, equipment, annual campaigns, regular operations, or capital campaigns. The Foundation also manages scholarship funds, provides technical assistance to guide

grantseekers through the fundraising process, and is involved with a number of initiatives that provide major support to address specific issues within Maine. Visitors to the MCF Web site will find general information about the Foundation, application procedures, a staff listing, donor information, a community leadership section, scholarship information, a news and events section, and contact information for other Maine-based philanthropic organizations.

MARYLAND

Community Foundation of the Eastern Shore (http://www.intercom.net/npo/commfnd/)

The Community Foundation of the Eastern Shore is dedicated to improving the quality of life in Worcester, Wicomico, and Somerset counties, Maryland. The Foundation manages and distributes monies from individual funds in the areas of education, health and human services, arts and culture, community development and conservation, and historic preservation. Grants are awarded to nonprofit organizations located within or serving the three counties for three general purposes: "as seed funding for special projects that meet priority needs; as expansion funding to enable successful programs to serve broader constituencies; and to strengthen small and moderate sized nonprofit agencies that are providing exemplary services within [Foundation] areas of interest." Grants are usually not made for long-term operating support, building and endowment projects, budget deficits, sectarian programs, or direct assistance to individuals, other than through scholarship funds. Visitors to the Foundation's Web page will find general information about the Foundation, application guidelines and instructions, and contact information.

Prince George's Community Foundation, Inc. (http://www.pgcf.org/)

Incorporated in 1981 as the Prince George's County Parks and Recreation Foundation, in 1994 it became the Prince George's Community Foundation. It serves the residents of Prince George County, Maryland. The Foundation awards grants and services to community-based, nonprofit groups, schools, and social services organizations that offer programs in the areas of human services, education, and children and youth. Contact information as well as application guidelines and a community resource directory can be found at the Foundation's Web site.

MASSACHUSETTS

The Boston Foundation (http://www.tbf.org/)

Founded in 1915, the Boston Foundation is one of the oldest and, with an endowment of more than $500 million, one of the largest community foundations in the country. The Foundation comprises more than 500 separate funds that have been established by hundreds of donors either for the general benefit of the community or for special purposes, such as giving that is targeted to a special need or the yearly support of specific nonprofit organizations. The current focus of the Foundation's discretionary grantmaking is the Building Family and Community Initiative, which gives priority to community-building strategies that help children and their families overcome poverty. The Foundation's special donor initiatives include the Fund for Arts and Culture, the Next Generation Program, the Boston

Lesbian and Gay Communities Funding Partnership, the Boston Community AIDS Partnership, the Fund for Self-Reliance, and the Fund for Preservation of Wildlife and Natural Areas. Special funding initiatives include the Arts and Audiences Initiative, the Vision Fund, the Boston Schoolyard Initiative, the Massachusetts Citizenship Fund, and the Bruce J. Anderson Foundation. In addition to information about these initiatives and the Foundation's discretionary grantmaking, the Foundation's Web site provides application procedures and guidelines (in English and Spanish), a selection of recent grants, excerpts from past issues of the Foundation's quarterly newsletter, and information for donors.

Community Foundation of Cape Cod (http://www.capecodfoundation.com/)
Established in 1989, the Community Foundation of Cape Cod serves the community of Cape Cod, Massachusetts. Areas in which grants are made include the arts, education, health and human services, conservation, the environment and community development. The Foundation also provides scholarships for local students through a number of scholarship funds. The Foundation's Web site provides news, grant guidelines, a list of scholarship funds, grants lists, and a form through which to request additional information.

Community Foundation of Southeastern Massachusetts (http://www.agmconnect.org/cfsem1.html)
The Community Foundation of Southeastern Massachusetts was established in the early 1990s. The Foundation "is not dedicated to one specific cause, it can aid local charities and nonprofit organizations in a variety of areas—from the arts to education, from the environment to helping the needy." Contact information can be found at the Foundation's Web site.

MICHIGAN

The Community Foundation for Muskegon County (http://www.cffmc.org/)
Founded in 1961, the Community Foundation for Muskegon County is committed to improving the quality of life for the residents of Muskegon County, Michigan. In addition to managing numerous individual funds earmarked for specific philanthropic purposes, the Foundation also awards grants from a pool of discretionary income. Discretionary grants are made to support community projects in the areas of arts, education, community development, health and human services, and youth issues. The Foundation's Web site provides descriptions of Foundation-administered grant programs, scholarships, and special Foundation initiatives, as well as general application information.

Community Foundation for Southeastern Michigan (http://comnet.org/comfound/index.html)
The Community Foundation for Southeastern Michigan serves the residents of seven counties in southeastern Michigan. Its main areas of interest are education, arts and culture, health, human services, community development, and civic affairs. The Foundation has an informative Web site, with very specific application guidelines, including a list of types of support the Foundation does not provide. The Foundation has a major interest in improving the already existing

cultural and economic infrastructure of its geographic area. Contact information, including a telephone number, is included at the Web site.

Community Foundation of Greater Flint (http://www.flint.lib.mi.us/cfflint/)
Through its support of "projects aimed at solving community problems or enhancing life in the county," the Community Foundation of Greater Flint is committed to improving the quality of life in Genesee County, Michigan. The Foundation makes grants through more than 100 funds in the fields of arts and humanities; advancing philanthropy; community services; education; conservation and the environment; and health, human, and social services. The Foundation also makes limited grants from discretionary funds, with special priority given to programs addressing issues of persistent and pervasive poverty and children under the age of ten. The Foundation does not make grants to individuals, for sectarian religious purposes, budget deficits, routine operating expenses of existing organizations, or endowments. Visitors to the Foundation's simple, straightforward Web site will find general information about the Foundation and its funding priorities, application guidelines, and information for potential donors.

Grand Rapids Foundation, The (http://www.grfoundation.org/)
Established in 1922, the Grand Rapids Foundation serves Grand Rapids, Michigan and its surrounding communities. The Foundation's fields of interest include education, arts and culture, health, environment, and human services. The Foundation offers grants and scholarships and provides detailed information about both at its Web site. Applications can be downloaded and contact information is provided.

Greater Rochester Area Community Foundation
(http://www.metronet.lib.mi.us/ROCH/gracf/gracf.html)
The Greater Rochester Area Foundation makes grants to individuals for educational scholarships, and to nonprofit organizations located in or serving the citizens of Rochester, Rochester Hills, and Oakland Township, Michigan. The Foundation manages and awards grants from more than 50 individual funds in the general areas of arts and culture, civic beautification, community development, education and scholarships, health and human concerns, recreation, science, and youth. The Foundation's Web site provides visitors with application information, a complete listing of individual funds and their specific areas of interest, annual report, and a listing of the Foundation's board of trustees.

The Midland Foundation
(http://www.midlandfoundation.com/MF/homepage.nsf)
The Midland Foundation promotes and enables community-wide philanthropic giving to enrich and improve the lives of residents throughout the greater Midland County area. Now one of the largest of the approximately 100 community foundations in Michigan, the Foundation restricts its discretionary grantmaking to 501(c)(3) nonprofit, educational nonprofit, or governmental nonprofit organizations and the projects which have a direct relevance to the people of Midland County and the surrounding area. While the Foundation does not make grants directly to individuals, it does administer two student loan funds and a general scholarship program for Midland County high school seniors or college students, as well as for adults who are resuming undergraduate work or who are retraining

to enter the job market. All grant requests must be submitted on the Foundation's grant application form, and applicants are encouraged to discuss their proposal with the Foundation's executive director prior to completing the application form. Visitors to the Foundation's Web site will find general information about the Foundation and its activities; general grant, student loan, and scholarship application forms in three formats (MS Word, WordPerfect, and PDF); relevant application deadlines and a deadline calendar; information for donors; and contact information.

Saginaw Community Foundation (http://www.SaginawFoundation.org/)

The Saginaw Community Foundation (SCF) is dedicated to improving the quality of life in Saginaw County, Michigan. Its donors are individuals, families, corporations, and organizations who establish permanent charitable funds within the Foundation. From arts education to human services and the environment, SCF supports all types of community projects. Guided by the wishes of its donors, SCF makes grants and awards scholarships to a wide variety of nonprofit organizations and individuals throughout Saginaw County. Visitors to the SCF Web site can find detailed information about its grants and download several grant applications. In addition, there is a special section for professional advisors.

MINNESOTA

The Minneapolis Foundation (http://www.mplsfoundation.org/)

Created more than 80 years ago to encourage and facilitate philanthropy in the Minneapolis-St. Paul area, the Minneapolis Foundation today seeks to improve the quality of life in the Twin Cities by making program or project-specific support grants, operating support grants, and capital support grants in the following areas: children, youth and families in poverty; public policy research; neighborhood capacity building; economic development and employment; low-income senior citizens; people with disabilities; health care for low-income citizens; and medical research and services for children's chronic diseases. Program details are fully explained in the Foundation's grant guidelines, which can be ordered from the Publications area of the Foundation's Web site. The site also offers brief descriptions of a dozen of the Foundation's programs and projects, press releases and a regional events calendar, information for prospective donors, financial statements and a copy of the Foundation's 990 form, listings of the Foundation's staff, board, and trustees, and contact information.

The Minnesota Foundation (http://www.mnfoundation.org/)

The primary mission of the Minnesota Foundation is to assist individuals, organizations, and communities statewide in developing local charitable trusts. The Foundation is affiliated with the Saint Paul Foundation (see below), which, generally speaking, serves the east metropolitan area of the Twin Cities. The Foundation does not make grants on a general unrestricted basis and, therefore, does not publish grant guidelines or application forms. Professional financial advisors will appreciate the link to the Planned Giving Design Center, which was created by the two organizations to provide financial advisors with resources they can use to advise their clients in matters of charitable gift and estate planning. The site also has a section for potential donors and provides contact information for those who'd like to learn more about the Foundation and its programs.

St. Croix Valley Community Foundation (http://www.pressenter.com/~scvcf/)
Founded in 1995, the St. Croix Valley Community Foundation serves the communities of St. Croix Valley in Wisconsin and Minnesota. Its fields of interest include education, arts, environment, civic affairs, and emergency human needs. The Foundation's Web site includes its annual report, board and staff lists, and a form to request more information.

The Saint Paul Foundation (http://www.tspf.org/)
The Saint Paul Foundation was established in 1940 with a $5,000 bequest from a Lithuanian immigrant named Annie Paper. Today, it's the largest community foundation in the state of Minnesota and a major philanthropic force in the city of Saint Paul. The Foundation recently approved grants in eight fields of interest: arts and humanities, civic affairs, education, environment and nature, health, human services, religion, and scholarships. Visitors to the Foundation's Web site will find grant and application guidelines; information for scholarship seekers and prospective donors; a separate section on the Foundation's Diversity Endowment Funds initiative; and contact information.

MISSISSIPPI

Foundation for the Mid South (http://www.fndmidsouth.org/)
The Foundation for the Mid South makes grants "to build the capacity of communities, organizations, and individuals" throughout the states of Arkansas, Louisiana, and Mississippi. Grants are made within the three primary program areas of economic development, education, and families and children. In addition to general information about the Foundation, visitors to the Web site will find detailed program descriptions, including types of funding provided within each program area; downloadable application forms in PDF format; and an interactive bulletin board through which regional grantseekers and grantmakers can communicate. Selections from the Foundation's annual report, including listings of grants by program area, are also available.

MISSOURI

Greater Kansas City Community Foundation (http://www.gkccf.org/)
Established in 1978 and today comprised of more than 500 charitable funds, the Greater Kansas City Community Foundation strives "to make a positive difference in the lives and future of the people in Greater Kansas City"—Jackson, Clay, and Platte counties in Missouri and Johnson and Wyandotte counties in Kansas—"through grant making, advocacy, support of the not-for-profit sector and promotion of philanthropy for the benefit of the community." In addition to a listing of the Foundation's board and officers, contact information, and links to other sites of interest, visitors to the site will find general descriptions of the Foundation's programs, a listing of scholarships available through the Foundation, information about important Foundation initiatives in the areas of early childhood education and homelessness, application guidelines, a list of publications, an online copy of

the Annual Report, an upcoming events list, and a section devoted to the services the Foundation provides to donors.

MONTANA

Montana Community Foundation (http://www.mtcf.org/)
Established in 1988, the Montana Community Foundation is a statewide charitable organization that administers more than 350 private and public funds encompassing the whole spectrum of philanthropy. The Foundation makes grants annually in five focus areas—arts and culture, basic human needs, economic development, education, and natural resources and conservation—and two additional categories: leadership development and tolerance. The MCF Web site provides a good overview of the Foundation and its activities; descriptions of its General Grants, Leadership Development, and Fund for Tolerance programs; grant application procedures and a grant application cover sheet; information for potential donors; a list of board members and staff; links to sites of interest; and contact information.

NEBRASKA

Grand Island Community Foundation (http://www.gicf.org/)
The Grand Island Community Foundation was established in 1960 to make a lasting difference in the quality of life for greater Hall County area citizens. The Foundation does not operate charitable programs itself, but rather, through partnering and coordination, assists in orchestrating charitable activities within the greater Hall County community. The principle vehicle for its activities in this area is the GICF "wish list," which leverages the GICF Web site and other emerging communications technologies to bring potential donors together with worthwhile charitable causes and organizations. The GICF Web site provides information about a number of endowed scholarship funds established by people and organizations wanting to assist Grand Island and Hall County area students in continuing their education beyond high school, a list of board members, the Foundation's mission and history, and contact information.

Lincoln Community Foundation (http://www.lcf.org/)
The Lincoln Community Foundation makes grants to enrich the quality of life in Lincoln and Lancaster Counties, Nebraska. The Foundation administers and disperses monies from a permanent unrestricted endowment, responding to emerging and changing community needs and sustaining existing organizations through grants for education, arts and culture, health, social services, economic development, and civic affairs. The Foundation also manages a number of individual funds established by donors with specific philanthropic interests. Visitors to the Foundation's Web site will find general funding guidelines and restrictions, application instructions (including the common application form accepted by a number of area grantmakers), information for donors interested in establishing funds, and a staff listing. Visitors will also find a listing of grants, excerpts from the Annual Report and a full description of grantmaking focus and programs.

Omaha Community Foundation (http://www.omahacf.org/)

The Omaha Community Foundation was created to enhance the quality of life for the citizens of the Greater Omaha community by identifying and addressing current and anticipated community needs, as well as raising, managing, and distributing funds for charitable purposes in the areas of education, health, and civic, cultural, and social services. The Foundation's three primary grantmaking programs are the Fund for Omaha, Neighborhood Grants, and the Women's Fund Community Initiated Grants. Each program has a different process and timetable, though all limit their grants to organizations—not individuals—serving the Greater Omaha area. In addition to general information about the Foundation's grantmaking, visitors to the OCF Web site will find a Planned Giving Design Center with resources that can be used in matters of charitable gift and estate planning, an electronic publications request form, and staff contact information.

NEW JERSEY

Princeton Area Community Foundation
(http://www.princetonol.com/groups/pacf/)

The PACF was established in 1991 to bring the services of a community foundation to the greater Mercer County area. Today, the Foundation seeks "to enter into partnerships with non-profit organizations that are actively involved in developing their community," while supporting "groups working to coordinate resources and strengthen relationships between residents, businesses and institutions in a neighborhood." In addition to a brief history of the Foundation and information about the New Jersey AIDS Partnership, the PACF Web site provides application guidelines; a listing of the Foundation's various unrestricted, donor-advised, memorial, special use, and scholarship funds; grants lists; brief trustee and associate profiles; and information for prospective donors.

NEW MEXICO

Albuquerque Community Foundation (http://www.swcp.com/~albcfdn/)

The Albuquerque Community Foundation manages a pool of charitable funds whose income is used to benefit the greater Albuquerque, New Mexico, community through grants to nonprofit organizations, educational programs, and scholarships. The general policy of the Foundation is to allocate funds to nonprofits (including educational institutions) whose purpose and continuing work is in the areas of arts and culture, education, health and human services, and environmental and historic preservation. ACF's well-organized Web site provides information about its grant policies and restrictions, detailed proposal guidelines, a section for prospective donors, board and staff listings, useful links to regional and national nonprofit resources, and contact information.

New Mexico Community Foundation (http://www.nmcf.org/)

Established in 1983, the New Mexico Community Foundation supports residents of the state of New Mexico, primarily in rural areas. The Foundation's focus is on "entrepreneurial enterprises which address environmental, water-related, youth service or other community resource use issues," as well as technical assistance in the forms of organization and business development, marketing design, and financial management. The Foundation's informative Web site contains detailed application guidelines and contact information.

Santa Fe Community Foundation (http://www.santafecf.org/)

Founded in 1981, the Santa Fe Community Foundation serves the general area of Santa Fe, New Mexico. Although priority is placed on projects and programs in the Santa Fe area, proposals from Rio Arriba, Los Alamos, Taos, San Miguel, and Mora counties are also eligible. The Foundation's fields of interest include arts, civic affairs, education, environment, and health and human services; it also offers technical assistance grants and lesbian and gay initiative grants. The Foundation's Web site provides detailed grant guidelines, a calendar with proposal deadlines, and contact information.

NEW YORK

Community Foundation for the Capital Region (http://www.cfcr.org/)

The Community Foundation for the Capital Region was established in 1968 to serve residents of in the area of Albany, New York. The Foundation gives grants to nonprofits and scholarships to individuals. The Foundation is primarily interested in funding for health services and welfare, but other areas are not excluded. The Foundation's Web site includes detailed descriptions of its grantmaking activities, as well as thorough contact information and application guidelines.

Community Foundation of Greater Buffalo (http://www.cfgb.org)

The Community Foundation of Greater Buffalo serves the area of Western New York. The Foundation's areas of interest include education, humanities, civic needs, community development, health, environment, science, and social needs. The Foundation's Web site contains grant guidelines, contact information, and a staff listing.

Long Island Community Foundation (http://www.licf.org/)

Founded in 1978, the New York-based Long Island Community Foundation serves as the Long Island arm of The New York Community Trust for the citizens of Nassau and Suffolk Counties. The Foundation "prefers supporting efforts that: start, change, or accomplish something specific and concrete; solve problems rather than alleviate their symptoms; address the needs of people who are disadvantaged, economically or otherwise; address problems that have significance for large numbers of people; are undertaken by smaller organizations with limited access to other resources; use the resources of the community to accomplish self-sustaining change." In addition, the Foundation believes "that strong arts organizations form an integral part of healthy communities." Answers to frequently asked questions, detailed application guidelines, and contact information can be found at the Foundation's Web site.

Northern Chautauqua Community Foundation (http://fdncenter.org/grantmaker/nccf/index.html)

The mission of the Northern Chautauqua Community Foundation is to enrich the area it serves. To that end, the Foundation, which was established in 1986, has five primary goals: to be a catalyst for the establishment of endowments to benefit the community both now and in the future; to provide a vehicle for donors' varied interests; to promote local philanthropy; to serve as a steward of funds; and to provide leadership and resources in addressing local challenges and opportunities. The Foundation's "folder" on the Foundation Center's Web site provides lists of recent grants and scholarships awarded by the Foundation, brief descriptions of the many funds it administers, financial statements, a short section on "How to Become a Community Philanthropist," and a roster of the Foundation's board, staff, and members.

Rochester Area Community Foundation (http://www.racf.org/)

The Rochester Area Community Foundation manages more than 500 funds that provide grants for a wide variety of arts, education, social service, and other civic purposes in the Genesee Valley region of upstate New York. Visitors to the Foundation's Web site can get a good sense of RACF's services, including grant guidelines and applications, program information, scholarship information, and a calendar of events.

NORTH CAROLINA

Community Foundation of Greater Greensboro (http://www.cfgg.org/)

The Community Foundation of Greater Greensboro "promotes philanthropy, builds and maintains a permanent collection of endowment funds, and serves as a trustworthy partner and leader in shaping effective responses" to issues and opportunities in the Greater Greensboro, North Carolina, community. Geared more to potential donors than grantseekers, the Foundation's Web site provides general information about the various funds and endowments managed by CFGG, grants information organized by category (grants from unrestricted endowment funds, grants from special interest endowment funds, and permanent revolving loan funds), answers to frequently asked questions, general financial information, profiles of recent donors and grant recipients, listings of the Foundation's board and staff, and current and previous issues of Horizon, the Foundation's newsletter.

The Community Foundation of Western North Carolina (http://www.cfwnc.org/)

Established in 1978 to benefit 18 mountain counties, the Community Foundation of Western North Carolina comprises more than 400 charitable funds with combined assets of over $50 million. The Foundation currently makes grants to support activities benefiting the arts, education, the environment, human services, and civic improvements. Typically, grants are made for one-year projects or programs and fall into two categories: seed grants that help an organization provide a new level of service to the community, and "signature" grants that show potential for producing significant long-term benefits for western North Carolina. In addition to a good deal of information about the Foundation's programs and affiliates, including the Cashiers Community Fund, the Fund for Haywood County, the Highlands Community Foundation, the McDowell Foundation, the Rutherford County Foundation, the Transylvania County Endowment, and the Yancey Foundation, the Foundation's Web site provides detailed application guidelines and procedures, recent grants lists by category, information for donors, an online version of the Foundation's quarterly newsletter, a calendar of upcoming events, and contact information.

Foundation For The Carolinas (http://www.fftc.org/)
With assets in excess of $200 million and annual giving of $25 million, the 40-year-old Foundation For The Carolinas is the largest community foundation in the Carolinas. Building A Better Future, the Foundation's major grantmaking program, awards grants only to organizations located in or serving the greater Charlotte area. Other grant opportunities are available through affiliated community foundations serving the Lexington area and Blowing Rock, Cabarrus, Cleveland, Iredell, and Union counties in North Carolina, and Cherokee, Lancaster, and York counties in South Carolina. Specialized grants programs operated by FFTC include the Salisbury Community Foundation (Salibury and Rowan counties), the African American Community Endowment Fund (Charlotte-Mecklenburg and surrounding communities), the Cole Foundation Endowment (Richmond County area), HIV/AIDS Consortium Grants (13 Charlotte area counties), and the Medical Research Grants program (North and South Carolina). In addition to a good deal of information aimed at potential donors, the Foundation's Web site provides general program information, guidelines, and deadlines; listings of senior management and board members; an electronic form for requesting copies of the Foundation's publications; and contact information.

Triangle Community Foundation (http://www.trianglecf.org/)
The mission of the Triangle Community Foundation is to expand private philanthropy in the communities of the greater Triangle area, including Wake, Durham, and Orange Counties, North Carolina. The Foundation is comprised of more than 230 individual philanthropic funds with combined total assets currently exceeding $34 million. The Foundation also distributes discretionary monies for new initiatives or one-time special projects in cultural affairs and the arts, community development, education, environmental issues, health, social services, and other areas that benefit residents of the region. Visitors to the Foundation's Web site will find eligibility guidelines, application procedures, a grants list, and featured articles from its current newsletter. Visitors with Active-X enabled browsers can also download an application form in Microsoft Word format.

NORTH DAKOTA

Fargo-Moorehead Area Foundation (http://rrnet.com/~pepp1/fmat/index.html)
Established in 1960, the Fargo-Moorehead Area Foundation serves the residents of Fargo and Moorehead area of North Dakota. The Foundation's fields of interest include arts, culture, civic improvements, education, health, recreation, youth, and human service. Contact and application information can be found at the Foundation's Web site.

OHIO

Akron Community Foundation (http://www.ohio.com/nonprofit/acf/)
The ACF was established in 1955 to serve the communities of Summit County, Ohio through grantmaking in civic affairs, culture and the humanities, education, and health and human services. Today it comprises more than 150 charitable funds holding a combined $73 million in assets. A number of those funds, such as the Women's Endowment Fund and the Medina County Fund, have been created

to address the needs of distinct populations or a specific region. The former, ACF's first affiliated fund, focuses on creating opportunities to support the educational, physical, emotional, social, artistic, and personal growth of women and girls. The MCF, another affiliate fund, is laying the groundwork for the establishment of a Medina County community foundation in the future. In addition to an overview of the Foundation's activities, the ACF Web site provides application guidelines, answers to frequently asked questions, information about its donor services, press releases, a calendar of Foundation-sponsored events, links to sites of interest, and contact information.

The Cleveland Foundation (http://www.clevelandfoundation.org/)

The Cleveland Foundation, the nation's oldest community foundation, celebrated its 85th birthday in 1999. The Foundation gives grants in support of projects in greater Cleveland or that benefit greater Clevelanders directly in the following categories: arts and culture, education, education development, health, neighborhoods and housing, and social services. It does not give grants to individuals, nor does it give support for membership drives, most fundraising projects, travel, police and fire protection, government staff positions, publications or audiovisual programs (unless they're part of a larger project), most requests for buildings, land or equipment, or religious organizations for religious purposes. (It does support religious organizations' non-religious programs, such as hunger centers or job training or child care.) In addition to detailed program guidelines and application procedures, the CF Web site provides information for donors and a planned giving design center, an electronic publications order form, information about the Anisfield-Wolf Book Awards (which recognize books that address issues of racism or expand our appreciation for human diversity), a listing of the Foundation's board and executive staff, and contact information.

The Columbus Foundation (http://www.columbusfoundation.com/)

Established in 1943 under the guidance of Harrison M. Sayre, the Columbus Foundation today is one of the largest community foundations in the country. Dedicated to improving the lives of people in central Ohio, the Foundation addresses pressing needs in the community through grantmaking focused on four strategic areas: making sure that all children enter school physically, emotionally, and developmentally prepared to learn; helping youth make a positive transition to young adulthood; building the capacity of families to provide safe, nurturing, and economically secure living environments; and making neighborhoods positive environments for living. The Foundation also gives consideration to the following areas: arts and humanities, conservation, education, health, social services, urban affairs, and advancing philanthropy. In addition to general information about the Foundation, visitors to the Web site will find proposal guidelines and a PDF version of the Foundation's proposal cover sheet; information about the scholarship funds it administers as well as its grantmaking strategies; a range of downloadable trust forms; the results of a community foundation survey; and an online version of Commentary, the Foundation's newsletter.

Community Foundation of Greater Lorain County (http://www.cfglc.org/)

The Community Foundation of Greater Lorain County was established in 1980 to serve the residents of Lorain County, Ohio. Every year the Foundation gives numerous contributions to the community through many funds. The Foundation's areas of interest include arts and culture, civic affairs, education, health, and social services. Diversity grants are awarded through its African American Community Fund and Hispanic Fund. The Foundation also awards scholarships and tries to address "gaps in services" through funds for program development, capacity building, preventive endeavors, and "projects that enhance greater self-sufficiency" for individuals and organizations. Application forms can be downloaded from its Web site.

Dayton Foundation (http://www.daytonfoundation.org/)
Established in 1921, the Ohio-based Dayton Foundation is "a community foundation designed for permanence and for the benefit of the Dayton/Miami Valley region." The Foundation supports a wide range of interests. Its goal is to support projects "not addressed by existing organizations or to support special efforts of already-established nonprofit organizations in the Miami Valley." Grantseekers are encouraged to call for application guidelines; the telephone number is given at the Foundation's Web site.

The Jackson Community Foundation (http://www.jacksoncf.org/)
The Jackson Community Foundation was founded in 1948 for the purpose of assisting the residents of Jackson County, Ohio. The Foundation provides support to the programs and services of nonprofits in areas such as the arts, community development, education, health, and human services. It "serves as a convener of individuals and organizations for the purpose of identifying community-wide challenges and opportunities as well as the resources to address both." Application guidelines and contact information are available at the Foundation's Web site.

Parkersburg Area Community Foundation
(http://fdncenter.org/grantmaker/pacf/index.html)
The Parkersburg Area Community Foundation is committed to serving the people of the Mid-Ohio Valley—Wood, Pleasants, Tyler, Ritchie, Doddridge, Gilmer, Wirt, Calhoun, Roane, Jackson, and Mason Counties in West Virginia and Washington County in Ohio—linking community resources with community needs. PACF focuses its grantmaking in the following areas: arts and culture, education, health and human services, recreation, and youth and family services. To be eligible for a grant from the Foundation, an applicant must be a private, non-profit, tax-exempt organization under section 501(c)(3) of the Internal Revenue Code, or they must be a public institution. The Foundation also administers more than 40 different scholarship funds, the majority of which are designated for students in Wood County, West Virginia. The Foundation's "folder" on the Foundation Center's Web site provides general information about the Foundation, detailed application guidelines and scholarship information, and general information about becoming a donor to the Foundation.

OKLAHOMA

Oklahoma City Community Foundation, Inc.
(http://connections.oklahoman.net/commfound/)
Established in 1969, the Oklahoma City Community Foundation serves the area of Oklahoma City, Oklahoma. The Foundation's areas of interest include arts,

culture, education, rural development, and others. The Foundation's Web site provides answers to frequently asked questions, a board of trustees listing, contact information, and community program descriptions with a telephone number for requesting guidelines.

PENNSYLVANIA

Greater Harrisburg Foundation (http://www.tghf.org/)

Established in 1920 by Donald McCormick, the Greater Harrisburg Foundation serves the five-county area of Cumberland, Dauphin, Lebanon, Perry, and Franklin in South Central Pennsylvania. Field of interest funds held by the Foundation include funds that specify the arts, services for children, education, homelessness and hunger, health, the environment, dental care for the disadvantaged, head and spinal injury prevention, services to girls, mental health, mental retardation, and services for the needy, among others. The Foundation's Web site provides answers to frequently asked questions, information on regional foundations, grant guidelines, and contact information.

The Philadelphia Foundation (http://www.philafound.org)

The Philadelphia Foundation serves as a vehicle and resource for philanthropy in Bucks, Chester, Delaware, Montgomery, and Philadelphia counties. It does this by developing, managing, and allocating community resources in partnership with donors and grantees, by building on community assets, and by promoting empowerment, leadership, and civic participation among underserved groups. The Foundation makes grants from over 250 individually named charitable trust funds, with assets totaling approximately $120 million. Grant distributions are made according to the charitable interests and specifications of the individual fund donors, but the Foundation also identifies emerging needs in the community and sets policies and priorities for distributing unrestricted dollars in the areas of children and families; community organizing and advocacy; culture; education; health; housing and economic development; and social services. To be eligible for any funding through the Foundation, organizations must have 501(c)(3) tax exempt status and be based in one of the five counties of southeastern Pennsylvania. The Foundation's Web site offers application guidelines, detailed information about the various individual funds under the Foundation's auspices, the Foundation's financial management policies, and listings of recipient organizations, its Board of Managers, and staff. The Foundation's Web site also includes a "What's New?" section, which contains recent press releases, and a donor information section.

Three Rivers Community Fund (http://www.fex.org/three/threeriv.html)

The Three Rivers Community Fund helps the communities of Southwestern Pennsylvania. The Foundation "provides a funding base for the empowerment and self-determination of disenfranchised groups." The Foundation generally supports groups of smaller size, not supported by the government or other foundations. Grant guidelines, application information, and contact information can be found at the Foundation's Web site.

PUERTO RICO

Puerto Rico Community Foundation (http://www.fcpr.org/)

Through its support of self-directed development of Puerto Rican community groups, the Puerto Rico Community Foundation "seeks to contribute to the growth of a healthier community, [acting] as a catalytic agent in fostering new and innovative solutions to the Island's problems." Although the Foundation concentrates its efforts on the needs of Puerto Ricans on the island, it collaborates with Puerto Rican communities in the United States as well. Visitors to the Foundation's bilingual Web site will find descriptions of its various programs, including the General Fund, the Permanent Fund for the Arts, the Community Housing Development Organizations Program, the Middle School Renewal Initiative, and the Institute for the Development of Philanthropy; a listing of the Foundation's board of directors and staff; and links to other philanthropic resources and organizations of interest on the Web.

RHODE ISLAND

The Rhode Island Foundation (http://www.rifoundation.org/)

Established in 1916 with a gift of $10,000, the Providence-based Rhode Island Foundation has grown to become one of the largest community foundations in the United States, with an endowment of more than $300 million. The Foundation focuses its discretionary grantmaking in the areas of children and families, economic/community development, and education—although it views those designations more as starting points than as hard and fast categories with fixed parameters. In 1997, it made the largest grant in its history—and possibly the single largest grant ever made by a community foundation in the U.S.—for a "Teachers and Technology" pilot project designed to give substantial computer training to at least one teacher from every school in the state. Visitors to the Foundation's Web site will find a nice history of the Foundation, detailed program descriptions and recent grants in each program area, application guidelines and eligibility requirements, information for donors, a financial overview of the Foundation, listings of the board and staff, and contact information.

SOUTH CAROLINA

Foundation For The Carolinas (http://www.fftc.org/)

With assets in excess of $200 million and annual giving of approximately $25 million, the 40-year-old Foundation For The Carolinas is the largest community foundation in the Carolinas. Building A Better Future, the Foundation's major grantmaking program, awards grants only to organizations located in or serving the great Charlotte area. Other grant opportunities are available through affiliated community foundations serving the Lexington area and Blowing Rock, Cabarrus, Cleveland, Iredell, and Union counties in North Carolina, and Cherokee, Lancaster, and York counties in South Carolina. Specialized grants programs operated by FFTC include the Salisbury Community Foundation (Salibury and Rowan counties), the African American Community Endowment Fund (Charlotte-Mecklenburg and surrounding communities), the Cole Foundation Endowment (Richmond County area), HIV/AIDS Consortium Grants (13 Charlotte-area counties), and the Medical Research Grants program (North and South Carolina). In addition to a good deal of information aimed at potential donors, the Foundation's well-organized Web site provides general program information, guidelines, and deadlines; listings of senior management and board members; an electronic form for requesting copies of the Foundation's publications; and contact information.

TENNESSEE

Community Foundation of Greater Memphis (http://www.cfgm.org/)

The Community Foundation of Greater Memphis was established in 1969 to serve communities in Eastern Arkansas, Northern Mississippi, and Western Tennessee. The Foundation supports a wide variety of causes through several funds. Among those listed are: serving children with disabilities and visually impaired individuals, organizing children's summer camps, and providing humane contraception for animals. This list is not exhaustive. Contact information, application guidelines, and staff and board listings can be found at the Web site.

The Community Foundation of Middle Tennessee (http://www.cfmt.org/)

The Community Foundation of Middle Tennessee was created to enhance the quality of life in the 39 counties of Middle Tennessee. In order to serve this community, the Foundation has identified several broad categories in which needs exist and in which grant requests are encouraged. These categories include arts and humanities, civic affairs and community planning, conservation and environment, education, employment and training, health, historic preservation, housing and community development, and human services for citizens of all ages. The Foundation is particularly interested in ideas that shed new light on the needs and aspirations of Middle Tennesseans, with emphasis on providing long-term solutions. The Foundation does not award grants for fundraising events, annual campaigns, capital campaigns (unless there is compelling evidence that such support is vital to the success of a program), general operating funds (unless similar evidence is presented), individuals, private schools, religious/sectarian causes, private foundations, debt retirement or restructuring, fundraising feasibility studies, biomedical or clinical studies, lobbying or political activities, advertising, trips and/or conference attendance, or to organizations or for purposes outside its service area. The Foundation's Web site provides a considerable amount of information about the Foundation's various funds (e.g., discretionary, donor-advised, scholarship, etc.), grant application guidelines, financial policies, listings of its staff and board of directors, and contact information.

TEXAS

El Paso Community Foundation (http://www.epcf.org/)

The El Paso Community Foundation was created 20 years ago to address community challenges in the southwest Texas border region. Today, it awards funds twice a year (in May and November) to grant applicants from area nonprofit organizations or from community activist groups in the following areas of interest: arts and humanities, civic affairs/public benefit, environment/animal welfare, education, health and disabilities, and human services. Priority is given to: 1) more effective ways of doing things and ideas that require risk-taking; 2) projects where a moderate amount of grant money can have an impact; and 3) projects that show collaboration with other organizations. Generally speaking, the Foundation does not fund capital campaigns, fundraising events, projects of a religious nature, medical or academic research, annual appeals and membership contributions, organizations that are political or partisan in purpose, travel for individuals or groups, ongoing requests for general operating support, and requests from organizations outside the El Paso geographic area. Visitors to the EPCF Web site will find a rundown of the various funds under its management, detailed grant guidelines, features about local history grants lists, and contact information.

Kerrville Area Community Trust (http://www.kact.org/)
In operation since 1981, the Kerrville Area Community Trust is a collection of individual funds and resources given by local citizens and organizations to enhance and support the quality of life in the Kerrville, Texas, area. The KACT Web site provides detailed information on the Trust and the community trust concept; answers to frequently asked questions about the Trust; summary of KACT grants made since 1982; grant application guidelines, policies, deadlines, and a downloadable grant application form; information about established KACT funds; a list of KACT publications; and the Trust's regional calendar of events.

Lubbock Area Foundation, Inc. (http://www.lubbockareafoundation.org)
The Lubbock Area Foundation was created in 1981 to help Texas South Plains residents realize their long-term philanthropic goals. The Foundation manages a pool of charitable funds, the income from which is used to benefit the South Plains community through grants to 501(c)(3) nonprofit organizations, educational programs, and scholarships. Grants, the typical range for which is $500-$2,500, are made for start-up funding, general operating support, program support, and/or demonstration programs. The Foundation does not make grants to individuals, for political purposes, to retire indebtedness, or for payment of interest or taxes. The LAF Web site offers information for prospective donors and grantseekers, including funding priorities and application procedures; a list of endowed scholarship funds within LAF; general information about the Foundation's Mini-Grants for Teachers Program and its Funding Information Library (a Foundation Center Cooperating Collection); and contact information.

San Antonio Area Foundation (http://www.saafdn.org/)
The San Antonio Area Foundation was established in 1964 as a memorial to local community leader, visionary, and philanthropist Nat Goldsmith. Today it manages more than $83 million in assets distributed among 280 component funds and one support foundation. The Foundation does not state its areas of interest on its Web site, and only reviews proposals from applicants whose Letters of Intent—submission of which is the first step in the Foundation's grant application process—have been approved. In addition to a brief history of and general information about the Foundation, visitors to the SAAF Web site will find scholarship and grant application instructions, information for donors, and a listing of the Foundation's board of directors.

Waco Foundation, The (http://www.wacofdn.org/)

Established in 1958, the Foundation serves the residents of Waco and McLennan counties in Texas. Its fields of interest include childcare, medical facilities, education, art and culture. Through its Mac Grant Scholarship Fund, the Foundation helps local high school graduates attend a community college. Grant application forms and guidelines can be downloaded from the Foundation's Web site, which also provides contact information.

VERMONT

Vermont Community Foundation (http://www.vermontcf.org/)

The Vermont Community Foundation was established in 1986 to address the needs of Vermont now and in the future by building charitable capital and by providing services, resources, leadership, and encouragement to donors and to the nonprofit sector. In its role as a grantmaker, the Foundation will consider any project that meets a clearly defined community need in Vermont. Categories of support include, but are not limited to, the arts and humanities, education, the environment, historic resources, health, public affairs and community development, and social services. The Foundation emphasizes small (typically under $10,000) one-time grants rather than continuing support. It does not make grants for endowments, annual operating or capital campaigns, religious purposes, individuals, or equipment (unless it is an integral part of an otherwise eligible project). In addition to detailed grant guidelines, lists of recent grants, information for potential donors, and a list of links to related resources, the VCF site provides general information about the Vermont Women's Fund and various TAP-VT technical assistance programs.

VIRGINIA

The Virginia Beach Foundation
(http://fdncenter.org/grantmaker/vbf/index.html)

The Virginia Beach Foundation is a community foundation serving the people of Virginia Beach and their neighbors. Founded in 1987, The Virginia Beach Foundation's mission is to stimulate the establishment of endowments to serve the people of Virginia Beach now and in the future; respond to changing, emerging community needs; assist donors in achieving their charitable giving objectives; and serve as a resource, broker, catalyst and leader in the community. At the site you will find a history of the Foundation, frequently asked questions, words from Foundation supporters and grantees, and donor information.

WASHINGTON

The Seattle Foundation (http://www.seattlefoundation.org/)

Established in 1946, the Seattle Foundation today works to improve the quality of life for people in the Puget Sound region by nurturing a greater sense of community in the region and serving as a catalyst for dialogue within the area's nonprofit community. The Foundation manages an endowment of more than $190 million. Grants are awarded quarterly to organizations in the areas of arts, culture, and the humanities; health; human services; the environment; and public/society benefit.

All applicant organizations must qualify as tax-exempt under 501(c)(3) of the IRS Code and be located primarily in King County. Visitors to the Seattle Foundation Web site will find general information about the Foundation and its activities, PDF versions of the Foundation's discretionary grant guidelines and an annual report, an electronic form for requesting other Foundation publications, information for potential donors, and contact information.

WEST VIRGINIA

Parkersburg Area Community Foundation
(http://fdncenter.org/grantmaker/pacf/index.html)
The Parkersburg Area Community Foundation is committed to serving the people of the Mid-Ohio Valley—Wood, Pleasants, Tyler, Ritchie, Doddridge, Gilmer, Wirt, Calhoun, Roane, Jackson, and Mason Counties in West Virginia and Washington County in Ohio—by linking community resources with community needs. PACF focuses its grantmaking in the following areas: arts and culture, education, health and human services, recreation, and youth and family services. To be eligible for a grant from the Foundation, an applicant must be a private, nonprofit, tax-exempt organization under section 501(c)(3) of the Internal Revenue Code, or they must be a public institution. The Foundation also administers more than 40 different scholarship funds, the majority of which are designated for students in Wood County, West Virginia. The Foundation's "folder" on the Foundation Center's Web site provides general information about the Foundation, detailed application guidelines and scholarship information, and general information about becoming a donor to the Foundation.

WISCONSIN

Milwaukee Foundation (http://www.milwaukeefoundation.org/)
Established in 1915, making it one of the first community foundations in the U.S., the Milwaukee Foundation today comprises nearly 550 individual funds with a combined $275 million in assets. The Foundation makes grants in six areas—arts and culture, education, employment and training, health and human services, community economic development, and conservation and historic preservation—and limits its grantmaking "to projects that offer a significant improvement" to the lives of the people living in Milwaukee, Waukesha, Ozaukee, and Washington counties. Grants made outside this area are based upon donor recommendations. Detailed criteria in each of these funding areas are available from the Foundation upon request. In addition to general information and a history of the Foundation, visitors to the Web site will find application procedures, examples of recent grants, a variety of information for prospective donors, an electronic form for requesting guidelines and the Foundation's annual report, and contact information.

St. Croix Valley Community Foundation (http://www.pressenter.com/~scvcf/)
Founded in 1995, the St. Croix Valley Community Foundation serves the communities of St. Croix Valley in Wisconsin and Minnesota. Its fields of interest include education, arts, environment, civic affairs and emergency human needs. The Foundation's Web site includes its annual report, board and staff lists, and a form to request more information.

WYOMING

Community Foundation of Jackson Hole
(http://www.jacksonholenet.com/CFJH/)

The Community Foundation of Jackson Hole is committed to "enhance[ing] philanthropy and strengthen[ing] the sense of community in the Jackson Hole [Wyoming] area [by providing] a permanent source of funding and other support for non-profit organizations and scholarship recipients." The Foundation assists donors in maximizing the impact of their charitable giving; manages permanent endowments in response to donors' wishes; provides and monitors competitive grants; and holds workshops for local nonprofit organizations. The Foundation's Web site provides comprehensive listings (alphabetically and by subject category) of Jackson Hole-area charitable organizations, the Foundation's annual report, and contact information for grantmaking guidelines and application forms.

Links and Abstracts of Web Sites of Other Grantmaking Public Charities

The Foundation Center continually strives to identify and describe other public charities that operate grantmaking programs along with their other activites. Be sure to check the "Grantmaker Information" area of our Web site at fdncenter.org for the latest listings.

The Abraham Fund (http://www.coexistence.org/)

The Abraham Fund promotes constructive coexistence between Jews and Arabs within Israeli society. Named for Abraham, the common ancestor of Jews and Arabs, the Fund was founded in 1989 as a funding source for programs—cultural, educational, health related, recreational, and vocational—aimed at developing coexistence opportunities. Visitors to the Fund's Web site will find a description of the Fund and its activities, a listing of coexistence projects (grants summary and list), newsletter excerpts, a message from the chairman, contact information for the Fund in the U.S. and Israel, links to related Web sites, and a quiz.

Academy of American Poets (http://www.poets.org/)

The academy provides support to American poets at all stages of their careers, and seeks to foster the appreciation of contemporary poetry. It is the largest poetry organization in the U.S. and it sponsors several national programs, including the administration of several poetry awards, prizes, and readings. Its Web site includes a feature on National Poetry Month, tips on getting published, and RealAudio spoken poetry files, in addition to information about the Academy, its programs, board members, and membership options.

Aid to Artisans (http://www.aid2artisans.org/)

Aid to Artisans, a nonprofit organization founded in 1976 to create economic opportunities for craftspeople around the world, offers design consultation, on-site workshops, business training, and links to markets where craft products are sold. Every year it awards 30–40 grants, ranging from $500 to $1,500 to emerging artisans and craft-based associations worldwide. Grant application information is located in the "Description of Services" directory. The ATA site also offers information about ATA's direct service programs, a bulletin board of events, a description of its work and projects, and listings of its officers, directors, and staff.

Alabama Law Foundation (http://www.alabar.org/allaw/alfstup.html)

The Alabama Law Foundation was established in 1987 to be the recipient of funds generated by the Interest on Lawyers' Trust Accounts (IOLTA) program. The Foundation distributes IOLTA grants each March in support of legal aid to the poor, to help maintain public law libraries, and to provide law-related education to the public. It also administers the Cabaniss Johnston Scholarship Fund and the Kids' Chance Scholarship Fund. The Foundation's Web site offers brief descriptions of its creation and programs.

Alaska Humanities Forum (http://www.akhf.org/)

The Alaska Humanities Forum seeks to enrich the civic, intellectual, and cultural lives of Alaskans through the humanities. The AHF grant program funds a variety of innovative humanities-based projects, including publications, films, lectures, exhibits, conferences, scholarly research, and public discussions. The Forum's Web site provides information about AHF's activities, along with grant guidelines and application forms in PDF format, a listing of grant recipients, and a collection of links to related resources on the Web.

Alzheimer's Association (http://www.alz.org/)

The Alzheimer's Association, which has more than 200 local chapters across the U.S., works to eliminate Alzheimer's disease through the advancement of research, and to enhance care and support services for individuals and their families. The "Progress" area of the Association's Web site outlines its research grants and conference grants programs, lists past grant recipients by year and state, and provides contact information for interested grantseekers. The Association's grants activities are administered by the Ronald and Nancy Reagan Research Institute established by President Reagan and his wife in 1995. The remainder of the Association's site is devoted to news, as well as facts, care, and medical issues of Alzheimer's disease.

American Association of School Administrators (http://www.aasa.org/index.htm)

The American Association of School Administrators, an international professional organization for educational leaders, focuses on preparing schools and school systems for the 21st century, on connecting schools and communities, and on enhancing the quality and effectiveness of school leaders. AASA offers numerous awards and scholarships, which are listed and described in various degrees of detail in the "Awards and Scholarships" area of the AASA Web site. The organization also operates two programs (Healthy School Environments, and School Health), and provides general descriptions of and contact information for each program on its site.

American Association of University Women (http://www.aauw.org/)

The American Association of University Women promotes education and equity for women and girls through a membership organization, the AAUW Educational Foundation, and the AAUW Legal Advocacy Fund. The Education Foundation funds research on girls and education, community action projects, and fellowships and grants for outstanding women around the globe. The Legal Fund provides funds and a support system for women seeking judicial redress for sex discrimination in higher education. AAUW's Web site clearly describes the organization's fellowships, grants, and awards and provides application instructions for each category. Visitors to the site will also find membership information, AAUW research, a detailed overview of public policy issues of concern to organization members, a call for papers, and contact information.

American Bar Foundation (http://www.abf-sociolegal.org/)

The Chicago-based American Bar Foundation supports basic empirical research into the theory and functioning of the law, legal institutions, and the legal profession. The Foundation sponsors in-residence fellowship programs for postdoctoral scholars, doctoral candidates, and minority undergraduate students. The Foundation's Web site outlines each of these programs in detail and provides a downloadable application form. The site also provides an overview of current areas of research, information for prospective donors, online versions of recent annual reports, and a directory of staff members with e-mail links.

American Cancer Society (http://www.cancer.org/research/index.html)

Since 1946 the United States has committed more than $2 billion to finding a cure for cancer. The American Cancer Society, the largest non-government funder of cancer research in the U.S. offers a variety of research grants, training grants for health professionals, fellowships, and a clinical research professorship. Detailed information on its programs, including application forms in multiple formats for downloading, is provided in the "Research" area of the ACS Web site. Visitors to the site will also find a listing (including e-mail addresses) of the extramural grants administrative staff, histories of funding by research area and by state, and a Cancer Resource Center, with information about different cancers and cancer treatments, statistics, alternative therapies, and a comprehensive set of links to related resources.

American Council of Learned Societies (http://www.acls.org/jshome.htm)

The ACLS is a federation of 61 national scholarly organizations that seeks to "advance humanistic studies in all fields of learning in the humanities and the related social sciences and to maintain and strengthen relations among the national societies devoted to such studies." ACLS administers several grant and fellowship programs, which are explained in detail at its Web site. Visitors to the site can also request, through an electronic order form, a brochure on the current year's competitions and will find, in addition, information about ACLS affiliates and publications and a nice list of links to funding, research, and institutional resources.

American Digestive Health Foundation (http://www.gastro.org/adhf.html)

The American Digestive Health Foundation was founded in 1994 to improve digestive health through financial support of scientific research, medical education, and consumer awareness. The Foundation funds many awards to individuals—all levels of students and established investigators—for research into gastroenterology and hepatology. The Foundation's Web site provides a searchable, online version of its current Research Awards Book, which includes application forms to print and mail, as well as information on industry scholar awards, and the Foundation's research funding newsletter, *Research In Focus.* The Foundation's Web site also offers information on digestive health, news, and its annual report.

American Federation for Aging Research (http://www.afar.org/)

Founded in 1981, the American Federation for Aging Research helps scientists launch and further their careers in aging research and geriatric medicine in order to promote healthier aging. To achieve its goal, AFAR administers eight grant programs a year: AFAR Research Grants; the AFAR/Pfizer Research Grants in Cardiovascular Disease and Aging Program; the Paul Beeson Physician Faculty Scholars in Aging Research Program; the Merck/AFAR Fellowships in Geriatric Clinical Pharmacology; the John A. Hartford Foundation/AFAR Medical Student Geriatric Scholars Program; the Glenn/AFAR Scholarships for Research in the Biology of Aging; the Merck/AFAR Research Scholarships for Medical and Pharmacy Students in Geriatric Pharmacology; and the John A. Hartford Foundation/ AFAR Geriatrics Centers of Excellence Program. The site describes these programs in details and provides an interactive form for requesting application forms. Visitors to the site will also find donor information, meetings and conference information, an electronic form for requesting publications, and a listing of AFAR's board members.

American Federation of Riders (http://www2.eos.net/jjseta/afr.html)

The American Federation of Riders, founded in 1982 and based in Cincinnati, Ohio, is a federation of motorcyclists dedicated to helping needy, orphaned, handicapped, abused, and/or neglected children, which it does through support of individual children and organizations. AFR has provided trust funds for orphaned children, medical grants to families, Christmas gifts and meals, and recently started a scholarship fund for college-bound high-school seniors. AFR's Web site describes its support in general terms, gives a history of the organization, and provides contact information.

American Floral Endowment (http://www.endowment.org/)

The American Floral Endowment funds research and educational development in floriculture and provides development funding for the advancement of the floral industry. The Endowment's research funding is focused on Thrips (TSWV/INSV control systems), post-harvest systems for fresh cut flowers, air/soil borne disease control systems for potted plants, and development of production protocols for Minor crops, potted plants, cut flowers, and bedding plants. The Foundation also offers scholarships and paid internships to horticulture students. Information about all funding programs, including some offered by related organizations, is provided at the Endowment's Web site, along with applications for downloading. The site also lists funded programs going back to 1991, the names of proposal reviewers, news, and donor information.

American Foundation for AIDS Research (http://www.amfar.org/)

The American Foundation for AIDS Research works to prevent death and disease associated with HIV/AIDS and to foster sound AIDS-related public policies—a goal it seeks to achieve through support of scientific and social research, advocacy, and public information programs. Requests for proposals are posted at AmFAR's Web site, along with contact information for its grant programs.

Visitors to the site will also find press releases, a publications catalog, information about upcoming events and conferences, and donor information.

American Health Assistance Foundation (http://www.ahaf.org)

The Foundation supports basic research grants on the causes of or treatments for degenerative diseases of aging for University of Florida personnel. The Foundation's Web site includes specific information on its research and grant programs, an application request form for the Alzheimer's Family Relief Program, and donor information.

American Heart Association (http://www.americanheart.org/catalog/Scientific_catpage69.html)

The American Heart Association provides education and information on heart disease and stroke, and supports scientific research that will help fight these life-threatening medical conditions. The AHA offers numerous national and regional-affiliate research programs. The "Science and Professionals" area of its Web site provides guidelines for all research programs and the application form for the national programs, which can be downloaded and/or submitted electronically. This large Web site provides a great deal of educational and scientific information on heart disease, links to AFA affiliates and other resources, online advocacy, and donor and volunteer information.

American Hotel Foundation (http://www.ei-ahma.org/ahf/ahf.htm)

The American Hotel Foundation serves the lodging industry by providing resources for projects that assure continued growth and opportunities for the industry. The Foundation awards scholarships to students pursuing an undergraduate degree in hospitality management and awards grants for research that will benefit the industry. The Foundation's scholarship programs are outlined at its Web site; however, scholarship recipients are selected by schools, not by the Foundation. The Foundation's research is described only briefly, but contact information is provided.

American Physicians Fellowship for Medicine in Israel (http://www.apfmed.org/)

The American Physicians Fellowship for Medicine in Israel, established in 1950, is an organization of North American physicians and others dedicated to advancing the state of medical education, research, and care in Israel. The core of APF's funding is a fellowship program for Israeli physicians training in the U.S. and Canada—40 physicians currently receive APF fellowship support. In recent years, APF has expanded its support to include various awards and programs benefiting the medical community in Israel. Funding areas include research projects, a trauma program, training for Russian immigrant physicians and pathology technicians, the Solomon Hirsh Nurse Fund, and programs focused on women's health, Jewish genetic diseases, and geriatric medicine. APF's Web site describes its programs and provides contacts for requesting more information. The site also provides information on recent APF fellows, news, donor and membership information, a discussion forum, and a listing of staff and board members.

American Psychological Foundation (http://www.apa.org/apf/)
The American Psychological Foundation, based in Washington, D.C., works to advance psychology as a science, a profession, and a means of promoting human welfare, which it achieves through support of research and education. APF's Web site has information on funding programs for students, education programs, scientific research, and minority fellowship programs. These are most easily located by going to the "Site Map" and following the links in the "General Information" area. APF's site lists its own funding and programs from other sources; most listings are fairly detailed and some provide application forms. Visitors to the site will also find publications, a members-only area, membership and employment information, news, and contact information by department.

American Society of Consultant Pharmacists Research and Education Foundation (http://www.ascpfoundation.org/)
The Foundation is the research and education affiliate of the American Society of Consultant Pharmacists. Its mission is to fund, coordinate, and conduct educational programs and research. The unique focus of the Foundation is the integration and application of knowledge regarding drug use in the elderly and the practice of long-term care and consultant pharmacy to optimize health care outcomes. The Foundation's areas of interest include geriatrics, the elderly, medications, drug therapy, long-term care, and pharmacy. Press releases, articles about consultant pharmacy, and information on the Foundation's grant and traineeship programs are available on their Web site.

Aplastic Anemia Foundation of America (http://www.aplastic.org/)
The Aplastic Anemia Foundation of America works to find the causes of and cures for aplastic anemia, myelodysplastic syndromes, and other kinds of bone marrow failure. To this end, the Foundation funds scientific research into these conditions. A brief description of its Research Awards program is provided at AAFA's Web site with contact information for requesting an application packet. The site also offers a newsletter, donor information, and related Web links.

Appalachian Community Fund (http://www.fex.org/applach/acfdesc.html)
The fund supports progressive community change in the central Appalachian states. Conceived as a unique partnership of community activists and donors, it works to build a new source of capital for community-based groups and to leverage money and resources to the region. The focus of grantmaking is social change, which is defined as working to redistribute wealth, power, and resources, and to eliminate barriers that keep people from participating fully in society. Social change also means focusing efforts on changing the circumstances and the social institutional systems that create barriers and inequities. Although this Web site was recently under construction, donor information, application guidelines, and a grantee list were already available.

Archstone Foundation (http://www2.archstone.com/Archstone/)
Established in 1985 as the FHP Foundation and renamed in 1996, the Archstone Foundation has refocused its grantmaking activities on "contribut[ing] toward the preparation of society in meeting the needs of an aging population." The Foundation's funding priorities for the immediate future include addressing the needs of caregivers of the elderly, end-of-life issues, and direct delivery of services to non-

institutionalized seniors, with an emphasis on Southern California. The Foundation's Web site offers general statements about its funding priorities and restrictions, application procedures, an "Announcements" area, a list of Foundation-sponsored publications, and contact information.

Arizona Humanities Council (http://www.azhumanities.org)

The Arizona Humanities Council, founded in 1973 as the state affiliate of the National Endowment for the Humanities, directs and supports programs that promote understanding of human thoughts, actions, creations, and values. AHC provides support in four program areas: heritage, books and reading, community dialogue, and teacher education. In addition to its Competitive Grants Program, AHC awards General Grants, Proposal Development Grants, Resource Center Grants, and Book Bucks. The programs are described at AHC's Web site with contacts for requesting application instructions. AHC's site also a list of Arizona humanities scholars, news, a calendar, resources, and donor information.

Arkansas Humanities Council (http://www.arkhums.org/)

The Arkansas Humanities Council, established in 1974 as the state affiliate of the National Endowment for the Humanities, promotes understanding, appreciation, and use of the humanities in Arkansas. To achieve its goal, the Council awards grants to groups and organizations to plan, conduct, and evaluate projects in the humanities. Funding is provided for public programs, research, publications, media projects, and planning, as well as occasional matching grants. Thorough guidelines are provided at the Council's Web site; however, prospective applicants are encouraged to consult with council program staff before submitting grant applications. Visitors to the site will also contains find descriptions of materials held in the Council's Resource Center.

Arthritis Foundation (http://www.arthritis.org/research/rga/)

The Arthritis Foundation, which was organized in 1948 as the Arthritis and Rheumatism Foundation until its name was changed in 1964, generated initial research into arthritis and now supports research to help find causes, treatments, and ways to prevent and cure the condition. The grants, training awards, and career development awards provided by the Foundation are detailed at its Web site with an application form to download (in PDF format). The "Research" area of the Foundation's Web site also provides information on its peer review process, "Study Section" members (grant application reviewers), and the Lee C. Howley Sr. Prize for Research in Arthritis—awarded for excellence in research.

Arthritis National Research Foundation (http://www.curearthritis.org/)

The Arthritis National Research Foundation, located in Long Beach, California, provides financial support to research studies aimed at discovering new knowledge for the prevention, treatment and cure of arthritis and other rheumatic diseases. The Foundation awards grants to fund salaries, supplies, and equipment directly related to research studies in the range of $20,000 to $50,000. Grant application instructions and a description of current research are available at the Foundation's Web site, along with donor information, an online newsletter, links to related Web sites, and an interactive form for contacting the Foundation.

Arts Council of Greater Kalamazoo (http://www.kazooart.org/)

The Arts Council of Greater Kalamazoo, founded in 1969, supports the arts in Kalamazoo County, Michigan. Funds are granted on the basis of high artistic quality and merit to artists and organizations in the region. The Council's Web site offers a list of grant programs and provides more detailed arts funding information in its *ACGK News* newsletter—available in HTML or PDF formats. Visitors to the site will also find membership information, press releases, events, information on Council activities, an artists registry, and contact information.

Arts Council of Northwest Florida (http://www.artsnwfl.org/)

The Arts Council of Northwest Florida supports quality, diversity, and economic growth in the region's cultural community. The Council awards grants to organizations to improve, extend, preserve, create, and plan cultural programs. Grant guidelines, the application form, and a grants calendar are available for download from the Council's Web site in Rich Text and Microsoft Word formats. The site also provides information on the Council's activities and programs, links to Northwest Florida cultural institutions, news articles, and donor information.

Arts Midwest (http://www.artsmidwest.org/)

Formed in 1985 through the merger of two organizations, the Affiliated State Arts Agencies of the Upper Midwest and the Great Lakes Arts Alliance, Arts Midwest provides funding, training, publications, information services, and conferences to arts and cultural organizations, artists, art administrators, and art enthusiasts in Illinois, Indiana, Iowa, Michigan, Minnesota, North Dakota, Ohio, South Dakota, and Wisconsin. Since its inception, the organization has distributed almost $8 million to artists and arts organizations through a variety of funding and training programs. At present, it manages several funding programs: The Heartland Arts Fund, Meet the Composer/Midwest, Jazz Satellite Touring Fund, and the Jazz Master Awards. The latter serves individual artists in Arts Midwest's nine-state region. The other programs assist presenters in the region in bringing Midwestern artists as well as national artists to their communities. Visitors to the AM Web site will find a variety of program, application, conference, and publication information.

ArtServe Michigan (http://artservemichigan.org/index2.html)

The organization serves, supports, and advocates for an enriched cultural environment, and promotes the arts as a valuable state and community resource. It assists and informs individuals and organizations in the state of Michigan through education, professional services, networking, support of artists and cultural organizations, volunteer assistance, and collaborations. Its Web site includes information on grants and awards for individual artists, a listing of the Board of Directors, news about arts advocacy, and more.

The Asia Foundation (http://www.asiafoundation.com/)

The Asia Foundation is a private, nonprofit, nongovernmental organization working to build leadership, improve policies, and strengthen institutions to foster greater openness and shared prosperity in the Asia-Pacific region. The Foundation currently has program priorities in four areas: Governance and Law, Regional Relations, Women's Political Participation, and Economic Reform and Development. Visitors to the Foundation's Web site will find detailed information on the

Foundation's programs in Bangladesh, Cambodia, China, Indonesia, Japan, Korean Peninsula, Malaysia, Mongolia, Nepal, Pakistan, Philippines, Sri Lanka, Taiwan, Thailand, and Vietnam; as well as its U.S.-administered programs, which are the Asian-American Exchange, Books for Asia, NGO-Business Environmental Partnerships, Luce Program, and the Washington D.C. Program. The Web site provides contact information, including e-mail addresses for representatives in each country and the U.S.; lists of trustees, officers, and senior staff in the U.S.; and Web resources in Asia.

The Asia Society (http://www.asiasociety.org/)

The Asia Society, founded in 1956 by John D. Rockefeller 3rd, is dedicated to fostering an understanding of Asia and communication between Americans and the peoples of Asia and the Pacific. Headquartered in New York City, the Asia Society has a presence in Hong Kong, Houston, Los Angeles, Melbourne, and Washington, D.C., Seattle, and Shanghai. The Asia Society's Web site provides a great deal of information on its programs, although much of it pertains to its operations. Some funding opportunities, with applications, can be found in the "Education" area of the Web site. This large site also provides information on the Society's many activities, its network, publications, press releases, regional centers, and membership information.

Astraea National Lesbian Action Foundation (http://www.astraea.org/)

The Astraea National Lesbian Action Foundation, established in 1977, provides financial support for organizations and projects that are lesbian led or focused and works to promote the economic, political, educational, and cultural well-being of lesbians. Grant guidelines can be found at the following link: http://www.astraea.org/grants. Visitors to the site will also find membership and volunteer information, events, news, and contact information.

Atlas Economic Research Foundation (http://www.atlas-fdn.org/)

The Atlas Economic Research Foundation, incorporated in 1981, helps to create, develop, advise, and support independent public policy research institutes by providing "intellectual entrepreneurs" with advice, financial support, workshops, and access to a network of leaders who share a commitment to achieving a free society. The Foundation's Sir Antony Fisher International Memorial Awards for Public Policy Institutes recognizes institutes that combine the talents of the academic and the entrepreneur. Application information is provided at the Foundation's Web site, along with lists of previous winners going back to 1990. The site also provides best practices "Nuts & Bolts" for independent public policy institutes, a virtual phone book, and upcoming conference information.

Averitt Express Associates Charities
(http://www.averittexpress.com/aecares.htm)

Averitt Express, a delivery service located in Cookeville, Tennessee, supports local and national health care organizations and charities. The "Averitt Cares" area of the company's Web site provides details of recent contributions and a list of giving since 1987. Contact information is provided.

Barberton Community Foundation (http://www.bcfcharity.org)
The Foundation supports projects that benefit the citizens of Barberton, Ohio by prudently managing their funds and spending the investment income for charitable endeavors, education, public health, public recreation and to lessen the burden of government. Visitors to their site will find grant and scholarship information, donor opportunities, and links to Barberton, Ohio area events and Web sites.

Mary Black Foundation, Inc. (http://www.upstate.net/mbf/)
The Foundation seeks to benefit and enhance the health status and wellness of citizens of Spartanburg County, South Carolina. Grants may support activities such as policy analysis, research and the dissemination of data; the development of pilot or model programs; and the promotion of public understanding of key issues relating to the community's well-being. The Foundation's Web site includes grants lists, application guidelines, program information, and a listing of the board of trustees and staff.

Blue Cross Blue Shield of Michigan Foundation
(http://www.bcbsm.com/foundation.shtml)
The BCBSM Foundation seeks to improve health care in Michigan by "enhancing the quality and appropriate use of health care; improving access to appropriate health services; and controlling health care costs." Its grant programs support research and community health care solutions, acknowledge excellence in research, and support medical education. The Foundation area of the BCBSM Web site provides clear and concise information on the Foundation's primary funding programs, including its Proposal Development Award, Matching Initiative Program, Physician-Investigator Research Award, Student Award Program, Request for Proposal Program, Excellence in Research Awards, and Investigator-Initiated Program. Applications for the above programs are available at the site in PDF format. The site also provides e-mail contact to program administrators, a select list of links, and an online version of the Foundation's most recent annual report.

Boston Adult Literacy Fund (http://www.tiac.org/users/balf/home.htm)
The Boston Adult Literacy Fund was founded in 1988 to provide access to basic education for adults in the Boston metro area and to raise awareness of the need for basic education and literacy. Grants are awarded to community-based literacy programs (ABE—Adult Basic Education, ESL—English as a Second Language, and high school credential programs—either GED or EDP). The Fund also awards scholarships to adults who have completed their basic education and wish to continue on to higher education or vocational training. In addition to descriptions of its programs, the BALF Web site provides a list of recent grant recipients, links to literacy-related Web sites, and contact information.

Bread and Roses Community Fund (http://www.fex.org/bread/bread.html)
Grants are provided to community-based social change organizations and projects. The Fund defines social change as working to redistribute wealth, power, and resources and to eliminate the barriers that keep people from participating fully in society. Priority is given to small groups that do not have access to traditional funding sources. Donor information, application guidelines, staff names, and application forms are among the offerings of this Web site.

Broadway Cares/Equity Fights AIDS (http://www.bcefa.org/)

Founded in 1988, Broadway Cares/Equity Fights AIDS leverages the talents and resources of the American theater community to raise funds for AIDS-related causes in the United States. BC/EFA also awards grants, usually in January and September, for direct care and/or services to people with HIV/AIDS. Projects funded in the past have provided meals, shelter, transportation, emergency financial aid, emotional/practical support, and/or payment of non-reimbursable medical expenses. Information on BC/EFA's grants program can be requested by telephone or e-mail. In addition to information on its activities, the BC/EFA Web site provides a listing of its affiliates, links to Web resources, a password-protected electronic callboard, and an e-mail list for receiving information and updates.

Bronx Council on the Arts (http://www.bronxarts.org/bronxhome.html)

The Bronx Council on the Arts serves the New York City borough of the Bronx by developing programs that provide for public participation in the arts, nurture arts organizations' development, publicize and promote the arts, and generate financial support and new initiatives. The Council offers several types of grants, all of which are described on the Council's Web site. The Community Arts Grants guidelines and application forms can be downloaded (in PDF format); however, grantseekers must contact the Council's Arts Services department for more information on the other programs. The site also outlines its arts activities, and provides membership, funding, staff, and contact information.

Brother's Brother Foundation (http://www.brothersbrother.com)

The Foundation promotes international health and education through the efficient and effective distribution and provision of donated medical, educational, agricultural, and other resources. Their Web site includes information about the Foundation's founder, Robert Andrew Hingson, newsletters, application forms, program information, volunteer opportunities, and information of specific relief efforts.

Nicole Brown Charitable Foundation (http://www.nbcf.org/)

The Nicole Brown Charitable Foundation, formerly the Nicole Brown Simpson Foundation and based in California, helps to fund organizations that protect families from domestic violence and offer long-term solutions for those affected by it. The Foundation's Web site lists donor and volunteer information, news, Web resources, and a listing of shelters.

California Council for the Humanities (http://www.calhum.org/)

The California Council for the Humanities is a non-governmental affiliate of the National Endowment for the Humanities, which looks for ways to make the knowledge and insights of the humanities available to all Californians. The CCH Web site offers two options for joining in humanities discussions—a "Citizenship, Culture, and the Humanities" e-mail discussion list and a Web-based "Humanities Forum"—as well as a calendar-style listing of programs funded by grants from CCH.

California HealthCare Foundation (http://www.chcf.org/)

The California HealthCare Foundation was established in May 1996 as a result of the conversion of Blue Cross of California from a nonprofit health plan to WellPoint Health Networks, a for-profit corporation. The Foundation is one of two philanthropies created by the conversion—the other is the California Endowment—and is charged with responsibility for gradually divesting the Foundation of WellPoint stock and transferring 80 percent of the proceeds to the Endowment, and for developing the Foundation's own independent grantmaking program with the remaining 20 percent of the funds. The Foundation's grantmaking is statewide and focuses initially on five program areas: managed care and special populations, California's uninsured, California health policy, health care quality, and public health. CHCF's well-organized Web site provides general program information, grant guidelines and limitations, a list of recent grants, RFPs (in MS Word and PDF format), an electronic form for ordering Foundation publications, a comprehensive set of links to health-related Web sites, a message from Foundation president Mark D. Smith, listings of the board and staff, and contact information.

Cancer Care, Inc. (http://www.cancercare.org/)
The organization helps cancer patients and their loved ones cope with the impact of cancer. Services which are provided include counseling for cancer patients and their loved ones; limited financial assistance to residents of New York, New Jersey, and Connecticut to help families with costs of home care, child care, and transportation for treatment; outreach; information and referral to home and child care services, hospices, hospitals, and other community resources; teleconference workshops; volunteer visitors to assist homebound patients and caregivers; and educational workshops. The Web site includes details about these and other services, a full annual report, and information about how to contribute.

Cancer Research Foundation of American (http://www.preventcancer.org/)
The Cancer Research Foundation of America, founded in 1985, supports education and research to help prevent cancer. Since its inception, the Foundation has funded more than 200 scientists at leading medical centers, recognizing scientific excellence, new and innovative projects, and young scientists interested in cancer prevention research. The Foundation's grant review process is approved by the National Institutes of Health. Grant and fellowship details, past recipients, and application forms to download (PDF format) or print from the browser are available in the "Prevention Science and Research" directory of the Foundation's Web site. The site also provides facts on preventing cancer, information on education programs, online versions of publications, and links to cancer resources on the Web.

Cancer Research Fund of the Damon Runyon-Walter Winchell Foundation (http://www.cancerresearchfund.org/)
The Cancer Research Fund was established in 1954 by radio personality Walter Winchell after his friend, journalist Damon Runyon, died from cancer. Winchell believed that "young scientists following their own best instincts would make the critical discoveries leading to the defeat of cancer." Following this belief, the Fund grants post-doctoral fellowships and scholar awards for biomedical scientists. The Fund's Web site provides detailed guidelines and application forms to view and print for both programs. The site also provides donor information and a "Scientist Spotlight."

Catholic Campaign for Human Development
(http://www.nccbuscc.org/cchd/index.htm)
Established in 1969 by the National Conference of Catholic Bishops, the Catholic Campaign for Human Development works to empower the poor and encourage their participation in the decisions and actions that affect their lives in order to move beyond poverty. It does this by supporting and funding community-controlled, self-help organizations, and economic development projects, as well as through transformative education. Guidelines for both types of projects are available on the CCHD Web site, as is a list of currently funded projects organized by state, local contact information (also by state), and a form for requesting more information.

Harry Chapin Foundation (http://www.harrysfriends.com/hcf/)
The Harry Chapin Foundation, founded to "address the problems of the disadvantaged and promote educational programs that lead to a greater understanding of human suffering," provides funding for community education, arts in education, and agricultural and environmental programs. The Foundation favors programs in the New York region, although it will consider national programs. The Foundation's Web site provides funding guidelines and a contact for application requests, as well as a biography of Harry Chapin, memorabilia, and a listing of board members.

Child Health Foundation (http://www.childhealthfoundation.org/)
The Child Health Foundation was established in 1985 to prevent and treat life-threatening communicable diseases in infants and children through support of clinical research, medical outreach, public education, and collaborative research partnerships. The Foundation's Web site provides excerpts from the CHF newsletter, an online version of the Foundation's most recent annual report, and general information about the Foundation's formal partnership agreements with a number of educational and medical organizations, including the University of Alabama, Hahnemann University (Philadelphia), City Hospital (Boston), Johns Hopkins Hospital and University (Baltimore), the University of Maryland (Baltimore), the Hospital Infantil Albert Sabin (Brazil), the International Centre for Health and Population Research (Bangladesh), the Instituto Investigación Nutriciónal (Peru), and the University of Virginia.

The Children's Charities Foundation (http://www.ccfdc.org/)
The Children's Charities Foundation was created to raise money for at-risk children and youth in the Washington, D.C. metropolitan area. The Foundation provides grants to organizations that strengthen children's health and welfare, support strong and cohesive families, and assist educational and recreational programs. The Foundation's Web site provides a list of organizations that received grants last year, information on its fundraising activities, and a mailing address.

Chinook Fund (http://www.fex.org/chinook/chinook.html)
The Fund's primary goal is to support progressive social change organizing and activism across Colorado. The Fund defines progressive social change work as efforts that challenge and attempt to alter existing economic and social relationships and institutions which are inequitable and undemocratic. This type of change requires an analysis of the root causes of social problems and their

solutions, followed by action and evaluation of the effectiveness of that action. The fund supports projects that are working for progressive social change through means such as community organizing, advocacy, and coalition work. The Fund's site, recently under construction, includes application guidelines and forms and the most recent newsletter, all in PDF format, as well as donor and contact information. In the future, the site promises to have board member listings, grants lists, events, links to related sites, and details about the Fund itself.

The Club Foundation (http://www.clubfoundation.org/)
The Club Foundation, a professional organization for the managers of private clubs, was established in 1988 to provide educational opportunities for future professionals of the club industry. Scholarships and grants are awarded to students enrolled in hospitality programs who are pursuing managerial careers in club management. The Foundation's straightforward Web site provides descriptions of its programs and contact information for requesting application forms.

Coalition for the Advancement of Jewish Education (http://www.caje.org)
The coalition seeks to advance Jewish education by supporting Jewish teachers; encouraging young people to go into the field professionally; and running national conferences and local in-service programs. The Coalition's Web site provides information about their annual conference, a job bank, newsletters, membership, and advocacy. In addition, information and an application form (in MS Word format) for the Spack Fellowship are available.

Coca-Cola Scholars Foundation (http://www.coca-cola.com/scholars/)
The Coca-Cola Scholars Foundation, created in 1986 to support higher education for communities where Coca-Cola Bottlers are located, awards 250 merit-based scholarships to high-school seniors annually. The Foundation area of Coca-Cola's Web site provides an outline of the program, application instructions, an interactive form that allows interested students to find out if they live in an eligible geographic location, and contact information.

College Art Association (http://www.collegeart.org/)
The College Art Association, founded in 1911, promotes scholarship and teaching in the history and criticism of the visual arts, and creativity and technical skill in the teaching and practices of art. CAA's Professional Development Fellowship Program helps artists to complete their M.F.A., Ph.D., or M.A. degree, to secure employment, and then subsidizes their first year's salary through matching grants to the institutions that hire them. CAA's Web site announces the current year's fellows in the "News" section, and there provides information for requesting application forms. CAA's Web site also lists opportunities for artists—awards, calls for entries and manuscripts, grants and fellowships, internships, online opportunities, publications, and residencies – offered by various organizations. Publications, conference information, and job opportunities are also available online.

Common Counsel Foundation (http://www.commoncounsel.org)
Common Counsel is a consortium of family foundations—current members include the Abelard Foundation, the Acorn Foundation, and the Penney Family Fund—and individual donors whose philanthropic interests include a broad range of economic, environmental, and social justice initiatives. The Foundation also

administers the Grantee Exchange Fund, a small grants program for community organizations seeking travel stipends and technical assistance funds, and coordinates two retreat programs: the Windcall Resident Program in Montana for social change community organizers and activists; and the Mesa Refuge, a Northern California center for writers addressing issues related to restructuring the economy and its relationship to people and nature. The CCF Web site provides general information about its residency programs and member foundations, lists of recent grantees, grant application guidelines and procedures, and information for donors.

The Conservation Alliance (http://www.outdoorlink.com/consall/)

The Conservation Alliance is a group of outdoor businesses that support grass-roots citizen-action groups in protecting rivers, trails, and wild lands—natural areas where outdoor enthusiasts recreate. Grants are made to organizations for projects focused on direct action to protect and enhance natural resources for recreation—not education or scientific research projects. Guidelines and application instructions are provided at the Alliance's Web site, along with a history of grantmaking; however, grantseekers are asked to contact the Alliance before submitting a proposal. The Alliance site also provides success stories, news, and membership information.

Cooper Foundation (http://www.cooperfdn.org/)

The Cooper Foundation, established in 1943 and located in Waco, Texas, provides financial support for experimental projects, research, surveys, and special community needs for which other financing is not available. Grants are made only to organizations in the Waco area, and the Foundation's Web site provides a listing of past grants. Interested grantseekers are instructed to submit the interactive form to request more information or contact the Foundation by phone.

Cottonwood Foundation (http://www.pressenter.com/~cottonwd/)

The Cottonwood Foundation is "dedicated to promoting empowerment of people, protection of the environment, and respect for cultural diversity." The Foundation focuses its modest grantmaking activities on "committed, grassroots organizations that rely strongly on volunteer efforts and where foundation support will make a significant difference." The Foundation typically awards grants in the $500 to $1,000 range to organizations in the United States and internationally that protect the environment, promote cultural diversity, empower people to meet their basic needs, and rely on volunteer efforts. In addition to general information about its activities, the Foundation's Web site provides grant guidelines, a downloadable grant application form, a list of grant recipients, and the Foundation's annual report.

Council of Independent Colleges (http://www.cic.edu/)

The Council of Independent Colleges, founded in 1956 and based in Washington, D.C., is an association of independent liberal arts colleges and universities that helps to enhance educational programs, improve administrative and financial performance, and increase institutional visibility. CIC offers funding and technical assistance programs, which are outlined in the "Programs & Services" area of its Web site. Additionally, CIC's Consortium for the Advancement of Private Higher Education (CAPHE) helps corporations and foundations stimulate meaningful reform by designing and administering directed-grant competitions, offering technical assistance to funders, and disseminating ideas resulting from its programs. The Web site provides detailed information about CAPHE, as well as membership and sponsor information, board and staff listings, and an online version of its most recent annual report (in PDF format).

Creative Capital (http://www.creative-capital.org/)

An outgrowth of the Andy Warhol Foundation, Creative Capital is oriented towards supporting individual artists in the visual, performing, and media arts. The organization provides audience development, marketing, and other forms of assistance tailored to individual projects in exchange for a share of the proceeds generated, which are then reinvested into the work of other artists. The organization's description, history, application and guidelines, list of staff and advisors, and a section of links to other arts resource organizations can all be found on its site. In addition, visitors may join a mailing list to receive updates.

Cystic Fibrosis Foundation (http://www.cff.org/)

The mission of the Cystic Fibrosis Foundation is to assure the development of the means to cure and control cystic fibrosis and to improve the quality of life for those with the disease. It is also a resource of public information about cystic fibrosis. This informative Web site includes news about cystic fibrosis research, links to local foundation chapters, donor information, as well as research program guidelines and deadlines.

Deaconess Community Foundation (OH)
(http://fdncenter.org/grantmaker/deaconess/)

Deaconess Community Foundation was created in 1997 following the sale of Deaconess Hospital of Cleveland in 1994 and two years of planning by Deaconess Health Systems. The Foundation provides resources that help organizations empower people in Greater Cleveland, Ohio to become self-sufficient, and is guided by the spiritual traditions of the United Church of Christ. Grants are provided to nonprofit organizations for charitable, health, education, welfare, community, or social services. The Foundation's Web site gives the history of the Foundation, grant guidelines and an application form, grants lists, and a listing of the board of trustees.

Delaware Humanities Forum (http://www.dhf.org/)

The Delaware Humanities Forum, an adjunct of the Delaware Humanities Council, supports educational programs in the humanities through its own programs and sponsorship of a range of activities, including lectures, conferences, radio and television broadcasts, interpretive exhibits, and book and film discussions. Descriptions of the Forum's programs, which include a Speakers Bureau, a Visiting Scholars Program, an Annual Lecture, and Workplace Programs are available on the Forum's Web site, along with information about grant eligibility requirements and deadlines, frequently asked questions, and downloadable guidelines and application forms in PDF format. Visitors will also find a calendar of events, an interactive form for ordering Forum materials, and contact information.

Detroit Lions' Charities (http://www.detroitlions.com/charities.html)

Established by the NFL's Detroit Lions, the Detroit Lions' Charities support education, civic affairs, and health and human services in the state of Michigan.

Programs currently funded by the DLC include learning initiatives for youth, housing for less fortunate families, mentoring projects, domestic violence education, athletic programs for youth, substance abuse programs, and a visiting lecturer series at a creative studies center. Visitors to the Lions' Web site will find a description of the DLC and its activities, funding request deadlines, a press release on current grants and annual giving totals, and contact information.

Do Something, Inc. (http://www.dosomething.org/)

Founded in 1993, Do Something provides leadership training, guidance, and financial resources to young people committed to strengthening their communities. The organization annually honors ten community leaders under the age of 30 with the "BRICK Award for Community Leadership." Do Something also awards grants of up to $500 to young people with an idea for a community project. Application forms for both programs can be printed from the Do Something Web site (the form for the latter program is also available on America Online by entering the keyword "Do Something").

Dollywood Foundation (http://www.dollywood.com/foundation)

The Dollywood Foundation was founded in 1988 by Dolly Parton and the Dollywood Company to develop and administer educational programs for the children of Dolly's native Sevier County, Tennessee, to inspire them to "dream more, learn more, do more, and be more." It provides a number of scholarships to local individuals. The Web site includes brief information about the scholarships, contact information, a history and mission, and details about their major project, the Imagination Library.

Murray Dranoff Foundation (http://www.dranoff2piano.org/)

The Foundation seeks to educate, involve, introduce, and invite the widest possible audience to the world of music, particularly four-hand chamber music for the piano. It is primarily devoted to the renaissance of this music and to preserving the literature for posterity. If your computer is equipped to play MediaPlayer files, background music will play on this site; however, you can still enjoy the site without this capability. All visitors will be able to access information on the founder, Murray Dranoff, competition guidelines and dates, and major donor information.

The Drug Policy Foundation (http://www.dpf.org/)

The Drug Policy Foundation was founded to provide alternatives to current drug policies, guided by the belief that the drug war is not working. The Foundation provides funding for advocacy, harm reduction, and public education projects. Guidelines to view or download, an application form, grants lists, and a helpful appendix are available at the Web site. In addition to grants information, the Web site provides an online newsletter, public policy and conference information, a press area, resources and links, chat rooms, forums, and an online store.

The Dunn Foundation (http://www.dunnfoundation.org/)

The mission of The Dunn Foundation is to promote the quality of the visual environment as a guiding principle for the growth and development of America's communities through education and philanthropy. This mission is fulfilled through increasing public understanding of the contribution community appearance makes to our quality of life, and by linking people to the tools they need to make positive aesthetic changes in their environment. Application guidelines, grants lists, grantmaking priorities, and information on the Foundation's "visual literacy" programs, Viewfinders and Suburban Streetscapes, are among the features offered on the Foundation's Web site.

Dystonia Medical Research Foundation (http://www.dystonia-foundation.org/dmrf.html)

The Dystonia Medical Research Foundation, based in Chicago, Illinois, supports research on dystonia, increases public awareness, and provides support to those affected by the disease. A brief description of the Foundation's research funding is provided at its Web site, along with information on its education and awareness activities, donor information, listings of its board of directors and scientific advisory board, and contact information. The Foundation also provides Spanish and French versions of its Web site.

Educational Foundation for a Free World (http://www.iserv.net/~edfreewd/)

The mission of the Educational Foundation for a Free World is to provide opportunities for college students from former Communist countries to study in the United States. Its site describes the organization's services, application requirements and procedure, and governing board.

The Enterprise Foundation (http://www.enterprisefoundation.org)

Launched by visionary developer Jim Rouse and his wife Patty in 1982, the Enterprise Foundation focuses its activities on providing "all low-income people in the United States the opportunity for fit and affordable housing." The Foundation's Web site offers extensive information about the plethora of loans, investments, training programs, and technical assistance supported by the Foundation and its subsidiaries. Visitors to the site can also access information on the Foundation's annual Network Conference; read various Foundation publications, news releases, and newsletters; and search the "Best Practices Database," which shares experiences, strategies, and techniques for assisting low-income people.

The Entertainment Industry Foundation (http://www.eifoundation.org/)

In 1942, Samuel Goldwyn founded the forerunner of The Entertainment Industry Foundation, The Motion Picture Charities Committee, to create an organization that would conduct a single unified campaign for all of the charitable giving within the industry. The Foundation still maintains its historical commitment to coordinate the philanthropy of the entertainment industry to achieve maximum social impact in the community thanks to the generosity of the people who work in the industry. Over the years, The Foundation has distributed more than $140 million raised by industry members to charitable organizations involved with children's health, community, the arts, the environment, homelessness, literacy, aging, and numerous other areas. Its Web site details their grantmaking process, donor information, current sponsors, a history of the organization, and event listings. It also provides a link to the National Women's Cancer Research Alliance (NWCRA), an organization co-founded by the Foundation and Lilly Tartikoff.

Entrepreneurs' Foundation (http://www.the-ef.org/)

The Entrepreneurs' Foundation was created in 1998 to encourage entrepreneurs in the Silicon Valley/Bay Area to reinvest in their communities. The Foundation works with young companies to help them develop and facilitate a three-year community involvement plan. In return, each company gives equity stock to the Foundation, which invests the capital gains from the appreciated stock in non-profit leaders who engage in "venture philanthropy" practices the application of venture capital strategies to philanthropic giving. The Foundation collaborates with existing funders to provide capital for expanding education and youth development programs. The EF Web site provides a helpful FAQ on the Foundation's brand of philanthropy, information about sponsors and participants, links to related "venture philanthropy" resources, and contact information.

Equity Foundation, Inc. (OR) (http://equityfoundation.org/)

Based in Portland, Oregon, the Equity Foundation works to promote the welfare of the gay, lesbian, bisexual, and transgendered communities and of the people of Oregon in general by providing support to nonprofit organizations throughout the state. The Foundation provides funding through its annual granting cycle and community outreach grants as well as through the administration of individual donor-advised funds and scholarship programs. Key issues for the Foundation include improving acceptance, understanding, and cooperation among people, and eradicating homophobia and other forms of discrimination; providing support for youth and family programs that strengthen g/l/b/t families; health and social services; and support for arts and cultural organizations whose programs are in alignment with the Foundation's mission and which enrich the entire community. The Foundation's Web site provides a thorough description of its grantmaking activities, a list of recent grants, information for donors, answers to frequently asked questions, brief bios of the Foundation's board and staff, and contact information.

The Eurasia Foundation (http://www.eurasia.org/)

The Washington, D.C.-based Eurasia Foundation is a privately managed grantmaking organization dedicated to funding programs that build democratic and free market institutions in the Newly Independent States of the former Soviet Union—Armenia, Azerbaijan, Belarus, Georgia, Kazakstan, Kyrgyzstan, Moldova, Russia, Tajikistan, Turkmenistan, Ukraine, and Uzbekistan. The Foundation concentrates its support in eight priority areas: business development, business education and management training, economics education and research, public administration and local government reform, NGO development, rule of law, media, and electronic communications. Visitors to the Foundation's Web site will find program descriptions and application guidelines; a searchable database of grants; a directory of Foundation offices, staff, and board members; links to Web sites of interest; job opportunities; news; and contact information.

Fidelity Investments Charitable Gift Fund (http://www.charitable-gift.org)

The Fund makes donor-advised grants primarily to U.S. tax-exempt charitable organizations. Its Web site, mainly directed at potential donors, includes donor information, contact information, an annual report, and grants lists.

First Nations Development Institute (http://www.firstnations.org/)

The First Nations Development Institute was formed in 1980 to help Native American tribes build sound, sustainable reservation communities by linking grassroots projects with national programs. Through its Eagle Staff Fund: A

Collaborative For Native American Development, the Institute offers grants in support of "holistic" economic development projects that consider communities' economic, environmental, spiritual, cultural, political, social, and health needs. In addition, the Institute's Oweesta Program provides technical assistance to communities in creating and controlling capital assets for financing reservation and community development. Detailed information on these programs, a list of related links, and contact information are available at the First Nations Web site.

FishAmerica Foundation
(http://www.asafishing.org/outreach/fish_america.htm)
Support is given primarily for hands-on projects that enhance fish populations, conserve and enhance waterways and fisheries, and promote fish habitat and water quality. The Foundation's Web site includes the application forms and guidelines, donor information, and a grants list.

A.J. Fletcher Foundation (http://www.ajf.org/)
Originally formed to provide operating support for A.J. Fletcher's Grass Roots Opera, which later evolved into the National Opera Company, the A.J. Fletcher Foundation today supports a broad range of "nonprofit organizations in their endeavors to enrich the people of North Carolina." The Foundation makes grants in five areas: Arts and Humanities, Organizational and Administrative Development, Education, Programs Benefiting Children and Youth, and Community Initiatives and Human Services. The Foundation's Web site provides a description of the Foundation, a biography of A.J. Fletcher, grants lists by giving area, grant guidelines and a downloadable application form. Visitors to the site can also read about the National Opera Company and another major beneficiary, the Fletcher School of Performing Arts.

Florida Humanities Council (http://www.flahum.org/)
Since its founding in 1971, the Florida Humanities Council has awarded more than eight million dollars to community and educational organizations in support of public programs centered in the following disciplines: philosophy, ethics, comparative religions, history, art criticism/art history, jurisprudence, literature, languages, linguistics, archaeology, cultural anthropology, and folklore/folklife. FHC's grantmaking is divided into three main categories:

Major Grants (all requests for more than $2,000, with an upper limit of $25,000 per grant); Mini Grants (grants up to $2,000); and Scholar/Humanist Fellowships (grants to individual scholars or humanists for research on humanities topics or themes announced by FHC). In addition to detailed program information and information about FHC activities and membership, visitors to the FHC Web site will find downloadable application and independent evaluator forms, a calendar of FHC-sponsored and -funded events, and links to dozens of state humanities councils and humanities resources on the Web.

The For All Kids Foundation, Inc.
(http://rosieo.warnerbros.com/cmp/allkids/allkids.htm)
The For All Kids Foundation, Inc., established by comedienne Rosie O'Donnell in February, 1997, awards grants to help support the intellectual, social, and cultural development of disadvantaged children throughout the United States. It also seeks to develop long-term relationships with donors and grant recipients based

on a shared vision that recognizes nonprofit organizations as vital agents in the communities they serve. The Web site gives an overview of the Foundation's history and mission, grant guidelines, a grants list, and information about upcoming benefit events for the organization.

Frameline, Inc. (http://www.frameline.org/)

Frameline is dedicated to the exhibition, distribution, promotion and funding of lesbian and gay film and video and presents the annual San Francisco International Lesbian & Gay Film Festival. Frameline's grant program is called the Completion Fund, which helps artists to complete their film and video projects. Fund guidelines are provided at Frameline's Web site. Visitors to the site will also find information about the festival, Frameline Distribution, membership, events, and resources.

Milton and Rose D. Friedman Foundation (http://www.friedmanfoundation.org/)

The Milton & Rose D. Friedman Foundation, established in September 1996 by two economists concerned about the quality of public schools, works to restructure the education system to encourage competition in the market for educational services and give parents more choices about the schools their children attend. The Foundation promotes the use of "educational vouchers"—providing to parents who wish to send their children to private schools "a sum equal to the estimated cost of educating a child in a government school, provided that at least this sum was spent on education in an approved school." The Foundation funds research into the judicial and legislative decisions on school choice and the social and economic impact of voucher programs. The Foundation's Web site offers opinions and answers to questions on this issue, and provides donor information, related Web sites, and an e-mail contact.

Fund for Santa Barbara (http://www.fex.org/santa/santades.html)

The Fund, which is a member of the Funding Exchange, supports projects that advocate, educate, and organize in order to examine and address the root causes of social, economic, and environmental problems. These projects work for issues such as: human rights, racial equity and ethnic heritage, protecting the environment, accessible health care, peace and nonviolence, responsible government, legal rights, progressive solutions, and community organizing. Their Web site describes their areas of funding interest, their grantmaking history, application guidelines, and contact information.

Fund for Southern Communities (http://www.fex.org/south/south.html)

The Fund, also a member of the Funding Exchange, provides financial support and human resources to grassroots organizations working for social and economic reform. Its Web site includes grants lists, application guidelines, and donor information.

Gay and Lesbian Medical Association (http://www.glma.org/)

The Association is dedicated to combating homophobia within the medical profession and in society at large, and to promoting the best possible health care for lesbian and gay patients. Through the Lesbian Health Fund, the organization supports medical research and both patient and physician education in several areas pertaining to lesbian health issues including reproductive health, mental health, family issues, and cancer in the lesbian community. Grantseekers should use the link to Lesbian Health Fund on the Web site in order to access application guidelines and forms, grants lists, the fund's advisory board listing, and donor information.

General Health System Foundation (http://www.generalhealth.org/foundation.html)

Based in Baton Rouge, Louisiana, the General Health System Foundation is committed to improving that community's access to health care services. GHS provides opportunities for education and assistance, as well as support for affiliates of the General Health System, a network of health care providers. The Foundation is described briefly on a page of the GHS Web site.

Georgia Humanities Council (http://www.emory.edu/GHC/ghc.html)

The Georgia Humanities Council, the state affiliate of the National Endowment for the Humanities, was founded in 1970 to support and conduct local and statewide educational programs in the humanities. In addition to descriptions of and guidelines for its four grant programs, the site also provides information about a range of humanities resources (Web sites, book discussion groups, video resources, etc.) and contact information.

German-American Academic Council Foundation (http://www.gaac.org/)

The German-American Academic Council Foundation works to strengthen German-American cooperation in the sciences and humanities through the joint activities of young scientists and scholars and by serving as a forum for Trans-Atlantic dialogue. GAAC funding supports a visiting lectureship series, research facilities for visiting scientists and scholars in Washington, DC, and cooperative research projects between German and U.S. or Canadian scholars. Program descriptions, deadlines, and contact information in both English and German are available at GAAC's Web site. The site also provides information about the Foundation's activities and projects, affiliated organizations, and a listing of GAAC staff.

Gifts In Kind International (http://www.GiftsInKind.org/)

Gifts In Kind helps businesses to effectively and efficiently donate their products to charities. Its donation programs include Clothe & Comfort, Healthy from the Start, Housing the Homeless, Youth Programs, Emergency Relief, Office Smart, Recycle Technology, and the Retail Donation Partner Program. Gifts In Kind's Web site asks those seeking product donations to locate a Coordinating Agency Partner in their geographic region, and provides a listing by state. For those unable to locate a CAP, an online application form can be filled out and submitted electronically. The site also provides donor and partnership information, as well as new products, programs, and reports.

Elizabeth Glaser Pediatric AIDS Foundation (http://www.pedaids.org/)

The Elizabeth Glaser Pediatric AIDS Foundation is dedicated to identifying, funding, and conducting basic pediatric HIV/AIDS research, with the goal of reducing HIV transmission from mother to newborn, prolonging and improving the lives of children living with HIV, and eradicating HIV from infected children. The Foundation conducts its own targeted research and awards several grants for individual research, including the Elizabeth Glaser Scientist Awards, Basic Research Grants, Scholar Awards, Short-Term Scientific Awards, and Student Intern Awards, all of which are briefly outlined at the Foundation's Web site. Visitors to the site will also find a brief history of the Foundation, facts about pediatric AIDS, listings of the Foundation's staff and various boards, Foundation-related news, and information for donors.

Glaucoma Research Foundation (http://www.glaucoma.org/)
The Glaucoma Research Foundation funds research to find a cure for glaucoma. Funding goes to research in the U.S. and in other countries, particularly collaborative projects across disciplines. Current research explores such subjects as genetic links to glaucoma, optic nerve analysis, new medications, and laser treatments. The "Research" area of the Foundation's Web site provides the grants policy, grantees list, program details, and information about its fellowship program. Visitors to the Web site will also find information on the disease, donor information, an interactive forum, a link to online donation opportunities, and contact information.

Global Fund for Women (http://www.globalfundforwomen.org)
The Global Fund for Women strives to advance female human rights and improve women's economic autonomy and access to communications in countries around the world. It does not fund in the United States, however, nor does it fund individuals. As a non-endowed foundation, it relies on the annual support of individuals, foundations, corporations, and other nongovernmental and multilateral organizations. The Fund's Web site provides program descriptions, a FAQ section, grant application guidelines and criteria, a listing of the Fund's board of directors and advisory council, detailed accounts of many of its recent activities, dozens of links to nonprofit resources and sites concerned with women's issues, and an appeal for support (accompanied by an interactive donation pledge form).

Golden Apple Foundation for Excellence in Teaching
(http://www.goldenapple.org/)
The Chicago-based Golden Apple Foundation promotes excellence in Pre-K–12 education through the work of excellent teachers. Chicago venture capitalist Martin J. ("Mike") Koldyke founded the organization, originally called the Foundation for Excellence in Teaching, in 1985 to publicly honor excellent teachers and provide them with the means to have an impact on their profession. Grants and awards are given to encourage and support the teaching profession. The Web site clearly describes each of the Foundation's programs, outlines the Foundation's mission, and provides press releases and information on upcoming events.

Good Samaritan Foundation, Inc. (http://www.gsfky.org/)
The Foundation provides grants for charitable and educational activities related to health care and health education in central and eastern Kentucky. Primary and preventative health care for low-income and uninsured people in underserved areas are a priority. The Web site includes donor information, a list of the board of trustees, program information, and a publication request form.

Group Health/Kaiser Permanente Community Foundation
(http://www.ghc.org/foundatn/foundatn.html)
The Group Health/Kaiser Permanente Community Foundation was founded in 1984 to support health research, clinical innovations, health promotion/education programs, and community-based public health projects that focus on healthcare for homeless families, infant mortality, immunizations, and the prevention of violence. The Foundation's page of Group Health's Web site provides examples of research grants, information on its endowment, and a listing of its board members.

Hawai'i Committee for the Humanities (http://www.planet-hawaii.com/hch/)
The Hawai'i Committee for the Humanities was founded in 1972 to promote and support public awareness in Hawai'i of the humanities (defined on the HCH's Web site as studies examining philosophy, ethics, comparative religion, history, archaeology and anthropology, literature, languages, and art history). HCH offers grants primarily to nonprofit organizations that operate humanities programs, although a limited number of smaller grants are temporarily available for research by individuals and preservation and publications projects by nonprofits. The Web site provides detailed information about its grant programs and downloadable applications and instructions in PDF format. The site also lists humanities resources and links to those with Web sites, information on Hawaii History Day and other programs, and contact information.

Haymarket People's Fund (http://www.fex.org/hay/haymark.html)
The Fund, which is a member of the Funding Exchange, is a progressive organization that makes grants throughout New England to grassroots groups which organize for peace, equality, and economic justice. Besides providing support and resources to grassroots organizations through grants, the fund does its best to provide technical assistance and referrals as well as encouraging coalition building and networking. It strives to maintain a multicultural organization controlled by activists representing constituencies served. Their Web site includes application guidelines, donor information, and grant application forms downloadable as WP5.1 and text-only files.

Headwaters Fund (http://www.fex.org/headwater/headwate.html)
Founded on the belief that the capacity for fundamental social change lies in the hands of ordinary people, the Headwaters Fund provides financial and organizational resources to grassroots organizations in the Minneapolis/St. Paul metropolitan area. The Fund tends to support smaller organizations (i.e., those with budgets under $200,000) whose programs address the root causes of social, political, environmental and economic injustice, and its grantmaking decisions are made by community activists, including people of color, women, poor and working class individuals, gays and lesbians, and people with disabilities. Visitors to the Fund's Web site will find grant guidelines, information about donor opportunities, and contact information.

Health Foundation of South Florida & Affiliates
(http://www.hfsf.org/index.html)
The Foundation supports primary health care services that meet the needs of indigent, disadvantaged, and medically underserved persons in southern Florida. The Foundation also provides funds for medical research and education. The Web site

includes the Foundation's history, mission/philosophy, and funding priorities, as well as a grants list, newsletters, and press releases.

Health Trust of Santa Clara Valley (http://www.healthtrust.org/)

The Health Trust of Santa Clara Valley was formed in 1996 with proceeds from the sale of the Good Samaritan Health System. The Health Trust makes grants to nonprofit organizations that provide direct preventive health and wellness services, and operates community health programs that fill gaps in current health prevention services. General support (i.e., "Good Samaritan") grants are limited to 10 percent of the funds distributed by the Trust; the other 90 percent of its giving is initiated through an RFP process and invited proposals. Good Samaritan grants support community-based health, prevention, and wellness projects, particularly for medically indigent children, the elderly, and vulnerable adults. The Health Trust Web site outlines the organization's various activities and grant programs (including those involving restricted funds), and also provides donor and volunteer information, a listing of board and staff members, and contact information.

Jimi Hendrix Family Foundation (http://www.jimihendrix.org)

The Jimi Hendrix Family Foundation funds charitable, religious, and educational organizations with programs concentrating on education, inner city assistance, international humanitarian aid, and Christian outreach. The Foundation's Web site includes contact information and details about its annual Electric Guitar Competition, its mission, and their Board of Advisors.

Holy Land Foundation for Relief and Development (http://www.hlf.org)

The Holy Land Foundation for Relief and Development focuses on national and international programs aimed at helping the needy, empowering the disadvantaged, and finding practical solutions for human suffering everywhere. It operates relief and development projects worldwide, as well as makes grants to nonprofit, non-political institutions that provide relief work and humanitarian services. Although their Web site primarily focuses on information about the Foundation's operating programs and donor information (including an online donation form), visitors can also access recent newsletters and information about the Foundation's areas of interest.

Hospice Foundation of America (http://www.hospicefoundation.org/)

The mission of the Hospice Foundation of America is to "provide leadership in the development and application of hospice and its philosophy of care for terminally ill people, with the goal of enhancing the American health care system and the role of hospice within it." The Foundation designs and implements programs that assist hospices and the terminally ill, and makes grants that are supportive of hospice concepts. Grants are not normally awarded for endowments, debt reduction, religious efforts, or to individuals. Priority is given to those communities from which the Foundation collects donations. The Web site serves as an online resource for hospice care, providing excerpts from the Foundation's own publications in addition to numerous links to online hospice resources. The online version of the Foundation's annual report provides descriptions of grant programs, grant guidelines, a listing of grants, Foundation history, board and staff lists, and contact information. Visitors to the site will also find information on an array of Foundation projects, as well as interactive order and donation forms.

The Whitney Houston Foundation for Children (http://www.whfoundation.com/)
The Whitney Houston Foundation for Children is dedicated to promoting a positive self-image in children and youth by providing opportunities for them to learn and express themselves in safe, supportive environments. The Foundation's Web site includes grant guidelines, application instructions, and donor information.

The Howard Hughes Medical Institute (http://www.hhmi.org/)
In addition to supporting more than 60 medical research laboratories worldwide, the Howard Hughes Medical Institute awards both institutional and individual grants to strengthen education in medicine, biology, and the related sciences. HHMI's grants program also supports the research of biomedical scientists outside the United States. Visitors to the Web site will find detailed program descriptions, application guidelines and requirements, a short history of the organization, press releases and the HHMI Bulletin, online versions of annual reports, a map of HHMI locations, and an interactive form that allows for direct communication with HHMI staff.

Humanities Council of Washington, D.C. (http://www.humanities-wdc.org)
The Humanities Council of Washington, D.C. is the District's affiliate of the National Endowment for the Humanities. The Council annually supports 60-70 humanities programs in the nation's capitol through its grants program. The Council's Web site provides grant information and deadlines, contact information, a calendar of events, information about its activities, newsletter subscription information, and donor information.

Idaho Humanities Council (http://www2.state.id.us/ihc/)
The Idaho Humanities Council partners with civic groups, citizens, and educators to expand public humanities programs in the state. It accomplishes this mission by supporting educational programs for the general public as well as various target audiences. Although the Council's Web site offers comprehensive information on its grants programs, applicants are "strongly advised to seek more detailed information through staff consultation before completing and submitting grant proposals," and an e-mail contact is provided for this purpose. The Council's Web site also provides news, information on programs for teachers, humanities resources and links of interest, and contact and donor information.

Independent Accountants International Education Foundation (http://www.iai.org/education/)
The Independent Accountants International Educational Foundation administers the Robert Kaufman Memorial Scholarship Fund to assist young people pursuing education in the field of accountancy. The scholarship program is described on the Foundation's page of the IAI Web site; the page also provides links to the scholarship application form and a list of last year's award winners.

Indiana Humanities Council (http://www.ihc4u.org/)
The Indiana Humanities Council supports the humanities in Indiana in cooperation with educational, cultural, and community organizations. IHC grant programs include International Awareness Grants, Humanities Initiative Grants, and Mini-Grants. IHC's Web site offers brief descriptions of its programs, listings of recent grant recipients, and e-mail contacts for requesting more information. The

IHC site also provides information on the organization's activities, articles about the humanities, and a listing of humanities resources—exhibits, books, films, speakers, performances, and curricula—available to Indiana residents.

Initiative Fund of Southeastern and South Central Minnesota (http://www.semif.org/)

The Initiative Fund is a regional economic and community development fund serving 20 counties in southeastern and south central Minnesota. The Fund awards program grants up to $30,000 twice a year, and mini-grants up to $2,000 on a monthly basis. The Fund also runs a loan program to help finance new business start-ups and to expand existing businesses. The Fund's Web site provides grant and loan guidelines and staff e-mail contacts for requesting more information. The site also provides online versions of publications, links to special projects, and resources.

International Center for Research on Women (http://www.icrw.org/)

The International Center for Research on Women, founded in 1976, focuses its funding and activities on women's productive and reproductive roles, family status, leadership in society, and management of environmental resources in developing countries. Funds are primarily available through the Promoting Women in Development (PROWID) Program and the ICRW's Fellows Program, which gives development researchers and practitioners from developing countries the opportunity to spend time in Washington, D.C. to conduct independent research, meet policymakers, and refine their skills in data analysis, computer applications, and program development. The ICRW's Web site provides fellowship details and an application form to submit electronically, as well as downloadable and interactive application forms. Contacts are provided for those interested in the PROWID Program. The ICRW site also provides news, information on its activities, publications, and listings of board, staff, and partners.

International Youth Federation (http://www.iyfnet.org/)

The International Youth Foundation promotes the positive development of children and youth, ages 5 to 20, around the world by supporting programs that focus on such areas as vocational training, health education, recreation, cultural tolerance, environmental awareness, and the development of leadership, conflict resolution, and decision-making skills. The Foundation's Web site provides recent grants lists, a listing of international partners, IYF programs, and an e-mail contact, as well as detailed information about its work.

The Henry M. Jackson Foundation (http://www.hmjackson.org/)

The Foundation was established to carry forward the commitment of the late Senator Henry M. "Scoop" Jackson to advancing education and public service. Its mission is to build bridges between the academic and policy worlds, between the public and private sectors, and between citizens and their government. Primary areas of interest include international affairs, human rights, public service, and environmental and natural resources. Information on the founder, application guidelines, grants lists, and contact information can be accessed from the Web site in both English and Russian.

Jewish Community Federation of Cleveland (http://www.jewishcleveland.org/)
The Federation acts to produce the resources, ideas, and commitment necessary to preserve and strengthen Jewish life in Cleveland; to identify needs and provide funding to agencies that can help address those needs; to empower individual Jews or Jewish families to live quality Jewish lives; to contribute to the creative survival of Jews in the U.S., in Israel, and throughout the world. The Web site is an excellent resource for links related to the Jewish community in Cleveland, including specific sections on children/youth, young adults and singles, and seniors. There is also a directory of executive staff and an executive summary of the Federation's strategic plan.

Elton John AIDS Foundation (http://www.ejaf.org/)
The London and Los Angeles-based Elton John AIDS Foundation was founded in 1992 by entertainer Elton John to fund programs that "provide services to people living with HIV/AIDS and educational programs targeted at AIDS prevention, and/or elimination of prejudice and discrimination against HIV affected individuals." Services supported by the Foundation include food banks and meal programs, legal aid, hospice and housing, counseling and support groups, education outreach programs, at-home care, and pediatric treatment centers. The Foundation's Web site provides a description of its programs, contact information for those seeking grants, and areas for purchasing merchandise or otherwise contributing to the Foundation.

Magic Johnson Foundation (http://www.magicjohnson.org/)
Originally established to raise funds for HIV/AIDS educational and prevention programs, the Magic Johnson Foundation now awards grants to community-based organizations involved with educational, health, and social programs for inner-city youth. The Foundation recently launched a National Breast Cancer Awareness Initiative that targets African-American Women, and it also operates a number of programs to support youth. These include the Youth Entrepreneurial Project, the Education Program, and the Fashion and Merchandising Scholarship Program. Grant guidelines and scholarship information are provided in the "About" area of the Foundation's Web site and online application and request-for-information forms are promised in the near future. The site also provides HIV/AIDS and general health information, a calendar of upcoming events, and donor and contact information.

Kansas Humanities Council
(http://www.cc.ukans.edu/kansas/khc/mainpage.html)
The Council provides support for humanities programs directed at the adult public of Kansas through Major Grants (over $2,000), Minigrants (up to $2,000), and the Heritage Program Grants. In addition to specific grant program information and guidelines, the Web site also provides links to other sites of interest and features on topics related to the state of Kansas.

Kentucky Humanities Council (http://www.uky.edu/~vgsmit00/khc/khc.htm)
The Kentucky Humanities Council, an independent, nonprofit affiliate of the National Endowment for the Humanities, provides grants and services to nonprofit organizations seeking to foster greater understanding of the humanities. The sort of programs traditionally funded by the Council include, but are not limited

to, conferences, lectures, radio and video productions, exhibits, teacher training and development of curricular materials, interpretive programs for festivals, book discussions, and planning for future projects. Visitors to the Council's Web site will find grant guidelines as well as information about its speakers bureau, living history performances, book discussion programs, a listing of board and staff members, and contact information.

Susan G. Komen Breast Cancer Foundation (http://www.komen.org/)

Founded in 1982 and best known as the sponsor of the 5K "Race for the Cure" runs to raise funds for national and local breast cancer initiatives, the Susan G. Komen Breast Cancer Foundation is the largest private funder of research dedicated solely to breast cancer in the United States. The Foundation's National Grant Program awards grants and fellowships in basic and clinical research, as well as grants for breast cancer education, treatment, and screening projects for the medically underserved. Descriptions of the Foundation's programs and downloadable application forms are available on the Web site, as is a list of Komen affiliates who award grants locally. Visitors to the site will also find information about "Race for the Cure," an online version of the Foundation's annual report, and "breastcancerinfo.com," which provides general health and breast cancer news and information, an online forum, and a calendar of events.

LCMS Foundation (http://www.lfnd.org)

The LCMS Foundation meets challenges crucial to the survival and growth of the Missouri Synod Lutheran Church. It works on issues like providing adequate numbers of pastors and teachers, providing schools and funds to educate professional church workers, and expanding mission efforts at home and abroad. To access programs used to accomplish these challenges, the Web site lists a category named "LCMS IN ACTION." For further information about the Foundation other categories can be accessed on the Web site.

Leukemia Society of America (http://www.leukemia.org/)

In addition to sponsoring a broad range of public conferences about leukemia treatment and research, the Leukemia Society of America supports worldwide research efforts—both in the lab and clinical applications—toward controlling and finding a cure for leukemia, lymphoma, and myeloma. Grant information, guidelines, and application forms in a mix of Word 6.0 and PDF formats are available in the "Research" area of the Society's Web site.

Liberty Hill Foundation (http://www.libertyhill.org/main.htm)

The Foundation, which is a member of the Funding Exchange, offers support primarily for grassroots organizations working to effect social change. Grants target those groups which lack access to government or traditional funding sources and which seek to involve and empower the people who are most affected by the uneven distribution of economic resources and political power. Grants are made through general and donor-advised funds, memorial gifts, and the Fund for a New Los Angeles, which addresses the problems of poverty, racism, and urban violence in Los Angeles, California. Web site visitors may access a full annual report, newsletters, detailed history and background information on the organization, program guidelines, and donor information.

The Charles A. and Anne Morrow Lindbergh Foundation
(http://www.mtn.org/lindfdtn/)
The Lindbergh Foundation awards grants to individuals whose "initiative and work in a wide spectrum of disciplines furthers the Lindberghs' vision of a balance between the advance of technology and the preservation of the natural/ human environment." The Foundation pursues its mission through three major programs: the presentation of Lindbergh Grants of up to $10,580 (a symbolic amount representing the cost of the "Spirit of St. Louis"); presentation of the Lindbergh Award to an individual for his or her lifelong contributions to the Lindberghs' shared vision; and the sponsoring of educational programs and publications which advance the Lindberghs' vision. In addition to a brief history of the Foundation, contact information, and application guidelines, the Foundation's Web site offers visitors a grant application to view and print, or to download in MS Word format; a list of Lindbergh Grants awarded; an online version of the Foundation's annual report; a listing of the Foundation's officers, board, and staff; and links to other sites.

LMC Community Foundation (http://www.lmccf.org/)
Established in 1998, the LMC Community Foundation was formerly the fundraising arm of the Lutheran Medical Center of Jefferson County, Colorado. The Foundation is committed to community health activities and health system support. Through this commitment the Foundation seeks to enable individuals and the community to achieve better health in all aspects of their lives. Programs and services are focused on children and youth, and seniors, as well as innovative activities that center on health and well being. Check the Web site home page for community programs, application and contact information. A list of the Board of Directors is available on the site.

Louisiana Endowment for the Humanities (http://www.leh.org/about.htm)
The Louisiana Endowment for the Humanities was founded in 1971 to foster a deeper understanding and appreciation of the humanities throughout Louisiana, and to broaden Louisianans' access to history, literature, philosophy, language, and culture. To that end, LEH develops its own projects and makes grants to nonprofit organizations for public projects such as documentary films, museum exhibits, radio programs, conferences, lecture series, library reading programs, books, and interpretive folklife festivals. The LEH Web site provides brief descriptions of its programs and provides an interactive form for requesting more detailed information, including grant guidelines.

Lymphoma Research Foundation of America (http://www.lymphoma.org/)
Founded by non-Hodgkins lymphoma survivor Ellen Glesby Cohen in 1991, the Lymphoma Research Foundation of America funds lymphoma research and educational information for lymphoma patients. Research grants are awarded annually to third-year researchers, and applications can be requested via e-mail through the Foundation's Web site, where the LRFA grants program is described and past recipients are listed. The site also provides information on the Foundation's activities; information about clinical trials; an online version of Lymphoma Update, the organization's newsletters; and links to various lymphoma-related resources on the Internet.

March of Dimes (http://www.modimes.org/)

President Franklin D. Roosevelt created the March of Dimes in 1938 at the height of the polio epidemic. With the advent of the polio vaccine in the late 1950s, the focus of the organization shifted to the reduction of birth defects and infant mortality rates through advocacy, education, and the support of community programs and research in genetics and neurobiology. The Foundation's Web site provides detailed information about its grants, scholarships, and application guidelines and an interactive form for contacting a local chapter of the March of Dimes. The site also offers a great deal of information about the Foundation's advocacy and education efforts and about various health issues affecting infants.

Mary's Pence (http://www.igc.apc.org/maryspence/)

Mary's Pence is dedicated to furthering the self-empowerment of all women and, through women's growth, the self-improvement of all humanity. In support of these goals, it provides seed money for creative programs designed to bring about systemic change in church and society, especially programs that are likely to help dismantle oppressive structures and to have liberating and long-lasting results. Support is reserved for ministries in the Americas that have been created and are managed by women, that are not sponsored by parishes or dioceses, and that do not receive significant funding from other sources. In addition to a detailed description of the organization's funding philosophy, the Mary's Pence Web site provides grant guidelines, a list of past recipients, information on how to get involved, and contact information.

Massachusetts Environmental Trust
(http://www.agmconnect.org/maenvtr1.html)

The Massachusetts Environmental Trust was established in 1988 through the settlement of a federal lawsuit over the pollution of Boston Harbor. The Trust funds grassroots environmental programs that will restore, protect, and improve the quality of Massachusetts waterways. The Trust recommends that grantseekers apply for funds within one of its eight defined grant programs, but will accept unsolicited proposals that do not fit within those parameters. Guidelines are provided at the Trust's Web site with links to the Massachusetts Common Proposal Format, required for at least two of the programs. Recent grant awards and contact information are also provided at the Trust's site.

MAZON: A Jewish Response to Hunger
(http://www.shamash.org/soc-action/mazon/funding.html)

MAZON, named for the Hebrew word for "food," was founded in response to the problem of hunger in the United States and abroad, providing meals and food to elderly Jews, families living in temporary shelter, hungry children; people with AIDS, refugees of international crises, and nonprofits serving these populations. MAZON primarily funds organizations working for longer-term solutions to hunger, to improve the reach and effectiveness of government food assistance programs, and to provide counseling, assistance, and training for low-income people. International grants make up seven percent of MAZON's grantmaking. Grant guidelines and priorities are detailed at MAZON's succinct Web site.

McKenzie River Gathering Foundation
(http://www.fex.org/mckenzie/front.html)
The McKenzie River Gathering Foundation was established in 1976 to provide funding in Oregon to grassroots groups challenging social, economic, and political inequities. The Foundation's grantmaking focuses on human and civil rights, racial justice, economic justice, environmental protection, peace, and international solidarity, with grant amounts in the $3,000–$5,000 range. The Foundation's Web site describes its mission and provides grant guidelines and contact information for administrators of its programs, as well as donor information and a link to the Funding Exchange Network, of which it is a member.

Meet the Composer (http://www.meetthecomposer.org/)
Meet The Composer was founded in 1974 as a project of the New York State Council on the Arts to increase artistic and financial opportunities for American composers, which it does by providing composer fees to nonprofit organizations that perform, present, or commission original works. Meet the Composer has several funding programs, which are detailed on its Web site with downloadable application forms and guidelines (in PDF format). Visitors to the site will also find news, free publications to order, links to related Web sites, and donor and contact information.

Michigan AIDS Fund (http://www.michaidsfund.org/)
Launched in 1990, the Michigan AIDS Fund seeks to "support efforts to stop the spread of HIV/AIDS and alleviate the suffering of those infected and affected by the AIDS epidemic." The fund is a coalition of foundations and funding partnerships. It awards grants and provides support to grassroots community-based service organizations with HIV/AIDS-related programs. There is an emphasis on collaborative projects. The Web site contains a section named "Our History of Collaboration" where you will find information about grantmaking that includes a description of the grantmaking program, application information, support opportunities and a contact name.

Michigan Humanities Council (http://mihumanities.h-net.msu.edu/)
The Michigan Humanities Council, the state's affiliate of the National Endowment for the Humanities, encourages and supports activities that bring humanities scholars and the public together to promote understanding and appreciation of the humanities. The Council's grants program funds collaborative projects that use the disciplines of the humanities to explore community issues, particularly in communities with limited humanities programming and resources. Grant guidelines and application forms, in Mac and IBM formats, are provided at the Council's Web site, along with grant announcements, a note from the director, Council newsletters, resources and events, and grants lists.

Mid Atlantic Arts Foundation (http://www.charm.net/~midarts/index.html)
One of six regional arts organizations in the continental United States, the Mid Atlantic Arts Foundation addresses the support of the arts in a multi-state region comprised of Delaware, the District of Columbia, Maryland, New Jersey, New York, Pennsylvania, the U.S. Virgin Islands, Virginia, and West Virginia. The Foundation, which is primarily concerned with providing increased access to quality arts programs, provides financial support, technical assistance, and

information to artists and arts organizations through a variety of programs and services. Visitors to the Foundation's Web site will find general program descriptions for the individual artist, visual arts, performing arts, jazz, and traditional and folk arts; some recent grant awards and descriptions; listings of the Foundation's board and staff; links to the nine Mid-Atlantic state arts agencies' Web sites; and an online version of ARTSINK, the Foundation's newsletter.

Mississippi Humanities Council (http://www.ihl.state.ms.us/mhc/index.html)

The Mississippi Humanities Council encourages and supports activities that make the humanities accessible to the people of Mississippi, primarily by awarding grants to nonprofits that plan and sponsor humanities activities. The Council's Web site provides grant program descriptions, guidelines, and contact information, as well as information about the Council, a calendar of events, and links to humanities resources and funding sources on the Web.

Missouri Humanities Council (http://www.umsl.edu/community/mohuman/)

The Missouri Humanities Council promotes community, citizenship, and learning through humanities programs. The Council makes grants primarily for family reading programs, cultural heritage development, Chautauqua programs (a form of history theater), and local initiatives. Guidelines and an application to print and mail are provided at the Council's Web site. The site also provides information on the humanities and the Council's activities, links to Missouri Web sites, a listing of board members, and contact information.

Montana Committee for the Humanities (http://www.umt.edu/lastbest/)

The Montana Committee for the Humanities, the state's affiliate of the National Endowment for the Humanities founded in 1972, offers grants for public programs in history, literature, philosophy, and other disciplines of the humanities, and awards fellowships for humanities research relating to Montana. MCH provides guidelines for these programs and for its "Packaged Programs," a speakers bureau and media collection, in the "Grant Info" area of its Web site, along with contacts for requesting additional information. The site also provides news, MCH committee information, and a listing of humanities resources.

Ms. Foundation for Women (http://www.ms.foundation.org/)

The Ms. Foundation for Women, founded in 1972, supports the efforts of women and girls to govern their own lives and influence the world around them by funding women's self-help organizing efforts, and supporting changes in public consciousness, law, philanthropy, and social policy. The Foundation awards grants through special RFP initiatives in three issue areas—Women's Economic Security; Women's Health and Safety; and Girls, Young Women and Leadership—and offers Movement Building Grants in two grant cycles. Grant guidelines, RFPs, and the application form for Movement Building Grants are provided in the "Women & Philanthropy" area of the Foundation's Web site. The site provides information on the Foundation's activities, "Take Our Daughters to Work Day," and collaborative funding information.

Muscular Dystrophy Association (http://www.mdausa.org/research/index.html)

The Muscular Dystrophy Association seeks to find the causes of and cures for 40 neuromuscular diseases through sponsorship of 400 research projects worldwide.

MDA provides research grants to professionals or faculty members at appropriate educational, medical or research institutions, who are qualified to conduct and supervise a program of original research. Grant guidelines are provided at the MDA Web site along with an application form. The site also lists current research grantees and projects, research developments, clinical trials, and scientific meetings, symposia, and workshops.

A.J. Muste Memorial Institute (http://www.nonviolence.org/ajmuste/)

The A.J. Muste Memorial Institute explores the link between nonviolence and social change by applying its resources to the nonviolent struggle for social justice and a peaceful future. The Institute awards grants for projects promoting its mission through peace and disarmament, social and economic justice, racial and sexual equality, and the labor movement. It also provides funding through its International Nonviolence Training Fund. Grant guidelines are available at the Institute's Web site along with contact information for interested grantseekers, a list of grantees since 1994, and details of its fiscal sponsorship program. The site also describes the "Peace Pentagon"—low-cost office space in New York City for activists—and provides information on publications, contributions to the Institute, and a biography of A.J. Muste.

NAFSA: Association of International Educators (http://www.nafsa.org)

NAFSA, a membership organization created in 1948, promotes the international exchange of students and scholars through training workshops and in-service training grants, grants for professionals to travel to NAFSA conferences, and a variety of overseas opportunities. The "Education and Training" area of the NAFSA Web site provides information on these programs. Visitors to the site can also find information on or about financial aid and re-entry job searching ("Students, Scholars, and…."); funding programs for study abroad ("Inside NAFSA"); and upcoming conferences and publications by NAFSA members.

National Blood Foundation of the American Association of Blood Banks (http://www.aabb.org/docs/nbf.html)

The National Blood Foundation was established in 1983 as a program of the American Association of Blood Banks to fund "basic and applied scientific research, administrative/research projects, professional education, technical training, and public education in all aspects of blood banking, transfusion medicine, and tissue transplantation." NBF's 1999 Scientific Research Grant Program provided $30,000 grants for projects dealing with scientific, administrative, or educational aspects of blood banking and transfusion medicine. Application forms (in PDF format) can be downloaded from the NBF Web site, or requested via phone or e-mail. In addition to information on the Research Grant program, visitors to the site will find a list of grant recipients since 1986, donor information, and board and staff listings.

National Catholic Community Foundation (http://www.nccfcommunity.org/)

The National Catholic Community Foundation was established in May 1997. Through several types of funds it offers a philanthropic vehicle to those in the community who wish to support charitable, religious, and cultural activities. It supports only those activities that are consistent with the Gospel of The Roman Catholic Church. Funding is both national and international. The descriptions of the fund types make clear the activities in which the Foundation is engaged. Select "site search" from the index on the home page to quickly locate areas to research on the Web site.

National Council for the Social Studies (http://www.ncss.org/awards/home.html)

Founded in 1921, the National Council for the Social Studies supports social studies education—geography, economics, political science, sociology, psychology, anthropology, and law-related education—at all levels. NCSS awards excellence in teaching, curricula, research, writing, and service. Grantmaking programs include the Grant for the Enhancement of Geographic Literacy, the Fund for Advancement of Social Studies Grant, and the Christa McAuliffe Reach for the Stars Award. Application information is provided at NCSS's Web site for these programs and for the Council's service and writing awards. This site is also a social studies resource offering information on NCSS's activities, professional development, publications, a discussion board, membership information and a "members only" area, curriculum standards, state and local councils, and teaching resources.

National Environmental Education and Training Foundation (http://www.neetf.org/)

Established in 1990 in Washington, D.C. by the U.S. Congress in the National Environmental Education Act, the Foundation seeks to "help America meet critical national challenges through environmental learning." The Foundation aims to achieve these goals through programs that focus on the links between learning about the environment and critical issues such as health care, excellence in education, consumers' right to know, our competitive edge in business, the promotion of individual responsibility and effective community involvement. Information concerning programs, achievement awards, Competitive Challenge Grants, and application procedures are listed on the Web site, as well as links to other sources, staff and contact information.

National Fish and Wildlife Foundation (http://www.nfwf.org/)

The National Fish and Wildlife Foundation was established by an act of Congress in 1984 to help conserve and sustain natural resources in the U.S., which it accomplishes through conservation education, natural resource management, habitat protection, ecosystem restoration, and public policy development. The Foundation makes "Challenge Grants" with federal funds matched by private dollars through five initiatives—Conservation Education, Fisheries Conservation and Management, Neotropical Migratory Bird Conservation, Wetlands and Private Lands, Wildlife and Habitat—and through special programs funded by corporate partners. The Foundation's Web site provides grant guidelines for its challenge grants; the Unified Request for Proposals describes its special programs and provides an application form in various word-processing formats. The site also provides news and donor information.

National Foundation for Advancement in the Arts (http://www.nfaa.org/)

The Miami-based National Foundation for Advancement in the Arts was founded in 1981 to identify emerging artists and assist them at critical junctures in their educational and professional development, and to raise appreciation for and

support of the arts in American society. The NFAA operates five programs in support of individual artists: the Arts Recognition and Talent Search, Presidential
Scholars in the Arts, the Scholarship List Service, Career Development for NFAA
Artists, and Career Advancement of Visual Artists. The NFAA Web site provides
e-mail contacts for all five programs and online registration for two, news items
of interest, and employment opportunities.

National Foundation for the Improvement of Education (http://www.nfie.org/)
The National Foundation for the Improvement of Education, created in 1969 by
the National Education Association, provides grants and technical assistance to
improve student learning in public schools. The NFIE's Leadership Grants under-
write professional development opportunities for teachers, education support personnel, and higher education faculty and staff to prepare them for collegial leadership. The Foundation's Web site provides guidelines for this grant program and an
application form to print out and mail. Visitors to the site will also find detailed
information on other NFIE initiatives, recent Leadership grantees, and a newsletter on a Microsoft partnership program called "Road Ahead."

National Foundation for Infectious Diseases (http://www.nfid.org/)
The National Foundation for Infection Diseases supports research toward understanding the causes of infectious diseases, preventing and curing them, and supporting educational programs. In addition to its own research and education activities, the Foundation awards grants and fellowships for research and specialization
in infectious diseases and the microbiological/immunological/epidemiological
sciences. Detailed information about the Foundation's fellowship and grant programs can be found in the "Fellowships" area of its Web site. Visitors to the Web
site will find various sources of information on infectious diseases (some areas are
for members only), as well as publications, conferences and press conferences,
and contact information.

National Gardening Association
(http://www2.garden.org/nga/edu/NGA-EDU6.HTM)
The Association, located in Vermont, is focused on the community garden movement. Through the use of "Grow Lab," the Association's science education program, students learn about science and the environment using plants and gardens
to stimulate inquiry-based learning. The Association awards 300 Youth Garden
Grants each year. A Garden Grant application can be downloaded or obtained by
mail. A menu on the home page will give an overview of the Web site.

National Geographic Society Education Foundation
(http://www.nationalgeographic.com/society/ngo/foundation/)
The National Geographic Society Education Foundation currently awards more
than three million dollars in grants annually to programs nationwide in support of
their mission "to revitalize the teaching and learning of geography in the nation's
K–12 classrooms." Ninety percent of the Foundation's grants budget is "earmarked for a state-based network of geographic alliances, grassroots organizations of classroom teachers and university geographers dedicated to improving
geography education." In addition to funding the alliances, the Foundation awards
grants to individual teachers who work with the alliances to implement innovative
educational strategies relating to geography. The Foundation also funds an urban

initiative program, which awards grants to address the special needs of urban schools, and offers discretionary grant endowments for geography education in Colorado, Mississippi, and Oklahoma. Visitors to the Foundation's Web site will find detailed descriptions of the Foundation's programs, application guidelines, a downloadable teacher grant application form, and a contact list for each state alliance.

National Hemophilia Foundation (http://www.hemophilia.org/)

The National Hemophilia Foundation is dedicated to preventing, treating, and finding the cures of inherited bleeding disorders through education, advocacy, and research. The Foundation's Web site provides information on its Nursing Excellence and Judith Graham Pool Research fellowships in the "Resources" directory under "Programs & Services." Contact information and a downloadable application form for the research fellowship are provided. The Foundation's Web site also provides information on bleeding disorders, events, publications, an online version of its annual report, a listing of board members, and related Web sites.

National Heritage Foundation (http://www.nhf.org/)

Established in 1968, the National Heritage Foundation seeks to renew our national heritage through charitable projects and activities. It offers resources and industry experience to provide the fledgling foundation with sustainable advantages. The Foundation's focus is on educational, scientific, religious, and charitable projects. The main page of the Web site outlines all the topics covered. It provides information on staff, history of the Foundation, and recent grants.

National Hispanic Scholarship Fund, Inc (http://www.hsf.net/)

Established in 1975, the National Hispanic Scholarship Fund, located in California, helps pave the way for young Latinos to gain access to higher education. Since its inception it has "awarded more than 36,000 scholarships totaling nearly $38 million." The Web site covers all aspects of searching for scholarships including financial aid advice. Applicants can apply on-line for awards. In addition to the Scholarship portal, there is a portal for Cyber Campus. This site provides a complete career counseling section in both English and Spanish. A list of the Board of Directors and links to other resources for scholarships can be accessed.

National Park Foundation (http://www.nationalparks.org/)

The National Park Foundation was established in 1967 to help conserve, preserve and enhance U.S. National Parks, and to support education and outreach programs. The Foundation's Competitive Grants program funds conservation, preservation, and education efforts; funds are distributed to parks as seed money or challenge grants. Grant guidelines are provided in the "NPF Programs" directory of the Foundation's Web site, along with sample grants and a contact for requesting more information. This area of the site also details the Foundation's research, education, and other special initiatives.

National Press Foundation (http://www.natpress.org/)

The National Press Foundation offers professional development programs and gives awards for excellence in the field of journalism. The Foundation grants fellowships for its development programs—conferences, briefings, and college-based programs—covering all expenses, including travel and accommodations.

Application information is provided at the Foundation's Web site, along with last year's award recipients, resources culled from Foundation programs, and contact information.

The NRA Foundation, Inc. (http://www.nrafoundation.org/)

Created in 1990, the NRA Foundation, Inc., located in Virginia, supports a wide range of firearm-related public interest activities. The Foundation's grants focus on youth programs, range improvement and development, public safety, education and training, wildlife and natural resource conservation and constitutional research and education. The Web site includes program descriptions, grant guidelines including application and contact information, and a list of the board of trustees.

National Society of Accountants Scholarship Foundation (http://www.nsacct.org/scholar.htm)

The NSA Scholarship Foundation, created in 1969 to ensure the future of the accounting profession, awards annual scholarships to second-, third-, and fourth-year college accounting students. The scholarship program is outlined at NSA's Web site, along with application instructions.

National Trust for Historic Preservation (http://www.nthp.org/main/frontline/departments/awards.htm)

The National Trust for Historic Preservation, founded in 1949, provides leadership, education, and advocacy to save diverse historic places and revitalize communities. The Trust gives several awards recognizing excellence in preservation and restoration. The "Awards" page of the Trust's Web site provides a brief description and contact telephone number for each award. Exploring the rest of the site, visitors will find a wealth of information on historic preservation, news, membership and donor information, and online publications.

New England Foundation for the Arts (http://www.nefa.org/)

One of six regional arts organizations in the continental United States, the New England Foundation for the Arts links the public and private sectors in a regional partnership to support the arts in Connecticut, Maine, Massachusetts, New Hampshire, Rhode Island, and Vermont. Organized on a "community foundation" model, the Foundation has three program areas: the Culture in Community Fund, to strengthen the role the arts play in community development; the Connections Fund, to expand knowledge concerning the roles, practices, and social impact of the arts; and the Creation and Presentation Fund, to enable the development and presentation of high quality artistic work. Most grants are made through the Creation and Presentation Fund's New England Arts Access programs providing support to artists for art-making and to arts organizations for presenting activities in the New England area. NEFA's Web site provides descriptions of the Foundation's programs; grant program descriptions, guidelines, and deadlines; a calendar of events; news; links to other Web sites related to the arts; and a staff list with e-mail addresses.

New Israel Fund (http://www.nif.org/home/)

The New Israel Fund supports activities and groups that defend civil and human rights, promote Jewish-Arab equality and coexistence, advance the status of women, nurture tolerance and pluralism, bridge social and economic gaps, seek environmental justice, and press for government accountability within Israel. "The NIF's primary strategy is building Israel's public interest sector: it nurtures the growing network of nonpartisan, nonprofit organizations that enable Israelis to advocate more effectively to improve their lives, the conditions in their communities, and the policies of their government." To further its objectives, NIF makes grants; supports Shatil, its "capacity-building center," which provides technical assistance to some 170 Israeli public-interest groups and promotes action by coalitions of like-minded organizations; trains civil-rights and environmental lawyers; and conducts public education globally about the challenges to Israeli democracy. NIF's Web site offers detailed information about its programs; links to NIF grantees; lists of board members and senior staff; NIF contact information worldwide; and information on volunteer and donor opportunities.

New Jersey Council for the Humanities (http://www.njch.org/)
The New Jersey Council for the Humanities, established in 1973 as the state affiliate of the National Endowment for the Humanities, encourages the public's use of the humanities and supports "projects that explore and interpret the human experience, foster cross-cultural understanding, and engage people in dialogue about matters of individual choice and public responsibility." NJCH awards grants of up to $10,000 ($15,000 for media projects), minigrants of up to $3,000, "Ready Grants" for NJCH Resource Center programs, and a number of awards. Grant guidelines and a downloadable application form are provided at NJCH's Web site, as well as nomination information for the awards. Visitors to the site will also find information on volunteering, resources, and NJCH activities and newsletter.

New Mexico Endowment for the Humanities (http://www.nmeh.org)
The New Mexico Endowment for the Humanities, the state affiliate of the National Endowment for the Humanities, was founded in 1972 and seeks to bring the humanities to public audiences throughout New Mexico. In addition to descriptions and guidelines for the types of grants awarded, the site contains a list of recently funded projects. The humanities resource center lists specific programs of value to the community. Links to other nonprofits are also found on the site.

New Mexico Women's Foundation (http://www.worldplaces.com/nmwf/)
The New Mexico Women's Foundation, which seeks social justice, economic equity, peace, and security for women and girls in the state of New Mexico, supports existing programs that enable women and girls to realize their dreams. Grants focus on women and a particular problem, population, or area of New Mexico. The Foundation's Web site briefly describes its grant program, provides a listing of grants awarded since 1990, and lists the Grants and Projects Committee members. Visitors to the site will also find a history of the Foundation, a description of its work, and a listing of board members.

New Visions for Public Schools (http://www.newvisions.org/)
New Visions for Public Schools works with the New York City school system, the private sector, and the New York community to improve the educational achievements of children. New Visions' programs include creating new schools, renovating school libraries, bringing technology to classrooms, and training teachers in

innovative instruction. Visitors to the New Visions Web site will find descriptions of the organization's programs, some of which award grants; an online version of its most recent annual report; a public bulletin board; a statistical snapshot of the New York City school system; and an excellent set of links to education-related (local and national) resources.

New York Foundation for the Arts
(http://www. artswire.org/Artswire/www/nyfa/)
Through its fellowships, residencies, sponsorships, loans, information and advocacy services, the New York Foundation for the Arts "works with artists and arts organizations throughout New York State and other parts of the country to bring the work of contemporary artists to the public." NYFA's charitable vehicles include the Artists' Programs and Services division, which provides cash grants, sponsors artists' projects, and provides financial and administrative services to individual artists and their organizations; and the Revolving Loans Program, which provides short-term loans to nonprofit cultural organizations. The Foundation also provides educational and informational services to benefit the arts. NYFA's Web site offers detailed program information and specific contact information for each program, as well as a number of links to other grantmakers in the arts.

Northland Foundation (http://www.northlandfdn.org/)
The Northland Foundation, located in Duluth, Minnesota, seeks to address economic, social, and human needs in a rural seven-county area of northeastern Minnesota to accomplish greater self-sufficiency for communities, organizations, families, and individuals. The Foundation achieves these goals through grants and business loan programs. Grants are awarded in four areas: Connecting Kids and Community, Aging With Independence, Economic Diversification, and Opportunities for Self-Reliance. The Foundation's Web site provides this information and e-mail contacts for interested grantseekers, as well as information on its other activities and a staff listing with e-mail links.

North Star Fund (http://www.fex.org/north/northsta.html)
Established in 1979 in New York, the Fund is a partnership of donors and activists dedicated to progressive social change which makes grants to community-based groups in New York City that are organizing around issues of social, economic, and political justice. People of color and multiracial organizations are encouraged to submit proposals. Applications are welcomed from new organizations, especially those working on emerging issues. Guidelines and grant descriptions, and staff members to contact for information are listed on the Web site.

Northwest AIDS Foundation (http://www.nwaids.org/)
The Northwest AIDS Foundation, founded in 1983 and located in Seattle, Washington, provides case management, housing assistance, emergency grants to people with AIDS, wellness information, prevention education, public policy advocacy, and grants to associate agencies and to other AIDS service organizations throughout Washington state. The Foundation's Web site provides information on financial advocacy and assistance for people with AIDS. Also at the site: AIDS legislation and education, volunteer and donor information, links to related Web sites, and contact information.

Orangewood Children's Foundation
(http://www.InOrangeCounty.com/orangemedia/sites/orangewood/default.asp)
The Orangewood Children's Foundation, based in Orange County, California, works to reduce child abuse and neglect and to see that abused and abandoned children are cared for and become well-functioning members of society. In addition to three direct service programs, the Foundation administers the Children's Trust Fund, providing grants and scholarships to former foster children for college and living expenses and funds for foster children's special needs, such as camp, sports programs, and counseling. Grants range from $60 for high school graduation expenses to $6,000 for college tuition and books. The Foundation's Web site provides an e-mail contact for requesting more information, as well as information on child abuse, its activities, and how to contribute.

Orthopaedic Research and Education Foundation (http://www.oref.org/)
The Foundation was created in 1955 in Illinois by leaders of the specialty to "support research and build the scientific base of clinical practice." Through its fundraising efforts it raises more than $4 million dollars each year. Since its inception the Foundation has provided over $34 million through more than 1,200 grants to fund research and education programs. The Web site contains a section for Grants & Awards. This is the entrance to information concerning programs, awards and grants available, and applications. Other sections of the site include a list of staff and links to additional sources of information.

The Gary Payton Foundation (http://www.gpfoundation.org/)
Established in 1996 by Gary Payton, an All-Star NBA point guard and Olympic Gold Medalist, the Foundation's mission is to benefit underprivileged youth. Funding is currently within the greater Seattle area. The Foundation supports opportunities in the areas of education, recreation, and overall wellness to at-risk youth who are deprived of basic options in life. Grant recipients, grant guidelines, a list of the board of directors and a section on Foundation events can be found on the Web site.

Peace Development Fund (http://www.peacefund.org/)
The Peace Development Fund, located in Massachusetts, was created in 1981 to fund a grassroots peace movement. Its mission is to strengthen a broad-based social justice movement by offering grants, training, and other resources in collaboration with other communities, organizations, trainers, and donors with whom they share a common goal. Funding is primarily focused on peace, community development, and citizen coalitions. Projects, types of grants, application information, and a recent list of grantees are accessible on the Web site.

Pediatric Brain Tumor Foundation of the United States
(http://www.ride4kids.org/)
The Pediatric Brain Tumor Foundation of the United States seeks to find the cause of as well as a cure for childhood brain tumors; aid in the early detection and treatment of such tumors; and provide hope to the families of children afflicted with brain tumors. The Foundation also supports the development of a national database on all primary brain tumors and provides funding for research on new therapies designed to extend the lives of stricken children. Although the Foundation's Web site is geared toward attracting new donors and participants in Ride 4 Kids, a

motorcycle fundraising event started in 1984 in Atlanta, Georgia, it does provide a list of recent grant recipients, a list of the board of directors, and contact information.

Pennsylvania Humanities Council (http://www.libertynet.org/phc/)
The Pennsylvania Humanities Council, the state affiliate of the National Endowment for the Humanities, conducts and supports "public humanities programs for adults who seek lifelong learning in history, philosophy, literature, and related subjects." The Council provides qualified nonprofit organizations with resources for developing humanities programs, including speakers, grants, and access to local scholars. The PCH Web site offers a brief description of its grant program and interactive forms for requesting more information or grants counseling.

The Pet Care Trust (http://petsforum.com/petcaretrust/)
The Pet Care Trust seeks to enhance public and professional understanding of companion animals and their value. The Trust awards grants to direct service programs to improve the health and welfare of pets; to research programs exploring various aspects of the health, care, and possession of companion animals; and to education programs that enhance the public's knowledge and professionalism among pet care professionals. The Trust's Web site lists grant recipients and provides contact information for further grant information. The site also provides a listing of the board of trustees, and selected program video clips.

Pharmaceutical Research and Manufacturers of America Foundation (http://www.phrmaf.org/)
The PhRMA Foundation promotes public health through support of scientific and medical research into improved medicines. The Foundation's funding helps to develop the careers of young scientists and researchers; establish an infrastructure of expertise in biomedical technology, scientific research, and outcomes measurement; and build alliances between industry and academia scientists. Foundation grants, fellowships, and faculty awards are available in the areas of Clinical Pharmacology, Basic Pharmacology, Bioinformatics, Pharmacology-Morphology, Pharmaceutics, and Pharmacoeconomics. Guidelines and application forms can be downloaded (in various formats) from the Foundation's Web site, which also provides listings of the Foundation's board, advisory committees, and benefactors.

Philanthrofund Foundation (http://www.scc.net/~philanth/)
The Philanthrofund Foundation provides financial and fundraising support to organizations that serve the needs and enhance the quality of life of the gay, lesbian, bisexual, transgender, and allied communities of the Upper Midwest—primarily in the state of Minnesota. Typical grants range from $1,000 to $2,000, and the Foundation keeps its definition of who is eligible for funding intentionally broad. The Foundation's Web site provides grant guidelines and application instructions, along with a listing of board members and last year's grant recipients.

The Ploughshares Fund (http://www.ploughshares.org/)
Founded at a time when global nuclear conflict seemed a real and immediate possibility, the Ploughshares Fund was designed to provide financial support to

people and organizations working to eliminate the threat of nuclear war. Plough-shares now focuses its support on combating the burgeoning trade in conventional weapons, the explosion of regional conflict in the aftermath of the Cold War, and the growing danger of nuclear weapons proliferation following the breakup of the Soviet Union. Ploughshares has made over 1,000 grants totaling more than $15 million. Visitors to the Foundation's Web site will find detailed information on its main areas of interest: banning land mines, preventing armed conflict, restraining the weapons trade, cutting Pentagon waste, cleaning up our radioactive environ-ment, and fighting nuclear terrorism and proliferation. A grants list—with links to grantee Web sites—is available, along with grant application guidelines, an inter-active subscription form for the Foundation's free newsletter, board and staff lists, and contact information.

Points of Light Foundation (http://www.pointsoflight.org/default.html)
Created in 1990 and merged with the National Volunteer Center in 1991, the Foundation is a nonpartisan, nonprofit organization dedicated to fostering volunteerism. It is located in Washington, D.C., and works throughout the nation through a network of more than 500 Volunteer Centers. "Connect America," the Foundation's initiative, was launched in response to the belief that disconnection and alienation are the root causes of social problems. The Foundation seeks to bring people together through volunteer service as a powerful way to combat these challenges. Major areas of the Foundation's work and several awards pro-grams are described at their Web site.

The Pride Foundation, (http://www.pridefoundation.org/)
The Foundation was chartered in 1985 in Washington by the Greater Seattle Busi-ness Association. Its mission is to "strengthen the lesbian, gay, transgender, and bisexual community today and to build an endowment fund for tomorrow." Pride funds a wide range of projects including arts and recreation, education and advo-cacy, HIV/AIDS education and support, lesbian health, youth and family services, etc. Lists and descriptions of scholarship and grants programs, application infor-mation, names of contact persons, and links to additional resources on granting can be accessed on the Web site.

Princess Grace Foundation - USA (http://www.pgfusa.com/)
Established in 1982 in memory of Princess Grace of Monaco, the Princess Grace Foundation–USA supports emerging young artists nationwide in the fields of the-ater, dance, and film. Students in their last year of schooling or training are eligi-ble for tuition assistance through scholarships, while young artists working in the areas of theater and dance qualify for apprenticeships and fellowships. The Foun-dation, which has awarded over $1.6 million in grants since 1984, also recognizes exceptional and continuing professional achievement through the awarding of Princess Grace Statuettes, its highest honor, to two or three recipients annually. The Foundation's Web site provides a fact sheet and background information about the Foundation, application guidelines, a list of recent grantees, and contact information.

Public Entity Risk Institute (http://www.riskinstitute.org)
The Institute was established in 1997 in Virginia, as the result of the settlement of a civil anti-trust lawsuit brought by states, private, and nonprofit organizations

against insurance companies which "alleged anti-trust violations by the firms in the availability and cost of liability insurance, particularly for local governments." PERI is primarily focused on small public entity risk issues but develops its programs and services with an awareness that small nonprofit organizations and businesses are concerned with issues similar to public entities. Its grants and research program targets risk management, impairment of the environment, and disaster management. The Web site contains a list of topics. Choose the onriskinstitute.org button for a summary of all the sections.

Ayn Rand Institute/The Center for the Advancement of Objectivism (http://www.aynrand.org/)

The Ayn Rand Institute was founded in 1985 by philosopher Leonard Peikoff to advance Objectivism, Ayn Rand's philosophy of reason, egoism, individualism, and laissez-faire capitalism. The Institute influences the public through opinion pieces and its own media projects; runs a "Campaign Against Servitude" opposing volunteerism; sponsors essay contests; supports college and university campus clubs; and produces materials and training on Objectivism. The Institute's Web site provides a fair amount of information on Objectivism and Ayn Rand, and describes the activities of the Institute.

The Donna Reed Foundation for the Performing Arts (http://www.frii.com/donna_reed/)

The Donna Reed Foundation for the Performing Arts was formed in 1987 in Denison, Iowa, to memorialize Ms. Reed's achievements and to perpetuate the actress's belief in the importance of education and the pursuit of one's dreams. The Foundation supports talented youth through national, state, and local scholarships; conducts workshops by industry professionals; and promotes stage plays, concerts, and other cultural activities. The Foundation's Web site provides information about the Donna Reed Scholarships for students of the performing arts, including a downloadable application form. The site also provides details and registration information for workshops, membership information, and press releases about the Foundation and its activities.

Resist, Inc. (http://www.resistinc.org)

Created in 1967 to support draft resistance and opposition to the Vietnam War, Resist, located in Massachusetts, has broadened and deepened its commitment to the social action movement. Resist supports groups to develop leadership, work on innovative grassroots campaigns, hire organizers, distribute literature and videos related to those campaigns, and demand justice on a variety of issues. The Web site provides grant guidelines, projects, a recent list of grantees, links to other resources, and a list of the board of directors and staff.

Rex Foundation (http://www.gl.umbc.edu/~jlockn1/rex.html)

The Rex Foundation, a charitable foundation established by members and friends of the Grateful Dead, "aims to help secure a healthy environment, promote individuality in the arts, provide support to critical and necessary social services, assist others less fortunate than ourselves, protect the rights of indigenous people and ensure their cultural survival, build a stronger community, and to educate children and adults everywhere." Virtually all the Foundation's grant recipients are preselected; therefore, unsolicited requests are not considered.

Jackie Robinson Foundation (http://www.jackierobinson.org/)

The Jackie Robinson Foundation, founded in 1973 by Rachel Robinson, helps young people in financial need to reach their potential through education. The Foundation awards four scholarships annually to minority students enrolled in higher education studies, and offers personal and career counseling, and assistance obtaining employment. The Foundation's Web site provides scholarship guidelines, and alumni and donor information.

Rockefeller Family Fund (http://www.rffund.org/)

The New York City-based Rockefeller Family Fund supports tax-exempt organizations engaged in educational and charitable activities of national significance. It does not usually fund projects pertaining only to a single community. In addition to general program descriptions, visitors to the Fund's Web site will find a list (by program and alphabetically) of recent grantees and links to those with Web sites, application procedures, a letter from the Fund's president, a listing of the Fund's trustees and staff, and information about the Rockefeller Technology Project, which helps grantees to learn about and effectively use new communication technology.

Rose Community Foundation (http://www.rcfdenver.org)

Founded in 1995 with proceeds from the sale of Rose Medical Center, the Foundation's work is focused on aging, child and family development, education, health and Jewish life in the greater Denver area. Within the Rose Community Foundation, the Rose Biomedical Research organization works to address significant health needs of the community. RBR seeks to conduct research to develop new medical devices to improve the quality and reduce the cost of care. A site map will enable you to quickly navigate the site.

The Rotary Foundation of Rotary International (http://www.rotary.org/foundation/)

As the philanthropic arm of Rotary International, the Rotary Foundation supports efforts to "achieve world understanding and peace through international humanitarian, educational, and cultural exchange programs." The Foundation sponsors activities in two main areas: the Humanitarian Programs, which fund projects designed to improve quality of life, primarily in the developing world; and the Educational Programs, through which the Foundation provides funding for students to study abroad each year, for university professors to teach in developing countries, and for exchanges of business and professional people. In addition to general program descriptions, visitors to the Foundation area of Rotary International's Web site will find information on the Foundation's history, support, and governance, including a list of trustees.

Albert B. Sabin Vaccine Institute at Georgetown University (http://www.sabin.georgetown.edu/)

The Albert B. Sabin Vaccine Institute was established to promote "rapid scientific advances in vaccine development, delivery and distribution worldwide." (Albert B. Sabin developed the original polio vaccine.) In the field of vaccine development, the Institute supports the academic development of scientists and physicians; provides grants for research, development, and testing; advocates for the integration of scientific advances and public policy; and promotes public awareness of vaccine research and the development of educational materials. The Institute's Web site offers brief descriptions of its programs and activities and contact information.

Stanley J. Sarnoff Endowment for Cardiovascular Science, Inc. (http://www.sarnoffendowment.org)

The mission of the Stanley J. Sarnoff Endowment is to interest medical school students in careers in cardiovascular research. The Endowment administers a Fellowship Program that is open to students currently attending medical school, and a Scholars Program, which is open to former Sarnoff Fellows. Details of both programs are outlined on the Endowment's Web site along with information about current and past Sarnoff Fellows and Scholars. The Fellowship application can be downloaded (in PDF format) along with sample essays from previous applicants. The site also provides a brief biography of Dr. Sarnoff, information about the Endowment's scientific board and board of directors, and contact information.

Detlef Schrempf Foundation (http://www.detlef.com/index.html)

The Foundation was established in 1996 in Washington state by Detlef Schrempf, a professional basketball player whose concern for children and belief in the value of a solid family life provided the basis for the organization. The Foundation funds events for various children's charities and youth organizations. Specific concerns of the Foundation are homelessness, housing, education, HIV/AIDS, and health services for children and youth. The Foundation's Web site provides information on fundraising accomplishments, current charities and charity guidelines, contact information, and an events calendar.

The Sierra Club Foundation (http://www.sierraclub.org/affiliated/foundation.htm)

The Sierra Club Foundation funds charitable, scientific, artistic, and educational endeavors of the Sierra Club and other environmental organizations. The page of the Sierra Club's Web site devoted to the Foundation offers a description of the organization and examples of funding projects.

Social Science Research Council (http://www.ssrc.org/)

The Social Science Research Council (SSRC), an independent, nongovernmental, not-for-profit international association, was created in 1923 to further the advancement of interdisciplinary research in the social sciences. The Council holds workshops and conferences and offers fellowships and grants, summer training institutes, scholarly exchanges and publications. The Web site contains grant and fellowship information, application information, descriptions of ongoing fellowship and grant programs, and links to related committees and organizations. For advice on how to write effective proposals, access Fellowships and go to that subsection.

Society of Manufacturing Engineers Education Foundation (http://www.sme.org/cgi-bin/smeefhtml.pl?/foundation/homepg.htm&SME&)

The Society of Manufacturing Engineers is a professional membership organization for career development. SME's Education Foundation makes grants of $50,000 to $500,000 that target "competency gaps" in manufacturing identified by SME's Manufacturing Education Plan. Programs should involve local industry and encompass interdisciplinary university education. The Education Foundation area of SME's Web site provides an outline of its grant program, including guidelines, application form, recent funding results, board members, donor information, related links, and contact information.

Sons of Italy Foundation (http://www.osia.org/sif/sif.html)

The Sons of Italy Foundation, established in 1959, supports programs to preserve Italian-American culture, encourage educational excellence, and support transatlantic initiatives for diplomatic, economic, and educational exchanges. The Foundation's Web site provides information on its National Leadership Grant Competition—comprising several scholarship programs—along with application forms to download and profiles of last year's scholarship winners. The Foundation's other philanthropic activities, described briefly on the site, include of medical research for genetic diseases, provision of homes for orphans, aid to victims of natural disasters, forums on international issues, strengthening of communities through law enforcement projects, and sponsorship of special programs of national and international significance.

South Dakota Humanities Council
(http://www.sdstate.edu/~whum/http/home.html)

The South Dakota Humanities Council, formerly known as The South Dakota Committee on the Humanities, was founded in 1972 as the state's affiliate of the National Endowment for the Humanities. It explores and promotes state, regional, and national programs centered on ideas, history, and culture. The Council's grant program funds projects that increase public appreciation and use of the humanities. Their Web site provides program guidelines which include application procedures, links to state humanities sites, information concerning speaker guidelines and application forms, grants awarded, and a list of the board of directors.

Southern Education Foundation http://www.sefatl.org/

The Southern Education Foundation was formed in 1937—the merger of four funds committed to developing educational opportunities for minorities and disadvantaged citizens following the Civil War—to help achieve equal educational opportunities for minority students. The Foundation operates programs with funding partners that focus on teacher preparation, student opportunity and performance, educational equity and opportunity, socioeconomic factors affecting equity, and community enrichment. The Foundation supports programs in collaboration with funding partners, which are listed at its Web site (with links to those with Web sites). Grant lists are provided for each program, along with information on the Foundation's activities, history, and contact information.

Special Libraries Association (http://www.sla.org/)

The Special Libraries Association seeks to be "a catalyst in the development of the information economy, and a strategic partner in the emerging information society." To that end, SLA has set research goals related to the topics of futures, current/user issues, measures of productivity and value, client/user satisfaction measures, and staffing. SLA awards grants through the Steven I. Goldspiel Memorial Research Fund to support research on and advancement of library sciences. SLA's Web site provides guidelines, an application form to print out, and information on recent recipients and their projects, publications, and links to other funding sources. Contact information for Research as well as the SLA Scholarship, can be found in "Association Information: SLA Unit Leadership: SLA Committees."

Spirits of the Land Foundation (http://greatspirit.earth.com/)

The Spirits of the Land Foundation supports education and activities benefiting state and federally recognized Indian tribes, bands, and nations, and supports scientific research to benefit humanity and earth. The Foundation's Web site provides news, Indian resources and business opportunities, Indian attractions in Oklahoma, and mailing addresses of tribes and leaders. Although the site doesn't provide much detail on the research it supports, contact information is provided.

St. Luke's Charitable Health Trust (http://www.sltrust.com/)

The St. Luke's Charitable Health Trust, located in Phoenix, Arizona, invests in the development and support of activities, programs, and organizations that improve the health of people in the Phoenix metropolitan area. In its grantmaking, the Trust places emphasis on prevention programs for children, youth and families; delivery of health services to the underserved; and building the capacity of communities to help themselves. The Trust awards community grants, "Bridge" grants for emerging programs, individual medical financial assistance, and issues RFPs for special initiatives. Application information for grants is provided at the Trust's Web site, along with a listing of recently awarded grants, proposal tips, and evaluation criteria.

TAPPI Foundation, Inc.
(http://www.tappi.org/public/foundation/foundation_main.asp)

Created in 1990 by the Technical Association of the Pulp and Paper Industry to support research and education, the TAPPI Foundation awards research grants to scientists and engineers for projects that will assist in securing the future of the paper and pulp industries. Research needs of the industry are available for download in PDF format on the Foundation's Web site, and the Foundation encourages proposal submissions from newcomers to the industry. The site also provides guidelines, the application in PDF format, research summaries for award recipients, and a funding evaluation form.

A Territory Resource Foundation (http://www.atrfoundation.org/)

Based in Seattle, Washington, A Territory Resource Foundation strives to "create a more equitable, just, and environmentally sound society for all" by providing limited financial support to activist, community-based organizations in the states of Idaho, Montana, Oregon, Washington, and Wyoming. In addition to grant guidelines and a list of recent grantees, visitors to the ATR Web site will find a brief history of the Foundation, a copy of the director's report, a short essay on socially responsible investing, and donor information.

Texas Council for the Humanities (http://www.public-humanities.org/)

The Texas Council for the Humanities, established in 1972, working with the National Endowment for the Humanities, encourages the people of Texas to engage in "critical reflection on their individual and collective lives by providing opportunities for lifelong learning in the humanities." TCH's grant program provides financial support to nonprofit organizations and institutions for public educational humanities programs through Packaged Programs and Speakers Grants, Community Projects Grants, General Grants, and Media Grants. TCH's Web site provides guidelines and a printable form for ordering application forms by mail or fax. The site also provides information about its activities, publications, and donors, as well as listings of board and staff members and related links.

Theatre Communications Group (http://www.tcg.org/)

Theatre Communications Group was founded in 1961 to provide artistic, administrative, and information services to theaters and independent theater artists. TCG collaborates with the National Endowment for the Arts to offer a residency program for playwrights and career development programs for directors and designers. Guidelines for these programs are provided at TCG's Web site. TCG also offers extended collaboration grants to fund research and developmental time for playwrights and collaborating artists, as well as National Theatre Artist Residency grants. Although information at the site on these programs and about the Foundation in general is limited, contact information, including e-mail, is provided.

The TIA Foundation (http://www.tia.org/whatsTIA/found.stm)

The TIA Foundation was founded in 1990 to benefit the U.S. travel industry by supporting education and research vital to the concerns of the industry. The Foundation awards yearly graduate and undergraduate scholarships. Although the Foundation's Web site does not provide application information, it does list its board members and contact information.

The Tides Foundation, (http://www.tides.org/)

Established in 1976, the Tides Foundation, located in California, supports community-based organizations on both a national and international basis and the larger progressive movement through innovative grantmaking. It seeks to promote social change by funding primarily in areas concerned with the environment, international affairs, economic public policy and enterprise development, social justice, and community affairs. The Foundation encourages nonprofit entities working toward social change to request their Guidelines for Grantseekers, which offer advice on preparing and funding a request. To request additional information a contact address is listed.

Richard Tucker Music Foundation (http://www.rtucker.com/)

The Richard Tucker Music Foundation helps to advance the careers of promising and talented American opera singers, and seeks to heighten public awareness of opera. The Foundation offers awards and grants for study, performance, and other career-related activities to singers at an advanced level of vocal training or nearing artistic acclaim. Nominations are solicited from a national panel of opera professionals. The Foundation's Web site describes these programs and provides lists of recipients, as well as a listing of board members, events and contact information.

Les Turner Amyotropic Lateral Sclerosis Foundation (http://www.lesturnerals.org/)

The Foundation was established in 1977 in Illinois, by Les Turner, a Chicago-area businessman who at the age of 36 was diagnosed with Amyotropic Lateral Sclerosis, commonly known as Lou Gehrig's disease. "The Foundation supports the ALS community in Chicago and its suburbs and is affiliated with Northwestern

University Medical School." The Foundation funds state-of-the-art research programs, a clinic, a tissue bank, support groups, communication and equipment banks, and educational programs. The Web site provides an overview of ALS, staff names, and an e-mail address for additional information.

An Uncommon Legacy Foundation, Inc. (http://www.uncommonlegacy.org)
The Uncommon Legacy Foundation, was founded in 1990 to enhance the visibility, strength, and vitality of the lesbian community. The Foundation awards scholarships to openly lesbian students with leadership potential, and funds projects and organizations that contribute to the health, education, and culture of the lesbian community. The Foundation's Web site provides grant guidelines and a downloadable application form in PDF format; scholarship guidelines, and a list of recent scholarship recipients; an online version of the Foundation's newsletter; and information for prospective donors.

United Hospital Fund (http://www.uhfnyc.org/)
Established in 1879, the fund was originally focused on New York City hospitals. Today that focus has been broadened to include all aspects of health care concerning New York City and the people it serves. The Fund is dedicated to providing reliable information and conducts research and analysis on health care that ultimately helps shape pubic policy. Through its grants and programs it targets issues like "shaping the financing and organization of an evolving health care system, improving access to care for vulnerable persons, advancing social values in the mission and governance of health care organizations, enhancing the quality of hospital care for patients and their families, developing services and systems for people with chronic health problems, and promoting volunteer leadership and participation." A recent grants list, descriptions of the grants and programs, and contact information can be accessed on their Web site.

United States Institute of Peace (http://www.usip.org/)
Founded in 1984, "the Institute aims to strengthen the nation's capacity to promote the peaceful resolution of international conflict. It meets this congressional mandate through an array of funded projects including grants, fellowships, conferences, workshops, library services, publications, and other educational activities." A description of the Institute's grants, fellowships, application guidelines, links, and a list of the board of directors can be accessed on the Web site.

Utah Humanities Council (http://www.utahhumanities.org)
The Utah Humanities Council, the state affiliate of the National Endowment for the Humanities, promotes learning through the humanities. UHC provides grants and technical assistance to nonprofit organizations and a limited number of individual grants to teachers and scholars. Grant programs include competitive grants to nonprofits up to $5,000, "quick grants" for smaller projects, Teacher Incentive Program grants of $500, and an annual $3,000 research fellowship. Guidelines and application forms (in PDF, WP 6, or MS Word 6 formats) can be viewed and downloaded at UHC's Web site. Visitors to the site will also find online versions of the most recent annual report (in PDF format) and newsletter; details of UHC's activities; and contact and donor information.

V Foundation (http://www.jimmyv.org/)

Founded by the late Jim Valvano and ESPN, the cable sports network, the V Foundation seeks to raise awareness of and support for cancer research. Although grant information on the Foundation's Web site is limited to a list of recent grant recipients, visitors to the site can read about the life and times of Jimmy "V," learn more about events staged in support of the Foundation, and sign up for e-mail updates about the Foundation and its activities.

Vanguard Public Foundation (http://www.fex.org/van/vanguard.html)

Established in 1972 in California, the Foundation is committed to social justice. It primarily funds projects without access to traditional funding sources because they may be thought to be risky, controversial, or of low priority. The Foundation's specific interests include "working on issues of civil rights, economic justice, workers' rights, women's rights, education, disability, health, housing, environment, cultural activism, indigenous peoples' rights and international solidarity." Grant guidelines, contact information and a staff list can be found on the Web site.

Virginia Health Care Foundation (http://www.vhcf.org/)

The Virginia Health Care Foundation funds local public-private partnerships that increase access to primary health care services for uninsured and medically underserved residents of the Commonwealth. VHCF supports projects that offer innovative primary care service delivery, increase primary care providers in target areas, incorporate telemedicine initiatives, and/or replicate VHCF's "Models That Made It"—programs that have proven to be cost effective and capable of sustaining themselves. The VHCF Web site offers descriptions of the Foundation's funding categories, answers to frequently asked questions, grant guidelines, a listing of board and staff members, and information for donors.

Washington Commission for the Humanities (http://www.humanities.org/)

The Washington Commission for the Humanities supports humanities projects—which it defines as "the stories, ideas and writings that help us make sense of our lives and enhance our ability to think creatively and critically about our world"—in Washington State. Grants are awarded for a range of programs and activities, including exhibits, public forums, school programs, reading and discussion series, and cultural events. The WCH Web site provides grant guidelines—applicants are encouraged to contact WCH before applying—along with information about past recipients. WCH also gives two annual awards, the Washington Humanities Award and the Governor's Writers Award, with eligibility requirements provided on the site.

West Central Minnesota Initiative Fund (http://www.wcif.org/)

The West Central Initiative was created to enhance the viability of the west central Minnesota region through six funding initiatives: quality employment, workforce, housing, community, family, and economic development. The WCI Web site thoroughly details these initiatives and also provides more than a dozen downloadable application forms in PDF format. Where applications are not available, e-mail links are provided for requesting the forms via regular mail. In addition to its funding programs, the WCI site provides a variety of regional information, including links to community home pages.

Western States Arts Federation (http://www.westaf.org/)

The Western States Arts Federation, also known as WESTAF, supports state arts agencies, arts organizations, and artists in the western United States to promote creative advancement and preservation of the arts. Its current work centers on arts policy research, information systems development, and the convening of arts experts and leaders. Most program information is available in the "News" section of WESTAF's Web site. WESTAF also publishes "ArtJob," a bi-monthly publication of national and international listings of arts employment and related opportunities in the Arts, which is available by subscription online or by regular mail.

Wheat Ridge Ministries (http://www.wheatridge.org/)

Wheat Ridge is an independent Lutheran charitable organization that provides seed money grants for new church-related "health and hope" ministries that address health-related issues through Christian service, or prevent conditions that keep people from living full lives. Wheat Ridge awards Major Grants, Special Short-Term Grants, and Congregation Health and Hope Grants. The Ministries' Web site provides proposal guidelines, grantwriting resources, and recipients, as well as news, Web, video, and fax resources, Wheat Ridge awards, and a listing of board and staff members.

The Woodrow Wilson National Fellowship Foundation (http://www.woodrow.org/)

The Woodrow Wilson National Fellowship Foundation encourages excellence in education by developing and funding programs that target the needs of new teachers and scholars, that encourage cooperation between academia and other sectors of society, that improve the status and representation of minority groups and women, and that maintain the vitality of teachers. The Foundation offers numerous fellowships, grants, and scholarships in the humanities, public policy and international affairs, women's studies, children and women's health, and teacher development, all of which are described in detail at its Web site. Visitors to the site will also find an online version of the Foundation's most recent annual report, information about upcoming Foundation-sponsored conferences, press releases, listings of board and staff, and contact information.

Wisconsin Humanities Council (http://www.danenet.wicip.org/whc/)

Founded in 1972 as an independent affiliate of the National Endowment for the Humanities, the council is a nonprofit, nonpartisan organization governed by a board comprised of volunteers from every part of the areas it serves. The Council seeks to support public programs that deepen the awareness of cultures, ideas and values in the humanities through an exchange of ideas between scholars and the people in the community. It addresses questions of importance to Wisconsin residents through its projects, speakers forum, resource center and grant programs. A recent list of funded projects, types of grants, grant guidelines, links to other humanities councils and to the University of Wisconsin Extension through which the Council operates can be accessed on their Web site.

Women's Funding Alliance (http://www.wfalliance.org)

The Alliance was founded in 1993 in Washington. The fund is a federation of 13 nonprofit member agencies and a community fund providing services and advocacy for women and girls. It is focused on critical issues like domestic violence, sexual assault, and discrimination. The community fund expands on this commitment by supporting organizations that are not addressed by the member agencies.

Women's Sports Foundation
(http://www.lifetimetv.com/WoSport/stage/INTERACT/)
The Women's Sports Foundation, founded in 1974 by Billie Jean King and other female athletes, is dedicated to increasing opportunities for girls and women in sports and fitness through education, advocacy, recognition, and grants. Visitors should follow the "Funding" link on the Web site's athletic shoe navigation tool to find detailed information on numerous grant and scholarship programs, some of which provide downloadable application forms.

The Tiger Woods Foundation, Inc.
(http://ww1.sportsline.com/u/fans/celebrity/tiger/course/foundation.html)
The Foundation was created in 1996 by Eldrick Tiger Woods who chose not to complete his undergraduate education at Stanford University in order to pursue his interest in professional golf. The Foundation is particularly focused on the welfare of children and families living in urban areas. Grantmaking is centered on children, family health and welfare, education, parenting and youth development. The menu on the Web site lists a Year in Review section, in which you will find a list of funded projects, and a policies and procedures section in which you will find application information and a list of staff and benefactors.

World Wildlife Fund (http://www.worldwildlife.org/)
The World Wildlife Fund, the largest privately supported international conservation organization in the world, directs its conservation efforts toward three global goals: protecting and saving endangered species (e.g., elephants, pandas, rhinos, tigers, whales) and addressing global threats to wildlife (e.g., global warming, worldwide deforestation, overfishing). The Fund's beautiful Web site provides a great deal of information on its activities around the world as well as on issues related to conservation. While grant information does not fall into a particular area of the site, recent grants lists can be found by entering the word "grant" into the site's search engine.

Wyoming Council for the Humanities (http://www.uwyo.edu/special/wch/)
The Wyoming Council for the Humanities fosters interaction between the public and humanities scholars on questions related to the "significant dimensions of our existence—personal, social, cultural, and political—from local, national, and international perspectives." The Council awards grants to Wyoming nonprofits to support public presentations that examine the humanities. Programs supported by WCH generally comprise lectures, panel discussions, conferences, seminars, exhibits, historical dramatizations, and/or community forums. Visitors to the WCH Web site will find information on the Council's activities, grant guidelines and downloadable application forms, a database of humanities scholars, an online newsletter, and information for prospective donors.

CHAPTER FIVE

Corporate Giving Information on the Web

This chapter will cover the following key points, while acknowledging that finding information specific to corporate giving on the Web requires more creativity than is required researching other giving sources.

- What is corporate giving?
- Company-sponsored foundations vs. direct corporate giving programs
- Using the Internet to find corporate grantmakers
- Researching corporate information
- Corporate giving on the Internet
- Utilizing the material
- Links and abstracts of corporate givers

In general, while some funding sources, the government for instance (see Chapter 6), provide an overwhelming amount of funding information to be sifted through on the Web, in the corporate world, you will have to sift through a lot of other information about various companies to locate information specific to their funding programs.

Corporate Grantmaking: An Overview

Companies large and small in the United States traditionally have provided philanthropic support to the communities in which they operate as well as to worthy charitable causes. The motivations behind individual corporations' giving vary widely and can be complex. Before delving into corporate giving research using the Web, a brief description of why and how corporations may give can offer grantseekers a better understanding of what to look for in undertaking this research.

Corporate giving usually entails a combination of altruism and self-interest. Unlike foundations and other charitable agencies, corporations don't exist to give. Their main responsibilities are to their employees, customers, shareholders, and the bottom line. They give to support employee services, to guarantee a supply of well-trained potential employees, to build community relations and community life, both local and national, to enhance company image, to return favors, to get tax deductions, and to influence policymakers and other opinion makers.

Companies understand the power of publicity and that charitable giving helps build a strong community image. That makes giving essential for good corporate business and citizenship. However, corporations expect concrete rewards for their generosity.

Many companies have begun to use the Internet as a means to advertise their philanthropic activities. By posting grantmaking activities on the Web, companies make the public aware that they are involved in improving the quality of life, particularly in areas of company operations. This exposure gives the company a positive image and improves public relations.

TRENDS IN CORPORATE GIVING

In recent years corporations have reshaped and rethought their giving programs, narrowing their focus to specific objectives, examining how grants are used, and thinking in terms of possible benefits. They also have developed additional non-cash giving programs.

Companies often favor causes in the public eye like education, with a focus on math, science, minority education, and school reform. Environmental issues, low-income housing, and preventive health maintenance are also popular areas of giving.

In addition, companies want to maximize the impact of their giving. Direct involvement with students and teachers, in projects like the Adopt-A-School program and other tutoring and mentoring programs, is one approach. Across the board, companies want to plan and manage, foster collaborative donor and non-profit efforts, and take on long-term projects. They also look to volunteerism in the bid for community standing.

COMPANY-SPONSORED FOUNDATIONS AND CORPORATE GIVING PROGRAMS

Companies provide support to nonprofits through private "company-sponsored" foundations, direct giving programs, or both. Company-sponsored foundations usually maintain close ties with their sponsoring company, and their giving reflects that corporation's interests. Most maintain relatively small endowments and rely on contributions from the company to support their programs. Some corporations build their foundations' endowments in fat years and tap into them in lean ones so that their giving levels remains fairly consistent.

Foundations must adhere to the appropriate regulations, including filing a yearly IRS Form 990-PF, which includes a report on contributions. These returns are publicly available from the IRS and at Foundation Center libraries and cooperating collections. They can be very helpful in researching individual corporate foundations.

As of fall 1999, new disclosure regulations were proposed. Under the proposed regulations, foundations are required to provide, at a "reasonable fee," photocopies of their three most recent tax returns—including 990-PF and 4720 forms—as well as their original application for tax-exempt status to anyone who requests them in person or in writing. As with other tax-exempt organizations, the requirements can be satisfied by private foundations making the documents "widely available" through the Internet. Foundations will not be required to fulfill requests when they are determined to be part of a campaign of harassment. Unlike other tax-exempt organizations, however, foundations will be required to make publicly available the names and addresses of their donors.

Direct corporate giving—all charitable activities outside the company's foundation—is less regulated than foundation giving. Corporations are not required to publicize direct giving programs or sustain prescribed funding levels. They also may give to nonprofits out of operating funds, and these expenditures won't show up in their giving statistics. Direct giving programs and foundations often share staff, adding to the confusion. For these reasons, finding information on direct company giving programs can be difficult.

"In-kind gifts" (such as donated products or loaned employee services) constitute an estimated 20 percent of corporate giving, although these numbers may be inflated due to the fact that many companies report their in-kind donations at market value rather than at their cost. Whatever the true percentage of corporate giving they represent, in-kind gifts are sometimes overlooked by organizations seeking company support.

For all the reasons noted above, most of the corporate giving information available on the Web concerns company-sponsored foundations. Foundations usually provide much more specific information concerning their grantmaking activities, including information on application addresses, contact persons, geographic limitations, fields of interest supported, types of support offered, and so on. One of the advantages to a company of using a direct giving program rather than a company-sponsored foundation is precisely that the company need not disclose how much or to whom they contribute. Therefore, to find out about direct corporate giving programs, grantseekers must use a little more strategy and a discerning selection process.

One of the basic handicaps is that companies often use their Web site primarily as a public relations tool. They may put up several pages concerning some of the grants they have given in the recent past and little else. Unfortunately, this kind of Web site can lead a grantseeker to believe that they are eligible for a grant when in fact they are not. Sites like these often generate hundreds, if not thousands, of applications to companies that do not accept unsolicited applications or who will not support the causes for which they are receiving applications.

THE COMMUNITY REINVESTMENT ACT

The passage of the Community Reinvestment Act (CRA) as a federal law in 1977 requires banks to help meet the credit needs of their entire community, including low- and moderate-income neighborhoods. Banks failing to do so may be denied permission by the government to expand their business locations, buy or merge with other banks, or engage in interstate banking. So, grantseekers looking for *loans* rather than cash or in-kind gifts should concentrate on banking firms in their communities.

It is debated within the philanthropic field whether these CRA loans represent a form of corporate giving at all. Some companies include their loans as part of their total charitable giving, at the same time that they earn interest on these investments.

The Community Reinvestment Act does not require banks to make unsound business decisions. Banks are not obliged to make loans to organizations or individuals believed to be a great risk. The CRA gives banks a general direction in order to serve the needs of the community in which they are located rather than direct them to make specific loans. CRA stimulates banks to make loans for low-income family housing, invest in community development, and support small businesses. Whether a true form of corporate charitable giving or not, we mention CRA loans here as an avenue of potential assistance for some people.

How to Find Corporate Funders

Corporate giving is often in fields related to corporate activities and in company communities. The grantseeker's search should focus on local businesses as well as major corporations. Corporate directories and corporate giving studies are key resources.

A company-sponsored foundation's tax return (Form 990-PF) is available through IRS district offices, at the foundation's office, through the attorney general for the state in which the foundation is chartered, and at Foundation Center libraries and cooperating collections. As noted earlier, according to the proposed regulations, corporate foundations—like any other private foundations—are required to provide at a "reasonable fee," upon written request, photocopies of their three most recent tax returns (Forms 990-PF and 4720) and their original application for tax-exempt status. Placing tax returns on the Web satisfies the "widely available" stipulation in the regulations.

In addition to the Web strategies outlined below, grantseekers should consult public libraries for regional and business indexes. The local Chamber of Commerce and Better Business Bureau may also have such guides. Do not overlook the yellow pages and staff community knowledge. In corporate grantseeking, personal contacts are invaluable. A grantseeker should consider their staff, board members, and volunteers as assets who may know corporate funders; they should be encouraged to investigate giving policies at these companies.

USING THE WEB

Many companies now maintain a presence on the World Wide Web, an important potential source for information about corporate community involvement and grantmaking activities.

Searching: Let Others Do the Searching for You

Several Web sites are good starting points for grantseekers on a quest for funding from corporate giving programs and company-sponsored foundations. Two are the Foundation Center's Corporate Grantmakers on the Internet (http://fdncenter.org/grantmaker/gws_corp/corp.html) and the U.K.-based Charities Aid

Foundation's CCInet (http://www.ccinet.org/frames/fpages.html). These sites have extensive lists of hypertext links to corporate giving programs and company-sponsored foundations. (See Chapter 2 for more detail on the Foundation Center's Web site.)

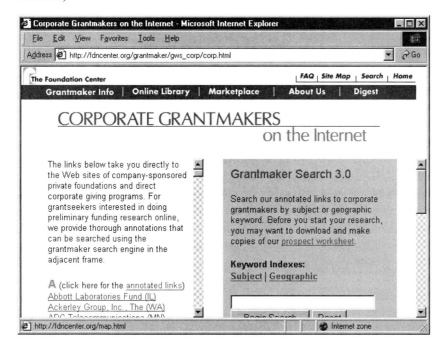

Another place to get started is the Council on Foundations' Web site (http://www.cof.org). This site includes a page addressing corporate grantmaking.

Other Web pages worthy of mention for corporate giving information include Internet Prospector's Corporate Giving page (http://w3.uwyo.edu/~prospect/corp-giv.html), which contains links to and descriptions of several corporate giving programs and company-sponsored foundations, and *Philanthropy News Network Online* (http://pj.org), which is full of interesting links to a corporate giving newsletter, a hypertext directory of company-sponsored foundations and corporate giving programs, and a hypertext list of other prospective research pages. The Northern California Community Foundation provides another good hypertext directory of foundations and corporate grantmakers (http://www.foundations.org/grantmakers.html).

Searching: Doing It Yourself Using a Search Engine

When searching for corporate giving information on the Internet, another way to find information you want is by using a search engine such as:

- About.com (http://about.com)
- AltaVista (http://www.altavista.com)
- AskJeeves (http://www.askjeeves.com)
- Excite (http://www.excite.com)
- Google (http://www.google.com)
- Hotbot (http://www.hotbot.com)
- Infoseek (http://www.infoseek.com)
- Lycos (http://www.lycos.com)
- Northern Light (http://www.northernlight.com)
- ProFusion (http://www.profusion.com)
- Yahoo (http://www.yahoo.com)

There are many others. Try each one out to see which search engine is most to your liking. The key to retrieving a reasonable number of sites that contain useful information, rather than a list of thousands of irrelevant Web sites, is choosing the proper wording and knowing the rules pertaining to the specific search engine you may be using at the time. There are differences in how they work and what you can expect from them.

The words you select can greatly improve the search results you get. Try to search initially with phrases like "corporate giving," "community relations," and "corporate contributions." Once you have gotten an idea about what kind of information is available on the Web, you may be able to further narrow your searches by adding words more specific to your needs (e.g., "arts corporate giving"). You may also want to try the same search using various search engines; you will often get vastly different results. Other terms to try are "in-kind gift," if looking for product donations, or "community reinvestment act" for those seeking loans.

Searching: Looking Within a Corporate Web Site for Grantmaking Information

A different strategy is required to research the corporate giving policies regarding a specific company. Often there is no "search" option within the Web site, although this feature is becoming more widely available. Therefore, you must search for the hypertext categories that may lead you to the information you need. Often these categories are within a menu list containing items such as "Products and Services," "Annual Report," etc. The categories most likely to contain the direct giving policies of the company are subjects like "Corporate Relations," "Corporate Information," or "About Us."

Frequently, the corporate giving program information is contained on a "page within a page." In other words, you have to go through a lot to get to it. The best way to circumvent this is to find the Web site's site map, a listing of all of the pages contained within the Web site. These listings are usually the simplest way to cut to the heart of the subject you are looking for and are often more reliable than the hit-or-miss process of doing a search within a Web site.

For more on searching within individual Web sites, see the section in this chapter called "Comparing Individual Corporate Web Sites."

RESEARCHING CORPORATE INFORMATION

In order to learn about a company's philanthropic efforts, it is often easier when basic information about the company itself is available, including: their areas of company operations, if the corporate giving program has geographic limitations; the products and services the company provides, when seeking in-kind gifts; a list of corporate officers, to help find a contact person when none is evident; and fiscal information, to give an idea about the possible size of the corporation's philanthropic efforts.

A good place to start when looking for any information about a public company, that is, a company whose stock is traded publicly, is the Security and Exchange Commission's (SEC's) EDGAR Database (http://www.sec.gov/edgarhp.htm). This is a text-only database that contains an archive of all the financial documents filed with the SEC since 1994.

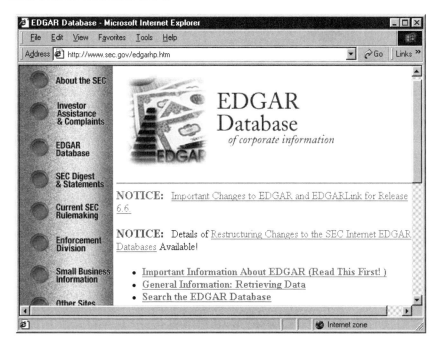

This site contains more information than one could ever want about a company and its operations. Thus, the main challenge is digging through a lot of irrelevant material to find the information you need.

Another valuable site to consider when researching corporate information is Yahoo!'s Company and Fund Index (http://biz.yahoo.com/i). This site provides a searchable database of information on most public companies in the U.S. and even offers a "backdoor" to the SEC's site, making a search of the EDGAR Database quick and easy.

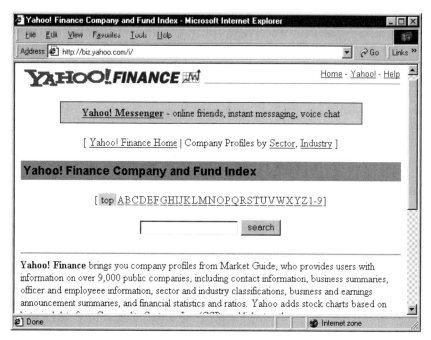

One of the most comprehensive sites for links to corporate information on public and private companies, not only in the United States but abroad as well, is aptly named CorporateInformation (http://corporateinformation.com). This site lists separate links for corporate information in over 100 countries.

Other helpful pages for information about businesses include Internet Prospector's Corporations page (http://w3.uwyo.edu/~prospect/company.html) and David Lamb's Prospect Research Page (http://staff.washington.edu/dlamb/). Both of these sites have many hypertext links to corporate directories and other sources of business information and either is a good starting point when looking for corporate information. Additionally, those wishing to receive corporate annual reports may want to visit the Investor Relations Information Network (http://www.irin.com). Here, annual report requests for over 3,200 companies may be submitted.

Most of the corporate information available on these sites is for publicly traded companies. To find information on privately held corporations takes more research and may require using a search engine, looking for the company in question by name.

Perhaps the quickest and easiest way to find corporate information, public or private, is to simply type the name of a company into your browser window and hope for success. Many companies have set up Web sites that can usually be accessed by using the "www.companyname.com" format.

For example, Bell Atlantic Corporation's Web site can be found at http://www.bellatlantic.com/. By clicking on the link called "About Us," a wealth of corporate information becomes available. Corporate officer profiles can be found within the "Executives" section, the company's annual report can be found within "Investor Information," and press releases can be found within "News Center."

ConAgra, Inc.'s Web site can be found at (http://www.conagra.com). By selecting "Company Profile," one can access corporate facts and figures within "ConAgra at a Glance," information regarding products and services within "Across the Food Chain," and a corporate timeline within "ConAgra History."

When having problems finding corporate Web sites without the aid of a search engine or online directory, try using different variations of a company's name. For example, the Web site for Minnesota Mining and Manufacturing Company can be found at (http://www.3m.com).

COMPARING INDIVIDUAL CORPORATE WEB SITES

Corporations present their giving information in widely varying formats. Some companies provide easy access to their philanthropic activities directly from their homepage while others may have information on their grantmaking programs hidden within other sections. Some companies provide no information at all while others combine corporate giving program information with foundation information on a single page. Grantseekers must be diligent in order to find the information they need from a corporate Web site and must examine the information given very carefully before applying for a grant.

Buried Information

It is often the case that a company provides philanthropic information within a section called, for example, "Corporate Information" or "About Us." An example of a Web site containing buried corporate giving information is Compaq Computer Corporation's site (http://www.compaq.com/corporate/community).

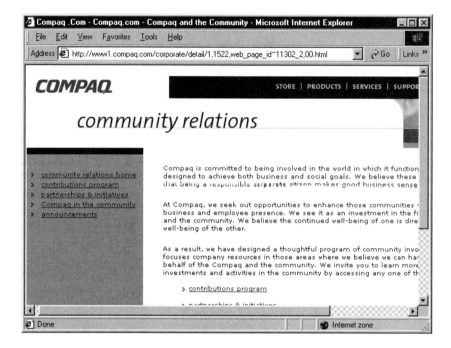

The data on the corporation's grantmaking activities is within the section refer-ring to "Community Relations," which is itself within the section called "Corpo-rate Info." The links can easily be followed from the company's homepage but a problem is that no reference to this path is mentioned. Less Web-savvy grantseekers could very well visit Compaq's Web site and not realize that philan-thropic information is available.

Like Compaq, the philanthropic information contained within Merck & Co., Inc.'s Web site (http://www.merck.com/philanthropy) is hard to uncover.

It is within the section called "Corporate Philanthropy Report," which can be found within "General Information," which is itself within "About Merck." Once again, the information is easily found if you know where to look, but Merck pro-vides no reference to the fact that this specific sequence of links must be followed.

Some companies provide site maps which can be used as a guide to find a hid-den page. For example, International Paper Company's homepage includes a link to a site map which clearly shows that the company has dedicated a page to phil-anthropic activities (http://www.internationalpaper.com/map). "Community Out-reach" is listed under the section called "Our World" and can be accessed easily with a click of the mouse.

More Transparent Sites

In comparison, Dollar General Corporation's homepage has a hypertext link directly to its "Community Initiatives" page (http://www.dollargeneral.com/ communit/communit.htm). This is the area containing information on its charita-ble contributions and represents what a grantseeker might find at a typical corpo-rate Web site.

Dollar General provides links to its guidelines for grantseekers, a description of one of its charitable programs, and selected profiles of individuals the company has helped. Grantseekers should never ignore such content and automatically send a proposal to the company's application address. Read the material carefully and use your judgment to decide whether you or your organization is a logical candidate for this program. An inappropriate application is a waste of time for both the candidate and the corporation.

Likewise, Norfolk Southern Corporation provides a link to its foundation directly from its homepage (http://www.nscorp.com/nscorp/html/foundation.html). Links to company-sponsored foundations are usually easier to spot than those to the more general and informal corporate giving pages. In this case, the hypertext category named "NS Foundation" leaves no doubt as to the type of information that awaits beyond.

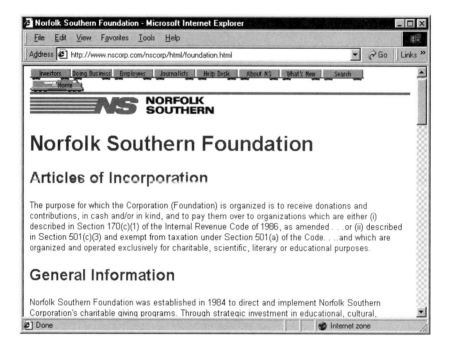

Norfolk Southern's foundation page contains a general synopsis of its grant-making activities and includes guidelines, application information, a description of its matching gifts program, and correspondence information. This is an excellent example of a well-organized corporate giving page and provides virtually all of the information that a grantseeker would initially need in determining whether a company might be an appropriate source of support.

It should be noted that many companies provide information regarding their environment- and health and safety-related initiatives. This is *not* relevant grantmaking information. Although many companies do indeed make grants to environmental organizations or to those that promote health and safety, this material usually refers to a company's efforts to reduce its impact on the environment or improve health and safety conditions for its employees. Use your best judgment to decide whether the information provided is of relevance to the grantseeker.

Combination Sites

Many companies make charitable contributions both directly and through a company-sponsored foundation. For a number of procedural, policy, or legal reasons, the foundation may not be able to support a worthy organization, and so the company will choose to provide support directly. Often, information on both arms of their charitable giving effort is combined on the Web, making it difficult for the grantseeker to differentiate between the two separate grantmaking bodies. Unfortunately, there is no easy solution to this problem. Grantseekers need to proceed with caution when visiting such sites and conduct further research to determine the appropriate approach. Sometimes both programs are administered out of the same office and by the same staff while at other times they act completely independently of one another. In some cases they each require separate proposals. Very often, the types of support provided and the geographic limitations established will vary widely. For instance, cash donations might be supplied by the foundation while in-kind support is handled exclusively by the company.

CIGNA Corporation's site (http://www.cigna.com/corp/contributions) contains information on both a company-sponsored foundation and a direct corporate giving program. In fact, the company announces this at the bottom of the page, something many companies forget or refuse to do. There is valuable information here on CIGNA's philanthropic endeavors, but one never knows for sure whether the information reflects donations made by the CIGNA Foundation or by the company itself. When in doubt, a telephone call to the company is probably the grantseeker's best bet.

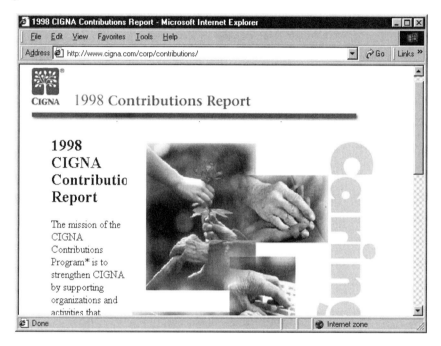

Utilizing the Material at Hand

THE SUBJECT, GEOGRAPHIC, AND TYPE OF SUPPORT APPROACHES TO GRANTSEEKING

There are several tried-and-true approaches to grantseeking research, each most appropriate for different situations. The subject approach leads grantseekers to corporations with an interest in funding programs in certain fields and businesses whose activities are related to their nonprofit programs. Some nonprofit/corporate relationships will be obvious: a sporting goods manufacturer expresses interest in an athletic program for disadvantaged youth; a musical instruments manufacturer supports a music appreciation program; a pharmaceutical company or alcoholic beverage manufacturer funds a drug education program.

Most corporate giving programs are limited to giving in communities where the company operates. Therefore, a grantseeker's research should include a company's areas of operation, including corporate headquarters, subsidiaries, divisions, joint ventures, and community plants and offices. A company will often support programs that provide direct service to employees and other community residents, that promise public recognition, and that improve customer relations in specific geographic areas.

A type of support approach can be equally productive. Corporations will often provide funds in a few specific ways: for capital improvements, for operating budgets, and by matching employee donations. Many also make noncash contributions. For example, a clothing manufacturer may have "irregulars" or extra clothing to donate to a homeless shelter. It's important to note that in-kind giving can be more indirect. Charities such as Gifts In Kind International (http://www.giftsinkind.org), Share Our Strength (http://www.strength.org), Volunteers of America (http://www.voa.org), and New York's City Harvest (http://www.cityharvest.org) act as pass-through organizations for corporations wishing to provide in-kind gifts, to see that the donations reach those who most need them in an efficient manner. Using these services, rather than applying to the company, giftseekers are encouraged to apply to the appropriate charity.

DO YOUR HOMEWORK

Learn about a corporation's funding before submitting a request. The funder may have an annual report or printed guidelines as well as information about the company and its giving on a Web page. These will help you target your appeal. Business reports present company philosophy and describe company plans for the community, providing vital background in linking a grant request to company interests. Economic conditions and business news should also be followed. A company laying off employees or running up a deficit may not be the one to ask for a donation.

Follow a corporate giver's guidelines to the letter, especially in regard to submission deadlines. Find out to whom the request should be addressed and the preferred format. At some companies, sponsorships and nonmonetary support may be handled by the marketing or public relations department; employee volunteerism may be coordinated in the human resources department. Different areas of company operations may have different contact persons. Some companies want a preliminary letter of inquiry, and a full proposal only after they have expressed an interest; others require full applications, and some ask for multiple copies of a proposal. Find this out in advance if you can.

PERSONAL CONTACTS

How important is it to know someone? In the electronic age, interpersonal contact is becoming less prevalent. With e-mail, fax machines, voice mail, and the World Wide Web all competing for attention, it is sometimes difficult to get in direct touch with someone you know, much less a stranger. Personal contacts can sometimes help, but their impact varies from organization to organization. Seeking grants from company foundations and direct corporate giving programs with specific philanthropy personnel and explicit guidelines for grantseekers is unlikely to require personal contacts. Personal contacts may be more important when seeking support from the companies with informal giving programs and no formal guidelines.

Nonprofit grantseekers with no personal contacts are not necessarily out of the running. They can begin to build relationships and establish contacts at a professional level. Write an introductory letter to the relevant contact describing your program and expressing interest in a meeting date. Send printed literature and articles that are relevant to your program; but be sure not to send any extraneous materials. Invite decision makers to see your organization in action and to attend special events. Ask whether you should send a preliminary letter of inquiry or a full proposal. Establishing rapport with a wary grantmaker can be difficult, but it isn't impossible. Cultivation should be taken on as a long-term effort.

If you receive a grant, send a letter of thanks and submit all agreed-upon reports, following the established timetable. Corporate funders will expect you to follow through and will notice a missed deadline. Keep them informed regardless of the agreement. You may want to suggest forms of recognition, such as programs and posters, reception and dinner honors, certificates, plaques, and newspaper coverage. However, grantmaker recognition depends on nonprofit resources as well as the desires of the corporation, and given the small size of most corporate donations, such formal recognition is not often required.

Even if you are rejected, continue to nurture the relationship. Thank those in charge for considering your request. Ask why you were not funded if they have not made this clear. Determine whether you will reapply in the next cycle.

Getting corporate support demands creativity, ingenuity, and persistence. Competition will be stiff, but the possibility of support cannot be ignored.

PRESENTING YOUR IDEAS TO A CORPORATE GIVER

A proposal must be honest, clear, concise, and appropriate in tone. Draw up a realistic budget, and be prepared to divulge all sources of income and how that money was used, since corporate grantmakers emphasize the bottom line. Many ask for evidence of fiscally responsible, efficient management. Be explicit. State program or agency goals, a plan of action, a timetable, and a method of evaluation. Be brief but comprehensive.

Highlight an innovative program, a program that tackles a new issue, or that addresses an unfulfilled need—without undue self-promotion. Nonprofits should consider asking not only for money and in-kind support. They should target local businesses for board members and volunteers, likely paths to further contributions. Nonprofit leaders should remember that a good relationship with one company may point the way to others or provide an actual introduction to other funding prospects.

First and foremost, the grantseeker should always consider the funder's motivation for giving. Establishing the connection with a corporate grantmaker's goals is the grantseeker's key to success. Focus on company self-interest more than benevolence. For example, a corporate giver may want to develop a trained pool of potential employees, support research, expand its markets, respond to related social issues, and increase sales. Consider what a business stands to gain from your program. Point out the potential benefits to the company in your proposal.

Links and Abstracts of Corporate Grantmaker Web Sites

The annotated list below includes both company-sponsored private foundations and direct corporate giving programs.

Abbott Laboratories Fund (http://www.abbott.com/community/abtfund.htm)
The Abbott Laboratories Fund makes grants to nonprofit organizations operating in "Abbott Communities" in the areas of human health and welfare; elementary, secondary, and higher education; and culture, the arts, and civic activities. The Fund generally favors requests for one-time contributions and for programmatic and operating purposes; its guidelines preclude it from making grants for individuals, purely social organizations, political parties or candidates, religious organizations, advertising, symposia and conferences, ticket purchases, memberships, or business-related purposes. In addition to general facts about the Fund's giving, at the site visitors will find general program guidelines and contact information.

The Ackerley Group, Inc.
(http://www.ackerley.com/ackerley_corporate/cgbody.html)
The Ackerley Group, a Seattle, Washington provider of multimedia advertising services, supports organizations that improve the communities in which the company does business. Areas of funding include youth services, the arts, human services, education, civic and community affairs, and the environment. The company's Web site lists guidelines, screening criteria, and restrictions, provides information on application procedure and review process, and includes contact information and a grant request summary sheet.

Adobe Systems Incorporated
(http://www.adobe.com/aboutadobe/philanthropy/main.html)
Adobe's corporate giving is centered around its "Philanthropy Council," a representative group of Adobe employees committed to supporting programs that improve the quality of life for everyone. The company specifically supports nonprofit organizations that service "disadvantaged youth, the homeless, minorities, the elderly, and victims of abuse; provide disaster relief, medical and hospice care, and meal services; provide education and literacy programs; support human rights; support the arts; protect the environment; and support animal rights." Both cash grants and equipment donations are available. The single page devoted to the company's philanthropic activities provides visitors with a brief description of program and application guidelines, downloadable application forms (in PDF format), information about Adobe's software donation program, and contact information.

Aetna Foundation, Inc. (http://www.aetna.com/foundation)
As the Hartford-based insurance giant's primary philanthropic vehicle, the Aetna Foundation focuses its activities in the areas of children's health, where it looks for initiatives that "focus on cardiac disease prevention and detection initiatives; and education, where it favors college preparation, school-to-career initiatives, and entrepreneurial education...for middle school students whose parents actively participate in the programs." The grant awards made by the Foundation reflect a geographic emphasis on organizations and initiatives in selected communities of strategic importance to Aetna Inc., and are limited to proposals submitted by invitation. Grant proposals are accepted year-round and must be submitted in writing. In addition to detailed application guidelines, visitors to the Foundation section of the company's Web site will find general program information, profiles of successful Foundation-sponsored initiatives, and a section devoted to the company's Voice of Conscience Award, created as a tribute to the late Arthur Ashe.

Additionally, the Foundation makes grants to participants in its Academic Medicine and Managed Care Forum for research that will directly improve practices impacting the quality of care and health outcomes for patients.

Agrilink Foods/Pro-Fac Foundation
(http://www.agrilinkfoods.com/corp/about/community)
Agrilink Foods, Inc. is a food processing and marketing cooperative headquartered in Rochester, New York. The Agrilink Foods/Pro-Fac Foundation provides grants to nonprofit organizations operating in communities where Agrilink has facilities or where Pro-Fac members are located. Primary giving areas are health, community services, education, youth, agricultural research, and cultural programs. Grant guidelines, restrictions, and contact information for various divisions and locations are included in the "Philanthropy and Community Service" section of the company's Web site.

ALZA Corporation (http://www.alza.com/cmnty.htm)
ALZA, a pharmaceutical company headquartered in Palo Alto, California, awards grants to nonprofits (of up to $5,000) through its corporate giving program for education, health and human services, science, cultural, and civic programs. Preference may be given to organizations that have ALZA employees serving as board members or volunteers. In addition, ALZA contributes to specific universities for their work in pharmaceutics and biosciences and maintains an employee matching gifts program. The "Community Relations" area of ALZA's Web site describes its funding areas and provides grant application procedures.

Ameren Corporation (http://www.ameren.com/ameren2/amerpags/comm.html)
Ameren, an energy provider based in St. Louis, Missouri, supports community groups and organizations through the Ameren Corporation Charitable Trust and a direct corporate giving program. Contributions focus on education, services for youth, services for the elderly, and the environment, and scholarships are offered at Missouri and Illinois colleges and universities to eligible customers in Ameren service territories. The "Community Services" area of Ameren's Web site describes the Trust's giving policy and provides grant application information and information on scholarship eligibility. The site also provides information on the non-grantmaking charitable activities and environmental programs.

American Express Company
(http://www6.americanexpress.com/corp/philanthropy)
The philanthropic program of the American Express Company includes the activities of the American Express Foundation and a direct corporate giving program, and encompasses both U.S. nonprofits as well as organizations outside the U.S. that can document nonprofit status. The company makes grants in three program areas: community service, with funding primarily supporting the volunteer efforts of employees and advisors in their local communities; cultural heritage, with the twin themes of protecting "the built and natural environment" and supporting "art and culture unique to countries and regions"; and economic independence, with an emphasis on supporting initiatives that "encourage, support or develop economic self-reliance." In addition to general program information and application guidelines, visitors to the company's Web site will find a list of grant recipients

and descriptions of major programs to which the company has recently made grants. An online version of the company's annual report is also available.

American Savings Bank Foundation, Inc. (http://www.americansavingsbank.com/found.asp)

In 1996, American Savings Bank formed the American Savings Bank Foundation to improve the quality of life in communities it serves, with special emphasis on children and education. The Foundation awards grants and scholarships within the 45 Connecticut towns served by the company. Visitors to the American Savings Bank Web site will find a listing of the towns served by the bank, a grant application form (in PDF format), and contact information.

Ameritech Corporation (http://www.ameritech.com/community/index.html)

Ameritech, the Chicago-based communications company, provides local phone, data, and video services in Illinois, Indiana, Michigan, Ohio, and Wisconsin. The company gives priority "to grants that improve education, economic development, and quality of life." Ameritech also considers organizational support for "projects and special programs which make communities where it operates better places to live, learn and work. . . ." The company posts a good deal of information about its contributions program on its Web site, including program guidelines and limitations, application procedures, and links to grantee organizations that have their own Web sites. The contributions report is available to download as a PDF file. Visitors to the Ameritech site can also access an online version of its annual report.

AMP Foundation (http://www.amp.com/about/foundation)

The AMP Foundation, the charitable organization of AMP Incorporated, a Pennsylvania manufacturer of electrical and electronic components, focuses primarily on education, with an emphasis on pre-college math and science. Special attention is also given to community-wide arts organizations and programs with an educational component. AMP's Web site includes details of the Foundation's support of education and technology, grant guidelines, contact information, and a grant application form.

AMR/American Airlines Foundation (http://www.amrcorp.com/corp_fdn.htm)

The AMR/American Airlines Foundation supports nonprofit organizations in the communities that AMR Corporation serves, particularly its hub cities of Dallas/Fort Worth, Texas; Chicago, Illinois; Miami, Florida,; and San Juan, Puerto Rico. The Foundation provides organizations with air transportation as well as monetary support, which is focused on four areas: community development, arts and culture, education, and health and welfare. The company's Web site provides grant guidelines and instructions for proposal submission.

AOL Foundation (http://www.aol.com/corp/phil)

America Online, Inc., based in Dulles, Virginia, "is a world leader in interactive services, Web brands, Internet technologies, and e-commerce services." The AOL Foundation's mission is "to pioneer the development of strategies and programs that leverage the power of the emerging global medium to benefit society by improving the lives of families and children, and empowering the disadvantaged."

The company's Web site provides facts about the Foundation, grant guidelines, and a listing of recent grant winners.

Apple Computer, Inc.
(http://www.apple.com/education/k12/leadership/funding/index.html)

The primary philanthropic activity of Apple is the donation of new computer equipment to K–12 schools. In the area of higher education, Apple helps institutions to use technology more effectively "to deliver learning experiences that are rich in communication, collaboration and construction of knowledge." The Cupertino, California-based company does not fund religious groups, political groups, or individuals, and does not make donations in support of raffles, fund-raising events, auctions, or door prizes. The Education section of the Apple Web site offers general information about Apple's support of K–12 and higher education; information about the Apple Education Grants program, the Apple Distinguished Schools initiative, the Apple Classroom of Tomorrow (ACOT) project, and other education-oriented initiatives; and a helpful FAQ section with, among other things, specific guidelines for contacting the company about its philanthropic programs.

Applied Materials, Inc.
(http://www.appliedmaterials.com/about/community.html)

Applied Materials, a California-based semiconductor production equipment company, "maintains a program of corporate philanthropy aimed at assisting organizations, programs and activities that benefit [its] community." Grants and other forms of support are awarded for specific programs falling into three major categories: Education, Civic, and Arts/Culture. The University Partnerships Program "is designed to foster an ongoing working relationship between [the company] and designated institutions." Applied Materials also donates used office and computer equipment primarily to K–12 public schools in communities where the company has plant sites. Visitors to the company's Web site will find grant guidelines, the Corporate Philanthropy Report, and contact information for California and Texas.

ARCO Foundation
(http://www.arco.com/Corporate/reports/foundation/home.htm)

As the philanthropic vehicle of the Atlantic Richfield Company, the ARCO Foundation "has shaped its grantmaking around the belief that corporate philanthropy and individual participation in the nonprofit world go hand in hand." The Foundation relies heavily on the personal involvement of company employees and retirees as volunteers and donors, and to reinforce employee and retiree support of community causes, the Foundation gives its Employee Programs—namely Matching Gifts and Volunteer Grants—precedence over regular grants in the allocation of available funds. The online version of the Foundation's annual report provides grantmaking objectives, priorities, and grants lists in five broad program areas (arts and humanities, community initiatives, education, the environment, and public policy); information about the Foundation's Employee Programs; application procedures; and regional contact information.

Ashland Inc. (http://www.ashland.com/community)
Ashland is a diversified company headquartered in Russell, Kentucky, with operations in specialty chemical production and distribution, motor oil and car care
products, and highway construction. The "In Our Communities" area of
Ashland's Web site outlines its charitable efforts, which are focused on education,
arts and culture, the environment, and health and human services in cities where
the company operates. The online Community Relations Annual Report provides
detailed information on Ashland's giving in each area.

**Aspect Telecommunications Corporation
(http://www.aspect.com/company/community.htm)**
Aspect Telecommunications, a supplier of call center products headquartered in
San Jose, California, created the Aspect Community Commitment Fund, a direct
corporate giving program, to support local nonprofits and schools (public and private) to help better educate children and youth. The Fund awards grants of $1,000
to $10,000 for projects that encourage "positive and healthy" learning by children
at the K–9 level, and primarily targets minorities, low- or no-income populations,
and the physically or mentally challenged. The "Community Commitment" area
of the company's Web site details the company's corporate giving program,
explains grant eligibility, and provides application instructions.

AT&T Foundation (http://www.att.com/foundation)
As the principal philanthropic arm of AT&T Corp., the AT&T Foundation makes
grants in the program areas of education, arts and culture, and civic and community service. While the scope of the Foundation's activities is global, the majority
of its funds support U.S.-based institutions. The Foundation also maintains a local
program to focus support on cities and regions with large concentrations of AT&T
employees and business operations. The company's Web site includes a separate
area for Foundation information where visitors will find detailed program
descriptions; application guidelines and procedures; complete grants listings for
each program area; and an interactive form for requesting additional information.

**Avon Products Foundation, Inc.
(http://www.avon.com/about/women/foundation/foundation.html)**
The Avon Products Foundation, located in New York City, supports organizations
addressing the needs of women worldwide. Funding is provided for women's programs that focus on health, education, community and social services, and arts
and culture. Although the Foundation accepts unsolicited proposals, funds are
more commonly awarded to pre-selected organizations. Guidelines are provided
in the Foundation section of the Web site, along with a sampling of grant
recipients.

**Baltimore Gas and Electric Company
(http://www.bge.com/aboutbge/contrib/contrib.html)**
Through "thoughtful social investments," Baltimore Gas and Electric Company's
corporate contributions program seeks to "enhance the health, welfare, financial
strength, and quality of life" of those living in communities where the company
operates. The nation's first gas utility supports the following program areas: education, health and welfare, cultural enrichment, civic and environmental improvement, and economic development in communities where the company has a

significant business interest. Visitors to the company's Web site will find program and application guidelines, a graphic illustrating its giving by program area, and contact information.

Bankers Trust Corporation
(http://www.bankerstrust.com/corpcomm/communi/index.html)

Through the BT Foundation and a direct corporate giving program, New York City-based Bankers Trust concentrates its philanthropic activities in seven program areas: community development, education, arts and culture, health and hospitals, environment, international, and a general category (i.e., public policy research and national and international emergencies). Bankers Trust also allocates funds to special categories and through employee programs. Although the company's activities are focused on major institutions either operating in or committed to improving the quality of life in New York City, it also has a "coordinated strategy of overseas philanthropy" in communities where it has employees or conducts business. The company's Web site provides detailed program descriptions; grant policies and guidelines; a report of contributions; *Community Focus,* a periodic newsletter about Bankers Trust's philanthropic efforts; and contact information.

Eddie Bauer, Inc. (http://www.eddiebauer.com/about/frame_comrelmain.asp)

Retailer Eddie Bauer, established in 1920, is an international company headquartered in Redmond, Washington. Eddie Bauer's corporate giving program supports education, the environment, community volunteerism, and the empowerment of women. The Eddie Bauer Scholars Program is aimed at college-bound youth with financial need and is offered at a number of institutions. Environmental support includes the Eddie Bauer/Global ReLeaf Tree project. Visitors to the company's Web site will find information on how to apply for monetary and merchandise donations.

Baxter International Inc.
(http://www.baxter.com/investors/citizenship/index.html)

Baxter International, located in Deerfield, Illinois, develops therapies and technologies for treating life-threatening conditions of the blood and circulatory system. Its principal philanthropic vehicle, the Baxter Allegiance Foundation, supports health care and social service systems and providers internationally, and is committed to environmental awareness. The Foundation's grantmaking program awards funds to improve health care in the United States, Europe, Latin America, and Mexico. The company's Web site describes the Foundation, offers examples of grantmaking, and provides contact information.

Bayer Foundation
(http://www.bayerus.com/about/community/com_foundation.html)

Bayer Corporation, headquartered in Pittsburgh, Pennsylvania, develops health care products, chemicals, and imaging technologies. The Bayer Foundation supports the communities where the company is located and awards grants in three areas: civic and community programs; science education and workforce development; and the arts, arts education, and culture. The company's Web site provides detailed grant guidelines, application instructions, and deadlines.

Bechtel Foundation (http://www.bechtel.com/buildingminds/bechfoun.html)

Bechtel Group, Inc., located in San Francisco, California, develops and manages capital projects and facilities worldwide. The Bechtel Foundation supports communities where the company has offices or major projects. Grants are typically directed to youth and educational programs—particularly math and science education—and engineering and business programs at selected colleges and universities. Although most grant recipients are pre-selected by Bechtel's office and project managers, the Foundation section of the company's Web site provides proposal guidelines for grantseekers whose projects fall into the Foundation's funding areas. Visitors to the site will also find highlights of the Foundation's recent giving.

Bell Atlantic Foundation (http://www.bellatlanticfoundation.com)

The Bell Atlantic Foundation provides "opportunities for non-profit organizations to apply new technology to the programs and services they offer," focusing its efforts on the communities from Maine to Virginia served by Bell Atlantic Corporation, particularly the children and young people of those communities. Most of the Foundation's support aims to make technology more available to students, teachers, service organizations, and cultural institutions with youth programs. Priority is given to activities in education, health and human services, arts and humanities, and community service that facilitate collaborations through network solutions and enhanced communications systems. The Foundation's sophisticated Web site is available in Java and non-Java versions. Visitors to the Web site will find summaries of giving by state, grants lists by state, an overview of the Foundation, grant guidelines, detailed program descriptions, contact information (e-mail is the preferred form of communication), news, and a list of the Foundation's board of directors. Grantseekers can locate their community relations manager by entering their zip code in a form on the Web site, and the Foundation encourages online submission of grant applications, guaranteeing a response within 48 hours.

BellSouth Foundation (http://www.bellsouthcorp.com/bsf)

The BellSouth Foundation seeks to improve outcomes and stimulate active learning for students in elementary and secondary education in nine southern states—Alabama, Florida, Georgia, Kentucky, Louisiana, Mississippi, North Carolina, South Carolina, and Tennessee. The Foundation focuses its efforts in three areas: developing individual capacity to improve learning; creating environments to improve learning; and promoting partnerships through technology to improve learning. BellSouth Corporation's Web site offers visitors a broad range of information about the activities of its Foundation, including online versions of two reports on the Foundation's grantmaking initiatives; detailed program descriptions; application guidelines, deadlines, and restrictions; and an interactive application form.

Ben & Jerry's Foundation, Inc.
(http://www.benjerry.com/foundation/index.html)

Ben & Jerry's Homemade, Inc. gives away a portion of its pre-tax earnings through its Foundation. The Foundation supports projects that are "models for social change" in three focus areas: children and families, disadvantaged groups, and the environment. The Foundation does not support basic or direct-service programs. The company's Web site provides basic information on grant restrictions and size; application procedures; recent grants lists; a letter of interest to view and print; information on other funding sources; and tips on writing a successful proposal. Visitors to the site can also access the Foundation's annual report.

Boston Globe Foundation, Inc.
(http://www.boston.com/extranet/foundation/home.stm)
The Boston Globe Foundation, one of the principal charitable arms of the Boston-based Globe Newspaper Company, focuses its grantmaking on children and youth in the Massachusetts cities of Boston, Cambridge, Somerville, and Chelsea and also funds community-based health and environmental organizations. The Foundation's Reactive Grantmaking program accepts grant proposals for program and operating support, particularly for programs targeted towards youth at a societal disadvantage due to race, class, ethnicity, disability, gender, or sexual orientation. Visitors will find application instructions, financial audit information (in PDF format), frequently asked questions, a description of Foundation initiatives, and links to related Web sites.

The Bristol-Myers Squibb Foundation, Inc.,
(http://www.bms.com/aboutbms/founda.html)
The Bristol-Myers Squibb Foundation provides financial support in keeping with Bristol-Myers Squibb Company's commitment to extending and enhancing human life. The Foundation awards grants in four program areas: biomedical research, women's health education, math and science education, and international local/community support where the pharmaceutical company has a presence. The Foundation area of the company's Web site delivers the Foundation's most recent charitable giving report in PDF format, which includes grant guidelines, and also contains a link to detailed information on the Foundation's Unrestricted Biomedical Research Grants Program, including application instructions.

The Brooklyn Union Gas Company,
(http://www.bug.com/commune/bunewy.htm)
Brooklyn Union's corporate giving program supports education and community service programs in the New York metropolitan area. The Educational Services Grants Program funds nonprofit, community-based organizations for programs "in line with the company's corporate education agenda." Other educational programs include the Ambassadors for Education program, the Brooklyn Union Engineering Explorer Program, and the Science In Industry Summer Academy. The company's community service support includes toy donations, employee volunteerism, and support of over 1800 local organizations. Businesses interested in expanding in or moving to Brooklyn Union's service area may find the company's economic development programs a good resource. Brooklyn Union's Web site details its various programs and provides contact information.

Brookshire Grocery Company
(http://www.brookshires.com/company/community/index.asp)
Through its corporate giving program, the Texas-based Brookshire sponsors many community services projects, including the Spirit of Christmas Food Drive, the Adopt-A-School Program, the Children's Miracle Network, and the United Way. The company's Web site provides contact information.

Canon U.S.A., Inc. (http://www.usa.canon.com/cleanearth/index.html)
Canon, headquartered in Lake Success, New York, manufactures imaging equipment and information systems. In 1990, the company established The Clean Earth Campaign, which "supports various environmental and recycling initiatives," including recycling and conservation in the workplace, the conservation of environmental resources, scientific research, and education and outdoors appreciation.

Carolina Power & Light Company (http://www.cplc.com/community)
Through the CP&L Foundation, Inc. and a direct corporate giving program, Carolina Power & Light, headquartered in North Carolina, supports programs that benefit its customers and employees, focusing on education, economic development, and the environment. The company's Web site provides descriptions of recent and ongoing projects and contact information.

Ceridian Corporation (http://www.ceridian.com/who_community.asp)
The primary emphasis of Ceridian's corporate giving program is on innovative policy initiatives and programs that help people balance the growing demands of work and home life. The Minneapolis-based information services and defense electronics company also emphasizes giving in the areas of health, education, and the arts. The "In the Community" section of the company's Web site provides general program information as well as application guidelines and an interactive application form. Visitors to the site can also access an online version of the company's annual report.

Chevron Corporation (http://www.chevron.com/community/index.html)
Chevron, the San Francisco-based petroleum and chemicals concern, has a long history of supporting communities where it does business and where its employees live and work. Those communities are scattered around the globe—from the Americas (Bolivia, Canada, Mexico, the U.S.), to Europe and Africa (Angola, Scotland, Wales, Zaire), to Asia and the Pacific (Australia, China, Indonesia, Kazakhstan, Papua New Guinea). Currently, the company focuses its giving in the areas of math and science education, with an emphasis on K–12; environmental conservation, with an emphasis on habitat preservation, wildlife protection, and environmental education programs; crime; and substance abuse. The "Community" section of the company's Web site offers a good deal of general program information, grant guidelines, a grants list organized by program area, answers to frequently asked questions, and a simple interactive application form.

CIGNA Corporation (http://www.cigna.com/corp/contributions)
Through the CIGNA Foundation and a direct corporate giving program, CIGNA, an insurance, health care, and financial services company located in Pennsylvania, seeks to "strengthen [itself] by supporting organizations and activities that improve the overall climate for business." Support is focused primarily on activities of concern to the health care, insurance, and financial services industries. Visitors to the company's Web site will find information on specific projects, a list of recent grants, grant guidelines, and contact information.

Cinergy Foundation, Inc. (http://www.cinergy.com/foundation/default.htm)
Cinergy Foundation is the philanthropic organization of Cinergy Corp. The Foundation seeks to improve the quality of life in Indiana, southwestern Ohio, and

northern Kentucky communities by supporting arts and culture, community development, education, and health and social services. The company's Web site provides thorough program descriptions and grant guidelines, application forms to download (in MS Word 7.0 and PDF formats), geographic considerations, examples of exemplary projects, a listing of Foundation officers, and contact information.

Cisco Foundation (http://www.precept.com/warp/public/750/fdn_home.html)

Cisco Foundation, the principal charitable arm of Cisco Systems, Inc., a provider of computer networking services located in San Jose, California, was established in 1997. The Foundation funds organizations that "fulfill basic needs within the community," such as education, food, and shelter. The company's Web site provides information about various Foundation programs and grant guidelines.

The Clorox Company Foundation (http://clorox.com/)

The Clorox Company Foundation is dedicated to improving the quality of life in communities where employees of the Clorox Company live and work—primarily in 23 "Clorox Cities" in the U.S., Canada, and Puerto Rico. The Foundation focuses its grants on programs that serve youth, core cultural and civic organizations, plant programs, and organizations in which Clorox employees are involved. Grants typically support innovative programs in their developmental stages. The company's Web site offers a brief description of the Foundation's philanthropic interests and activities, contact information, and links to the Web sites of organizations receiving support from the Foundation.

Coca-Cola Scholars Foundation, Inc. (http://www.thecoca-colacompany.com/scholars/index.html)

Coca-Cola Company established its Coca-Cola Scholars Foundation in 1986 to support higher education for communities where Coca-Cola bottlers are located and awards 250 merit-based scholarships to high school seniors annually. The Foundation area of the company's Web site provides an outline of the program, application instructions, an interactive form that allows interested students to find out if they live in an eligible geographic location, and contact information.

Columbia Gas of Pennsylvania, Inc./Columbia Gas of Maryland, Inc. (http://www.columbiagaspamd.com/html/community_services.html)

Columbia's corporate giving program, defined as a social and economic investment in its community, provides cash contributions and employee volunteer services to individuals and organizations. Key areas of focus are humanities education, community development and safety, and health and human services in the company's service territory. The company's Web site provides grant guidelines and information on areas of interest.

The Comcast Corporation (http://www.comcast.com/about/commun.htm)

Comcast, located in Pennsylvania, develops, manages, and operates broadband cable networks. A significant portion of support is made in the areas of education, civic and community, culture and arts, and health and human services in local company communities. The company provides cash grants, in-kind contributions, and employee volunteer services. Comcast's Web site provides application guidelines.

Compaq Computer Corporation
(http://www.compaq.com/corporate/community)
Compaq is a personal computer manufacturer headquartered in Houston, Texas, where it currently focuses its grantmaking in the areas of education, health, social services, and the arts. Its current grantmaking strategy is described in the "Community Relations" area of the company's Web site along with success stories for each giving category and guidelines.

Computer Associates International, Inc. (http://www.cai.com/charity)
Computer Associates, located in New York, designs, develops, and markets computer software. Through its corporate giving program, the company provides cash grants, matching gifts, and employee volunteer services. Visitors to the company's Web site will find links to specific charitable initiatives.

The ConAgra Foundation, Inc., (http://www.conagra.com/commun.html)
Through its Foundation, ConAgra, Inc., a diversified international food company based in Omaha, Nebraska, seeks to improve the quality of life in communities where the company's employees work and live. To that end, the ConAgra Foundation focuses its resources in the areas of education, health and human services, arts and culture, sustainable development, and civic and community betterment. The company's Web site provides very general information about the Foundation's guidelines, restrictions, and deadlines, as well as contact information for written requests only.

Cooper Industries, Inc.
(http://www.cooperindustries.com/about/giving/toc.html)
Houston-based Cooper Industries, a diversified manufacturing company with 40,000-plus employees in 24 countries, makes contributions through the Cooper Industries Foundation and a direct corporate giving program in the areas of community development, the environment, education, health and human services, arts and culture, and workplace safety in communities where it has a strong presence. The company's Web site provides a good deal of information about charitable activities, including guidelines and application procedures, grants of $1,000 or more arranged by program area, a listing of the communities in which Cooper Industries has operations, and an online version of the company's annual report.

Corning Incorporated Foundation
(http://www.corning.com/employment/quality_of_life/foundation.html)
The Corning Foundation is the philanthropic organization of Corning Incorporated, a New York manufacturer of communications products, specialty materials, and consumer products. The Foundation was established in 1952 and "develops and administers projects in support of educational, cultural, community, and selected national organizations." Resources are directed foremost to projects that improve the quality of life in or near Corning locations. Corning's Web site describes the various types of organizations that receive support and provides grant guidelines.

Credit Suisse First Boston Foundation Trust
(http://www.corp.csfb.com/corp/about/html/csfb_-_foundation_trust.htm)

Credit Suisse First Boston operates a private investment banking and securities company in New York City. The company's principal philanthropic arm, the Credit Suisse First Boston Foundation Trust, supports educational initiatives and programs for inner-city youth, mostly in New York. The company's Web site provides application guidelines.

Datatel Scholars Foundation
(http://www.datatel.com/scholars_foundation/index.html)

The Datatel Scholars Foundation is the philanthropic organization of Datatel, Inc., a provider of information service solutions to higher education. The Foundation awards scholarships to students planning to attend higher learning institutions that are Datatel client sites. The Foundation area of the company's Web site describes the Datatel and Angelfire scholarships and provides application instructions and contact information.

Dayton Hudson Foundation (http://www.dhc.com/dhf)

The Dayton Hudson Foundation "strives to enhance the quality of life in the Twin Cities metropolitan area by creating partnerships with local arts and social action organizations." The focus of the Foundation, the charitable organization of Dayton Hudson Corporation and one of the largest foundations in the U.S., is on the professional nonprofit arts and on programs that help people reach economic independence. Visitors to the company's Web site will find information on the types of programs the Foundation sponsors, a summary of the Foundation's giving commitment, and a description of the Masterworks Awards.

Deere & Company (http://www.deere.com/aboutus/general/support.htm)

Through the John Deere Foundation and a direct corporate giving program, Deere, also known as John Deere, awards grants and gives support to a variety of nonprofit organizations nationwide, with an emphasis on human services, community development, educational issues, and cultural opportunities. The "Corporate Contributions Program" page of John Deere's Web site provides general information about the company's contributions program, Foundation policies and procedures, and contact information. A link to the *JD Journal* provides a somewhat more detailed look at the scope and impact of various Foundation-sponsored initiatives. HTML and/or PDF versions of John Deere's annual report are also available at the site.

The Dell Foundation
(http://www.dell.com/corporate/vision/comm_init/foundation/index.htm)

Through the Dell Foundation, Dell Computer Corporation, headquartered in Austin, Texas, seeks to fund innovative programs serving children and their communities in central Texas. The company's Web site provides an article on recent grant recipients, examples of contributions made in past years, and information on various Foundation initiatives.

Detroit Edison Foundation
(http://www.detroitedison.com/discover/community/foundation.html)

Detroit Edison Foundation, the principal philanthropic vehicle of the primary energy supplier of southeastern Michigan, supports civic and community organizations, cultural activities, education programs, and health and human service agencies. The Foundation area of the Detroit Edison Company's Web site offers a brief description of the Foundation and an online version of its annual report, available as a .PDF file.

R. R. Donnelley & Sons Company
(http://www.rrdonnelley.com/public/community)

R.R. Donnelley & Sons, an international printing and information management company headquartered in Chicago, Illinois, supports activities that promote the written word, serve children and youth at risk, and enhance the quality of life in communities served by the company. The company's Web site provides descriptions of its funding areas, grant guidelines, application instructions, a listing of R.R. Donnelley & Sons geographic locations, an online version of the Community Relations annual report (in PDF format), and contact information.

The Dow Chemical Company Foundation
(http://www.dow.com/about/charitable/charity.html)

The Dow Chemical Company is a worldwide provider of chemicals, plastics, energy, agricultural products, consumer goods, and environmental services. The Dow Chemical Company Foundation focuses its funding on community needs in locations where Dow Chemical has a presence; pre-college science education; university-level science, engineering, or business programs; and improving the environment. Preferential treatment is given to charitable contributions requested by Dow Chemical employees, but the Foundation does accept unsolicited proposals. The company's Web site describes the Foundation and provides instructions for submitting a proposal.

Dreyer's Grand Ice Cream Charitable Foundation
(http://www.dreyers.com/thecompany/main_foundation_intro.html)

The mission of the Dreyer's Grand Ice Cream Charitable Foundation is "to promote a family, school and community environment which enables young people to develop their individual initiative and talents to the maximum extent in order for them to become contributing members of their community and caretakers of the community's values and ideals for the next generation." Through its grant program, the Foundation supports projects that benefit young people in the Oakland, California/East Bay Area, with particular priority given to low- and middle-income youth and minority youth. Visitors will find program guidelines and application procedures for the grant program, as well as a number of other Foundation-sponsored programs, including the Employee Community Involvement Fund, the "Dream the Dream" Competition, and small grant and product donation opportunities.

E. I. du Pont de Nemours and Company
(http://www.dupont.com/corp/community.html)

E.I. du Pont de Nemours, located in Delaware, "is committed to improving the quality of life and enhancing the vitality of the communities in which [it operates]

. . . by supporting community sustainability efforts." Community progress, the environment, and education are central concerns of the company. The "Community Relations" section of the company's Web site details the types of programs most likely to receive support and provides application guidelines.

Eastern Enterprises Foundation (http://www.efu.com/foundation.html)

Eastern Enterprises is a natural gas and marine transportation concern with operations in Massachusetts and Ohio. The Eastern Enterprises Foundation awards grants from $1,000 to $5,000 to service area programs that can improve the quality of life for youth in the long-term. The company's Web site provides application guidelines.

Eastman Kodak Company (http://www.kodak.com/US/en/corp/community.shtml)

Eastman Kodak, an imaging company headquartered in Rochester, New York, designs its philanthropic programs and initiatives to instill employee pride, build public trust, foster education, respond to community needs, and enhance the company image. The company's primary funding areas include community revitalization, education, and health and human services. The "Community Relations and Contributions" area of Eastman Kodak's Web site thoroughly describes its corporate giving program and provides grant guidelines, highlights of giving in Rochester, recent quarterly recipient lists, special projects and awards, scholarship information, and information on the company's support for diversity and volunteerism.

Eaton Corporation (http://www.eaton.com/corp/contribute/index.html)

Eaton, headquartered in Cleveland, Ohio, is a manufacturer of products for industrial, vehicle, construction, commercial, and semiconductor markets. Eaton's corporate giving program comprises cash grants, a matching gifts program, and support of the United Way. Grants are focused on education and community improvement. Organizations considered for funding include educational, health, human service, civic, arts, and cultural organizations, and accredited colleges and universities. The company's Report of Contributions, available in PDF format, details its giving activities and funding areas and provides guidelines, a listing of company communities, staff and Corporate Contributions Committee lists, a letter from the chairman, and information on volunteerism.

eBay Foundation (http://pages.ebay.com/aboutebay98/foundation/index.html)

The eBay Foundation—described as "clever, unique, passionate, and eclectic"—was established in June 1998 by eBay Inc., a personal online trading community. The Foundation supports community organizations that seek to provide long-term tools, hope, and direction to those who wish to learn new skills. The company's Web site provides a list of recent donations, the Foundation's Guiding Principles, and application guidelines.

Educational Communications Scholarship Foundation (http://www.eci-whoswho.com/highschool/scholar)

Founded in 1968 by the directory publisher Educational Communications, Inc., the Educational Communications Scholarship Foundation today awards $1,000 scholarships to 250 outstanding high school students each year. The company's

Web site provides a searchable database of previous scholarship winners by state or year.

Electronic Data Systems Corporation (http://www.eds.com/about_eds/en/overview/about_eds_community.shtml)

Electronic Data Systems, an information technology provider headquartered in Plano, Texas, primarily supports education efforts in communities where the company has a presence and makes cash, volunteer, and technology contributions. In addition to awarding grants to organizations in local communities, grants are provided through the Technology Grants program, which provides $1,500 to teachers wishing to purchase information technology products, training, or services. The company's Web site describes these programs and provides application instructions for each, as well as a recipient list for Technology Grants. Visitors will also find information on volunteer activities and technology contributions.

Ernst & Young Foundation (http://www.ey.com/about/foundation.asp)

Through the Ernst & Young Foundation, a public charity, Ernst & Young, a New York auditing, accounting, tax, and management consulting firm, supports institutions and associations of higher education mainly in the areas of accounting, information systems, tax, and business. Visitors to the company's Web site will find a list of established programs and activities and contact information.

Exxon Corporation (http://www.exxon.com/exxoncorp/community/index.html)

Exxon supports charitable organizations in the U.S. through a direct corporate giving program and the Exxon Education Foundation. Direct contributions concentrate on the following program areas: the environment; public policy and public research; united appeals and civic and community-service organizations; arts, museums, and historical associations; and education. The Exxon Education Foundation provides funds to launch new activities or to expand existing programs in mathematics education; elementary and secondary education; and undergraduate science, technology, engineering, and mathematics. The "Community Focus" area of Exxon's Web site offers thorough program descriptions and grant application guidelines; *Dimensions,* a report on Exxon's contributions, including the Exxon Education Foundation report, which provides a grant summary and grants list; reports on special funding areas; and an online version of *Intersection,* the Foundation's newsletter.

Fannie Mae Foundation (http://www.fanniemaefoundation.org)

The mission of the Fannie Mae Foundation is "to expand decent and affordable housing opportunities and improve the quality of life in communities throughout the United States." The Foundation supports national and local nonprofit organizations dedicated to helping more families afford homes, provides prospective buyers and immigrants with information on the home-buying process, conducts local home-buying fairs as well as research on a broad range of housing and urban issues, and supports organizations addressing housing and community development issues across the country. In addition to detailed information on the Foundation's initiatives, the Web site provides complete grant program guidelines, current RFPs, and information about the Maxwell Awards for Excellence. Grant applications can be downloaded as PDF files or requested through an interactive form. An online version of the Foundation's annual report provides lists of program-related investments; national and local grants; Washington, D.C. grants; and officers and board members.

Farmers Group, Inc. (http://www.farmersinsurance.com/fi4500.html)

Farmers Group, the third largest insurer of autos and homes in the U.S., makes contributions in the areas of education, safety, health and human services, civic services, and arts and culture. The company's Web site provides links to information on various programs and initiatives, a break-down of participation by state, a partial list of recent grants, and application guidelines.

The Fieldstone Foundation (http://members.aol.com/mmfieldsto/index.htm)

As the philanthropic vehicle of Fieldstone Communities, Inc., a home builder based in southern California, the Fieldstone Foundation is primarily interested in programs serving children and families. The Foundation funds capacity building of nonprofits through leadership programs; school retention programs; and prevention of drug and alcohol abuse, child abuse, and community violence. It also supports organizations that provide child care services, emergency assistance for youth and families, positive alternatives for youth, and positive responses to diversity. Contributions are made primarily within southern California, and to national organizations that earmark Foundation funds for use in these communities. Visitors to the Foundation's Web site will find a listing of the Foundation's grants; grant guidelines and criteria; information on the Fieldstone Leadership Network, which provides technical and management training to nonprofits in Fieldstone communities; a listing of the Foundation's staff and board members; and contact information.

FMC Foundation (http://www.fmc.com/community/foundation/foundation.html)

Chicago-based FMC Corporation is one of the world's leading producers of chemicals and machinery for industry, government, and agriculture. The company's principal charitable giving arm, the FMC Foundation, contributes more than $1.5 million annually in five major areas—health and human services, education, community improvement, urban affairs, and public issues—to nonprofit organizations in FMC communities, as well as to national organizations working on issues relevant to FMC's businesses. Visitors to the company's Web site will find brief descriptions of the Foundation's philosophy and purpose; program descriptions and guidelines; detailed submission requirements; and basic contact information.

Ford Motor Company Fund (http://www.ford.com/default.asp?pageid=83)

Detroit's Ford Motor Company established the Ford Motor Company Fund in 1949. The Fund supports charitable, scientific, literary, cultural, environmental, educational, and health care organizations in communities where the company operates. The company's Web site includes extensive application guidelines.

Freddie Mac Foundation (http://www.freddiemacfoundation.org)

The Freddie Mac Foundation, the principal charitable arm of Federal Home Loan Mortgage Corporation, is dedicated to helping children, youth, and families at risk. The Foundation provides funds to nonprofit organizations in the Washington, D.C., area and in cities where regional offices are located, and supports programs with a national scope. Giving areas include building strong families, developing the early child, foster care and adoption, building constituencies for children, assisting teen parents, and expanding child care. The Foundation's Web site provides grant guidelines, geographic locations of the company, information on special leadership initiatives and volunteerism, news, the Foundation's annual report (in PDF format), and a message from the chairman.

Gannett Foundation, Inc. (http://www.gannett.com/map/foundation.htm)

The Gannett Foundation, the philanthropic organization of Gannett Co., Inc., a news and information concern headquartered in Alexandria, Virginia, funds programs to improve the education, health, and quality of life of people living in company communities. The Foundation seeks to fund programs that provide creative solutions to the issues of education and neighborhood improvement, economic development, youth development, community problem solving, assistance to disadvantaged people, environmental conservation, and cultural enrichment. The Foundation page of Gannett's Web site provides grant guidelines, an application form, a list of company locations, recent grantees, and contact information.

The Gap, Inc. (http://www.gap.com/onlinestore/gap/company/community.asp)

Through its Community Relations program, The Gap gives cash grants and contributions of merchandise to nonprofit organizations in program areas of particular concern to company employees. While The Gap makes grants in a variety of areas of importance to its communities, including health and human services, education, and arts and culture, it has a special interest in supporting environmental projects. The Gap also makes contributions of t-shirts, sweatshirts, and gift certificates. Visitors to the "Our Community" section of the company's Web site will find general program descriptions, funding limitations, application instructions, and contact information.

James & Marietta Gargiulo Foundation (http://www.jmgscholarship.com)

Each year, the James & Marietta Gargiulo Foundation offers an $8,000 memorial scholarship to a graduating high school senior entering the first year of college. The Foundation was established by SOFCO-Mead, Inc. to honor the founders of the company. Applicants must live in the New York, Massachusetts, Pennsylvania, Ohio, or Vermont counties serviced by SOFCO-Mead. Visitors to the Foundation's Web site will find application guidelines, a list of past scholarships winners, and an application form.

GE Fund (http://www.ge.com/fund)

The GE Fund places education at the crux of its international grantmaking efforts, with support to programs in the areas of science and engineering, pre-college education, public policy, international programs, management, and arts and culture. An online version of the Fund's annual report, featured within General Electric Company's well-organized Web site, includes a letter from the Fund's president, profiles of the Fund's major initiatives, program descriptions, grants lists, and application guidelines.

Genentech, Inc. (http://www.gene.com/Company/Responsibility)

Genentech is a biotechnology company headquartered in San Francisco, California, that uses human genetic information to develop, manufacture, and market pharmaceutical products. The company makes charitable contributions through the Genentech Foundation for Biomedical Sciences and the Genentech Foundation for Growth & Development for research and science education and through a direct corporate giving program supporting Genentech communities. The "Corporate Responsibility" area of the company's Web site provides a brief description of its programs and contact information for each. Additionally, a Material Request Form can be filled out and submitted online by researchers wishing to receive proteins and antibodies free of charge through the Research Contracts and Reagents Program.

General Mills, Inc. (http://www.genmills.com/explore/community)
Through the General Mills Foundation and a direct corporate giving program, General Mills focuses its funding on four areas: arts and culture, education, family life, and health and nutrition. The "Community Involvement" area of the company's Web site provides a description of the Foundation's objectives, a report on corporate citizenship, an overview of grant allocations, a directory of staff and General Mills locations, and a downloadable application form (in PDF format).

General Motors Corporation
(http://www.gm.com/about/info/world/philanthropy/home.html)
General Motors, ranked among the top corporations in philanthropy, targets its support to education, health, community relations, public policy, arts and culture, and environment and energy through the General Motors Foundation, Inc., the General Motors Cancer Research Foundation, Inc., and a direct corporate giving program. The "GM Philanthropic Report" section of the company's Web site details its investment in the communities in which it operates and provides links to descriptions of programs and initiatives and application guidelines.

GTE Corporation (http://www.gte.com/AboutGTE/Community/index.html)
The GTE Foundation, one of the country's 20 largest corporate philanthropies, gives nearly $25 million annually to educational, scientific, and charitable organizations on behalf of GTE and its business units. As a corporation, the telecommunications giant is concerned about America's ability to produce a well-educated, highly productive workforce and has committed significant resources to improving education, with special emphasis on mathematics and science. The company's Web site offers information about GTE's philanthropic efforts in education, health and human services, the arts, and community involvement, and a brief description of the Foundation itself, including contact information.

H & R Block, Inc. (http://www.handrblock.com/community.html)
The H & R Block Foundation is the principal charitable organization of H & R Block, which offers tax preparation and financial services. By "building stronger communities through people," the Foundation aims to improve the metropolitan Kansas City area, home of the company's world headquarters. Funding is focused on the following areas: the arts, education, health and human services, and volunteerism. The "Community Involvement" section of the company's Web site provides a general overview of funding interests.

John Hancock Mutual Life Insurance Company
(http://www.jhancock.com/company/community/index.html)

John Hancock, headquartered in Boston, Massachusetts, focuses its funding on Boston's public schools and inner-city and minority youth. Its funding priorities are affordable housing, education, emergency shelters, employment and job training, intercultural/interracial relations, performing arts, social services, transitional and permanent housing, violence prevention, and youth development. The "Community Relations" area of John Hancock's Web site describes its funding activities in some detail and provides application instructions and brief descriptions of its special initiatives.

Hawai'ian Electric Industries Charitable Foundation
(http://www.hei.com/heicf/heicf.html)

The Hawai'ian Electric Industries Charitable Foundation awards grants to 501(c)(3) organizations in the state of Hawai'i in the categories of community development, education, environment, and family services. The company's Web site provides financial highlights from its annual report, a message from the company's president, summaries of giving for each program area, and general guidelines and application information.

Hewlett-Packard Company (http://webcenter.hp.com/grants)

Hewlett-Packard's Web site offers application guidelines and selection criteria for the primary components of its corporate giving program: the University Grants Program, which emphasizes the donation of equipment over cash; the National Grants Program, primarily supporting K–12 education; U.S. Education Matching, which provides cash matching to universities and equipment matching to educational institutions of all levels; U.S. Local Grants, which support local organizations and K–12 education; and the European Grants Programs, designed to help fulfill Hewlett-Packard's European citizenship objective. Visitors to the site will also find a corporate philanthropy overview and annual report, program and application guidelines, grant and product request forms to download as PDF or text files, and philanthropy contacts at Hewlett-Packard.

Hilton Hotels Corporation
(http://www.hilton.com/corporate/charitable/index.html)

Hilton Hotels, headquartered in Beverly Hills, California, operates hotels and casinos around the world. The company's corporate giving program concentrates on education, health, youth programs, civic affairs, and public policy. Organizations with a national constituency and programs in communities where the company has a major presence are preferably supported. The "Charitable Contributions" section of the company's Web site provides application guidelines and an application form.

The Home Depot, Inc.
(http://www.homedepot.com/cgi-bin/prel80/compinfo/community/index.jsp)

The Home Depot, a chain of home improvement stores headquartered in Charlotte, North Carolina, focuses its charitable giving on affordable housing, at-risk youth, and the environment. The "Community Involvement" area of the company's Web site provides a Social Responsibility Report that outlines the corporate giving program and provides application instructions, a list of charitable activities by program area, and a description of the company's environmental program.

Independence Community Foundation (http://www.icfny.org)

The Independence Community Foundation was founded in 1998 by Independence Community Bank Corp. of Brooklyn, New York. Grants and investments are marked for neighborhood renewal, education, arts and culture, and community quality of life initiatives for New York City and Nassau County. The Foundation's Web site provides examples of funded programs and application guidelines.

International Business Machines Corporation (http://www.ibm.com/ibm/IBMGives/index.html)

International Business Machines, also known as IBM, is guided by a new corporate strategy that aims to combine the company's "technology and people in effective partnerships to bring solutions to the systemic problems that impact society, business, and our quality of life." The four key elements in all new contributions are IBM technology and service, IBM expertise, IBM partnerships, and rigorous measurement. The "Philanthropy" section of Big Blue's Web site offers a listing of "Recent Events" (i.e., press release-style narratives about the company's recent charitable endeavors); a statement of the company's new corporate giving strategy and a summary of its current philanthropic initiatives, including K–12 education, reinventing education, workforce development, adult education and job training, and the environment; and examples of funding to IBM communities worldwide. A snazzy online version of the company's annual report is also available.

Inland Foundation, Inc. (http://www.iccnet.com/content/social/default.htm)

Indianapolis-based Inland Paperboard and Packaging, a wholly-owned subsidiary of Temple-Inland Inc., places a substantial emphasis on action-oriented social responsibility. The company embraces the values of its founder, entrepreneur and philanthropist Herman Krannert, and his wife, Ellnora, who were committed to improving educational and cultural opportunities for all people. The Inland Foundation, established in 1951, makes grants in the areas of health and welfare, education, art and culture, and civic issues. The company's Web site provides visitors with a strong sense of the company's mission, its activities vis-a-vis its stewardship of the environment, and initiatives that comprise its Partners in Education program.

Intel Corporation (http://www.intel.com/intel/community)

The focus of Intel's giving and outreach programs is on bettering education, supporting Intel communities, improving life with technology, and protecting the environment. The Intel Foundation funds programs which "advance math, science and engineering education, promote women and under-represented minorities entering science and engineering careers, and increase public understanding of technology and its impact on contemporary life." All information on the company's philanthropic activities is provided at its Web site under the heading "Intel's Community Involvement." The "Grant Information" section in this area offers grant guidelines, downloadable application materials (as MS Word executable files—you don't need MS Word to view them), additional information on local community grant programs, and links to information on research grants, scholarships, and fellowship programs. An online version of Intel's annual report is also available.

IPALCO Enterprises, Inc.
(http://www.ipalco.com/ABOUTIPALCO/Community/Community.html)
IPALCO, a multi-state energy company headquartered in Indianapolis, Indiana, supports programs that focus on education, the environment, health and welfare, and the arts. IPALCO administers the Golden Apple Award, which recognizes outstanding teachers who integrate math, science, and technology into classroom subjects. The company's Golden Eagle Grants program funds projects aimed at resource conservation and environmental awareness. IPALCO's charitable efforts are briefly described at its Web site.

Johnson & Johnson
(http://www.johnsonandjohnson.com/who_is_jnj/sr_index.html)
Johnson & Johnson, a manufacturer of health care products, believes that "improving the health and welfare of children around the world is an integral part of [its] business." Contributions are allocated to children, health care, education, the environment, local communities, and research. The "Social Responsibility" section of the company's Web site provides a link to the Contributions Annual Report.

K N Energy Foundation
(http://www.kne.com/pages/community/foundation.htm)
The K N Energy Foundation, the charitable organization of K N Energy, Inc., an energy services company headquartered in Lakewood, Colorado, focuses its funding on programs involving education, arts and culture, civic and community development, and youth. The Foundation area of the company's Web site provides grant guidelines, a printable application form, the Foundation's funding history, information on a separate funding initiative called K N for Kids, contact information, and a map of company locations.

Koch Industries, Inc. (http://www.kochind.com/community.asp)
Koch Industries operates businesses in chemicals, gas liquids, agriculture, mineral services, and capital services worldwide and maintains a 43-state presence in the U.S. The company strives "to make a positive impact in [its] communities by giving [its] time and financial resources to organizations, programs and activities that recognize the role of the free market in advancing a free and prosperous civil society." Koch Industries is particularly interested in supporting educational programs that promote the application of economic and scientific principles to problem solving; projects that apply innovative solutions to solve local environmental problems; and projects that promote self-sufficiency, responsibility, tolerance, and respect. The company's Web site includes examples of recent grants and application guidelines.

Sara Lee Foundation (http://www.saraleefoundation.org)
Sara Lee Foundation is the principal philanthropic vehicle of the Chicago, Illinois-based Sara Lee Corporation. The Foundation focuses its funding on programs that support women, culture, hunger, and people in need. In addition, the Foundation administers three awards programs honoring exceptional

organizations involved in those focus areas. The Foundation's Web site thoroughly describes its funding programs and community involvement, offers samples of grants awarded in each funding area, and provides grant application and award nomination procedures.

The Limited, Inc. (http:limited.com/whoweare/)

The Limited supports organizations that respond to the needs of women, children, education, and communities where the company is located. The "Philanthropy" section of the company's Web site provides descriptions of grant categories, grant guidelines, contact information for making inquiries, and listings of grant recipients.

Lincoln National Corporation (http://www.lfg.com/who/communit.htm)

The Lincoln National Foundation, Inc., the principal charitable giving arm of Lincoln National, is committed to enhancing the quality of life in communities where company employees live and work and focuses its grantmaking on arts and culture, education, and human services. Additionally, the company's affiliate offices make charitable contributions through a direct corporate giving program separate from the Fort Wayne, Indiana-based Foundation. The company's Web site outlines the Foundation's funding goals and provides grant guidelines and contact information.

The Lubrizol Foundation (http://www.lubrizol.com/aboutlubrizol/lz_foundation/index.htm)

The Lubrizol Corporation, located in Ohio, formulates chemicals for transportation and industrial systems. The Lubrizol Foundation, the company's philanthropic organization, seeks to support the company's interests and values by awarding grants to educational institutions and charitable groups concerned with education, youth, health, human services, and civic and cultural activities in the Cleveland, Ohio, and Houston, Texas, areas. The company's Web site provides the Foundation's annual report and application guidelines.

Lucent Technologies Foundation (http://www.lucent.com/news/about/community/foundation.html)

Lucent Technologies, Inc., a communications technology company headquartered in Murray Hill, New Jersey, supports education and community needs through the Lucent Technologies Foundation. The company's Web site briefly describes the Foundation's giving objectives and provides a collection of articles and press releases about the support it offers.

McDonald's Corporation (http://www.mcdonalds.com/community/index.html)

McDonald's supports charitable activities focused on children, the environment, education, and health. Most of the company's grantmaking is administered by Ronald McDonald House Charities, which helps children through two programs: Education and Social Responsibility and Healthcare and Medical Research. The company's Web site provides information on scholarships, application instructions, links to information on McDonald's environment and health initiatives, and a link to the Ronald McDonald House Charities Web site.

The McGraw-Hill Companies, Inc.
(http://www.mcgraw-hill.com/corpinfo/philanthropy/index.html)
McGraw-Hill supports "innovative programs that increase the abilities of people around the world to learn, to grow intellectually, to master new skills and to maximize their individual talents for school, work and community." The "Corporate Contributions and Community Relations" section of the company's Web site provides a history of philanthropy at McGraw-Hill, its mission statement, descriptions of its programs, and contact information

McKesson HBOC, Inc. (http://www.mckhboc.com/webpage_templates/
commout_front.php3?page_name=community_outreach)
McKesson HBOC, headquartered in San Francisco, California, is a provider of health care products and services to retail pharmacies, hospitals, and health care networks. The company's principal charitable arm, the McKesson Foundation, Inc., supports health-related, social, educational, civic, and cultural projects primarily focused on youth and located in the San Francisco Bay Area. The company's Web site describes the Foundation's funding philosophy; provides grant guidelines and sample grants; and offers information on educational matching gifts, scholarships, special youth initiatives, and volunteering.

The Medtronic Foundation (http://www.medtronic.com/foundation/index.html)
The Medtronic Foundation is the principal worldwide philanthropy and community affairs vehicle of Minneapolis-based Medtronic, Inc., a manufacturer of medical equipment and devices. Most of the Foundation's grant dollars are spent in three areas: education, with an emphasis on K–12 science education through its STAR (Science and Technology Are Rewarding) program; health; and community affairs, which includes human services, civic, and arts grants. In all three areas, priority is given "to programs that benefit people of color and those who are socioeconomically disadvantaged." The company's Web site offers program descriptions, grant guidelines and application procedures, an application form to print out, a list of Foundation grants, a listing of Medtronic communities, a selection of press releases, and a handy interactive correspondence page. Visitors can also browse an online version of Medtronic's annual report.

Merrill Lynch & Co., Inc. (http://www.ml.com/woml/phil_prog/index.htm)
Merrill Lynch, a global financial management and advisory company headquartered in New York City, promotes education by supporting scholastic programs and academic institutions, and supports cultural arts, environmental, human service, health, and civic organizations. Grants are awarded to regional programs in New York state and to national organizations. The "Corporate Responsibility" area of the company's Web site provides an overview of Merrill Lynch's charitable activities, a global record of giving, grant guidelines, information about scholarships and employee programs, success stories, and news.

Metropolitan Life Foundation
(http://www.metlife.com/Companyinfo/Community/Found/index.html)
Metropolitan Life Insurance Company's Web site provides visitors with detailed program guidelines and limitations, application procedures, and contact information for the Metropolitan Life Foundation, which awards grants in the areas of health, education, culture, civic affairs, and anti-violence.

Micron Technology, Inc. (http://www.micron.com/resources/resources.htm)

Micron Technology, a manufacturer of computer products headquartered in Boise, Idaho, supports projects and programs focused primarily on educational programs related to math and science in the states of Idaho and Utah. The company considers requests from schools, organizations, and universities for grants, personal computers, and decommissioned manufacturing equipment. Guidelines and electronic application forms can be found within the "Resources" area of the Micron Technology Web site. Visitors will also find information on the company's K–12 Resource program, the company's environmental policy, maps to company locations, and contact information.

Microsoft Corporation (http://www.microsoft.com/giving)

Microsoft supports organizations in its communities of operation, primarily the Puget Sound region of Washington state where its headquarters are located and where most of its employees reside. Community grants are made in the areas of human services, education, arts and culture, the environment, access to technology, and civic activities. The world's largest software manufacturer also makes cash and in-kind contributions nationally to K–12 and higher education institutions. The "Community Affairs" section of Microsoft's Web site offers brief program descriptions, application guidelines, giving highlights, and information on its employee giving and Libraries Online! programs.

The Millipore Foundation
(http://www.millipore.com/corporate/mf.nsf/docs/42YSSX)

The Millipore Foundation's objectives are to foster advances in science and technology related to Millipore Corporation business objectives, which include developing purification products for the microelectronic, biopharmaceutical, and analytical laboratory markets; to improve the quality of life in those communities in which Millipore employees live and work, particularly in its headquarters city of Bedford, Massachusetts; and to stimulate volunteerism and active community involvement by Millipore employees. Through its Grants Program, the Foundation supports projects in the areas of education and research, social services, health care, and the arts. Visitors to the company's Web site will find a brief overview of the Foundation, program guidelines, application instructions, and contact information. There is an online version of the company's annual report, and the Foundation's annual report is available for downloading as a PDF file.

Minnesota Mining & Manufacturing Company
(http://www.mmm.com/profile/community/index.html)

Through the Minnesota Mining and Manufacturing Foundation, Inc. and a direct corporate giving program, Minnesota Mining & Manufacturing, a St. Paul, Minnesota manufacturer, seeks to "build on successes in [its] communities." Support for education focuses on higher education in science, technology, and business; support for health and human services focus on organizations that improve quality and address gaps in service delivery systems. Major arts organizations receive general operating or program grants to enhance the cultural life of company communities and local civic agencies are granted assistance in economic and community development and job training. The company's Web site details its areas of interest, provides examples of programs that are presently being funded or were funded in the past, and includes a Contributions Summary.

Mitsubishi Electric America Foundation (http://www.meaf.org)

The Mitsubishi Electric America Foundation is dedicated to the "improvement of quality of life and the empowerment of disabled youth." Its Web site details the Foundation's history and mission, and includes extensive program descriptions, application guidelines, and recipient information on grants awarded by the Foundation. Visitors to the site will also find a list of Foundation staff and officers and Foundation contact information.

Monsanto Company
(http://www.monsanto.com/monsanto/mediacenter/background/97_building.html)

The mission of the Monsanto Fund, the principal philanthropic arm of the Monsanto Company, is "to enhance the value of Monsanto by improving the quality of life in communities of particular importance." The Fund's annual budget of approximately $11 million is distributed for science education, the United Way, arts and culture, and other charitable purposes. Approximately 25 percent of the Fund's annual contributions support programs to improve the quality of life in Monsanto's plant communities. Visitors will find general program goals, descriptions of recent grants, and a handful of links to recent grant recipients. The site also offers an online version of the company's annual report.

The Montana Power Company
(http://www.mtpower.com/community/welcome.htm)

Through the Montana Power Foundation, Inc. and a direct corporate giving program, Montana Power bestows grants to projects and activities affecting the areas surrounding its local and regional offices. The "Community Relations" section of the company's Web site is designed to keep customers and nonprofits up to date on the company's activities in its communities and provides application guidelines and an application form.

MONY Foundation (http://www.mony.com/AboutMONY/InsideMONY/Foundation)

The MONY Foundation is the principal charitable organization of the New York City-based MONY Life Insurance Company. The Foundation "seeks out innovative, strategically effective, community-based programs for economic support." The Foundation is a leader in funding AIDS programs, especially direct services for AIDS patients, and it also cultivates innovation in public service, particularly by fostering partnerships with schools and universities. The company's Web site provides a general overview of the Foundation's endeavors.

J. P. Morgan & Co. Incorporated
(http://www.jpmorgan.com/CorpInfo/CRA/CommunityDevel.html)

J.P. Morgan, the global financial services firm established more than 150 years ago, makes charitable contributions to a wide range of organizations involved in the arts, education, the environment, health and human services, international affairs, and urban affairs through both the J.P. Morgan Charitable Trust and a direct corporate giving program. J.P. Morgan's Community Relations and Public Affairs Department, which is responsible for the firm's relationships with nonprofit organizations, supports "recognized and competent groups" with financial grants, donations of equipment, volunteer services, technical advice, and other services. The department also supports the company's efforts to comply with the Community Reinvestment Act. The J.P. Morgan Web site offers general information about the firm's charitable activities, back issues of *Capital Ideas,* a biennial newsletter, and contact information.

The Nalco Foundation
(http://www.nalco.com/About_Nalco/AN-Foundation/an-foundation.html)
Nalco Chemical Company, based in Naperville, Illinois, produces specialty chemicals and services for water and industrial process treatment. The Nalco Foundation makes grants to nonprofit organizations in the areas of education, community and civic affairs, health, and culture and arts. Geographic regions eligible for grants include Illinois, mainly the metropolitan Chicago area and DuPage County; Carson, California; Freeport and Sugar Land, Texas; Garyville, Louisiana; Jonesboro, Georgia; and Paulsboro, New Jersey. The Foundation area of the company's Web site offers a brief description and contact information for requesting grant guidelines.

NEC Foundation of America
(http://www.nec.com/company/foundation/index.html)
The NEC Foundation of America was established in 1991 by NEC Corporation and its United States subsidiaries to promote the company's corporate philosophy: the integration of computers and communications to help societies worldwide move toward deepened mutual understanding and fulfillment of human potential. The particular focus of the Foundation is on organizations and programs with national reach and impact in one or both of the following areas: science and technology education, principally at the secondary level, and/or the application of technology to assist people with disabilities. Visitors to the company's Web site will find extensive information about the Foundation's activities, including funding guidelines, application procedures, deadlines, and restrictions; a list of recent grant recipients indexed by organization type, geographic location, and grant purpose; and a financial statement.

New England Financial (http://www.nefn.com/Content/AboutUs/comminv.cfm)
New England Financial, an insurance and investment company headquartered in Boston, Massachusetts, supports public education and makes grants to nonprofit organizations in the areas of education, health care, social service, housing, and culture. The "Community Involvement" area of the company's Web site provides a brief description of its funding strategy, examples of organizations awarded grants, and contact information.

NewDeal Foundation (http://www.newdeal.org)
The NewDeal Foundation aims to promote computer literacy and internet access for all through the facilitation of pilot programs in computer technology, the research and advocacy of technology access issues, and the donation of computer labs and software. The Foundation's Web site provides a mission statement, a list of current pilot programs, information on sponsors and partners, and application guidelines.

Newport News Shipbuilding Inc.
(http://www.nns.com/overview/98_community_affairs/community.htm)
Newport News, based in Newport News, Virginia, supports educational and cultural arts programs, as well as civic, health, and human services organizations.

Grants are generally made in the geographic locations of company plants, primarily in the state of Virginia. The "Community Affairs" area of the company's Web site describes its giving strategy, provides a breakdown of charitable giving, and lists grant recipients in various categories.

Oracle Corporation (http://www.oracle.com/corporate/giving)

Oracle, a California-based provider of software and services for information management, contributes funds for environmental protection, endangered animal protection, medical research, primarily in cancer, AIDS, and neuroscience, and K–12 math, science, and technology educational programs. The company's Web site provides a list of recent grant recipients, a grant application form, and further information on Oracle's charitable activities.

Pacific Gas & Electric Company
(http://www.pge.com/about_us/communities/giving.html)

Through its corporate contributions program, Pacific Gas & Electric makes grants exclusively to nonprofit organizations in northern and central California, primarily in two areas: job training and economic development; and education. It also makes a limited number of grants for emergency preparedness and response, environmental stewardship, and civic and cultural activities. Although the company prefers to fund special projects and new or existing programs, it does make grants for general operating support and, on a limited basis, for capital campaigns. Grants typically range from $1,000 to $15,000. In addition to a general description of the company's philanthropic programs, visitors will find a rundown of its grant application procedures and contact information.

Panasonic Foundation, Inc.
(http://www.panasonic.com/MECA/foundation/foundation.html)

Matsushita Electric Corporation of America is a manufacturer of digital electronics products for the home and office and supports a variety of programs primarily focused on education. The Panasonic Foundation, the principal charitable vehicle of the company, assists school districts and state departments of education with reform efforts, but does not provide grants. The company's Web site provides a narrative of the Foundation's charitable efforts and information on its educational programs.

Patagonia, Inc.
(http://www.patagonia.com/enviroaction/earthtax/earthtax_body.ehtml)

Patagonia, an activewear designer and distributor, donates 1 percent of sales—its "Earth tax"—to grassroots environmental organizations through its Environmental Grants Program. The "Enviro Action" section of the company's Web site explains its strong commitment to protecting undomesticated lands and waters; lists by category organizations that have received recent grants, and provides contact information.

J. C. Penney Company, Inc.
(http://www.jcpenneyinc.com/company/commrel/index.htm)

J.C. Penney makes grants to national organizations in the areas of health and welfare, education, civic betterment, and arts and culture. Special attention is given to the support and promotion of volunteerism and the improvement of pre-college education, with a focus on the areas of K–12 reform, restructuring, and dropout prevention. Funding emphasis is given to projects that serve a broad sector of a particular community, national projects that benefit local organizations across the country, organizations that provide direct services, and organizations with a proven record of success. Grants for projects with a local scope, hospitals, museums, and individual colleges and universities are made by local units of the company. Visitors to the "Community Relations" area of the company's Web site will find general funding guidelines, application procedures and limitations, and the company's Community Partners Annual Report.

Pfizer Inc. (http://www.pfizer.com/pfizerinc/philanthropy/home.html)

Through its "Venture Philanthropy" program, pharmaceutical giant Pfizer makes grants to nonprofit organizations within the broad categories of health, education, and community and cultural affairs. Through both product donations and cash grants, Pfizer's health program seeks to "expand access to compassionate, high-quality health care, especially for those most at risk of poor health outcomes." The goal of its education program is to "excite students, primarily K-12, about science and to increase their understanding of scientific principles and the importance of scientific progress." Through its community and cultural affairs program, the company "is committed to strengthening and enhancing the quality of life in communities" where Pfizer operates, particularly New York City. Visitors to the "Venture Philanthropy" section of Pfizer's Web site will find extensive descriptions of the company's philanthropic philosophy, general program descriptions, listings of selected grant recipients in each program area, and application instructions.

The Pillsbury Company Foundation
(http://www.pillsbury.com/community/foundation.html)

The Pillsbury Company Foundation, the grantmaking organization of food supplier Pillsbury, awards grants to programs that help prepare and empower economically disadvantaged young people in company communities. Grants support direct service programs that fall into two categories: Caring Adults and Kids and Skills for Self-Sufficiency. The Foundation area of Pillsbury's Web site describes these funding initiatives and provides a phone number for more information.

Polaroid Foundation, Inc.
(http://www.polaroid.com/polinfo/foundation/index.html)

Polaroid Foundation is the philanthropic organization of Polaroid Corporation, a manufacturer of instant imaging products headquartered in Cambridge, Massachusetts. The Foundation supports programs in the Massachusetts communities of greater Boston and greater New Bedford that help disadvantaged children and adults develop measurable skills. The Foundation area of the company's Web site provides guidelines and an application form for grant proposals. Visitors will also find information on the Foundation's Volunteer Action Fund, college scholarships for children of employees, product donations, and matching gifts.

Principal Life Insurance Company (http://www.principal.com/about/giving)

Principal, also known as Principal Financial Group, is an insurance company headquartered in Iowa. Through the Principal Financial Group Foundation, Inc. and a direct corporate giving program, the company makes charitable contributions of cash, employee volunteer services, and in-kind gifts. The Foundation was established in 1987 to strengthen company communities in the areas of housing, health and human services, education, and culture. Visitors to the company's Web site will find the Report to the Community, application guidelines, and an application form.

The Procter & Gamble Company
(http://www.pg.com/docCommunity/activity/index.html)

Procter & Gamble makes charitable contributions worldwide in excess of $50 million annually. Roughly 60 percent of the company's annual contributions support education, through grants to colleges and universities, public policy research programs, economic education organizations, and Procter & Gamble's scholarship program for employee children. Procter & Gamble also makes grants to health, social service, civic, cultural, and environmental organizations. Visitors to the "P&G Community Activity" section of the company's Web site will find a brief description of the company's philanthropic interests and a brief accounting of its contributions by interest area.

The Prudential Insurance Company of America
(http://www.prudential.com/community/cmzzz1000.html)

Founded in 1875, New Jersey-based Prudential today relies on two vehicles to further its philanthropic goals: the Prudential Foundation, which awards grants in support of early childhood education, professional development for teachers, school leadership development, school-based health and human services, arts education and conflict resolution, youth development, and the teaching of job entry skills; and a direct corporate giving program. Information about the company's philanthropic activities is gathered in the "Community Center" section of Prudential's Web site, which also offers areas devoted to the company's Spirit of Community Initiative, the goal of which is to encourage young people to become involved in making their communities better places to live; and the Helping Heart Program, which helps voluntary emergency medical service squads purchase semi-automatic cardiac defibrillators.

Quantum Corporation
(http://www.quantum.com/quantum/corporate/community/community.htm)

Quantum, a California-based supplier of digitized mass storage products, awards two kinds of grants: Capacity for the Extraordinary grants, which support teacher/professional development for K–12 public schools, and Capacity for Caring grants, which support local initiatives that are of interest and importance to the company's communities. Grants are limited to certain areas of California, Massachusetts, and Colorado. The "Community Relations" section of the company's Web site offers application guidelines, advice to grantseekers, and examples of Quantum's other community involvements.

Reynolds Metals Company Foundation
(http://www.rmc.com/gen/about/foundation.html)

The Reynolds Metals Company Foundation is the principal charitable organization of Reynolds Metals Company, a producer of aluminum products headquartered in Virginia. The Foundation's major area of interest is business education, which comprises one half of its donations, but support is also targeted to health and human services, civic, and cultural and arts organizations. Grants are limited to the areas in which the company operates. The company's Web site provides application guidelines and a list of Foundation directors and staff.

Rohm and Haas Company (http://www.rohmhaas.com/company/CSI/index.html)
Rohm and Haas is a chemical technology manufacturer located in Pennsylvania. The company's corporate giving program, which addresses the needs of company communities, provides grants to organizations concerned primarily with health and human services or education, and secondarily for civic and community improvement or arts and culture. The Rohm and Haas Web site includes application guidelines.

Rite Aid Corporation (http://www.riteaid.com/commun.htm)
Rite Aid, a chain of pharmacies headquartered in Harrisburg, Pennsylvania, supports programs and projects in communities served by the company. Funding is focused on health and medical programs, social services, education, the arts, and civic services. The "In the Community" area of the company's Web site provides funding criteria and request procedures.

SAFECO Corporation (http://www.safeco.com/about/corporate/relations.asp)
SAFECO Corporation, an insurance company headquartered in Seattle, Washington, focuses its charitable support on strengthening neighborhoods in areas of company offices throughout the U.S. The company creates partnerships with organizations to build safe and vigorous neighborhoods, maintain engaged and proud neighborhoods, and support economically secure and prosperous neighborhoods and funds programs that promote stable and friendly neighborhoods. The company's Web site provides contact information and a list of SAFECO office locations.

SBC Foundation (http://www.sbc.com/Community/SBC_Foundation/Home.html)
The SBC Foundation, the philanthropic unit of SBC Communications Inc., seeks to help "communities search for lasting solutions to critical and complex problems." To that end, the Foundation focuses on education, community economic development, health and human services, and culture and the arts. Most grants are directed toward a five-state region—Texas, Missouri, Kansas, Oklahoma, and Arkansas—but the Foundation does support a number of relevant initiatives that are national in scope. The company's Web site provides visitors with a thorough, user-friendly overview of the grantseeking process, including grantmaking guidelines, a grant application form, and contact information.

S. C. Johnson & Son, Inc. (http://www.scjohnson.com/community)
S. C. Johnson, headquartered in Racine, Wisconsin, is a manufacturer of home cleaning, storage, personal care, and insect control products and a supplier of products and services for commercial, industrial, and institutional facilities. Through the S. C. Johnson Wax Fund, Inc. and a direct corporate giving program, the company supports programs focused on education; medical, health, and environmental protection; and social, cultural, and community concerns. Scholarships and fellowships are also provided. The "Building Better Communities" area of the company's Web site briefly describes its giving initiatives.

Sears, Roebuck and Co. (http://www.sears.com/company/pubaff/commun.htm)
Sears, Roebuck, a general merchandising concern, directs its community activities and giving to organizations or programs that directly address women, families, and diversity issues. Gilda's Club, established in 1995, provides meeting places for people living with cancer and their loved ones and the Get Back Give Back program helps clothe needy children. The company's Web site provides a link to detailed information on its Gilda's Club initiative.

Sega Youth Education & Health Foundation (http://www.sega.com/foundation)
The Sega Youth Education & Health Foundation, also known as the Sega Foundation, is committed to improving the lives of young people, and has a particular interest in children's education and health. The Foundation area of Sega of America, Inc.'s Web site offers a good deal of information about Foundation-funded projects and initiatives, past, present, and future. The Foundation initiates most of its funding discussions with nonprofit organizations, but it accepts unsolicited proposals for small grants, typically ranging from $500 to $2,500. Site visitors will find thorough funding information, grant application and eligibility guidelines, and lists of grants.

Shell Oil Company Foundation
(http://www.countonshell.com/nonShock/index.html)
Shell Oil Company, located in Houston, Texas, is a producer of crude and refined oil, natural gas, and chemicals. The Shell Oil Company Foundation is committed to making a difference in the communities where company employees live and work. The Foundation supports qualified organizations that provide "broad-based support in areas such as equal opportunity, health and human services, civic involvement, the arts, and education." The company's Web site provides detailed descriptions of support areas and contact information. Follow the links with "community" in the title to reach the Foundation's page.

Siemens Foundation (http://www.siemens-foundation.org/index.htm)
Siemens Corporation is a holding company located in New York, New York. The Siemens Foundation seeks to "stimulate, support and encourage the pursuit of education," especially in the fields of technology, math, and science. The Foundation's Web site provides links to information on regional competitions, the Siemens Westinghouse Science & Technology Competition, and the Siemens Awards for Advanced Placement and an application form (in PDF format) for the Siemens Westinghouse Competition.

Silicon Graphics, Inc. (http://www.sgi.com/company_info/oommunity)
Silicon Graphics is a computer equipment manufacturer headquartered in Mountain View, California. Through a direct corporate giving program, the company makes charitable contributions to nonprofit organizations involved with arts and culture, education, the environment, and health and human services. The "Community Relations" area of the company's Web site provides links to a Corporate Responsibility Statement, information on the company's B.R.I.T.E. Award, a B.R.I.T.E. Award application form (in PDF format), and recent Giving Reports.

The Skadden Fellowship Foundation, Inc.
(http://www.sasmf.com/fellows/default.html)

Skadden, Arps, Slate, Meagher & Flom is a legal services firm located in New York, New York. The Skadden Fellowship Foundation was established in 1988 as an "affirmation of the firm's commitment to public law." The Foundation awards 25 fellowships per year to graduating law students and outgoing judicial clerks who provide legal services to the elderly, poor, homeless, and disabled. The company's Web site provides contact information and application guidelines.

Skidmore, Owings & Merrill Foundation
(http://www.som.com/html/som_foundation.html)

Skidmore, Owings & Merrill is an architectural firm located in Chicago, Illinois. The Skidmore, Owings & Merrill Foundation is committed to helping young architects and engineers broaden their professional education by offering annual traveling fellowships in different disciplines. The company's Web site provides detailed information on various fellowship programs and contact information.

Sonoco Foundation (http://www.sonoco.com/sonoco_foundation.htm)

The Sonoco Foundation, the philanthropic conduit for South Carolina-based Sonoco Products Company, focuses its giving on education, health and welfare, arts and culture, and the environment in locations where the company has operations. The majority of its grants are awarded to United States institutions with a local, rather than a national, perspective. Visitors to the company's Web site will find general policy, program, and application guidelines, the grant application format, program and support limitations, and contact information.

Southwire Company (http://www.southwire.com/community)

Southwire, a wire and cable manufacturer, supports education and environmental programs in several counties in Georgia, Illinois, Mississippi, Alabama, and Kentucky. The company's Web site describes its education grant and environmental award programs and provides online application forms.

Sprint Corporation (http://www.sprint.com/sprint/overview/commun.html)

Commitment to community, with an emphasis on "support of local and regional organizations in which the corporation has a major presence," is the basis for Sprint's corporate philanthropy. Through the Sprint Foundation and its direct corporate giving program, Sprint supports education, arts and culture, community improvement, and youth development. The "Community Service" area of the company's Web site includes information on Sprint's employee giving programs, a brief overview of the Sprint Foundation's activities, application guidelines, and contact information. An online version of the company's annual report is also available and can be downloaded as a PDF file.

State Farm Companies Foundation
(http://www2.statefarm.com/foundati/found.htm)

State Farm Insurance Cos., located in Bloomington, Illinois, sells casualty and life insurance. Founded in 1963, the State Farm Companies Foundation supports higher education through scholarship programs and grants to colleges and universities. Additional funding is aimed at community, human service, and health agencies in locations where State Farm employees maintain a presence. The company's Web site provides application guidelines and contact information.

Levi Strauss & Co. (http://www.levistrauss.com/index_community.html)
Through the Levi Strauss Foundation and a direct corporate giving program, Levi Strauss seeks to create "positive change in [its] communities by awarding grants, encouraging employees to volunteer their time and standing behind critical, controversial issues." The majority of resources are directed toward poor and underserved people across the nation and centered on AIDS prevention and care, economic empowerment, youth empowerment, and social justice. The "Giving Programs" section of the company's Web site provides links to application guidelines and information on employee giving.

Sun Microsystems, Inc.
(http://www.sun.com/corporateoverview/corpaffairs/giving.html)
Through its Community Development Grants Program, the Sun Microsystems Foundation, Inc. "invests in communities that are often characterized by low income, high unemployment, and disturbing school drop-out rates." Grants are awarded in the areas of education (grades 7–12 in the United States and secondary schools S1-S6 in Scotland) and employment and job development in the southern San Francisco Bay Area, California, the Merrimack Valley of Massachusetts, and the West Lothian District of Scotland. Visitors to the company's Web site will find information on the Program's funding criteria (including limitations), application guidelines, and an online version of the company's annual report.

Texaco Inc. (http://www.texaco.com/support/index.html)
Texaco, a provider of energy and energy products worldwide, supports programs that prepare children for the study of math and science. The Texaco Foundation makes grants through two specific programs: Education and Music and Science Discovery. A third, broad program provides funding for arts and culture, primary health care for children, the environment, and economic education in countries where Texaco operates. The company's Web site describes the Foundation's giving philosophy, provides guidelines and application instructions, and includes press releases of recent donations and scholarships.

Texas Instruments Foundation
(http://www.ti.com/corp/docs/company/citizen/foundation/index.shtml)
The Texas Instruments Foundation is the principal charitable vehicle of Texas Instruments Incorporated, a digital signal processing solutions company based in Dallas, Texas. The Foundation supports educational and research institutions, as well as organizations and projects in communities where the company has major facilities. In addition to education and research, funding is available for health, welfare, civic, and cultural projects committed to systemic change. The Foundation area of the company's Web site describes the Foundation's giving strategy, provides grant guidelines, and offers examples of funded programs.

Toshiba America Foundation (http://www.toshiba.com/new/taf.shtml)
As the principal charitable arm of Toshiba America, Inc., a leading consumer electronics company, the Toshiba America Foundation focuses on the improvement of classroom teaching in grades 7–12, especially in the areas of science,

mathematics, and technology. Although the Foundation welcomes proposals from communities across the United States, it "feels a special responsibility toward those communities where the Toshiba America group companies have a corporate presence." In addition to information about the Foundation's current program interests, the company's attractive, well-organized Web site provides a summary of projects funded by the Foundation during the last 12 months, detailed instructions on preparing a grant application, a proposal format outline and sample proposal cover page, and contact information.

Toyota USA Foundation
(http://www.toyota.com/times/commun/feature/founhome.html)
With a primary emphasis on improving the teaching and learning of mathematics and science, the Toyota USA Foundation is committed to improving the quality of K–12 education in the United States. Grants are made to accredited colleges, universities, community colleges, and vocational or trade schools, and to nonprofit organizations engaged in pre-collegiate math and/or science education. K–12 public and private schools may not apply directly to the Foundation, though they may be the recipient of an independent nonprofit agency's funding request. In addition to contact information and a general overview of its activities, visitors to the company's Web site will find detailed application guidelines and restrictions, highlights of recent grants and a list of past Foundation grantees, and a grant application form.

U S WEST Foundation (http://www.uswf.org)
The U S WEST Foundation seeks to "strengthen the link between developments in the communications world and the kinds of projects it funds" through its Major Initiative and Community Outreach programs. The Foundation's Major Initiatives include Widening Our World, a mobile interactive school teaching people how to interact through computer and telecommunication technologies; Connecting People Through Communications Technologies for Education, an information technology training program for teachers; Connecting People to Economic Growth, supporting programs designed to nurture small businesses and other economic development efforts; and Creating Content for the Future, improving lives of individuals with multimedia technologies. Through its Community Outreach program, the Foundation supports nonprofit organizations in the areas of arts and culture, civic and community improvement, education, and human services. The Foundation's Web site provides general guidelines for RFPs, deadlines for each program area, and contact information for regional program officers.

U.S. Bancorp Piper Jaffray Companies Inc.
(http://www.piperjaffray.com/pj/pj_ci.asp)
U.S. Bancorp Piper Jaffray, an investment firm based in Minneapolis, Minnesota, contributes to civic and charitable causes through the U.S. Bancorp Piper Jaffray Companies Foundation and a direct corporate giving program. The Foundation awards general operating and capital grants for programs that support families working toward self-sufficiency and the development and education of children. The "Community Involvement" area of the company's Web site describes its philanthropic activities and provides Foundation grant guidelines, an application form (in .PDF format) to download, and contact information.

United Airlines Foundation (http://www.ual.com/airline/Our_Company/civic.asp)
UAL Corporation is a provider of air transportation located in Elk Grove Township, Illinois. The United Airlines Foundation is committed to defining, developing, implementing, and communicating its longstanding commitment to community service by sponsoring and supporting charitable organizations, programs, and activities that improve the quality of life in company communities. Support is aimed at education, health, and community through cash grants, air travel, and employee volunteer services. The company's Web site provides detailed information on each of its areas of interest.

United Technologies Corporation (http://www.utc.com/commun/index.htm)
United Technologies, a diversified $23 billion Fortune 500 conglomerate, makes grants to tax-exempt 501(c)(3) organizations in the areas of education, health and human services, cultural arts, and civic involvement. The company focuses its grantmaking in communities where it has a substantial corporate presence, including Hartford, East Hartford, Stratford, Windsor Locks, and Middletown, Connecticut; Syracuse, New York; Dearborn, Michigan; Bloomington, Indiana; West Palm Beach, Florida; and Washington, D.C. The application form available on the company's Web site must be filled out and submitted by July 15 of the current year for projects to be considered for the next year's budget. The "Community" area provides visitors with general descriptions of each area of support, guidelines and limitations for grant and matching gift programs, summaries of funded projects, and appropriate contact information.

The UPS Foundation
(http://www.community.ups.com/community/leading/foundation.html)
United Parcel Service of America, Inc., located in Atlanta, Georgia, provides parcel delivery and international air express services. The UPS Foundation, established in 1951, is dedicated to the resolution of social problems and supports programs involved with family and workplace literacy, food distribution, and increased nationwide volunteerism. The Foundation also supports "high-impact educational and urgent human needs programs." The company's Web site provides links to information on the Foundation's Neighbor to Neighbor volunteer program and UPS Region/District Grant Program.

USX Foundation, Inc. (http://www.usx.com/usxci.htm)
USX Corporation, headquartered in Pittsburgh, Pennsylvania, is a producer of oil, natural gas, and steel products. The USX Foundation was founded in Delaware in 1953 as the United States Steel Foundation to support educational, scientific, charitable, civic, cultural, and health needs. The Foundation awards grants to organizations for education; health and human services; and public, cultural, and scientific affairs. From the company Web site you can download a PDF file that provides a summary of giving, including financial statements, describes grant programs and lists recipients by giving category, includes grant application guidelines, and lists trustees, officers, and staff.

Vastar Resources, Inc. (http://www.vastar.com/fi/direct-charitables.html)
Vastar Resources is an oil and gas producer headquartered in Houston, Texas. Through a direct corporate giving program, the company makes charitable contributions to nonprofit organizations involved with arts and culture, the humanities,

education, the environment, and health and human services. Support is given primarily in areas of company operations. The company's Web site provides contact information and application guidelines (in PDF format).

Wal-Mart Foundation (http://www.walmartfoundation.org)

Wal-Mart Stores, Inc., located in Bentonville, Arkansas, operates a regional chain of discount department stores and wholesale variety stores. The Wal-Mart Foundation is dedicated to improving education, health and human services, and the environment through a variety of awards and scholarships. In addition, the Foundation has developed a four-part community-wide commitment to supporting educational programs for children and supporting and encouraging local community and environmental activities. The Foundation's Web site provides application guidelines and a monetary breakdown of recent giving.

Walgreen Co. (http://www.walgreens.com/)

Walgreen is a drug store operator headquartered in Deerfield, Illinois. Through a direct corporate giving program, support is given on a national basis. The company also gives through the Walgreen Benefit Fund. The company's Web site provides descriptions of its charitable initiatives and links to information on its Tutoring Programs and a school partnership. Search through the company Web site to find these various initiatives.

Weyerhaeuser Company Foundation (http://www.weyerhaeuser.com/community/foundation)

Weyerhaeuser Company, a supplier of forest products based in Washington state, established the Weyerhaeuser Company Foundation in 1948 to improve the quality of life in company communities and to increase understanding of forests and the products they provide. The Foundation supports education and programs that promote responsible natural resource management, and dedicates 30 percent of its giving to industry-related projects. The Foundation area of the company's Web site describes these giving activities and provides guidelines, a list of eligible locations, and an electronic application form.

Whirlpool Foundation (http://www.whirlpoolcorp.com/whr/ics/foundation)

Through the Whirlpool Foundation, Whirlpool Corporation, the appliance manufacturer, seeks to "improve the quality of family life primarily in [Whirlpool] communities, worldwide." The Foundation particularly likes to partner with "organizations that target women and family life issues." Visitors to the company's Web site will find general descriptions of the Foundation's areas of interest, information on the Foundation's women's studies research, a sampling of recent grants, and contact information.

CHAPTER SIX

Government Resources on the Web

In an environment of government cutbacks and the call for balanced budgets, the abundance of government grants for nonprofits and individuals may come as a surprise to some. Also surprising may be the U.S. government's notable presence on the Internet, which attests to the wealth of resources for grantseekers at all levels as well as to the government's interest in keeping pace with technological change.

Because printed government documents and information tend to be dense and laborious to search through, the Internet is an ideal place to conduct such research. Online government resources of interest to grantseekers include general information about the government, databases and statistics about philanthropy, legal and financial information, funding availability announcements, and guides to proposal writing. Although government resources on the Internet are plentiful and therefore potentially overwhelming, a number of Web sites exist whose creators—often at universities or nonprofit organizations—have culled, categorized, organized, and annotated government and government-related sites. These sites vary greatly in design, amount and type of information, and usefulness to grantseekers. This chapter is intended to suggest starting points and, especially, to help identify those sites most useful for grantseekers.

Start at the Top

The top is a logical place to start to get the broadest possible view of resources. The legislative and judicial branches of the federal government have Web sites, as do many departments, agencies and state and local governments. The Interactive Citizens' Handbook (http://www.whitehouse.gov/wh/html/handbook.html)

provides access to information from the White House, the President's cabinet, independent federal agencies and commissions, as well as the legislative and judicial branches.

This site is also a place to start your search for general government resources. Follow the link to the Government Information Locator Service (GILS) (http:// www.gils.net/index.html), an index to all government information.

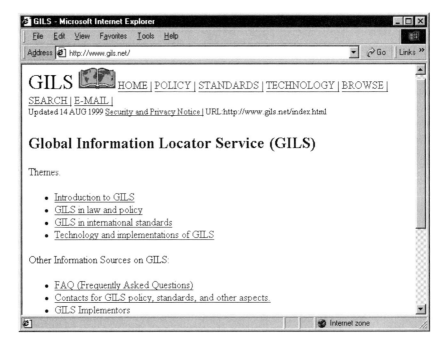

The House of Representatives site (http://www.house.gov/) and the Senate site (http://www.senate.gov/) include access to information about legislation recently passed and that under consideration.

The frequently updated databases of THOMAS, the official site of the U.S. Congress (http://thomas.loc.gov/), include information on congressional activity, committee reports, and the legislative process.

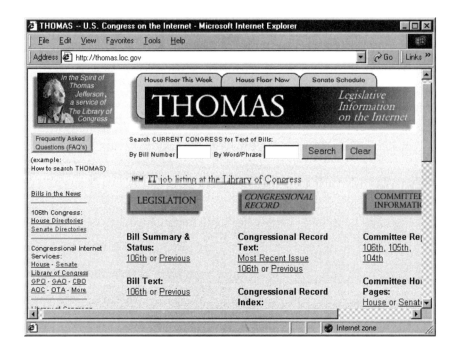

GENERAL GOVERNMENT INFORMATION SITES

In addition to the official government branch home pages, many government departments and nongovernmental organizations compile and list links, providing entrance to government and related sites. The Library of Congress's Internet Resource Page series (http://lcweb.loc.gov/global/executive/fed.html), for example, has a comprehensive set of links organized by departments and agencies. Here are some other places to start:

Federal Web Locator (http://www.infoctr.edu/fwl/)

A service provided by The Center for Information Law and Policy, this site offers a comprehensive search engine using keywords or "federal quick jumps" to find an agency or organization.

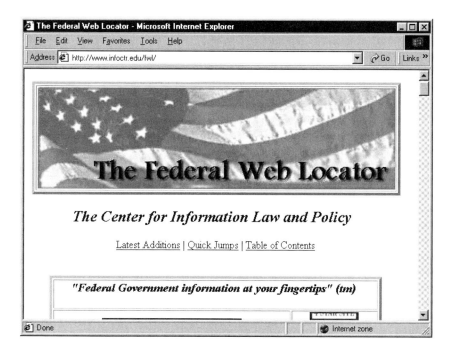

This site is "intended to be the one-stop-shopping point for federal government information on the World Wide Web. This list is maintained to bring the cyber citizen to the federal government's doorstep."

FedWorld (http://www.fedworld.gov/)

Sponsored by the National Technical Information Service, this is a comprehensive, easy-to-use resource for government databases and general government information.

GovBot (http://ciir2.cs.umass.edu/Govbot/)

Developed by the Center for Intelligent Information Retrieval, the GovBot database consists of over 800,000 Web pages from U.S. government and military sites and can be searched by means of a simple form with keywords.

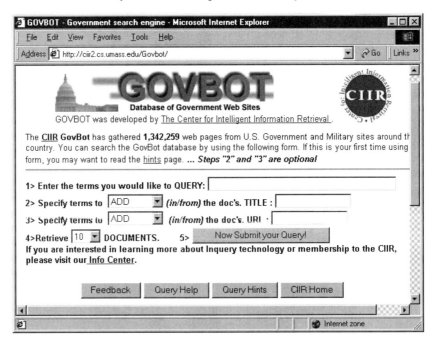

**World Wide Web Virtual Library: US Government Information Sources
(http://iridium.nttc.edu/gov_res.html)**
This site, maintained by the National Technology Transfer Center, is similar to the
Federal Web Locator but on a smaller scale (about 1,000 government links).

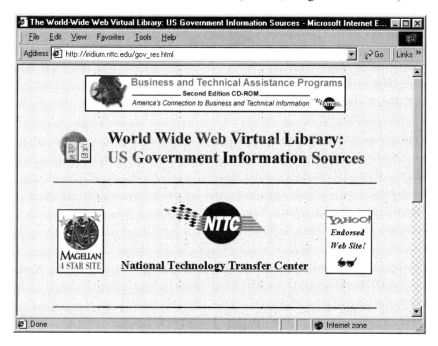

**Louisiana State University's Libraries List of U.S. Federal Government
Agencies (http://www.lib.lsu.edu/gov/fedgov.html)**
This site provides a comprehensive list of links to government departments, agencies, and related organizations right on the first page so that you can simply search
or scan for relevant words or appropriate departments.

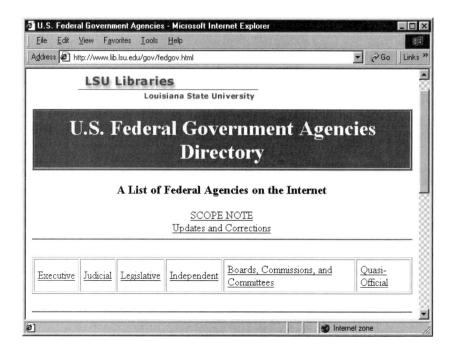

University of Texas Health Center United States Government and Grant Resources (http://psyche.uthct.edu/ous/Govt.html)
This site provides useful links organized in categories such as Foundations and Grant Information, Minority Funding Opportunities, U.S. Federal, State, and Local Grant Funding Opportunities, and specific grantmaking foundations, government departments, and institutes.

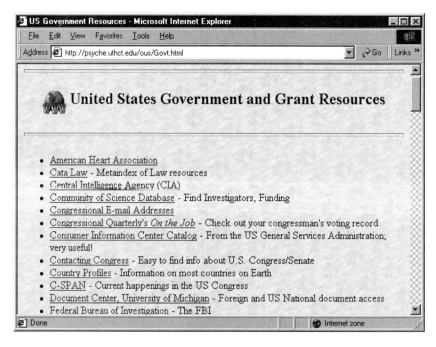

The Foundation Center's Links to Nonprofit Resources – Government Resources (http://fdncenter.org/onlib/npr_links/index.html)

The Government Resources section of "Links to Nonprofit Resources" in the Foundation Center's Online Library provides easy access to sites highlighted in this chapter in addition to several specific federal and state agencies of interest to grantseekers and nonprofit organizations. (See Chapter 8 for more on the Center's "Links to Nonprofit Resources.")

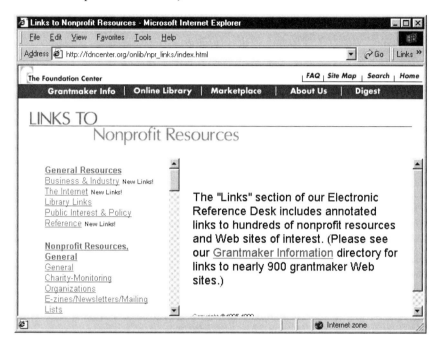

Federal Acquisition Jumpstation (part of NASA Acquisition Internet Service) (http://nais.nasa.gov/fedproc/home.html)

This site, which links to Internet sites of federal procurement information, is designed for the business community but is also relevant to grantseekers because it delineates how the government spends its money. It also includes specific grantmaking bodies.

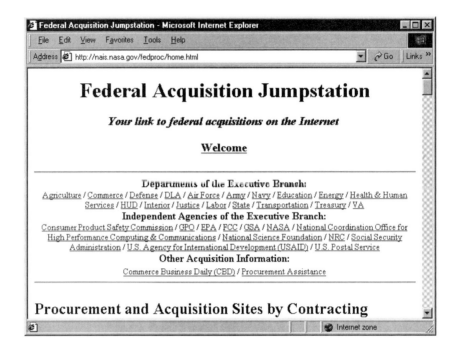

Federal Gateway (http://www.fedgate.org)

This search engine, which includes links to federal, state, and local government sites, bills itself as "America's one-stop resource for government information." It includes a unique section on commonly used government abbreviations and acronyms.

The Federal Information Center (http://fic.info.gov)

This site provides information about federal agencies, programs, and services. It includes a section on federal loans, grants, and assistance with links to general resources and specific government agencies.

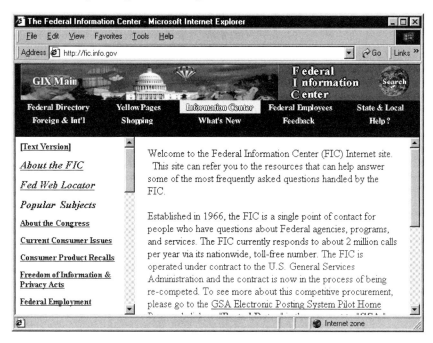

Google Special Searches-Government (http://www.google.com/unclesam)

Search the government category within this popular search engine.

STATE AND LOCAL GOVERNMENT INFORMATION SITES

The government Internet presence extends deep into all levels and, therefore, so can your grantseeking. To find state and local government resources, try these sites:

State and Local Government on the Net
(http://www.piperinfo.com/state/states.html)
This site consists of links to each state (plus tribal governments), and in turn each state page provides links to the branches, departments, boards, and commissions that have Web sites. This site can be helpful in searching for local grantmaking bodies such as arts councils.

StateSearch (http://www.nasire.org/StateSearch/index.cfm)
This site is "designed to serve as a topical clearinghouse to state government information on the Internet." Linking to a subject area results in a list of all departments, listed by state, that are involved in that subject and have a Web presence.

Library of Congress: State and Local Governments
(http://lcweb.loc.gov/global/state/stategov.html)
This site offers a combination of the previous two sites—a meta-list of links to state and local government information. (e.g., National City Government Resource Center, a site providing access to cities' government information) and links to each state's Web pages.

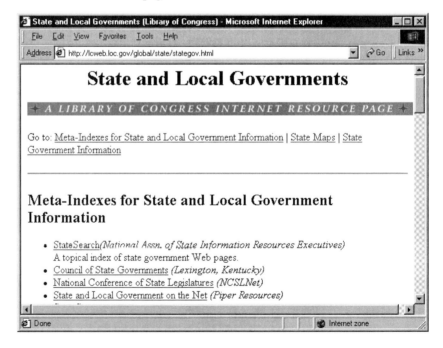

U.S. State and Local Gateway (http://www.statelocal.gov)
An interagency project in collaboration with the National Partnership for Reinventing Government, this Web site was developed to give state and local

governments easy access to federal information. It organizes its links to grants, loans, and contracts by subject category in an easy-to-read chart.

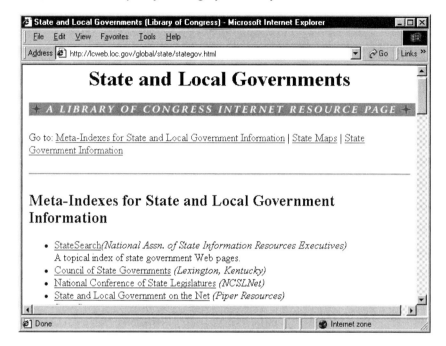

Focusing Your Research on Government Funding

Government-related sites can contain an enormous amount of information, much of it not very useful to the focused grantseeker. As with corporate Web sites (see Chapter 5), grants and funding information is often buried within a site and can easily be missed. In addition, funding information may not be situated in one area of the site but rather by department or subject matter. Because most of these sites are so information-rich, many of them have internal search engines and grantseekers should make a habit of using them. By using the search terms "grants," "funding," "opportunities," or even "research and development," in addition to keywords describing the particular subject matter of interest, you are less likely to miss relevant information.

The majority of grants offered by the government—especially at the federal level—are in the fields of education, health and scientific research, human services, environment, agriculture, and industry, though they are not limited to these subject categories. The government also funds historical research, arts and humanities. Looking at the more specialized departments, grants are awarded in a wide range of disciplines. Federal funders generally prefer projects that serve as prototypes or models for others to replicate, whereas local government funders look for strong evidence of community support for the project.

Though a fair number of individual awards exist, the majority of government grants (as is true for private grants as well) are awarded to eligible nonprofit organizations, not to individuals.

GENERAL GOVERNMENT GRANT INFORMATION SITES

There are a number of general sites that focus specifically on government funding, which can be very useful to grantseekers.

NonProfit Gateway (http://www.nonprofit.gov)

This is the starting point for nearly one-stop shopping for federal information, including grants. Created by the White House Office of Public Liaison, the site provides extremely valuable and easy-to-use information and services from federal agencies.

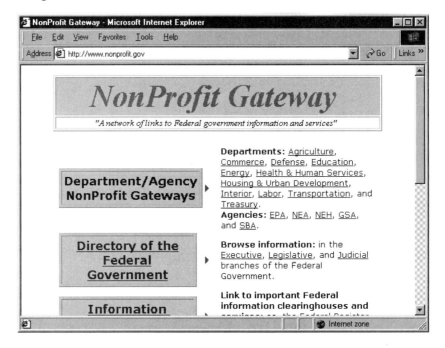

You can link to related Web sites hosted by federal departments and agencies, search for grant programs, and get information about federal laws that apply to nonprofits. The most useful feature of the site is the set of charts that list government cabinet departments and agencies and note whether or not they offer grants. Bullets in the charts link to the department or agency's Web site and directly to the grantmaking section of each site. The "Nonprofit Resources" section provides similar charts which indicate government agencies and departments which offer opportunities for nonprofits to partner with them or which have volunteer programs. This site also offers a "Master Search" of over 530,000 government Web sites.

Federal Register (http://www.access.gpo.gov/su_docs/aces/aces140.html)

This is the official daily record of the federal government. It has the most current and comprehensive information regarding government-funded projects and funding availability. You will also find postings of proposed regulations and agency meetings. The Federal Register is an essential stopping point in the grantseeker's journey because it provides information on all government grants. Other departments often link to this site in their grants information, and their own compilations may not be as current.

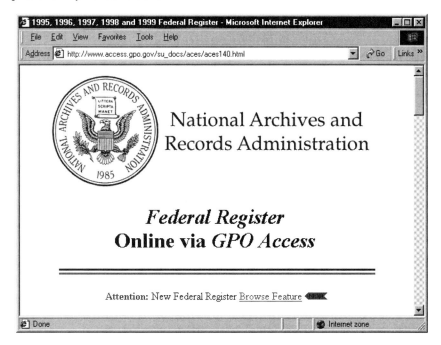

You can search the database in a variety of ways, guided by detailed instructions and sample searches. Although there is no section devoted entirely to grants or requests for proposals (RFPs), grantseekers can enter key words to generate a list of potential funding notices. The official term is "Notice of Funding Availability" or NOFA. Grantseekers can search the Register back to 1994, although the 1994 version does not include subject field identifiers. The default is to search the current year only, but you can check off multiple years. An additional feature is the capability to browse the daily tables of contents for the Register back through 1998, which can be very useful if you are looking for a specific agency or department's notices (the table of contents is listed alphabetically by government agency).

EZ/EC Notices of Funding Availability (http://ocd.usda.gov/nofa.htm)
As noted above, although comprehensive, the Federal Register is not solely dedicated to serving the grantseeker. So a visit to this site, developed by the Empowerment Zone and Enterprise Community Program Offices of the U.S. Department of Agriculture and the U.S. Department of Housing and Urban Development, allows grantseekers to customize a search for Notices of Funding Availability (NOFA), thereby making the Federal Register database more relevant and manageable. You can search for NOFAs by keywords such as "Housing" and "Youth," or by specific agency or department.

Catalog of Federal Domestic Assistance (CFDA) (http://www.gsa.gov/fdac/)
This site is part of the General Services Administration and provides information on a wide variety of financial and non-financial assistance programs, projects, services, and activities.

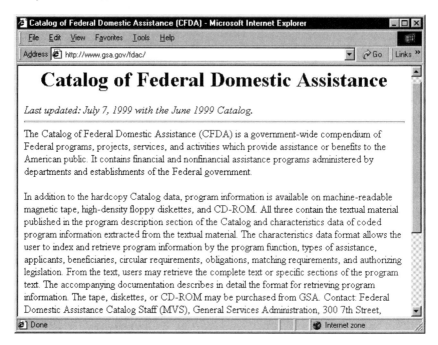

This is probably the government resource most familiar to grantseekers, with good reason. You can submit a simple query and receive clear, detailed information, including eligibility requirements, application procedures, and examples of funded projects. Suggested keywords to use are "grants," "money," or "assistance," along with topic words describing your program interests.

Federal Information Exchange (FEDIX) (http://web.fie.com/fedix/index.html)
This page is run by several federal agencies and provides access to information on government research and education grants, programs, contracts, and more. The site is comprehensive and easy to use.

You can search by audience (e.g., Higher Education and Research Organizations, Elementary/Secondary Schools, Minority Federal Opportunities) or subject and you can also receive targeted funding opportunities via e-mail. Other features include news updates and a Grants Keyword Thesaurus, which can be downloaded by eligible nonprofit institutions after free registration.

You can also connect to MOLIS (http://web.fie.com/web/mol/index.htm), the Minority Online Information Service, which serves minority populations in the education and research communities.

GrantsNet (Department of Health and Human Services) (http://www.hhs.gov/progorg/grantsnet/)

The Department of Health and Human Services has an exemplary Web site for grantseekers. Visitors to the GrantsNet portion of the site will find relevant headings, including "How to Find Grant Information," "Search for Funding," "How to Apply," "Useful Grants Management Information/Resources," as well as links to other federal grant programs.

The site also includes useful information regarding how the department administers grants, and a directory of key grants management personnel in other departments. GrantsNet guides the grantseeker to specific funding opportunities within each of the many agencies that make up HHS, and also encourages the use of the CFDA and the Federal Register (see previous descriptions).

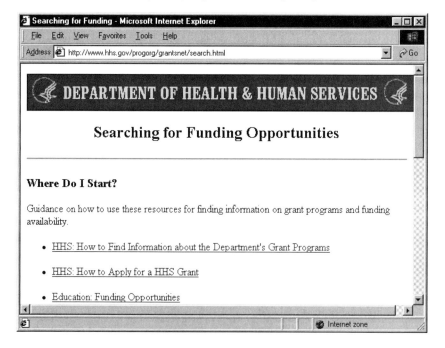

The HHS Partner Gateway (http://www.odphp.osophs.dhhs.gov/partner/funding.htm), also a service of the Department of Health and Human Services, is "an easily navigable roadmap to HHS resources" that highlights Web pages with grant information if you are seeking funding for projects in this area. Other useful sections of the Gateway include links to sample projects funded by HHS, tools for putting together federal grant applications, and a database of abstracts, reports, and other completed and on-going evaluative research of DHHS.

GPO Access Browse Topics: Grants and Awards
(http://www.access.gpo.gov/su_docs/dpos/topics/grants.html)

One of the collections of "Electronic Titles: Government Information Products Available via the Internet" made available through the GPO (Government Printing Office) Access' Pathway Services, this is a meta-list of government Web sites having to do with grants and awards.

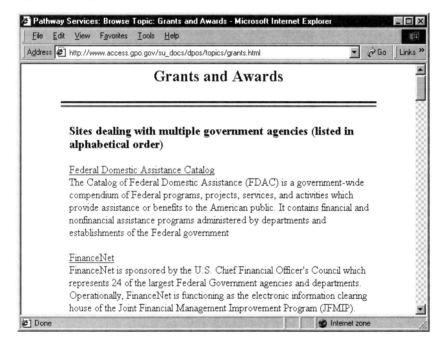

In addition to profiling comprehensive sites such as the Catalog of Federal Domestic Assistance (previously mentioned), grantseekers will appreciate the list of links to funding information from specific government agencies. Also included is a "Special Awards" section which lists awards given by government agencies (i.e., the Presidential Awards for Excellence in Mathematics & Science Teaching).

Narrowing Your Focus on Funding Information

Like FEDIX, the following sites list resources specifically geared towards government grant information and therefore help reduce searching time.

Grants Web (http://sra.rams.com/cws/sra/resource.htm)
This is a comprehensive, well-organized site, created by The Society of Research Administrators, which highlights government grantmaking areas with links to federal agencies and their funding programs. The site also features links to the application forms of specific agencies.

Grants Information Service (Penn State) (http://infoserv.rttonet.psu.edu/gis/)
This site provides links to several searchable government databases, most of which have been previously mentioned here, in addition to several university gateways and new, featured databases. This site links directly to funding opportunities from the National Science Foundation and the National Institutes of Health.

University of Michigan Documents Center
(http://www.lib.umich.edu/libhome/Documents.center/fedgt.html)
Annotated links provide access to some of the major government databases and grantmaking sites, such as the Federal Register, a few searchable university databases, Education Department Grants, etc. Again, this site provides access to most of the previously mentioned sites but is well-organized and worth visiting.

The National Adjunct Faculty Guild At-a-Glance Guide to Grants (http://www.sai.com/adjunct/nafggrant.html)

This site has two useful sections, "Databases of Funding Opportunities" and "Indices of Grant-Related Sites," which include links to federal and state grant catalogs, several of which require subscription or university affiliation, but again, worth a visit.

Texas Research Administrators Group (TRAM) (http://tram.east.asu.edu/)

TRAM offers a variety of useful resources on their Web site, hosted by Arizona State University East. One of the most interesting features is the Electronic Agency Forms section, where you can download copies of application forms accepted by certain government agencies. You can also search a database of funding opportunities, which are culled from the Web sites of agencies such as NASA, NIH, the EPA, etc. They also include links directly to various funding agency Web sites.

Specific Subject Areas

Grantseekers who have a very clearly defined project in a specific discipline or subject area may choose to go directly to the government department or agency that would be most likely to offer such funding. A project may even be developed with a particular funder in mind. The Web sites of most of the myriad government agencies have some information about funding. They usually provide links to the general grant information sites described in the previous section. The following are some of the federal government departments and agencies commonly known to provide funding assistance. (URLs indicate grants/funding information pages, not the departmental home page.)

DEPARTMENTS

Department of Agriculture
(http://www.reeusda.gov/1700/funding/funding.htm)
The Cooperative State Research, Education, and Extension Service of the USDA administers a variety of grant programs available to researchers, educators, and small businesses.

Department of Education (http://www.ed.gov/funding.html)
The "Funding Opportunities" section of the Department of Education's Web site contains information about student financial assistance and links to a host of grants and contracts information.

Department of Housing and Urban Development
(http://www.hud.gov/fundopp.html)
This site provides information about various types of grants, including community development, affordable housing, and research.

Department of Justice (http://www.usdoj.gov/08community/08_1.html)
The funding information offered on this site includes the ADA Technical Assistance Grant Program, Office of Justice Programs Grants, and Community Oriented Policing Services (COPS) Grants, Programs, and Activities.

Department of Transportation (http://www.dot.gov/ost/m60/grant/)
Grants for planning, design, and construction of transportation improvements are generally made to state and local governments (with some to Indian tribes, universities, and nonprofit organizations). There is also a limited amount of funding available for research and development projects.

INDEPENDENT AGENCIES

Environmental Protection Agency (http://www.epa.gov/ogd/grants.htm)
This revised site offers plentiful information on funding opportunities through links to general government funding sites and to an interactive grantwriting tutorial.

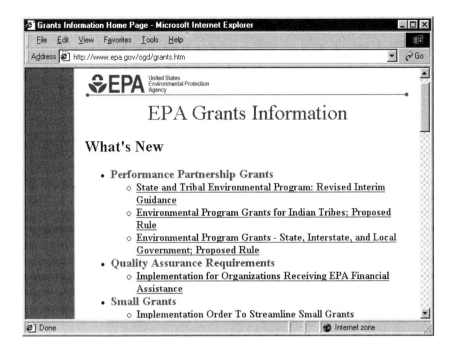

National Archives (http://www.nara.gov/nara/nhprc/)

The National Historical Publications and Records Commission (NHPRC) makes grants to archives, educational organizations, libraries, historical societies and other nonprofit organizations for identifying, preserving, and providing public access to records, photographs, and other materials that document American history.

National Endowment for the Arts (http://arts.endow.gov/)
National Endowment for the Humanities (http://www.neh.fed.us/)

These are two very well known and thus highly competitive grantmaking programs. Their main purpose is to fund projects, so both sites are worth browsing.

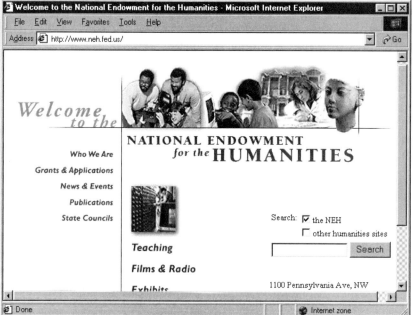

National Institutes of Health (http://www.nih.gov/grants/)

This is an easy-to-use site with clear information about funding for health and research projects.

National Science Foundation (http://www.nsf.gov/home/grants.htm)

This is an attractive, user-friendly site. The Foundation is an independent U.S. government agency responsible for promoting science and engineering through research and education projects.

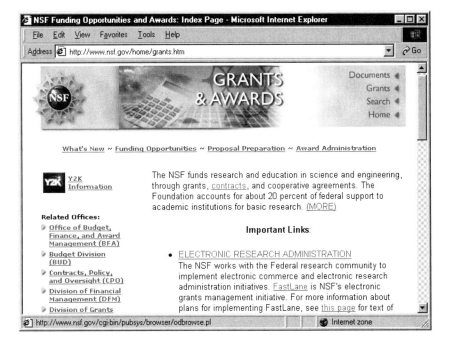

National Telecommunications and Information Administration (http://www.ntia.doc.gov/)
This site offers grants, training, information, and research services in the telecommunications arena.

Small Business Administration (http://www.sbaonline.sba.gov/financing/)
This is a well-known independent governmental agency that assists small businesses through a variety of financial assistance programs. The Web site is easy to navigate, with concise descriptions explaining the variety of routes available to financing a small business (check under the headings "Starting Your Business"; "Financing Your Business"; and "Expanding and Growing Your Business").

Smithsonian Institution (http://www.si.edu/organiza/offices/fellow/start.htm)
The Smithsonian offers predoctoral, postdoctoral, and graduate student fellowship programs, the Minority Internship Program, and the Native American Internship Program.

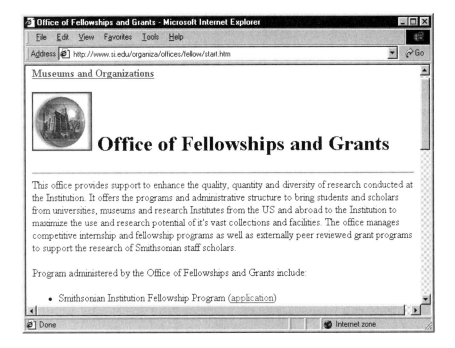

SUBORDINATE AGENCIES

Agency for Health Care Policy and Research (http://www.ahcpr.gov/fund/)
Funding Opportunities on this site describes the agency's research agenda and financial assistance for research projects. The focus is primarily on opportunities for investigator-initiated research grants.

Office of Juvenile Justice and Delinquency Prevention (OJJDP)
(http://ojjdp.ncjrs.org/)
This site offers comprehensive information on the grants and funding process of OJJDP, as well as statistics, publications, and national resources on juvenile justice issues.

Office of Minority Health Resource Center (http://www.omhrc.gov/)
We show the main Web page here, but this site includes a database of funding and grant resources for minority health projects, providing information on private and public foundations, pharmaceutical and insurance organizations, and federal, state, and community resources.

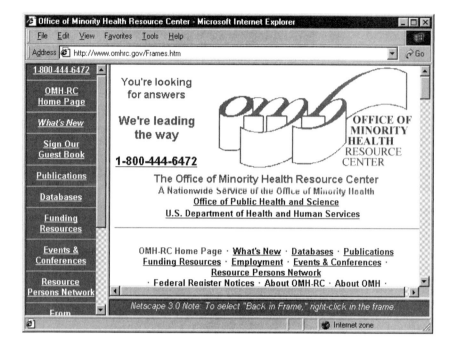

**Substance Abuse and Mental Health Services Administration (SAMHSA)
(http://www.samhsa.gov/GRANT/GFA_KDA.HTM)**
This site has an online version of the booklet *Tips for SAMHSA Grant Applicants*
used in their Grant-Writing Technical Assistance Workshops as well as ample
information on several programs offering discretionary grants.

Other Government Resources

In addition to online grant announcements, you may find the following government-related sites useful both in your grants search and in gaining a better understanding of the nonprofit sector and its relationship to the government.

FedStats (http://www.fedstats.gov/)
This site provides a variety of statistics produced by more than 70 agencies in the
federal government, such as the National Center for Education Statistics and the
Federal Assistance Awards Data System.

**Information for Tax-Exempt Organizations
(http://www.irs.ustreas.gov/prod/bus_info/eo/index.html)**
This is a very useful site for tax information. Visitors can learn about the various
types of exempt organizations and the exemption process, and can also conduct a
search for any exempt organization. There are a number of links to explore on this
page.

**State Agencies that Monitor Charities
(http://philanthropy.com/free/resources/general/stateags.htm)**
The Chronicle of Philanthropy provides a directory of Web sites for the various
state agencies which regulate charities and fundraising within their states.

Another helpful source for state regulations is the directory of homepages of states attorney general (http://www.naag.org/aglinks.htm), offered by the National Association of Attorneys General (NAAG). (Add image for NAAG)

The Federal Election Commission (FEC) (http://www.fec.gov)

The FEC's Web site offers a wealth of information on contributions to presidential and congressional campaigns (not including the Senate). Visitors can view campaign finance disclosure filings going back to 1993-94, and search a database of selected contributions by individual contributor or PAC name (going back to 1997-98). This Web site is especially useful for grantseekers researching an individual's giving patterns.

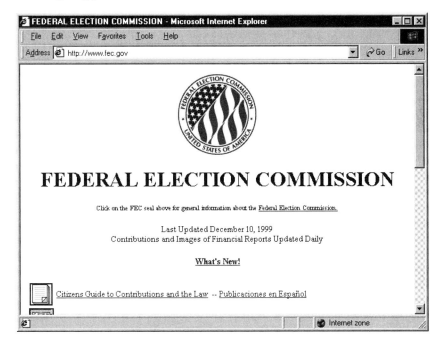

U.S. Census Bureau (http://www.census.gov/)

A wealth of statistical information about the U.S., its people, its communities, its businesses, and its geography can be found at this site.

Conclusion

This list of resources is by no means exhaustive, but rather a guide to some user-friendly points along the grantseeking journey. As with any grant search, it is essential to start out with a clear idea of what is needed. This proves especially true when combing through the profusion of government resources. As a rule, it is a good idea to contact the agency you are considering applying to in order to obtain the most up-to-date information on its programs and procedures.

CHAPTER SEVEN

Databases on the Web

Many grantseekers use Internet search engines as an integral component of their investigations. Because the Internet itself is indexed by search engine services, you could say that it is a sort of database, albeit sprawling and without the important data consistency provided by a single-source database. However, a variety of specific nonprofit, government, and corporate databases, some of them completely free, are available on the Web. Such publicly accessible databases generally offer keyword searching in one or more searchable fields and can be effectively utilized by even the most inexperienced researcher. Additionally, veteran information service providers, some of whom have utilized database technology for decades, have begun making their databases available online via the Internet, often modifying their search technology in the process—introducing natural language searching and combining data sources, for example—to ease access by novice researchers. As a result of these Web-based modifications, database searching, once the sole province of research professionals, has become an option for a wide and varied audience of grantseekers. The Web has brought the search and retrieval of organized data sets within reach of a much wider audience.

Internet databases cover a wide spectrum—from the funding-specific that let you search on consistently fielded data as a way to identify potential donors, to the more general and news-oriented types which may help you find potential donors but which certainly will help you conduct further research on the prospects you have identified from other resources. In this chapter, we describe various databases of nonprofit, corporate, and government resources that are of interest to grantseekers as well as databases of general interest to grantseekers. While there is some overlap with other chapters (in particular, Chapter 5 about corporate funding research and Chapter 6 concerning government resources), this chapter focuses specifically on searchable databases.

Nonprofit and Foundation Databases

There are several databases containing information on nonprofits that can be very useful to the grantseeker in providing names, addresses, and financial information for foundations and other nonprofit grantmakers. The source for some of these services is publicly available IRS information. (See Chapter 6 to learn more about the wealth of government information available via the World Wide Web.)

Foundation Finder—Foundation Center (http://lnp.fdncenter.org/finder.html)

If you know the name or partial name of any of the approximately 50,000 private and community foundations in the U.S., Foundation Finder will provide you with that foundation's address, contact person, and basic financial information, as well as link you to its Web site if a URL exists.

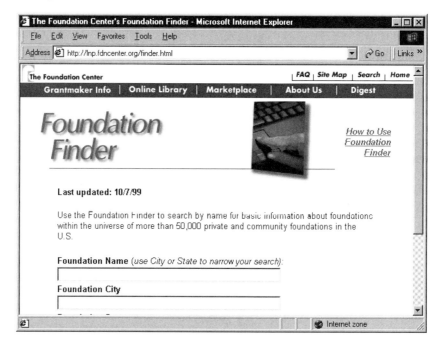

Foundation Directory Online—Foundation Center (http://www.fconline.fdncenter.org/)

The *Foundation Directory Online* is a searchable database containing information on 10,000 of the largest U.S. foundations. This fee-based service ($19.95 per month or $195 per year) allows detailed searches. Grantmakers included in the database each hold assets of $3 million or more, or distribute $200,000 or more in grants each year. Together, these foundations hold total assets in excess of $304 billion and donate over $14 billion yearly. In addition to full descriptions of the grantmakers' giving activities and contact information, the database contains 35,000 selected grants. Grantmaker records in *The Foundation Directory Online* contain the same information found in the Foundation Center's flagship print publication, *The Foundation Directory*.

By entering specific search criteria in as many as seven fields, you can perform targeted searches that will help you identify prospective funding sources for your nonprofit organization. When conducting your searches, you have the option of sorting your results in either ascending or descending order by the foundations' total annual giving amount, or in alphabetical order.

Nonprofit Locator—Internet Nonprofit Center
(http://www.nonprofits.org/loc/index.html)
The Internet Nonprofit Center's Nonprofit Locator allows you to find any nonprofit organization in the U.S. by searching a database of over one million tax-exempt entities.

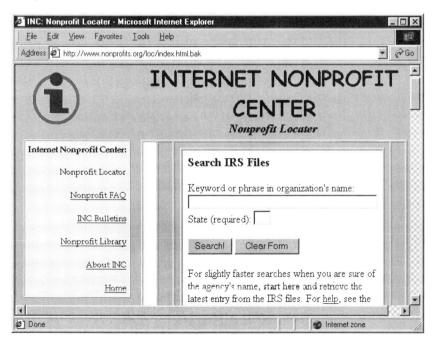

Using keywords from the organization's name, you can find the address of a particular organization, find organizations in your area, or check the exempt status of an organization. (Data is from the IRS, and explanatory information on the IRS fields and codes is accessible from the Nonprofit Locator site.) You may want to find organizations concerned with a certain issue by typing a short word or phrase that is likely to occur in the organization's name. The Locator also permits zip code searches to find nonprofits in a particular geographic area. It includes access to maps and a search engine to find organization Web sites.

Action Without Borders (http://www.idealist.org)

Action Without Borders is a nonprofit organization that promotes the sharing of ideas, information, and resources to "help build a world where all people can live free, dignified and productive lives." Through the site's searchable indexes, visitors can access a global directory of 17,000 nonprofit and community organizations including nonprofit news sites, jobs and volunteer opportunities, and resources for nonprofit managers. Search by organization name, location, or mission keyword.

GuideStar (http://www.guidestar.org)

GuideStar's database contains information on American nonprofit organizations. All of these organizations are classified by the IRS as 501(c)(3) nonprofit organizations. This group includes public charities, private nonoperating foundations, and private operating foundations (operating foundations generally focus on specific foundation-administered programs). Financial data are taken from the IRS Business Master File and/or the Form 990, a public report filed with the IRS by all 501(c)(3) public charities with revenues exceeding $25,000. A GuideStar Report flagged with a gray icon includes asset and income information from the IRS Form 990. A GuideStar Report flagged with a blue icon includes financial and basic program information from the IRS Form 990, direct input from the individual organization about its goals, accomplishments, and program monitoring systems, and comments from its executive director.

State Home Pages and Secretaries of State WWW Sites (http://w3.uwyo.edu/~prospect/secstate.html)

The Internet Prospector has created a page of links to corporate and nonprofit corporation databases contained on state Web pages. These database listings frequently contain lists of donors, officers, and trustees and are sometimes searchable by keyword as well as by foundation name.

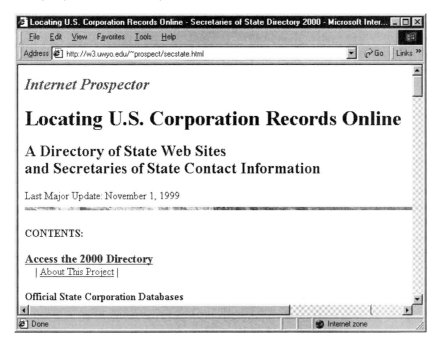

European Foundation Centre (http://www.efc.be)

The European Foundation Centre is an organization founded in 1989 by seven large European foundations. It primarily serves grantmakers. The goals of the center are: "to represent the interests of member organisations at the level of third parties such as national governments and European Union institutions; to convene and coordinate meetings and facilitate networking; and to provide a relevant and current information base to reinforce member organisation programmes and initiatives."

FinAid (http://www.finaid.org)

This award-winning site was started in 1994. It has a reputation of objectivity and thoroughness. The site caters to high school, college, and graduate students. It contains information about scholarships, fellowships, loans, and military aid. In addition to the databases, the site also offers a variety of useful tips, making it a good place on the Web to start a scholarship search. The site cooperates with FastWeb (http://www.fastweb.com), which is a free scholarship database.

FOUNDATION GRANTS DATABASES

A number of foundations offer fully searchable Web sites. The Ford Foundation, W.K Kellogg Foundation, Charles Stewart Mott Foundation, and Pew Charitable Trusts have gone one step further and provided grantseekers with specialized databases of their grant awards.

Ford Foundation (http://www.fordfound.org)

To access the database click on "Grants Database" on the top bar. You can search the database by the following five fields: Keyword(s), Subject, Location, Organization, Year. The results window includes descriptive text about grants.

Kellogg Foundation Online Database of Current Grants—W.K. Kellogg Foundation (http://www.wkkf.org)

To access the database, visitors to the homepage should select "grants" and then "search database." The grants database is organized around the W.K. Kellogg Foundation's program interests—Health; Food Systems and Rural Development; Youth and Education; Higher Education; and Philanthropy and Volunteerism. Funding for the specific initiatives of Leadership; Information Systems/Technology; Capitalizing on Diversity; and Family, Neighborhood, and Community Development is represented throughout these programming interests. You can direct a search of the database (by grantee name, location, program information, timeframe, and purpose) or you can browse by thematic coding, country, or grantee name.

The Mott Grants Database—The Charles Stewart Mott Foundation (http://www.mott.org/grants/search.html)

The Mott Grants Database contains detailed fact sheets on each grant made by the Foundation in recent years. Two ways are provided to search for specific grant information. The first allows users to search by keyword. The second method of searching allows users to search on specific fields, such as the project description or state location of the grantee.

Pew Charitable Trusts "Search Grants" Database—The Pew Charitable Trusts (http://www.pewtrusts.com)

The Pew Charitable Trusts Web site allows visitors to search all of its grants from the previous three years. A synopsis of the purposes, the amount, and the recipient of each grant is provided. A more expanded table containing the recipient contact's name, the relevant dates, and a longer grant description is available. The database search can be made extremely specific by narrowing it through the given categories.

REGIONAL FOUNDATION DATABASES

Nonprofit Resource Center of Texas (http://www.fic.org)

This is a membership organization that offers technical assistance, consultation, and training opportunities for board members, staff, and volunteers of nonprofit and philanthropic organizations. This site includes access (for a fee) to the Database of Texas Foundations which contains profiles of over 1,700 foundations. Search by areas of interest and types of support. The database is updated throughout year.

The Greater Kansas City Council on Philanthropy (http://www.kcphilnet.org)

This is a professional organization that has provided a local forum for the exchange of information on philanthropy and fundraising since 1975. This site offers (for a fee) the Directory of Greater Kansas City Foundations, a quarterly updated directory of nearly 500 area funders, including who is on their boards, the types of programs they fund, grant recipients, grants awarded, and procedures for submitting a funding request.

Donors Forum of Chicago (http://www.donorsforum.org)

The Donors Forum, an association of Chicago-area grantmaking institutions, promotes effective philanthropy through its educational, collaborative, and networking efforts. The main offering at the Forum's no-frills Web site is an updated 1994 version of its foundation grants database, searchable by foundation name, recipient, beneficiary type, support type, and grant purpose. Search results are displayed in plain-vanilla ASCII, but with approximately 7,500 grants made by some 50 Chicago-area funders, the Forum's database is worth exploring.

OTHER DATABASES FOR GRANTSEEKERS

There are also small number of database services specializing in information for grantseekers. These services are offered by people with a particular focus on nonprofits and who also offer database management software and other electronic services geared to the needs of charitable organizations.

Prospect Research Online (PRO) Rainforest Publications Books (http://www.rpbooks.com)

The Prospect Research Database offers access to a full range of corporate data geared to the needs of grantseekers, such as company history, proxy statement information, lists of officers and directors, and links to various stock markets, EDGAR and SIC codes, and links to corporate Web sites. Each PROfile includes recent financial reports, announcements regarding senior officers, mergers, acquisitions and buy-outs, as well as information about corporate giving programs. There is an annual subscription fee. A free guided tour is available.

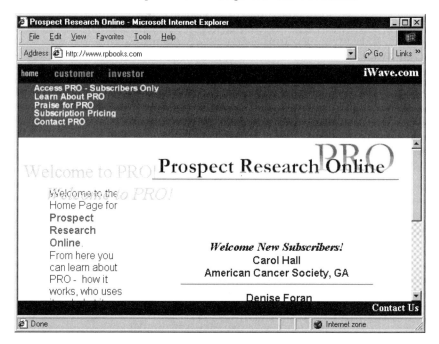

Corporate Funding Information

Corporate information on the Web is vast and varied. Many corporate information database services offer a variety of free and fee-based content. Some information available for free at certain sites will require fees at other sites, particularly those of database vendors.

Going directly to a company's Web site is the best way to locate corporate giving information. (See Chapter 5 for more information about corporate grantseeking on the World Wide Web.) There are many free search services for locating company Web pages, including:

Domain Name Search (http://www.internet.org)
Companies Online (http://www.companiesonline.com)

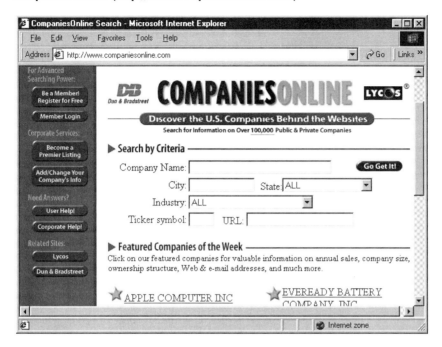

CORPORATE FINANCIAL INFORMATION

Hoovers Online (http://www.hoovers.com)

An easy-to-use site with links to over 4,000 corporate Web sites and over 14,000 Company Capsules. Free Company Capsules provide news and information—company profile, key personnel, full stock quote, selected press coverage—on more than 14,000 public and private enterprises. Subscribers (two options: personal or multi-user) get the same information but in much greater depth and detail. Hoovers also contains capsules on a number of large non-publicly traded U.S. enterprises, including not-for-profits, foundations, health care companies, cooperatives, and universities.

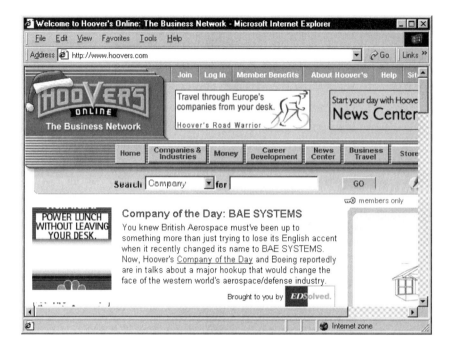

EDGAR Database of Corporate Information (http://www.sec.gov/edgarhp.htm)
The Securities and Exchange Commission's EDGAR (Electronic Data Gathering,
Analysis, and Retrieval) system contains basic but often hard-to-find corporate
information (e.g., fiscal data, officers, subsidiaries, recent merger and acquisition
activity, etc.). EDGAR on the Web allows visitors to retrieve publicly available
filings submitted to the SEC from January 1994 to the present.

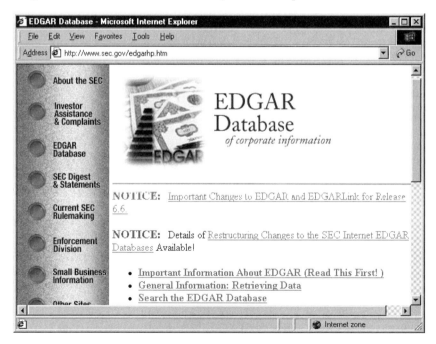

Edgar Online (http://www.edgar-online.com)

The same database as above, but the interface is more user-friendly. Edgar Online is fee based.

Inc. Online (http://inc.com/)

Inc. Online is an information resource for entrepreneurs and small business owners who are serious about growing their businesses. In addition to the most recent edition of *Inc.* and an archive of 5,000-plus articles on a wide variety of topics, the site offers a searchable database of America's 500 fastest-growing companies.

CORPORATE NEWS ONLINE

BusinessWire (http://www.businesswire.com)

This site includes searchable company press releases by date, industry, or company. It also includes selected corporate profiles and related URLs.

PR NewsWire (http://www.prnewswire.com)

This site includes searchable company press releases, with a one-year archive and company news on call.

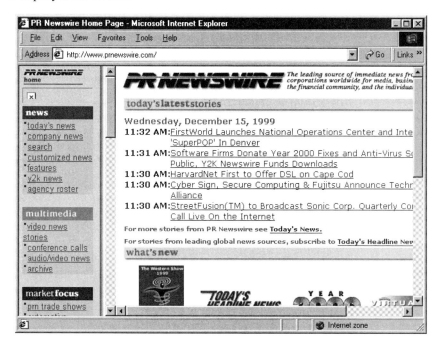

Forbes Toolbox (http://www.forbes.com/tool/html/toolbox.asp)

Forbes magazine has made available in database format a variety of its lists of wealthy individuals and of companies. (The 500 Largest Private Companies in the U.S., 400 Richest People in America, Technology's Richest 100, etc.)

Newspaper Searching

Newspaper search sites are generally searchable by keyword. Articles are available until the source site deletes them (typically one day). Archived information is generally available only for a fee from the source publication or online vendor. Many regional business newspapers are now available online (indexed at most of the major news sites) and provide excellent information on local philanthropists, corporate giving, foundations, etc.

American Journalism Review (http://www.ajr.org)
This site includes worldwide links to some 3,500 news organizations online. You can also search other news sites from here (Total News, Newsindex.com, newsbots.com, etc.).

General Information Databases

Database vendors offer for-fee access to an enormous variety of databases. Most for-fee information vendors, including those that specialize in funding information, offer their database information in a variety of electronic formats, including CD-ROM and direct modem access (requiring software installation). Indexed print versions are also available for many directories. The choice of format depends largely on cost effectiveness (frequency of use, expense of support systems, etc.).

Web access offers users a great deal of flexibility. For-fee database searches can, however, be quite expensive. The World Wide Web has expanded rapidly, and the cost of data now varies greatly. While fee-based services are often very comprehensive and therefore efficient, the same information can sometimes be found through other sources for less cost (or even for free).

Fee-based services typically require only a user name and password for access from any online location. Internet database vendors offer pricing options which can be tailored to a user's particular needs, such as short-term, narrowly focused searches. Additionally, databases are updated on a regular basis, some daily. The major database vendors tend to simplify their search structures for Web presentation, gearing them toward a broad end-user audience. Experienced researchers may therefore prefer the wider range of search options available in direct dial-up services.

Other major database vendors offer legal and government documents, newspaper and periodical articles, and a wide variety of corporate information, including company profiles. These services are generally updated daily and offer easy-to-use search interfaces and a wide variety of search parameters. Newspaper searches, for example, can be restricted by date, source, geography, etc. You can search a single newspaper or thousands of sources at once. (Although many major and mid-sized newspapers now offer Web editions, they do not generally make archived information available. Those that do, such as the Los Angeles Times, frequently charge a single-use or subscription fee.)

The DIALOG Corporation (http://www.dialog.com/info/home)

Knight-Ridder Information, Inc., formerly known as DIALOG Information Services, had been a source for online information for over 25 years with over 200,000 corporate users in 100 countries. Knight-Ridder Information, Inc. recently merged with M.A.I.D to form the Dialog Corporation, which offers hundreds of databases representing a broad range of disciplines: company directories, news sources, general reference, biographical information, etc.

A complete list of online databases is available at DIALOG Web (see below). The online access rates vary by database (prices include output and search time costs, as well as telecommunications charges). There are annual service fees and start-up fees. Training is provided as online tutorials and/or guided tours.

DIALOG Web

This is a tool for intermediate and advanced online searchers. It offers a browser-enabled interface to the full DIALOG command language, an index to most of the DIALOG databases, plus a guided search component for search assistance. Other than an enhanced graphical Web interface, there are some features unique to DIALOG Web, which include a free database directory that lets you browse DIALOG databases by subject with a "Search DIALINDEX" feature that helps you find the exact databases for your topic.

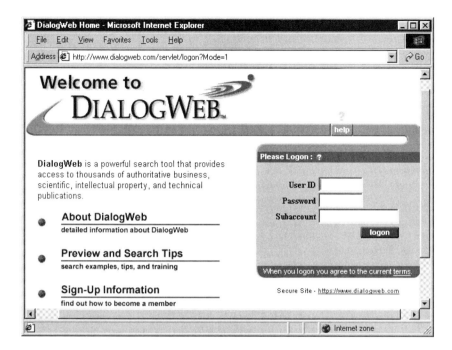

DIALOG Select

This service is designed for novice end-users, utilizing pre-defined search forms where users enter keywords and use pull-down menus to set up their searches. No prior search expertise is required.

Grantmaker/Grant Information on DIALOG

There are two Foundation Center databases provided via the DIALOG service. The "Foundation Directory" database is known as "File 26" and the "Foundation Grants Index" is known as "File 27." The two files can be used in conjunction through software functionality provided through the DIALOG service.

Foundation Directory—File 26 (available on DIALOG Web and DIALOG Select) is a comprehensive database providing descriptions of more than 50,000 grantmakers, including private grantmaking foundations, community foundations, operating foundations, and corporate grantmakers. Records include entries from the following Foundation Center print publications: *The Foundation Directory*; *The Foundation Directory, Part 2*; *Guide to U.S. Foundations: Their Trustees, Officers, and Donors*; and *National Directory of Corporate Giving*.

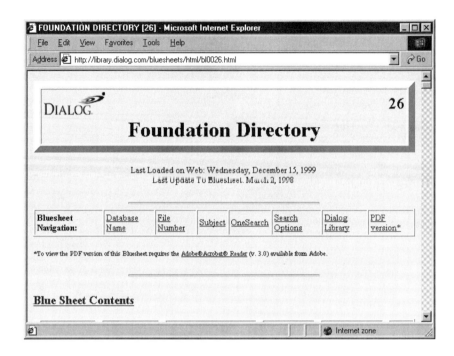

Use File 26 to identify foundations that provide funding for a specific subject area; identify foundations that provide certain types of support; identify grantmakers in a specific city, state, or zip code; determine on which foundation boards, if any, a certain individual serves; identify company-sponsored foundations and corporate giving programs; find additional information about foundations whose grants appear in File 27; find detailed information about a specific foundation or corporate giving program; create a list of the largest foundations that support a specific subject area or give in a specific geographic area. Full records (available for approximately 30,000 of the nation's largest foundations) include foundation name and address, parent company (for company-sponsored foundations); lists of donors, officers, and trustees; purpose and activities statements; grantmaking program descriptions; financial information, including assets and total giving; giving limitations statements; application information; a list of publications available from the foundation; fields of interest (descriptors); indication of whether grant records for a particular foundation exist in File 27. File 26 contains brief records for about 20,000 smaller foundations which include foundation name and address; donor, officers, and trustees; financial information, including assets and total giving, geographic focus; indication of whether or not the foundation accepts applications.

The file covers one year's data, based on the most currently available fiscal year. The file is reloaded annually, with a semi-annual update. Search and retrieval time is $0.50 per minute. Costs for displayed records are shown in the title list.

The Foundation Grants Index—File 27 (available only on DIALOG Web) is an index of grants of $10,000 or more awarded to nonprofit organizations by over 1,000 of the largest foundations in the U.S. (While these comprise a small subset of the foundations included in File 26, their grants represent over 50 percent of the total dollars awarded by all U.S. private, corporate, and community foundations during the latest year of record.) Information in File 27 includes grants found in the print *Foundation Grants Index* beginning with those included in the 1989 Edition. Each record in File 27 represents one grant. Grant records include the following elements: name/state of the foundation awarding the grant; geographic focus of the grantmaker; recipient organization (name, city, state); recipient type (hospital, museum, university); recipient auspices (religious, government, private non-sectarian); purpose of the grant and year authorized; amount (and duration) of the grant; intended beneficiaries (if specified); type of support represented (capital, research, etc.); fields of interest (descriptors).

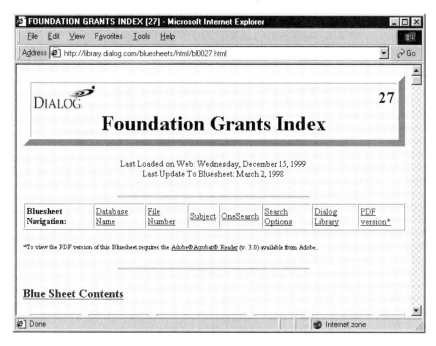

Use File 27 to find grants awarded in specific subject areas; locate grants that serve certain populations; examine a foundation's grants in one subject area; find grants awarded to organizations similar to your own; locate grants awarded to organizations in your city or state; identify the largest grants in a subject area. After locating appropriate grants in File 27, search for the grantmaking organizations in File 26. New grant records are added five times each year. No grants to individuals are included in the Grants Index. Search and retrieval time is $0.50 per minute. Costs for displayed records are shown in the title list.

The Center classifies grants according to its Grants Classification System, derived from the National Taxonomy of Exempt Entities (NTEE). The NTEE standardizes language used to describe the activities of the nonprofit sector. (See the Foundation Center's Grants Classification Manual and Thesaurus, Internet Edition at http://www.fdncenter.org/about/taxonomy/index.html for more information on the Grants Classification System.)

Use the *DIALOG User Manual and Thesaurus* (available from the Foundation Center) as an aid to the most cost-effective searching of Files 26 and 27. The *User Manual* contains a fully revised and expanded list of subject terms and shows you how to retrieve facts from the Center's databases quickly, easily, and efficiently.

GRANTS Database—File 85 (available on DIALOG Web) is provided from Oryx Press and is also available on KEDSnet on the World Wide Web (http://www.knowledgeexpress.com/).

The GRANTS Database offers access to information on more than 8,500 funding programs available through over 3,000 nonprofit organizations, foundations, private sources, and federal, state, and local agencies in the United States and Canada.

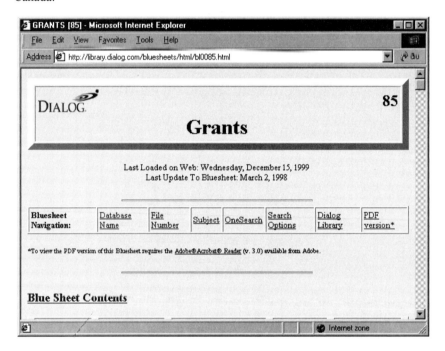

The GRANTS Database is searchable by title, sponsoring organizations, keyword, program type, or any combination of 20 searchable fields. It is updated monthly. Use the Grants Subject Authority Guide to become familiar with the 2,422 subject terms used to index the database. The database also features "see" and "see also" references to help users target the most appropriate files.

Other DIALOG Databases

Files on grants and grantmakers comprise a small percentage of the information available on DIALOG (as elsewhere on the Web). The DIALOG corporate and biographical databases are extensive and varied and can be extremely useful to grantseekers. Because information on corporate funding is subject to somewhat less stringent reporting standards than information on company-sponsored foundations, it can be more difficult to locate. Corporate information on DIALOG (DIALOG Corporate Information, Standard & Poor's American Business Directory, Corporate Descriptions, etc.) can be searched geographically, providing you with a potentially enormous list of companies to research to find prospective sponsors for your project or organization. Archived business newspapers and journals as well as press releases can be used to narrow the search, giving indications of past corporate giving and likely company giving interests. Stock prices and other indicators of corporate wealth also can be used in the formulation of a realistic charitable solicitation. (See Chapter 5 for more on corporate grantseeking on the Web.)

The lists of top executives included in many corporate profiles also provide you with lists of potentially wealthy individuals in your geographic area. Because individual giving accounts for approximately 80 percent of all charitable funding, the biographical resources available on DIALOG provide a huge pool of possible funders. Biographical information, such as alumni affiliations, foundation or charity board membership, and volunteer involvement can be used in conjunction with corporate indicators of wealth, such as stock proxy listings and professional affiliations, to develop a fairly comprehensive potential donor profile. (You can cross-reference names with the officer, trustee, and donor search capacity of File 26.) Running an archived newspaper search on an individual's name in conjunction with search words such as "donate," "give," etc. can return information on past charitable donations.

DIALOG offers many comprehensive corporate and biographical databases, including:

Corporate
- DIALOG Corporate Information (Directories, News Sources)
- American Business Directory (531, 532)
- Standard & Poor's Corporate Descriptions plus News (133)
- Business Dateline (635)
- Commerce Business Daily (194, 195)
- Corporate Affiliations (513)
- DIALOG Company Name Finder (416)
- Trade & Industry Database (148)
- Moody's Corporate Profiles (555)
- Dunn & Bradstreet Dunn's (515, 519, 516)
- Financial Times Full Text (622)
- Harvard Business Review (122)

Biographical
- Biography Master Index (287)
- Bowker Biographical Directory (236)
- Standard & Poor's Register—Biographical (526)
- Marquis Who's Who Database

Check the full list of DIALOG databases by name accessible from the Databases page of DIALOG Web.

LEXIS-NEXIS on the World Wide Web (Mead Data Central) (http://www.lexis-nexis.com)

LEXIS-NEXIS provides online access to legal, news, and business information services. There are 7,300 databases between the two services. More than 9.5 million documents are added each week to the more than one billion documents online. Information on LEXIS-NEXIS is organized into "libraries." LEXIS-NEXIS information is accessible with a user name and password.

The LEXIS-NEXIS service offers three options of searching: FREESTYLE, Boolean, and Easy Search. The FREESTYLE feature is a plain English search feature that allows the user to search both legal and non-legal materials all in one commercial database. Experienced searchers most often select the traditional

Boolean search option for precision searching of specific data sets. The Easy Search feature, on the other hand, uses online menus and screen prompts to assist novice users in formulating precise search requests and then to select the best parts of the database to search for the user.

The LEXIS Service

The LEXIS service contains major archives of federal and state case law, continuously updated statutes of all 50 states, state and federal regulations, and an extensive collection of public records from major U.S. states and counties. The LEXIS service has 40 specialized libraries covering all major fields of practice, including tax, securities, banking, environmental, energy and international. Although the LEXIS service is not directly related to grantseeking research needs, a subscriber to the LEXIS service also has access to the NEXIS service and its related services.

The NEXIS Service

The NEXIS service is a news and business information service which contains more than 13,500 sources. These include regional, national, and international newspapers, news wires, magazines, trade journals, and business publications. The NEXIS service also offers: brokerage house and industry analyst reports; business information from Dunn & Bradstreet; public records such as corporate filings, company records, and property records; and tax information.

Useful NEXIS Libraries for Grantseekers

The People Library (PEOPLE) brings together information sources concentrating on biographical or people-related news, issues, and events. This library allows you to use custom file selection. Within the PEOPLE library you will find a combined news and biographical information set called ALLBIO. This includes Gale biographies from January 1990 (Newsmakers from January 1985), Marquis Who's Who biographies, and the most recent edition and selected full-text articles from major newspapers and periodicals, including the *Washington Post, Los Angeles Times,* and *New York Times.*

The Assets Library (ASSETS) provides access to real estate assessment records and current deed transfer information gathered from county assessors' and recorders' offices in selected counties (metropolitan areas) nationwide, U.S. Federal Aviation Administration Aircraft Registrations, Florida Boat Registrations from Florida Department of High Safety and Motor Vehicles, U.S. Coast Guard Merchant and Recreational Vessel Registrations, and Texas Motor Vehicle Registrations. The information available in this library can be useful in providing indicators of the wealth of a potential funder.

The Entertainment Library (ENTERT) combines facts pertaining to the entertainment industry such as: litigation, credits, grosses, contracts, company profiles, biographies and industry profiles, along with a variety or daily and weekly news sources. This library allows you to use custom file selection. It contains some biographical information sources.

There are a number of corporate libraries. (See Chapter 5 for suggestions on how to plumb other resources in your corporate grantseeking efforts.) Several are described below.

The Company Information Library (COMPNY) contains business and financial information, including thousands of in-depth company and industry research reports from leading national and international investment banks and brokerage houses. The materials may be searched in individual files, such as brokerage house reports, or in group files organized by subject, such as SEC filings.

The Dunn & Bradstreet Library (D&B) provides a vast base from which information can be obtained on more than 50 million domestic and international businesses. This library allows you to use custom file selection.

The Corporation Library (INCORP) provides access to records on active and inactive limited partnerships and limited liability companies, and corporations registered with the office of the Secretary of State or other appropriate agency. These records include information extracted by the State's staff from articles of incorporation, annual reports, amendments, and other public filings. "Doing Business As" records titled in over 1,000 counties nationwide are also provided.

The Business/Finance Library (BUSFIN) contains a wide variety of sources that provide business and finance news, including business journals as well as investment and merger and acquisition news sources. This library allows you to use custom file selection.

Other LEXIS-NEXIS Features and Products

EdgarPlus, offered on the LEXIS-NEXIS services through an agreement with Disclosure Incorporated, allows access to SEC filings and a series of SEC products developed from EDGAR (Electronic Data Gathering, Analysis and Retrieval system) data.

Martindale-Hubbell is a professional directory database of over 900,000 lawyers and law firms in 150 countries. Listings are updated monthly and include such details as contact data, areas of practice, education, clients, languages, and representative cases.

Dow Jones Interactive (Formerly Dow Jones News/Retrieval) (http://ip.dowjones.com)

Dow Jones Interactive, based on the Dow Jones News/Retrieval service, is an online business news and research tool that provides access to breaking news from 3,800 sources, a custom news-tracking tool that automatically filters news and information based on an individual's needs, and a financial center that covers more than 10 million public and private companies around the world. Dow Jones provides access to the local newspapers formerly available through UMI's DataTimes. In addition to UMI content, Dow Jones is the exclusive online source of the combined same-day, full-text editions of the *Wall Street Journal, New York Times, Washington Post, Financial Times,* and *Los Angeles Times.* Dow Jones offers a wide variety of flexible pricing plans (based on per article usage), including monthly flat-free pricing.

ProQuest Direct (UMI) (http://www.umi.com/proquest)

ProQuest Direct provides "one of the world's largest collections of information," including summaries of articles from over 8,000 publications, with many in full-text, full-image format. ProQuest Direct offers a free trial period.

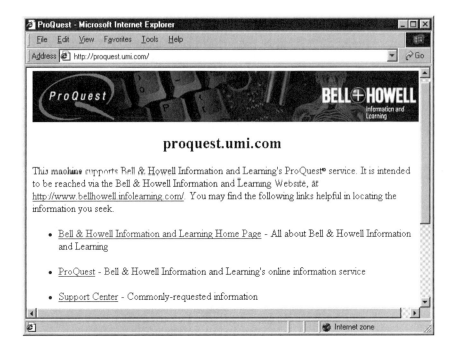

Useful ProQuest Database Files for Grantseekers:
The list of available databases is accessible from the Guided Tour page.

ABI/INFORM provides in-depth coverage of business conditions, trends, corporate strategies and tactics, management techniques, competitive and product information, and a wide variety of other topics.

Business Dateline contains fully searchable full-text articles, in ASCII format, from more than 450 North American business tabloids, magazines, daily newspapers, and news wire services. Each record also includes complete bibliographic, geographic, and indexing information. Current material is from 1994 forward, with retrospective coverage on tape available from 1985. The database covers a variety of subject areas, including employment opportunities; benefit packages and compensation plans; businesses and industries in particular locations; corporate strategies, mergers, acquisitions, and expansions; marketing trends and new products; local effects of regulation and legislation; and more.

Business Periodicals provides coverage of business and management publications available, with three different editions to choose from. The database links full images of articles from the most important and popular ABI/INFORM sources. Each edition contains abstracts and indexing to articles from top publications, plus cover-to-cover page images from about half of the cited journals. Coverage for current subscriptions begins in 1992, with backfile availability to 1971. Full-image coverage begins in 1988.

Wilsonline (H.W. Wilson Company) (Readers Guide to Periodical Literature) (http://www.hwwilson.com)
H.W. Wilson's Information Retrieval System for the World Wide Web, WilsonWeb, provides several search tools for accessing information in Wilson databases. You can search for records pertaining to a topic of interest, then show, print, and download those records. WilsonWeb's interface is customizable. WilsonWeb offers a free trial.

Useful Wilson Databases for Grantseekers

The Wilson offerings include lists of Index and Abstract Databases and Full-Text Databases.

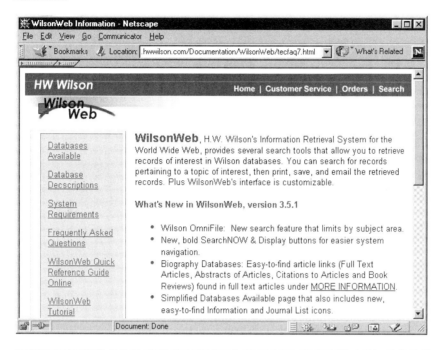

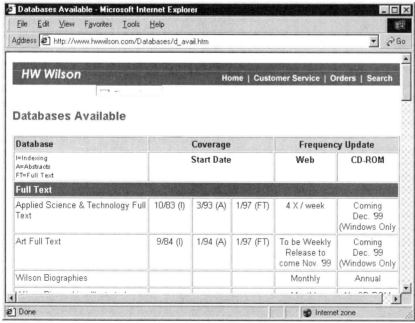

H.W. Wilson's Biography Index Database cites biographical material appearing in more than 2,800 periodicals indexed in other H.W. Wilson databases and additional selected periodicals; some 2,100 books annually of individual and collective biography; and incidental biographical material in otherwise non-biographical books. Periodicals indexed are selected from all subject areas represented by other H.W. Wilson databases. Biographical subjects indexed range from antiquity to the present and represent all fields and nationalities.

H.W. Wilson's Business Periodicals Databases cover 400 English-language general business periodicals and trade journals, plus the *Wall Street Journal* and the business section of the *New York Times.* Topics include management, accounting, advertising and marketing, construction, entertainment and media, information technology, mergers and acquisitions, occupational health and safety, public relations, and small business. Users can access citations via SIC codes.

Wilson Business Abstracts includes abstracts of periodicals from June 1990 and indexing from July 1982. Wilson Business Abstracts Full-Text includes full-text coverage of 158 periodicals back to January 1995.

GaleNet (Gales Research, Inc.) (http://galenet.gale.com)

This subscription service requires a user name and password in order to access any Web pages.

Useful Gale Databases for Grantseekers

Associations Unlimited contains information for approximately 440,000 U.S. national, regional, state, local, and international nonprofit membership organizations in all fields, and U.S. 501(c)(3) nonprofit organizations. Subsets of Associations Unlimited are also available.

U.S. National Associations contains information for approximately 23,000 U.S. national nonprofit membership associations in all fields. Features include full contact information, description, SIC descriptors, convention dates, and more.

U.S. 501(3) Nonprofit Organizations contains information for approximately 300,000 U.S. 501(c)(3) nonprofit organizations, agencies, and service programs as registered with the U.S. Internal Revenue Service.

The Biography and Genealogy Master Index is an index to more than 10 million biographical sketches in over 1,000 current and retrospective biographical dictionaries, covering both contemporary and historical figures throughout the world.

Gale Business Resources integrates some 30 print volumes of Gale's business reference works. It contains listings for some 200,000 U.S. companies, extensive essays for 54 industrial categories, industry statistics, market share reports, and company rankings. In addition, company histories are available for 1,500 of the most prominent businesses in the United States. Gale Business Resources also provides access to the complete text of U.S. Securities and Exchange Commission Reports for 1,100 top U.S. companies and the U.S. Industrial Outlook.

Community Information Exchange
(http://www.comminfoexch.org/database.htm)

The Community Information Exchange is a national, nonprofit information service founded in 1983 that provides community-based organizations and their partners with the information they need to successfully revitalize their communities. The Exchange provides comprehensive information about strategies and resources for affordable housing, and economic and community development. The Exchange provides information in easy-to-search databases containing case studies about innovative and replicable strategies, describes funding and financing sources, identifies technical assistance providers, and abstracts printed resources such as how-to guides and sample legal documents. Bulletin boards feature the latest funding announcements, including those from the Federal Register, and timely news items. The databases are available on a subscription basis for PCs, CD-ROMs, and local area networks (LANs). They were due to be placed on the Web, and so we include them here.

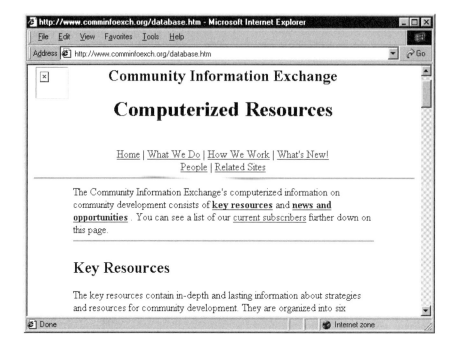

Target America (http://www.tgtam.com)
The Target America Database offers comprehensive information (financial, employment, address, etc.) on the wealthiest five percent of the U.S. population.

Database Services for Academic Professionals

There are also a number of grants databases, primarily intended for academic professionals, that offer access to a variety of government and private funding sources. These services are fee-based, but some also offer free information.

IRIS—Illinois Researcher Information Service
(http://carousel.lis.uiuc.edu/~iris/about_iris.html)
A unit of the University of Illinois Library at Urbana-Champaign, IRIS contains records on over 7,000 federal and non-federal funding opportunities in the sciences, social sciences, arts, and humanities. The file is updated daily. The Online Periodical Service (OPS) is a full-text database of selected items from the Commerce Business Daily and abstracts of research-related items from the Federal Register. The service is available free of charge to the University of Illinois at Urbana-Champaign community. It is available to other colleges and universities for an annual subscription fee.

Community of Science (http://www.cos.com)
This site is maintained by a consortium of research institutions as a repository of scientific information searchable through the Internet. It offers several searchable grant databases for both private and federal funding. The Funding Opportunities Database is a good place to start. It includes grants in non-science areas.

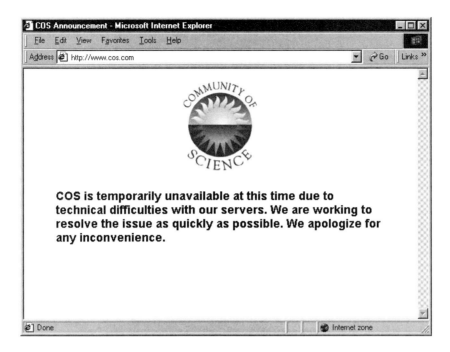

For federal grant database searching, this Web site provides access to the Federal Register and the Commerce Business Daily. Also note that searching federally funded research in the U.S. will provide summaries of research grants and projects from five agencies: the National Institutes of Health, the National Science Foundation, the U.S. Department of Agriculture, the Small Business Innovation Research awards, and the Advanced Technology Program of the National Institute of Standards & Technology. (See Chapter 5 for more on the wealth of government information on the Internet.)

SPIN (Sponsored Programs Information Network) (http:// www.infoed.org/spin1.stm)

SPIN is the Sponsored Programs Information Network provided by InfoEd, Inc. This service includes funding for research, fellowships, exchange programs, travel, equipment, collaborative projects, and more. The Web version requires a subscription. This service includes searching by deadline, academic discipline, and more. Federal and non-federal grants are listed with free access to key federal databases.

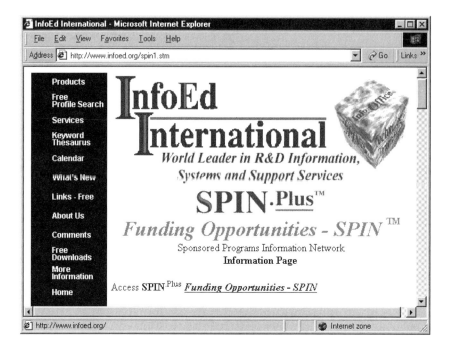

Conclusion

Initial exploration and assessment of the usefulness of these and other Web databases will require an investment of time and perhaps money. However, in conjunction with other Web resources, you may find a wealth of information useful to your grantseeking efforts.

CHAPTER EIGHT

Other Useful Sites for Grantseekers

How do you find out whether the foundation prospect you're interested in is on the Web? Although you can certainly start by searching on its name with a search engine like HotBot or AltaVista, remember that other people have done the job for you. Many Web sites now function as "portals" to the Web at large, sites that attempt to organize Web information and make it accessible in one location. As described in Chapter 2, the Foundation Center continues to design and organize its own Web site to function as such a specialty portal, providing access to the world of philanthropy, as well as providing information resources and guidance on how to do funding research and then to approach potential funders.

(See Chapter 2 for a description of the many resources and links available at the Center's Web site [http://fdncenter.org], Your Gateway to Philanthropy on the world Wide Web.)

There are hundreds of annotated links to various types of grantmakers in the Grantmaker Information section of the Foundation Center's Web site. There is also a fairly large section of foundation links available through Yahoo, a (http://dir.yahoo.com/Society_and_Culture/Issues_and_Causes/Philanthropy/Organizations/Grant_Making_Foundations/). If you need to locate information about a particular organization, or if you'd just like to browse for prospects, the resources that follow point the way to extensive online information about potential funders. This chapter introduces in detail some useful Web resources for grantseekers, which you'll find listed in the Links to Nonprofit Resources section of the Online Library found at the Foundation Center's Web site (http://fdncenter.org/onlib/npr_links/index.html).

One interesting note: 1999 saw the proliferation of web sites through which people could donate money to charities, either directlly or as a percentage of online purchases. These could be possible sources of contributions for your organization. There arc scveral different operational models. Rather than describe any of these sites in detail in the beginning of the chapter, we list them under "Giving Online" on page 425 so that you can explore this new phenomenon first-hand.

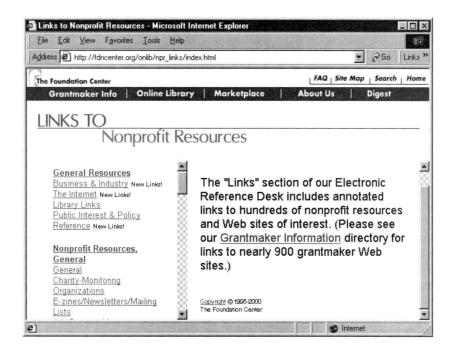

We continue to add to these categorized lists of sites and prepare annotations for them to aid in your exploration of funding opportunities and helpful resources. The comprehensive list of nonprofit resource links taken from the Center's Web site is included at the end of this chapter, organized into categories. We have condensed and revised this list because some of these sites are discussed in greater detail in other sections and chapters. However, some overlap remains, reflecting the hyperlinked nature of the Web environment.

A Selection of Useful Sites

Below are our recommendations for useful Web sites for grantseekers. The categories we have used to organize the sites we describe in some detail are to a certain extent arbitrary; that is, many of the resources could fit into two or more categories, based on their features and content. What these sites have in common is that they reward deeper investigation. They are resources that you'll want to return to time and again in searching for online information about foundations, grants, fundraising, and nonprofit management. Our goal is not to be comprehensive—which often isn't practical when dealing with the Web—but to point the way to a manageable number of useful sites. Please refer to the more complete listing at the end of the chapter to make additional selections of sites of particular interest to you.

Funder Information

Council on Foundations (http://www.cof.org)

The Council, a nonprofit membership organization of foundations and corporations, offers a wealth of information at its Web site, which is organized into broad categories. The Council also links to affinity groups of grantmakers and has a community foundation locator.

FundsNet (http://www.fundsnetservices.com)

This site includes links to hundreds of foundations, corporations, and grantmaking public charities online. The Funders area offers links alphabetically, by grantmaker type and by area of grantmaking emphasis, within broad categories like arts, communities, education, health, and religion. This part of the site is especially helpful for grantseekers browsing for new prospects, and some of the links include a short note about the funder's mission or guidelines. The goal is comprehensive coverage of what's currently available on the Web from grantmakers, but the site also includes links to information on fundraising, proposal writing, government agency resources, and more. Best of all, the site is updated daily, and there's almost always something new.

Michigan State University Grants and Related Resources
(http://www.lib.msu.edu/harris23/grants/grants.htm)

The amount of information available on these pages is nearly overwhelming, but Jon Harrison of the University of Michigan Libraries has created a site that is well organized and cleanly designed. You won't get lost.

Most valuable here are the annotated lists of resources (print, electronic, and online) for grant information in particular subject areas, from Arts and Cultural Activities to Religion and Social Change. For each subject area, Harrison gives abstracts of useful print resources, descriptions of databases, and hyperlinks to online information. There is a substantial section of information on grants to individuals, including financial aid. Harrison also has assembled an impressive bibliography, with links, on techniques of grantsmanship, including lots of information on fundraising research and proposal writing.

National Charities Information Bureau (http://www.give.org/)
For 81 years, the National Charities Information Bureau (NCIB) has helped donors to give wisely to charitable organizations.

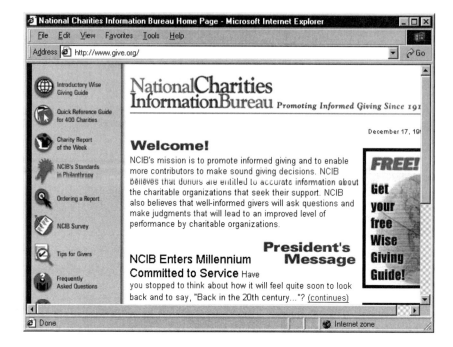

NCIB's basic philosophy is that the public is entitled to accurate information about the organizations that seek its support. NCIB does not recommend that people contribute to one organization rather than to another. They believe that well-informed givers will ask questions and make judgments that will lead to an improved level of performance by charities. The site contains their searchable Wise Giving Guide based on the NCIB's Standards in Philanthropy

National Assembly of State Arts Agencies (http://www.nasaa-arts.org)
Sponsored by the National Endowment for the Arts, this site is a clearinghouse of Internet information for arts organizations.

State arts agencies are important funding sources for both arts nonprofits and individual artists (usually through sponsorship programs), and visitors will find a comprehensive collection of links to state arts agency Web sites as well as notices of arts events and conferences nationwide.

University of Virginia-Prospect Research
(http://www.people.virginia.edu/~dev-pros/)
This site contains a comprehensive list of useful Internet sites, which includes links to biographical resources, corporate sites, Internet directories, foundations and grants, and much more. It also provides suggestions for conducting international research and finding assets on the web. Check out the campaign contributions search engines provided for most states.

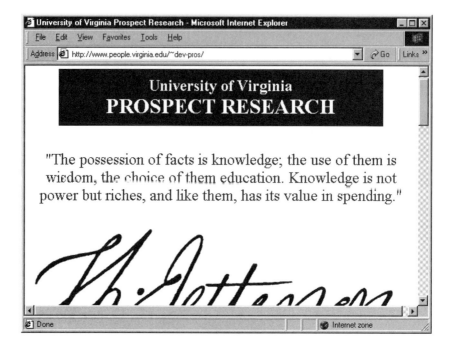

National Directory of Computer Recycling Programs
(http://www.microweb.com/pepsite/Recycle/recycle_index.html)
Of course, nonprofits don't live by foundation grants alone. If your organization is looking for a free or low-cost technology upgrade and you don't mind working with equipment that isn't brand new, you might want to stop by the Parents Educators and Publishers (PEP) site.

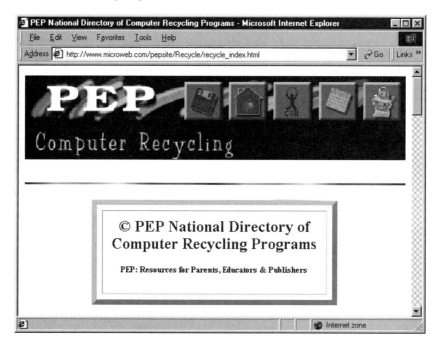

This site, maintained by Anne Bubnic, includes a directory of organizations that facilitate donations of computer hardware and software to schools and community-based nonprofits. Annotated entries describe each program's eligibility requirements, with complete contact information, including links to Web sites and e-mail addresses, when available. A wide variety of organizations are represented, and resources are classified by geographic scope, from international to state level.

Nonprofit News and Current Awareness

One of the most valuable features of the Web is the fast access it provides to current information about new developments affecting philanthropy, nonprofits, and fundraising. Stopping by some of the following sites on a weekly basis can help to keep your organization apprised of grant proposal deadlines, training opportunities, and pending legislation that could impact your operations. The Web also offers you a way to learn about what organizations like yours are doing with programs and services, special events, fundraising, and public relations, making it possible to network with people who are working on similar issues the world over. Visiting the Web sites of other organizations active in your field of interest is a great way to see what seems to work (and what doesn't) in using the Web to promote services, recruit volunteers, and even raise money. Some of the sites that follow will lead you to nonprofits like yours, others will give you the opportunity to make information about your organization available on the Web.

Chronicle of Philanthropy (http://philanthropy.com)
Like its biweekly print analog, The *Chronicle of Philanthropy's* Web site is full of useful information for grantseekers.

The site is organized into broad topic areas—Gifts and Grants, Fund Raising, Managing Non-Profit Groups, and Technology—and offers, among other items, a summary of the contents of the *Chronicle*'s current and previous issues, the full text of selected stories, award and RFP deadlines, job opportunities in the non-profit sector, and information about forthcoming conferences and workshops. The annotated links section is one of the best for finding nonprofit resources on the Internet. Visitors can also sign up for free updates via e-mail about changes at the site as well as breaking news stories.

Nonprofit Online News (http://www.gilbert.org/news)

Michael Gilbert of the Gilbert Center maintains this site, where he posts one to three news items per day, Monday through Friday. Visitors will find notices of meetings and conferences, links to new online resources for nonprofits, full-text articles about the sector, and especially, information about how nonprofits can use the Web as a resource for sharing information and making themselves more visible. The focus is on timely issues, and the news items tend toward the Web-centric.

GuideStar (http://www.guidestar.org)

In a partnership with Lexis/Nexis, the GuideStar News Service posts the full text of current news stories from newspapers around the country on charitable giving, tax regulations, prominent philanthropists, and nonprofit organizations. The stories are searchable by topic, location, or revenue.

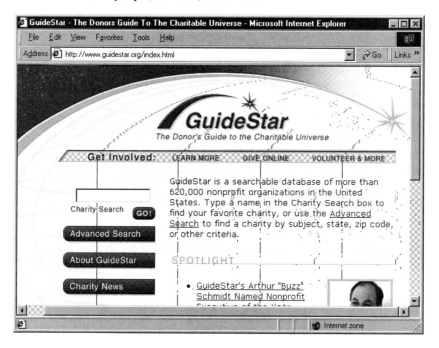

As noted in Chapter 7, GuideStar also provides a free, searchable database of information on the programs and finances of U.S. nonprofit organizations. GuideStar information is drawn from the IRS Business Master File or from Form 990 and may include a description of the organization and a summary of revenues and expenses. The goals of this service are to inform donors and promote nonprofit accountability. Thus, organizations are given the opportunity to supply GuideStar with additional information about their programs, services, and financial status. Simply click on Just for Nonprofits on the home page to get started.

Action Without Borders (http://www.idealist.org)

Idealist, a project of Action Without Borders, (formerly the Contact Center Network) is a searchable directory of over 17,000 nonprofit organizations in 130 countries. You can search for nonprofits by subject, geographic area, name or mission.

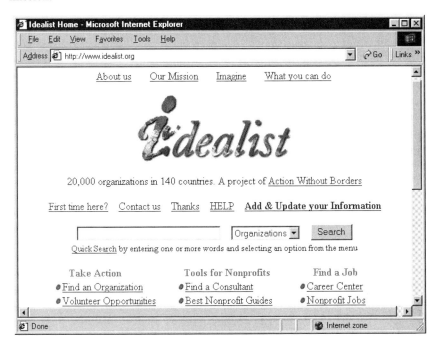

There are plenty of links here, but what's really nice about Action Without Borders is that nonprofits without Web sites of their own can submit information about their mission, programs, and services for posting. Raising your organization's profile in cyberspace is just a few mouse clicks away. Action Without Borders also includes links to nonprofit news, jobs and volunteer opportunities, and resources for nonprofit managers.

Internet NonProfit Center (http://www.nonprofits.org/)

The Center aims to provide, fast, free, and easy access to information on nonprofit organizations, wise giving practices, and issues of concern to donors and volunteers.

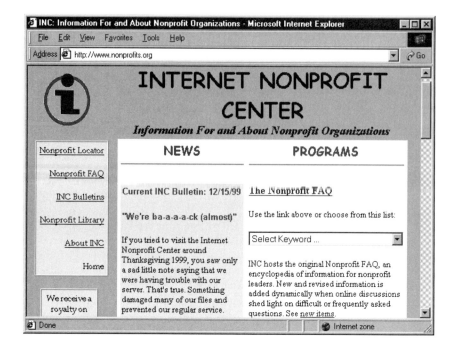

Major components of the site include a "library," which offers essays and data about the nonprofit sector, and a Nonprofit Locator that provides financial information from IRS filings on more than a million charities. It is searchable by keyword and state. The Nonprofit FAQ contains extensive information and advice about nonprofits arranged in five main areas.

Impact Online (http://www.impactonline.org)

"Turning good intentions into action" is the motto of this organization, based in Palo Alto, California. Impact Online aims to use the Internet to promote community involvement by means of a searchable database of volunteer opportunities in major cities.

The site also allows nonprofits to post information about themselves in order to recruit volunteers. Through its "Virtual Volunteering" program, Impact Online seeks to expand the reach of voluntarism by matching nonprofits with individuals who can help out via a computer at home or at work.

Fundraising Tips and Training

Another advantage of the Internet is the opportunity it provides for consulting professionals in the nonprofit field. The Internet has been about sharing information since its very beginnings, and a great deal of expertise in areas like fundraising, taxation, legal issues, and nonprofit management is readily available. This is also true, of course, of the wide variety of mailing lists, bulletin boards, and discussion groups available online, which are discussed in detail in Chapter 10. Think of the Web as a constantly growing storehouse of knowledge that your organization can explore at some of the sites that follow.

The Grantsmanship Center (http://www.tgci.com)
The Grantsmanship Center specializes in training nonprofit managers and fundraisers, and its site offers the full text of stories from the Center's magazine, along with grant announcements and funding news from federal government agencies. A bulletin board area for fundraising tips has been added.

The Alliance (http://www.allianceonline.org/)

The Alliance for Nonprofit Management (the Alliance) is the result of the 1998 merger of the Support Centers of America and the Nonprofit Management Association.

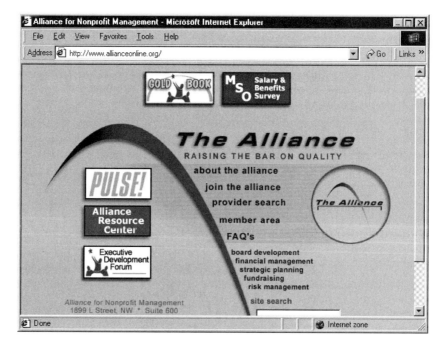

The Alliance, whose slogan is raising the bar on quality, has an excellent FAQ section in four broad subject areas, including board development, financial management, fundraising and strategic planning. You can also subscribe to PULSE, the Alliance's free online newsletter.

National Center for Nonprofit Boards (http://www.ncnb.org)

If you've wondered how to get the members of your board to take a more active role in your organization's fundraising efforts, you will find useful resources and publications at the NCNB's Web site.

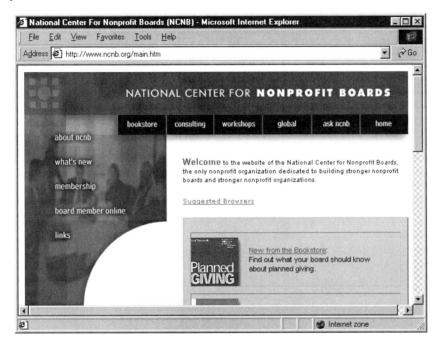

The NCNB FAQ section includes information about recruiting and communicating with board members, forming nonprofits, resolving board conflicts, and developing board job descriptions. For visitors who need further information, there is an electronic query form for submitting questions to NCNB staff.

Association of Professional Researchers for Advancement (http://weber.u.washington.edu/~dlamb/apra/APRA.html)

APRA is a membership organization for professional fundraising researchers, and its Web site features "prospecting resources" links (including the PROSPECT-L discussion list and its archives; see Chapter 10) and information about APRA's mission, membership, and events.

National Society of Fund-Raising Executives (http://www.nsfre.org)

The National Society of Fund Raising Executives is the premier professional organization for nonprofit fundraisers, and its site is primarily for the use of NSFRE members. In addition to the full text of its Code of Ethical Principles and Standards of Professional Practice, visitors will find NSFRE's directory of fund-raising consultants, with contact information and areas of specialization.

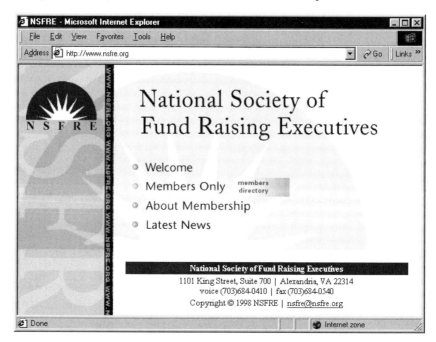

David Lamb's Prospect Research Page
(http://weber.u.washington.edu/~dlamb/research.html)
Lamb, a development officer at the University of Washington, has attempted to "separate the wheat from the chaff" in describing truly useful Internet sites for researching corporations, foundations, and individual donors. His page includes links to directories of doctors, dentists, lawyers, and airplane owners, as well as to online news sources and fee-based information providers like Dialog. What's nice about the Prospect Research Page is that Lamb has distilled the overwhelming number of potential sources of information on the Internet into a relatively small selection of sites, which he has thoughtfully annotated. The casual visitor can tell that he or she is in capable hands.

The Nonprofit FAQ (http://www.nonprofit-info.org/npofaq/index.html)
Brought to you by the Internet Nonprofit Center, the Nonprofit FAQ gathers items from discussions on e-mail lists, in Usenet and other sources. This set of frequently asked questions is divided into five broad categories; organization, management, regulation, resources, and development.

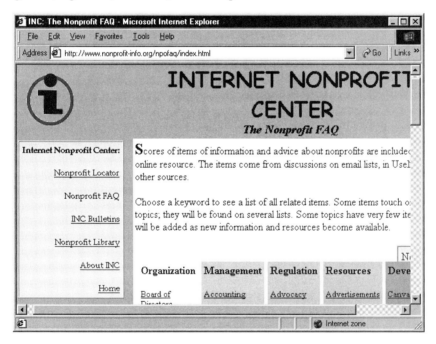

You get to see what professionals in the field have to say on topics like special events, direct mail, corporate sponsorship, and enlisting celebrity support for your organization.

Grantscape (http://www.grantscape.com)
The Web site of Aspen Publishers, Grantscape offers a "Funder of the Day," links to other sites and services, and Grantseeking 101, an overview of the process of fundraising research, proposal development, and good grantsmanship practices

Grants for Individuals

Most foundations and corporations make grants to nonprofit organizations rather than to individuals. It shouldn't be surprising that most of the available online information for grantseekers focuses on funding for charities rather than for artists, writers, and researchers. One of the best starting places for the individual grantseeker is the Michigan State University Grants and Related Resources page (http://www.lib.msu.edu/harris23/grants/grants.htm), previously introduced in the "Funder Information" section of this chapter. The MSU site includes a separate section for individuals that covers print resources as well as many federal, state, and university-based funding sources online. It is a very good place to browse for new Web-based resources. Some additional places to visit follow.

ArtsWire (http://www.artswire.org)

ArtsWire, a membership organization devoted to arts advocacy that is sponsored by the New York Foundation for the Arts, offers funding information for individual artists each week in the Current section of its Web site. Current includes late-breaking details on fellowships, residencies, exhibition spaces, arts events, and job listings. The site also includes an archive of Current postings going back to 1995.

Art Deadlines List (http://custwww.xensei.com/adl/)
Richard Gardner's Art Deadlines List is a monthly compilation of information about juried competitions, contests, jobs, internships, scholarships, residencies, fellowships, casting calls, auditions, tryouts, festivals, and grants for artists in the visual, literary and performing arts. Posted to the site is a free version of the list, which is also available via e-mail as a paid subscription service.

FinAid: The Financial Aid Information Page (http://www.finaid.org)
Sponsored by the National Association of Student Financial Aid Administrators and created by Mark Kantrowitz, FinAid is the most comprehensive Internet resource available on funding for education in the United States.

The site runs the gamut from general information about public and private sources of scholarships and loans to scam alerts to FastWEB, a searchable database of funding. It would be difficult to pose a question about financial aid and not find a detailed response here.

FastWEB.com (http://fastweb.com)
Since 1995, FastWEB has helped students find college scholarships. A student's background is matched with the eligibility requirements for scholarships from around the country. The factFOCUS section gives advice on admissions, scholarships, jobs, career planning, money, and financial aid.

International Resources

At this point, the Web's promise for creating a global network that links international nonprofits with prospective sponsors has yet to be fully realized. Online information for organizations is heavily concentrated in Europe and North America, areas of the world with well developed philanthropic and telecommunications infrastructures. FundsNet, previously cited in the Funding Information section of this chapter, offers a collection of links to online information about grantmakers active outside the United States at (http://www.fundsnetservices.com/internat.htm). The sites that follow may be useful as well.

European Foundation Centre (http://www.efc.be/)
Visitors to this simply designed page will find information about the Foundation Center's European counterpart, including links to foundations and corporations active on the Continent, and advice about research and cultivation of potential funders. There is also a searchable database of European grantmakers.

UK Fundraising (http://www.fundraising.co.uk/)
A wide variety of information for charities and fundraisers in the United Kingdom is made available here by the Charities Aid Foundation. The information offerings range from monthly news features to book reviews and statistical information about the nonprofit sector. Check the "Grants and Funding" section for useful links. "Fundraising Online" features examples of how to use the Web to publicize your organization, attract donations and in-kind gifts, and recruit members and volunteers.

Charity Village (http://www.charityvillage.com)
The online resource for all things nonprofit in Canada, this site combines news headlines, conference listings, job opportunities, a directory of Canadian organizations by subject area, and links to online publications and mailing lists. The Sources of Funding section has links to Canadian foundations, databases of funding for research, and grants opportunities from Canadian government agencies.

German Charities Institute (http://www.dsk.de)

This site is a clearinghouse of information on German and international charities which features a searchable directory of over 5,000 organizations, an immense collection of links, and information about everything from volunteer opportunities to e-mail discussion groups on philanthropy and social issues. Much of the information is available in English.

CONCLUSION

The Internet is growing so rapidly that it could be a full time job keeping current with what's available. Surfing for new Web sites, while time consuming, is an essential part of that process. Many of the sites we've reviewed will help keep you posted about new online resources, but it's important not to understate the value of simply spending time on the Web yourself. The Links to Nonprofit Resources section of the Foundation Center's Web site is a great jumping off point for further exploration. We'll continue to use that space to inform you about new sites of interest as well as changes to some of your old favorites. Below we reproduce those listings of links from the Center's Web site, condensed and revised for a print presentation.

Links and Abstracts of Nonprofit Resources on the Foundation Center Web Site

BUSINESS & INDUSTRY

(See Chapter 5 for more about corporate information available on the Web.)

Council of Better Business Bureaus (http://www.bbb.org/index.html)

Besides serving as a gateway to more than 150 local Better Business Bureaus throughout the U.S. and Canada, the CBBB Web site provides instant access to business and consumer alerts, charity reports and standards (through its Philanthropic Advisory [Service], and other helpful resources. It also has begun to accept consumer complaints, which it forwards to the appropriate local BBB.

Business for Social Responsibility (http://www.bsr.org/)

Business for Social Responsibility (BSR) serves companies around the world that work towards promoting ethical values, people, communities, and the environment while sustaining commercial success. BSR helps its members create value for investors, customers, employees, local communities, and other stakeholders by providing professional assistance with socially responsible business policies and practices. One of the BSR Web site's outstanding features is its Global Business Responsibility Resource Center, a free service to site visitors which contains basic information regarding a wide range of corporate responsibility topics, along with company examples and links to other helpful sites.

EDGAR Database of Corporate Information (http://www.sec.gov/edgarhp.htm)

The Securities and Exchange Commission's EDGAR (Electronic Data Gathering, Analysis, and Retrieval) system is a goldmine of basic but often-hard-to-find corporate information (e.g., fiscal data, officers, subsidiaries, recent M&A activity, etc.). EDGAR on the Web allows visitors to retrieve publicly available filings submitted to the SEC from January 1994 to the present.

iHelpSupport.com (http://www.ihelpsupport.com)

iHelpSupport.com, a service of NicheNET Inc., is a free program that offers nonprofit organizations the opportunity to receive a portion of the revenue generated from online purchases by the public.

Hoover's Online (http://www.hoovers.com/)

Hoover's, the Austin, Texas-based publisher of corporate information, may not be the "Ultimate Source for Company Information," as it bills itself, but it sure is a good one. The site's offerings come in two flavors, free and fee-based. The former center around Hoover's Company Capsules, which provide news and information—company profile, key personnel, full stock quote, selected press coverage—on more than 11,000 public and private enterprises. Subscribers (two options: personal or multi-user) get the same—in much greater depth and detail. This site offers coverage of more than 1,500 nonpublic companies including nonprofits and foundations.

Inc. Online (http://www.inc.com/)

Brought to you by the folks at *Inc.* magazine, the award winning Inc. Online is a great resource for entrepreneurs and small business owners who are serious about growing their businesses. In addition to the most recent edition of *Inc.* and an archive of 5,000-plus articles on a wide variety of topics, the site offers interactive worksheets, case studies, online tutorials, a searchable database of America's 500 fastest-growing companies, and great links to other small business-related resources on the Net.

Small Business Knowledge Base (http://www.bizmove.com)

A vital online resource for entrepreneurs, this small business information clearinghouse includes extensive content areas dealing with virtually every aspect of successfully starting and managing a small business. Site visitors may also subscribe to a free online newsletter containing relevant tips and tricks.

U.S. Small Business Administration (http://www.sbaonline.sba.gov/)

As an independent agency of the U.S. government, the SBA assists small businesses in order to encourage free enterprise and improve the nation's overall economy. Visitors to the site can retrieve exhaustive information about what the agency offers, including a variety of financial assistance programs. The SBA site also includes a section devoted to laws and regulations affecting small businesses, a "business card" registration center and links to other government resources. Easy to navigate, concise descriptions explain the variety of routes available to financing a small business.

THE INTERNET

Download.com (http://www.download.com)

Hosted by CNET, this site serves as a virtual warehouse of software and shareware of all kinds. Application types include Business, Education, Games, Home & Personal, Internet, Multimedia & Design Development Tools, Utilities, Drivers, PalmPilot, Windows CE, and Linux.

Electronic Frontier Foundation (http://www.eff.org/)

The not-for-profit EFF is a high-profile clearinghouse for news and information about Internet-related issues such as free speech, encryption, privacy, and intellectual property rights. One of the four most-linked-to sites on the Web. This site also contains daily news updates and opportunities to participate in Internet advocacy.

Internet Law & Policy Forum (http://www.ilpf.org/)

The ILPF was conceived as "a neutral venue in which to develop solutions to the challenging legal and policy questions of the Internet." Issues currently being addressed by the Forum include online certification of commercial transactions, digital signatures, and content blocking and regulation. This site also offers listings of Internet law resources, conferences and an archive of press releases.

The 'Open Source' Page (http://www.opensource.org/index.html)

The "open source" movement is dedicated to the proposition that computer source code developed in an open, non-proprietary environment is chiefly responsible for the global popularity of th e Internet. Examples of open source software in commercial use include Apache, which runs 50 percent of the world's Web servers; the Perl programming language, in which most CGI applications are written; BIND, the software that provides the domain name service (DNS) for the Internet; and sendmail, the most widely used email transport software on the Net. The 'Open Source' Page explains the roots of the movement and where it's headed.

Technology Resource Institute (http://www.tripl.org/)
TRI works with public libraries to ensure that communities have access to the Internet, and helps to train local library personnel in the use of emerging communications technologies.

Technology Tip Sheets for Nonprofits (http://www.coyotecom.com/tips.html)
Tip sheets to help organizations and individuals reap money-saving, program-enhancing benefits from technology. Basic customer database principles, Web development and maintenance, and Internet-related advice and suggestions can be found at this site.

Technology Resource Institute (http://www.techresource.org/)
TRI works with public libraries to ensure that communities have access to the Internet, and helps to train local library personnel in the use of emerging communications technologies. This site also provides listings of training opportunities, and other Web-based resources.

World Wide Web Consortium (http://www.w3.org/)
Under the direction of Tim Berners-Lee, the creator of the World Wide Web, the WC3 has played a leading role since 1994 in developing and articulating the specifications and protocols at the heart of the Web. A touchstone in the evolution of the Web, and a vitally important resource for Web developers.

LIBRARY LINKS

American Library Association (http://www.ala.org/)
The 57,000-member ALA, the oldest library association in the world, has been a leader in defending intellectual freedom and promoting quality library and information services for more than a century. Today, the association's interests and activities range from copyright and intellectual property issues, to library education and professional development. A great resource for library professionals as well as anyone interested in the critical role libraries and librarians will play in the emerging information-based economy.

Association of Research Libraries (http://www.arl.org/)
The programs and services of the ARL promote equitable access to, and effective use of, recorded knowledge in support of teaching, research, scholarship, and community service.

CAUSE (http://www.educause.edu/)
This membership organization, which recently consolidated with Educom, is dedicated to managing and using information resources in higher education.

Foundation Center Historical Foundation Collection (http://www.ulib.iupui.edu/special/mss005.html)
The Historical Foundation Collection, covering materials for the period 1896–1996, collected by the Foundation Center, was established as a manuscript collections of The Ruth Lilly Special Collections and Archives at the Indiana University-Purdue University Indianapolis (IUPUI) in 1997. The site generally describes

the four components of the collection: IRS tax documents, historical information files, annual reports, and sets of Foundation Center directories, and it provides a detailed list of the available annual reports. Reference queries can be made by telephone, fax, email, or from the Web site.

IUPUI Special Collections Philanthropy Studies (http://www-lib.iupui.edu/special/ppsl.html)

The Ruth Lilly Special Collections and Archives houses the Joseph and Matthew Payton Philanthropic Studies Library among its Manuscript Collections. Reference queries can be made by telephone, fax, email, or from the Web site. It also compiles and maintains the Philanthropic Studies Index, an online, searchable bibliography to literature, primarily periodicals and research reports, on voluntarism, nonprofit organizations, fundraising, and charitable giving.

Library Power (http://www.dewittwallace.org/focus/library/index.htm)

A project of the DeWitt Wallace-Reader's Digest Fund, Library Power works to improve teaching and learning in public schools through strengthening library services.

Libri Foundation (http://www.teleport.com/~librifdn/index.html)

The Libri Foundation is a national nonprofit organization that donates new hardcover children's books to small rural public libraries in the U.S. through its "Books for Children" program.

Library of Congress (http://lcweb.loc.gov/)

The entire Library of Congress catalogue searchable online, as well as information on the LC's programs and services.

Technology Resource Institute (http://www.techresource.org/)

TRI works with public libraries to ensure that communities have access to the Internet, and helps to train local library personnel in the use of emerging communications technologies. This site also provides listings of training opportunities, and other web-based resources.

POLICY INSTITUTES

Hoover Institution on War, Revolution and Peace (http://www-hoover.stanford.edu/)

Before he became 31st president of the United States, Herbert Hoover founded the Hoover Institution, a public policy research center at Stanford University devoted to the advanced study of domestic and international affairs. Recognized as one of the first "think tanks" in the U.S., the Institution boasts one of the world's most complete libraries on political, economic, and social change in the 20th century. The Hoover Institution Web site offers information on the organization's research program, publications, and library collections, as well as subscription information for its electronic mailing lists.

NIRA's World Directory of Think Tanks (http://www.nira.go.jp/ice/tt-info/nwdtt96/)

The Japan-based National Institute for Research Advancement provides a no-frills site with basic information on more than 250 policy organizations in 65 countries. Information available for each organization can include executive personnel, organizational history, areas of research, geographic focus, availability of research findings, and funding sources. Contact information is also available, as are individual Web site links (when available). Although the site lacks a master index, this is an excellent place to start for those interested in policy institutes and their work.

RAND (http://www.rand.org/)

RAND (an acronym for Research and Development) researchers assist public policymakers at all levels, private sector leaders in many industries, and the public at large in efforts to strengthen the nation's economy, maintain its security, and improve its quality of life. RAND's Web site offers information about the organization's research activities, technical capabilities, publications, educational opportunities, and board of trustees, along with a "Hot Topics in RAND Research" area.

REFERENCE

Ask.com (http://www.ask.com)

This unique site combs the Web for answers to specific questions posed by the user. In addition to its own indexed links, it also retrieves results from four major search engines.

Fast Area Code Look-Up (http://www.555-1212.com/aclookup.html)

Brought to you by the folks at 555-1212.com, Fast Area Code Look-Up does exactly that: Plug in the name of a city, add the name of a state or (Canadian) province, and voila!—it supplies that pesky area code you can never remember. Also works in reverse (though less well): Enter an area code and Fast Look-Up gives you abroad geographical location and the names of major cities in that location.

InfoPlease.com (http://www.infoplease.com)

A colossal online reference center, InfoPlease.com empowers users to conduct keyword searches that retrieve facts from its almanacs, encyclopedia, and dictionary. Topics include current events, "today in history," science and technology, people, the US and world, business and economy, lifestyles and interests, entertainment and sports, and society and culture.

National Center for Charitable Statistics—Resources on Nonprofits and Philanthropy (http://nccs.urban.org/resource.htm)

Visitors to this site can download microdata on nonprofit organizations, view or download database documentation and data dictionaries, and download blank IRS forms from which most of the data is collected.

The Ultimates (http://www.theultimates.com)
The be-all-end-all of contact information directories, this site offers visitors the chance to simultaneously search multiple Internet-based White Pages, Yellow Pages, and e-mail directory databases. It also includes access to several online mapping services for travel route planning.

U.S. Census Bureau (http://www.census.gov/)
The Census Bureau's sprawling site is the source of social, demographic, and economic information about the U.S. on the Web. Offerings include all Census Bureau publications (in PDF format) released since January 1996; statistical profiles for states, congressional districts, and counties; current economic indicators; state and county maps created on the fly; and much, much more. Who would have guessed that statistics could be this much fun?

GENERAL

Catalog of Federal Domestic Assistance
(http://www.gsa.gov/fdac/default.htm)
The Catalog of Federal Domestic Assistance provides information on a wide variety of financial and non-financial assistance programs, projects, services, and activities. Programs are administered by departments and establishments of the federal government and are available to the public. Visitors to the site submit a simple query and receive clear, detailed information, including eligibility requirements, application procedures, and examples of funded projects.

Federal Information Exchange, Inc. (http://web.fic.com/fedix/index.html)
FEDIX provides free access to information on government research and education grants, programs, contracts, and more. Supported by selected federal agencies under a cooperative agreement forged by the Department of Energy and the Office of Science Education and Technical Information, the FEDIX Web site is comprehensive and easy to use. Visitors can search by audience or subject and can also receive targeted funding opportunities via e-mail. Other features include news updates and a Grants Keyword Thesaurus, which can be downloaded by eligible nonprofit institutions.

Federal Register (http://www.access.gpo.gov/su_docs/aces/aces140.html)
The no-frills Federal Register site provides access to presidential documents, executive orders, rules, and proposed rules from federal agencies and organizations. Visitors to the site can search the database in a variety of ways, and detailed instructions and sample searches are provided to facilitate the process. The exhaustive information on governmentally funded projects and funding availability is especially helpful.

Grants Information Service (http://infoserv.rttonet.psu.edu/gis/)
A collection of links to (mostly) government sources of funding for research, instruction, and continuing education projects from the folks at Penn State's Office of Sponsored Programs.

OMB's Nonprofits and Technology Project
(http://www.ombwatch.org/ombwatch/npt/)
The goal of the Nonprofits and Technology Project is to improve communications linkages within thenonprofit sector to strengthen public policy participation. Through the project, OMB Watch will offergrants to nonprofits in the range of $5,000 to $25,000 to help fund innovative and creative applications of technology to the field of public policy participation.

THOMAS: Legislative Information on the Internet
(http://thomas.loc.gov/home/thomas2.html)
The online arm of the U.S. Congress Library, offering up-to-date information on the legislative activities of both Houses, and searchable databases of current and historical legislative documents of the U.S.Congress.

WWW Virtual Library: U.S. Federal Government Agencies
(http://www.lib.lsu.edu/gov/fedgov.html)
A meta-index of federal agencies on the Internet.

WWW Virtual Library: U.S. Government Resources
(http://iridium.nttc.edu/gov_res.html)
A searchable meta-index of federal agencies on the Internet.

FEDERAL AGENCIES

(See Chapter 6 for more detail on government Web sites.)

Administration on Aging (http://www.aoa.dhhs.gov/)
An exhaustive online resource for senior citizens and issues concerning aging and senior health.

Administration for Children and Families (http://www.acf.dhhs.gov/)
Information on the vast array of programs and services offered by this division of DHHS, dedicated to promoting the economic and social well-being of families, children, individuals, and communities.

Agency for Health Care Policy and Research (http://www.ahcpr.gov/)
Grantmaking DHHS agency, dedicated to generating and disseminating information that improves the health care system.

Centers for Disease Control and Prevention (http://www.cdc.gov/)
Includes comprehensive program and application information for the CDC's many health-related funding opportunities.

Department of Health and Human Services (http://www.os.dhhs.gov/)
The DHHS Web site provides consumer and policy information, searchable databases, employment opportunities, and links to related government agencies.

Health Resources and Services Administration (http://www.hrsa.dhhs.gov)
An overview of programs, services and grant opportunities from this DHHS agency.

Indian Health Service (http://www.ihs.gov/)
Dedicated to raising the health status of American Indians and Alaska Natives, the Web site of this DHHS agency provides information on the agency's activities, and serves as an online resource for Native American communities.

Internal Revenue Service (http://www.irs.ustreas.gov/prod/)
This highly regarded site provides comprehensive tax information and has a site-wide search engine.

National Endowment for the Arts (http://arts.endow.gov/)
The NEA's elegant Web site provides information on the endowment's programs and funding guidelines and serves as a comprehensive resource for the arts community and its supporters.

National Endowment for the Humanities (http://www.neh.fed.us/)
Program information and application guidelines for the NEH's grantmaking programs in the humanities.

National Institute on Alcohol Abuse and Alcoholism (http://www.niaaa.nih.gov/)
One of 18 agencies that comprise the National Institutes of Health, NIAAA supports and conducts biomedical and behavioral research on the causes, consequences, treatment, and prevention of alcoholism and alcohol-related problems.

National Institutes of Health (http://www.nih.gov/)
Comprehensive information on the NIH's activities and programs, including grants and funding opportunities.

National Science Foundation (http://www.nsf.gov/)
The NSF is dedicated to fostering science and engineering research and education nationwide. As you'd expect from the agency that step-fathered the Internet into adolescence, the NSF Web site is comprehensive, well organized, and fast. Site includes program and grants and awards info in biology, education, engineering, the geosciences, math and physical sciences, polar research, social and behavioral sciences, and much more.

National Telecommunications & Information Administration (http://www.ntia.doc.gov/)
Includes application guidelines and a listing of recent grants awarded through its Telecommunications and Information Infrastructure Assistance Program.

Oak Ridge Institute for Science and Education (http://www.orau.gov/orise.htm)
The Institute supports national and international programs in education, training, health, and the environment.

**Substance Abuse and Mental Health Services Administration
(http://www.samhsa.gov/)**
The Web site of this DHHS agency provides information on its programs, events
and funding opportunities, and serves as an online resource for substance abuse
prevention.

U.S. Census Bureau (http://www.census.gov/)
The Census Bureau's sprawling site is the source of social, demographic, and economic information about the U.S. on the Web. Offerings include all Census
Bureau publications (in PDF format) released since January 1996; statistical profiles for states, congressional districts, and counties; current economic indicators;
state and county maps created on the fly; and much, much more. Who would have
guessed that statistics could be this much fun?

STATE AGENCIES

Nebraska Arts Council (http://www.gps.k12.ne.us/nac_web_site/nac.htm)
The NAC promotes the arts, cultivates resources, and supports excellence in artistic endeavors for all Nebraskans. Still under construction, the NAC Web site provides general information about its grant programs and application requirements;
an artists directory; links to other art councils (community and state), state organizations, and art museums on the Web; and contact information.

North Carolina Arts Council (http://www.ncarts.org/)
The mission of the NCAC is to enrich North Carolina's cultural life by supporting
the arts. The Council is a catalyst for the development of arts organizations, and
awards grants and offers technical guidance statewide. The Council's colorful
Web site provides, among other items, program and grant information; links to
various arts organizations, government agencies, and regional and national arts
partners; and contact information for 285 North Carolina arts organizations organized by county and by type of art group.

North Dakota Council on the Arts (http://www.state.nd.us/arts/)
Established in 1967 by the state legislature, the NDCA is responsible for the support and development of the arts and artists in North Dakota. In addition to making grants based on recommendations from artists and arts administrators, the
Council administers the Cultural Endowment Fund, through which it secures private and public funds to enhance existing programs. The Council's Web site provides program information, application instructions, grant writing tips, related
arts resource links, and contact information.

Ohio Arts Council (http://www.oac.ohio.gov/)
Established in 1965 to "foster and encourage the development of the arts and assist
the preservation of Ohio's cultural heritage," the OAC funds programs to make
arts activities available to the public and also supports Ohio artists through 25 different grant programs. The Council's Web site provides information about all
OAC programs, complete grant guidelines, an impressive search engine, links to
both state and national arts resources, and e-mail links to staff members.

**South Dakota Arts Council
(http://www.state.sd.us/state/executive/deca/sdarts/sdarts.htm)**
The SDAC encourages and supports artists, strengthens arts organizations and arts education programs, and increases South Dakotans awareness of the arts. As a state agency of the Department of Education & Cultural Affairs, the Council makes grants to schools, individuals, and arts organizations. Grantseekers will especially appreciate the Council's online program guide, which includes detailed grant application guidelines and a handy glossary of terms.

INTERNATIONAL

Charities Aid Foundation (http://www.charitynet.org/index.html)
CAF, a British nonprofit whose aim is to encourage charitable giving in the United Kingdom as well as internationally, sponsors the Charitynet Web site, "a resource centre for the non-profit sector and its contributors." The site includes contact information for thousands of charities and serves as a technical assistance provider to both funders and nonprofits. Of special interest is the site's Corporate Community Involvement Resource Center, an alpha list of links to more than 100 corporate (U.S.-based and multinational) Web sites with charitable giving information.

CIVICUS (http://www.civicus.org/)
An international alliance dedicated "to strengthening citizen action and civil society throughout the world."

ConflictNet (http://www.conflict.inter.net/)
ConflictNet is committed to promoting the resolution of conflict through non-adversarial processes. Its resources include news, editorials, chat groups, and an entry point to over 200 discussion lists on various issues around the world.

Disaster Relief.Org (http://www.disasterrelief.org/)
An easy-to-navigate clearinghouse for worldwide disaster aid and information.

International Donors' Dialogue (http://www.internationaldonors.org/)
Almost everything you wanted to know about international philanthropy, from the clever, passionate folks who started the San Francisco-based IDD in 1996. The IDD Web site offers a list of international projects that need urgent, immediate action; a selection of worthwhile projects in need of funding arranged by region, organization, or issue; a calendar of conferences, films, workshops, and site visits; helpful answers to frequently asked questions about international philanthropy; and more. Check it out. You'll be inspired.

International Law Institute (http://www.ili.org)
The International Law Institute works toward finding practical solutions to the legal, economic, and financial problems of the international community. Its mission is carried out through scholarly research, publishing, and practical legal training and technical assistance regarding various components of international law, economic policy, and practice. The organization's site features news, descriptions

of its courses and publications, and includes a long list of related links, broken down by subject area.

International Research & Exchanges Board (http://www.irex.org)
The International Research & Exchanges Board is a private, nonprofit organization dedicated to promoting advanced field research and professional training programs between the United States and the countries of Central and Eastern Europe, Russia,Ukraine, Central Asia, the Caucasus, Eurasia, China, and comparable contiguous societies. With its traditional base in the university research community, and in collaboration with partners from the policy, corporate, media, and private foundation sectors, IREX sponsors and supports programs of advanced field research, professional training, international conferences, seminars, and comparative analysis.

Internet Law & Policy Forum (http://www.ilpf.org/)
The ILPF was conceived as "a neutral venue in which to develop solutions to the challenging legal and policy questions of the Internet." Issues currently being addressed by the Forum include online certification of commercial transactions, digital signatures, and content blocking and regulation.

Internet Prospector (http://w3.uwyo.edu/~prospect/inter.html)
Check out IP's resources for international prospect research.

NGO Global Network (http://www.ngo.org)
Links to non-governmental organizations associated with the United Nations.

Novartis Foundation for Sustainable Development (http://www.foundation.novartis.com/)
Established in December 1996, and formerly known as the Ciba-Geigy Foundation for Cooperation with Developing Countries, the Novartis Foundation supports a variety of projects in developing countries—among them Bangladesh, Bolivia, Brazil, China, Laos, Mali, Senegal, and Tanzania—in the areas of agricultural, health care, and social development.

Organization for Economic Co-operation and Development (http://www.oecd.org/)
The OECD, an international think tank whose headquarters are located in Paris, France, incorporates 29 member countries within an organization that provides governments a setting in which to discuss, develop, and perfect economic and social policy. Its Web site includes statistics, news and events, publication information, an online bookstore, and a site-wide search engine.

The Peace Corps (http://www.peacecorps.gov/home.html)
The Peace Corps, a volunteer aid organization, currently serves 80 countries and includes programs in education, the environment, health, business, agriculture, and other fields.

ReliefWeb (http://www.reliefweb.int)
ReliefWeb is a project of the United Nations Office for the Coordination of Humanitarian Affairs (OCHA). It strives to improve humanitarian relief efforts

through the timely dissemination of reliable information on prevention, preparedness, and disaster response. In addition to current news regarding international
emergencies, the site provides financial figures on humanitarian assistance in the
last five years, a list of recent natural disasters worldwide, job openings, and a
directory of humanitarian organizations.

Soros Foundations Network (http://www.soros.org)

A clearinghouse of information about and gateway to the dozens of Soros programs and organizations that support the development and maintenance of "open
societies" in countries around the world.

United Nations (http://www.un.org/)

The United Nations, an umbrella organization of international agencies, committees, and task forces, conducts worldwide efforts encompassing peace and security, economic and social development, international law, human rights, and
humanitarian aid. Its vast, multilingual site provides detailed information about
various facets of the organization and its work, a list of conferences and events,
access to several of its online databases and documents, news, and a publications
index.

USAID (http://www.info.usaid.gov)

The United States Agency for International Development is an independent government agency that provides economic development and humanitarian assistance
to advance U.S. economic and political interests overseas. The USAID Web site
offers numerous links to governmental and non-governmental organizations concerned with international development.

Village Banking (http://www.villagebanking.org)

Village Banking is a program of the Foundation for International Community
Assistance (FINCA), which supports the economic and human development of
families trapped in severe poverty by creating "village banks" peer groups of 30 to
50 members, predominantly women, based on microcredit. The site offers a
detailed explanation of how the program works, program locations and statistics,
news, and job opportunities and internships.

The World Bank (http://www.worldbank.org/)

The sometimes-controversial World Bank strives to reduce poverty and improve
living standards by promoting sustainable growth and investment in developing
countries. The World Bank Group includes the International Bank for Reconstruc-
tion and Development, the International Development Association, the International Finance Corporation, the Multilateral Investment Guarantee Agency, and
the International Centre for the Settlement of Investment Disputes. The Bank's
Web site offers an imposing smorgasbord of economic facts and general information about the dozens of countries in which the Bank and its sister institutions do
business.

USAID (http://www.info.usaid.gov/)

The United States Agency for International Development is an independent government agency that provides economic development and humanitarian assistance
to advance U.S. economic and political interestsoverseas. The USAID Web site

offers numerous links to governmental and non-governmental organizations concerned with international development.

AFRICA

Africa News Online (http://www.africanews.org/)

A one-stop source for up-to-date information on all of Africa, with reports from Africa's leading newspapers, magazines, and news agencies. An invaluable resource.

ACCORD (African Centre for the Constructive Resolution of Disputes) (http://www.accord.org.za/)

ACCORD was founded with the goal of ending the political and social turmoil ravaging South African countries in the wake of apartheid. By making efforts to popularize and institutionalize the process of peaceful negotiation, and to create partnerships between members of society, government, and the business sector, the organization strives to facilitate the progression towards a stable democracy.

Novartis Foundation for Sustainable Development (http://www.foundation.novartis.com/)

Established in December 1996, and formerly known as the Ciba-Geigy Foundation for Cooperation with Developing Countries, the Novartis Foundation supports a variety of projects in developing countries—among them Bangladesh, Bolivia, Brazil, China, Laos, Mali, Senegal, and Tanzania—in the areas of agricultural, health care, and social development.

EUROPE/EURASIA

European Foundation Centre (http://www.efc.be/)

Information about the Foundation Center's European counterpart, including a list of links to foundations and corporate funders active on the Continent.

International Research & Exchanges Board (http://www.irex.org/grant-opps/index.htm)

Washington, D.C.-based IREX was founded in 1968 to administer academic exchanges between the U.S. and Soviet Union. Since then, its efforts have expanded to encompass professional training, institution building, technical assistance, and policy programs with the Newly Independent States, Central and Eastern Europe, and Mongolia and China. The "Grants & Fellowships" section of this information-rich site includes opportunities for international and U.S. scholars, and reports on library and archive access in a host of far-flung locales. The site also offers a database-driven links section showcasing the best of the World Wide Web.

National Forum Foundation (http://www.nff.org/)

Information on NFF's internship and volunteer programs and the NGO Regional Networking Project. Visitors to this site can also access the Freedom Forum's NGONet , an online database on Central and Eastern European NGOs.

Regional Environmental Center for Central and Eastern Europe
(http://www.rec.org/Default.shtml)
Comprehensive Web site offering information on REC's programs and grant-making activities, as well as several searchable databases.

NGONet (http://www.ngonet.org/)
NGONet provides information to, for, and about non-governmental organizations (NGOs) active in Central and Eastern Europe. Visitors to the NGONet site will find resources for funders, grantseekers, organizations looking for project partners, and jobseekers.

ASIA

Asia-Pacific Philanthropy Consortium Information Center
(http://iews.yonsei.ac.kr/appcic)
Based in Korea, the Asia-Pacific Philanthropy Consortium Information Center (APPC-IC) was established to generate and exchange information within the Asia-Pacific region about philanthropy and nonprofit issues. The Center's searchable database of regional foundations includes grantmakers in Australia, Hong Kong, Korea, Japan, the Philippines, and Thailand. Its Web site also features an organizational history and description, news, projects under development, and related links.

CANADA

Council of Better Business Bureaus (http://www.bbb.org/index.html)
Besides serving as a gateway to more than 150 local Better Business Bureaus throughout the U.S. and Canada, the CBBB Web site provides instant access to business and consumer alerts, charity reports and standards (through its Philanthropic Advisory Service), and other helpful resources. It also has begun to accept consumer complaints, which it forwards to the appropriate local BBB. An important service, and a nice site.

Charity Village (http://www.charityvillage.com/)
An excellent source of news, information, nonprofit resources, and discussions for the Canadian nonprofit community. Updated daily

In Kind Canada/In Kind Exchange (http://www.inkindcanada.ca)
A collaborative effort between In Kind Canada, which distributes donated goods and services to other Canadian charities, and Charity Village, the award-winning Canadian Web site.

Ontario Arts Council (http://www.arts.on.ca/)
The OAC supports artists and arts organizations throughout the province of Ontario, and awards grants based upon a unique peer assessment process that "gives artists and arts organizations a voice in how funds are distributed." Visitors to the OAC Web site will find a thorough description of its grant programs, application procedures, eligibility requirements, and deadlines. Excerpts from past

Council newsletters are also available, providing a clear picture of the OAC community and how it is affected by government policy.

Science's Next Wave (http://www.nextwave.org/)

Billed as "an electronic network for the next generation of scientists," the Next Wave site features profiles of and practical career advice for young scientists, as well as links to numerous scientific organizations and funding sources. Lots of material written by and of interest to Canadian scientists.

The Trillium Foundation (http://www.trilliumfoundation.org/)

The Trillium Foundation was established in 1982 "to ensure that a portion of the proceeds of the Ontario Lottery Corporation is directed toward social issues" in Ontario. The focus of the Foundation is on "the development of a new social vision which provides opportunity, and promotes both individual and collective responsibility." Through its grants program, the foundation encourages innovation and experimentation, cross-sector collaboration, citizen participation, and systemic change." English- and French-language versions.

GERMANY

German Charities Institute (http://www.dsk.de/)

More than 25,000 pages on German charity, philanthropy, and volunteering, including extensive listings of German and international nonprofit resources. German and English versions.

Lycos Germany (http://www.lycos.de/)

The German-language edition of the popular search engine.

Yahoo! Deutschland (http://www.yahoo.de/)

The German-language edition of the popular Web directory.

IRELAND

The Wellcome Trust (http://www.wellcome.ac.uk/)

The Trust spends hundreds of millions annually on research in biomedical science and the history of medicine, making it the largest non-governmental source of funds for biomedical research in Europe. Grantsare made to researchers in the UK and the Republic of Ireland, and for a variety of purposes, including programmatic, training, travel abroad, and equipment. Loads of information here in two flavors—frames-based and text-only.

ITALY

Vialardi di Sandigliano Foundation (http://www.gvo.it/VdSF/torrione_atrium.html)

Dedicated to the conservation of the medieval castle complex of Torrione, in northern Italy, and to creating and administering nonprofit activities and collaborative projects that make a significant contribution to preserving history and tradition.

JAPAN

Japan Center for International Exchange (JCIE) (http://www.jcie.or.jp/)

An independent nonprofit organization dedicated to strengthening Japan's role in international networks of policy dialogue and cooperation. Major components of the Center's Web site include Global ThinkNet, a cluster of JCIE-sponsored activities designed to broaden policy research and dialogue on issues pertaining to Japan's relationships with other countries; and CivilNet, which is designed to advance the cause of the nonprofit sector in the Asia Pacific region, with a special emphasis on the development of civil society in Japan. The CivilNet portion of the site is the gateway to information about the Asia Community Trust(ACT), a Japan-based charitable trust committed to financially supporting the grassroots efforts of NGOs involved in sustainable social and economic development across Asia.

MEXICO

Fundacion Mexico Unido (http://www.m3w3.com.mx/MexicoUnido/)

The United Mexico Foundation promotes the appreciation of Mexico's traditional cultural values through grants, mutual benefit programs, and the efforts of volunteers, with the focus on children, teachers, and women. Visitors to the site will find a mission statement in English and Spanish and contact information.

SPAIN

Fundesco (http://www.fundesco.es/)

A nonprofit institution set up by Telefonica de Espana, promoting research into, and use of, telecommunications and information technologies. Spanish and English versions.

SWEDEN

Lycos Sweden (http://www.lycos.se/)

The Swedish-language edition of the popular search engine.

UNITED KINGDOM

Scottish Community Foundation (http://www.caledonian.org.uk/)

A non sectarian, non-political charitable trust in its second year of operation that raises funds around the world to help the work of charities in Scotland.

Charities Aid Foundation (http://www.charitynet.org/index.html)

CAF, a British nonprofit whose aim is to encourage charitable giving in the United Kingdom as well as internationally, sponsors the Charitynet Web site, "a resource centre for the non-profit sector and its contributors." The site includes contact information for thousands of charities and serves as a technical assistance provider to both funders and nonprofits. Of special interest is the site's Corporate Community Involvement Resource Center, an alpha list of links to more than 100 corporate (U.S.-based and multinational) Web sites with charitable giving information.

The Commonwealth Foundation (http://www.oneworld.org/com_fnd/)
Intergovernmental organization supporting exchange, training opportunities, and the sharing of skills, experience, and information in the British non-governmental sector.

UK Fundraising (http://www.fundraising.co.uk/)
Comprehensive resource for charities and nonprofit fundraisers in the UK.

The Wellcome Trust (http://www.wellcome.ac.uk/)
The Trust spends hundreds of millions annually on research in biomedical science and the history of medicine, making it the largest non-governmental source of funds for biomedical research in Europe. Grants are made to researchers in the UK and the Republic of Ireland, and for a variety of purposes, including programmatic, training, travel abroad, and equipment. Loads of information here in two flavors—frames-based and text-only.

NONPROFIT FUNDRAISING—GENERAL

Foundations On-Line (http://www.foundations.org/othersites.html)
Links to various foundations and grantmakers, fundraising software vendors and consultants, not-for-profit attorneys, and related sites.

Internet Prospector (http://w3.uwyo.edu/~prospect/)
Internet Prospector is a unique Web site/service that, every month, gathers and presents the efforts of as many as eight researchers from across the country who "mine" the Internet to report on sites useful to prospect researchers. Organized into a number of broad categories (Access, Archives, Corporations, Ethics, Grants, International, News Online, and People), the site offers a wealth of annotated links to news and information resources, online directories, grantmaker Web sites, and search engines. For those who prefer their information in more manageable chunks, the IP crew publishes a monthly e-newsletter that summarizes their most recent finds.

EDUCATION

The Chronicle of Higher Education (http://chronicle.com/)
Published weekly, the online version of the *Chronicle* is an award-winning source of news and information for college and university faculty and administrators and includes lists of recent gifts and grants to higher education, new software titles, and appointments and promotions in the academic world. "Academe Today," a free online service available to subscribers of the print version of the *Chronicle,* provides daily updates on federal grant opportunities in addition to other features. Limited grant and award deadline information is available to non-subscribers.

Nonprofit Resources, General

GENERAL

About.com Guide to Nonprofit Charitable Organizations (http://nonprofit.about.com/index.htm)
A mini-Web site within the comprehensive About.com site (formerly the Mining Company) that serves as a useful guide to resources and information about nonprofit organizations, foundations, jobs, educational opportunities, and the latest developments in the field. Visitors can search feature archives as well as the entire About.com site, participate in chats, and receive newsletters via e-mail.

The Chronicle of Philanthropy http://philanthropy.com/
Like its biweekly print analog, the *Chronicle of Philanthropy*'s Web site is full of useful information for fundraisers, grantmakers, nonprofit managers, and others.

FundsNet Online Services (http://www.fundsnetservices.com/)
A comprehensive, somewhat randomly organized directory of funders and funding resources on the World Wide Web. Lots of links, some annotated, arranged alphabetically and/or by subject area. Also offers a section, organized by subject area, in Spanish.

Grants Web (http://infoserv.rttonet.psu.edu/gweb.htm#index)
Links to a wide range of grants-related Internet sites and resources. Includes funding opportunities and grants databases.

GuideStar (http://www.guidestar.org)
GuideStar offers a searchable database of nonprofit organizations, philanthropic news, and a resource exchange. Nonprofits can post (for free) classifieds, news, and other information.

HandsNet on the Web (http://www.igc.apc.org/handsnet/)
A national nonprofit organization that promotes information sharing, cross-sector collaboration, and advocacy among individuals and organizations working on a broad range of public interest issues.

Idealist (http://www.idealist.org)
Searchable network of over 17,000 nonprofits from around the world. Includes a global directory of Public Internet Access Points.

IGC's Activism/Internet Resource Center (http://www.igc.org:80/igc/issues/activis/index.html)
A comprehensive directory of links to nonprofit resources on the Internet. The "activist toolkit" includes links to a number of e-zines, Web-based publications, and helpful legislative directories.

Impact Online (http://www.impactonline.org/)
Offers a searchable database of opportunities for volunteers in ten cities, as well as an online newsletter, a directory of nonprofits, volunteering tips, and a "Virtual

Volunteering" program for those who wish to contribute time via e-mail/computer.

Internet Nonprofit Center (http://www.nonprofits.org/)

A project of the Evergreen State Society in Seattle, Washington, the INC is oriented toward providing information to and about nonprofit organizations. Its newly redesigned Web site provides two valuable and popular features—a Nonprofit FAQ database and Nonprofit Locator database—which had previously resided at separate URLs.

INDEPENDENT SECTOR (http://www.indepsec.org/)

INDEPENDENT SECTOR, the D.C.-based coalition of corporate, foundation, and voluntary organization members, has developed a site that reflects its wide-ranging outreach efforts. Standard Web site components (e.g., mission statement, contact information) are complemented by the site's program modules: government relations (with information on pending legislation affecting the sector); management/ethics; research (with a searchable database compiled by the National Center for Charitable Statistics); membership; and public information and education.

IUPUI University Special Collections (http://foyt.iupui.edu/special/)

The Special Collections department at the University Library of Indiana University-Purdue University Indianapolis (IUPUI) encompasses the Manuscript Collections, University Archives, and Rare Books—located in the Ruth Lilly Special Collections and Archives—and the Joseph and Matthew Payton Philanthropic Studies Library (PPSL). (The Manuscript Collections' "Philanthropy" section houses the Foundation Center Historical Foundation Collection, 1896–1994.) Special Collections also compiles and maintains the Philanthropic Studies Index, a reference to literature, primarily periodicals and research reports, on voluntarism, nonprofit organizations, fundraising, and charitable giving.

National Center for Charitable Statistics (http://nccs.urban.org/)

NCCS, a program of the Center on Nonprofits and Philanthropy at the Urban Institute, is the national repository of data on the nonprofit sector in the United States. Newly available at the Center's Web site are fact sheets on the number and types of nonprofits in the U.S. circa 1989, 1992, and 1994; and the number of tax-exempt organizations registered with the IRS, 1989-1995. Also available are individual state profiles (i.e., number and basic financial information) taken from NCCS' *State Nonprofit Almanac 1997;* an introduction to the Center's various databases; examples of various IRS forms (e.g., 990, 990-PF) in Adobe Acrobat (PDF) format; and a nice collection of links to Internet sites of interest.

Nonprofit Outreach Network, Inc.(http://www.norn.org/)

Organizational site dedicated to helping other nonprofit organizations utilize the power of the Internet and World Wide Web to disseminate information.

Nonprofit Prophcts
(http://www.kn.pacbell.com/wired/prophets/prophets.res.topics.html)

A comprehensive index of annotated links to resources for investigating problems/research organized by topic. Categories include the environment/ecology;

global conflict/politics; family issues; homelessness, hunger, and poverty; disasters; and major online news sources.

CHARITY-MONITORING ORGANIZATIONS

National Charities Information Bureau (http://www.give.org/)

The mission of NCIB is "to promote informed giving and charitable integrity, to enable more contributors to make sound giving decisions and . . . to encourage giving to charities that need and merit support." In addition to "Tips for Givers" and a biweekly report on a "Featured Charity," NCIB's Web site has a number of interesting features, including an online reference guide to more than 300 public charities; a help desk; and an interactive order form that can be used to request e-mail updates on new additions to the site.

E-ZINES/NEWSLETTERS/MAILING LISTS

(See Chapter 9 for a full listing of nonprofit journals; see Chapter 10 for more on mailing lists.)

American Philanthropy Review's CharityChannel
(http://charitychannel.com/forums/)

Claiming over 20,000 nonprofit sector subscribers, CharityChannel's 20 online discussion groups cover a variety of topics relevant to fundraising and to the philanthropy community in general. Each forum includes a searchable archive.

Board Café
(http://www.supportcenter.org/publications/board_cafe/boardcafe.html)

A monthly electronic newsletter for members of nonprofit boards published by the Support Center for Nonprofit Management. Each issue includes numerous "Little Ideas," as well as one "Big Idea" that can be applied to your board work.

The Chronicle of Philanthropy (http://philanthropy.com)

Like its biweekly print analog, the *Chronicle of Philanthropy*'s Web site is full of useful information for fundraisers, grantmakers, nonprofit managers, and others. Visitors can also sign up for free e-mail updates about changes at the site as well as breaking news stories.

Internet Prospector (http://w3.uwyo.edu/~prospect/)

Internet Prospector is a unique Web site/service that, every month, gathers and presents the efforts of as many as eight researchers from across the country who "mine" the Internet to report on sites useful to prospect researchers. Organized into a number of broad categories (Access, Archives, Corporations, Ethics, Grants, International, News Online, and People), the site offers a wealth of annotated links to news and information resources, online directories, grantmaker Web sites, and search engines. For those who prefer their information in more manageable chunks, the IP crew publishes a monthly e-newsletter that summarizes their most recent finds.

Philanthropy News Digest (PND)
(http://www.fdncenter.org/pnd/current/index.html)
This free weekly online journal is a Web-based electronic publication of the Foundation Center Online. Content includes a compendium, in digest form, of philanthropy-related articles and features gathered from print and electronic media outlets nationwide. Abstracts summarize the content of each original article, and include complete citations (to assist in locating the complete original article through a library or document delivery service). Many abstracts include "FCnotes," providing the most current financial information on mentioned grantmakers from the Foundation Center's database, and "Other Links" connect readers to Web sites adding in-depth coverage on featured topics. A timely pullout quote of the week begins each journal issue, and there are book, CD-ROM, and philanthropic Web site reviews. The RFP Bulletin, which is updated in conjunction with the weekly posting of PND, provides information on current funding opportunities, and the "Job Corner" offers listings of available positions at U.S. foundations. Subscribe to the free PND Listserv and receive the journal weekly via e-mail Tuesday evenings, at the same time the current issue is posted to the Web. Subscribe at the PND home page (http://fdncenter.org/pnd/current/index.html). The PND archive page also lists the eight most recent issues of the journal as well as providing access to prior issues dating back to 1995. A search engine allows readers to perform keyword searches of all archived issues

Philanthropy News Network (http://www.pj.org/)
A comprehensive source of nonprofit news, information, and links. Features include Philanthropy Links (formerly Ellen's List), the Meta-Index of Nonprofit Organizations, and an e-newsletter. Also a good regional source of nonprofit job openings and listings.

JOB OPPORTUNITIES

ACCESS (http://www.accessjobs.org)
Established just as public use of the Internet was beginning to explode, ACCESS continues to serve as a clearinghouse for employment, internships, volunteering, and career development in the nonprofit sector.

Action Without Borders—Nonprofit Internships
(http://www.idealist.org/IS/intern_search.html)
A one-stop shopping source for internship opportunities around the United States and around the world. Visitors can conduct a keyword search of the database and subscribe to an internship mailing list for daily updates on new postings.

American Philanthropy Review Career Search Online
(http://charitychannel.com/career_search)
Hosting on its "CharityChannel" approximately 20 different discussion forums on various topics of interest to the nonprofit community, the *American Philanthropy Review* also maintains job listings in a database searchable by position title, location, or organization. Each position in the database is also posted to all the discussion lists.

CareerPath.com (http://www.careerpath.com)
Combining the classified sections of several leading newspapers across the U.S. with Web postings from individual employers, this site is one of the hottest destinations for jobseekers with Internet access.

The Chronicle of Higher Education Career Network (http://chronicle.com/jobs/)
A valuable resource for professionals seeking employment in the field of higher education, this site contains job announcements that are updated weekly and offers career-related advice.

The Chronicle of Philanthropy—Job Openings (http://www.philanthropy.com/jobs.dir/jobsmain.htm)
Like its biweekly print analog, the *Chronicle of Philanthropy*'s Web site is full of useful information for fundraisers, grantmakers, nonprofit managers, and others. Job hunters can also benefit from searchable online position listings at a variety of nonprofit organizations in each issue.

Community Career Center (http://www.nonprofitjobs.org/)
The Career Center provides a place for employers and prospective employees in the nonprofit sector to find each other. Employers can post jobs and candidates can submit their credentials. Also provides information on other services available for nonprofit managers.

Idealist—Nonprofit Jobs (http://www.nonprofitjobs.org)
Searchable database of nonprofit jobs around the world. Visitors can search the database, subscribe to a free job e-mail list, and nonprofits can register and post job openings at no charge.

Monster.com (http://monster.com/)
One of the first and biggest online job boards, Monster.com allows jobseekers to search nationwide listings by geographic location, field of interest, company, or keyword, and even contains international listings. In addition, users can receive custom job tracking and store their resumes and cover letters online.

Nonprofit Career Network (http://www.nonprofitcareer.com/)
Created to fill the needs of the nonprofit sector, the Nonprofit Career Network is a "one-stop resource center" for jobseekers looking for employment within a nonprofit organization and for nonprofits seeking qualified candidates. Visitors can post jobs or resumes, search national job listings, consult a nonprofit organization directory and corporate profiles, and find out about job fairs, conferences, and workshops going on around the country. Internships and volunteer information for a handful of nonprofit organizations is also available.

Opportunity NOCs (http://www.opportunitynocs.org)
Jobseekers can conduct free searches through a large database of available nonprofit jobs online, and nonprofit organizations can post help wanted classified ads. Opportunity NOCs also features a nonprofit library and career resource center. This resource for those seeking careers in the arts, health, social services, education and other public sector, social enterprise jobs has been published by the Management Center of San Francisco since 1986.

Philanthropy News Network—Nonprofit Jobs (http://jobs.pj.org)

A comprehensive source of nonprofit news, information, and links. Its Nonprofit Jobs area enables prospective employees to search current listings by region or title, and encourages employers to post announcements of open positions as they become available.

SERVEnet (http://www.servenet.org/)

SERVEnet, an online program of Youth Service America, is designed to encourage more citizens to become actively engaged in their communities by volunteering; to provide volunteer-based nonprofit organizations the best resources available to them in a quick and easy manner; and to match the skills, experience, and enthusiasm of dedicated volunteers with nonprofit organizations who need their participation. The site includes a zip code search feature for national volunteer opportunities.

NEWSGROUP

Nonprofit FAQ (http://www.eskimo.com/~pbarber/npofaq/index.html)

The frequently asked questions file, divided into 21 topics, for the newsgroup soc.org.nonprofit. Categories include start-up and management issues, fundraising, marketing, nonprofit organizations and the Internet, education and training, and general theoretical discussions.

GIVING ONLINE

Animal Funds of America (http://www.animalfunds.org)

A site where donors interested in national animal welfare charities can find one they wish to support. Donations can be made online to any charity via check, credit card, or gift of stock. AFA is a membership organization that reviews and certifies its members annually.

Canadian Government (http://www.communitystorefronts.com)

Created by the government of Canada, this site encourages the use of the Internet for charitable donations.

Charities Today (http://www.charitiestoday.com)

Provides analytical information about charities to potential donors and supporters.

Children's Charities of America (http://www.childrenscharities.org)

Donors will find national children's charities that have been certified and reviewed annually. Donations can be made online.

Conscious Change (http://www.donate.net)

Nonprofit organizations can find assistance with design to generate contributions via the World Wide Web.

Conservation and Preservation Charities of America (http://www.conservenow.org)
A portal site for donors wishing to locate a national environmental charity to support. Donations online are accepted.

Do Unto Others (http://www.duo.org/)
This site features national and international relief and development charities, which are reviewed and certified annually. Donations can be made online via check, credit card, or gift of stock.

Educate America! (http://www.educateamerica.org)
Certified national education charities who can accept donations online.

eGrants (http://www.egrants.org)
Internet and e-commerce tools to help nonprofit groups raise the funds they need.

Entango (http://www.entango.com/)
Entango provides secure online donation Web sites for nonprofit organizations.

etapestry (http://www.etapestry.com/)
Fundraising software that can run over the Internet or on the Intranet.

Give On-Line (http://www.giveonline.org)
An Internet utility for making secure financial contributions to charitable organizations.

GiveToCharity.com (http://www.givetocharity.com/)
This site provides an international secure donation service for nonprofits in an alphabetic and searchable database.

Grant Match (http://www.GrantMatch.com)
GrantMatch.com is a U.S. and Canadian Internet portal for nonprofits to list their desired grants in a central clearinghouse forum.

GreaterGood.Com (http://www.greatergood.com)
Based in Seattle, this company manages shopping villages branded with each nonprofit's own name and graphic identity.

Health and Medical research Charities of America (http://www.hmr.org)
This sites lists certified national charities in the health and medical research fields.

Helping.org (http://www.helping.org/)
A service of the AOL Foundation, Helping.org allows visitors to find volunteer and giving opportunities in their own communities.

Human and Civil Rights Organizations of America (http://www.hcr.org)
A site where donors will find national human rights charities.

icharity.net (http://www.icharity.net)
Offers nonprofit organizations the ability to raise funds online, distribute electronic messages and manage mailing lists.

Independent Charities of America (http://www.independentcharities.org)
Charities are categorized by type of service and reviewed annually. Donations can be made online.

Local Independent Charities of America (http://www.lic.org)
A place for donors to find local charities. Donations can be made online.

Military, Veterans & Patriotic Service Organizations of America (http://www.mvpsoa.org)
Certified national charities with a military emphasis. Donations online.

Nonprofit Online News (http://www.gilbert.org/news/features/feature0021.html)
This article summarizes a conference session which explored methods and techniques for online fundraising.

Nonprofit Zone (http://www.nonprofitzone.com)
Information systems for nonprofit organizations.

Online Fundraising Resources Center (http://www.fund-online.com)
This site has links, classes, articles, and a book on the topic.

RemitNet, Inc. (http://www.remit.net/)
This company provides payment service for electronic commerce.

seeUthere.com (http://www.seeuthere.com)
This company offers special event coordination services. The online service includes the creation of a Web event page and a Web organization page that will create invitations sent though e-mail or direct mail.

signup4U.com (http://www.signup4u.com)
Here you can build customized event forms with the ability to collect donations.

TEN97 (http://www.ten97.com)
TEN97 produces fundraising and promotional events for worthy causes. They enlist the support of celebrities, corporate sponsors, nonprofit organizations, the media, the public, and a group of specialists.

The Hunger Site (http://www.thehungersite.com/)
You may visit this site once a day and donate enough food for one person for one day. Sponsored by several corporations.

Virtual Foundation (http://www.virtualfoundation.org/)
The Virtual foundation is an online philanthropy program that supports grassroots initiatives worldwide.

WeCareToo (http://wecaretoo.com)
This site assists nonprofit organizations by giving them free World Wide Web publicity and help in raising funds.

Women, Children & Family Service Charities (http://www.womenandchildren.org)
Donors can find certified national charities working to improve the lives of women and families. Donations can be made online.

WEB DEVELOPMENT/HOSTING/SOFTWARE

Charity Village (http://www.charityvillage.com/charityvillage/lib8.html)
Created and maintained by the Toronto-based Hilborn Group, publishers of *Canadian Fundraiser,* the excellent Charity Village site offers a number of directories with information on software for nonprofits. The site's "Software" section lists about a dozen products along with brief product descriptions and appropriate contact information. From there, jump to the "Professional Building" section of the site for listings of "products and services especially for the nonprofit community" under such categories as donor management, direct mail, fundraising, and grant writing.

Download.com (http://www.download.com)
Hosted by CNET, this site serves as a virtual warehouse of software and shareware of all kinds. Application types include Business, Education, Games, Home & Personal, Internet, Multimedia & Design Development Tools, Utilities, Drivers, Palm Pilot, Windows CE, and Linux.

Flatiron WebWorks (http://www.flatiron.org/)
A nonprofit organization "dedicated to creating and promoting affordable Internet presence and customized World Wide Web pages for small business and nonprofit organizations." Site offerings include a mission statement, client list, and detailed price sheet.

The Nonprofit Software Index (http://pirate.shu.edu/~kleintwi/tnopsi/tnopsi.html)
Hosted by Seton Hall University's Center for Nonprofit Service, this low-graphics, frames-based site lists software packages in a variety of categories, including fundraising, financial, personnel, and volunteer management. Each entry includes a detailed description of the software, system requirements, and company contact information.

Rockefeller Technology Project (http://www.rffund.org/techproj/index.html)
The Technology Project is a collaboration of funders interested in helping grantees learn about, and effectively use, new communication technology. The Project's no-frills Web site provides examples of several nonprofits organizations' innovative sites, as well as links to resources for activists and organizations providing technical assistance.

Technology Tip Sheets for Nonprofits (http://www.coyotecom.com/tips.html)
Tip sheets to help organizations and individuals reap money-saving, program-enhancing benefits from technology. Most of the material is geared to not-for-profit and public sector organizations.

UK Fundraising (http://www.fundraising.co.uk/software.html)
Howard Lake's highly regarded UK fundraising site has a section on fundraising software that lists more than 20 products. A brief description of the product, links to developers' Web sites, and links to sites with additional information on software for nonprofits are also included.

VOLUNTARISM

Points of Light Foundation (http://www.pointsoflight.org/)
The Washington, D.C.-based foundation was founded in 1990 with a mission to engage more people more effectively in volunteer community service. The Foundation's beautifully designed Web site offers useful information for volunteers, would-be volunteers, and organizations that employ or train volunteers.

Nonprofit Resources, by Program Area

AGING

Administration on Aging (http://www.aoa.dhhs.gov/)
An exhaustive online resource for senior citizens providing a resource directory, statistics on aging, an Eldercare Locator, and links to related sites.

American Association of Retired Persons (http://www.aarp.org)
Helping older Americans achieve lives of independence, dignity and purpose, advances the interests of its members through advocacy efforts on issues related to Medicare, health insurance, housing, consumer rights, Social Security, tax reform, and transportation. AARP has added an entire section devoted to Computers & Technology to its site.

Project on Death in America (http://www.soros.org/death/)
Dedicated to transforming the culture of dying in the United States. Now into its second three-year funding cycle, the project is focusing on several major initiatives while maintaining a commitment to educationand training for health care professionals. The PDIA Web site provides information about project initiatives, press releases and research, and amicus briefs, as well as an excellent annotated list of links to other sites.

SeniorNet (http://www.seniornet.org/)
Provides training for and access to computer technology for older adults (age 50 plus). The site offers online courses on a variety of technology—related topics, virtual roundtable discussion groups, discounts on computer hardware/software, a "Showcase" where members can describe various computer- and online-supported projects and display original digital works of art, and links to sites of interest.

SPRY Foundation (http://www.spry.org/)
Helps older adults plan for a healthy and financially secure future by conducting research and developing education programs. An information-rich site.

ARTS—GENERAL

Americans for the Arts (http://www.artsusa.org/)
A creation of the American Council for the Arts, Americans for the Arts supports the arts and culture nationwide through resource, leadership, and public policy development, information services, and education.

The Artsnet Homepage (http://artsnet.heinz.cmu.edu/)
Offers information on and links to development resources, career services, discussion forums, arts management resources, and art sites on the Internet.

Arts Wire (http://www.artswire.org)
A comprehensive "self-service" database of cultural resources on the Web funded and operated by the New York Foundation for the Arts. Offerings include a conferencing system and a free weekly digest of arts news, exhibits, job openings, and funding opportunities from around the country.

Association for Independent Video and Filmmakers (http://www.aivf.org)
AIVF is a national service organization for independent media, serving as a clearinghouse for information on all aspects of filmmaking. The organization sponsors events nationwide, publishes several books and a monthly trade magazine called *The Independent,* and engages in advocacy efforts. Visitors to the Web site can participate in online discussions, search classified ads, and find out about job openings and internships.

The Estate Project for Artists With AIDS (http://www.artistswithaids.org/)
The Estate Project is part of the Alliance for Arts, a nonprofit arts service organization dedicated to policy research, information services, and advocacy for the arts in New York State. EP's Web site offers information on arts news, artists' resources, specific strategies for arts preservation, lists of grants that have been awarded in the arts, and information and/or links to relevant arts organizations, many of which are national in scope. The site is geared toward the special needs of artists with AIDS, but provides information useful to others involved with the arts communities and information on how to donate to the project.

Intermedia Arts (http://www.intermediaarts.org/)
The mission of Minneapolis-based Intermedia Arts, a nonprofit multidisciplinary art center, is to help "build understanding among people through art" by providing artist support, programs, and community education in the upper Midwest region. Among other features, visitors to the Web site will find an artist opportunities page that offers guidelines for fiscal sponsorship and a list of funding opportunities nationwide.

National Alliance for Media Arts and Culture (http://www.namac.org)
Founded in 1980, NAMAC is a nonprofit association of more than 160 organizations whose purpose is to further the media arts in all its forms: film, video, audio, and interactive. The group's Online Support Center provides a central place where media arts organizations and media makers can connect, locate profiles of the nation's major media arts groups, find current news and useful resources, and share their experiences. The site also provides job and event listings, advocacy information of relevance to the field, and an archive of NAMAC's quarterly newsletter.

National Association of States Arts Agencies (NASAA) (http://www.nasaa-arts.org)
The membership organization of America's state and jurisdictional arts agencies. "Arts Over America" section provides a directory of regional and state arts agencies (listings for each agency include Web site link, mailing address, phone number, and name and e-mail address of the executive director), as well as an annotated list of selected Web sites and links to major funders in the arts.

National Endowment for the Arts (http://arts.endow.gov/)
An elegant site that serves as a comprehensive resource for the arts community and its supporters. The site includes a "gateway" for nonprofits in search of information about grants, government services, regulations, and taxes, and also posts announcements of grants, competitions, awards, arts-related news and interviews, and legislative updates. NEA publications—many of which are free—can be ordered through the site.

National Endowment for the Humanities (NEH) (http://www.neh.gov)
The NEH supports learning in history, literature, philosophy, and other areas of the humanities through its support of research, education, documentaries, museum exhibits, and preservation. The information-packed NEH site is a good place to find out about funding opportunities, cultural events, and publications and exhibits of interest nationwide.

National Gallery of Art (http://www.nga.gov/home.htm)
Created in 1937 for the people of the United States, the National Gallery began with the private art collection of financier and art collector Andrew Mellon, and today houses a growing number of world-class art collections. The NGA's elegant Web site is an outstanding example of the marriage of good design with compelling information. Art scholars can visit the Academic Programs section, which includes the Center for Advanced Study in the Visual Arts and the Conservation Division, to explore available fellowships. A variety of volunteer and internship opportunities are also available.

Nebraska Arts Council (http://www.gps.k12.ne.us/nac_web_site/nac.htm)
The NAC promotes the arts, cultivates resources, and supports excellence in artistic endeavors for all Nebraskans. Still under construction, the NAC Web site provides general information about its grant programs and application requirements; an artists directory; links to other art councils (community and state), state organizations, and art museums on the Web; and contact information.

North Carolina Arts Council (http://www.ncarts.org/)

The mission of the NCAC is to enrich North Carolina's cultural life by supporting the arts. The Council is a catalyst for the development of arts organizations, and awards grants and offers technical guidance statewide. The Council's colorful Web site provides, among other items, program and grant information; links to various arts organizations, government agencies, and regional and national arts partners; andcontact information for 285 North Carolina arts organizations organized by county and by type of art group.

Ohio Arts Council (http://www.oac.ohio.gov/)

Established in 1965 to "foster and encourage the development of the arts and assist the preservation of Ohio's cultural heritage," the OAC funds programs to make arts activities available to the public and also supports Ohio artists through 25 different grant programs. The Council's Web site provides informationabout all OAC programs, complete grant guidelines, an impressive search engine, links to both state and national arts resources, and e-mail links to staff members.

Open Studio: The Arts Online (http://www.openstudio.org/)

A partnership between the D.C.-based Benton Foundation and the National Endowment for the Arts, Open Studio is focused on building community through public service media by providing access to the arts via the Internet, helping local arts groups and artists to become information providers online, and by offering free Internet access to the public at dozens of arts-related institutions around the country.

South Dakota Arts Council
(http://www.state.sd.us/state/executive/deca/sdarts/sdarts.htm)

The SDAC encourages and supports artists, strengthens arts organizations and arts education programs, and increases South Dakotans awareness of the arts. As a state agency of the Department of Education & Cultural Affairs, the Council makes grants to schools, individuals, and arts organizations. Grantseekers will especially appreciate the Council's online program guide, which includes detailed grant application guidelines and a handy glossary of terms.

North Dakota Council on the Arts (http://www.state.nd.us/arts/)

Established in 1967 by the state legislature, the NDCA is responsible for the support and development of the arts and artists in North Dakota. In addition to making grants based on recommendations from artists and arts administrators, the Council administers the Cultural Endowment Fund, through which it secures private and public funds to enhance existing programs. The Council's Web site provides program information, application instructions, grantwriting tips, related arts resource links, and contact information.

CHILDREN, YOUTH, & FAMILIES

Administration for Children and Families (http://www.acf.dhhs.gov/)

Information on the vast array of programs and services offered by this division of DHHS, dedicated to promoting the economic and social well being of families, children, individuals, and communities.

Child Welfare League of America (http://www.cwla.org/)

The Child Welfare League of America is devoted to the well-being of America's children and their families. In addition to action alerts, statistics, and information about work the organization is doing, the CWLA Web site offers links to CWLA member organizations.

Children Now (http://www.childrennow.org/)

This colorful, well-organized site devoted to the nurturing, safety, and rights of children offers news, job listings, volunteer opportunities, and a wealth of related links, many of which lead to funding opportunities in children's issues.

Children, Youth and Family Consortium, University of Minnesota (http://www.cyfc.umn.edu/)

The CWLA Consortium's Electronic Clearinghouse at the University of Minnesota is an electronic bridge to information and resources on children, youth, and families. Among other things, visitors to the site will find a listing of events and activities, an experts' file, a list of CWLA publications, discussion groups, and links to related resources.

Children's Defense Fund (http://www.childrensdefense.org/)

A leader in child advocacy, CDF provides a wealth of information and news about children's issues at its Web site. The site also offers state-by-state statistics, half a dozen electronic mailing lists, and the Parents Resource Network, a collection of links to Web sites that offer parents information on caring for their own children and on getting involved in group efforts to help children in their communities or states.

HandsNet (http://www.handsnet.org)

Membership organization of more than 5,000 public interest and human services organizations. Feature articles and "Action Alerts" provide daily news updates on human services issues and legislation. Recently introduced Web site features include the "Virtual Training Institute" and the "Webclipper" news delivery service.

KidsHealth.org (http://kidshealth.org/)

Created by the medical experts at the Nemours Foundation. Offers up-to-date health and medical information for the parents of children and teens as well as numerous interactive educational features.

Mediascope (http://www.mediascope.org)

The aim of Mediascope is to sensitize researchers, the government sector, and the producers and consumers of film, television, the Internet, video games, and music to social and health issues, particularly as they relate to children and adolescents, and to promote the production of constructive and responsible work without compromising creative freedom. The organization's Web site features sections for parents and educators, journalists, entertainment industry professionals, and public policymakers, researchers, and activists. Its "Media Policy Clearinghouse" resource area includes an extensive list of materials relating to media usage and issues.

National Parent Information Network (http://www.npin.org/respar/texts.html)
The "Resources for Parents" section of the National Parent Information Network offers a huge number of child-related links arranged alphabetically and by subject area. Built for speed, the site is extensive and well organized.

Quest International (http://www.quest.edu/)
Quest International strives to "empower and support adults throughout the world to nurture responsibility and caring in young people where they live, learn, work, and play." The organization serves more than two million children in some 30 countries, and its founder, Rick Little, was recently honored by the Council of Foundations with the 1997 Robert W. Scrivner for creativity and risk-taking in grantmaking. The Quest Web site offers extensive information about the organization itself, a collection of articles on and about community-based service-learning, a workshop calendar, a bulletin board for threaded discussions, and links to dozens of relevant Web sites.

Save the Children (http://www.savethechildren.org/)
Save the Children works in over 35 developing countries around the world to provide education and aid to communities in need. Areas of focus include health and nutrition, education, economic opportunity, and emergencies.

UNICEF (http://www.unicef.org/)
The United Nations Children's Fund (UNICEF) advocates and works for the protection of children's rights by collaborating with other United Nations bodies, governments, and non-governmental organizations (NGOs) to offer community-based services in primary health care, basic education, and sanitation in developing countries. In addition to organizational information, UNICEF's Web site provides a newsline, statistics, and job postings, among other features.

COMMUNITY DEVELOPMENT

Coalition for Healthier Cities and Communities
(http://www.healthycommunities.org/)
The Coalition is a network of hundreds of community partnerships working to improve the health and quality of life of the country's communities. Through its Web site, CHCC is compiling a database of people, organizations, and initiatives dedicated to the sustenance of healthy communities around the nation. The site also offers a library of materials, tools, and resources; press releases and a calendar; and a password-restricted area where visitors can contribute and share stories and lessons with others.

Communities and Community Development Corporations
(http://www.citynet.com/friendship-pgh/cdc/inttop20.html)
Listings of the top 20 U.S. and top 20 international economic development Web sites, plus some 90 other sites that didn't make the top 20 U.S. list, as ranked by students in the University of Pittsburgh's Urban and Regional Planning Program. Includes documentation on procedures and criteria.

Department of Housing and Urban Development (HUD) (http://www.hud.gov)
Information about various types of grants, including community development, affordable housing, and research.

Habitat for Humanity International (http://www.habitat.org)
Habitat for Humanity International aims to eliminate homelessness and poor housing conditions around the world by building and rehabilitating simple, decent houses with the help of volunteer labor and tax-deductible donations of money and materials. Habitat houses are sold to homeowner families at no profit and financed with affordable, no-interest loans. The site features basic information about the organization in 12 languages, a list of local affiliates, testimonials from Habitat volunteers and homeowners, news, and events.

National Congress for Community Economic Development (http://www.ncced.org)
A membership organization of more than 800 community development corporations (CDCs), which support their community's economic development through grants, loans, donations, and income-generating projects. The "Hot Flash" section lists funding opportunities and awards programs, and the "State Associations" section gives contact information for state-based coalitions of CDCs across the nation.

National Low-Income Housing Coalition (http://www.nlihc.org)
The National Low-Income Housing Coalition (NLIHC) seeks to address America's affordable housing crisis through education, organization, and advocacy. Its site contains citizen action alerts, news, publications, recommended reading, events, legislative committees and reports, a state coalition directory, answers to frequently asked questions, and related links. Of special interest is the NLIHC's annually updated *Advocate's Resource Guide*, the full text of which is available online.

NeighborWorks Network (http://www.nw.org/)
The NeighborWorks Network site "promotes the creation of healthy communities through affordable housing, home ownership and investments in neighborhood revitalization through local partnerships of residents, nonprofits, lenders, business community and local government." Comprehensive and well organized, the site includes extensive information about a range of programs, coalitions, and organizations, including the Neighborhood Reinvestment Corp., the Neighborhood Housing Services of America, and the Rural NeighborWorks Alliance. A handy table of contents, site-wide search engine, conference calendar, and library of links organized alphabetically and/or by category round out the features at this very useful site.

ELEMENTARY & SECONDARY EDUCATION

Children's Educational Opportunity Foundation (http://www.ceoamerica.org)
Serves as the national clearinghouse for privately funded school voucher program information, and provides support services for existing programs and funding for new programs through the Children's Scholarship Fund.

Computers 4 Kids (http://www.c4k.org/)
C4K accepts donated computers, refurbishes them, and donates them to schools and organizations in need. The site has a list of needed equipment, grant information, downloadable application forms, and news of upcoming events.

Education Week (http://www.edweek.org/)
A clearinghouse of information about education reform, schools, and the policies that guide them, brought to you by Editorial Projects in Education Inc., the publishers of *Education Week* and the monthly *Teacher Magazine*. Offers online versions of both publications, a Daily News section (access to the best articles written about education in newspapers around the country), a series of special reports, and a great links section.

Eduzone (http://www.eduzone.com/)
Resources, scholarships, grants, education news, and free home pages for teachers and educators.

ERIC: Clearinghouse on Elementary and Early Childhood Education (http://ericeece.org/)
This site out of the University of Illinois at Urbana-Champaign provides access to the Educational Resources Information Center (ERIC), a comprehensive national database of education-related literature administered by the National Library of Education.

LETSNet (http://commtechlab.msu.edu/sites/letsnet)
LETSNet (Learning Exchange for Teachers and Students Through the Internet), a product of the Michigan State University College of Education, helps teachers to effectively harness the World Wide Web's instructive potential in the K–12 classroom. Resources include lesson plans, curriculum standards and guides, pointers to e-mail discussion lists, and many other online materials from teachers who have successfully utilized the Internet as a way to fulfill their teaching objectives.

National Education Association (http://www.nea.org/)
America's oldest and largest organization committed to advancing the cause of public education. Offers links to local and state affiliates and new school-based Web sites, as well as information on school funding and grants for study abroad, pilot programs, TV specials, and education in cyberspace.

National Education Service (http://www.nes.org/)
The NES site includes an online teaching journal and newsletter, information about professional development opportunities, links to education resources, and access to a chat network with peers and authors in the field.

The 21st Century Teachers' Network (http://www.21ct.org/)
Comprising leading education organizations, the 21st Century Teachers' Network is a nationwide initiative designed to encourage teachers to work with their colleagues to develop new skills for using technology in their teaching. The Network's Web site offers news, grant and professional development information, links to research findings, and updates on specific events around the country.

The Well-Connected Educator (http://www.techlearning.com/index2.html)
An interactive publishing forum for the K–12 community where participants can read, write, and talk about educational technology.

THE ENVIRONMENT

Amazing Environmental Organization Web Directory (http://www.webdirectory.com/)
The name says it all. An enormous searchable directory of environmental organizations on the Web.

Conservation Action Network (http://takeaction.worldwildlife.org/)
A new electronic advocacy network created by the World Wildlife Fund. The network disseminates concise information on issues such as endangered species, global warming, forest protection, and fisheries conservation, and uses emerging communications technologies to facilitate communication between concerned individuals and members of Congress, state legislators, newspaper editors, corporations, foreign government leaders, and international agencies.

Earth Pledge Foundation (EPF) (http://www.earthpledge.org)
Promotes the principles and practices of sustainable development in the fields of art, architecture, community development, agriculture, food, tourism, education, and media.

Earth Share of Washington (http://www.esw.org/esw/)
A federation of 66 environmental nonprofits working to conserve and protect the environment internationally, nationally, and locally in Washington State. The user-friendly Earth Share Web site provides eco tips, information on workplace giving and volunteer opportunities, a speakers' bureau, and links to member organizations.

EcoNet (http://www.igc.org/igc/econet/index.html)
Provides news on environmental issues and timely Action Alerts on opportunities for public involvement.

Environmental Defense Fund (http://www.edf.org/)
Founded in 1967 by volunteer conservationists on Long Island, New York, who wanted to ban the pesticide DDT, the EDF today focuses on a broad range of regional, national, and international environmental issues. An inspired—and inspiring—action-oriented site.

Environmental Grantmaker Association (http://www.ega.org/)
A voluntary association of foundations and giving programs concerned with the protection of the natural environment.

Environmental "NewsLink" (http://www.caprep.com/index.htm)
News service with a comprehensive list of links to government agencies. An excellent place to track environmental legislation.

Environmental News Network (http://www.enn.com/)
Daily news updates on all aspects of environmental activity on the Web.

Environmental Protection Agency (http://www.epa.gov)
Includes material on virtually every aspect of U.S. environmental policy and protection.

Goldman Environmental Prize (http://www.goldmanprize.org/)
A small but elegant site devoted to the world's largest prize program honoring grassroots environmentalists. Founded in 1990 by philanthropists Richard and Rhonda Goldman, the Goldman Environmental Prize and $125,000 is awarded annually to an activist from each of the planet's six inhabited continental regions.

National Audubon Society (http://www.audubon.org/)
The Audubon Society is dedicated to conserving and restoring natural ecosystems for the benefit of humanity and the earth's biological diversity.

The Nature Conservancy (http://www.tnc.org/)
The Nature Conservancy operates the largest private system of nature sanctuaries in the world, and preserves threatened species by buying and putting into trust the habitats they need to survive. A great "green" site.

The Wilderness Society (http://www.wilderness.org/)
The Washington, D.C.-based Wilderness Society is dedicated to fostering an American land ethic and to preserving wildlife and natural ecosystems in the U.S., including prime forests, parks, rivers, deserts, and shore lands. The organization's Web site includes hot topics and news, multiple levels of links to original educational content, an annual report, job openings, and links to related sites, broken down by category.

HEALTH

Agency for Health Care Policy and Research (http://www.ahcpr.gov/)
Grantmaking DHHS agency, dedicated to generating and disseminating information that improves the health care system.

Centers for Disease Control and Prevention (http://www.cdc.gov)
Includes comprehensive program and application information for the CDC's many health-related funding opportunities.

Dana Alliance—BrainWeb (http://www.dana.org/brainweb)
A vast collection of links to sites recommended by professionals containing information on various brain diseases and disorders.

Department of Health and Human Services (http://www.os.dhhs.gov/)
The DHHS Web site provides consumer and policy information, searchable databases, employment opportunities, and links to related government agencies.

Health Resources and Services Administration (http://www.hrsa.dhhs.gov/)
An overview of programs, services and grant opportunities from this DHHS agency.

Indian Health Service (http://www.tucson.his.gov/)
Dedicated to raising the health status of American Indians and Alaska Natives, the Web site of this DHHS agency provides information on the agency's activities, and serves as an online resource for Native American communities.

National Institutes of Health (http://www.nih.gov/grants/)
The federal government's principal biomedical research agency and a terrific online resource for NIH grant and fellowship information.

MedWeb (http://www.medweb.emory.edu/MedWeb/)
Created by the folks at Emory University's Health Sciences Center Library, MedWeb is billed as a Biomedical Internet Resource. The site's Grants and Funding area offers a lengthy, well-organized list of links to funding opportunities, newsgroups, libraries, and medical and health organizations, as well as a variety of grantseeking and grantwriting resources. Many of the grantwriting links are also of interest to general grantseekers.

New York State Conference of Local Mental Hygiene Directors (http://www.clmhd.org/)
The New York State Conference of Local Mental Hygiene Directors is a statewide membership organization composed of local mental hygiene directors and commissioners throughout all 57 state counties and the Cityof New York. Its site provides a listing of members and their counties, a page of useful related links, and includes a "members only" section.

Office of Minority Health Resource Center (http://www.omhrc.gov/)
Established in 1985 by the U.S. Department of Health and Human Services, OMH-RC exists to promote improved health among American minority groups. The site contains an impressive amount of easily navigable material, including news releases, publications, and a database of funding and grant resources to help support minority health projects. Visitors can also browse OMH-RC's Funding Resource Guide, which was developed with grantseekers in mind.

HIGHER EDUCATION

American Council on Education (http://www.acenet.edu/)
The ACE site features information about training and programs, international initiatives, women and minorities in education, upcoming events, and products and services. Also offers a clearinghouse on post-secondary education for individuals with disabilities through the HEATH Resource Center.

Beyond Bio 101: The Transformation of Undergraduate Biology (http://www.hhmi.org/BeyondBio101/)
A colorful, well-designed report from the Howard Hughes Medical Institute based on the experiences of many of the 220 colleges and universities that, since 1988,

have been awarded grants by the Institute's Undergraduate Biological Science Education Program. The 88-page report can be read online, or it can be downloaded to your hard drive and read offline.

The College Board (http://www.collegeboard.org)
An association of schools, colleges, universities, and other educational organizations dedicated to putting college within the reach of all students. Web site features include "Scholarship Search," a database of 3,400 award programs, and "College Applications Online," a comprehensive guide to the application process.

College Is Possible (http://www.CollegeIsPossible.org)
Offers guidance about preparing for, choosing, and paying for college. Serves parents, students, and education professionals on behalf of the Coalition of America's Colleges and Universities.

EDUCAUSE (http://www.educause.edu/)
EDUCAUSE, a membership organization created by the merger of Colorado-based CAUSE and the Washington, D.C.-based Educom, focuses on "the management and use of computational, network, and information resources in support of higher education's missions of scholarship, instruction, service, and administration." Visitors to the Web site can learn about award and fellowship opportunities, upcoming conferences, and current issues in the field; post appropriate job openings; download extended excerpts from relevant print publications; and join any of a dozen or so online discussion lists.

The Chronicle of Higher Education (http://chronicle.com)
Published weekly, the online version of the *Chronicle* is an award-winning source of news and information for college and university faculty and administrators and includes lists of recent gifts and grants to higher education, new software titles, and appointments and promotions in the academic world. "Academe Today," a free online service available to subscribers of the print version of the *Chronicle,* provides daily updates on federal grant opportunities in addition to other features. Limited grant and award deadline information is available to non-subscribers.

Federal Information Exchange, Inc.(http://web.fie.com/fedix/)
FEDIX provides free access to information on government research and education grants, programs, contracts, and more. Supported by selected federal agencies under a cooperative agreement forged by the Department of Energy and the Office of Science Education and Technical Information, the FEDIX Web site is comprehensive and easy to use. Visitors can search by audience or subject and can also receive targeted funding opportunities via e-mail. Other features include news updates and a Grants Keyword Thesaurus, which can be downloaded by eligible nonprofit institutions.

FinAid: The Financial Aid Information Page (http://www.finaid.org/)
The most comprehensive collection of links to information about student financial aid on the Web. Includes name and subject indexes as well as links to mailing lists and newsgroups, financial aid calculators, and FastWEB, a free scholarship search service.

International Research & Exchanges Board (http://irex.org)

The International Research & Exchanges Board is a private, nonprofit organization dedicated to promoting advanced field research and professional training programs between the United States and the countries of Central and Eastern Europe, Russia, Ukraine, Central Asia, the Caucasus, Eurasia, China, and comparable contiguous societies. With its traditional base in the university research community, and in collaboration with partners from the policy, corporate, media, and private foundation sectors, IREX sponsors and supports programs of advanced field research, professional training, international conferences, seminars, and comparative analysis.

National Science Foundation (http://www.nsf.gov/)

The NSF is dedicated to fostering science and engineering research and education nationwide. As you'd expect from the agency that step-fathered the Internet into adolescence, the NSF Web site is comprehensive, well organized, and fast. The site includes program and grants and awards info in biology, education, engineering, the geosciences, math and physical sciences, polar research, social and behavioral sciences, and much more.

PEP Directory of Computer Recycling Programs
(http://www.microweb.com/pepsite/Recycle/recycle_index.html)

Sponsored by Children's Software Revue and Custom Computers for Kids, the PEP (Parents, Educators, and Publishers) directory on the Web is a comprehensive guide to organizations that supply low-cost or donated computer equipment to nonprofits and schools. The annotated index is arranged by state, and also includes national and international listings.

Science's Next Wave (http://www.nextwave.sciencemag.org/)

Billed as "an electronic network for the next generation of scientists," the Next Wave site features profiles of and practical career advice for young scientists, as well as links to numerous scientific organizations and funding sources.

HIV/AIDS

Bailey House (http://www.baileyhouse.org/)

A clearinghouse for information on programs and trends in AIDS housing from the second oldest AIDS organization in New York City.

The Body (http://www.thebody.com)

A comprehensive HIV/AIDS information site offering information on giving and getting help, as well as treatment information from experts, policy updates, and bulletin board communities.

CDC HIV/AIDS Resources (http://www.cdcnpin.org/cgi-bin/
WebIC.exe?template=p_result.wi&conffile=pub_cnfg.wi&action=
browse&theme=hiv_aids)

Access to four searchable databases: Resources and Services (19,000+ organizations); AIDS Daily Summary with abstracts of HIV/AIDS-related articles; funding; educational materials. There are FAQ's, free online publication orders, links to a national hotline, and the latest information on clinical trials and treatment programs. Spanish path available.

The Estate Project for Artists With AIDS (http://www.artistswithaids.org/)

The Estate Project is part of the Alliance for Arts, a nonprofit arts service organization dedicated to policy research, information services, and advocacy for the arts in New York State. EP's Web site offers information on arts news, artists' resources, specific strategies for arts preservation, lists of grants that have been awarded in the arts, and information and/or links to relevant arts organizations, many of which are national in scope. The site is geared toward the special needs of artists with AIDS, but provides information useful to others involved with the arts communities and information on how to donate to the project.

Gay Men's Health Crisis (http://www.gmhc.org/)

Founded by volunteers in 1981, Gay Men's Health Crisis offers AIDS education and political advocacy nationwide and direct services to men, women, and children with AIDS, as well as their families, in New York City. GMHC's Web site is divided into eight areas: HIV Alert, What Can You Do?, Who Can You Talk To?, Stopping HIV, Living with HIV or AIDS, AIDS Library, the Press Room, the Geffen Center, and Careers and Internships. Each area summarizes the issues specific to it and directs visitors to practical information.

MINORITIES

Coalition for Asian-American Children and Families (http://www.cacf.org/)

Established to challenge myths, break barriers, and advocate for change, the CAC&F's Web site contains avaluable directory of resources for members of the Asian-American community.

Council of Latino Agencies/Consejo de Agencias Latinas (http://www.consejo.org)

Composed of approximately 30 member organizations in the nation's capital, the CLA promotes awareness of available services geared towards bettering the quality of life in the Latino community.

Foundation Funding Sources for Tribal Libraries (http://www.u.arizona.edu/~ecubbins/founfund.html)

Provides links to funding sources for North American Indian tribal libraries.

Indian Health Service (http://www.ihs.gov/)

Dedicated to raising the health status of American Indians and Alaska Natives, the Web site of this DHHS agency provides information on the agency's activities, and serves as an online resource for Native American communities.

National Association for the Advancement of Colored People (http://www.naacp.org/)

The largest civil rights organization in the United States serving to ensure the political, educational, social, and economic equality of minority group citizens.

Its site includes a description of programs, an online newsletter, and a map to locate local units.

NativeWeb Resource Center (http://www.nativeweb.org/resources)

A comprehensive collection of Web links oriented towards the Native American community and those who want to learn about Native culture.

Office of Minority Health Resource Center (http://www.omhrc.gov/)

Offers a large amount of easily navigable material, including news releases, online publications, grants announcements, a funding resource guide, news of upcoming events and conferences, links to OMH-RC databases for funding opportunities, and organizations and programs.

World Development Board—Multicultural Resources (http://www.wdb.org/multcult.htm)

A comprehensive list of Internet destinations with special sections for every major minority group in the United States.

PUBLIC SAFETY, DISASTER PREPAREDNESS & RELIEF

Disaster Relief.Org (http://www.disasterrelief.org)

An easy-to-navigate clearinghouse for worldwide disaster aid and information.

SCIENCE & TECHNOLOGY

Accent Productions (http://www.cloud9.net/~wmason/accent)

Provides free Web site design services to nonprofit organizations and worthwhile causes operating on a tight budget.

American Association for the Advancement of Science (http://www.aaas.org)

Provides up-to-date information on scientific research and education. Links to science funding organizations in the United States and around the world. Includes access to "Science's Next Wave," an electronic networking resource for the "next generation of scientists," and "GrantsNet," a database of funding opportunities for training in the biological and medical sciences.

Beyond Bio 101: The Transformation of Undergraduate Biology Education (http://www.hhmi.org/BeyondBio101/)

A colorful, well-designed report from the Howard Hughes Medical Institute based on the experiences of many of the 220 colleges and universities that, since 1988, have been awarded grants by the Institute's Undergraduate Biological Science Education Program. The 88-page report can be read online, or it can be downloaded to your hard drive and read offline.

CompuMentor (http://www.compumentor.org)

Works to provide appropriate technical assistance to institutions that serve low-income populations, primarily through a mentor volunteer program. Also provides services in other formats including staff consulting, software distribution (free catalog, "Software Offering," can be ordered online), production and dissemination of written materials, and online support.

ebase (http://www.ebase.org)

Integrated database template designed to help nonprofits effectively manage interactive communications with their members, donors, and citizen activists. Available for downloading free of charge from Desktop Assistance.

iComm (http://www.icomm.ca)

Dedicated to providing free Internet access, Web space, and technical support to nonprofits, charities, and community organizations around the world.

National Science Foundation (http://www.nsf.gov/)

The NSF is dedicated to fostering science and engineering research and education nationwide. As you'd expect from the agency that step-fathered the Internet into adolescence, the NSF Web site is comprehensive, well organized, and fast. The site includes program and grants and awards info in biology, education, engineering, the geosciences, math and physical sciences, polar research, social and behavioral sciences and much more.

OMB's Nonprofits and Technology Project (http://www.ombwatch.org/ombwatch/npt/)

The goal of the Nonprofits and Technology Project is to improve communications linkages within the nonprofit sector to strengthen public policy participation. Through the project, OMB Watch will offer grants to nonprofits in the range of $5,000 to $25,000 to help fund innovative and creative applications of technology to the field of public policy participation.

Rockefeller Technology Project (http://www.techproject.org)

The Technology Project is a collaboration of funders interested in helping grantees learn about, and effectively use, new communication technology. The Project's no-frills Web site provides examples of several nonprofit organizations' innovative Web sites, as well as links to organizations providing technical assistance, activist resources, and technology news.

Science's Next Wave (http://www.nextwave.org/)

Billed as "an electronic network for the next generation of scientists," the Next Wave site features profiles of and practical career advice for young scientists, as well as links to numerous scientific organizations and funding sources.

SeniorNet (http://www.seniornet.org/)

A national nonprofit organization dedicated to building a community of computer-using seniors who use their new skills for their own benefit and to benefit society. The site provides a listing of SeniorNet Learning Centers by state, round table discussions and e-mail pen pals, information on computer discounts, and more.

Technology Tip Sheets for Nonprofits (http://www.coyotecom.com/tips.html)
Tip sheets to help organizations and individuals reap money-saving, program-enhancing benefits from technology. Most of the material is geared to not-for-profit and public sector organizations.

SUBSTANCE ABUSE

The Alcoholic Beverage Medical Research Foundation (http://www.abmrf.org)
Supports research on the effects of alcohol on health, behavior and prevention of alcohol-related problems. The site provides grant guidelines, a journal on the issue, and links to other resources.

Join Together Online (http://www.jointogether.org/)
Join Together Online works to reduce substance abuse and gun violence across the nation. The JTO Web site provides considerable information in the areas of public policy and community action, as well as funding news, grant announcements, foundation profiles, and link to hundreds of related Internet sites.

National Institute on Alcohol Abuse and Alcoholism
(http://www.niaaa.nih.gov/)
One of 18 agencies that comprise the National Institutes of Health, NIAAA supports and conducts biomedical and behavioral research on the causes, consequences, treatment, and prevention of alcoholism and alcohol-related problems.

Phoenix House (http://www.phoenixhouse.org/)
The nation's leading nonprofit drug abuse service organization has developed a comprehensive Web site loaded with news and links to related resources.

PREVLINE: Prevention Online (http://www.health.org/)
Offers electronic access to searchable databases, substance abuse prevention materials that pertain to alcohol, tobacco, and drugs, and funding opportunities.

Substance Abuse and Mental Health Services Administration
(http://www.samhsa.gov)
SAMHSA awards grants in the areas of substance abuse treatment and prevention, collects and analyzes relevant statistics and data, and makes public and private policy recommendations to finance substance-abuse related services. The governmental organization also sponsors "PREVLINE: Prevention Online," a site providing searchable databases and substance abuse prevention materials.

WOMEN & GIRLS

Ann Castle's Home Page (http://www.hamilton.edu/personal/acastle/)
A terrific bibliography and resource list compiled by the woman who researches and edits The Slate 60.

Feminist Internet Gateway (http://www.feminist.org/gateway/master2.html)
A comprehensive list of women's sites.

Institute for Women's Policy Research—Resources for Research on Women's Lives (http://www.iwpr.org/RESOURCE.HTM)
This comprehensive list of national organizations, categorized by subject area, is a valuable resource for information on women's lives and issues.

WomensNet (http://www.igc.org/igc/womensnet)
WomensNet supports women's organizations worldwide by providing and adapting telecommunications technology to enhance their work.

Women's Philanthropy Institute (http://www.women-philanthropy.org/)
The WPI is a nonprofit educational organization that brings together philanthropists and fundraisers to educate, encourage, and empower women as philanthropists.

Women's Wire (http://www.womenswire.com/talk/)
A very good women's news resource.

Philanthropy Resources

GENERAL

American Association of Fund-Raising Counsel (AAFRC) (http://www.aafrc.org)
The Web site of the AAFRC, whose membership is composed of consulting firms that advise nonprofits on fundraising matters, leads visitors to useful data regarding trends in philanthropy and the distribution of the types of sources and recipients of giving.

American Philanthropy Review (http://charitychannel.com/)
A rich site featuring reviews of nonprofit periodicals, books, and software written by nearly 100 volunteers from the fundraising field, e-mail discussion forums (over 20,000 participants), and an online career search feature.

Charities Today (http://www.charitiestoday.com/)
Serving as a guide to individual charity organizations and the field of philanthropy as a whole, the Charities Today site includes its "Encyclopedia of Charities," which profiles individual charity organizations, and its "World of Philanthropy," which contains news and information of general interest to the public and charitable sectors.

The Chronicle of Philanthropy (http://philanthropy.com/)
Like its biweekly print analog, the *Chronicle of Philanthropy*'s Web site is full of useful information for fundraisers, grantmakers, nonprofit managers, and others.

Council on Foundations—Affinity Groups Listing
"Affinity groups" are coalitions of nonprofits focused on a specific area of interest, and tend to be oriented towards grantmakers who want to fund efforts in those particular areas. Some groups primarily engage in networking and information exchange among members, while others emphasize advocacy efforts centered

around an issue or cause within philanthropy and beyond. The Council on Foundations site includes a list of affinity groups in a variety of fields, along with a summary of their work, key staff member contact information, and links to their individual Web sites.

Council on Foundations—Community Foundation Locator (http://int1.cof.org/council/map.html)
This extremely useful tool from the COF provides links to foundations that provide aid to specific communities not only in all 50 states, but also in Australia, Canada, Costa Rica, England, New Zealand, and the Philippines

GuideStar (http://www2.guidestar.org)
GuideStar offers a searchable database of nonprofit organizations, philanthropic news, and a resource exchange. Nonprofits can post (for free) classifieds, news, and other information.

INDEPENDENT SECTOR (http://www.independentsector.org/)
Committed to promoting philanthropy, volunteering, and citizen action, this coalition group brings together nonprofit organizations, foundations, and corporate giving programs. The site gives an overview of IS programs and includes a section on the basics of lobbying by charitable organizations. A media section includes facts and figures on the size and scope of the nonprofit sector and a statistical overview of the IS 1996 survey on giving and volunteering. "Giving Voice to Your Heart" is a starter kit to help guide visitors in their public relations efforts. The IS publications catalog can be searched electronically for material of interest.

Internet Prospector (http://http://w3.uwyo.edu/~prospect)
This nonprofit service to the Prospect Research Community is located on the University of Wyoming server and produced by volunteers nationwide who "mine" the Net for prospect research nuggets for nonprofit fundraisers. You'll find an online newsletter and archives of past issues, a directory of U.S. secretary of state incorporation records, search engine prospecting and test results, and tips for foundation searches.

National Commission on Philanthropy and Civic Renewal (http://www.hudson.org/ncpcr/)
Chaired by former Tennessee governor and Education secretary Lamar Alexander, the National Commission on Philanthropy and Civic Renewal is dedicated to the proposition that "'less from government, more from ourselves' is a sound basis on which to care for the needy and revitalize communities." Among other items, visitors to the NCPCR Web site will find a copy of the Commission's charter; a full text version of the Commission's report, "Giving Better, Giving Smarter: Renewing Philanthropy in America"; and links to research and Web resources that reflect the Commission's agenda.

National Committee for Responsive Philanthropy (http://www.ncrp.org/)
Convinced that, in "the Age of Newt," nonprofit advocacy groups have been targeted by Congress while mainline philanthropic organizations watch from the sidelines, the National Committee for Responsive Philanthropy is committed "to making philanthropy more responsive to socially, economically and politically

disenfranchised people, and to the dynamic needs of increasingly diverse communities nationwide." In addition to information about the Committee's projects and publications, the NCRP Web site offers a selection of reports on such topics as "Philanthropy's Responsibilities to the Public and Private Sectors," "10 Powerful Trends That Are Transforming the Media World," and "Corporate Giving for Racial/Ethnic Populations."

Philanthropy Roundtable (http://www.philanthropyroundtable.org/)

The Philanthropy Roundtable is a national association of grantmakers founded on the principle that "voluntary private action offers the best means of addressing many of society's needs, and that a vibrant private sector is critical to creating the wealth that makes philanthropy possible." The Web site features the journal, Philanthropy, which includes hot relevant topics in the philanthropy field, as well as other Roundtable publications and Roundtable-sponsored conferences and events.

REGIONAL ASSOCIATIONS OF GRANTMAKERS

Forum of Regional Associations of Grantmakers (http://www.rag.org)

The Forum of Regional Associations of Grantmakers (RAGs) is a membership association of 29 of the nation's largest RAGs. RAGs themselves are associations of area grantmakers who collaborate to enhance the effectiveness of private philanthropy in their communities. The Forum assists RAGs in providing local leadership to grantmakers on the issues of public policy, promoting the growth of new philanthropy, technology, and measuring effectiveness and impact. The Forum of RAGs site includes a section that lists contact information for each individual RAG in the United States.

Associated Grantmakers of Massachusetts (http://www.agmconnect.org)

AGM is a statewide association of more than 90 corporate and foundation grantmakers whose mission is to "support and advance effective and responsible philanthropy throughout the Commonwealth." The Association's Janet C.Taylor Library, a Foundation Center Cooperating Collection, maintains an extensive collection of publications that focus on local and national grantmaking, fundraising, and nonprofit management. AGM's Web site offers detailed descriptions of the services it provides to grantmakers and nonprofit organizations in the Bay State, information on events of interest to grantseekers and grantmakers, a catalogue of AGM books and videos for sale, extensive links to online nonprofit and philanthropy resources, and contact information.

Association of Baltimore Area Grantmakers (http://www.rag.org/abag)

ABAG's nice, one-page site provides a list of the grantmakers who are members, information about the Association's regional state initiatives, member services, and contact information. It also includes ABAG's Common Grant Application Format and a list of area grantmakers who currently use the form.

Conference of Southwest Foundations (http://www.rag.org/csf/csfindex.html)

The Dallas-based CSF holds two major meetings yearly and presents several educational programs throughout the year for its member foundations from Texas,

Oklahoma, Colorado, Arizona, New Mexico, and Arkansas. The one-page CSF Web site offers a short history of the Conference, an overview of its services to grantmakers, and a calendar of upcoming Conference-sponsored events.

Connecticut Council for Philanthropy (http://www.ctphilanthropy.org/)

The mission of the CCP, a membership association of the state's grantmaking institutions, is to support and promote effective philanthropy. To that end, CCP's Web site provides information about its services; news from and about its members; a short list of publications it makes available to the public; and a set of links to other philanthropic organizations on the Internet.

Coordinating Council for Foundations (http://www.hartnet.org/~ccf)

The mission of the CCF, a membership association of Hartford-area grantmaking institutions, is to support and promote effective philanthropy. To that end, CCFF's Web site provides information about its services; news from and about its members; a downloadable version of its common grant application form; a short list of publications it makes available to the public; and a set of links to other philanthropic organizations on the Internet.

Council of Michigan Foundations (http://www.novagate.net/~cmf/)

The membership of CMF comprises private, community, and corporate foundations and giving programs in Michigan. The Council assists Michigan grantmakers in their work in order to enhance philanthropy through education, networking, technological assistance, information on philanthropic issues and research, and advocacy. The no-frills CMF site provides information on membership, library services, fax-on-demand service, and grantseeking information.

Delaware Valley Grantmakers (http://www.libertynet.org/dvg/)

DVG, a membership organization comprised of private, trustee-managed, corporate and community foundations, charitable trusts, federated funds, and corporate giving programs, promotes philanthropy in the Delaware Valley area, acts as a clearinghouse of information, and educates grantmakers, recipients of grants, and the general public on the role of private philanthropy in improving the quality of life for all persons. In addition to statements of its mission, purposes, and values, DVG's Web site provides visitors with a listing of members and their telephone numbers, a list of DVG-sponsored publications, and links to member organizations that have established Web sites of their own. Visitors to the site can also download DVG's common grant application form and its common report form.

Donors Forum of Chicago (http://www.donorsforum.org/)

The Donors Forum, an association of Chicago-area grantmaking institutions, promotes effective philanthropy through its educational, collaborative, and networking efforts. The main offering at the Forum's no-frills Web site is an updated 1994 version of its foundation grants database, searchable by foundation name, recipient, beneficiary type, support type, and grant purpose. Search results are displayed in plain-vanilla ASCII, but with approximately 7,500 grants made by some 50 Chicago-area funders, the Forum's database is worth exploring.

Donors Forum of Ohio (http://www.dfo.org/)

An association of foundation and corporate grantmakers whose purpose is to strengthen and enhance philanthropy in Ohio. DFO's Web site offers an overview of its services to grantmakers; a PDF (AdobeAcrobat) version of Ohio: State of Philanthropy, 1998, the Forum's first-ever attempt to chronicle charitable giving in the State; a calendar of meetings for grantmakers; and links to member Web sites and other sites of interest.

Grantmakers of Western Pennsylvania (http://lm.com/~gwp)

An association of grantmaking foundations, corporations, and charitable trusts whose mission is to improve the effectiveness of its members to meet the needs of the people, organizations, and communities of Western Pennsylvania. The GWP Web site offers an overview of the organization's services to grantmakers; separate value and mission statements; basic information about the funding resource library at the Carnegie Library of Pittsburgh (a Foundation Center Cooperating Collection); a downloadable version of GWP's common grant application form; a calendar of upcoming GWP-sponsored events; and contact information.

Indiana Donors Alliance (http://www.indonors.com)

The Indiana Donors Alliance, a membership association serving Indiana's grantmaking community, acts as a catalyst for philanthropic action "by providing information and education, by facilitating communication and collaboration, and by encouraging new opportunities for giving and volunteering." Offerings at its Web site, include a mission statement; a calendar of IDA-sponsored workshops and conferences; information about the *Directory of Indiana Foundations,* its flagship publication; and links to other sites.

Metropolitan Association for Philanthropy (http://www.mapstl.org/)

MAP, a regional association of grantmakers in metropolitan St. Louis, serves both donors and donees to facilitate more effective philanthropy in the St. Louis region. The Association's Web site offers information about the MAP library (a Foundation Center Cooperating Collection) and various MAP programs; listings of MAP members and publications available from the Association; an interactive "Nonprofit Profile Form"; and a number of links to related sites.

Minnesota Council on Foundations (http://www.mcf.org/)

Founded in 1969, the Minnesota Council on Foundations is a regional membership association of more than 155 public, private, and corporate foundations dedicated to strengthening and increasing participation in philanthropy in Minnesota and neighboring states. The MCF Web site is a good starting point for the latest news and information on grantmaking organizations, people, and trends in Minnesota; general grantseeking resources; listings of nonprofit events and grantmaker job opportunities in the region; and links to other online resources. The site also offers a downloadable version of the Minnesota Common Grant Application Form.

Minnesota Council of Nonprofits (http://www.mncn.org/)

The Minnesota Council of Nonprofits, a statewide membership organization that shares information, services, and research in order to educate its members and the community, advocates for "the unique role of nonprofits in society." In keeping with its mission, the Council's Web site is chock-full of useful links and resources, including a weekly Minnesota legislative update; a nonprofit job board and a separate nonprofit bulletin board; and links to a number of searchable databases.

New York Regional Association of Grantmakers (http://nyrag.org/)

NYRAG is a membership organization of private grantmakers in the New York City tri-state area. Its work is guided by three strategic goals: to improve the practice of philanthropy, to increase and diversify philanthropy, and to provide and encourage leadership for collaborative action. NYRAG's Web site includes information about member services, a Peer Networks program, legislative outreach and monitoring, and City Connect, NYRAG's initiative to foster information-sharing and coalition-building among city government, private funders, and the nonprofit community. The site also includes highlights of recent activities, announcements of job openings at member organizations, and information about programs they co-sponsor for nonprofits.

Pacific Northwest Grantmakers Forum (http://www.pngf.org/)

The Pacific Northwest Grantmakers Forum (PNGF), a professional association of grantmakers whose funding extends throughout Alaska, Idaho, Montana, Oregon, and Washington, sponsors conferences, professional development workshops, gatherings of grantmakers who share funding interests, and meetings focused on various societal issues. Its Web site provides resources for grantseekers as well, including its member directory, tips on grantwriting, the Common Grant Application, and links to sites of interest to grantseekers.

Southeastern Council of Foundations (http://www.secf.org/)

The Atlanta-based SECF seeks to advance the expansion and effective stewardship of the Southeast's philanthropic resources on behalf of all citizens. The SECF Web site provides an overview of the Council's services to grantmakers; information about and online application forms for its Peer Assistance Network; online versions of recent issues of *Interchange*, the Council's monthly newsletter; a calendar/announcements section that includes legislative updates and news alerts; and links to member Web sites and other sites of interest.

Southern California Association for Philanthropy (http://www.scap.org/)

Created in 1973, the Southern California Association for Philanthropy (SCAP) is a nonprofit association of private sector grantmakers committed to increasing the impact of philanthropy in Southern California. SCAP currently has more than 120 member organizations, including corporations, family and independent foundations, community foundations, and other private sector funders. In addition to general organizational info, SCAP's Web site provides a listing of its member organizations and member guidelines, a calendar of SCAP-sponsored workshops and meetings (with an online registration option), a directory of local resources for grantseekers, and a dozen or so links to other sites of interest.

Washington Regional Association of Grantmakers (http://www.wag.org/)

An association of grantmakers in and around the District of Columbia. The WRAG web site provides a calendar of upcoming meetings for members, a review of the prior year's activities, announcements of current job openings at its member organizations, the common Grant Application Format, and a list of grantmakers that accept the Format. In addition, the site also includes pages devoted to the Community Development Support Collaborative (a WRAG project) and the Washington AIDS Partnership.

CHAPTER NINE

Online Journals

The range of information that is available on the World Wide Web is vast and growing daily. There are publications that simply post their print contents online, and journals and newsletters created specifically for the Web. You'll find foundation-sponsored publications, government-sponsored journals relating to topics on the federal, state, and local levels, and newsletters researched and written by private companies and individuals. No longer do you have to wait for a monthly print newsletter to arrive in your "snail mail" box, or wait until the first of the month for a favorite magazine to appear on the newsstand. Some of the online publications are posted daily, some bi-weekly, some monthly, some several times a year. (All should indicate how often the content is updated.) More and more frequently these online publications are becoming available as "listservs." This means that if you have an e-mail address, you can subscribe to the publication (directly from the Web site, or by sending your e-mail address to the listed e-mail address of the publication) without logging onto the Internet. (See Chapter 10 for more on joining mailing lists.)

Although some of the publications require a user name and password, most are open for free access. Content ranges from well-researched, in-depth features to abstracts of notable articles and library indexes. Many of the journals include photographs, colorful graphic images, and links to other philanthropy-related Web sites. Some are collections of news notes, grants and program listings, and upcoming events—gathered on a site devoted to user groups, bulletin boards, and online forums.

Below is a listing of some of the philanthropy-related journals now on the Web, with a brief description of each; the "L" next to some of the titles indicate that a listserv is available. Specific pages for some of the sites containing these journals are mentioned in other chapters. Here we try to focus on the online journals themselves.

Journals On The Web, Listed Alphabetically

About.com: Nonprofit Charitable Organizations – L (http://nonprofit.miningco.com/msubmed.htm)

This informative page (formerly "News About Nonprofits") is an "About.com Guide" to "Nonprofit Charitable Organizations," on the New York City-based Mining Company Web site (http://home.miningco.com). The Mining Company is an Internet network in over 200 countries with hundreds of expert topic-specific guides. Subject areas are grouped into 38 channels (including Early Childhood Educators and the Health Care Industry), each led by a guide who has either formal training or life experience in his or her particular subject matter. Each guide "mines" the Internet for pertinent information, highlights sites that are noteworthy, presents regular features, hosts special live chats, manages forums and discussions, maintains bulletins boards, recommends books and videos, publishes newsletters, and responds to e-mail.

The guide for "Nonprofit Charitable Organizations" is Stan Hutton, who has been a nonprofit manager, consultant, grantwriter, and volunteer. Content includes a valuable listing of online publications in the area of philanthropy with brief descriptions and an Archives for recent years, relevant news headlines and features, hand-picked Net Links for exploring the nonprofit sector, job listings (from hotjobs.com), and a site-wide search engine.

Subscribe online for the "Nonprofit Charitable Organizations" newsletter, or for another of the service-wide newsletters. You can also fill out a form to share the site with a friend.

Aris Funding Reports: Creative Arts and Humanities Report, "Subject Headings" (http://www.lib.msu.edu/harris23/grants/ariscart.htm)

This Web newsletter provides subject indexes (divided by "Art," "Humanities," and "General" subjects, with page numbers) of issues of the San Francisco-based *Creative Arts and Humanities Report* (*CAHR*); complete volumes are located at Michigan State University (MSU) Main library, and are available via interlibrary loan. (MSU students , faculty, and staff can access the full text of each issue from the Web site.) *CAHR* provides current information on funding opportunities, programs, and policies in the humanities (i.e., humanistic and social and community applications), as well as creative arts (i.e., performing and visual arts), agency activities, new programs (i.e., private and public). The indexed bi-monthly online issues date back to February 15, 1995. You can subscribe to complete print issues from Aris (415) 558-8133, or request an interlibrary loan.

Ark Online (http://www.arkonline.com)

This site is described as the "online magazine for people who care about animals"; the "ark" in the title is highlighted with graphics of Noah's ark. Weekly content is focused on the Portland, Oregon, area, although news stories are welcomed nationwide. You'll find articles relating to animals in the areas of shelters/adoptions, animal abuse, animal testing, memorials/pet loss, legislative issues (e.g., the 1997 Pet Safety & Protection Act). You'll also find artwork from artists supporting animal welfare issues and links to other animal welfare sites, such as *Animal Alert News* (http://animalalertnews.com).

ArtsWire CURRENT (http://www.artswire.org/Artswire/www/current.html)
Archives of past issues (http://www.artswire.org/Artswire/www/current/archive.html)

This weekly online journal of arts news is a project of ArtsWire, a national computer-based network which serves the arts community; ArtsWire is a program of the New York Foundation for the Arts (with major support provided by the List Foundation), and is on the server of the Master of Arts Management Program of Carnegie Mellon University.

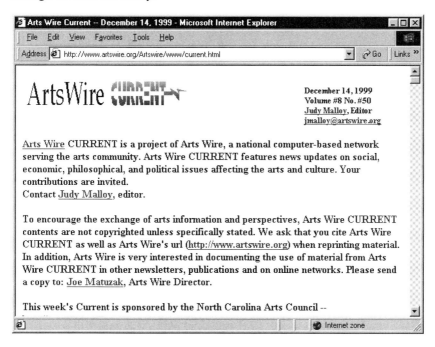

The journal includes news updates on philosophical, political, social, and economic issues which affect the arts and culture. News topics in a 1999 issue ranged from a floor debate on cultural funding in the House to funding opportunities for artists. Also featured is the ArtsWire WebBase, paragraph descriptions of and links to other Web sites of artists and art organizations who are ArtsWire members. And there is a section titled "Conferences, Symposia, Lectures," with descriptions of events, time, date, place, and contact. Other pluses are a "Call For Entries" section—requests for articles to be submitted to other journals, "Funding News"—a searchable database of current funding opportunities for artists and arts groups (with contacts), and "Jobs" (descriptions and contacts). An "Elsewhere on the Net" section updates readers on Internet news relating to the arts and film showings. Free subscription is available via e-mail (instructions available on-site), although membership ($60/year for individuals; $100/year for organizations) in ArtsWire supports the publication of *ArtsWire Current.*

Board Cafe—L (http://www.supportcenter.org/publications)
Subscribe online to this electronic newsletter delivered by e-mail or fax, the second week of each month. The publication is co-published by the National Center for Nonprofit Boards, based in Washington, D.C. (with the mission of strengthening nonprofit organizations by strengthening their boards of directors), and the

Nonprofit Development Center of the Support Center for Nonprofit Management (a consulting and training organization with regional focus and national reach, with offices in San Francisco and San Jose, California). Content includes news, opinions, and information to help board members contribute and get the most out of their board service.

Canadian FundRaiser (http://www.charityvillage.com/charityvillage/cfr.html)

This Toronto-based online "journal of record" for Canada's fundraising professionals actually has space on the server of Charity Village, a large and inclusive Web site targeted to the Canadian nonprofit community (see listing, this chapter). The eight-page bi-weekly print edition of *Canadian FundRaiser* is available through subscription ($197 CDN+GST=$210.79 for one year/24 issues); log on to the Charity Village site and a large banner ad links you to information for subscriptions for small charities at a 54 percent savings (just $97 Canadian + GST). Subscribers also receive special-topic issues and "Careers and Coming Events Bulletins." Content includes "timely, usable fundraising news, ideas, and information" in the areas of corporate giving, postal matters, accountability, planned giving, media, and public relations, as well as a listing of coming events and a "People on the Move" section. All content is directed to those involved with developing and managing fundraising programs. Tips help readers remain competitive among the 70,000+ registered charities in Canada—all seeking a share of the $6 billion expected to be donated by Canadians this year. Articles range from the topics of "Charitable Gaming" to "Volunteer Recruitment." Writers are practitioners, consultants, and academics in the Canadian fundraising community, and contributions are welcome.

Charity Village NewsWeek—L (http://www.charityvillage.com)

This weekly newsletter appears within Charity Village, the charming Ontario, Canadian-based site with colorful icons and a "main street" to meander down. Enjoy the 3,000 pages of news, jobs, information, and resources targeted toward executives, staffers, donors, and volunteers in the nonprofit sector of Canada. *Charity Village NewsWeek* includes a timely in-depth cover story, a section of "Newsbytes" or shorter stories, a weekly "Spotlight" on a nonprofit organization, and calls for proposals. You'll also find a Volunteer Bulletin Board, a "People on the Move" section announcing new job titles in the philanthropic field, "Career Opportunities" detailing available nonprofit jobs, a "What's Your Opinion" section inviting site-user feedback about a recent statement or event relevant to nonprofits, an "Op/Ed Page," a "HelpLink" for in-kind exchanges of goods and services, a "Free Stuff" section (brochures and publications), and a "Coming Events" section listing professional development conferences and seminars.

Village Vibes, the free weekly e-mail newsflash, will keep you up to date on what's new at Charity Village. Also within the Charity Village site, you'll find a Library with entertaining and succinct reviews of books from the nonprofit sector, and a Research Section containing how-to articles in 55 subject areas (ranging from Accountability and Nonprofit Management to Women and Philanthropy) from *Canadian FundRaiser* and *Charity Village NewsWeek.* (Full text reprints of articles are available for a fee; search by subject or key words.) An online bookstore offers philanthropic titles through Amazon.com (most at a 10 percent discount), and there are lists and links to "Online Resources for Nonprofits" and

"Online Publications for Nonprofits," including online discussions and directories. You'll also find reviews of software, videotapes, and audiotapes.

Charity World (http://www.fundraising.co.uk/mags/chworld/chworld.html)

This URL takes you to a Web site that simply describes a two-in-one information service produced by the Surrey, England-based Tolley Publishing Co. Ltd. Tolley publishes the magazines *Charity World* and *Charity World Bulletin,* which provide news, information, and guidance to the charity field on investment, trusteeship, fundraising, and technical subjects.

Chicago Philanthropy (http://www.chicagophilanthropy.com)

This is the "Quarterly Publication For the Midwest Philanthropic Community," based in Chicago, Illinois, available by subscription only. Content focuses on the people and programs of the philanthropic and nonprofit sectors in the greater Chicago area and in the Midwest. It includes news, trends, profiles of area corporate or foundation grantmakers and nonprofits, grant opportunities, people on the move, columns, and articles. Online, you'll find highlights of the current and past issues, with full text of selected articles. Subscribe online.

The Chronicle of Higher Education—L (http://chronicle.com)

This Washington, D.C.-based print publication targeted to university and college faculty members and administrators offers daily online news and information in the field of higher education to subscribers (sign up online or download the order form: $75/year, 49 issues). Articles are organized by category (information technology, publishing, money, government and politics, grants, community colleges, international, opinions and arts). There is also an online information bank (updated weekly) of facts and figures, scholarly books, coming events, grant and fellowship deadlines, in-depth issues, and "people in academe."

The site also offers developments in information technology, links to higher education resources, daily updates on grant opportunities, and job announcements (available every Friday morning before the print publication is mailed). Access the full text of each current issue every Monday morning and search nine years of issues in the archives. You can subscribe from the site to daily e-mail briefings on higher education news. Free to nonsubscribers online: Colloquy, an open forum; job announcements from the previous issue; and selected articles on information technology.

The Chronicle of Philanthropy—L (http://www.philanthropy.com)

This is an abbreviated online version of the bi-weekly print publication the *Chronicle of Philanthropy,* considered the "newspaper of the nonprofit world."

Log onto the Web site and you'll find a tabloid-like newspaper layout, a home page with four-color news photographs, excerpts from stories appearing in the recent print edition of the *Chronicle of Philanthropy,* a search engine which allows you to browse the site by topic (Gifts and Grants, Fundraising, Managing Nonprofit Groups, Technology), "Updates" from the contents of the current issue of the *Chronicle of Philanthropy* or from previous issues. You can also search an archives of articles from the past year or search two years of grant listings that were printed in the *Chronicle.* And, you'll find a listing of upcoming conferences in the field, news of workshops and seminars, and links to other philanthropic Internet sources. Job postings are updated the Monday following each issue date. Contributions for news articles and letters to the editor/opinion pieces are welcome. Subscribe online from the site via e-mail, snail mail, or phone ($67.50/year, 24 issues; $36/six months, 12 issues). And subscribe to the *Chronicle's* free e-mail list to receive updates on what's new in the newspaper and on the site, plus special bulletins when major philanthropic news stories break.

Consumer Information Center (http://www.pueblo.gsa.gov)
This is the Web site of the Consumer Information Center of the U.S. General Services Administration, based in Pueblo, Colorado, and publisher of helpful and service-oriented consumer brochures on everything from safe drinking water to safer sunning. Most relevant to the nonprofit field are links in the "Money" category to publications such as "Establishing a Trust Fund," "Doing Your Taxes," "Inheritance," "Making Chartable Contributions," "Making a Will," and "Planning Your Estate." The site also includes "Highlights of Federal Consumer Publications" in the form of online press releases. A search engine will help you navigate the site (search by keyword or concept). There are also links to the Web sites of other federal agencies, programs, and resources, organized by categories ranging from education and health to money.

Council on Foundations Newsletters
(http://www.cof.org/newsroom/newsletters/index.htm)

The Washington, D.C.-based Council on Foundations (COF) publishes four news-letters, sent free to all members or accessible online. The *Community Foundation Quarterly* offers information for community foundations—news and notes, a "Legal Corner," a calendar, a note from the Council; read the current issue or access issues dating back to Winter 1998. *Council Columns* is a monthly newsletter with coverage of Council news—including trends, conferences, a calendar, a section on new members; read full text of content online, dating back to April 1998. The quarterly *Family Matters* discusses current issues for family foundations, including legal matters, news, a calendar, call-in meetings, conferences; read the current issue online. And *International Dateline* is a quarterly resource for international grantmakers, written by COF's International Programs staff; read the current issue online, and access issue content back to Fall 1997.

Don Kramer's Nonprofit Issues—L (http:/www.nonprofitissues.com)

This bi-monthly print publication based in Dresher, Pennsylvania, is described as "A Newsletter of Nonprofit Law You Need to Know," edited by Don Kramer. Mr. Kramer, a partner in a Philadelphia law firm who has worked with nonprofits of all sizes, is a teacher, writer, publisher, board member, and one of the founders of the Pennsylvania Association of Nonprofit Organizations. Content is targeted to nonprofit executives and their advisors, and includes recent issues and news about federal and state cases, recent regulations and rulings affecting the work of non-profit organizations. Specifically, you'll find coverage of federal tax law issues, employment law, foundation liability, volunteer law, corporate governance, funding rules, charitable giving, insurance, copyright/trademark issues, and a "non-profit bookshelf." Online, you'll find tables of contents and highlights of the cur-rent and past issues, plus reference pages that summarize rules and regulations controlling nonprofit activity. Subscribe online and receive a special six-month rate for first-time subscribers ($64/nonprofit rate, $74/standard rate); yearly rates: $129/nonprofits, $149/standard rate. Also register for "Friday with the Editor," a monthly seminar conference call with the publication's editors ($39/subscribers, $49/nonsubscribers), to discuss topics in the current issue or anything relevant to your organization. You can also subscribe online to an "e-mail update" and mail-ing list, alerting you to site changes, new publications, and other offers.

EnetDigest (Government on the Web)—L (http://www.enetdigest.com)

This site includes a bi-monthly electronic guide to Internet resources worldwide in the areas of the environment, natural resources, and agriculture compiled by Kathy E. Gill, a public affairs professional in the natural resources sector (food, agriculture, forest and paper products) with experience as writer, publications designer, and Webmaster. Each issue offers annotated links to sites divided into the categories of "Agriculture, Environmental and Natural Resources," "General and Government," "Mailing Lists," and "Web Tools." There is an archives of back issues dating from 1996, and the site has a search engine to assist with navigation (search by keywords). Criteria for sites selected for links include content and browser compatibility. There are also links to government agency Web sites in the above-mentioned subject areas, organized by continent. The site is also a member of the Amazon.com associates program, offering books in these subject areas for sale online (most at a 10 percent discount). Subscribe free from a link from the home page.

FastWEB (http://www.fastWEB.com)

Founded in 1995, this site is a wealth of free information for students, parents, and educators researching financial aid and scholarship information for colleges nationwide. The goal is to use the Internet to help students find college scholarships, matching individual backgrounds with eligibility requirements. Content is divided into six channels. Before accessing the database of over 4,000 colleges, students must register in the "fastSEARCH" area. The "fastTOOLS" area offers helpful tools such as a total college cost calculator, a student loan predictor, a loan analyzer. The "fastFOCUS" area presents an archives of tips from nationwide experts on career planning, employment, money management, admissions, scholarships, financial aid. The "fastLIFE" area includes a daily news summary from Reuters News Service, plus weather and horoscope reports. The "fastBREAK" is an area that can be individually designed to include movie trailers and reviews, music downloads, entertainment news, trivia, puzzles, games and tips. And the "fastBUY" area allows students to purchase used or rented text books online (no more waiting in line at the campus bookstore) or choose from 46,000 hardware and software products.

501(c)(3) Monthly Letter (http://www.nishna.net/501c3/)

This monthly newsletter is described as "The best little newsletter in fundraising." Founded in 1980 by Margaret Stewart Carr, it was purchased in 1988 by Jim and Marilyn Kennedy and is today published by Great Oaks Communications Services in Atlantic, Iowa. Subscribe online ($46/year) for the print edition, and receive a password (in six weeks) for the online version (you can also access issues back to January 1997). Content includes articles by leaders in the nonprofit sector, ranging from grants to postal rate savings. Best online feature: "Issue in Progress," which previews features in the upcoming issue as they are completed, prior to the mailing of the entire publication.

Foundation News & Commentary—L (http://www.cof.org/foundationnews)

This bi-monthly print publication, published by the Washington, D.C.-based Council on Foundations (COF), has an electronic presence on the Web site of COF, offering highlights from the Tables of Contents of the complete print issues, dating back to March/April 1995, and links to the complete text of selected articles. You'll also find an Author Index, a Subject Index, as well as a "People" section detailing job changes in the foundation world—compiled from press releases and news media, many previously published in the print version of the publication.

The target audience: trustees and staff of donor organizations, grantseekers, financial advisors, policymakers, anyone interested in the philanthropic field. Editorial content focuses on the grantmaking community and includes round-ups of trends and news in the philanthropic field, and interviews with leaders in the nonprofit area. It also offers news, analysis, commentary and ideas—all conducive to effective grantmaking. Content includes a cover story, features, research and color charts, quick news takes, "Clips" (a round-up of abstracts of news stories grouped by media outlet), a letters section called "Feedback," book reviews; new book and CD-ROM releases; and news from "Affinity Groups" (special interest groups within COF) and RAGs (regional associations of grantmakers). You'll also find a helpful "Government Update" and "Verbatim" (a round-up of timely quotes from foundation executives). There is also a searchable job bank (search by job category, state/region, keyword) with an e-mail notification listserv. Job postings and subscription are free for COF members; subscribe to the print publication (annual subscription, $48) via the phone number posted on the home page. You can e-mail staff members from on the site and fill in an order form for COF books.

Foundation Watch—L (http://www.capitalresearch.org/fw)

This monthly newsletter is published by the Washington, D.C.-based Capital Research Center (CRC), which focuses its studies on reviving the American traditions of charity, philanthropy, and voluntarism, and identifies private alternatives to government welfare programs. Its research is channeled into seven newsletters, including *Foundation Watch,* which monitors the activities of private foundations and analyzes their impact on American society. Specifically, their focus is the cultural activities of the Ford, Rockefeller, and MacArthur Foundations, and the responsibility of donor commitment to the decline of federal funds for the arts and humanities. Online you'll find selected articles (such as "A TV Network of Their Own: How the Great Foundations Established PBS") dating back to March 1996, with links to the Web sites of private foundations. If you contribute $75 to CRC, you'll receive all seven newsletters free for one year (a $150 value). Also sign up online (http://www.capitalresearch.org) for a mailing list and e-mail updates on CRC's work.

A Fund Raiser's Newsletter from Joyaux Associates (http://www.lib.msu.edu/harris23/grants/newsy.htm)

This is a periodic free print bulletin, available by request (subscribe from online form or phone number), published by the Rhode Island-based nonprofit consulting firm Joyaux Associates. It features news on fundraising, management, and nonprofit organization boards and is available on the "Grants and Related Resources" Web site of Michigan State University Library, compiled by Jon Harrison. Published approximately twice a year, the site location also includes an archives linking to issues dating back to October 1993. The Summer 1999 newsletter features abstracts from timely stories on philanthropy from publications ranging from the *Chronicle of Philanthropy* and *American Benefactor* to *Board & Administration* and the *Los Angeles Times.* There are also brief descriptions of books and links to Web sites with volunteerism resources, and advocacy.

Funding Digest (fdOnline Service)—L (http://www.rtipub.demon.co.uk)

This 13-year-old, 60-page United Kingdom monthly digest, available by subscription only and based in Newcastle upon Tyne, is actually considered a fundraising information service—focused on the needs of charities, voluntary organizations, local authorities, other nonprofit bodies, and the agencies and information services who advise them. The editorial content includes new sources of grant aid (or awards) from companies, trusts, government, corporate sponsorships, and individual donors—for local, regional, and national projects throughout the United Kingdom and for United-Kingdom-based organizations overseas. News items detail the total amount of funds available and for what purpose, and list contacts, application closing dates, tips on application preparation and approach. Online, you can download a text or PDF file of a sample issue. Information is organized in the categories of Funding, European News, National Lottery, and Government Watch.

Single-user subscriptions (for small charities and organizations, for internal use) are 120.00 pounds/year. Enhanced Multiple-user subscriptions (for large organizations, information services) are 240.00 pounds/year, and may be received on computer disc or via e-mail, allowing recipients to pass information to users within an organization and edit and reprint the information in their own publications. Multiple-user subscribers receive approximately 50 quarterly New Trusts supplements every three months, with news about newly formed charitable trusts. Subscription forms can be downloaded from the site in PDF format.

The new *fdOnline* Internet service sends fundraising information, updated several times a month, directly to your e-mail box. You receive a password granting access to a research database, and to articles and information with links to other sites, e-mail addresses, and contacts. An index provides funder information and comes with a regularly updated CD-ROM with copies of the *fdOnline* site and relevant software. Download a sample issue of *Funding Digest* in text or PDF format.

The Fundrai$er's Guide Online (http://www.fundraisers-guide.com)

This online publication, based in Fayetville, Arkansas, is published by the Arkansas Support Network, Inc. (http://www.supports.org/), founded in 1988 with the mission of supporting the presence and participation of children and adults with developmental disabilities in the home and community. Described as a fundraising newsletter for small nonprofits, the content includes a collection of ideas and expertise from other nonprofit administrators, following the philosophy that "we're all in this together." Print subscriptions are $32/year; online, you can access a "hot topic" of the month and book-of-the month" (e.g., "cause-related marketing"), articles from the current issue, issues dating back to May 1999, and a message board.

Fund$Raiser Cyberzine—L (http://www.fundsraiser.com)

This three-year-old online monthly cyberzine, based in Belding, Michigan, offers fundraisers "the latest and most complete news and ideas in fundraising." It is available free on the Web; join the listserv online and receive monthly notification of the posting of each new issue, along with notes about what's new on the site.

View each issue's index from the Web site. Content includes an FAQs section about the cyberzine; a publisher's editorial about a timely issue in the field of philanthropy; excerpts of fundraising chatter taken from Usenet newsgroups each month by the publication's editors; basic fundraising features ("Fundraising 101"); news about fundraising raffles; products and software; creative fundraising activities; publications and related Web sites; a Yellow Pages section with links to fundraising resources, consultants, and providers; how-to information from fellow fundraisers on planning fundraisers and organizing a group; and announcements of fundraising events nationwide. The target audience includes small-to-medium nonprofit groups (ranging from booster clubs and sports teams to church groups) seeking to raise funds.

Giving Forum Online (http://www.mcf.org/mcf/forum/index.html)

This free quarterly newspaper is published by the Minnesota Council on Foundations (MCF), a regional association of grantmakers based in Minneapolis. Content includes information and news on Minnesota philanthropy, grantmaking, and research. Online you'll find highlights of the latest issue plus the full text of selected articles (a cover story, community section, a Q&A profile of a foundation executive). Access the complete text of popular past articles, listed by title (reprints available for a fee from MCF), and subscribe from the site.

The Grant Advisor Plus—L (http://grantadvisor.com)

This is the new online subscription service for academic faculty and graduate students ("grant seekers") at U.S. colleges and universities, offering the 16-year-old newsletter *The Grant Advisor,* which reports grant and fellowship opportunities for U.S. institutions of higher education (ranging from federal agencies to foundations) and their faculty.

The Sterling, Virginia-based newsletter is published monthly (except July); each issue reviews 20-25 programs, describing eligibility requirements, criteria, funding amounts, contacts, as well as the "Deadline Memo"—over 300 listings of fellowship and grant opportunities for the coming four months, divided into eight academic divisions (fine arts, humanities, sciences, social sciences, education, international, health-related, unrestricted/other). Listings include links to Web sites offering funding sources and fellowships, and text from the *Federal Register* grant listings and National Science Foundation online documents. As a subscriber you can also access the service's database search engines, searching by funding agency acronym, keywords, academic divisions, program listings, or do an article search. Or, access "The Grant Works," hundreds of essays (in PDF format) with tips for seeking grant money in higher education. Sign up for a free 30-day trial subscription from the Web site, or subscribe from the site to a one-year online subscription, $398; one-year print subscription via first-class mail, $198). Subscribers receive free monthly e-mails alerting them that the new issue has been posted online. IP (Internet Provider) Access allows transparent connection from campus system or Password Access (connection from any computer worldwide).

Grantmakers in Health Bulletin (http://www.gih.org/bulletin/bulletin.htm)

This bi-weekly newsletter is published 24 times a year by Grantmakers in Health (GIH), the Washington, D.C.-based organization with the mission of helping foundations and corporate giving programs improve the nation's health by building the skills, knowledge, and effectiveness of grantmakers in the field of health philanthropy; through its work, it fosters communication and collaboration among grantmakers and others.

The bulletin features breaking news in health philanthropy, including grants, surveys, studies, people, conferences. Once a month, in "Grantmaker Focus," the activities and accomplishments of a "founding partner" are profiled. "Issue Focus" examines a single health issue and its implications for health grantmakers. You can access 1999 issues and past issues back to January 13, 1997, through a searchable archives, and view them all in PDF files. Subscribe to a print edition by phone, fax, or e-mail.

Grants and Related Resources
(http://www.lib.msu.edu/harris23/grants/grants.htm#periodicals)
This invaluable section of the Michigan State University Libraries site
(www.lib.msu.edu) includes a listing of links to grant guides arranged by subject
areas. "Foundation Collection Guides" are listed under "Subject," ranging from
"Grants for Individuals," "Federal Grants Guides," "Grants from Nonprofits,"
"Grantsmanship Techniques," and "Publisher Directories." "Web Resources"
(related to funders, financial aid, fundraising) range from "Funding Newsletters" and "Academic Financial Aid" to "Job Information"; "Prospect Research
Sources"; "Conferences, Meetings, and Workshops"; "Academic Newsletters";
and "Nonprofit Newsletters."

The Grantsmanship Center Magazine
(http://www.tgci.com/publications/magazine.htm)
This quarterly publication (circulation 200,000+) is free to the staffs of nonprofit
and government agencies worldwide (delivered to office addresses) in print format or electronically via the Web. The magazine is on the site of the Los Angeles-
based Grantsmanship Center (TGCI), a 27-year-old source of training and information for the nonprofit sector—in the areas of proposal writing, grantsmanship,
and fundraising.

The magazine offers information on how to plan, manage, staff, and fund the
programs of nonprofit organizations and government agencies. There are also
daily grant announcements and news from the *Federal Register,* daily contract
solicitations from *Commerce Business Daily,* listings of federal grant programs
from the *Catalog of Federal Domestic Assistance,* and an index of links to
grantmaking foundations' Web pages (divided by arts, community, or international foundations; corporate foundations and donors; associations of grantmakers; grantmaking private foundations or public charities). Access articles
from recent issues on Agency Management, Proposal Writing/Grantseeking,
Foundation/Corporate Funding, Government Funding, Fundraising, Nonprofit
Business Ventures, Internet Issues, Consulting, Nonprofit Law, International
Funding.

TGCI has also compiled an archives of *Federal Register* grant announcements,
searchable by subject or by date. You can link to the *Catalog of Federal Domestic
Assistance* and its search engine, and there are grantmaker services and training
areas. There are also links to agencies and funding sources on the state and international levels, and links to community foundations.

HandsNet on the Web—L (http://www.handsnet.org)
This 12-year-old national, nonprofit organization, based in Washington, D.C., has
a mission of "Empowering organizations to integrate effective online communications strategies to strengthen their programs and policies for children, families
and people in need." The site includes news notes and features on timely surveys,
data, legislation, and budget issues ranging from managed care and welfare
reform to HIV prevention and neighborhood preservation. There are also alerts on
pending legislation, with links to pertinent sites and direct e-mail to relevant
sources. The new WebClipper Service ($99/year) sends members daily e-mail
updates on issues they specify, ranging from welfare reform to affordable housing; information comes from searches of Web sites singled out by experts in each
field. Sign up online for a free 30-day trial; you'll also be able to consult the

online *Professional Directory,* publish your new report in the Publications Center for distribution to thousands of online colleges, and check a calendar of upcoming conferences.

Hearts and Minds: Inspiration and Information for Change (http://www.heartsandminds.org)

This New York City-based nonprofit, nonpartisan, and nonsectarian organization has a mission of increasing the positive impact of individuals on the world through volunteering effectively and building effective organizations and individuals. A clearinghouse of information, it motivates people to get involved and offers information on how to make volunteering and donations more effective. The Web site has photos, graphics, and features written "from the heart and mind"—personal accounts and advice on subjects such as the environment, poverty, campaign reform. There are self-help and volunteering links, donating resources, inspirational quotes and ideas, a listing of New York City cultural events, a socially responsible food section, and better health/insurance links. You'll even find a political humor page—with quotes, advertisements, links, a comic strip. There are also links to "creative, free, and low-cost ideas for nonprofits." Also new: a section on the spirit, Web pages in Spanish. Soon to come: video reviews; new print publications; public service advertising campaigns for the homeless, the environment, racism.

Horizon—L (http://www.horizonmag.com)

This is the monthly online magazine of the Washington, D.C.-based Enterprise Foundation, a national nonprofit housing and community development organization. The publication's official mission is to raise awareness and expand discussion about community revitalization, "inciting interest and inspiring action in communities." Amidst the handsome four-color photographs and graphics are features on community programs and organizations and national campaigns, as well as profiles of local heroes and neighborhoods. There are also synopses of new books and reviews of films about community. The "Media Cuts" section includes highlights from recent magazine and newspaper articles offering insight into community building and action needed, and there are links to more relevant resources. Also online: alerts to volunteer opportunities to improve communities nationwide, issue-related polls. Subscribe at the site to free e-mail messages highlighting the features of each new issue. An archives offers abstracts of key features dating from 1997, a letters section invites comments on articles, and a discussion page includes success stories and information from readers. There is a also a site-wide search engine. The site permits you to e-mail an article to a friend, or call up a "printer-friendly version."

Ideas in Action (http://www.idealist.org/newsletter.html)

This electronic newsletter is published every three to four weeks by the Idealist, a global clearinghouse of nonprofit and volunteering resources on the Web, a project of the New York City-based Action Without Borders, which has a mission of sharing ideas to build a world where people live free, dignified, productive lives. The group also trains nonprofits to use the Internet in their work. Newsletter content is targeted toward those who work for or support nonprofit and voluntary organizations. Online you'll find a mixture of news and helpful resources, plus links to ten past issues. Subscribe online for the newsletter, and for daily e-mail job and internship alerts.

Internet Prospector—L (http://w3.uwyo.edu/~prospect)

A free monthly newsletter appears on the site of this five-year-old "Nonprofit Service to the Prospect Research Community," located on the server of the University of Wyoming Web site in Laramie, Wyoming. *Internet Prospector* is produced by volunteers nationwide who mine the Net for prospect research "nuggets" targeted to nonprofit fundraisers/"information miners," who are seeking tools to access corporate, foundation, biographical, international, and online news sources.

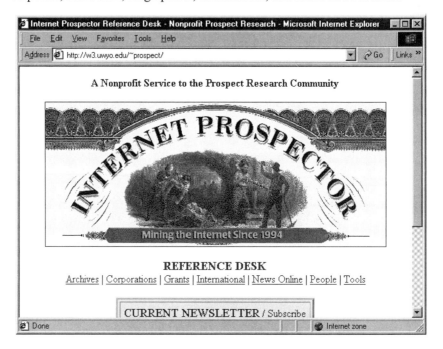

The site is heavy with mining and gold prospecting imagery, sepia-toned and four-color graphics from the Gold Rush era, and mining puns (e.g., burros transport your prospect "nuggets," and the phrases "Dig It!" and "Strike pay dirt" are used repeatedly). The newsletter includes news organized under the headings Corporations, Foundations/Grants (organized by U.S. private funding, grants and sponsored research, nonprofit information links, fundraising news online), International (private and government), People (biographical resources and a Reference Desk), News Online, International (i.e., Asia Guide), Tools (e.g., "The Play Is The Thing," a guide to streaming audio and video players; a salary calculator; maps online), Special Projects (i.e., "Trademarks and Patents"). You can also link to the search engines of major news sites (i.e., ABC News, the *Boston Globe,* the *Miami Herald* in Spanish), people locators, and specialized directories, and there are summaries of the search conventions of many online search engines, and news of related Web sites and centers and their services.

There is also an archives of the past 12 issues of the newsletter. Subscribe to an e-mail version of the newsletter online (each issue is sent the first week of the month) or to PRSPECT-L (a listserv for prospect researchers, based at Bucknell University).

Join Together: Online—L (http://www.jointogether.org)

This site is a Boston-based national resource center and meeting place for communities working together with the goal of reducing substance abuse (e.g., illicit drugs, excessive alcohol, tobacco) and gun violence. It is a project of Boston University School of Public Health, funded by the Robert Wood Johnson and Joyce Foundations. The site offers current news releases and features, with links to related articles and resources. You'll also find a featured photo essay and summaries of research reports. A "News Finder"—site-wide search engines in the areas of Funding, Prevention, Government & Law, Media & Communications, Product/Substance, Public Policy, Community, Treatment, The Problem, Location (State, International)—accesses over 20,000 news items over four years, allowing you to search by keyword or subject. Forums are available for discussing issues, support, or technical access, and for planning strategies and action. You can subscribe from the site to *JTO Direct,* a digest of the most important national news, funding news, and alerts (delivered via e-mail daily or weekly), and can also build "JTO News" into your own Web site. A "Legislative Toolbox" provides rosters of elected officials (on the federal and state level) and Congressional committees, with search engines to locate your representatives and an online form to send direct e-mails. You can also check today's Senate/House schedules, this week's committee schedules, current bill status, a "Key Vote Spotlight," legislative alerts and updates.

Leader to Leader (http://www.josseybass.com/JBJournals/ltl.html)

This is a quarterly report sponsored by the Peter F. Drucker Foundation for Nonprofit Management (http://www.pfdf.org/), with content focusing on management, leadership, and strategy, written by top leaders—executives, management authors, consultants, social thinkers. The editorial offers an insight into exactly what leaders are planning for, the major challenges ahead, and how they are dealing with change. From the site, you can link to the tables of contents to back issues dating to 1996, and view the full text of selected features online. Subscribe online to the print edition ($149/year).

Michigan Nonprofit Inter@ctive—L (http://comnet.org/interactive)

This free five-year-old online newsletter for the nonprofit community in Michigan is located on the Michigan Comnet site. Michigan Comnet is a free online and information-sharing network for individuals and organizations concerned with increasing communication and information sharing within the nonprofit public-service sector. Those actively engaged in public service in the state are urged to register and benefit from guest-access services. There is an archive of past issues dating to September 1996. A monthly print newsletter focuses on one topic and spotlights relevant Web sites on Comnet.

As a Comnet member, you can have your organization's Web site hosted on the Comnet server, add your organization to the *Directory of Organizations* or be listed in the *Directory of Individuals,* access both directories and the *United Way Community Services—Help Book,* post announcements in the "News and Announcements Forum," or host/participate in an e-mail discussion list. The main Comnet site includes links to health care, funding, education, human services, business, government, nonprofit, and political activism resources, as well as to a community calendar, and employment and volunteering opportunities.

News Spotlight (GuideStar) (http://www.guidestar.org/news/)

This section of the GuideStar site is devoted to "News on Charity and Philanthropy," including headlines and text on philanthropists, charitable giving, tax regulations, and nonprofit organizations. Each news item has a headline, date, source, and a link to full text. You can also link to "Nonprofit Management News" (the business side of nonprofits). GuideStar is an initiative of Philanthropic Research Inc., a 501(c)(3) public charity founded in 1994 with the mission of helping to "improve the effectiveness of the nonprofit sector through the collection and presentation of exhaustive information about nonprofit organizations." From the News Spotlight, you can link to profiles of nonprofit organizations, and a "Cartoon Gallery" filled with artwork and humor pertaining to the nonprofit sector.

Nonprofit News *(OMB Watch)*—L
(http://www.ombwatch.org/www/ombw/html/npi.html)

This site, described as "News Analysis on Issues Affecting Nonprofits," is actually part of *OMB Watch,* initiated during the Reagan administration, which actually proposed a rule to "defund the left"—which would have been a large segment of the nonprofit community. *OMB Watch* considers itself to be at the forefront in the fight against proposals limiting nonprofit advocacy rights, and works to increase nonprofit access to communications technology. From the *OMB Watch* site, you can review the latest legislative issues facing nonprofits, and access news on nonprofit advocacy. You can also link to Activist Central, an "On-line Grassroots Mobilization Center and Congressional Directory," and subscribe to the "Nonprofit Advocacy" listserv (for regular e-mail updates).

Nonprofit Online News: News of the Online Nonprofit Community—L
(http://www.gilbert.org/news)

This monthly compilation of "Current News Features" in the nonprofit sector is a program of the Seattle, Washington-based Gilbert Center, with the mission of helping nonprofits communicate successfully, particularly via the Internet. Included are opinions and observations by Michael Gilbert, a nonprofit communication consultant and former nonprofit executive and board member. News features range from announcements of upcoming conferences and featured speakers to notes about interesting features on philanthropic sites, news reports and surveys, books, and links to relevant articles and sites. Soon to come: more customizable news channels from the Gilbert Center, via their soon-to-be launched "Nonportal" service, a noncommercial portal to the nonprofit sector, with interfaces to other online nonprofit sites (following the "Potlatch" vision: "We are each valued in accordance with how much we give away.").

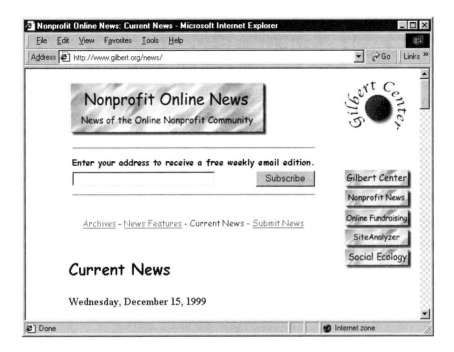

A site archives gives you access to back issues dating to August 1997. And through the feature "Nonprofit Site Analyzer," Gilbert regularly surveys nonprofit Web sites in particular subject areas (e.g., children and youth, disabilities) to determine average age of site, links, content, "vitality," accessibility. News items in the areas of computer-mediated communications, resources for nonprofit organizations, and experiences of nonprofits online are welcome. Enter your address online to receive a free weekly e-mail edition of *Nonprofit Online News,* or join the new *Online Fundraising* mailing list.

Nonprofit World (http://danenet.wicip.org/snpo/newpage2.htm)

This is the four-color print journal of the Madison, Wisconsin-based Society for Nonprofit Organizations (SNO), published since 1983 as a national leadership, management, and governance-focused magazine. Subscription information is available on the SNO site ($79/six issues or free with SNO membership: organizations, $99/year; individuals, $50/year). You will also find a list of headlines for the current issue. Articles from the May 1983 through 1996 issues are available on "Nonprofit World on CD-ROM" ($54, nonmembers; $47, members), or through purchase of back issues ($15/copy). The SNO site also includes an "Index of Articles" (such as "Protecting Your Organization Against Financial Misuse") appearing in *Nonprofit World* since its founding, organized by topics ranging from Accounting to Volunteers. And the site offers a free online "Career Opportunities" section, listed alphabetically by state and job title, and a Resource Center of books, videos, and audio cassettes. SNO also sponsors the Learning Institute, which distributes educational training programs for those in the nonprofit sector via satellite, along with other electronic and print training tools, and the site offers a vendor/contacts area.

The NonProfit Times On-Line (http://www.nptimes.com)

This print newsletter (published 52 times a year), located in Cedar Knolls, New Jersey, presents excerpts from its contents online—"hard-hitting and useful information on the business of managing your nonprofit organization"—first viewed via a newspaper-like home page with highlighted headlines linking to complete nonprofit news features. The target audience is nonprofit executive managers (34,000 subscribers to date).

On the Web, you'll have access to lead stories from the current issue and back issues dating to May 1995, letters to the editor, an online advertiser directory, links to other nonprofit sites, classified ads/job listings, and a "Newsmakers of the Month" section. Although you can view the complete table of contents, the entire issue is available only through print subscription (information and subscription form available on-site); $59/18 issues including a "Direct Marketing Edition"; $98/36 issues; $89/year, Canada and Mexico; $129/year, international. As a subscriber, you also get access to TeamWorks, the publication's Interactive News Forums in areas such as Fundraising, Association Member Development, Volunteerism, Nonprofits and Technology, Current Events, Nonprofit Management, Administrative.

Non-Profit Nuts & Bolts—L (http://www.nutsbolts.com)

This online version of the eight-page monthly print newsletter based in Oviedo, Florida, presented in quick digest format, is directed to nonprofit professionals and includes "how-to management tips to build a better organization." On the Web there is a listing of the complete tables of contents (30–35 features) for current and back issues, with access to the full text of selected articles. There is also an articles index arranged by 12-month periods, by topics, ranging from "Board Relations" and "Technology" to "Volunteer Management." And there are links to online nonprofit publications, resources, and lists of free publications from various nonprofit sources, directories of nonprofit organizations, listservs, newsgroups, and discussion groups, nonprofit job listings and volunteer opportunities nationwide, upcoming conferences and seminars, and product and service providers. Soon to come: "Sample Suite," an area for sharing documents. A "Free Stuff" section includes free resources—reprinted from past issues (brochures, checklists, etc.; readers are invited to add their own). Tips and experiences in the nonprofit management area are welcome in the form of article submissions. "Share Your Stuff" invites readers to respond to a monthly question (i.e., "What creative ways do you use to publish your organization's 'wish list'?"). To gain access to the complete text of each issue, you must subscribe (information available at site, $89/12 issues; special online offer). From the site, nonprofit organizations can also request a free sample issue, and join the free *E-mail Updates* list to receive notices about what's new in the newsletter and on the nonprofit resources list, as well as updates on nonprofit management tips, news releases, site enhancements.

Oneworld—L (http://www.oneworld.org)

This site, accessed from over 120 countries, represents a partnership of over 500 organizations working for human rights and sustainable development by harnessing the democratic potential of the Internet. It is the Internet "arm" of One World Broadcasting Trust, a London-based charity in the United Kingdom launched in 1995 and a registered charity since 1997, with the mission of advancing information, tools, resources, and links about global development issues (from poverty to education) through creative and collaborative media uses.

The site is a "gateway to development issues"—a supersite comprised of separate Web sites created for each development partner. The "News" section functions as a daily newswire; content is focused on global justice and environmental issues, and is updated daily and searchable by topic and country. Also online: facts on global campaigns, job and volunteering opportunities, articles and press releases from partners. The "Think Tank" invites professional debate on global issues such as the banning of landmines; this is the area for academics and experts from colleges from over 100 countries to debate and offer research, policy, and practice in five areas, including ethnicity and conflict. Other site features: photos and paintings illustrating key concerns about global justice, a message board and live chat, live interviews, an open "Speakeasy" forum; "blast," a youth magazine and site authored by "Tiki the Penguin" on how to live without wasting the Earth. In "Spotlight," expert writers worldwide speak out on the "big issues." A One World Radio News Service offers text news summaries or RealAudio highlights (free to members). "Outlooks" offers news of Africa, Europe, Latin America, and South Asia. Individual membership is free to those concerned with global justice; members receive regular e-mail updates from One World partners on key issues. Organizations in the areas of social justice, human rights, or sustainable development pay annual membership fees ranging from $250-$975, based on size; register for a free three-month trial online.

Par' a.digms: The Pursuit of Non-profit Excellence (http://www.libertynet.org/~rhd/Paradigms/Paradigms2)

This is a virtual posting board for the nonprofit community (with graphics resembling a college bulletin board) devoted to nonprofit service. In keeping with the title (defined as "a pattern, example, or model"), the site includes an online forum for announcing and discussing projects and exchanging strategies (anyone can create a topic), and hosts a searchable directory of project models, as well as discussions on issues important to the nonprofit field. Nonprofit groups are encouraged to post news (no fee) about innovative projects; there is a database of posted projects, including funding, budget, contact, success, innovations. Send your comments and suggestions to staff via the direct e-mail forms online.

Philanthropy (http://www.philanthropyroundtable.org)

This is the bi-monthly magazine, located on the site of the Philanthropy Roundtable, a Washington, D.C.-based national association of individual donors, corporate giving representatives, foundation staff and trustees, trust and estate officers. Its founding principle is that voluntary private action presents the best means of addressing many of society's needs. The group also believes that a vibrant private sector is critical to creating the wealth that makes philanthropy possible. Click on "This Month in *Philanthropy*" to review the magazine's content, which includes features, reviews, commentary, grants announcements, staff changes, profiles, tax-related issues. Online you can see the cover of the current print issue and access complete text, as well as the content of past issues dating to Winter 1997. Subscribe to the print edition by phone or fax ($40/year).

Philanthropy in Texas Online (http://www.philanthropyintexas.com)

This monthly online magazine is an electronic extension of the Dallas-based bimonthly print magazine *Philanthropy in Texas,* with the mission of "informing and educating the fundraising executive, development director, volunteer board member, donor, and trust and grant community about charitable giving as it relates to Texas." The online publication features excerpts of features, special event listings, and the print magazine's complete fundraising section. In each issue (and online) there is a Philanthropy Datebook with announcements of upcoming benefits and symposia, organized by city, as well as news and features in the areas of Tax Law, Estate Planning, Capacity Building. Advertising is accepted in the print and online editions. The magazine also sponsors the "Texas Philanthropy Hall of Fame." A downloadable subscription form is available at the site ($57/year).

Philanthropy News Network Online—L (http://www.pj.org/)

This daily Web news service is part of the Philanthropy News Network (PNN), whose mission is "helping people understand, support, and work in the nonprofit world." PNN was established as *Philanthropy Journal* by Todd Cohen, former business editor of *The News & Observer.* Cohen first launched the print publication the *Philanthropy Journal of North Carolina* in 1993, published by the News and Observer Foundation. The name of the print publication was changed to the *Philanthropy Journal* in 1995, and became the Philanthropy News Network three years later, when *The News & Observer* was sold to the Sacramento, California-based McClatchy Newspapers, Inc. (The print publication is no longer published.) PNN also produces *Philanthropy Journal Alert,* a free, twice-weekly electronic newsletter for the nonprofit sector (with notes on fundraising, grants, corporate funding, legal and governmental issues, trends in the areas of technology and nonprofits, volunteering, and foundations, and sneak peeks at new features, national nonprofit job listings, tax news, resources, and surveys of the nonprofit sector). And it produces *Nonprofits & Technology,* a free monthly national print newspaper for nonprofits (with content focusing on technology planning, the benefits of cyberfundraising, virtual volunteering, finding money online, publishing on the Web). It also hosts "Nonprofits & Technology," regular nationwide conferences focusing on how nonprofits are using computers and the Web.

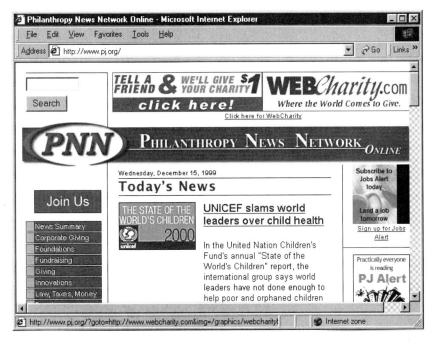

The online journal's home page is designed to resemble the front page of a newspaper, with article abstracts a link away from the full text of each piece. There is a daily national news summary and articles are organized by topic, under the headings Fundraising, Giving, Innovations (about novel programs and unique developments), Law, Taxes & Money, People. An archives in each area allows readers to access back issues dating to February 17, 1997, and links to other non-profit sites. The "WebTalk" sections includes real-time interviews with professionals and authors in the philanthropic field; transcripts are posted to the site after each event. You'll also find a discussion area where experts answer your questions on technology, fundraising, leadership, etc., and there is news about conferences and nonprofit jobs (searchable by region or category). Subscribe online to the free weekly e-mail newsletter *Nonprofit Job Alert,* or post a resume. PNN also presents the North Carolina Philanthropy Award, and sponsors a fellowship program in philanthropy.

Philanthropy News Digest (PND) – L
(http://fdncenter.org/pnd/current/index.html)

This is the free weekly online journal of the Foundation Center Online. Content includes a compendium, in digest form, of philanthropy-related articles and features gathered from print and electronic media outlets nationwide. Abstracts summarize the content of each original article, and include complete citations (to assist in locating the original article through a library or document delivery service). Timely pull-out quotes of the week begin each journal issue, and there are book, CD-ROM, and philanthropic Web site reviews. Also review the "RFP Bulletin," a weekly listing of current funding opportunities offered by foundations and grantmaking organizations, organized by categories ranging from Arts to Youth/Families. You'll also find the "Job Corner," a collection of positions open at domestic U.S. foundations, and the new "NPO Spotlight," highlighting the activities and interests of a different nonprofit organization weekly. Take a weekly quiz to test your knowledge of current philanthropy current events, based on the content of each issue. A PND search engine allows you to search the archives of complete issues, grouped by year and dating back to January 9, 1995, by name or keyword. Individual abstracts can be accessed (and printed) by clicking on a headline in the table of contents. The PND archives page also lists the nine most recent issues of the journal, in chronological order; the full text of each is just a link away. Subscribe to the free PND-L, and receive the journal weekly via e-mail Tuesday evenings (when the new issue is posted online); instructions are available on the PND home page.

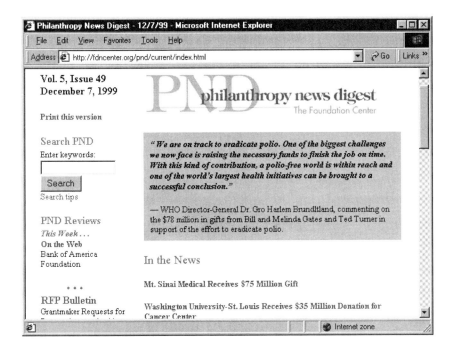

Planned Giving T.O.D.A.Y (http://www.pgtoday.com)

Called "The Practical Newsletter for Gift-Planning Professionals," this monthly, subscriber-based 12-page print newsletter from Edmonton, Washington, launched in 1990, focuses on planned giving issues relevant to nonprofit organizations and those who support them. It is targeted to gift-planning professionals with the goal of "helping them enable others to give generously, prudently, and joyfully," offering "education, information, inspiration, and professional linkage." Its publisher and editor is G. Roger Schoenhals, former foundation director, college teacher, editorial director, and author of seven books on planned giving. The publication now is only available via subscription and first-class mail (to 6,000 readers in the U.S. and Canada), but online you will find the current issue's table of contents, the complete text of selected articles, and each month's "On My Way" column, profiling an individual in the planning giving community. Also online is a "Planned Giving Bookshelf" with brief descriptions (order online) and links to other philanthropic sites. Content of the newsletter includes how-to articles, reports, reviews, and essays; marketing ideas; interviews; case studies; and humorous anecdotes. Subscribe online to the newsletter ($169/12 issues). Subscribers also receive the *PGT Marketplace,* a supplement with news about services, products, job opportunities, and training events for charitable gift planners.

The Planned Giving Web Letter (http://www.recer.com/news/index.htm)

This monthly Maryland-based "cyber-newsletter," produced by Recer Companies, a Maryland-based estate planning/planned giving communications firm specializing in services to financial services organizations and nonprofit organizations, is described as the first Web newsletter targeting the planned giving and estate-planning informational needs of nonprofit executives. The founder and principle officer is Dan Recer, Ph.D., nonprofit executive and consultant for more than 20 years. His motto for the site: "Every Donor: A Potential Planned Giver."

His credo, a favorite of Oliver Wendell Holmes: "Put Not Your Trust in Money, Put Your Money in Trust." The content includes clever features such as "How to Disinherit Your Son-in-Law . . . and Stiff the IRS," and a monthly drawing to win a copy of a selected book relevant to planned giving. The site also includes an archives of complete newsletter issues dating back to August 1996, information about the company's seminars on identifying potential donors within the community, and an offer to design and host Web sites to assist nonprofit organizations in publicizing their planned giving programs for current and future donors.

Prospect Research Online (PRO)—L (http://www.rpbooks.com)

This is an online subscriber-based service for the nonprofit sector that compiles corporate research, major gift announcements, executive biographies, searchable donor/board lists (over 1,500 from nonprofit organizations nationwide, sorted alphabetically, by state, by category), all delivered "PROactively." Complete access to all services is via password (information on nonprofit and corporate rates at site; rates begin at $1,495/user). Content includes the PRO Newsroom, a listing of the week's most important stories assembled from press releases, annual reports, newspapers, newsletters, and Web sites. Under "Corporate Research," there are corporate profiles, histories, and biographies; corporate and foundation reports, press releases, proxy statements, lists of officers and directors, donor and board lists, links to various stock markets and corporate Web sites, contacts and giving guidelines.

The "Virtual Library" includes an archive dating to 1996 with over 7,000 articles on philanthropy. News is culled from over 40 newspapers and newswires, corporate and foundation press releases, and nonprofit Web sites, and includes gift and grant information, and special events (search by topic and geographic area).

Subscribe to the service online and to the "Alumni & Hot Prospect Alerts" listserv (to help target promising donors). Weekly, as a subscriber, you will also receive a "What's New Report" (a weekly e-mail update highlighting new companies and corporate information, with headlines of news in the PRO newsroom), new "Donor and Board" lists, the "Executive Alert" (a summary by state of people changing jobs), new "Corporate Snapshots" (operating information, biographies on private companies and executives), and the "IPO Watch" (a report from the fundraisers' prospective on companies that have gone public, with biographical information about officers, directors, major shareholders).

Pulse! (http://www.allianceonline.org/pulse.html)

This national online San Francisco-based newsletter, described as "The Online Newsletter of the Nonprofit Management Support Community," is delivered via e-mail monthly, providing readers with a timely summary of what's happening in the nonprofit sector and the management support community. Content includes a brief digest of current happenings within the sector, new ideas, conferences, awards, and postings on relevant resources (including books, videos, and Web sites).

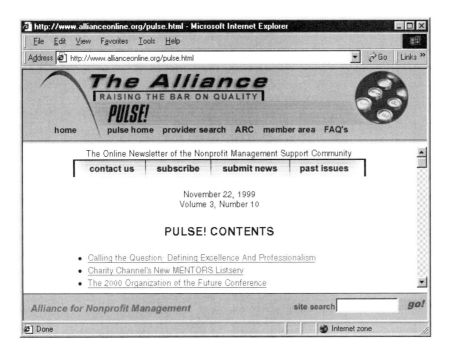

The newsletter is a free service of The Alliance, the Washington, D.C.-based organization resulting from the 1998 merger of the Support Centers of America (a network of nonprofit management support organizations and providers offering training, consulting, and information resources), the Nonprofit Management Association (a "learning community" with the mission of improving leadership and management skills in the nonprofit sector through the development of management-support professionals), and the Alliance for Nonprofit Management (with the mission of developing excellence in nonprofit management). The Alliance's mission is to "challenge and strengthen those who deliver management and governance support services to nonprofit organizations." Subscribe free or submit news from the site. Access complete contents of issues dating back to January 7, 1997, through the Michigan State University Libraries site (http://www.lib.msu.edu/harris23/grants/pulse.htm).

Show Me the Money—L (http://www.4pawsfundraising.com/Show_Me.html)
This monthly online is published by 4 Paws Fundraising, a Waldport, Oregon company that specializes in raising money for animal welfare organizations (most recently for the Free Willy Keiko Foundation, which returned the killer whale "Willy" to the sea). *Show Me the Money* offers fundraising tips for animal nonprofit fundraising. Online you'll find the complete current issue, and back issues dating to April 1999. Content ranges from secrets for direct mail packages and how to profit from a Web site, to the best products to retail and the most effective adoption/foster home ads, how to start a virtual adoption program, and information on where the money is. From the home page, subscribe to a free weekly fundraising listserv, offering "Hot Tips" and ideas.

Village Life News Magazine—L (http://www.villagelife.org/info/contents.html)
This weekly online Ellicott City, Maryland-based publication, launched in 1996, was one of the first Internet-based Christian news magazines. It is located on the site of Village Life, a nonprofit religious communication service created by Kaleidoscope Ministries Ltd., which has a mission of providing "objective clarity and hope to the news and an environment encouraging the open discussion of issues of interest to people of faith."

Magazine contents include the "human side" of daily news, a cover story on a current social issue (such as independence for the developmentally disabled or psychologists testifying in child custody suits), a Christian news archives, features, "Oldies But Goodies" (past news and feature stories), and "Carousel" (music, movie, and video reviews, plus features on travel with a religious focus). You can link to the Disaster News Network (http://www.disasternews.net/), which offers daily updates on U.S. humanitarian responses to disasters, sponsored by Church World Service and 11 other faith-based disaster response organizations (sign up for e-mail updates). The Village Life site also includes a chat forum on Christian music, movies, and values; a search engine for past articles (sorted by subject or keywords); a guestbook; a direct e-mail form; and press releases. And the Volunteer Now database lists local volunteer opportunities in more than 25 locations nationwide. Subscribe online for a free e-mail edition of the "Village Scoop," previewing changes at Village Life. (Listservs send contact information and story ideas to news media representatives and announce new online stories to subscribers.)

Virtual Verve—L (only) (http://www.serviceleader.org/vv/vverve.html)
This free monthly electronic newsletter encourages the development of opportunities to be completed by volunteers who work and report by home or work computers. It is part of the Virtual Volunteering Project (http://www.serviceleader.org/vv/index.html), which has a mission of encouraging and assisting in the development of volunteer activities to be completed off-site, via the Internet, and to help volunteer managers use cyberspace to work with all volunteers. The newsletter's content focuses on the benefits of funding and involving volunteers through the Internet. There are links to Virtual Volunteering's resources, and there is advice for those who want to volunteer virtually. Subscribe online or by e-mail; the electronic newsletter is mailed the first Tuesday of each month (except December).

Volunteer Today—L (http://www.volunteertoday.com)
Described as "The Electronic Gazette for Volunteerism," this monthly online magazine is directed to those interested in volunteer management. The site has witty cartoon graphics relating to volunteering. Features in the current issue are highlighted, with links to full-text articles organized by news, events, recruiting and retention, training, links to "Internet sites you'll love," resources (book reviews), a section of books to order. There's even an "ask the expert" column ("Connie" is a volunteer manager, consultant, trainer). Register on-site and receive an e-mail "heads-up" that there are new postings online. There are also directions on-site for subscribing to *VT News,* an e-mail newsletter that will let you know when each new newsletter is posted.

Who Cares: A Journal of Service and Action—L (http://www.whocares.org)
This free quarterly online journal (actually published five times a year) is produced by Who Cares Inc., a Washington, D.C.-based nonprofit organization by
the same name that "helps people grow, create, and manage organizations for the
benefit of the common good and foster a sense of community among social entrepreneurs nationwide." Described as "A Toolkit for Social Change," editorial is targeted to managers, directors, volunteer coordinators, entrepreneurial social-
change organizations, small-to-medium-sized nonprofit organizations, corporate
foundation representatives, and socially responsible business leaders, with the
goal of developing leadership, management, and entrepreneurial skills. Online
you'll find highlights of the current issue plus the full text of selected articles.
There are also highlights of press releases and past issues dating back to January/
February 1998, as well as internship opportunities. Subscribe online, free; the
long-term goal is to "put *Who Cares* in the hands of everyone."

Whole Earth (http://www.wholeearthmag.com)
This is the current incarnation of the renowned 25-year-old publication founded
by Stewart Brand as the *Whole Earth Catalog* in 1968, once described as the
"Space Age Walden." In 1971, it was published as the *Co-Evolution Quarterly,*
which became the *Whole Earth Review* in 1985. The content now exemplifies
"exploration, curiosity, independence, communication, living fearlessly, principles, tools, and ideas." More specifically, editorial focuses on restoring the local
ecosystem, citizen advocacy, socially responsible investing, tools for practicing
knowledge and creating comments according to your values. There are articles,
book reviews, links to other resources, online discussions/message boards, a marketplace with a special subscription rate ($14/year; subscribe online). Published
by the Point Foundation, the publication, based in San Rafael, California, has a
vision of "what's needed to change ingrained patterns and stale assumptions, take
back your power and put it to use." The magazine also founded "The Well," a
computer teleconferencing system that pioneered community networking online.
A cover shot and selected articles from the current issues can be accessed online
(by title, issue); search all articles by title and issue. Issues of the *Whole Earth
Catalog,* published every six to eight years (one is due for the Millennium), can be
direct-ordered online.

Women's Road Map (http://www.lib.msu.edu/harris23/grants/wrm.htm)
This free bi-monthly "Technical Assistance Newsletter" is published by the Michigan Women's Foundation, founded in 1986 and based in Livonia. Funded by the
Chrysler Corporation Fund, the newsletter is part of the Foundation's Management Assistance Program. Its goal is to improve the management of women's
organizations and enable them to compete more successfully in the nonprofit
world. Content includes articles such as "Thinking Like A Donor" (what they
want, think, expect). Access back issues online dating to February 1991.

CHAPTER TEN

Interactive Services for Grantseekers: Bulletin Boards, Discussion Groups, Mailing Lists

Interactive Communication on the Internet

INTRODUCTION

The rapid growth of the Internet has increased enormously the ability of grant-seekers to share information, advice, and techniques with colleagues through electronic mail, newsgroups, forums, and live chats. Like an ongoing mini-conference, participants can learn efficiently from each other about useful directories, books and software, upcoming conferences and meetings, fundraising strategies, job announcements, and more. Electronic mail is currently the most utilized form of interactive communication on the Internet—it's the most universal Internet function, it's easy to use, and it can be used in a variety of ways. When setting out to discuss interactive communication on the Internet, e-mail quite naturally became the primary focus of this chapter.

Grantseekers can communicate with each other on a wide range of nonprofit-related topics by subscribing to key mailing lists. By simply e-mailing a command to the appropriate e-mail address, a grantseeker may join what is really a discussion group and begin to receive automatically any messages posted to that list, as well as respond to messages and inquiries posted by others. There are also several relevant newsletters to which a grantseeker may subscribe electronically, newsletters that are also delivered via e-mail.

DISCUSSION GROUP BASICS

"Mailing list," "listserv," and "discussion group" are all terms used interchangeably to describe a community of subscribers to an electronic mailing list. Mailing list manager software—such as Listserv (actually a brand name), Listproc, Majordomo, Mailbase, or Mailserv—is used by the list owner to set up and administer the list. Subscribers, on the other hand, only need e-mail access to participate. Every mailing list has two e-mail addresses. There is an administrative address for subscribing, unsubscribing, and other useful commands, which will be described below. (When sending an e-mail to an administrative address, keep in mind that it is only being read by a computer. Although the commands are simple, misspellings and even slight deviations from the prescribed format will prevent your message from getting through correctly.) The second address is the one you use to send messages to the entire list of subscribers. Keep this important distinction between the addresses in mind in order to avoid sending an administrative message to all the other subscribers or posting your comments to a computer that won't receive them. If you wish to communicate directly with the person that manages the mailing list—often referred to as the list owner, list manager, or list administrator—you will need to send your message to that individual's personal e-mail address.

Another important distinction in mailing lists is whether the list is unmoderated or moderated. Unless it is stated otherwise, it is safe to assume that a list is unmoderated. This means that there is no filter on what gets posted to the list. This does not, however, mean that anything goes. Most lists have a ban on advertising and other specific rules as to what constitutes suitable subject matter. Violate these rules and you will likely hear from the list manager. You may also be barraged by negative messages from other subscribers, "flamed" in Internet speak. If the violation is particularly egregious or persistent, the list manager can and will "unsubscribe" you.

If you subscribe to a moderated list, your messages are forwarded to the list owner, who then decides whether or not they will be posted. The moderator also reserves the right to edit your material. The moderator is usually an individual, a volunteer, or a group of volunteers. There are various reasons that lists may be moderated. Often, the list owner wants to keep the discourse tightly focused. Another reason might be that a list with heavy volume is receiving too many administrative commands which are being sent mistakenly to the posting address for all subscribers to read. Subscribers may become annoyed and begin leaving the list as a result. A moderated list will introduce a slight delay in receipt of messages, though rarely more than one day.

FINDING LISTS

There are several ways to find suitable mailing lists. Immediately below are directories of mailing lists of interest to grantseekers. Once you are on a mailing list, you are bound to read about other related lists which may interest you. If you are seeking a list on a specific topic and you are already on a related mailing list, it is a legitimate query to post to the rest of the subscribers. There are also several excellent Internet sites, most of which are searchable, that contain directories of lists. You may use the indexes provided or try terms like fundraising, foundations, nonprofit, or philanthropy as key word searches. The following sites will be helpful:

Liszt Search (http://liszt.com)

Liszt is a mailing-list spider; that is, it queries servers from around the world and compiles the results into a single directory. This method ensures that the data Liszt provides is always up-to-date, since it comes directly from the list servers each week. Liszt's main directory contains over 90,000 mailing lists.

Tile.net (http://www.tile.net)

Tile.net, a Web site by Lyris Technologies, Inc., accepts paid advertisements and describes itself as a "Comprehensive Internet Reference to Discussion Lists, Newsgroups, FTP Sites, Computer Product Vendors, and Internet Service and Web Design Companies."

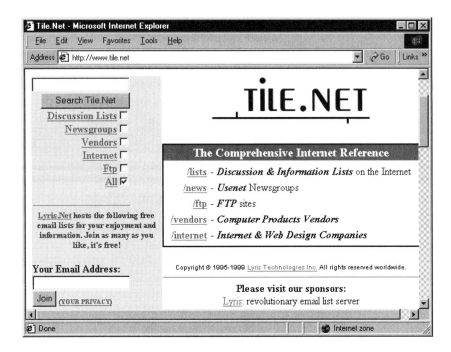

Inter-Links Internet Access
(http://www.alabanza.com/kabacoff/Inter-Links/listserv.html)
This Web area is an Internet navigator, resource locator, and tutorial provided as a public service by Robert K. Kabacoff. It contains a wide range of reference information, including a search engine for discussion lists. The help files found in the mailing lists at this Web site are especially useful, covering such topics as: "What is a Mailing List," "Subscribing, Unsubscribing, and Posting," and "Other Mailing List Commands."

Publicly Accessible Mailing Lists (http://www.Neosoft.com/internet/paml)

The resources section of the Neosoft homepage, developed by Stephanie and Peter DaSilva, contains a search engine and links to many useful mailing list sites. Click on the index and then in the index screen that comes up, click on "Subjects" for an alphabetical index of categories of mailing lists.

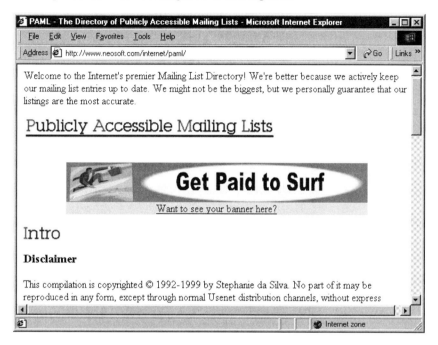

There are also several excellent Web sites that contain lists of discussion groups of interest to the nonprofit sector. These lists include the name of the list, a brief description, and the subscription and posting addresses for the list. One example is a page on a Web site operated by Jon Harrison, the Foundation Center Cooperating Collection Supervisor at Michigan State University. His list can be found at http://www.lib.msu.edu/harris23/grants/maillist.htm.

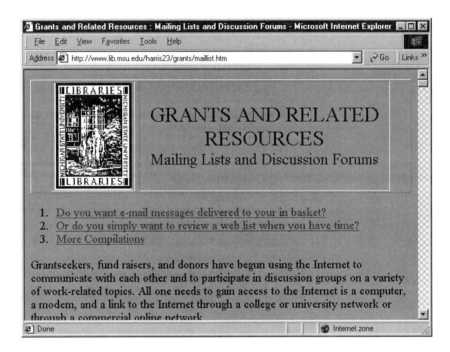

Charity Village, a web site for Canadian Charities and nonprofits, contains a valuable list of discussion groups among its 1,000+ pages of information. The list can be found at (http://www.charityvillage.com/charityvillage/stand.html#list).

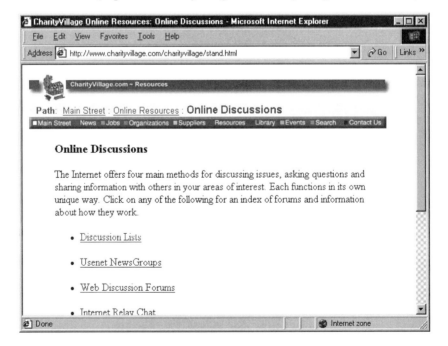

Once you find a specific list of interest to you, you may want to get more information about it to determine if it is really what you want. In most cases you may request information directly from the list by e-mailing the following message to the list administrative address: "info <list name>" (without the brackets or quotes). Leave the subject of your message blank. In addition, many lists have an archive of previous postings, sometimes searchable, in a Gopher file on the Internet or at a World Wide Web site. You may look in the archives to determine the level of activity and the type of discussions that have come before. Finally, you may subscribe to the list and view the messages that you receive to determine if the subject matter is relevant to you. Keep in mind that a subscription address can change.

HOW TO SUBSCRIBE

To subscribe to a list, send an e-mail to the list subscription address (administrative address) and leave the subject or "re:" line blank. In the body of the message, type: "subscribe <list name>" (without the brackets or quotes). Some lists require that you include your first and last name after the list name. The subscribe command varies slightly depending on the mailing list management software used by the list owner. Shortly after sending your subscription request, you will receive an e-mail acknowledging your subscription. You should read the instructions that you receive and *print out and save them in a paper file.* The acknowledgment normally includes a description of the list, appropriate subject matter, rules and additional commands that you may wish to use in the future—especially "unsubscribe."

SENDING A MESSAGE: DO'S AND DON'T'S

Before long you will be ready to post a message. But wait, don't be in a hurry! "Lurk" for a week or so, i.e., listen in for a while. One of the most valuable aspects of discussion groups is the fact that you have time to consider other postings and your own comments. Therefore, try to focus on sending concise, productive, and relevant comments or questions, not emotional ones. Be sure that your contribution is on target. Consider going to the list's archive, if it exists, to see if your topic has already been covered. Long-time subscribers can become impatient with novices that ask questions that have been repeated over and over in the past. If you are in a hurry, apologize up front before posting what could be an "old" topic and ask for advice about where to find the prior discussion.

Before responding to any posting to a list, think about whether you want to respond to an individual directly or post your response to the whole list. Hitting the reply button will normally mean that you are responding to the entire list. A typical mistake that a beginner makes is posting a private comment to the whole list. This can prove embarrassing. You can avoid embarrassment by making it a rule to keep personal comments or confidential information out of any e-mail. It may be unwise, for example, to send your resume over the Internet. Job announcements are frequently posted to mailing lists. We've seen people attach their resume and respond with the reply button, sending it to the entire list.

You should name the subject of your message carefully. Some lists have specific subject categories that you should use. These will be included in the initial instructions you receive upon acknowledgment of your subscription. Follow the rules. It will make it a lot easier for other subscribers to delete unwanted messages.

There is also the issue of advertising. Most lists specifically forbid advertising, although some lists actually invite it. Don't delude yourself into thinking that you are simply supplying information to a community of subscribers. An advertisement will always be recognized for what it is. If you are still unsure about how your communication will be construed, you can e-mail a message to the list owner and ask if your message would be acceptable.

A few other tips that will help you to be a productive member of your new list community include:

If you ask a broad question, invite other subscribers to send their messages directly to you and offer to provide feedback to the list in the form of a summary.

Be careful with humor, subjective comments, insults, etc. It is very easy to be misunderstood in this medium. You also risk being unsubscribed or censured by the other subscribers.

Don't post irrelevant, whimsical, pick-me-ups. Many subscribers will resent receiving unwanted messages in their e-mail box.

SOME LISTS TO INVESTIGATE

Grantseekers on the Web should not miss the American Philanthropy Review's Web Site at http://www/charitychannel.com.

CharityChannel™ features an impressive collection of discussion lists for non-profit professionals. Currently there are over 25,000 participants using the lists. With the help of many volunteers, Stephen D. Nill has developed and promoted these forums with clear instructions on how to use the lists, subscribe, unsubscribe, receive in digest forms and access archives. At Charity Channel™, you can simply click on the discussion forums link for a table of available groups. You may subscribe directly from the Web site or via standard e-mail commands.

To subscribe from the Web you must register first, and it's a good idea to choose the option to automatically save your password.

When you subscribe to a list from the Web site, an e-mail will be sent to you asking you to reply by e-mail or click on the URL in the message in order to verify the subscription (this will prevent others from using your e-mail address to subscribe). You will receive a message indicating that your subscription has been accepted. From that point onward, messages posted to the list will arrive in your e-mail box. You don't need to go to the Web site to participate in the forum. You may want to visit the Web site, however, for easy access to any of the lists archives or to subscribe to other lists.

Several of the CharityChannel™ lists are described below along with a compilation of other mailing lists of interest to development professionals, prospect researchers, and grantseekers. Each example includes the name of the mailing list, a brief summary, subscription and posting addresses, archive address (if one exists), and other useful information, where available, such as whether the list is moderated and the volume of its "traffic." When subscribing to a mailing list, always leave the "subject" line blank. Remember, too, that a subscription address can change.

ALUMNI-L

This unmoderated list is dedicated to the interchange of ideas and information among alumni relations professionals at colleges, universities, and independent schools. Topics include alumni education, working with boards and volunteers, alumni training and workshop programs, activities of the Council for Advancement and Support of Education, cooperation with one's development office, and more. Traffic is fairly heavy on this list. It is not unusual to receive five to ten messages per day.

To subscribe to Alumni-L, just send an e-mail message to listserv@ brownvm.brown.edu. In the body of your message type: subscribe alumni-l <firstname lastname>. To post a message to the list, send your e-mail to alumni-l@brownvm.brown.edu. The list managers are Paul Chewning (chewning@ ns.case.org) and Andy Shaindlin (shain@umich.edu). The address of the archive is http://www.pacificgroup.com/html/listserv.htm.

CFRNET

Cfrnet is an unmoderated discussion group for people involved in building partnerships among educational institutions and corporations and foundations. Issues may include solicitation strategies, stewardship programs, proposal writing, prospect tracking, corporate giving, gift-in-kind programs, and student recruitment by companies.

To subscribe to Cfrnet, send an e-mail message to cfrnet-request@ medicine.wust1.edu. In the body of your message type: subscribe CFRNET <firstname lastname>. To post a message to the list, send your e-mail to cfrnet@ medicine.wust1.edu. The list manager is Patricia Gregory (gregoryp@msnotes.@ medicine.wust1.edu). The address of the archive is http://www.pacificgroup.com/ html/cfrnet.

CHARITYTALK

This popular list was established in 1994 as TALK-AMPHILREV, for those who are interested in hearing from people outside of their particular area. It invites people from almost every segment of the nonprofit sector to participate. Fund development professionals, nonprofit CEOs, college presidents, consultants, accountants, and academics are all encouraged to contribute their expertise to a wide range of topics. It is not unusual to receive five to ten messages in a single day from this list. Brief, "tasteful" commercial messages are permitted.

To subscribe to Charitytalk, just send an e-mail message to listserv@ charitychannel.com. In the body of your message type: subscribe charitytalk <your name>. To post a message to the list, send your e-mail to charitytalk@ charitychannel.com.

The list is administered by CharityChannel™. You may also subscribe or access archives on the Web at http:www.charitychannel.com/forums.

CONSULTANTS

Originally established in 1997, as consult-l, Consultants list is now among the CharityChannel™ forums. It's audience has remained the same—fundraising consultants or those people interested in consulting. The purpose of the list is to discuss issues related to philanthropy and its associated services. Points of discussion may include such business aspects of consulting to nonprofit organizations as marketing, client/consultant relations, fees and collection, ethics, strategies, and resources.

To subscribe to Consultants, just send an e-mail message to listserv@ charitychannel.com. In the body of your message type: subscribe consultants. To post a message to the list, just send your e-mail to consultants@ charitychannel.com.

The list is administered by CharityChannel. You may also subscribe or access archives on the Web at http:www.charitychannel.com/forums.

FUNDLIST

This list is primarily for fundraising professionals with an emphasis on education. Fundlist is heavily used, with a wide range of topics in the areas of annual campaigns, planned giving, development, ethics, policy/procedures, and many others. The list often generates 20–25 messages per day.

To subscribe to Fundlist, send an e-mail message to listproc@listproc.hcf.jhu.edu. In the body of your message type: sub fundlist <firstname lastname>. To post a message to the list, send your e-mail to fundlist@listproc.hcf.jhu.edu. The list manager is Stephen A. Hirby (listmaster@listproc.hcf.jhu.edu). The address of the archives is http://www.pacificgroup.com/listserv/fundlist.htm.

FUNDSVCS

This list is for those interested in the more technical aspects of fundraising services. It is designed as a companion to, and not a replacement for, Fundlist. Fundsvcs is a "nuts & bolts" oriented discussion, which includes discussion of federal tax and accounting regulations, computer systems and procedures, and donor communications.

To subscribe to Fundsvcs, send an e-mail message to listserv@lists.duke.edu. In the body of your message type: sub fundsvcs <firstname lastname>. To post a message to the list, send your e-mail to fundsvcs@acpub.duke.edu. The list manager is John H. Taylor (fundsvcs-owner@duke.edu). The address of the archives is http://www.pacificgroup.com/html/fundsvcs.htm. A more current archive is also found at http://lists.duke.edu/archives/fundsvcs.html. You will need to register in order to access it.

GIFT-PL

Gift-pl is the electronic mail forum for gift planners that involves the development and dissemination of information in the field of gift planning. This forum is provided by the National Committee on Planned Giving (NCPG).

To subscribe to Gift-pl, send an e-mail message to listserv@indycms.edu. In the body of your message type: sub gift-l <firstname lastname>. To post a message to the list, send your e-mail to gift-pl@indycms.edu. The list manager is Barbara Yeager (byeager@indyunix.iupui.edu).

GIFTPLAN

Formerly pg-amphilreview, this list was established in March 1997 by the *American Philanthropy Review* and is now among the CharityChannel™ forums. It focuses mainly on issues of planned giving in the U.S. and Canada. It is much broader in scope than Gift-pl, a forum provided by the National Committee on Planned Giving.

To subscribe to gift, send an e-mail message to listserv@charitychannel.com. In the body of your message type: subscribe giftplan<your e-mail address>. To post a message to the list, send your e-mail to giftplan@charitychannel.com.

The list is administered by CharityChannel. You may also subscribe or access archives on the Web at http://www.charitychannel.com/forums.

GRANTS

Introduced by *American Philanthropy Review* in November 1997, Grants focuses on all aspects of grants and foundations. Grantseeking in any field, foundation formation, foundation funding, and foundation administration are all suitable topics. As soon as it was launched, the list quickly gained in popularity all over the United States across many nonprofit fields. With the support of the users, the list editors decided to lightly moderate the list on an experimental basis in order to maintain the quality of the postings.

To subscribe to Grants, send an e-mail message to listserv@charitychannel.com. In the body of your message type: subscribe grants <firstname lastname>. To post a message to the list, send your e-mail to grants@charitychannel.com.

The list is administered by CharityChannel. You may also subscribe or access archives on the Web at http://www.charitychannel.com/forums.

HEPID

One of many lists from the Higher Education Processes (HEPROC) Network Group, Hepid is focused on institutional advancement, including fundraising, publications, media relations, and the wide range of related topics. For more information about this list, HEPROC, and other HEPROC lists, visit HEPROC's Web site at http://heproc.org.

To subscribe to Hepid, send an e-mail message to listserv@heproc.org. In the body of your message type: subscribe hepid-d <firstname lastname>. To post a message to the list, send e-mail to hepid@heproc.org. The list owner is Carl Reimann (educ@heproc.org) of R&R Publishers.

HILAROS

The purpose of Hilaros is to provide a forum for discussion among Christians in fundraising. The list complements other development lists. Topics include a Christian perspective in fundraising, sharing ideas and information to help one another in this work, asking for suggestions from others on the list, and prayer requests.

To subscribe to Hilaros, just send an e-mail message to majordomo@ mark.geneva.edu. In the body of your message type: subscribe hilaros. To post a message to the list, send your e-mail to hilaros@mark.geneva.edu. The list owner is Cliff Glovier (hilaros-owner@mark.geneva.edu).

PRSPCT-L

Prspct-l is a discussion list for prospect researchers and development professionals in education and service organizations. Participants share resources and techniques for a wide range of topics, including rating prospects, ethics, job announcements, and foundations. This is a busy list, full of research leads.

To subscribe to Prspct-l, send an e-mail message to listserv@bucknell.edu. In the body of the message type: subscribe prspct-l <firstname lastname>. To post a message to the list, send your e-mail to: prspct-l@bucknell.edu. The list owner is Joe Boeke (boeke@bucknell.edu). The address of the archive is gopher:// gopher.bucknell.edu:70/11/services/listserv/prspct-l.

ROOTS-L (http://www.rootsweb.com/)

Roots-l is the first and largest mailing list for people who are interested in genealogy. Roots-l is a heavy volume list and messages are pre-screened due to a recent poll of subscribers who overwhelmingly supported the move after too many listserv commands were sent to the posting address. The Rootsweb homepage contains more information about this list as well as links to several genealogical databases.

To subscribe to Roots-l, just send an e-mail message to roots-l-request@ rootsweb.com. In the body of your message type: subscribe. To post a message to the list, send your e-mail to roots-l@rootsweb.com. The list owner is Rootsweb (roots-l-request@rootsweb.com).

MANAGING YOUR MAIL

You need to know several commands to keep your electronic mailbox from overflowing, to find previous postings on a subject, and even to conceal your subscription to a list. When you subscribe to a mailing list, your subscription is usually acknowledged. With the acknowledgment, you will receive a message containing the basic commands that you need. If that information is not sufficient, more information on list commands can be found by sending a message to the administrative address of the list and typing "help" in the body of your message.

Since there are five major mailing list manager software packages in use, there are variations in the commands used. For an easy-to-follow chart of the basic mailing list commands for the various list management software programs, see the Case Western University Law Library Web site page maintained by James Milles (http://lawwww.cwru.edu/cwrulaw/faculty/milles/mailser.html#commands). There is a handy chart there that you can print out in its entirety.

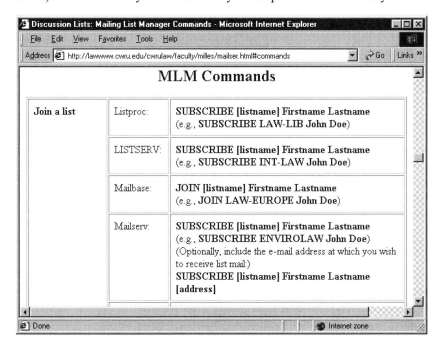

A quick overview here of the most common commands will include digest, postpone, index, and conceal. If you have subscribed to a list with fairly heavy volume, such as Prspct-l, you may send an e-mail to the administrative address (listserv@bucknell.edu) and in the body of the message type in "set prspct-l mail digest." This will allow you to receive batches of messages periodically rather than individually. The list manager determines the interval at which the digest will be sent—often daily or weekly. To undo this command, send a message to the administrative address again and type the following in the body of your message, "set <listname> nodigest or set <listname> mail." The digest command, usually included in your initial instructions after you sign on, is available for mailing lists that are managed by Listproc, Listserv, and Majordomo, but not Mailbase or Mailserv.

Lists that are handled by Listproc, Listserv, and Mailbase (but not Mailserv or Majordomo) also offer the option of postponing your mail if you will be away for a period of time. Send an e-mail to the administrative address with the following words in the body of your message: "Set <listname> mail postpone" (for Listproc lists); or "set <listname> nomail" (for Listserv lists); or Suspend mail <listname> (for Mailbase lists). When you wish to receive messages once again, you must send a new command to the administrative address. The command for Listserv-managed lists is "set <listname> mail." For Mailbase it is "resume mail <listname>." Since Listproc has at least three different commands for resuming receipt of messages, you may need to send a "help" message ahead of time to the administrative address of the list, in order to get the correct command.

The index command, available from all list manager software, allows you to obtain a list of archived files for the list. The command is the same for all lists. Send an e-mail to the administrative address of the list with the word "index" in the body of the message.

"Conceal" is another useful command. All mailing lists have a command whereby others may request that a list of the subscribers be sent to them via e-mail. In most cases this includes the e-mail address and first and last name of the person (i.e., no more than the information you provide when subscribing). With Listproc and Listserv, you have the option of sending a "set <listname> conceal yes" or "set <listname> conceal" command in order to conceal your address, so that it will not be included in any subscriber lists that are requested by others.

E-MAIL NEWSLETTERS, DIGESTS, AND OTHER PUBLICATIONS

Another use of the term "mailing lists," refers to one-way communications, such as newsletters, digests, journals and bulletins to which you may subscribe to receive on a regular basis via e-mail. We will review some examples of philanthropy-related electronic publications that are available for free. Many publications are available in World Wide Web versions (see Chapter 9). These usually have more graphics and links but lack the convenience of automatic delivery to your e-mailbox.

Philanthropy News Digest's PND-L is an e-mail version of a Web-based publication produced by the Foundation Center. It is a weekly digest of nonprofit-related developments culled from national and regional media. Many of the articles include "FC Notes," which provide information from the Foundation Center's database regarding grantmakers mentioned in the original article. The current issue as well as archives of issues dating back to 1995 are available at the Center's Web Site at http://fdncenter.org. To subscribe to the *Philanthropy News Digest,* send an e-mail message to listserv@lists.fdncenter.org with the words "subscribe PND-L <your name>" in the body of your message. You may also subscribe directly from the Center's Web site.

The *Chronicle of Philanthropy* is an example of a well-established print publication in the nonprofit sector that offers free electronic subscriptions to abridged news alerts. Free updates of the *Chronicle,* announcements about what's new in the paper or at the *Chronicle*'s Web site, and special bulletins when major news breaks are available through a mailing list. To sign up, send a message to chronicle-request@philanthropy.com. In the body of your message include "subscribe chronicle <your name and organization>."

Philanthropy News Network Online, a weekly newsletter, was originally the electronic offshoot of the printed magazine, *Philanthropy Journal of North Carolina.* The new incarnation of this popular online publication can be accessed in its Web version, *Philanthropy News Network Online* at http://pj.org, or received by e-mail. To subscribe, send an e-mail message to pjalert-on@mail-list.com. In the body of the message type "subscribe." To cancel your subscription, send a message to the same address with the word "unsubscribe" in the body of the message.

Some other electronic newsletters of interest to grantseekers include the Internet Prospector and *Pulse!,* the National Online Newsletter for Nonprofit Management Support Organizations. The Internet Prospector is a monthly electronic newsletter that publishes information on Internet resources for prospect researchers. To subscribe send an e-mail to chlowe@uci.edu. In the body of the message type "subscribe Internet prospector." The newsletter is also delivered monthly to the entire prspct-l mailing list. The current newsletter, archives, and additional information are available on the Internet Prospector site on the World Wide Web at http://w3.uwyo.edu/~prospect/.

PULSE!, a free service of Support Centers of America and the Nonprofit Management Association, has been distributed twice a month since Spring 1997. *PULSE!* provides readers with a timely synopsis of what's happening in the nonprofit sector and the management support community, as well as providing related postings about interesting ideas and relevant resources. You can subscribe directly from the Support Centers Internet site and find archives, at http://www.igc.org/sca/pulse.html.

Most read-only newsletters are enhanced by the use of "hotlinks." To take advantage of these automatic links to Web sites that are imbedded in the e-mail message, you will need an up-to-date version of e-mail software or a current Web browser that will allow you to receive your e-mail, open it, and read it in your browser.

NEWSGROUPS, ON-LINE FORUMS, AND LIVE CHATS

Newsgroups, on-line forums, and live chats are more examples of interactive communication available to the grantseeker on the Internet. In Usenet newsgroups, people with similar interests can chat about their favorite topic, exchange ideas, and so on, as they would on a mailing list. Newsgroups, however, do not operate by e-mail and are not moderated or owned by anyone. To access a newsgroup, you need to have a "Newsreader"—software that is usually included with your ISP software. You then go to the Usenet site where you can view previously posted messages, which you will find organized by topic. To participate, you post a message, technically referred to as an "article," of your own. Before starting a new thread (topic), you are advised to read the newsgroup's FAQs to see if the topic has already been thoroughly covered.

Each newsgroup has a name that signifies the subject matter covered. For example, newsgroups of interest to the nonprofit sector include soc.org.nonprofit, alt.activism., alt.society.civil-liberties, to name just a few. Usenet newsgroups are hosted by a wide range of organizations from government agencies and large universities to high schools and businesses. Among the periodic postings in newsgroups, you will find listings of active newsgroups. An official Usenet primer is available from *Deja News* on the Web at http://dejanews.com/info/primer1.shtml. This document also contains a "Newsgroup Directory" link. Or you can visit http://tile.net, the Web site discussed earlier, which will allow you to search for newsgroups.

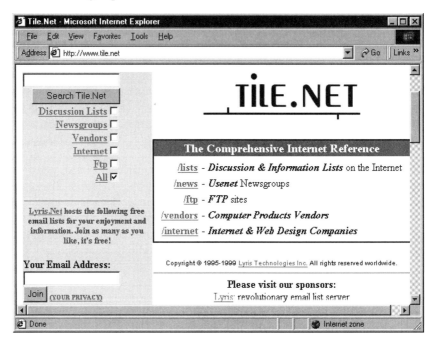

Like newsgroups, the online forums available at many nonprofit-related Web sites allow you to review ongoing discussions organized by topic. It is not necessary to have any additional software besides your Internet browser to participate in such forums. Web-based forums can be very convenient because your e-mail box won't fill up with messages that are not of interest to you. If you are seeking information or a dialog on a specific subject, you can start your own "thread" (topic), or go to the appropriate forum to see if it has been covered.

For a forum to be successful, however, its existence must be well publicized in print and through mailing lists, or the Web site must be compelling enough to attract repeat visitors. *The American Philanthropy Review* Web site (http://charitychannel.com) is particularly active in this area and offers a number of forums, described earlier.

Another example of a successful Web-based forum can be found at the Interaction Web site.

Interaction: American Council for Voluntary International Action is a coalition of 150+ nonprofit organizations worldwide. It has an active forum of interest at their Web site (http://www.interaction.org).

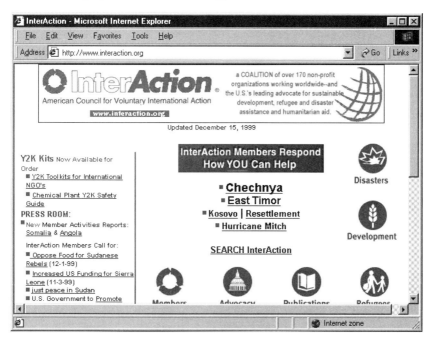

The forum on this site is called "Global Connections: A National On-line Conversation About the Changing World." It is necessary to register to use the forum, as is usually the case. A password is required. Instructions for getting a password are available at the site.

Live chats are yet another opportunity to get together online with colleagues to discuss topics of mutual interest. Chats are usually hosted at a Web site and, even more than forums, require a good deal of pre-publicity in order to be a success. Participants must come to a certain site at a specified date and time to engage in a "real time" conversation on a specific topic. Special guests are sometimes available to answer questions on the topic. Live chats have been especially popular on large commercial providers of Internet services, such as America Online, where the content is highly organized. In the nonprofit sector, this medium is particularly effective in membership-based organizations, where a structure exists to get the word out to potential participants.

Conclusion

Clearly, grantseekers can take advantage of a number of methods to interact electronically. Primarily e-mail based at this time, these interactions can be productive, inexpensive, and very convenient. Some of the other interactive capabilities (e.g., live chat and real-time conferencing) require more planning and organizing and may therefore be more suitable for specialty uses. However, many grantseekers and fundraisers have found that an easy way to get started communicating with one's colleagues is to subscribe to a mailing list and then "listen in" on the conversation for a time. If you are not interested, you can unsubscribe and try another. Once you are involved in a mailing list or a newsgroup, you will find frequent postings covering technical advice and pointing the way to the growing resources available over the Internet.

A Brief History of Internet Time

If you never thought your life would be affected by something called "packet switching," think again.

In 1962, in helping the Department of Defense figure out how to safeguard its ability to communicate after a nuclear war, in a Rand Corporation study Paul Baran proposed a computer system with no central authority, a system with no individual computers upon which all the other computers would depend. In this system there would be no key parts easily targeted for attack. Mr. Baran also proposed that the system would send messages broken into smaller pieces of data called packets. Each packet would have its own destination address and could travel by itself through any route available on the system, even at a different time, and rejoin other packets at a common destination point. In this way, the system would deliver a coherent, complete message, no matter what damage may have occurred to various parts of the overall computer system in the meantime.

In a relatively short time, this basic concept—a radical egalitarianism of computers and data—has evolved in unforeseen ways to give all of us the opportunity of finding any information that someone, in any part of the world, chooses to make available. This basic concept spawned the Internet and the World Wide Web.

This appendix will present a very brief history of this evolution simply because it is fascinating: the very nature of Mr. Baran's concept made accurate prediction of its consequences and impact impossible, and still does.

Internet History, Up to a Point

The Pentagon's Advanced Research Projects Agency (ARPA) put the Rand Corporation study to the test, beginning in the late sixties, and created ARPANET so that scientists around the world could use each other's computer systems. As it turned out, these scientists began communicating with each other, not just with each other's computers. This new system had facilitated person-to-person communication.

In the seventies, standards were developed that would let different kinds of computers make use of ARPANET. Robert Kahn and Vinton Cerf were central to this effort. (The accepted lore has it that Mr. Cerf diagrammed key aspects of the new system architecture on the back of an envelope in the lobby of a San Francisco hotel.) The details of the packet-switching concept were worked out and standardized into what is known as TCP/IP (Transmission Control Protocol/ Internet Protocol). The TCP/IP protocols created the information packets and handled the addressing necessary to route them to the right place on a decentralized computer network. By the early eighties, TCP and IP were firmly established as the protocols used by the ARPANET. Any computer that used TCP/IP could join what began to be known as the "internet." No one owned TCP/IP and so more people were able to participate. They couldn't be kept out.

In the mid-eighties, the National Science Foundation (NSF) created NSFNET, basically connecting more powerful computers to what now became known as "the Internet." The system's overall capacity grew quickly, and the original ARPANET section of the Internet disappeared. This now beefier Internet accommodated a growing number of connections, called nodes, particularly at universities, where there were lots of computers and people who knew how to use them. For a time NSF was the primary backbone of the whole Internet (a particular segment of the overall Internet network is called a "backbone"). Now there are many. Also in the eighties, the different Internet "domains" were created along with the "domain names" that contain the suffixes denoting different types of institutions: ".gov" (government), ".mil" (military), ".edu" (education), ".com" (commercial), ".org" (nonprofit), ".int" (international), and ".net" (computers set up specifically to connect people to the Internet at large).

ADDRESSING THE INTERNET

With all this democracy of computers and access, one of the things that makes the Internet possible is the organized assigning and maintaining of IP addresses. IP addressing can be complex because of the number of computers and files involved. To simplify the way people could contact another computer, the first name server was developed at the University of Wisconsin in 1983, around the time TCP/IP became the standard protocol suite for the Internet.

The first domain name server was introduced in 1984, when there were 1,000 computer hosts on the Internet. The name server simplifies the addressing process by providing for the translation between the common-language domain names and the numerical computer addresses. Within the Internet, this means translating from a name such as "fdncenter.org" to an IP address such as "204.5.210.11." Now the end-user no longer had to know the exact path to another computer in order to contact that computer.

Over the next decade, use of the Internet got more sophisticated. The network population was changing in both number and character. By 1993 there were 1,000,000 host computers on the Internet. This kind of growth required that the Internet, though unregulated in a strict sense, maintained integrity of services central to its continued operation and growth. In 1993, the National Science Foundation sponsored the creation of InterNIC to provide specific Internet services, which included a complete Domain Name System (DNS). InterNIC defined the DNS as:

> A distributed database of information that is used to translate domain names, which are easy for humans to remember and use, into Internet Protocol (IP) numbers, which are what computers need to find each other on the Internet. People working on computers around the globe maintain their specific portion of this database, and the data held in each portion of the database is made available to all computers and users on the Internet. The DNS comprises computers, data files, software, and people working together.

The Evolution of Essential Internet Services

Before establishment of the DNS, the hostname-to-address mappings had been maintained by the NIC (Network Information Center) in a single file, which was downloaded by all the hosts on the Internet. Local organizations were administering their own names and addresses, but had to wait for the NIC to make changes in the central file to make the changes visible to the Internet at large. Created to address limitations, the DNS is a set of protocols and distributed databases. Like the Internet itself, there is no dependence on a central computer. The DNS provided standard formats for resource data, standard methods for querying the database, and standard methods for name servers to refresh local data from other name servers.

In addition to translating names to addresses for hosts that are on the Internet, the DNS provides for registering DNS-style names for other hosts reachable (via electronic mail) through gateways or mail relays. The records for such name registrations point to an Internet host (one with an IP address) that acts as a mail forwarder for the registered host. This gives electronic mail users a uniform mail addressing syntax and avoids making users aware of the underlying network boundaries.

InterNIC Registration Services, located at Network Solutions, Inc. (NSI), was created by a cooperative agreement from the National Science Foundation to provide registration services for the Internet community via telephone, electronic mail, and U.S. postal mail. InterNIC Registration Services worked closely with domain administrators, network coordinators, Internet service providers, and other various users in its registration activities.

The IP allocation functions had been subsidized by domain name registration fees. The U. S. government also provided funding to InterNIC for handling IP allocation functions. In 1997, after more than a year of Internet infrastructure meetings and various discussions in the Internet community, there was agreement that the management of domain names and of IP numbers should be separate activities. As a result, the American Registry for Internet Numbers (ARIN), a non-profit organization, was established for the purpose of administration and registration of Internet Protocol (IP) numbers to the geographical areas formerly managed by InterNIC.

In December 1997, ARIN assumed responsibility for IP address allocation and network registration functions previously performed by InterNIC. NSI, through InterNIC, cooperated in the launch of ARIN in initiating discussions and proposals to bring IP numbering in the Americas under a model like that of the Reseaux IP Europeens (RIPE) and the Asia Pacific Network Information Center (APNIC). These organizations are also supported by their respective members. ARIN is an independent, nonprofit organization responding to its membership.

ARIN officially opened for operation on December 22, 1997, through the authorization of the National Science Foundation and the transfer by the Internet Assigned Numbers Authority (IANA) of authority of IP number administration from Network Solutions, Inc./InterNIC to ARIN. Imposition of fees is required because the U.S. government no longer funds IP number administration, an activity becoming increasingly more cost-intensive and commercial. The fee schedule of ARIN was in line with the other two IP Registries, RIPE in Europe and APNIC in the Asia Pacific region. With the addition of ARIN, there were three geographically aligned IP Registries which coordinate management activities and are supported by user funding.

Changes in how IP numbers are administered aren't visible to most end users. IP addresses are mostly registered by ISPs (Internet Service Providers) and then distributed to end users. NSI had retained management of domain names. The Domain Names Supporting Organization (DNSO) was formed to work with the Internet Corporation on Assigned Names and Numbers (ICANN), a nonprofit corporation, created in 1998, charged with privatizing the administration of the Internet's addressing system. By early 1999 NSI was having performance and data integrity problems in the provision of these services, in part because of the large number of domain name requests, including a large number of fraudulent ones. Besides plain malfeisance, the practice of "cybersquatting" proliferated. (Cybersquatting is when a person registers a domain name that most logically belongs to another group or company, in order to then sell that name to that group or company at a profit.)

NSI's government-mandated monopoly on the registration of domain names ending in .com, .net, and .org ended in April 1999, when five companies were selected to present competitive proposals for offering the domain name services provided by NSI. The goal was to transition the DNS from proprietary control to a competitive market for domain name registration. Even as the five new companies were to operate a shared registration system, NSI took steps to maintain control of the registry. This ongoing process has been contentious, with the Justice Department involved, largely because domain name registration is one of the more dependable income-generating activities in cyberspace.

This involved description of the evolution in the provision of essential Internet services is included to show that, although available to all and owned by no one, maintaining the Internet is not costless and depends on the cooperation, commitment, and expertise of many people around the world.

INTERNET FUNCTIONALITY

The original Internet (pre-World Wide Web) provided a number of different capabilities, briefly described below. (Many of these were subsequently incorporated into the Web environment, working seamlessly within popular Web browsers, See Chapter 1.)

E-mail

Personal messaging was from the outset the most widely used Internet function. Practically everyone could have a use for it. All it required was a computer, a little facility with it, and someone else with these two things.

Usenet

Usenet is a world-wide distributed discussion system. It consists of a set of "newsgroups" with names that are classified hierarchically by subject. "Articles" or "messages" are "posted" to these newsgroups by people on computers with the appropriate software—these articles are then broadcast to other interconnected computer systems via a wide variety of networks. Some newsgroups are "moderated." In moderated newsgroups, the articles are first sent to a moderator for approval before appearing in the newsgroup.

Because of the nature of Usenet, there is no way for any user to enforce the results of a newsgroup vote (or any other decision, for that matter). Therefore, for your new newsgroup to be propagated widely, you must not only follow the letter of the guidelines; you must also follow its spirit.

If you want to start a newsgroup idea, read the "news.groups" newsgroup for a while, at least six months, to find out how things work. A new newsgroup is unlikely to be widely distributed unless its sponsor follows the newsgroup creation guidelines. (Guidelines require that a new newsgroup pass an open vote run by neutral volunteer votetakers).

Telnet

Telnet is the generic name for logging onto a remote computer and making use of programs that reside there, as if you were actually using that computer.

File Transfer Protocol (FTP)

FTP was and still is one of the most useful of Internet functions. It lets a person download computer files from (and, less often, upload computer files to) any Internet host that is set up to allow this. FTP can require a password, but many FTP sites allow files to be downloaded by anyone. (This kind of "open season" FTP is known as Anonymous FTP.) The downloading of free software programs is probably the most well-known FTP practice. This ability was particularly important in the early days of the Internet when it was put together and operated by a smaller number of knowledgeable computer users, who basically built the Internet by sharing their experience and knowledge as they used it. A tremendous amount of information, both computer programs and text, was originally made available on the Internet via FTP for anyone with the equipment and ability to access it. FTP sites were searchable by using a program generically referred to as Archie, a nickname for Archive Server.

Gopher

In 1991 a team at the University of Minnesota developed a system whereby files were made available on the Internet and a menu system allowed users to locate information they wanted wherever it was on the Internet. The term "Gopher" referred to the state animal of Minnesota, as well as the University of Minnesota (whose teams are called the "Golden Gophers"), and euphoniously referred to the term "gofer," someone who fetches. Various locations established Gopher servers containing various files they wished to make available. Client software treated these many Gopher servers as connected. Gopher menus grew and users were able to "bookmark" those sites and files they were to visit regularly. Following on the name "Archie," in 1992 a program called "Veronica" was created that was able to search the growing "Gopherspace" for specific words appearing on Gopher menus. The results of Veronica searches looked themselves like Gopher menus and so Gopherspace became even more transparent to the user. As Gopherspace continued to grow, it became a practical necessity to search only parts of it. Veronica searches looked across the whole array of Gopher servers and the results could be unwieldy. As a result, a program called "Jughead" was developed at the Computer Center at University of Utah and released in 1993. Because Jughead generally searched higher level menus, rather than looking for words in all Gopher menus, it was good for doing more general research.

Wide Area Information Service (WAIS)

In 1991, another development appeared which extended a person's ability to search through material being made available on the Internet. Unlike the Archie software that searched for FTP archive files, or the Gopher/Veronica/Jughead software which searched through the growing number of Gopher menus, the Wide Area Information Service (WAIS) employed software that would search the entire text of all the articles, papers, etc. that were placed on WAIS servers. Initially the material made available was from the technical and scientific community around the world. In light of what was to happen to Internet functionality a short time later, it's fair to say that the WAIS search capabilities brought before a more general audience some new concepts for searching archived material: relevancy rankings and Boolean searching.

A WAIS search looked for keywords wherever they appeared in text, and the results of these keyword searches could include things out of context, things that fell outside of the intentions of the searcher. So the software tried to rank the items in results lists according to how well the items matched up with the keywords. The user could then pick and choose among the results list items based on how "relevant" they seemed relative to each other. Boolean searching allows the user to combine search terms in different ways when a search is performed, so that a search could be made more general or more specific, depending on the user's needs and the nature of the material. Boolean searching was already well known to experienced computer users, but the Internet was distributing this concept more broadly, along with information.

Getting good results from WAIS searches involved a higher level of conceptualization from the user for a number of reasons. The software did the picking and choosing by looking at text hidden from the user, rather than presenting various levels of menus (as in Gopherspace) for user review and selection. This in turn required that the user have more familiarity with the material being searched; one had to understand in advance the nature of the text to be searched in order to choose appropriate search terms. The system also depended on having enough different information sets which shared common concepts and issues. This made it particularly useful for the technical and scientific communities, where this condition pertained.

World Wide Web: The Internet Takes Off

The World Wide Web was developed by Tim Berners-Lee in Switzerland at CERN (European Laboratory for Particle Physics) in 1991. The key capability that created this new-thing-unto-itself, was a fairly simple implementation of "hypertext," a function which lets you jump from one document or file on the Internet to another, one that presumably is related to the first. Documents could now be created which included hypertext "links" that took users directly to other documents. Below we reproduce a version of the original World Wide Web vision of Berners-Lee, written around 1992. This prophetic synopsis was taken from the Web site of the World Wide Web Consortium (W3C) (http://www.w3.org), another organization dedicated to allowing the Web not only to keep going and growing, but developing in more sophisticated and useful ways.

This is an interesting presentation because it describes the Web specifically from the "viewer" (or "client") side and from the "information provider" (or "server") side. Concurrent developments on both sides would continue to spur the Web's rapid growth. In fact, the Web has exhibited "client-server" architecture to the world at large. That is, at least for those without previous experience of being connected to a network at an office, corporation, university, etc., the World Wide Web exemplified the oft-quoted adage, "The network is the computer."

WORLD WIDE WEB—EXECUTIVE SUMMARY OF THE ORIGINAL VISION

The WWW project merges the techniques of networked information and hypertext to make an easy but powerful global information system. The project represents any information accessible over the network as part of a seamless hypertext information space.

The WWW was originally developed to allow information sharing within internationally dispersed teams, and the dissemination of information by support groups. Originally aimed at the High Energy Physics community, it has spread to other areas and attracted much interest in user support, resource discovery and collaborative work areas. It is currently the most advanced information system deployed on the Internet, and embraces within its data model most information in previous networked information systems.

In fact, the Web is an architecture which will also embrace any future advances in technology, including new networks, protocols, object types and data formats. Clients and servers exist for many platforms and are under continual development.

Reader view

The WWW world consists of documents, and links. Indexes are special documents which, rather than being read, may be searched. The result of such a search is another ("virtual") document containing links to the documents found. A simple protocol ("HTTP") is used to allow a browser program to request a keyword search by a remote information server.

The web contains documents in many formats. Those documents, which are hypertext (real or virtual), contain links to other documents, or places within documents. All documents, whether real, virtual or indexes, look similar to the reader and are contained within the same addressing scheme.

To follow a link, a reader clicks with a mouse (or types in a number if he or she has no mouse). To search an index, a reader gives keywords (or other search criteria). These are the only operations necessary to access the entire world of data.

Information Provider View

The WWW browsers can access many existing data systems via existing protocols (FTP, NNTP) or via HTTP and a gateway. In this way, the critical mass of data is quickly exceeded, and the increasing use of the system by readers and information suppliers encourage each other.

Providing information is as simple as running the WWW server and pointing it at an existing directory structure. The server automatically generates the hypertext view of your files to guide the user around.

To personalize it, you can write a few SGML hypertext files to give an even more friendly view. Also, any file available by anonymous FTP, or any internet newsgroup can be immediately linked into the web. The very small start-up effort is designed to allow small contributions. At the other end of the scale, large information providers may provide an HTTP server with full text or keyword indexing. This may allow access to a large existing database without changing the way that database is managed. Such gateways have already been made into Oracle, WAIS, and Digital's VMS/Help systems, to name but a few.

The WWW model gets over the frustrating incompatibilities of data format between suppliers and readers by allowing negotiation of format between a smart browser and a smart server. This should provide a basis for extension into multimedia, and allow those who share application standards to make full use of them across the Web.

This summary does not describe the many exciting possibilities opened up by the WWW project, such as efficient document caching, the reduction of redundant out-of-date copies, and the use of knowledge daemons. . . .

Copyright © 1997 World Wide Web Consortium, (Massachusetts Institute of Technology, Institut National de Recherche en Informatique et en Automatique, Keio University). All Rights Reserved.

In many ways the hypertext function, which spawned the World Wide Web, was the natural extension of the "classic" Internet capabilities described briefly earlier. But it also marked a clean break with this past, allowing a true quantum leap in global interconnectivity and communication. But a couple of things had to happen to bring about this accelerated evolution.

Hypertext was a marvellous development. Now people could zoom through the chutes and ladders of a growing World Wide Web by jumping from link to link. The question immediately became, link to what? In the beginning, adding hypertext links to documents was a painstaking process. Further growth of the Web would depend both on the ease with which people could make hypertext information available and the ease with which people could access it. From this point forward, the development of both hypertext authoring and viewing capabilities became intertwined in an upward-leading spiral. Authoring would become a simpler process and allow a tremendous proliferation of content available on the Web, and viewers would become more point-and-click oriented to make viewing that content easier. By the mid-90s, the ability to "surf" the Web, a term first heard in 1992, was within the grasp of considerably more people.

HYPERTEXT MARKUP LANGUAGE (HTML)

At the heart of Tim Berners-Lee idea for a network of hypertext documents was the development of the tagging system required to create the hypertext documents and the links that would knit them together. He looked to the already existing Standard Generalized Markup Language (SGML), an international standard (ISO 8879) for tagging electronic text that allows another user or machine to know how the text should look, how it should be presented. This standard formatting language (a "metalanguage") could be used across all computer networks and systems.

By consistently using standard format tags for document elements, not only could electronic text be presented consistently on any device, but the documents could be "structured" using SGML tags. For instance, tables of contents could be automatically generated by presenting just the different levels of headings from a long text document. With SGML, information about the document was sent along with the text of the document so that machines could read and present the material consistently.

Berners-Lee used a small piece of the full SGML to create the original Hypertext Markup Language. HTML is really just one "Document Type Definition" (DTD), any number of which can be created using SGML. Restricting the Web markup language basically to one document type helped get it adopted rapidly, when people were primarily posting only very simple text documents to the Internet.

The system was beguilingly simple. Cross-platform capability was key, with standard format tags allowing consistent presentation of documents. The system also needed to include an addressing scheme that would allow creation of hypertext pointers, so the Internet addresses were incorporated into the tagging system. Also required was a transport mechanism that would let documents move across networks. This was developed to become the HyperText Transport Protocol (aka "http"), and "http" became the most common prefix used in Internet addresses. All these requirements were met by the "language" that became known as HTML. Similar to the adoption of TCP/IP, in which an "open" system can be open only if standards are developed and then accepted by a majority of users, HTML became the standard language of content generation on the Web. To become available to the widest group of users, the various Web viewing programs (known as "browsers") being developed needed to support the HTML standard, that is, they had to recognize HTML tagging in order to present documents appropriately.

THE WORLD WIDE WEB CONSORTIUM AND THE DEVELOPMENT OF STANDARDS

The World Wide Web Consortium (W3C) was founded in 1994 to develop common protocols for the evolution of the World Wide Web. The W3C is vendor-neutral, working with the global community to produce specifications and software that is made freely available throughout the world.

HTML was an important area of activity for the W3C when it began in 1994. Tim Berners-Lee's original HTML (now known as HTML 1) was extremely simple. However, by 1994 there were many "extensions" to HTML and the language was becoming complex and unwieldy. More to the point, Netscape, Microsoft, and other browser vendors had begun implementing different HTML features. In 1994, under the auspices of the Internet Engineering Task Force (IETF), HTML 2 was developed to specify the commonly used HTML tags and extensions. Going further, the Consortium felt it necessary to address the resulting incompatibilities, and in 1995 formed the HTML ERB (Editorial Review Board) to bring vendors together to prepare a common standard for HTML.

The original HTML was a simple subset of SGML. The same simplicity that had aided its rapid adoption as a standard quickly began to feel like a limitation. As Web publishing became so widespread, and people started talking about "Web design," there was great interest in restoring the full capabilities of a complete SGML-like system to the Web environment through the development and standardization of an expanded markup language. The W3C created a working committee of a variety of industry groups and vendors to develop a new system. In February 1998, the W3C released the specification for XML 1.0, the first version of an enhanced system for "defining, validating, and sharing document formats on the Web." XML stands for Extensible Markup Language.

XML—BACK TO SGML ROOTS

HTML had proved too simple for the more complex Web applications people wanted to develop. However, SGML was very complex and therefore hard to learn completely. XML is an attempt to strike the right balance between those two extremes. The excerpts below from a W3C press release describe the potential for XML to further advance the capabilities and scope of the World Wide Web. Many different DTDs can be created within XML (e.g., specific industries can create complex applications of interest only to their industry group). Existing HTML tagging can still be used as long as it is "well formed," that is, it meets some standards for consistency.

> XML 1.0 is a subset of an existing, widely used international text-processing standard (Standard Generalized Markup Language, ISO 8879:1986 as amended and corrected) intended for use on the World Wide Web. XML retains ISO 8879's basic features—vendor independence, user extensibility, complex structures, validation, and human readability—in a form that is much easier to implement and understand. XML can be processed by existing commercial tools and a rapidly growing number of free ones. . . . . XML is primarily intended to meet the requirements of large-scale Web content providers for industry-specific markup, vendor-neutral data exchange, media-independent publishing, one-on-one marketing, workflow management in collaborative authoring environments, and the processing of Web documents by intelligent clients. It is also expected to find use in metadata applications. XML is fully internationalized for both European and Asian languages, with all conforming processors required to support the Unicode character set. The language is designed for the quickest possible client-side processing consistent with its primary purpose as an electronic publishing and data interchange format.
>
> *Copyright © 1997 World Wide Web Consortium, (Massachusetts Institute of Technology, Institut National de Recherche en Informatique et en Automatique, Keio University). All Rights Reserved.*

After users have created their own specific tags for text information, that one file of tagged data can be used to create multiple presentations of that information (through the use of "style sheets" created according to the developing standards of Extensible Style Language, aka XSL), to transfer that data across any computer platform, or to add metadata (information about information) to Web documents and other files. Various researchers are proposing specifications for XML search engines so that XML tagged files can be searched at various levels without additional keywords or indexing needing to be created.

This brief discussion of the development of HTML and XML displays once again the rapidly expanding potential of the Web for serving a diverse global audience. Already, various DTDs (Document Type Definitions) are being developed using XML, and it is being used widely to facilitate business-to-business e-commerce. Support for XML rapidly is being incorporated into most software applications, even though for some time to come most Web surfers will be using their browsers to look at documents created using HTML tags.

What's Next

The software language known as Java made its first appearance on the Internet timeline in 1995. Created by Sun Microsystems, Java represented a significant development which at least holds the potential to revolutionize life on the Web. A description of Java (published by Jones Digital Century in 1997) explains its potentially revolutionary aspects:

> Because Java is platform-neutral, it facilitates the building of software that can run seamlessly across all computers on the Internet, and on private intranets. Java allows developers to embed small software applications, called applets, into HTML documents that can be sent to, and used by, users on any operating system. . . . It is possible that in the future, Java-enabled sites will be able to perform the functions of most home and business software, and even to serve as telephones or VCRs. Early proponents have therefore suggested that Java applications could some day replace the larger applications on computer hard drives, essentially establishing the Internet as a universal operating system.

Widespread acceptance of client-side Java may depend on performance advances in the World Wide Web generally, and some observers feel that Java will be used primarily in the market for hand-held computer devices, but it could potentially revolutionize the way people use computers over the Web.

Another new approach to computing over the Internet arose during 1999. In this computing model, end users don't purchase software applications that they then have to load and maintain on local systems with lots of disk space and memory, nor do they rely on client machine and overall Internet performance to make Java an efficient computing model. Rather, a software provider operates the application software on central servers and end users access the application functionality through their Web browsers. In this new model, software vendors become "application service providers" (ASPs) and end users are freed from the costs and headaches of maintaining costlier equipment and applications at their sites. Here again, general Web performance issues may determine when this model becomes a practical alternative.

PROPRIETARY COMPETITION OR OPEN SOURCE?

Like the debate over whether delivery of Java applets to client desktops fundamentally can alter the composition of the software business, it is unclear whether the ASP approach poses any immediate threat to current arrangements in the industry; that is, with Microsoft dominating the PC world through the hammerlock the Windows operating system has on the desktop. However, other forces were at work with the potential to alter things: Justice Department rulings that could force Microsoft to change business practices; the Netscape-AOL merger, which included the participation of Sun Microsystems, the creator of Java; the growing popularity of the "open source" Linux operating system; and the development and acceptance of other open standards such as XML. People were getting used to the debates surrounding these developments when AOL seemed to absorb Time Warner in their collosal "merger." (Whereas media companies had been scrambling to acquire Web portals, here was an Internet company acquiring a media company.)

Technological advances and the development of standards are both continuous processes. In fact, technology advances are inevitable, whereas the acceptance of standards can be difficult, especially if it affects industry economics. In fact, it often seemed like Microsoft against the world, or the world against Microsoft—at least until the proposed AOL–Time Warner "merger" threatened to create another behemoth to fear and loathe. It's interesting to consider whether current industry alliances, and perhaps the open source movement itself, don't owe their existence in some measure to the dominant presence of Microsoft. And Microsoft seems skilled at coopting open standards, or at least tactically delaying their broad acceptance, in order to find a way to take advantage of them within their own array of products and services. They slowed down the availability of a single Java standard by distributing a somewhat proprietary version, which the courts briefly forbid them to do before that decision was reversed. They pushed into the XML realm by incorporating support for XML into Explorer 5.0 and aggressively trying to establish their BizTalk as the standard format for e-commerce. In fact, all the major portal players seem to be positioning themselves to become "e-commerce aggregators" in the manner best exemplified in the public's eye by Amazon.com. It is hard to predict accurately what is around the next corner.

THE BANDWIDTH PROBLEM

And then there is the question of who will get rich selling the increased bandwidth that a fast-performing Web and its users demand. Different technologies are being offered, and decisions slowly being made as to who can offer which services to consumers, and at what prices. And the debate is raging about the efficacy of government regulation. Any incremental bandwidth gains are used up immediately by higher traffic levels, much of it multimedia. In any case, a quantum leap in the amount of bandwidth generally available has to be accomplished before the Web can become all the things it promises to be, hopefully to all people.

APPENDIX B

Bibliography: Grantseeking on the Internet

The following reading list is selected from the Foundation Center's bibliographic database, which is available on our Web site as *Literature of the Nonprofit Sector Online*. Be sure to check *LNPS Online* (www.fdncenter.org/onlib/lnps/) regularly to keep abreast of new publications. Simply input the term "Internet" from the subject list.

"1999 Technology Guide for Nonprofits." *Chronicle of Philanthropy*, vol. 11, March 25, 1999, p. 11–4.

"2000 Non-Profit Software Guide." *Fund Raising Management,* vol. 30 (October 1999): p. 25–37.
Annual guide to fundraising software for nonprofits.

Allen, Nick, Mal Warwick, and Michael Stein, eds. *Fundraising on the Internet: Recruiting and Renewing Donors Online.* Berkeley, CA: Strathmoor Press, 1996.
Focuses on how nonprofits can acquire new donors through the Internet. Topics discussed include online tools, translating direct mail and telephone fundraising techniques to an electronic medium, fundraising opportunities online, and useful Web sites for fundraisers. Provides a glossary of Internet terms.

Barth, Steve. "Pulling Gifts into your Web." *Currents*, vol. 24, September 1998, p. 32–7.
> Analyzes the practice of fundraising via the Internet on college campuses. Also includes some tips on successful Internet fundraising.

Bergan, Helen. *Where the Information Is: A Guide to Electronic Research for Nonprofit Organizations.* Alexandria, VA: BioGuide Press, 1996.
> Bergan explains in nontechnical language how electronic resources can help nonprofit organizations identify and cultivate potential donors, find grant funding, and manage daily operations. Chapters cover CD-ROMs, DIALOG, CompuServe, America Online, e-mail, using the Internet, and Internet resources of interest for nonprofits. Provides sections that list the names and addresses of vendors and groups that are involved in making electronic technology available for use by nonprofit organizations. Includes bibliography and index.

Blum, Debra E. "Charities Fail to Tap Internet's Potential to Spur Action and Giving, Study Finds." *Chronicle of Philanthropy,* vol. 11 (23 September 1999): p. 32.
> Discusses the findings of a new survey of "socially engaged Internet users" and "online activists," which indicates that charities are not utilizing the full potential of the Internet to stimulate giving and activism.

Corson-Finnerty, Adam, and Laura Blanchard. *Fundraising and Friend-Raising on the Web.* Chicago, IL: American Library Association, 1998.
> Intended for library administrators, but with approaches that will succeed for any nonprofit, the book offers advice on such topics as developing and measuring the impact of a Web site; creating donor recognition in cyberspace; delivering your site directly to potential donors on disk or CD-ROM; and fundraising with digital cash. Throughout, examples currently on the Web are provided. A CD-ROM disk is included.

Demko, Paul. "On-Line Solicitors: Tangled Web." *Chronicle of Philanthropy,* vol. 10, January 29, 1998, p. 23–4.
> Discusses the Web sites that are raising money for charities through the Internet, and the subsequent questions about whether they should be regulated.

Demko, Paul, and Jennifer Moore. "Charities Put the Web to Work." *Chronicle of Philanthropy,* vol. 10, October 8, 1998, p. 1, 41–4.
> Nonprofit organizations are increasing their use of the Internet to tell their stories, and also in their day-to-day operations.

Dickey, Marilyn. "E-mailing for Dollars." *Chronicle of Philanthropy,* vol. 10, September 10, 1998, p. 23–4.
> Recounts successful fundraising efforts accomplished through various uses of e-mail.

Dickey, Marilyn (comp.) "Internet Sites that Click for Charity Researchers Seeking Donors." *Chronicle of Philanthropy,* vol. 11 (23 September 1999): p. 30–1.
    Listing of Web sites useful to fundraisers.

Dickey, Marilyn. "Sold, to the Man at the Mouse." *Chronicle of Philanthropy,* vol. 11, October 22, 1998, p. 23–5.
    Nonprofit organizations are beginning to use Internet auctions as a way to raise money and to reach people globally who have never supported their organization. Experts also offer advice on ways to avoid problems.

Dickey, Marilyn and Holly Hall. "The Pitfalls of Mining the Internet." *Chronicle of Philanthropy,* vol. 11 (23 September 1999): p. 29, 32.
    Discusses current issues surrounding prospect research on the Internet. Experts remark that although the Internet is making it easier and less expensive to obtain information on potential donors, many charities are not utilizing it as effectively as they could be. The increasing involvement of professional researchers in fundraising efforts and the issue of donor privacy is also discussed.

Ellis, Susan J. "Virtual Volunteering." *501(c)(3) Monthly Letter,* vol. 19 (September 1999): p. 3, 5.
    Discusses virtual volunteering, through which individuals can contribute their time and expertise to nonprofit organizations via the Internet. Gives detailed examples of the types of technical assistance and direct client services that can be provided by virtual volunteers.

Ford, Eugene. "Virtual Philanthropy Gets Needed Funds to Remote Countries." *Nonprofits & Technology,* vol. 2 (September 1999): p. 6.
    Profiles the Virtual Foundation, an online philanthropy program that supports international grassroots initiatives. The Virtual Foundation posts project proposals on its Web site, where they can be read and funded by online donors. It was founded in 1996 by ECOLOGIA, an international nonprofit that focuses on environmental issues.

Foundation Center. *National Guide to Funding for Information Technology,* 2nd ed. New York, NY: Foundation Center, 1999.
    Provides information on 606 grantmaking foundations, 36 direct corporate giving programs, and 64 public charities that have shown a substantial interest in information technology, either as part of their stated fields of interest or through actual grants of $10,000 or more in the last year of record.

Frenza, JP and Leslie Hoffman. "Fundraising on the Internet: Three Easy Strategies for Nonprofits." *Nonprofit World,* vol. 17, July–August 1999, p. 10–3.
    The suggested strategies are to become a nonprofit beneficiary of one of the "shop for a cause" Web sites; to establish a simple but secure Web page with a one-page form for collecting donations; and to create an online catalog to sell products.

Frenza, JP, and Leslie Hoffman. "Organizing Your Web Site Content." *Nonprofit World*, vol. 15, November–December 1997, p. 14–6.
> Provides tips on how to arrange Web site content in a way that will make sense for users' needs.

Fuisz, Joseph. "Internet Causes Dramatic Changes in Fund Raising World." *Fund Raising Management,* vol. 30 (October 1999): p. 22–4.
> Discusses the impact of the Internet on fundraising, and explores the possibility of partnerships between nonprofits and online commercial enterprises.

Greer, Gayle. "Online Fundraising: The Time is Now." *Fund Raising Management,* vol. 30 (August 1999): p. 26–9.
> Encourages nonprofit organizations to utilize the Internet as a fundraising tool and a means of building relationships with donors.

Grobman, Gary M. and Gary B. Grant. *The Non-Profit Internet Handbook.* Harrisburg, PA: White Hat Communications, 1998.
> Comprehensive information about the uses of the Internet for nonprofits, devoting one chapter to fundraising. Includes case studies, issues to consider, and citations and reviews of numerous Web sites.

Grobman, Gary M. and Gary B. Grant. *The Wilder Nonprofit Guide to Getting Started on the Internet: How to Use the Internet's Best Features to Uncover Valuable Information and Help your Nonprofit Be More Profitable.* St. Paul, MN: Amherst H. Wilder Foundation, 1999.
> Basic handbook with information about the Internet, how to connect, use e-mail, join mailing lists, newsgroups, and other online tools. Includes glossary.

Grobman, Gary M., Gary B. Grant, and Steve Stoller. *The Wilder Nonprofit Guide to Fundraising on the Internet: How to Use the Internet to Raise Funds and Sharpen Your Fundraising Skills.* St. Paul, MN: Amherst H. Wilder Foundation, 1999.
> Handbook lists Web sites and Internet tools that assist in fundraising efforts. Instructions on how to join listservs, access journals, conduct prospect research, use e-mail to solicit support, and create a Web site are included. Following chapters list and review useful foundation and charity sites.

Hair, Dr. Jay D. "Fund Raising on the Internet: Instant Access to a New World of Donors." *Fund Raising Management,* vol. 30 (October 1999): 16–8.
> Discusses the advantages of having an online shopping village attached to a nonprofit organization's Web site.

Johnston, Michael. *The Nonprofit Guide to the Internet: How to Survive and Thrive*, 2nd ed. New York, NY: John Wiley & Sons, 1999.
>   Surveys the hardware and software needed to get online and discusses reasons for nonprofits to utilize the Internet. Explores and gives examples of fundraising, and fundraising research, online. Explains how to use a Web site for marketing and public relations purposes. Includes a resource list, glossary, and index.

King, Karen N. and Julia K. Nims. "Yes, the Internet Sounds Great, But Is it Really for Us?" *Nonprofit World*, vol. 16, March–April 1998, p. 5–8.
>   Details the value of the Internet, specifically for small nonprofits. Lists URLs for Web sites specifically geared to the interests of nonprofits.

Lane, Carole A. *Naked in Cyberspace*: *How to Find Personal Information Online.* Edited by Helen Burwell and Owen B. Davies. Somerville, MA: Pemberton Press Books, 1997.
>   One chapter on prospect research indicates how to use public records, telephone directory databases, motor vehicle records, news and biographical database to search for wealth prospects.

Lyttle, Jeni. "New Dimensions for Fundraising." *Nonprofits & Technology,* vol. 2 (October 1999): p. 1, 3.
>   Some fundraisers are creating virtual tours of their planned facilities in order to raise capital funds.

Moore, Jennifer. "A Web of Confusion." *Chronicle of Philanthropy,* vol. 11 (21 October 1999): p. 37, 39.
>   Discusses the annual meeting of the National Association of State Charity Officials, at which nonprofit representatives urged charity regulators to clarify federal and state requirements regarding fundraising on the Internet.

Moran, Amanda M., ed. *CyberHound's Guide to Associations and Nonprofit Organizations on the Internet.* Detroit, MI: Gale Research, 1997.
>   Provides entries for 2,500 Web sites of associations and other nonprofit organizations. Entries contain the URL; site description; updating frequency; site establishment date; geographic area and time span covered; language; target audience; contact information; and ratings of site content, design, and technical merit. Includes bibliography, glossary of Internet terms, and indexes of organization name, contact person, and subject.

Notess, Greg R. *Government Information on the Internet*, 2nd ed. Lanham, MD: Bernan Press, 1998.
>   Covers more than 1,500 U.S. government Internet resources. Organized into eighteen subject categories, and indexed by primary and alternative access URLs, Superintendent of Documents number, publication title, agency, and subject.

"Old-line Charities Succeed with New Approaches to Attracting Donors."
Chronicle of Philanthropy, vol. 12 (4 November 1999): p. 49.
> Some of the charities in this year's Philanthropy 400 are using newer
> techniques for fundraising, including the Internet, payroll deduction plans,
> and inventive means of solicitation.

Reinhard, William (ed.) *The Grantseeker's Handbook of Essential Internet Site,*
3rd ed. Gaithersburg, MD: Aspen Publishers, 1999.
> Contains descriptions of more than 500 Internet sites of interest to
> grantseekers. Each description includes the resource's address and login or
> subscription instructions where applicable. Sites are arranged in the
> following categories: corporations, foundations and associations,
> government, research, and resources. Includes indexes by site name, and
> by major giving category for corporations and foundations.

"Researching Funding Sources on the Web." *Grassroots Fundraising Journal,*
vol. 17, August 1998, p. 12–3.
> Provides Web addresses for foundation, corporate giving, government,
> individual donor, and business Internet sites.

Robinson, Andy. "Direct Mail Alternatives: Finding New Donors in Manageable
Numbers." *NonProfit Times*, vol. 13, April 199, p. 45–6.
> Discusses techniques for small community organizations for recruiting
> new contributions.

Roufa, Mike. "Can Nonprofits Really Raise Money on the Internet?" *Nonprofit
World,* vol. 17, May–June 1999, p. 10–2.
> Explains what e-commerce is and how nonprofit organizations are using
> the Internet to raise funds.

Vimuktanon, Atisaya. "Non-Profits and the Internet." *Fund Raising
Management,* vol. 28, October 1997, p. 25–8.
> Explores the use of the Internet to increase visibility and enhance
> fundraising for nonprofit organizations.

INDEX